Meanings of Madness

Meanings of Madness

Richard J. Castillo
University of Hawaii—West Oahu

Brooks/Cole Publishing Company

I(T)P® An International Thomson Publishing Company

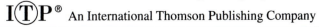

Pacific Grove • Albany • Belmont • Bonn • Boston • Cincinnati • Detroit • Johannesburg • London • Madrid
Melbourne • Mexico City • New York • Paris • Singapore • Tokyo • Toronto • Washington

Sponsoring Editor: *Marianne Taflinger*
Marketing Team: *Lauren Harp, Deborah Petit, Alicia Barelli*
Editorial Assistant: *Scott Brearton*
Production Editor: *Nancy L. Shammas*
Manuscript Editor: *Kay Mikel*
Permissions Editor: *Cat Morrison*

Interior Design: *Vernon T. Boes*
Cover Design: *Lisa Thompson*
Art Editor: *Lisa Torri*
Typesetting: *Archetype Book Composition*
Cover Printing: *Phoenix Color Corporation*
Printing and Binding: *R. R. Donnelley & Sons/Crawfordsville*

For more information, contact:

BROOKS/COLE PUBLISHING COMPANY
511 Forest Lodge Road
Pacific Grove, CA 93950
USA

International Thomson Editores
Seneca 53
Col. Polanco
11560 México, D. F., México

International Thomson Publishing Europe
Berkshire House 168-173
High Holborn
London WC1V 7AA
England

International Thomson Publishing GmbH
Königswinterer Strasse 418
53227 Bonn
Germany

Thomas Nelson Australia
102 Dodds Street
South Melbourne, 3205
Victoria, Australia

International Thomson Publishing Asia
221 Henderson Road
#05-10 Henderson Building
Singapore 0315

Nelson Canada
1120 Birchmount Road
Scarborough, Ontario
Canada M1K 5G4

International Thomson Publishing Japan
Hirakawacho Kyowa Building, 3F
2-2-1 Hirakawacho
Chiyoda-ku, Tokyo 102
Japan

Printed in the United States of America

10 9 8 7 6 5 4 3 2 1

Library of Congress Cataloging-in-Publication Data

Castillo, Richard J., (date)
  Meanings of madness / Richard J. Castillo.
    p.   cm.
  Includes bibliographical references and index.
  ISBN 0-534-34560-3
  1. Cultural psychiatry.   I. Title.
RC455.4.E8C384   1997
616.89—dc21   97-19078
                    CIP

ABOUT THE AUTHOR

Richard J. Castillo is a medical anthropologist specializing in the cross-cultural study of psychopathology and psychotherapy. He received his B.A. (*magna cum laude,* Phi Beta Kappa) in Philosophy (1983) and his M.A. in Asian Religions (1985) from the University of Hawaii–Manoa. He received his M.A. (1989) and Ph.D. (1991) in Medical and Psychiatric Anthropology from Harvard University. Dr. Castillo is currently Associate Professor of Psychology at the University of Hawaii–West Oahu and a Clinical Associate Professor of Psychiatry at the University of Hawaii School of Medicine.

Dr. Castillo is a Fellow of the American Anthropological Association and a member of the National Institute of Mental Health Group on Culture and Diagnosis that served as cultural advisers on the composition of DSM-IV. His principal research interests are in cultural factors affecting the dissociative disorders and the relationship of dissociative symptoms to schizophrenia and other psychotic disorders. His other works include *Culture and Mental Illness: A Client-Centered Approach* (1997, Brooks/Cole). He resides in Honolulu where he enjoys Hawaii's multicultural environment.

CONTENTS

PREFACE

This book is intended as a companion volume for *Culture and Mental Illness: A Client-Centered Approach.* However, this book can be read by itself as a main text or in conjunction with other works on the subject. Twenty-three articles are arranged in fifteen chapters. Most of the articles are recent, although a few articles that are considered to be "classics" in the field have also been selected. Most of the articles are ethnographic or clinical case studies illustrating cultural influences on various aspects of mental illness and treatment. There are also theoretical articles, review articles, and an epidemiological study. Some of the most influential authors in the fields of anthropology, psychiatry, psychology, and neuroscience are included: Arthur Kleinman, Horacio Fabrega, Byron J. Good, Laurence J. Kirmayer, Nancy Scheper-Hughes, Allan Young, Wolfgang G. Jilek, Theodore Lidz, Wen-Shing Tseng, L.A. Rebhun, James K. Boehnlein, J. David Kinzie, Marina Roseman, Theresa D. O'Nell, Larry G. Peters, Margery Wolf, and Roger W. Sperry. This book provides a brief but comprehensive series of case studies relevant to culture and mental illness.

Each chapter begins with an introduction that highlights the central points made by each author. Chapter topics include: (1) Culture and Psychiatry, (2) Culture and Clinical Reality, (3) Culture and Personality Development, (4) Sociocultural Assessment of Mental Illness, (5) Culture and Psychotherapy, (6) Culture and Personality Disorders, (7) Culture, Social Organization, and Sexuality, (8) Culture and Eating Disorders, (9) Culture and Substance-Related Disorders, (10) Culture and Anxiety, (11) Culture and Somatization, (12) Culture and Depression, (13) Culture and Dissociation, (14) Culture and Schizophrenia, and (15) Culture, Mind-Brain, and Mental Illness. This book is intended for advanced undergraduate and graduate level courses in anthropology, psychology, psychiatry, nursing, and social work programs.

Acknowledgments

Special thanks go to my mentor at Harvard University, Arthur Kleinman, for his inspiration and guidance. His teachings have led the way toward a new client-centered psychiatry. I am also deeply indebted to my colleagues in the National Institute of Mental Health Group on Culture and Diagnosis who consulted on DSM-IV: Juan E. Mezzich, Arthur Kleinman, Horacio Fabrega, Jr., Delores Parron, Bryon J. Good, Gloria Johnson-Powell, Keh-Ming Lin, Spero Manson, Roberto Lewis-Fernandez, Carlos A. Gonzalez, Ezra E. H. Griffith, Roland Littlewood, Laurence J. Kirmayer, Mitchell Weiss, Marvin Karno, Janis H. Jenkins, Peter J. Guarnaccia, Dona L. Davis, Gilbert Herdt, Renato D. Alarcon, Edward F. Foulks, Charles C. Hughes, Ronald C. Simons, Ronald M. Wintrob, Joseph Westermeyer, Glorisa Canino, Ian Canino, William Arroyo, Cheryl Ritenbaugh, Catherine Shisslak, Nicolette Teufel, Tina K. Leonard-Green, Raymond Prince, Armando R. Favazza, Candace Fleming, Atwood Gaines, James Gibbs, David J. Hufford, J. David Kinzie, Francis Lu, Enrique Madrigal, Theresa O'Nell, Wen-Shing Tseng, and William H. Sack. Their extremely valuable work in promoting cultural awareness in the study and diagnosis of mental illness has made this book possible.

I am also indebted to my colleagues on the Cultural Psychiatry Task Force in the Department of Psychiatry at the University of Hawaii School of Medicine for their many valuable insights on various aspects of culture and mental illness, including Wen-Shing Tseng, Jon Streltzer, Iqbal Ahmed, Danilo Ponce, Dykes Young, Junji Takeshita, David Bernstein, Alan Buffenstein, Patricia Harrison, Gary Cohen, Steve Chaplin, R. Andrew Schulz-Ross, Barry Carlton, and Leslie Matsukawa.

Richard J. Castillo

INTRODUCTION

This book takes a broad view of "madness" or what we now call mental illness, including the contemporary concepts of psychosis, depression, anxiety, substance abuse, abnormal sexual behavior, somatization, dissociation, eating disorders, and personality disorders. The symptoms of madness or mental illness occur in all cultures around the world but have different meanings in different cultural contexts, both for the mentally ill and for the families and societies in which the mentally ill live. In one cultural context, madness may be associated with demonic possession or the effects of witchcraft and sorcery. In another culture, madness may be seen as a genetically inherited brain disease.

Do these cultural differences make any real difference in the experience of mental illness, proper treatment, or outcome? Evidence suggests that the meanings of madness do have a significant impact on the subjective experience of madness, the idioms used in the expression of madness, the indigenous diagnosis, the indigenous treatment, and the outcome. Thus, the cultural meanings associated with madness are central to the problem of madness.

Cultural meaning systems create cultural entities, that is, objects that exist solely because of the collective social agreement that something counts as that entity. Among the cultural entities created by various cultures are categories of mental illness. Because of this cultural construction, madness possesses meaning in several different ways. Psychiatrist and anthropologist Arthur Kleinman (1988) has identified four ways in which mental illnesses have meaning.

The first way that mental illnesses have meaning is through the symptom as a symptom. A symptom is an indicator of illness. A particular experience, that is, a sensation, thought, emotion, or behavior, only becomes a *symptom* (an indication of illness) when it is cognized as such. Cognizing something as a symptom is an interpretation. The interpretation or cognitive construction of the event takes place within a cultural meaning system. A particular event is experienced as a symptom because the cultural meaning system defines it as an indicator of illness. This is important because the construction of an experience as a symptom can in itself cause further suffering in the form of fear, sadness, stigmatization, and so on.

Because different cultures have divergent meaning systems, there are differences in what counts as a symptom and what the symptom signifies. Even though the cultural schemas predict what kinds of symptoms will occur, and those symptoms are consequently experienced, the symptoms are considered to be completely natural and independent of human intentionality. The symptoms become reified and are observed to be natural entities happening on their own.

The second way that mental illnesses have meaning is through cultural significance. This refers to the meanings projected onto the mentally ill by the surrounding society, which then structures the experience of suffering by the patient. These meanings include what the society thinks about the ill person, about his or her particular mental disorder, and about mental illness in general. These meanings and their consequences become part of the lived illness experience of the patient. This is especially true in societies where mental illness is seen as particularly stigmatizing. The patient is forced to live with the meanings imposed by the culture. This can have important influences on the subjective experience of illness as well as on the course and outcome.

The third way mental illnesses have meaning are through personal and social relationships. This refers to the interpersonal relations and social life of the mentally ill person. Interpersonal relationships, particularly family and occupational relations, possess meanings that can exacerbate or shape the suffering associated with mental illness.

The fourth way that mental illnesses have meaning is through the explanatory model. This refers to the ways a set of cultural schemas explain the cause of mental illness, why the onset occurred when it did, the effects of the illness, what course the illness will take, and what treatments are appropriate. These meanings can affect the diagnoses of clinicians as well as the subjective experiences of mental patients.

Mental illness or madness can possess a variety of meanings. This book examines those meanings.

Looking back at madness during earlier times in western culture, it is clear that the cultural meaning systems existing in those times gave meaning to the symptoms and, thus, structured madness. For example, in medieval Europe the cultural schemas structured madness around the central concepts of demonic possession and witchcraft. The Christian Church provided society's view of nature. Therefore, life in the world was seen as a constant struggle between the forces of God and Satan. The mentally ill were culturally defined as either demonically possessed or the victims of witchcraft. This was the culture-based clinical reality of madness in medieval Europe.

However, this clinical reality was not merely a belief system. The cultural meaning system validates cultural entities, including God, Satan, witches, angels, and demons. These cultural entities were part of the daily lived experiences of people in this time and place. Demons and witches were as real to them as anything is to us in the modern world. Because cultural learning is structured in the neural networks of the brain, God, Satan, witches, angels, and demons were not merely believed in—they were encountered and personally experienced on an everyday basis. Thus, in subjective experience, idioms of distress, indigenous diagnoses, treatments, and outcomes, the patients of those times *were* possessed by demons and victimized by witchcraft.

The change from a medieval to a modern view of mental illness in western culture should be viewed as the evolution of madness based on an evolution of the general culture. The scientific and political revolutions of the 17th and 18th centuries changed western culture. No longer were the mentally ill defined as being possessed. Moreover, the patients themselves generally no longer experienced themselves as being possessed. That is, the subjective experience of madness had changed as well as the diagnoses. Instead of being "possessed," they were now "psychotic." This was the evolution of the possessed into the schizophrenic, an evolution of clinical reality based on an evolution of culture.

In the medieval world, demons were a lived reality. This medieval reality has its contemporary counterparts in many of today's nonindustrialized societies where people are still commonly possessed by various types of gods, demons, and ghosts, or are the victims of witchcraft. Anthropologists have been studying mental illnesses in these nonindustrialized societies for several decades. Generally, it has been found that the mental illnesses existing in these societies are structured by the indigenous set of cultural schemas. Some of the mental illnesses are in fact cultural entities. They exist only in a particular context and are structured by the indigenous meaning system. These mental illnesses have been labeled *culture-bound syndromes*. Some of these culture-bound syndromes are included in the appendix of DSM-IV (APA, 1994).

Significantly, the folk healing methods for these contemporary premodern forms of mental illness are sometimes effective. It is not necessary to diagnose a "possessed" patient with schizophrenia and provide medications to obtain a good outcome. Numerous reports have demonstrated that so-called witchdoctors, shamans, religious healers, and so on are capable of getting good clinical results. They are treating the subjective meanings in the mind of the patient, rather than only their disease.

This book takes an essentially anthropological viewpoint on mental illness, utilizing anthropology's deliberately holistic perspective and methodology, combining neurobiological, psychological, social, and cultural theories and data. The book specifically attempts to embrace a holistic, client-centered perspective on mental illness. In a *client-centered psychiatry,* rather than diagnosis and treatment of a *disease,* diagnosis and treatment are concerned with a *person*—with thoughts, emotions, a social context, and a cultural identity.

References

American Psychiatric Association. (1994) *Diagnostic and statistical manual of mental disorders* (4th ed.) Washington, DC: American Psychiatric Press.

Kleinman, A. (1988) *The illness narratives: Suffering, healing and the human condition.* New York: Basic Books.

CHAPTER ONE

Culture and Psychiatry

In recent decades, psychiatry has been heavily influenced by the neurosciences, and many psychiatrists have emphasized a primarily biological basis for most mental disorders. From the 1960s to the mid-1980s, many researchers believed that mental disorders were caused primarily by "chemical imbalances" in the brain, stemming from genetic abnormalities. This conception arose primarily because of the limited success obtained from treating mental disorders with psychotropic medications. In this biomedical paradigm, mental disorders were conceptualized as brain diseases, and psychiatrists focused on treating the disease. This approach is referred to in this book as *disease-centered psychiatry*.

However, an anthropological perspective on mental illness does not support a purely biological basis for mental illness. Attributing mental disorders primarily to diseases in the brain has been found to be too simplistic an explanation to accommodate recent research findings or to serve as a basis for consistently successful treatment. It is now known that the psychotropic medications currently in use treat symptoms, not diseases (Guttmacher, 1994). An emphasis on treating a disease rather than treating the patient can result in dehumanization of the patient in psychiatric practice (Brody, 1995; Fleck, 1995).

Some of the information that has been found to be most important in spurring a move beyond the boundaries of disease-centered psychiatry has come from cross-cultural studies of mental illness. For example, the finding that the duration of schizophrenia is shorter, the course more benign, and the outcome better in nonindustrialized societies than in industrialized societies has caused many researchers to reassess their conceptions of schizophrenia (Jablensky et al., 1992; Leff et al., 1992; Sartorius et al., 1986; Waxler, 1979; WHO, 1973, 1979). These cross-cultural findings on schizophrenia are contrary to expectations if schizophrenia is conceptualized as a genetically based, incurable brain disease. The data from cross-cultural studies have been convincing enough for psychiatric anthropologists and other cross-cultural researchers to be involved for the first time in the composition of the *Diagnostic and Statistical Manual of Mental Disorders* (DSM-IV) (APA, 1994).

Realization has slowly dawned that the etiology, structure, course, and outcome of mental disorders are far more integrated than previously imagined. It is now becoming clear to most re-

searchers that mental disorders need to be defined in a holistic manner. Interactions in the sociocultural environment and the effects of diagnosis and treatment on a human brain with plastic (modifiable) neural networks combine with other factors to produce an actual illness experience in a given patient (Castillo, 1995; Fabrega, 1993; Gaines, 1992; Good, 1992; Kleinman, 1988; Lu, Lim, & Mezzich, 1995).

The traditional biomedical paradigm in psychiatry is now being expanded to include the neurobiology of adaptation and learning. This theoretical expansion includes the effects of neuronal changes in the brain resulting from treatment, as well as the effects of individual and cultural learning on the brain. For example, it has been discovered that individual learning and memory storage change the neuronal structure of the brain (Kandel & Hawkins, 1992). Because culture determines many aspects of learning, cultural learning also has a biological basis in the brain and, therefore, in mental disorders. Thus, it is possible to conceptualize a biological basis for cultural differences in mental disorders.

The likelihood of culture-based differences in the brain argues for an essentially anthropological viewpoint of mental illness, utilizing anthropology's deliberately holistic perspective and methodology, which combines neurobiological, psychological, social, and cultural theories and data. This book specifically embraces a cross-cultural, client-centered approach to assessment and diagnosis. In a client-centered psychiatry, rather than diagnosis and treatment of a *disease*, diagnosis and treatment are concerned with a *client*—with the client's thoughts, emotions, social context, and a cultural identity.

Anthropologists have long had an interest in mental illness (Marsella, 1993). However, until recently anthropology has had little direct impact on psychiatric theory. Psychiatry mostly ignored anthropology until the 1980s because of the assumption of the psychic unity of humankind. This is the assumption that all people have the same basic brain structure; therefore, people universally have the same basic mental processes. It was assumed that even though all people do not think the same things, they still think in the same basic way.

However, recent findings in the neurobiology of learning, memory, and cognition clearly indicate that this is not true. Findings of neurobiological differences for learning and memory on the cellular and molecular levels of the brain confirm the biological basis of individuality of consciousness (Kandel & Hawkins, 1992). It follows that the same neurobiological processes operating in learning to create individual differences in the psychobiology of the brain and mind also operate at the collective level to create biological differences in the brain across cultures. Thus, the psychic unity of humankind can no longer be assumed on the basis of biological sameness. This has profound implications for the study of mental disorders.

Disease-centered psychiatry assumed the psychic unity of humankind. In the disease-centered paradigm, because the normal brain was thought to be structured and to function the same in all people, any differences in brain structure or functioning could be assumed to represent brain disease. Thus, until the discovery of neuronal adaptability in the brain, there was little need to include brain plasticity in conceptions of mental illness. However, we now know that neural structures in the brain are altered by adaptations to emotional stress and trauma, medications, psychotherapy, personal experience, and cultural learning. All of these can affect the neural networks of the brain and therefore the etiology, structure, and outcome of mental disorders.

The psychic unity of humankind was a basic assumption, sometimes even in anthropology, until the late 1970s. The cognitive revolution in the behavioral sciences changed that. Researchers discovered that learned cognitive schemas of an individual actually construct to some extent his or her subjective experience of the world (Neisser, 1976). Furthermore, the subjective construction of experience can be dramatically different in the same situation among different individuals. The discovery was also made that cognitive schemas are dependent to a very large extent on cultural learning (D'Andrade, 1984). This meant that cultural schemas are formed within the mind-brains of cultural groups. These cultural schemas can cognitively construct a particular behavior as an episode of mental illness. A different set of cultural schemas may cognitively construct a similar situation as something normal and normative. These differences in cognitive construction result from cultural learning and are based in plastic neuronal structures.

In this chapter, two highly influential psychiatrists adopt essentially anthropological viewpoints in their discussion of psychiatry and mental illness. The first paper is by noted psychiatrist Theodore Lidz, who concludes that an inappropriate interpretation of neuroscience has led many in psychiatry to ignore the psychosocial causes of mental illness and focus primarily on biological factors. He attributes this trend to "a misapprehension of the human biological make up and, particularly, the nature of human adaptive capacities." He notes that genetic evolution occurs when a species adapts to changes in its environment.

The evolution of humans can be traced back to Australopithecines who lived three million years ago. Homo sapiens evolved at least 40,000 years ago, and their early fossil remains reveal that the physique of early Homo sapiens differs considerably from the Australopithecines, particularly in the size of the cerebral cortex and the large forebrain of Homo sapiens. However, the evolution of Homo sapiens over the past 40,000 years has been very limited in terms of genetic changes. This is because the evolution of a large cerebral cortex, especially a highly developed forebrain, has allowed Homo sapiens to develop a means of adaptation that is far quicker and more flexible than genetic evolution—that is, cultural evolution. Homo sapiens adapt to changing environments not so much by changing their genes as by changing their patterns of thought and behavior. Essentially, evolution has provided humans with a highly adaptable and reprogrammable brain that allows us to be highly flexible and responsive to the environment. Further, because humans have learned to live in large groups, we adapt to our environment collectively, thus creating distinct cultures. Cultures provide not only customs of thought and behavior but also patterns for how to experience and understand life in the world. Therefore, all humans have both a genetic and a cultural inheritance. Human thought and behavior cannot be properly understood without recognizing this developmental fact.

Neuroscience research has made it clear that life experiences program and reprogram the highly flexible human brain. The implications of this are that looking for exclusively genetic explanations for normal or abnormal behavior of any given individual is inappropriate. The great adaptability of the human brain in response to its environment makes it far more likely that an individual's behavior will be based on learning and psychosocial adaptation rather than on genetic inheritance. According to Lidz, modern psychiatry has tried to simplify this complexity by inappropriately reducing matters to genetically caused abnormalities in the brain that can be corrected pharmaceutically.

The second article in this chapter is by noted cross-cultural psychiatrist Horacio Fabrega, Jr. He reviews the concept of cultural relativism coming from anthropology and applies it to psychiatric illness. He points out the implications of cultural relativism and the differences with the psychic unity of humankind perspective of biological determinism that has been paradigmatic in psychiatry in recent decades. He concludes that mental disorders should be construed in biocultural terms; that is, mental illness involves brain mechanisms and processes that reflect enculturation and the internalization of cultural schemas, including interpretations of reality and conceptualizations of the self.

REFERENCES

American Psychiatric Association. (1994). *Diagnostic and statistical manual of mental disorders* (4th ed.). Washington, DC: American Psychiatric Association.

Brody, E. B. (1995). Editorial. The humanity of psychotic persons and their rights. *Journal of Nervous and Mental Disease, 183*, 193–194.

Castillo, R. J. (1995). Culture, trance, and the mind-brain. *Anthropology of Consciousness, 6*, 17–34.

D'Andrade, R. G. (1984). Cultural meaning systems. In R.A. Shweder & R. A. LeVine (Eds.), *Culture theory: Essays on mind, self, and emotion* (pp. 88–119). Cambridge: Cambridge University Press.

Fabrega, H., Jr. (1993). A cultural analysis of human behavioral breakdowns: An approach to the ontology and epistemology of psychiatric phenomena. *Culture, Medicine and Psychiatry, 17*, 99–132.

Fleck, S. (1995). Dehumanizing developments in American psychiatry in recent decades. *Journal of Nervous and Mental Disease, 183*, 195–203.

Gaines, A. D. (1992). From DSM-I to III-R; voices of self, mastery and the other: A cultural constructivist reading of U.S. psychiatric classification. *Social Science and Medicine, 35*, 3–24.

Good, B. J. (1992). Culture and psychopathology: Directions for psychiatric anthropology. In T. Schwartz, G. M. White, & C. A. Lutz (Eds.), *New directions in psychological anthropology* (pp. 181–205). Cambridge: Cambridge University Press.

Guttmacher, L. B. (1994). *Concise guide to psychopharmacology and electroconvulsive therapy*. Washington DC: American Psychiatric Press.

Jablensky, A., Sartorius, N., Ernberg, G., Anker, M., et al. (1992). Schizophrenia: Manifestations, incidence and course in different cultures: A World Health Organization ten-country study. *Psychological Medicine, Monograph Supplement Vol. 20*.

Kandel, E. R., & Hawkins, R. D. (1992). The biological basis of learning and individuality. *Scientific American, 262* (3), 78–86.

Kleinman, A. (1988). *Rethinking psychiatry: From cultural category to personal experience*. New York: Free Press.

Leff, J., Sartorius, N., Jablensky, A., Korten, A., et al. (1992). The international pilot study of schizophrenia: Five-year follow-up findings. *Psychological Medicine, 22*, 131–145.

Lu, F. G., Lim, R. F., & Mezzich, J. E. (1995). Issues in the assessment and diagnosis of culturally diverse individuals. In J. M. Oldham & M. B. Riba (Eds.), *Review of psychiatry, volume 14* (pp. 477–510). Washington, DC: American Psychiatric Press.

Marsella, A. J. (1993). Sociocultural foundations of psychopathology: An historical overview of concepts, events, and pioneers prior to 1970. *Transcultural Psychiatric Research Review, 30*, 97–142.

Neisser, U. (1976). *Cognition and reality: Principles and implications of cognitive psychology*. New York: W. H. Freeman.

Sartorius, N., Jablensky, A., Korten, A., Ernberg, G., et al. (1986). Early manifestations and first-contact incidence of schizophrenia in different cultures: A preliminary report on the initial evaluation phase of the WHO collaborative study on determinants of outcome of severe mental disorders. *Psychological Medicine, 16*, 909–928.

Waxler, N. E. (1979). Is outcome for schizophrenia better in nonindustrialized societies? The case of Sri Lanka. *Journal of Nervous and Mental Disease, 167*, 144–158.

WHO. (1973). *International pilot study of schizophrenia*. Geneva: World Health Organization.

WHO. (1979). *Schizophrenia: An international follow-up study*. Chichester, NY: Wiley.

THEODORE LIDZ, M.D.[1]

Genetic and Psychosocial Evolution and the Future of Psychiatry

The decade of the brain has yielded notable advances in knowledge of the neurotransmitters and the structure and functioning of the brain. Unfortunately, it has led many investigators and teachers to believe that advancing knowledge of the brain eliminates the need to teach and understand such matters as personality development, interviewing skills, and psychodynamic principles. Moreover, the financial support for brain research has reduced funds for investigations into the nature and treatment of schizophrenic disorders. The problem derives less from a conflict between a biological and a psychosocial orientation than from a confusion of "brain" with "mind" due to a misapprehension of the human biological make up and, particularly, the nature of human adaptive capacities.

I believe that the situation can be clarified by a brief review of human evolution which may also help overcome the growing division in the theories that guide research as well as the practice of psychiatry.

Let us recall that in order for an evolving organism to be able to live in a different environment, or change its means of adapting to its environment, it must mutate into a somewhat different organism. Although mutations are very common, changes in the structure of a complex organism into that of a different species is an extremely slow process. We can pick up the line of human precursors in a type of Australopithecus that lived during the Pleistocene period some two to three million years ago; it not only had a skull with teeth resembling those of later prehominids, but it also used an axe-like tool (Washburn and Lancester, 1968). The slow pace of biological evolution is evident from the fact that *Homo sapiens* emerged just 30,000 to 40,000 years ago. The line of development to the human did not emerge from random mutations, but largely or even primarily from those that increased the capacity for tool bearing and the development of that tool of tools, language. Although the physique of proto-man kept changing, the more significant changes were in the size and complexity of the brain, notably of the cerebral cortex and its forebrain. With the emergence of *Homo sapiens,* further genetic evolution virtually, though not completely, came to a halt because a far quicker and more malleable way of adapting to new environments and finding new ways of utilizing the environment had gradually emerged. During these past 30,000 years, the human as a biological organism has changed little from our Stone Age progenitors, but humans *as persons* have changed enormously.

Oversimplifying somewhat, humans no longer needed to change to suit a new environment, but rather changed the environment to suit human needs and expanded their adaptability and aspirations by the use and invention of tools. The development of language was critical. Aside from greatly increasing cooperation between individuals and the development of structured societies, learning became cumulative. While all higher animals depend upon learning from others, primarily through following example, speech permitted the learning of an individual to be transmitted across generations. In contrast to genetic evolution, in which acquired characteristics cannot be transmitted to the next generation, humans could and did transmit what they learned to subsequent generations. Rather than starting anew, individuals could build on the experiences of their progenitors. Groups who lived proximately developed cultures, that is, common ways of understanding their world, and living together in it. These ways could change with the experience of an individual or of the group. Further, through the use of language, persons could fragment past experiences, draw converging lines through the present to project a future, and, by imaginative trial and error, decide on a course of action without committing themselves to actual irrevocable actions. Indeed, words that name objects provide a degree of predictability, for the proper critical attribute of a noun conveys its use or usages. Rather than being largely drive impelled or conditioned, humans became future oriented and could seek to direct themselves into the future.

[1]Sterling Professor of Psychiatry, Emeritus. Yale University School of Medicine, New Haven, Connecticut.

SOURCE: From *Journal of Nervous and Mental Disease, 182* (11), November 1994 601–603. Copyright © 1994 Williams & Wilkins. Reprinted with permission.

There is no reason to ponder, as so many thinkers have, how experiences and intangible thoughts, emotions, and beliefs can affect the manner in which the body functions. Each experience, including every thought, must register neuronally: we are influenced by perceptions of experiences and not by occurrences themselves which remain external to us. Involving a person's brain, they affect him at every level of integration. Experiences do not affect the genes, and thus do not become an intrinsic part of subsequent generations. But, they can become part of future generations by becoming part of the culture that a child assimilates, or by being taught by elders, notably the parents. Indeed, though we can define *Homo sapiens* in various ways, in essence it is the species that cannot develop into a functioning individual or even survive without assimilating a culture.

Stated somewhat differently, humans, genetically endowed to maintain their essential physiological homeostasis within certain environmental conditions, can, in contrast to other organisms, modify their environment to meet their physiological requirements (these capacities depend, of course, on a host of other genetically endowed requisites).

Unless one appreciates that humans have both genetic inheritance and a cultural heritage that are inextricably interrelated, human functioning can never be understood correctly. The genetic endowment can change, but slowly, through mutations; however, because it derives from a fusion of two different genetic lines, it gives rise to infinite variations of physique and temperament. The *basics* of cultural endowment, in contrast, are primarily mediated by the parents and the family and can change from generation to generation or even within a generation, as with migrations into a different culture. However, there is no assurance that specific parents are capable of conveying the culture or will provide suitable figures for the child to internalize. Nor will they necessarily provide the essential haven the child needs during the years of immaturity and dependency, or prepare their offspring to emerge from the nidus of the family to live in the broader society. The culture is a major factor in how people experience life, the way they think, whether they have a historical past to utilize or as the Indigines of New Guinea and the Aborigines of Australia, an indefinite mythic past of supernatural forbears. The culture not only conveys a way of life but, in a sense, programs how its members understand and experience life. As Leslie White has written (White, 1960), "In contrast to all other living organisms, if we wish to learn why a *typical* individual behaves as he does, we must concern ourselves not with their bodies, the neuromuscular-sensory-glandular systems, but with the culture into which they have been born and to which they respond . . . a new world created, an extra-somatic cultural environment, and it is this which determines the behavior of peoples (collectively) living within it and not their bodily structure."

Students of human evolution have increasingly realized over the past hundred years, and particularly since the centennial of Darwin's *The Origin of Species* (Tax, 1960) that the current state of humans cannot be explained by genetic mutation alone; their development depended on an intertwining of genetic and psychosocial or cultural factors. Since the emergence of *Homo sapiens,* people have reached their current condition primarily through cultural developments and the capacity for foresight—a process that has accelerated over the past three or four hundred years. A landmark event was the publication of Francis Bacon's *Novum Organum* (Tax, 1960), which recognized the vast potentialities for the future if people would use their minds as a tool to work upon nature to modify it for human purposes.

Sir Julian Huxley, for example, one of the leading scholars of the evolutionary process, wrote, "After man's emergence as truly man . . . man's evolution is not biological, but psychosocial; it operates by the mechanism of cultural tradition. Accordingly, major steps in the human phase of evolution are achieved by breakthroughs to new dominant patterns of mental organization, or knowledge, ideas, and beliefs—ideological instead of physiological or biological organization. There is a succession of successful idea systems instead of a succession of successful bodily organizations" (Huxley, 1960, p. 251). And further, "mind—our word for the mental activities and properties of organisms—eventually broke through, to become the basis for further evolution, though the character of evolution became cultural instead of genetic or biological . . . exploration of the mind has barely begun. It must be one of the main tasks of the coming era" (p. 252). Although Huxley's remarks may seem exaggerated, we now see that the capabilities of the human brain no longer suffice to enable certain expansions of adaptability. Instead, we find ourselves increasingly dependent on a tool, the computer, to carry out cognitive processes beyond the brain's capabilities, an adaptation that has probably ushered in a new era in human experience.

The study of the brain has preoccupied recent psychiatric research, but the brain is not the mind, though its evolution has made possible the development of the adaptive mind. The mind has to do with the assimilation of a culture, of parental teachings and attitudes, with the impact of bodily drives on feelings and directives, and with all of an individual's life experiences, including relationships to others. It is particularly important for psychiatrists to remember that humans alone are not only aware of the ultimacy of death, but have the capacity to choose between life and death. When life seems unbearable, this capacity can lead to panic reactions when individuals fear that suicidal wishes will outweigh desires to live, or to depressive states when resentments toward a person one needs, or hopelessness about one's future, provokes wishes for surcease from the tribulations of life.

Perhaps a few sentences written by the anthropologist A. I. Hallowell (1960) on the dilemmas brought on by the evolution of the mind will sharpen the relevance of the presentation for psychiatrists:

"Speech, through the use of personal pronouns, personal names, and kinship terms made it possible for an individual to symbolize, and thus objectify, himself in systems of social action. Self-related activities, both in the past and future, could be brought into the present and reflected upon. . . . Since self-objectification involves self appraisal in relation to sanctioned moral conduct, we can see the social as well as the individual adaptive values of unconscious psychological processes such as repression, rationalization and other defense mechanisms. Culturally constituted moral values impose a characteristic psychological burden, since it is not always easy . . . to reconcile idiosyncratic needs with the demands imposed by the normative orientation of the self."
(1960 vol. 2, p. 357)

He goes on to cite Freedman and Roe (1958):

"Incompatible aims and choices which are desirable, but mutually exclusive, are inevitable conditions of human development. This discrepancy between possibility and restriction, stimulation and interdiction, anger and constriction underlies that qualitatively unique characteristic of the human being: conflict."

Disturbances of thought, emotions, and behavior brought on by defects of the brain and by transient impairments of cerebral functioning due to toxic conditions, are but a limited part of the field of psychiatry. Psychiatry is more concerned with the mind that the brain made possible and the experiences that influence the mind and thereby brain functioning. It has to do with the culture in which individuals develop and which, in a sense, programs the brain, and the life experiences that register in the brain, that differ for all individuals, and which inevitably cause conflicts with the delimitations cultures require as well as between contradictory desires and aims. Individuals most frequently resolve conflicts by reliance on tradition, or by the use of their own intellect, experiences, and feelings, but they may reach impasses psychiatrists seek to help them out of by opening a path into the future. What a person learns from experience, including that which is transmitted by the culture, can be modified through understanding and guidance. Through the study of the human condition, human development, and conscious and unconscious conflicts, psychiatry can increase its ability to offer the needed understanding and guidance. Some of us have observed how some peoples, such as the Fijians, have changed within two generations from being among the fiercest cannibals, whose shores sailors avoided, to become one of the most friendly and trustworthy of peoples, eager for education, and even capable of waging war with highly sophisticated laser-directed weapons rather than the wooden clubs their grandfathers used early in the century.

The brain is so complicated that neuroanatomists and neurophysiologists can despair of ever completely working out its pathways and neurochemistry, but the task of understanding the complexity of a life and the problems that arise in its course is not only great, but difficult to grasp and sometimes ineffable because it is intangible. It is, indeed, no wonder that psychiatrists seek to simplify their tasks by hoping to explain matters as due to abnormalities in the brain or in its functioning that can be corrected pharmaceutically.

REFERENCES

Freedman LZ, Roe A (1958) Evolution and human behavior. In A Roe, CG Simpson (Eds), *Behavior and evolution* (p. 461). New Haven: Yale University Press.

Hallowell AI (1960) Self, society, and culture. In S Tax (Ed), *Evolution after Darwin: Proceedings of the University of Chicago Centennial Conference.* Vol. 2, *The evolution of man.* Chicago: The University of Chicago Press.

Huxley J (1960) The evolutionary vision. In S Tax (Ed), *Evolution after Darwin: Proceedings of the University of Chicago Centennial Conference.* Vol. 3, *Issues in evolution.* Chicago: The University of Chicago Press.

Tax S (1960) *Evolution after Darwin: Proceedings of the University of Chicago Centennial Conference.* Vol. 1, *The evolution of life.* Chicago: The University of Chicago Press.

Washburn SL, Lancester JB (1968) Human evolution. In *The international encyclopedia of the social sciences,* Vo. 5 (pp. 215–221). New York: Macmillan and The Free Press.

White L (1960) Fours stages of minding. In S Tax (Ed), *Evolution after Darwin: Proceedings of the University of Chicago Centennial Conference.* Vol 2, *The evolution of man.* Chicago: The University of Chicago Press.

HORACIO FABREGA, JR., M.D.[1]

Cultural Relativism and Psychiatric Illness

Psychiatry has had a long-standing association with sociology and, especially, cultural anthropology. These social sciences have been influential in developing the concept of cultural relativism and applying it to psychiatry, sometimes in a challenging way and with much detriment. The concept has been used by some antipsychiatrists in attempts to discredit psychiatric practice. Contemporary psychiatrists endorsing a form of biological determinism have tended to either disregard the concept or judge it as trivial if not nonsensical. This study describes the concept of cultural relativism, reviews its applications to illness, and analyzes its implications from a historical and theoretical point of view. Its varied aspects, power, and limitations are discussed.

Psychiatry is part of the Western biomedical tradition and seeks universal generalizations about illness. In general medicine, for example, claims are made about diabetes that apply to persons of diverse cultural backgrounds and psychiatry seeks such claims for its own domain. In many respects this is possible, but in others it is not, most dramatically when it involves the manifest appearance and social consequences of psychiatric illness. Such phenomena are said to differ significantly in different "cultures." The concept of cultural relativism and its implications has always operated as a potential obstacle to the universalistic claims of psychiatry, and recent research findings and theoretical writings have served to vividly reinforce this (Kleinman, 1986; Kleinman and Good, 1985; Littlewood and Lipsedge, 1985; Murphy, 1982). This paper reviews the concept of cultural relativism as it applies to psychiatry. It will discuss the bases and implications of cultural relativism, clarify the dilemmas and contradictions surrounding its use, and suggest ways in which the problems that it raises can be dealt with so as to advance the science of psychiatry.

[1]Departments of Psychiatry and Anthropology, University of Pittsburgh, School of Medicine, Western Psychiatric Institute and Clinic, 3811 O'Hara Street, E-1123, Pittsburgh, PA 15212.

WHAT IS CULTURAL RELATIVISM AND HOW DOES IT APPLY TO PSYCHIATRY?

Cultural relativism refers to the differences in beliefs, feelings, behaviors, traditions, social practices, and technological arrangements that are found among diverse peoples of the world. Such differences are related because they are believed to result from differences in culture. Culture can be defined as "consisting of learned systems of meaning, communicated by means of natural language and other symbol systems having representational, directive, and affective functions, and capable of creating cultural entities and particular senses of reality. Through these systems of meaning, groups of people adapt to their environment and structure interpersonal activities" (D'Andrade, 1984, p. 116). Thus, culture influences basic characteristics of humans, such as beliefs, emotions, the idea of self, and presumably the illnesses to which humans are susceptible.

Two positions need to be distinguished in thinking of cultural relativism and psychiatric illness. One is that of the outside Western observer who is knowledgeable about a psychiatric illness that can be conceptualized, reliably measured, and studied across societies as a function of cultural differences (an etic perspective). Any *parameter of illness* (cause, manifestation, distribution, course, and response to treatment) can be the object of an etic study. These studies are classically undertaken by epidemiologists who may be termed universalists, because they seek cross-cultural generalizations. An example is the cross-cultural study of depression or schizophrenia. Second, there is the position of one knowledgeable about cultural differences in life ways who intends to study a particular people with respect to medical phenomena (an emic perspective). In this instance, the parameters of the illnesses singled out by the people themselves (folk illnesses) might be studied using the theory of biomedical psychiatry or (perhaps more appropriately) that of the peoples themselves (the so-called ethnotheory). Emically oriented researchers, usually cultural anthropologists, are generally thought of as relativists because the idea of cultural differences has power to them.

Given these generalizations, one may characterize cultural relativism as involving the claim that at least some, if not all, of

SOURCE: From *Journal of Nervous and Mental Disease, 177* (7), 1989, 415–425. Copyright © 1989 Williams & Wilkins. Reprinted with permission.

the parameters of psychiatric illness among a people, are variable, different, and more or less unique precisely as a function of their culture. Cultural relativistic challenges are usually targeted at those espousing an etic perspective (*i.e.,* "universalists") and concentrate mainly on parameters of manifestations, course, and distribution, but in theory such challenges should also be made with respect to other parameters. The challenges grow out of empirical studies that have provided an appreciation of the differences in cultural perspective of a people in the areas of illness and medical practice. A cultural relativistic challenge is tautologically trivial when it merely stipulates that only native illnesses (and not Western biomedical ones) are culturally valid in a particular non-Western society. It is the cultural relativistic challenges to etically generated universal psychiatric claims (*e.g.,* the manifestations and course of schizophrenia) that have cogency.

Psychiatric illnesses are abstract "objects" or constructions that are constituted of the scientific knowledge base of the Western tradition of medicine (Fabrega, 1987). Science, medicine, and illness "objects" are viewed as empirically derived, reflecting what is "real" and "in" nature; that is, as objective, neutral, culture-free, and value-free (scientific objectivism). These are the bases for the claim that medical science and its objects and categories are "universal." However, as cultural relativists are quick to point out, science is a product and key component of the Western cultural tradition. Biomedical science is constituted by that culture and its knowledge and practice feed back into it. In brief, a distinctive culturally grounded epistemology (*i.e.,* theory of knowledge) and ontology (*i.e.,* nature and relations of being or entities) are fused together in the Western biomedical tradition. Hence, many relativists view psychiatric illness objects with suspicion; because they reflect a distinctive cultural tradition, they are held to have little or no warrant in and for people of highly contrastive cultural traditions. They claim that the illnesses of such people can hardly be qualified as psychiatric and do not resemble Western varieties of psychiatric illnesses. These two traditions, scientific objectivism and cultural relativism, are not only opposed but contradictory, for each invalidates the other when pushed to its extremes. These traditions would thus appear to be incommensurable.

WHY IS THE CONSTRUCT OF CULTURAL RELATIVISM PERTINENT TO PSYCHIATRY?

All medical disciplines, in their clinical/pragmatic aspects, deal with whole persons. Because the thrust of general biomedicine is to partition humanity into ever more basic and abstracted systems (*e.g.,* organs, tissues, chemical processes), this has led to criticisms that seek to restore its true "biopsychosocial" basis (Engel, 1977). However, psychiatry has a special emphasis on

the whole behaving person because attributes of illness importantly implicate social (symbolic) behavior (Fabrega, 1974a, 1975a). Even if a key lesion or biological marker were found for each psychiatric illness, the social and symbolic importance of psychiatric illness would not diminish because realizations of psychiatric illness have far different meanings and consequences in modern contemporary society than, for example, realizations of diabetes or pneumonia, because the core of the self is affected by them. Moreover, since its inception, the discipline of psychiatry has been involved with illness problems that blended with a variety of other social problems related to deviance; cultural conventions continue to be important in marking out psychiatry's proper boundaries within medicine and other social institutions (Scull, 1979).[2]

In summary, both psychiatric illness and culture meaningfully implicate humans as holistic and symbolic creatures. No abstracted structure or lower order system can meaningfully be substituted for the whole person, nor can an understanding of the essential attributes of the person be obtained through explanations that disregard a person's integrated and symbolically rooted complexity and connectedness to social institutions. It it these shared features of psychiatry, personhood, psychiatric illness, and culture that render the construct of cultural relativism central to psychiatry.

SOME DIFFERENCES IN THE UNIVERSALIST AND RELATIVIST APPROACHES

A fundamental element of the rationale of an etically oriented biomedical universalist is the use of symptom categories, illness criteria, and diagnostic inventory protocols that are explicit, discrete, abstract, and context independent. Stated differently, the researcher deals with experience-distant concepts and follows the methodological traditions of scientific objectivism. The rationale and methods of the International Pilot Study of Schizophrenia (IPSS; Sartorius et al., 1977), illustrate this. Suffice it to say that the IPSS has pointed to what appear to be invariant properties of psychoses and raised tantalizing questions regarding its course and duration.

In arguing for the importance of specific social and cultural factors in the content, experience, expression, trajectory, or distribution of a psychiatric or other illness, an emically oriented researcher (*i.e.,* a relativist) is committed in part to a qualitative and descriptivist approach and methodology. Because the latter is not widely appreciated it will be described briefly. A relativist re-

[2]H. Fabrega. Anglo-American psychiatry as an object for a critical medical anthropology. Paper presented at the Wenner-Gren Foundation Conference on Medical Anthropology, 1988.

quires rich behavioral and phenomenological data. Subtle ways in which perceptions of self and other are altered in the context of psychiatric illness, as an example, are required. The manner in which reality is now experienced and interpreted needs to be explicated, and this means probing subtle changes in the way in which the self and the behavioral environment are construed. Alternatively, the changed way in which emotion is elicited, experienced, and expressed needs to be clarified as well as its meaning to the actor and to others in the behavioral environment. Analysis of the discourse of the ill individual, as an example, will need to be recorded and carefully analyzed. In addition, the behavior of the person showing psychopathology will need to be carefully monitored, as well as the reactions of others to his/her intentions, motives, and actions. Monitoring of the latter is critical, inasmuch as others interpret the ill person's behavior and label it with native categories and theories, seeking to resolve the psychopathology in line with native cultural conventions of health, well-being, and illness. A shaping or constructing of the psychopathology takes place that bears the impact of culture and social context in an important way. An emphasis on details of behavior, intricacies of altered beliefs and emotional reactivity, interpretations of bodily perceptions and changes, and conduct and interpretation of social action in real settings means that linguistic science, semiotics, and semantic theory will need to be marshalled and used along with qualitative scrutiny of interpersonal behavior using field work techniques. The attempt of the analyst is to capture the way in which language is used; the body is talked about; the outside world of persons, physical objects, and possible preternatural agents is conceptualized and engaged; and how the whole of this in the context of illness or personal disequilibrium is made a social episode, drama, or event.

In summary, a person seeking to document cultural differences in psychopathology is committed to an exegetical analysis; that is, one that allows full interpretation. An idiographic *vs.* a nomothetic approach and methodology are required, which shifts the researcher away from exclusive reliance on discrete and context-independent items of behavior and especially from traditional categories of psychopathology, to more general and open ended methods that allow capturing the symbolic world of the person. Such a world includes theories of self, body, objects of the behavioral environment and, more generally, the purpose and rationale of social life. All such theories and rationales are held to affect "psychopathology" and its social consequences.

HOW HAS CULTURAL RELATIVISM BEEN APPLIED TO PSYCHIATRY?

The application of cultural relativism to psychiatry has a long history. The initial thrust came from culture and personality theorists who were concerned with psychological characteristics of

persons of diverse backgrounds and who emphasized behavioral differences (LeVine, 1983). Because of the centrality of the concept of personality in the "old" dynamic psychiatry, such cross-cultural studies were viewed as relevant and informative. Culture and personality theorists used the ideas of normal and abnormal behavior, the latter often standing for psychiatric illness. They emphasized the following logically derived categories: a) behavior that was definitely considered abnormal in our society but might be considered normal in others; b) behavior that was considered normal in our society but might be considered abnormal in others; c) behaviors that might be considered normal in all societies; d) behaviors that might be considered abnormal in all societies; e) abnormal behaviors or normal behaviors, considered as such, that would be seen in one or some but not in all societies.

Some of the characteristics of earlier studies that relied on these categories and applied the idea of cultural relativism to psychiatry can be briefly summarized. They tended to emphasize global aspects of behavior and to neglect specific Western illness entities; native theories of self, emotion, behavior, and illness were minimized; few details of the actual behaviors that signalled "abnormal behavior" or illness were reported; and Western psychological theories were dominant. Because of the psychoanalytic emphasis, some parameters of psychiatric illness were not considered relevant (*e.g.,* neurobiology, epidemiology) and others were disregarded (*e.g.,* course, response to treatment). The main challenge concentrated on manifestations and ontology (what sort of "objects" were they?). Although these researchers offered very suggestive inferences about normal *vs.* abnormal behavior, the weaknesses of these studies and their relative neglect of clinically vital issues failed to make a strong immediate impact within psychiatry. As a result, the challenge of cultural relativism was initially minimized because it seemed general, impressionistic, and far (exotically) removed from the study of "real" illness conditions.

A related important tradition also focused on social and cultural aspects of behavior, but dealt with Western (Anglo-American) societies. This consisted of the work of Blumer (1969), Garfinkel (1967), Goffman (1963), and Mead (1934) in sociology, all of whom drew attention to symbolic and interactional factors that entered into the creation, maintenance, and consequences of behavior. To these researchers, implicit and taken for granted meanings, symbolic conventions, and the social labeling of behavior in Western societies were all important in explaining its character and meaning. Their emphases also argued for cultural relativism because implicit meanings and labels depend on cultural conventions.

In summary, it was researchers from anthropology and sociology who challenged the universalistic pan-human claims of psychiatry and contributed to the influential role that the social sciences came to play in psychiatry. A culmination of this trend can be seen in the emphases that led to the new fields of "social"

and "community" psychiatry, and in the writings of enthomethod-
ologists and labeling theorists to the effect that even Western
psychiatric illnesses, as manifested in contemporary Western societies, were somehow socially created through the application of
culturally derived labels and theories. The reasoning seemed to
imply not only that social equivalents of Western psychiatric illness were different cross-culturally, but that the *Western illnesses
themselves* were not valid but merely products of social and cultural conventions.

The writings of some psychiatrists' most forceful critics,
which borrowed and in some instances refined many of the ideas
and assumptions of social scientists, appeared during this period
and contributed to the view that cultural relativistic claims made a
universalist science of psychiatry suspect if not illegitimate
(Laing, 1968; Scheff, 1966; Szasz, 1961). In other words, the
claims of the cultural relativists were in certain respects extended
far beyond their original confines: from the *legitimate* claim of
possible differences in personality, social behavior, illness pictures, and other parameters of illness because of cultural differences, the derived *illegitimate* claim was that Western psychiatric
illnesses are but products of social labels and cultural conventions
and hence are (psychobiologically) fictive. Some social scientists
and critics did not heed the basic distinction of Lemert (1951) between primary deviance (what was biologically produced, the
original malady or deviation) and secondary deviance (the social
elaboration of the primary deviance through the operation of labels, symbolizations). This gave their writings a rhetorical force
(but also a scientific naivete) that in the public arena undermined
the universalistic claims and professional integrity of psychiatry.
Many researchers have made abundantly clear that both concepts,
of primary as well as secondary deviance, are equally pertinent
and necessary to a full (*e.g.,* biological, social, and cultural) understanding of psychiatric illness and, that, more specifically, an
acknowledgment of the power of the concept of secondary deviance in no way undermines the centrality of biological factors
in psychiatric illness (the primary deviance; Edgerton, 1969;
Waxler, 1974).

A turning point in the growing socially influential critique of
"vulgar" cultural relativistic thinking with respect to psychiatry
can be discerned in the writings of Brody (1964), Leighton et al.
(1963), and Wallace (1961). Brody's paper was very far ranging
and proved extremely influential because it reflected a command
of both psychiatric knowledge and the fundamental axioms of social science. In it he critically discussed how concepts from anthropology, sociology, and medicine interlocked in the definition
and explication of normal *vs.* abnormal behavior. He acknowledged that concepts such as schizophrenia had a cultural basis but
also that the illness behaviors that they glossed might have universalistic meanings, although the behaviors might require a cultural
(emic) interpretation. Wallace's essay on the possible role of diet

and ecology in the genesis of native psychiatric and folk illnesses
among Alaskans underlined the problems of a narrow purely cultural or psychological approach and drew emphasis to the need of
paying attention to local, culturally specific as well as biological
and generic universalistic factors in any understanding of what
passes for a psychiatric illness.

Leighton et al. brought a culturally sensitive yet strict epidemiological approach to cross-cultural psychiatry. They concentrated
on Western nosological entities among the Yoruba and indicated
that such entities were valid there in the Nigerian setting because
native understandings and conventions of illness incorporated the
behaviors in question and, moreover, they were able to diagnose
the conditions in their field epidemiological study. The psychiatric
studies of Beiser et al. (1976), Murphy (1976), and Hughes
(1985), all early associates of Leighton, constituted forceful statements of the universalistic position with respect to psychiatric illness. What these latter researchers showed is that descriptions of
Western psychiatric illnesses (such as schizophrenia) are cross-
culturally valid. Not only can the Western criteria of psychiatric
illness be used to realistically and meaningfully diagnose persons
in other cultures (the etic perspective is valid and empirically fea-
sible), but the peoples themselves judge and respond to the (illness) behaviors in question in a manner that clearly identifies
them as abnormal and as medical (the emic perspective supports
the universality of psychiatric illness). The thrust of these researchers, then, was to invalidate the illegitimate claims of vulgar
cultural relativists pertaining to normal and abnormal behavior
(see above); but because of their heavily epidemiological and
hence narrow focus (see below), they tended to weaken the legitimate claims implicit in the construct of cultural relativism.

The universalistic assertions of cross-cultural and epidemiological psychiatrists need to be seen in relation to contemporary neurobiological emphases. Typical of this universalistic trend are the
rationale and findings of the IPSS (Leff, 1981; Sartorius et al.,
1977, 1986). Through reliance on quintessential Anglo-American
and Western European nosological psychiatric diagnostic criteria,
these researchers are able to confidently diagnose psychiatric illness in diverse settings and convince themselves and most of their
critics that such illnesses have the same configuration. However,
interesting differences regarding the duration and course of illness
in developed *vs.* underdeveloped nations have been uncovered,
and these have so far eluded full understanding. The IPSS symbol-
izes two important but contradictory themes: a) because of the
apparent ease of cross-cultural diagnosis, a theme emphasizing
universalistic claims within psychiatry that appears to strongly
weaken if not obliterate the challenges posed by the concept of cultural relativism; and b) because of the demonstration of national
differences in duration and course and a failure to explain these, a
theme that weakens the relevance of a pure biomedical approach to
the understanding of psychiatric illness cross-culturally.

EXPLAINING CULTURAL VARIATION IN PSYCHOPATHOLOGY IN BIOMEDICAL PSYCHIATRY

In the theory of biomedical psychiatry, local, particularistic, and/or specific cultural factors do not play a central role in the way the manifestations of psychiatric illness are explained (see below for contrast). Such illnesses are considered an outcome of the way disease mechanisms operate on substrates that are generic to homo sapiens. Manifestations glossed as anxiety, depressive mood, and disordered thinking, for example, are conceptualized as having an anatomical, chemical, and physiological base in the central nervous system. In other words, generic (pan-human) neurological properties of the hominoid way of life constitute the basic template in and through which psychiatric illness manifestations are believed to be produced. The indicators of the major disorders are held to be culture free. The rationale followed to ascertain cases in epidemiological research relies heavily on such indicators and underestimates the importance of behavioral phenomena that may reveal the operation of (unexpected, unsearched for) cultural influences (Fabrega, 1974b; Kleinman, 1977).

Ironically, however, it is not altogether true that biomedical psychiatrists make no use of the role played by social and cultural factors. The hominoid way of life is quintessentially social and cultural, and brain maturation necessarily involves an enculturation that produces a symbolic mode of existence (Geertz, 1962; Hallowell, 1960; Washburn, 1961). Indeed, biomedical psychiatric theory appears to incorporate a basic anthropological tenet about the biocultural unity of humans that is also integral to the thinking of sociobiologists (Wilson, 1975). Moreover, biomedical psychiatry has pointed to differences in the psychopharmacological responses of cultural groups that suggest physiological differences between them, although what these differences are due to and their possible relevance for understanding the role of culture on psychopathology are currently unclear (Lin et al., 1986). In summary, it is the possible extent and significance of the more local, particularistic, or specific cultural differences (which are superimposed on biocultural commonalities derived from evolution) that appear underemphasized in biomedical psychiatry.

Universalistic psychiatry has played down the apparent uniqueness of culture-bound syndromes (*e.g.,* amok, witiko psychosis) through the use of concepts such as personality, hysteria, and pathoplasty (Littlewood and Lipsedge, 1985; Yap, 1974). These concepts are used to explain the processes that account for the variegated appearances of such syndromes. Controversy exists as to whether culture-bound syndromes are truly psychiatric entities or merely exotic "folk" medical illnesses and whether, if they are psychiatric in nature, they are atypical variants of recognized Western disorders or truly unique. By defining such syndromes as behavioral and "poorly understood," some psychiatrists have been able to preserve the basic tenets and assumptions that posit a universal psychopathology (Manschreck and Petri, 1978).

A recent formulation of culture-bound syndromes invokes the idea of underlying universal and hence biologically grounded *behavioral taxa* as a way of ordering and classifying them (Simons and Hughes, 1985). It is suggested that brain-encoded mechanisms produced by human evolution created a limited number of behavioral ways (taxonomic profiles) in which maladaptation can be realized and that these behavioral taxa underlie the disorders. Many seemingly different culture-bound syndromes are really alike, reflecting the same underlying biological constraints. In this formulation, culture and language are viewed as providing only the surface content and coverings of basic humanoid forms of behavior that condition the syndromes. Such a formulation is similar if not identical to one that posits that disorders such as schizophrenia and depression are to be thought of as associated with underlying pan-human regularities (*e.g.,* "depressive taxa"), also conditioned by human evolution, to which local or specific cultural influences add but trivial and superficial trappings. Finally, one must appreciate that the reasoning here is consistent with that involving universals in the facial expression of emotion, perception of color and sound in newborns, folk biological classifications, and universals in personality descriptors. All of these regularities raise the question of brain mechanisms underlying human psychological behavior (Fabrega, 1977, 1981a, b). Nevertheless, in the alleged differences between biology and culture (roughly analogized as structure-form *vs.* content-meaning), one finds seemingly irreconcilable disagreements between universalists and relativists (*e.g.,* Kenny, 1983; Simons, 1980). Many culture-specific behavioral *reactions,* of course, do not constitute illness, by either local or outside observer-imposed criteria (*i.e.,* emic *vs.* etic); nor can they easily be equated with underlying neurobiological (disease) changes. Some are better seen as social (or symbolic) inversions, with the reactions exaggerating or reversing (thus indirectly affirming) pre-existing models of behavior and providing the individual and group with social benefits or at least with a means of expressing socioculturally induced stress, thus helping to resolve social crises (Fabrega and Mezzich, 1987; Littlewood and Lipsedge, 1985).

THE WESTERN PICTURE OF PSYCHIATRIC ILLNESS

A common phenomenology of the self and subjectivity anchors the study of psychiatric illness in contemporary biomedical psychiatry. Such a phenomenology was implicit in the early descriptions of psychiatric illness and has received its most visible expression in the formulations of theorists who have developed and used the Present State Examination (PSE; Wing et al., 1974).

Its queries illustrate this "Western picture" of the self and of psychiatric illness, for when carefully analyzed they presuppose a culturally distinctive model of a healthy and sick person. Key ideas, such as "physical health," "relaxing," "anxiety," "control over thinking," and "feeling depressed" are integral to a Western phenomenology. The items that involve delusions all imply, in addition to the notions of beliefs ("mental" attributes of the self), a specific ontology of the world, forces, or agencies that operate in it, and matters involving the control of human action and worldly happenings that are obviously conditioned by European culture and society (Fabrega, in press).

Given the quintessentially Western picture, if not bias, of self and schizophrenia in biomedical psychiatry generally and in the instruments used to ascertain schizophrenia in cross-cultural studies more specifically, the claims of success in epidemiological studies that rely on this cultural model are remarkable. A brief review of the difficulties encountered by Gillis et al. (1982) in their study of the Xhosa-speaking in Cape Town will prove instructive. The authors begin with a cautionary note: "The biggest problem lies in getting an understanding of the intent of the question which often has to be put in the spirit of the inquiry rather than the prescribed letter of the PSE . . ." (Gillis et al., 1982, p. 144). This warning orients the reader to the need for a more narrative/ explanatory (indeed educational if not indoctrinative) mode of elicitation, as opposed to a strictly interrogatory mode, that will allow probing sharply into self-awareness and interpretation. Gillis et al. also a) refer to many "linguistic distinctions which are second nature to Westerners," but not easily made in the Xhosa language, the emphases of which "may not lie in the same areas as in English"; b) point out the difficulty of properly metaphorizing the emotional experience of depression; c) acknowledge the impropriety of analogizing the self with a physical space in which thoughts move "round and round" ["Tribal people cannot comprehend the term 'worry' (item 4) and indicate that "in Xhosa one worries with one's heart"]; d) the notion of higher mental functions, of "concentration," of "thoughts drifting," and of "states of mind" simply have "no close translation" or, they found "impossible to get the idiomatic phraseology of . . ." (p. 144). Their admonition: "The question, 'Do you constantly have to question the meaning of the universe?' is virtually incomprehensible for the African universe is completely meaningful within the context of their beliefs" (p. 144) points out graphically the matter of ontology and causal bases/interpretations of reality and of differences in the "behavioral environments" of a people (see above). The "concepts of derealization" proved difficult to get across to the Xhosa and "the notion of delusional mood . . . is often beyond the tribal Xhosa." In addition to such purely linguistic and cognitive difficulties, Gillis et al. discuss problems related to reality/life experiences/environmental factors as well as cultural factors. With regard to the latter, consider the following remarks: a) "Many of

the difficulties in administering the PSE arise out of a different world view" (p. 145); b) ". . . a positive reply to the question (involving control by forces or powers other than oneself) does not necessarily indicate ideas of influence or control [since] . . . everyone is directly or indirectly affected . . . by beliefs and activities connected with [mystical] power . . ." (p. 145); and finally, c) with respect to the Xhosa-speaking native, "One has to bear in mind that ancestors live in the same psychic world as the individual and their influence can be tangible [insofar as the ancestors] call him by name and the voice may be extremely difficult to distinguish from an auditory hallucination" (p. 145).

In spite of these differences in linguistic and cultural background, Gillis et al. were of the "unanimous opinion" that their interviewers, although challenged by such differences, were able "to produce definite answers to the prescribed questions" (p. 146). Furthermore, "our experience with the PSE has also brought us to the important conviction that the experiential events of psychiatric disturbances and the elements of psychiatric illness defined by it exist in the Xhosa, *and do not differ from those amongst English speaking peoples* . . . (and any differences in the manner by which they are expressed or described) . . . are ascribable to cultural [*vs.* universalistic, biomedical, physiological?] factors" (p. 147, emphasis added).

From conclusions such as these, one is led to believe that language and cognition are unproblematically separated from each other and from culture, and that the latter is something external that merely beclouds the universal brain/mind events that characterize the individualistic self in its secularized and "scientific" (realistic or naturalized) world and during states of psychiatric illness. Although the problem has been viewed differently by specialists in linguistics and cultural anthropology (as well as in philosophy and Marxists' and neo-Marxists' accounts of knowledge more generally), a full account of these issues cannot be pursued here (Comaroff, 1982; Taussig, 1980). What is at stake in claims such as the above is the very difficult problem of unraveling relations between language and culture: The former can be thought of as the mechanics of saying something, the latter as how and when to say something that is appropriate and meaningful. A competent native speaker has learned the mechanics of producing grammatically correct sentences and, more importantly, how to use this mechanism in light of the common cultural understandings of his group. A knowledge of the world and a knowledge of what co-members know and expect in a specific social situation constitute the the internal map or model that guides the competent native speaker to utter comprehensible sentences. To understand what people say, thus, requires far more than knowledge of the language per se. In brief, the correct interpretation of queries about psychopathology requires full understandings of a native's linguistic knowledge and his/her cultural knowledge (Keesing, 1979). The cultural part involves knowledge of persons, spirits, or outside agents that influence the self, social situations in which this can occur, etc., as well as models of the self that are not dualistic or models of the world that do not rest on linear causal chains. The model of self in the PSE is Western European, but it is applied to people with far different models. In brief, given the disqualifications necessary to make the PSE "work" in this setting, disqualifications that include basic assumptions in its rationale, one is led to question the value of affirming its validity as a diagnostic tool. Psychiatrists from the "Third World" have argued cogently for the inclusion of clinical phenomena less mentalistic in content and for an awareness and rectification of the biases of Western psychiatric nosologies (Lambo, 1965; Wig, 1985).

THE EPISTEMOLOGICAL BIAS OF WESTERN BIOMEDICAL PSYCHIATRY

There is little doubt, then, that in some ways a culturally specific epistemological bias is operative in the Western conceptualization of psychiatric illness. In this section, we seek to further contextualize this bias. To begin, there exists an epistemological bias in the explanation of behavior and in the conceptualization of the self documented by cultural anthropologists, linguists and philosophers. The role of language and metaphor in constituting a domain and rendering it important as a cultural object has been explicated by Lakoff and Johnson (1980), who use a variety of mentalistic objects to illustrate their thesis. Lutz (1985) has suggested that the discipline of psychology is grounded in and a product of Western notions of self—a Western ethnopsychology, as it were. In light of such generalizations, one can say that the symbols upon which individuals draw to explain subjectivity and behavior and, more generally, to express their sense of personal integrity and the disturbances that mar it, are rooted in culturally constituted themes and objects. In Anglo-American societies, the mentalistic/psychological sphere is dominant. Many social historians have grappled with the problem of when and how such ways of conceptualizing self and human behavior developed, seeing these as outcomes of historically rooted experiences involving religious, legal, and political issues (Davis, 1986; Morris, 1972; Ullman, 1967; Weintraub, 1978). Social historians of psychiatry have provided rich and tantalizing views of ways that Western cultural suppositions may have colored psychopathology (Kroll and Bachrach, 1984; MacDonald, 1981).

Exactly where and how cultures and languages locate and explain phenomena, such as essential attributes of awareness, the self, and the meanings/rationale of behavior, will vary greatly despite uniformities built into the structures of the body, the physiology of the brain, and the physical habitat (Fabrega, 1981a, b). A psychological epistemological bias is a mode of explanation in which subjective experiences and internal nonmaterial aspects of the self are given priority. When applied to psychiatric illness,

such a bias means an emphasis on cognition, emotion, and related mentalistic structures, events processes, or attitudes as the critical parameters of psychiatric illnesses—in short, our concept of psychopathology. Kirmayer (1984) has termed this epistemological bias "psychologization."

Schizophrenia and depression, as examples, are psychiatric illnesses that are largely defined and identified in terms of parameters of thought and emotion. Whether schizophrenia and depression primarily affect or are manifest in these spheres can be argued. Because psychiatric illnesses are manifest in whole persons, it is reasonable to assume that manifestations of such illnesses will span many different systems and spheres of behavior. In this light, the somatic sphere is one that appears de-emphasized in Anglo-American psychiatry. The range of factors (historical and cultural) that make somatization an important domain of medicine and psychiatry in contemporary China have recently been emphasized, and they illuminate by contrast peculiarities and idiosyncracies of Anglo-American society (Kleinman, 1986). The somatic sphere is one that traditionally, and in light of recent modern historical developments, the Chinese (and their medical care system) have heavily emphasized, whereas the mentalistic sphere is comparatively underemphasized. Phenomena we term depression have for these reasons a different appearance in China. Whether the manifestations of schizophrenia may also show striking somatic sorts of symptoms cross-culturally is not clear, but even Western researchers draw attention to the neurological aspects of schizophrenia (Kolakowska et al., 1985; Manschreck et al., 1982; and Marsden, 1982).

CULTURAL RELATIVISM AND SOMATIZATION

The idea of somatization as a special type of illness or source of explanation for a medical problem is something of an anomaly when one examines it in relation to the idea of cultural relativism and in an ethnomedical (comparative) point of view. In recent times, such phenomena were conceptualized as specious if not fictive medical problems, and they still carry such associations to some extent. This is so because modern biomedicine has evolved a theory that stipulates that underlying physical *disease* changes are the primary or basic (*i.e.,* ontologically "real") changes that account for "surface" illness pictures, and somatization phenomena typically cannot be related to such changes. Among peoples in nonindustrial or non-Western societies the idea of specious or unauthentic medical problems is not meaningful and is not encountered (Hughes, 1968). For such people, perceived changes in the "territory" of the body are basic clues to understanding how the outside and spiritual worlds function, and conceptualizations about the latter territories usually explain its dysfunctions

(Fabrega, 1976a). In short, changes in bodily perceptions and reports of bodily symptoms and complaints are accepted as determinative of a "real" medical entity. In all types of societies hidden things (*e.g.,* spirits, viruses, genes, sorcery) play a role in accounting for illnesses, and culture stipulates their reality. If the documentation of "unseen" factors is necessary in order to validate an illness as real, then it is possible to invalidate some of them if such factors are judged not to be present. However, the idea of specious or unauthentic illness has gained ascendancy in societies dominated by biomedical science. It follows that a theory of illness that invokes unseen or hidden agencies constitutes a necessary but not sufficient condition for the idea of a fictive or unauthentic illness (or for the idea of somatization itself) to prevail, and aspects of our culture, social structure, political economy, and the role of physicians and scientists in all of this play a role as well.[2]

The fact that culture determines what is real about a medical problem raises the question of an epistemological basis for an ontology of so-called folk illnesses. Culture-bound "psychiatric" syndromes are types of folk illnesses (natively defined, treated, theorized about, etc.) but by convention (in line with the psychologization bias of Western psychiatry), they have been viewed as psychiatric. In contrast, other folk illnesses, for example, Susto in Latin America, are viewed as nonpsychiatric in nature, presumably because of their general, somatic, and social existential components (Rubel et al., 1984). However, culture shapes somatization and influences the production of illness in many ways: through definitions of persons and selves, which emphasize the body; by creating stressors, which promote and condition somatic and behavioral responses; by elaborating ethnophysiological and ethnopsychological theories of illness; by sanctioning behavioral models of illness; and by constituting practitioner roles and medical practices geared to the culturally defined illnesses. Hence, one can conclude that many folk illnesses (not just the "psychiatric" ones) are to some extent culturally formed and behaviorally produced and of relevance to a cultural psychiatry in just the same way that somatization phenomena are "psychiatric." Some folk illnesses, of course, including Susto, unequivocally have an organic base and cannot be explained as "cultural somatization," and this is certainly not being claimed. The basic point is that the "psychologization" bias within traditional psychiatry has narrowed the focus of what is considered relevant in cross-cultural studies. If psychiatry is thought to embrace the study of somatization, then folk illnesses are also its purview.

Just as somatization phenomena and folk illnesses reflect local particularistic and specific cultural influences (cultural relativism), they also reflect more generic biological ones (universalism). This is the case because such medical problems underscore ethological and evolutionary concerns, reinforcing the notion of the biocultural unity of humanity. In other words, an individual with a "somatization problem" or a folk illness is showing com-

promised adaptation, which is reflected in an illness picture that blends the psychological and somatic; moreover, such responses are natural in that they have a biocultural and ethnomedical rationale. To make this point is but to argue for the appropriateness of a holistic model in medicine (Engel, 1977).

In summary, this discussion has emphasized three interrelated concepts: a) the Western epistemological bias, b) somatization, and c) cultural relativism. The first cautions that the heavy emphasis on emotion and cognition in accounts of psychiatric illness stems from the Western cultural tradition. The second draws attention to the basic importance of bodily responses in illness generally, noting that such responses are integral to the way social and environmental stress and maladaptive behavior are realized. The third indicates that the appearance, meaning, and consequences of psychiatric illness or any illness differ as a function of culture. This symbolic/conceptual core constitutes the self and its behavioral environment and facilitates (or inhibits) response tendencies in many "levels" and/or "systems" of the person through complementary influences in brain organization and function, local interpersonal contexts, and the prevailing social structure and political economy.

THE CURRENT STATUS OF THE CONCEPT OF CULTURAL RELATIVISM

It was indicated earlier that the rationale and methods of the universalists and relativists are somewhat at odds. So are their objectives. The former seeks a cumulated base of scientific knowledge that provides understanding of psychiatric illness in a general (universal, etically extended) frame of reference. This enterprise is intrinsic to our discipline. Understanding and clarifying the etiology of an illness are crucial first steps toward its prudent control and, eventually, its elimination. Epidemiological science is a central tool in this enterprise.

The relativist, on the other hand, seeks detailed, multilayered, and culturally valid descriptions of illness and related phenomena and relies on different sciences. Analyzing the rationale and mode of operation of ethnomedical systems is a dominant concern. Relativists tend to believe that medical values are culturally grounded so that any one ethnomedical system, including the Western one, seeks something different from another; hence, all should be judged in context and valued accordingly (Fabrega, 1976b). The "hard" relativist eschews biomedical concepts, assumptions, and goals and feels that they are products of a culturally determined epistemology rooted in the social structure, political economy, and materialist ideologies of modern Western capitalist societies. The agenda of biomedicine is likely to be judged as ill-conceived and pernicious, because it has no warrant in another culture and cannot be imposed there without destroying its viability and integrity. To the extent that hard relativists circumscribe epistemologies and ontologies and see them as incommensurable, they endorse a cultural determinism (Spiro, 1986).

Given these opposing views of concepts, methods, rationales, and objectives, it is not surprising that the concept of cultural relativism and its application with respect to the study of psychiatric illness and medical systems more generally has been seen not only as ambiguous and obscure but also as challenging, provocative, and ultimately stultifying to the claims and pursuits of universalists within psychiatry. A basic need is that of a universal set of categories, metalanguage, and/or theory that would enable one to transcend cultural differences and build a cumulated ethnomedical science. The value of concentrating on illness and its manifest behavioral appearance while acknowledging the reality of biology has been emphasized (Fabrega, 1975b, 1976c).

If the assertions of a hard relativist were to be dominate, the enterprise of biomedical psychiatry would be undermined and a universal science of psychiatric illness (and of ethnomedicine more generally) could not evolve. Contemporary researchers in the field of cultural psychiatry who ascribe power to cultural relativism (relativists) are actually also universalists insofar as they take seriously some of the basic tenets of biomedical psychiatry and seek to study psychiatric illness and related behavioral - disorders cross-culturally. They are likely to endorse a systems approach and to see the "realities" of an illness or behavioral disorder in different levels, including neurobiology. In other words, there is something real and "biological" about depression, schizophrenia, and, for example, hormonal and autonomic nervous system changes associated with the climacterium. How these are understood and played out in a society, however, is also real but differs cross-culturally; the task is to clarify why and how this is so. The discovery of a root lesion or biological marker for a psychiatric disorder would in no way deter the efforts of contemporary cultural psychiatrists from explicating the influence of cultural factors in affecting what a disorder looks like and how it is brought about or played out. As relativists they are committed to the idea that particularistic and local cultural and social factors influence cause, manifestations, duration/outcome, and distribution of psychiatric phenomena in a special way. They claim, moreover, that many Anglo-American psychiatric illness entities as currently formulated are themselves (Western) culture-bound and are being inappropriately exported as though they were universal.[2] Thus, taking a relativistic perspective seriously, contemporary cultural psychiatrists propose dialectical, integrative, and biopsychosocial models of psychiatric illness, with culture operationalized as a research variable. In other words, the possibility of cultural influences is always entertained when studying any parameter of illness, and the researcher views culture as one of several relevant variables. Biomedical formulations of behavior disturbances constitute a good starting model of the way human adaptive behavior can be altered in the context of inherited vulnerabilities and environmental and social stress which inevitably are associated with changes in biological systems.

The drift of biomedical psychiatry is toward neurobiological explanations of psychopathology. Thus, the cognitive changes of schizophrenia are attributed to deficits in attention regulation and information processing. These in turn result from impairments of the mesolimbic system. The neurovegetative changes of depression and menopause are attributed to changes in subcortical neuroendocrine systems. Pushed to its extreme, this is the position of biological reductionism. To a relativist, it is also a form of cultural determinism and offers incomplete explanations. One who endorses a contemporary relativistic (not a determinist) perspective will explain part of such "physiological behavior" as a result of alterations in the experience of personhood (or selfhood). In other words, just as one may hold that neurobiological changes are fundamental features of psychopathology and/or psychiatric illness, one can hold that an altered phenomenology of the self in the context of prevailing cultural conventions is also fundamental. For example, schizophrenic "psychopathology" reflects an alteration of the ability of the self to orient symbolically in its culturally created and structured world (Fabrega, in press); neurovegetative symptoms of depression flow from the altered meanings life now has for the altered "depressed" self (Kleinman and Good, 1985); the "menopause" picture devolves from changes in self-perception of women due to failure to conceive, given the cultural conventions of their society about women and social worth or purpose (Lock, 1986). Even basic neuropsychological changes should be construed in biocultural terms; that is, as involving brain mechanisms and processes that reflect an enculturation in which native symbolic rules and schemata shape interpretations of reality, including conceptualizations of the self (Fabrega, 1977, 1979, 1981a, b). Suffice it to say that one who endorses a cultural relativistic, in contrast to a rigidly universalistic, position acknowledges the importance of neurobiological phenomena, but sees the basic ground of psychopathology as consisting of *both* cultural/symbolic and biological/neurological phenomena. Attemps to establish the "essential" basis or "real nature" of a disorder are judged as theoretically flawed.

REFERENCES

Beiser M, Benfari RC, Collomb H, Ravel JL (1976) Measuring psychoneurotic behavior in cross-cultural surveys. *J Nerv Ment Dis* 16:10–23.

Blumer H (1969) *Symbolic interactionism: Perspective and method.* Englewood Cliffs, NJ: Prentice-Hall.

Brody EB (1964) Some conceptual and methodological issues involved in research on society, culture, and mental illness. *J Nerv Ment Dis* 139:62–74.

Comaroff J (1982) Medicine, symbol and ideology. In P Wright, A Treacher (Eds), *The problem of medical knowledge* (pp 49–68). Edinburgh: Edinburgh University Press.

D'Andrade RG (1984) Cultural meaning systems. In RA Shweder, RA LeVine (Eds), *Cultural theory: Essays on mind, self, and emotion* (pp 88–119). Cambridge, MA: Cambridge University Press.

Davis NZ (1986) Boundaries and the sense of self in sixteenth-century France. In TC Heller, M Sosna, DE Wellbery (Eds), *Reconstructing individualism: Autonomy, individuality and the self in western thought* (pp 53–63). Stanford, CA: Stanford University Press.

Edgerton, RB (1969) On the recognition of mental illness. In SC Plog, RB Edgerton (Eds), *Changing perspectives in mental illness* (pp 49–72). New York: Holt, Rinehard and Winston.

Engel G (1977) The need for a new medical model: A challenge for biomedicine. *Science* 196:129–136.

Fabrega H (1974a) *Disease and social behavior: An interdisciplinary perspective.* Cambridge, MA: MIT Press.

Fabrega H (1974b) Problems implicit in the cultural and social study of depression. *Psychosom Med* 36:377–398.

Fabrega H (1975a) The position of psychiatry in the understanding of human disease. *Arch Gen Psychiatry* 32:1500–1512.

Fabrega H (1975b) The need for an ethnomedical science. *Science* 189:969–975.

Fabrega H (1976a) The biological significance of taxonomies of disease. *J Theoret Biol* 63:191–216.

Fabrega H (1976b) The function of medical care systems. *Perspect Biol Med* Autumn:108–119.

Fabrega H (1976c) Towards a theory of human disease. *J Nerv Ment Dis* 162:299–312.

Fabrega H (1977) Culture, behavior and the nervous system. *Ann Rev Anthropol* 6:419–455.

Fabrega H (1979) Neurobiology, culture, and behavior disturbances: An integrative review. *J Nerv Ment Dis* 167:467–474.

Fabrega H (1981a) Culture, biology and the study of disease. In HR Rothschild (Ed), *Biocultural aspects of disease* (pp 54–95). New York: Academic.

Fabrega H (1981b) Cultural programming of brain-behavior relations. In JR Merkingas (Ed), *A neuropsychiatric emphasis in brain behavior relationships* (pp 1–63). Lexington, MA: Heath.

Fabrega H (1987) Psychiatric diagnosis: A cultural perspective. *J Nerv Ment Dis* 175:383–394.

Fabrega H (in press) The self and schizophrenia: A cultural perspective. *Schizophr Bull.*

Fabrega H, Mezzich JE (1987) Adjustment disorder and psychiatric practice: Cultural and historical aspects. *Psychiatry* 50:31–49.

Garfinkel H (1967) Studies in ethnomethodology. Englewood Cliffs, NJ: Prentice-Hall.

Geertz C (1973) The growth of culture and the evolution of mind. In C Geertz, *The interpretation of cultures* (pp 55–83). New York: Basic.

Gillis LS, Elk R, Ben-Arie O, Teggin A (1982) The Present State Examination: Experiences with Xhosa-speaking psychiatric patients. *Br J Psychiatry* 141:143–147.

Goffman E (1963) *Behavior in public places: Notes on the social organization of gatherings.* New York: Free Press.

Hallowell AI (1960) Self, socity and culture in phylogenetic perspective. In S Tax (Ed), *Evolution after Darwin: The evolution of man* (Vol 2, pp 309–371). Chicago: University of Chicago Press.

Hughes CC (1968) Ethnomedicine. *International encyclopedia of the social sciences* (Sec 1, pp 87–93). New York: Macmillan.

Hughes CC (1985) Culture-bound or construct bound? The syndromes and DSM-III. In RC Simons, CC Hughes (Eds), *The culture bound syndromes* (pp 3–24). Boston: Reidel.

Keesing RM (1979) Linguistic knowledge and cultural knowledge: Some doubts and speculations. *Am Anthropol* 81:14–36.

Kenny MG (1983) The Latah problem revisited. *J Nerv Ment Dis* 171:159–167.

Kirmayer LJ (1984) Cultural affect and somatization. *Transcultural Psychiatr Res Rev* 21:159–188, 237–262.

Kleinman A (1977) Depression, somatization and the new cross-cultural psychiatry. *Soc Sci Med* 11:3–10.

Kleinman A (1986) *Social origins of distress and disease.* New Haven, CT: Yale University Press.

Kleinman A, Good B (1985) *Culture and depression: Studies in the anthropology and cross-cultural psychiatry of affect and disorder.* Berkeley: University of California Press.

Kolakowska T, Williams AO, Jambor K, Ardern M (1985) Schizophrenia with good and poor outcome. III: Neurological 'soft' signs, cognitive impairment and their clinical significance. *Br J Psychiatry* 146:348–357.

Kroll J, Bachrach B (1984) Sin and mental illness in the middle ages. *Psychol Med* 14:507–514.

Laing RD (1968) *The politics of experience.* Harmondsworth: Penguin.

Lakoff G, Johnson M (1980) *Metaphors we live by.* Chicago: University of Chicago Press.

Lambo TA (1965) Schizophrenic and borderline states. In VA DeReuck, R Porter (Eds), *Transcultural psychiatry* (pp 62–74). Boston: Little, Brown.

Leff J (1981) *Psychiatry around the globe: A transcultural view.* New York: Marcel Dekker.

Leighton AH, Lambdo TA, Hughes CC, et al (1963) *Psychiatric disorder among the Yoruba.* Ithaca, NY: Cornell University Press.

Lemert E (1951) *Social pathology.* New York: McGraw-Hill.

LeVine RA (1983) *Culture, behavior and personality.* Chicago: Aldine.

Lin K-M, Poland RE, Lesser IM (1986) Ethnicity and psychopharmacology. *Cult Med Psychiatry* 10:151–165.

Littlewood R, Lipsedge M (1985) Culture bound syndromes. In K Granville-Grossman (Ed), *Recent advances in clinical psychiatry* (pp 105–142). Edinburgh: Churchill Livingstone.

Lock M (1986) Ambiguities of aging: Japanese experiences and perceptions of menopause. *Cult Med Psychiatry* 10:23–46.

Lutz C (1985) Ethnopsychology compared to what? Explaining behavior and consciousness among the Ifaluk. In GM White, J Kirkpatrick (Eds), *Person, self and experience: Exploring Pacific ethnopsychologies* (pp 35–79). Berkeley, CA: University of California Press.

MacDonald M (1981) *Mystical bedlam.* Cambridge, England: Cambridge Press.

Manschreck TC, Maher BA, Rucklos ME, Vereen DR (1982) Disturbed voluntary motor activity in schizophrenic disorder. *Psychol Med* 12:73–84.

Manschreck TC, Petri M (1978) The atypical psychoses. *Cult Med Psychiatry* 2:233–268.

Marsden CD (1982) Motors disorders in schizophrenia. *Psychol Med* 12:13–15.

Mead GH (1934) *Mind, self and society.* Chicago: University of Chicago Press.

Morris C (1972) *The discovery of the individual 1050–1200.* New York: Harper & Row.

Murphy HBM (1982) *Comparative psychiatry.* New York: Springer-Verlag.

Murphy JM (1976) Psychiatric labeling in cross cultural perspective. *Science* 191:1019–1028.

Rubel AJ, O'Neil CW, Collado-Ardon R (1984) *Susto, a folk illness.* Berkeley, CA: University of California Press.

Sartorius N, Jablensky A, Korten A, et al (1986) Early manifestations and first-contact incidence of schizophrenia in different cultures. *Psychol Med* 16:909–928.

Sartorious N, Jablensky A, Shapiro R (1977) Two-year follow-up of the patients included in the WHO international pilot study of schizophrenia. *Psychol Med* 7:529–541.

Scheff TJ (1966) *Being mentally ill.* Chicago: Aldine.

Scull A (1979) *Museums of madness.* New York: St. Martins Press.

Simons RC (1980) The resolution of the Latah paradox. *J Nerv Ment Dis* 168:195–206.

Simons RC, Hughes CC (Eds)(1985) *The culture-bound syndromes.* Boston: Reidel.

Sprio ME (1986) Cultural relativism and the future of anthropology. *Cult Anthropol* 1(3): 259–286.

Szasz T (1961) *The myth of mental illness.* New York: Hoeber-Harper.

Taussig MT (1980) Reification and consciousness of the patient. *Soc Sci Med* 14b:3–13.

Ullman W (1967) *The individual and society in the middle age.* Baltimore: Johns Hopkins University Press.

Wallace AFC (1961) Mental illness, biology, and culture. In FLK Hsu (Ed), *Psychological anthropology: Approaches to culture and personality* (pp 255–295). Chicago: Dorsey.

Washburn SL (Ed) (1961) *Social life of early man.* Chicago: Aldine.

Waxler NE (1974) Culture and mental disease: A social labeling perspective. *J Nerv Ment Dis* 159:379–395.

Weintraub KJ (1978) The value of the individual: Self and circumstance in autobiography. Chicago: Chicago University Press.

Wig NN (1985) Standardized assessment in developing countries. *Acta Psychiatr Belg* 85:429–433.

Wilson EO (1975) Sociobiology: The new synthesis. Cambridge, MA: Balknap Press of Harvard University Press.

Wing JK, Cooper JE, Sartorius N (1974) *The description and classification of psychiatric symptoms: An instruction manual for the PSE and category system.* Cambridge, England: Cambridge University Press.

Yap PM (1974) In MP Lau, AB Stokes (Eds), *Comparative psychiatry: A theoretical framework.* Toronto: University of Toronto Press.

CHAPTER TWO

Culture and Clinical Reality

Clinical reality refers to the cognitive construction of reality in the clinical setting. Clinical reality is created by the clinician and the patient within a clinical context employing their learned cultural schemas.

Culture affects the clinical reality of mental illness in five ways (based on Kleinman, 1980):

1. Culture-based subjective experience
2. Culture-based idioms of distress
3. Culture-based diagnoses
4. Culture-based treatments
5. Culture-based outcomes

The first way that culture affects the clinical reality of mental illness is through *culture-based subjective experience*. This refers to the tendency of cultural schemas to structure an individual's experience of illness. For example, a person raised in western culture might view a depressive illness in biological terms even though no specific brain disease causing a major depressive episode has been identified. As is stated in DSM-IV, "No laboratory findings that are diagnostic of a Major Depressive Episode have been identified" (APA, 1994, p. 323). Nevertheless, a patient could view him- or herself as having such a problem. This is because of culture. Western culture tends to emphasize the biomedical paradigm, which defines depression as a biological problem.

The second way that culture affects the clinical reality of mental illness is through *culture-based idioms of distress*. Idioms of distress are the ways patients behave to express that they are ill. Physical actions, including seeking out clinical care, and mannerisms, figures of speech, and cognitive emphasis on certain symptoms while ignoring others are all idioms of distress. For example, westerners are more likely than persons in some other cultures to place more importance on depressive symptoms rather than on somatic symptoms, and to seek out a psychiatrist (Kleinman, 1988a).

The third way that culture affects the clinical reality of mental illness is through *culture-based diagnosis*. This refers to the way clinicians assess and diagnose a mental disorder in a manner that is consistent with their own cultural background and culture-based professional training. For example, American psy-

chiatrists and Japanese psychiatrists are likely to view the same patients differently.

The fourth way that culture affects the clinical reality of mental illness is through *culture-based treatment*. This refers to the appropriate treatment for an illness as defined by the indigenous clinical reality or the clinician's own clinical paradigm. In the case of a western psychiatrist treating a client with depression, the appropriate treatment defined by the clinical reality is most likely to be antidepressant medications or electroconvulsive therapy.

The fifth way that culture affects the clinical reality of mental illness is through *culture-based outcomes*. This refers to the outcomes that occur because an illness has been cognitively constructed and treated in a particular cultural fashion. For example, if a person suffering from a depressive illness related to social stress or loss of important relationships is treated exclusively for a brain disease, the outcome may be less than optimal.

The biomedical paradigm tends to decontextualize and dehumanize a client's emotional processes, ignoring traumatic life events and reducing personal and emotional problems to an imbalance in brain biochemistry. Kleinman, Eisenberg, and Good (1978) have referred to this dehumanization of patients' emotional lives as a "veterinary" style of clinical practice. The mental patient is reduced to nothing more than a "broken brain," without regard to environmental circumstances, emotional trauma, or shattered relationships (Fleck, 1995).

Researchers have learned that clients may cognitively construct an experience of mental illness one way as the doctor or folk healer cognitively constructs it in a different way, based on their different cultural schemas. The client could experience the illness as one particular kind of problem, and the clinician could diagnose it as something entirely different. This is the distinction made by medical anthropologists between the ideas of illness and disease.

The term *illness* refers to the subjective experience of the patient. It is the subjective experience of being sick, including the experience of symptoms, suffering, help seeking, side effects of treatment, social stigma, explanations of causes, diagnosis, prognosis, as well as personal consequences in family life and occupation (Kleinman, 1988b).

19

In contrast, the term *disease* refers to the diagnosis of the doctor or folk healer. It is the clinician's definition of the patient's problem, always taken from the paradigm of disease in which the clinician was trained. For example, a disease-centered psychiatrist is trained to diagnose brain diseases, a psychoanalyst is trained to diagnose psychodynamic problems, and a nonwestern folk healer might be trained to diagnose such things as spirit possession or sorcery. In each case, the clinician's diagnosis is the "disease."

In medical anthropology there is no assumption that only disease-centered psychiatrists can diagnose "real diseases." In medical anthropology, the clinician's diagnosis as well as the patient's personal illness experience are perceived to be cognitive constructions based on cultural schemas.

The first article in this chapter is by psychiatrist and anthropologist Arthur Kleinman. It is an example of how one person's mental illness was cognitively constructed in a particular culture-based clinical context and is in effect a mini-ethnography of psychiatric practice in the United States. Kleinman demonstrates how the cultural context influences the professional values and definitions of disease of the psychiatrist, and also defines and constrains treatment choices.

The second article in this chapter is by cross-cultural psychiatrist Wen-Shing Tseng et al. In this article, a comparison of assessment and diagnoses of social phobia in Japanese and Japanese-American clients was made between Japanese psychiatrists in Tokyo and American psychiatrists in Honolulu, using videotaped diagnostic interviews. The Japanese psychiatrists tended to diagnose social phobia for the Japanese cases but not for the Japanese-American cases. In contrast, the American psychiatrists tended to ignore the ethnic background of the patients and diagnosed a variety of disorders. Thus, the clinical reality constructed by these two groups of psychiatrists differed significantly based on their differing cultural backgrounds and clinical training. Clinical reality is a cultural construction of the client's problem.

REFERENCES

American Psychiatric Association. (1994). *Diagnostic and statistical manual of mental disorders* (4th ed.). Washington, DC: American Psychiatric Association.

Fleck, S. (1995). Dehumanizing developments in American psychiatry in recent decades. *Journal of Nervous and Mental Disease, 183,* 195–203.

Kleinman, A. (1980). *Patients and healers in the context of culture: An exploration of the borderland between anthropology, medicine, and psychiatry.* Berkeley: University of California Press.

Kleinman, A. (1988a). *Rethinking psychiatry: From cultural category to personal experience.* New York: Free Press.

Kleinman, A. (1988b). *The illness narratives: Suffering, healing and the human condition.* New York: Basic Books.

Kleinman, A., Eisenberg, L., & Good, B. (1978). Culture, illness, and care: Clinical lessons from anthropologic and cross-cultural research. *Annals of Internal Medicine, 88,* 251–258.

ARTHUR KLEINMAN

How Do Professional Values Influence the Work of Psychiatrists?

Psychiatry provides us with the very terms in which our problems are constituted, through its elaboration of the norms and images of healthy mental life, and its characterization of the features of pathology. These enable us to identify what is unhealthy, to classify and measure the problem, and to construe it as remediable. Mental life is now a domain that can be comprehended through, and may be arranged by scientific expertise.

> Nikolas Rose,
> *Psychiatry*

Neither domination or impotence may be ascribed to either the professions or their disciplines.

> Eliot Freidson,
> *Professional Powers*

Ten years ago, I conducted an ethnography of psychiatric practice in a North American city. Working with several senior clinical practitioners, I observed them practice, interviewed and followed the treatment of selected patients, and collected the practitioners' life histories. I also spoke with their colleagues and with their family members. Since 1980, I have done the same with a much larger group of psychiatrists in China. In this chapter, I draw upon both sets of ethnographic experiences to portray the work of psychiatrists within the ethos of professional values in two radically different societies. The comparison should help differentiate the lines of influence from profession and those from the broader society to the practitioner.

The following transcript is from an audiotape of a North American psychiatrist's initial interview with a patient. The patient, Bill Smith, is a 40-year-old white male physician who works in the hospital where the psychiatrist, Jake Kamin, a 45-year-old white male, also practices. They know each other, though not well, through professional contact. I provide the complete interview followed by a description of the psychiatrist's note in the clinical record. I then contrast these with an entry from the patient's personal diary and a description of how

this case will enter the professional literature via an article prepared by Dr. Kamin for publication in a medical journal.

THE CLINICAL INTERVIEW*

Bill: I set this appointment up with your secretary as I mentioned on the phone, Jake, to, to . . . to talk about what is going on in my life. Something's wrong, terribly wr . . . wrong.

Jake: Tell me about it, Bill. Start from the beginning.

Bill: The beginning Jake. I mean when was the . . . ah . . . beginning? This thing must go very far back. Way back. But I guess . . . you would say . . .

Jake: Well, why not begin with the way you are feeling now, and when that began, and what it's like? OK?

Bill: OK. I guess it's much worse now than it's ever been. I . . . ah . . . feel empty, broken, dead to things. I think I . . . I mean I know I'm depressed, very depressed. (Bill Smith starts to cry—slowly and then with increasing force.)

Jake: That's OK Bill, I can see how you feel. It's OK to cry. Tell me about it.

Bill: Oh, gosh, I don't know. It's everything. I just had my fortieth birthday last week, and I . . . I felt so lonely, so dejected. You see . . . I feel disappointed in myself. My personal life, my family, even my career. I've felt this way before, for the

*The names Bill Smith and Jake Kamin are pseudonyms to protect the anonymity of the protagonists. For this reason I have also altered identifying details, deleted reference to proper names, and made other small changes in the transcript and in the descriptions of case write-up, diary entry, and research manuscript that follow. In transcribing the audiotape, I did not include all the speech sounds, such as sighs, or mispronunciations, or overlapping speech. To do so would have rendered the transcript too cumbersome to read. I have noted those pauses, "ahs," repetitions, and stutterings which seemed prominent and potentially significant.

last few months, but never so bad. I just felt . . . I, well, I felt there was no sense in going on. (*Bill Smith cries again, though silently now. Jake Kamin puts is hand on Bill's arm.*)

Bill: Thanks. I'm OK. What I wanted to say is that . . . ah . . . things got so bad, so bad that I thought I'd be better off dead. I don't mean I would take any action. I wasn't suicidal, only I felt I might just as well be dead.

Jake: I see. It must be pretty bad.

Bill: It is. I feel like things have gone terribly wrong. There's not much left in my marriage. I'm not the father I wanted to be. My research isn't going anywhere. I feel like I made a terrible mistake dropping clinical practice for full-time research. I'm up for a tenure decision and I don't think . . . I mean I know I'm not going to get it. There are other things too.

Jake: And when did it begin to get this bad?

Bill: Oh, about two months ago I started to feel down and very irritable. Next thing I knew I was having trouble sleeping, getting up real early, 4 A.M., and not being able to get back to sleep. Then I started to get very anxious, worried about all kinds of things, frightened. I'm not that kind of person. And our sex life came to an end. She wanted to, but I just had no interest. I gave up the long walks we used to take. I even stopped coming into the lab at nights and on weekends.

Jake: How was your appetite?

Bill: About the same.

Jake: Did you have difficulty concentrating? For instance, on your research, or teaching, or when reading for pleasure?

Bill: I stopped reading for pleasure. And I have had some problem, a kind of slowness reading research papers. . . .

Jake: You mentioned you felt anxious. Can you tell me more about that?

Bill: Well, I began feeling tension. First in my arms and neck, then all over and all the time. I felt like I had drunk too much caffeine.

Jake: Did you have any episodes in which you felt a sense of panic come out of the blue, a feeling of something terrible about to happen, like you might die or lose control or something like that and also felt shaky, sweating with palpitations, tingling, numbness, you know?

Bill: No, nothing like that.

Jake: Which part of the day is worse for you?

Bill: Mornings are. I feel a bit better as the day progresses.

Jake: And you have felt, it seems . . . I mean, helpless, or hopeless?

Bill: Both. I feel hopeless all right. But I don't feel like anyone can help me either. I know I can't help myself.

Jake: Worthless?

Bill: Yeah, real worthless. Useless you could say.

Jake: Have you lost pleasure in things?

Bill: For sure. I don't get pleasure out of the lab work, it's become onerous, a terrible task. Playing with the kids—I used to love to be with them, all I want now is to be alone. Marsha and I don't go out anymore. She wants to; I can't see the point. Even watching sports on the TV; I've lost interest.

Jake: Have you . . . I mean have you had episodes like this before? Before a few months ago.

Bill: Not like this. I'm . . . I've felt down when Dad died last year, but not like this. And I've had some disappointments in the past; grants being turned down, work going poorly, my son John's school problems; but not like this.

Jake: Did you have similar problems after your dad died?

Bill: Kind of for the first month or so, then they slowly went.

Jake: Have you ever had any psychiatric problems or treatment?

Bill: Never.

Jake: Anyone in the family?

Bill: Well, Marsha has been seeing a counselor the last few years. Maybe that's part of the problem. She has changed so much. She's more independent. Seems to love me less. And spends less time with us. I've been taking more care of the kids and the house.

Jake: How about your folks, or sibs or the wider family?

Bill: Sorry, I don't get you?

Jake: I'm asking if there is a family history of mental illness or depression?

Bill: No, no one. I mean John, my son John has had dyslexia . . . I guess that's some kind of psychiatric problem. But not serious problems.

Jake: Go ahead, I interrupted. You were telling me how you feel.

Bill: Yeah! I'm not so sure there's much more to say. I feel . . . I feel depressed and irritable, angry, and I've been having headaches. I've had sinus headaches for years, but they've gotten bad again in recent weeks.

Jake: Any other symptoms with them?

Bill: No. And they aren't all that bad, or different than before.

Jake: And it all started?

Bill: That's the thing, Jake. I'm not sure when it all began. I'd say two or three months like this, but only this bad the last month or so. Before that . . . well, let's see. My father died a year ago last month. The anniversary was pretty tough. That upset me a great deal at first. All those archaic feelings returned. You know what I mean. You remember back to when you were a kid. All those feelings of love, disappointment, hate. I mean we had a . . . complex, ambivalent relationship . . . And it all came back last month and things got much worse. But there are other problems that made me feel bad even earlier.

Jake: All of that is important and we want to get into it later, but are you saying you began to feel depressed after your father's death and it just got worse and worse? Before I thought you said the symptoms disappeared for a while, then came back?

Bill: Not exactly like that. I grieved and then it wasn't so bad, but it kept coming back. The sleep and energy and depression disappeared until a few months ago. Troubled and ambivalent feelings . . . ah . . . about my dad went away, came back, went away; but other things were going on also.

Jake: Like what?

Bill: Things have been bad with Marsha for years. We have been married fifteen years. Everything went pretty well the first five years. Then when we first moved here, ten years ago almost, I got so very busy with my work we grew distant to each other. She had the three kids and the house and the dogs, and her parents were getting old and sick, and then John developed the learning problem. Marsha always had wanted to go back to school, but there . . . there wasn't any time. And then . . . well, then . . . then I had an affair. Nothing very serious. But I had a college student as a lab tech and we were there in the lab at night and on weekends. We . . . well we started becoming lovers. Then Marsha found out. All hell broke loose. She, I mean Marsha, threatened to kill me and herself and the kids. I mean she went after me with a kitchen knife, screaming that I had ruined her life. She was in her nightgown and her hair was all wild and she was wild, crazy. She threatened to leave. She did leave for a few days. I came back to my senses. What was I doing playing around with a college student and ruining my family?

That is when . . . ah . . . the rot set in. Things have never been the same since. I guess it's my fault . . . yeah, it was my fault. I hurt her . . . bad, and our marriage too.

Jake: And that has continued up to now?

Bill: I'm not sure what you mean by continued. Things got better for a while. Then we started having fights. Marsha got depressed, blamed me, went to see a counselor, then another, the one she is seeing now. She began to change. She went back to school, spent less time with me and the kids. We became distant. Not much of a sex life. It always had been good up till then, but over . . . over the years it's kind of died. Now we don't have any. Ironically now she is more interested than me.

The last few years we have had other . . . ah . . . concerns. John's school problem has gotten worse. And he's real aggressive with the other kids. Marsha and I have fought a lot over time and responsibilities. She rightly wants more time, time to study [*she is in a doctoral program in art history*] and to be by herself. Well, that means I have to stay with the kids and I should be in the lab or traveling to meetings. It has had a real effect on my work.

When my father died, well it all came to a head. She took it very hard too. I left for a few days. Or she kicked me out of the house. We had a big fight one night after being at a party. I drank a bit too much and I guess got angry at her. She threw all those things up to me. How I had ruined our marriage. Ruined her chances. Hurt the kids. Even John's problem. Then she told me I never loved anyone, not . . . not even my father. I . . . I lost my head. I slapped her and pushed her around. I cried and cried and asked her to forgive me. But she went wild again. She told me to leave. So I packed up—I think it surprised me even more than her—and left. I went to live in a small rental apartment for a few weeks. It was terrible, desolate, empty. I spent all my time blaming myself, feeling guilty and ashamed. And I kept thinking how she said . . . ah . . . I never loved my dad. Then I begged her to let me come back. To start over. But the rot was there. Do you know what I mean? It was never the same. She was cold, distant. She said I had hurt her too much. Me . . . I also felt distant. Something had spoiled our marriage.

Jake: I'm sorry to break in Bill, but you mentioned that the fight started after you had been drinking. Has alcohol been a problem?

Bill: No, no. I have a drink now and again. But not often. After my dad's death I got drunk a few times—once at that party, an . . . another time when I was by myself in the rental apartment.

Jake: Go ahead.

Bill: Well, there's not much more to add.

Jake: You said earlier that you are upset about your work, your research.

Bill: Yeah. You know I'm forty. When my birthday came around, I looked back on all the things we talked about. And I began to see that I hadn't achieved what I wanted, what I expected to. It's hard to talk about this. I know you're a psychiatrist . . . but you're also an academic, and a very productive clinician and administrator. Full-time research is different. You only do one thing. Well, me . . . I started out like a house on fire and then slowly over time, it petered out. I haven't made any major discoveries. My best work is five or six years behind me. Oh, I get grants all right to keep the lab going, and I have a few trainees of real quality. But the ideas, the original ideas—they don't come like they used to. And I haven't done what I wanted to. I always wanted to make a major discovery, a major breakthrough. Nobel Prize quality. That was my fantasy. I drove myself to do it. I felt I had to. All my life was taken up in my work, and daydreams about a signal success. Something so important everyone would honor me. I guess a lot of us come to see that it isn't going to be that way. That the dreams we have are not to be realized. That we have come to middle age only to discover we are not . . . ah . . . what we thought we were. Then there is disappointment and loss—

yes, a real sense of lost opportunities, lost direction, even the future is obscure. And we ourselves, what? Much less brilliant, less powerful . . . less energy and less everything than we thought we had. How then to live . . . to work? As a second-rate academic? Just holding on until the race is run? I'd never been that way. But all of a sudden I felt like my courage had slipped away. I felt terribly lonely. My Dad, he . . . he was a failed inventor. He was supposed to be brilliant. But nothing much came of his inventions. He got bitter and old. And I had the feeling he thought my mother and I regarded him as a failure. I saw the same thing for me. I never worried about tenure before. All of a sudden I could see that I might not get it. Why give it to someone who clearly is not as productive as he once was? The field I feel is . . . ah . . . moving beyond me. I'm . . .

Jake (interrupting): This is all very interesting and important Bill, but I need to ask you some things specifically before we finish up today. OK?

Bill: Okay, I was just trying to give you an idea of what has been happening. . . .

Jake: You mentioned earlier feeling it would be better to be dead. Have you made plans to take your life or been preoccupied with suicide?

Bill: No. I'm not suicidal.

Jake: But you did say you'd rather be dead? Or rather you felt that way?

Bill: Sometimes. But not now. And I've never thought of seriously taking my life or made plans.

Jake: Could you tell me if you did make such plans?

Bill: I think I could, but I haven't.

Jake: OK, OK. Let me ask you about thoughts you may have had recently. Have you had any strange thoughts, like belief your body was rotting or that you had a serious medical problem?

Bill: No.

Jake: I'm trying to get at any delusions.

Bill: No, none. In some ways I think depression has made me see things more clearly, more honestly with less self-protection.

Jake: No hallucinations or suspicions?

Bill: No; none.

Jake: During this period or before, ever had any manic symptoms? You know, grandiose thoughts hyperenergetic, giving away money, thinking you were very special?

Bill: No, no mania. I wish I had more energy. I always thought I was special, don't we all? But as I said, my problem seems to be not that idea but . . . but beginning to feel the opposite that I'm not as special as I thought.

Jake: Anyone in the family with depression?

Bill: No, I already said no one, except for Judy.

Jake: Bill, you said your father's death really affected you greatly?

Bill: It did.

Jake: Was he depressed before he died or in the latter part of his life? I ask because you said he was bitter.

Bill: Well, he seemed lonely, easily hurt, and disappointed. I don't think he was depressed like I am now. But he wasn't happy or optimistic.

Jake: Did he have any particular symptoms before he died?

Bill: He died from a CVA and he had had a few episodes of syncope and frequent headaches.

Jake: I see. You mentioned your ambivalent feelings about him. We can talk about these next time in detail, but can you briefly tell me what you meant when you used the word "ambivalent"?

Bill: Well, just that. I loved him. He was my father. And I have lots of warm feelings about him. But I also have negative feelings. He was a real Puritan. A taskmaster. Driven and driving. He had such ridiculously high expectations of me. And he seemed never satisfied. And then he seemed . . . at the end I mean . . . such a failure. I had the feeling that was me too. That somehow he had set us both on a disastrous course.

Jake: And these were the ideas that kept coming back?

Bill: Yes.

Jake: And they are still strong now?

Bill: They are.

Jake: Do you feel that this depression could be a thing that grew out of your grief and the difficult feelings you had for your . . . your dad?

Bill: I guess . . . guess so. I hadn't thought of it only that way. I . . .

Jake: The anniversary of his death seems to have really affected you.

Bill: It did. The whole thing came back along with all the other things going on in my life. But I felt just like when he died.

Jake: Well, I think that does it. You can see as well as I that you've got a major depression. Now depression is a treatable disorder, a biological problem. We have excellent meds for it, and I think we should start one now. I want to talk to you too about the things you mentioned, especially your father's death, because that could very well be connected. I mean short term . . . that is, a few sessions of psychotherapy can really help, but meds are what will get you better. Now, have you had any allergies or bad reactions to drugs?

Bill: No, but I know you need to take medication for this condition. I'm willing to do it, but I want to talk to someone about all these things I feel . . . pent up inside. I've never talked to anyone. I feel the need to talk it out. I know you guys think it's a brain disorder, but whatever it is, it's so deeply affected my life, I need to deal with these things. Is that the kind of thing you do, Jake?

The interview continued for another five minutes, while Dr. Kamin and Smith agreed on a course of tricyclic antidepressant drug and weekly psychotherapy sessions for five or six weeks. Below I record Dr. Jake Kamin's note in the clinical record as he wrote it down immediately after Dr. Bill Smith left the office.

THE WRITE-UP IN THE PSYCHIATRY RECORD: THE PROFESSIONAL CONSTRUCTION OF A CASE

40-year-old white male physician with several months of depression, hopelessness, helplessness, anhedonia, irritability, guilt, insomnia, and energy and concentration disturbances. Associated anxiety. Not acutely suicidal but has had some suicidal thoughts. No plans. No delusions or hallucinations. No family history. No prior episodes. No mania. Sinus headaches, chronic, amplified by depression. No other medical problems. No alcohol or drug abuse.

Bereavement 13 months ago following death of father. Grieving with ambivalence and modeling of father's symptoms seems to have extended into depression. Depression deepening over past few months, with greatest increase over past month since anniversary of father's death. Worse past month. Work, marital, family problems contributory.

Impression

Axis I: Major Depressive Disorder secondary to bereavement (prolonged and pathological).
Axis II: No personality disorder.
Axis III: Chronic sinus headaches.
Axis IV: Severe bereavement reaction, 4/5.
Axis V: Reasonably good level of functioning, some work-related problems and chronic mental tensions, worsening. But able to cope.

Plan*

(1) Doxepin, begin at 50mg, bring up to 150mg qhs over course of 1 week
(2) A few psychotherapy sessions to do grief work.
(3) ENT consult to rule out serious sinusitis and ? CNS effects.
(4) See in 1 week.

Jake Kamin, M.D.

*Doxepin is an antidepressant; qhs means each night at bedtime. ENT stands for an ear, nose and throat physician. CNS is central nervous system (i.e. the brain).

PATIENT'S DIARY

That night Dr. Bill Smith returned home and wrote a lengthy entry in his diary, from which I have selected the brief excerpt printed below.

I don't think he heard me. I wanted him to listen to me not for the diagnosis but for my story, my story. I know I'm depressed. But I wanted him to hear what is wrong. Depression may be the disease, but it is not the problem. The problem is my life. "The center doesn't hold. Things fall apart." It's falling apart. My marriage. My relationship with my kids. My confidence in my research. My sense of purpose. My dreams. Is this the depression? Maybe it caused the depression. Maybe the depression makes it worse; or seem worse. But the problems also have their own legitimate reality. This is my life, no matter if I am depressed or not. And that is what I want to talk about, to complain about, to make sense of, to get help to put back together again. I want this depression treated, all right. There is something more I want, however. I want to tell this story, my story. I want someone trained to hear me. I thought that was what psychiatrists do. Someone ought to do it, ought to help me tell what has happened. But all he seemed interested in was the diagnosis and my dad's death. I'm sure that is part of it, but so much else is going on. I need to talk to someone about my whole world not just one part of it.

PROFESSIONAL DISCOURSE

Dr. Smith's "case" entered the official professional discourse on two occasions. Dr. Smith became part of the aggregate statistics that Dr. Kamin reported to his psychiatric colleagues at a case conference as cases in his practice of major depression secondary to bereavement. In that presentation Dr. Smith's name did not appear. But in several of the slides, he was described as one of the cases reported by Dr. Kamin. In these slides, Dr. Smith's insomnia, lack of energy, guilt, and anhedonia are catalogued along with other vegetative complaints of depression. He is left out of the cases with suicidal plans or suicidal acts. But he is included in the cases with significant anxiety symptoms and those with anniversary reactions during which they experienced symptoms that the deceased had experienced. Although details of his bereavement response figure in the aggregate figures, little else from his life history is measured or counted.

Dr. Smith's case also appears in the aggregate statistics Dr. Kamin cites in a manuscript that he has prepared and plans to submit for publication to a professional journal. In that professional paper, Dr. Smith's case is used along with many others to

support Dr. Kamin's conclusions about the relationship of bereavement to depression. Dr. Smith's story is written up as a
brief vignette illustrative of Dr. Kamin's thesis that bereavement
is an important cause of depression, and that anniversary reactions play a special role in the progression of bereavement into
clinical depression. A paraphrase of the vignette goes as follows:

Dr. X is a 40-year-old white male with symptoms of major
depressive disorder. Symptoms of grieving recurred in the
tenth month of bereavement and greatly worsened at the time
of the anniversary. One month later a full-blown DSM-III
major affective disorder was present, and he made his first
contact with a health professional. Although many of the
same symptoms were present the first month after his father's
death, they diminished over the next six months before exac-
erbating. At the time of the anniversary reaction, Dr. X described characteristically "archaic feelings," including
disturbing images from childhood and feelings of love, disappointment, hate, and the complexity and ambivalence of
their relationship. Dr. X experienced bad headaches, which
his father had experienced prior to the CVA that caused his
death. He attributed the exacerbation of his depressed symptoms to the anniversary reaction as well as other problems in
his life. Dr. X also complained of the same feelings of loneliness, emptiness, dejection, and self-disappointment that I
have described in the preceding cases, and which his father,
like the fathers in the other cases, also had experienced in his
final period. Like those cases too he had a great need to see
all aspects of his life as affected and affecting him. And indeed there were other significant recent life event stressors in
his marriage, family relations, and work (including multiple
losses, real and symbolic) along with inadequate social support and self-defeating coping.

THE ROLE OF PROFESSIONAL NORMS IN CLINICAL WORK

Dr. Kamin is a senior clinician, board-qualified in psychiatry,
something of an expert in the treatment of depressive disorders,
especially clinical depressions complicating bereavement, for
which he has a well-deserved local reputation. He is a forty-five-
year-old white male, who at the time he treated Dr. Smith was in
the midst of difficult divorce proceedings with his wife of sixteen years over the custody of their three children. Dr. Kamin is
on the clinical faculty of the department of psychiatry at the
medical school, which means that he is out of the tenure track
for full-time researchers and in a special track for part-time medical academics who are principally clinicians and clinical teachers. He administered, at the time of the interview, a subunit in a

division of the department of psychiatry in one of the medical
school's affiliated teaching hospitals, the hospital where Dr.
Smith's laboratory is located.

Dr. Kamin's own father died five years before, during a period
when he was experiencing marital problems. Although he never
sought treatment, in retrospect he believes he became depressed
for a period of months following the anniversary of his father's
death. Like his father, who died of a heart attack, Dr. Kamin experienced chest pains at the anniversary, pains that were severe
enough to make him feel he too was suffering a heart attack. The
medical evaluation convinced him he was not experiencing a
heart disorder, but rather psychosomatic symptoms symbolically
related to his father's death. From that time he began to specialize
in this problem. Dr. Kamin has been greatly influenced by the literature on this theme. He believes that helping patients grieve
their real and symbolic losses is what psychotherapy for complicated bereavement is about. Dr. Kamin also has strong convictions about what constitutes competent professional practice in
the diagnosis and treatment of depression.

"Before giving a dynamic or behavioral or social interpretation of depression, it is essential to do as good a job at description of the symptoms as possible so that you get the diagnosis
right. I'm first and foremost a descriptive psychiatrist, and I see
my first task as getting the phenomenology right. If that leads to
a diagnosis of a treatable psychiatric disorder say, major depression or panic disorder or manic-depressive disorder or schizophrenia, then the next step is the prescription of specific
medication. For after all this is a disease of brain and endocrine
system."

"I prescribed Doxepin for Dr. Smith, and after six weeks he
was symptomatically very much improved. We spent four or five
sessions talking about his life problems and especially about his
father. I got him to grieve. Then when things looked much better,
I referred him for longer-term psychotherapy. You know, to deal
with other problems in his marriage and work. But frankly, at
that stage my thinking was he no longer was suffering from depressive disease. I don't feel Dr. Smith was completely satisfied
with our visits, even though he thanked me for the symptomatic
improvement. I think he had a lot to get out and work through. I
sent him to someone whom I felt would do a good job on that aspect of things, the life problems and kind of midlife crisis. (I
don't like the term, but that's what it amounted to.) Frankly, I
haven't heard further from him or his therapist. I've been so
busy I haven't had time to really think about him until today."

Later in the same interview, Dr. Kamin told me that after the
grief-oriented short-term psychotherapy, he felt Dr. Smith had
no further need for psychotherapy. He made the referral for
long-term therapy only because Dr. Smith insisted that he do so.

The structure of the initial interview illustrates a point made
earlier in this book: Dr. Smith presents *illness*—a chaotic mix-

ture of symptom complaints, coping responses, life problems, his own interpretations—and out of this patient-centered narrative Dr. Kamin configures a psychiatric disease. He does this by organizing the interview to provide answers to questions that are based upon the diagnostic criteria for making a psychiatric diagnosis of major depressive disorder. He also rules out, through these questions, other clinical hypotheses: psychosis, alcoholism, manic-depressive disorder, and an organic mental disorder related to sinusitis. Along the way he listens intently for certain kinds of data, most notably those which confirm his theoretical speculation concerning the relationship of depression to bereavement. The patient feels that in constructing the disease, Dr. Kamin has neither fully elucidated the anguish of his illness experience nor allowed him to express the range and depth of the problems that beset him. Dr. Smith does not feel that the turmoil in his life story is being heard.

From a professional perspective, Dr. Kamin's evaluation is likely to be viewed positively by descriptive psychiatrists but not nearly so positively by those with greater interest in the process of psychotherapy. The former are likely to see his clinical work as competent, the latter as at best marginal. Indeed, I suspect most psychotherapists would criticize Dr. Kamin for just those interrogative interventions that obstruct the flow of the patient's account which descriptive psychiatrists would regard as essential in applying rigorous diagnostic criteria to define a disease. (Psychotherapists would also criticize Dr. Kamin's lack of self-reflexive insight into the personal source of his own interpretive "interests," i.e., countertransference.)

It is important that Dr. Kamin rule out suicidal intent. After all, clinical depression for a small but significant percent of patients is a mortal disorder. If not properly assessed, tragedy may result. It is also important that he interrupt the patient's life narrative to determine if a treatable disorder is present. An "unconstrained interview," without interrogation or interruption, might do justice to the patient's life story but would be a serious and dangerous impediment to the evaluation and treatment of the disease. Somehow, the psychiatrist has to do both. Conflict among therapists centers on what constitutes the proper balance.

In his case description, academic presentation, and written report, Dr. Smith's case undergoes even greater reduction. It is fit into a framework to support Dr. Kamin's main thesis; but left out are all those areas of his patient's life that to the patient and doubtless to readers with a different conceptual framework would seem essential. The reduction to an aggregate statistic seems to do an injustice to the subtle complexity of this life story. It would seem to lack validity not because what Dr. Kamin writes isn't true, but because the context of Dr. Smith's life is left out and the vignette seems a distortion organized around a single determinative cause. After all, a family therapist might see the marital difficulties as the chief and earliest source of Dr. Smith's

later problems. And a developmentally oriented psychiatrist might emphasize the career conflict and midlife stress (cf. Lazare 1973; Gaines 1979). Finally, there is the fiction that all scientific and professional presentations commit in which findings are presented in "objective" terms that leave out contradiction, alternative possibilities, and self-reflective aspects of the case (Mulkay 1981). For example, Dr. Kamin's personal experience of past grief and of pending divorce would seem to significantly influence those answers he regards as significant and those he appears to disregard. He constructs the evidence to fit his concerns; whereas I could reconstruct the case in a rather different way as an example of a tightly integrated vicious cycle creating demoralization and amplifying distress.

The movement from illness to disease to case report and onward to research knowledge is a movement of social construction guided by professional norms of how to conduct an interview, what to regard as evidence, how to sift and marshal that information to support a clinical judgment, and how to write up a typical case and research article. This construction is indeed constrained by the patient's experience. Dr. Kamin neither fabricates that experience nor is insensitive to it. Within that constraint, however, there is ample opportunity to develop the "case" in one direction or another. Personal experience of the practicing psychiatrist both in the clinic and in his home influence that direction, as Dr. Kamin's life situation illustrates. Professional norms, moreover, are not a simple reflection of a homogeneous professional system shared by all members (see Freidson 1986). Dr. Kamin is primarily a practitioner. His job is to apply the official knowledge of his profession to individual cases. That always involves a transformation of what Freidson calls "formal knowledge" into "working knowledge."

Dr. Smith, in contrast, is a researcher, a creator of new knowledge. That knowledge also undergoes change in moving from the laboratory to the research literature (Latour and Woolgar 1979) and from that literature into textbooks. In the course of this transformation, the uncertainties, controversies, and fragmentary nature of research data are ironed out and a "classical" textbook picture of a case of a given disease emerges with a consistency, simplicity, and total structure quite at odds with both the messy research findings and the "blooming, buzzing" confusion of real life as lived by a particular person. For the practitioners who further rework this knowledge in the crucible of practice, it is essential to recognize both the transformed nature of the textbook presentation and the metaphoric leap between that formal knowledge and the working knowledge fashioned in experience.

Dr. Kamin is also a clinical administrator, and as such has a responsibility to his institution (the teaching hospital where both he and his patient practice) that cross-cuts his professional interests. The administrative and research side to professional norms become especially powerful in organizing a treatment plan. Here clinical experience, model of psychopathology, and professional psychiatric values concerning the possibility and significance of suicide are intensified by Dr. Kamin's administrative responsibilities (he feels compelled to do something quickly for a member of the hospital's professional staff for whose psychiatric problems he feels a special medical responsibility) and by his research interests (he is collecting cases to investigate depression following bereavement) to urge rapid and technically powerful "biomedical" treatment with an antidepressant drug and the use of psychotherapy in a highly delimited, short-term mode. Dr. Kamin told me later that in treating medical colleagues, it is important to impress them with the biomedical side of psychiatry, about which he feels most are suspicious. Thus, treatment becomes an opportunity for raising the specialty's marginal status in the profession and that of his clinical unit in the hospital. This plan conflicts with Dr. Smith's wish for existential confession and life course review—and it is not the only effective way to treat depression.

Individual practitioners are influenced to treat patients in a particular way not only by their institutions and their personal interest but also by the school of psychiatry to which they feel allegiance and by the official standards set by their professional association. Psychiatry is split into often irreconcilably opposed "schools"—biological, psychoanalytic, behavioral, social, and so forth. Each school has its own institutional centers, its own academic luminaries and rank-and-file members, and its own journals, meetings, societies, and "classics." Each school teaches a different view of human nature (cf. Schwartz 1986) and a distinctive value paradigm for professional practice (cf. Gaines 1979, 1982). The "classics" are journal articles and books that set out the latest information in distinctive formats, in keeping with each school's ideology, for researchers, students, and the lay public. What holds these schools together is the professional organization of psychiatry into a national association (the American Psychiatric Association) that lobbies for its members' interests in national and local political economies and that influences such key questions as licensing and, together with the American Board of Psychiatry and Neurology, another national association, the setting of standards of practice. The last few years have made explicit what has long been a less openly admitted function of the national association—namely, to protect the control of its members over a specially sheltered sector of the market, the treatment of mental illness (cf. Freidson 1986). But the shelter is not complete, and the association's influence is not determinative. Other professions—psychology, social work, and a myriad of forms of psychotherapists—contend for their market share. The association's influence is indirect, through the agencies of federal and state governments, the courts, via numerous consulting committees, and more recently through a wide variety of publications and public relations efforts which aim at influencing public opinion.

The profession's influence is greater than this sketch suggests, however. Through its official diagnostic criteria (DSM-III), the profession provides the formal standard for accessing psychiatric disorder that is used by the courts, by the disability system, and in clinical work generally. It is upon this official taxonomy of formal knowledge that Dr. Kamin draws to interpret Dr. Smith's disease and to justify its treatment. The American Psychiatric Association is now planning a manual of treatment that will specify the range of appropriate treatments for mental illnesses. That manual could codify treatment much as DSM-III codified diagnosis. Because of sharp disagreements among psychiatrists over which therapies are most suitable, which provoked fears that the psychiatrist's legal right to prescribe would be restricted, it should come as no surprise that this treatment manual has stimulated intense debate over whether its status should be official or not. At the APA's Annual Meeting in 1987, it was decided, in deference to the strong opposition, that the manual would be unofficial (Jonathan Pincus, personal communication, May 11, 1987).

It is all too easy to point to the potentially dark side of treatment standards and regulations without acknowledging their positive contribution. After all, in the absence of standards, practitioners are licensed to treat according to their own therapeutic biases and remunerative preferences. We are all too familiar with the results, i.e., unwarranted surgery, endless psychotherapy, therapeutic fads, and so forth. There is a genuine dilemma between useful and flexible standards that protect the public and rigid regimentation on the basis of received wisdom that locks both care giver and patient into an iron cage of orthodoxy. This dilemma is sharper now for all professions, not just psychiatry. And the problem almost certainly will become worse in the 1990s, because of a broad societal movement toward ever more elaborately refined standards.

It is important, as Freidson (1986) cautions, not to overemphasize the power of the profession. The patient, his social circle, public opinion, and other professional (primary case, psychology, social work) institutions and bureaucratic (the hospital, the HMO, the university) organizations influence psychiatric practice, as our case illustrates. The profession, moreover, incorporates spectacular diversity. Other psychiatrists would have responded to Dr. Smith rather differently. And the patient leaves the encounter still very much the master of his fate. At its worst, professionalization of Dr. Smith's life problems produces insensitive and inhumane treatment. At its best, it assures technically competent help with remediable problems. Much of the time it falls somewhere in between.

The profession is also not the only influence, as we have seen, on the practitioner. Personal experience and institutional concerns are often very influential. Shared cultural orientation also plays a role. It is inconceivable that Dr. Smith would have expressed his personal problems as fully if he were a member of a non-Western society. Rather, his headaches might have provided him with a more indirect somatic idiom for expression and response to his social problems. (This occurs frequently even in our own society.) The patient's responses offer resistance to the practitioner's orientation, resistance that often turns the treatment of different patients in unpredictable directions. For example, Dr. Smith, though a laboratory researcher, will not accept a solely biomedical explanation (and treatment) for a problem he believes emerges from his life situation. Nor is he as convinced as Dr. Kamin is that the chief causative factor is grief following his father's death. He insists on referral for long-term therapy—a form of care Dr. Kamin feels is, in this kind of case, unnecessary and in general ineffective. Because of his patient's urging, Dr. Kamin makes a referral he would not otherwise have made.

In this complex mélange of interests, however, professional norms do exert important effects, ones often hidden to the practitioner. While too anxious a concern with reflection on the nature of that influence may conceivably paralyze the psychiatrist as a clinical actor, too much denial blinds him to pressures which are not always in the best interest of patient care. Dr. Kamin is deeply interested in Dr. Smith's disease; he is not as concerned with Dr. Smith's illness experience. For the patient, particularly if he suffers from a chronic condition, the opposite is often true. Overly narrow and routinized professional medical standards of how to technically treat depression, the disease, may dehumanize the patient (and the practitioner). Care organized by such standards can be ineffective or even contribute to the downward spiral of demoralization. A medical perspective may restrict the sphere of intervention to too limited a target. Treating the problem as a social tension in Dr. Smith's relationships, or in fact, as a cultural one, in Dr. Smith's American upper-middle-class pro-

fessional world, might encourage a broader set of interventions applicable to the treatment of a class of similar cases: such as marital counseling, family therapy, counseling on academic issues, legal referral, or psychotherapy that explores adult development conflicts. These interventions may even offer opportunities to prevent the long-term consequences of the cultural pressures that beset many mid-career professionals like Dr. Smith. The historical development of the psychiatric profession has witnessed transformations in the salience of the patient's narrative and the diagnosis of the disease for the clinical construction of a therapeutic approach. (Scull, ed., 1981). At present the pendulum is swinging away from the former and more toward the latter.

REFERENCES

Lazare, A. (1973). Hidden conceptual models in clinical psychiatry. *New England Journal of Medicine, 288*, 345–350.

Gaines, A. (1979). Definitions and diagnoses: Cultural implications for psychiatric help seeking and psychiatrists' definitions of the situation in psychiatric emergencies. *Culture, Medicine and Psychiatry, 3*, 381–418.

Gaines, A. (1982). Cultural definitions, behavior and the person in American psychiatry. In A. Marsella & G. White (Eds.), *Cultural conceptions of mental health and therapy.* Dordrecht, Holland: D. Reidel.

Mulkay, M. (1981). Action and belief or scientific discourse? *Philosophy of the Social Sciences, 11*, 163–171.

Freidson, E. (1986). *Professional powers.* Chicago: University of Chicago Press.

Latour B., & Woolgar, S. (1979). *Laboratory life: The social construction of scientific facts.* Thousand Oaks, CA: Sage.

Schwartz, B. (1986). *The battle for human nature.* New York: Norton.

Scull, A. (Ed.) (1981). *Madhouses, mad-doctors, and madmen: The social history of psychiatry in the Victorian era.* Philadelphia: University of Pennsylvania Press.

WEN-SHING TSENG, M.D.,[1] MASAHIRO ASAI, M.D.,[2] KENJI KITANISHI, M.D.,[3] DENNIS G. MCLAUGHLIN, PH.D.,[4] AND HELEN KYOMEN, M.D.[1]

Diagnostic Patterns of Social Phobia

Comparison in Tokyo and Hawaii

A comparison was made of the diagnosis of social phobia by Japanese psychiatrists in Tokyo and American psychiatrists in Hawaii. A brief segment of videotaped interviews and written case histories of four Japanese patients from Tokyo and two Japanese-American patients from Hawaii, who were clinically diagnosed with social phobia, were presented to the clinicians for their diagnosis. Japanese psychiatrists tended to diagnose social phobia congruently for the Japanese cases but not for the Japanese-American cases. American psychiatrists tended to diagnose various categories including anxiety disorder and avoidant personality disorder, in addition to social phobia, disregarding the ethnic background of the patients. This illustrates that the diagnostic pattern for social phobia varied considerably between psychiatrists of these two countries. The reasons considered are the patient's cardinal symptom manifestation, style of problems presentation, as well as the clinician's professional orientation and familiarity to this particular disorder.

—*J Nerv Ment Dis* 180:380–385, 1992

There has been increased awareness among cultural psychiatrists that, in contrast to psychotic disorders, anxiety disorders or somatoform disorders tend to be influenced by sociocultural factors in terms of how the disorders are comprehended, diagnosed, and treated by the clinicians (Good and Kleinman, 1985; Tan, 1988; Tseng and McDermott, 1981). This is exemplified by the disorder of social phobia.

The diagnostic term "social phobia" that appeared in DSM-III (American Psychiatric Association [APA], 1980) was not described in DSM-II (APA, 1968) nor in ICD-9 (WHO, 1978). This, in a way, may reflect the fact that this disorder is less frequently observed among the Western population or is less identified by the clinician. Therefore, there was no great need for such a diagnostic term in the past (Liebowitz et al., 1985). In contrast to this, social phobia has gained great attention among Japanese psychiatrists since the turn of this century. This disorder has been publicized by the Japanese under the name *taijin-kyofu-sho* ("anthrophobia" in English translation, meaning phobia of interpersonal relations), which indicates that such a disorder was considered rather prevalent among the Japanese population (Kasahara, 1987; Kimura, 1983).

In fact, it was reported that among all neurotic patients who visited the psychiatric outpatient clinic of Kogomi Hospital at Tokyo between 1979 and 1980, 10% had been diagnosed as having anthrophobia (Iwai, 1982). Among college students at Kyoto University who received psychiatric care at the student health service and were diagnosed as neurotic, 19% had been classified under the category of social phobia (Kasahara, 1974). At Kora-Kosei-In, well known for treating anthrophobia, between 1940 and 1952, 37% of their neurotic patients had been diagnosed as having social phobia (Kora, 1955). The percentage of social phobia cases reported by Japanese psychiatrists varied considerably according to the

[1]Department of Psychiatry, John A. Burns School of Medicine, University of Hawaii, 1356 Lusitana Street, Honolulu, Hawaii 96813. Send reprint requests to Dr. Tseng.

[2]Department of Neuropsychiatry, School of Medicine, Keio University, Tokyo, Japan.

[3]Department of Psychiatry, School of Medicine, Jikei University, and Morita Therapy Institute, Jikei Daisan Hospital, Tokyo, Japan.

[4]Research and Evaluation, Mental Health Division, Department of Health, State of Hawaii, Honolulu, Hawaii.

place, institution, and time. Yet, social phobia is a commonly diagnosed disorder in Japan in contrast to the situation in other societies (Tseng et al., 1986).

Historically, Japanese psychiatrists have used the diagnostic term of *taijin-kyofu-sho* (anthrophobia), rather than social phobia, for the disorder. According to Japanese psychiatrists, *taijin-kyofu-sho* is a "neurotic" disorder characterized by "the presence of extraordinarily intense anxiety and tension in social settings with others, a fear of being looked down upon by others, making others feel unpleasant, and being disliked by others, so that it leads to withdrawal from or avoidance of social relations" (Kasahara, 1975). As subtypes of this disorder, various diagnostic terms for the disorders have been elaborated and used, including erythrophobia, eye-sight phobia, body smell phobia, dysmorphobia, laliophobia, etc.

Many Japanese psychiatrists tend to take the view that *taijin-kyofu-sho* is a special kind of social phobia observed more frequently among Japanese patients and emphasize that anthrophobia is characterized by a special set of symptoms. Based on the clinical severity, some Japanese psychiatrists (Kasahara, 1987) recognized four types of social phobia, namely transient type, which breaks out temporarily in life, usually for adolescents; neurotic type, which is related to nervous temperament (*shinkeishitsu*); severe type, which involves delusions or ideas of reference; and secondary type, which is a phobic disorder associated with schizophrenia. Attempting to rediagnose the disorder of anthrophobia into DSM-III categories, Japanese psychiatrists (Mori and Kitanishi, 1984) revealed that the anthrophobic disorder of the neurotic type can be recategorized into social phobia as defined in DSM-III, whereas the anthrophobic disorder of the severe type cannot be easily categorized into any disorders existing in DSM-III.

Until recently, anthrophobia was considered by Japanese psychiatrists to be deeply rooted in Japanese culture (Takano, 1977). As pointed out by behavioral scientists, Japanese patterns of behavior are characterized by extreme sensitivity and concern about social interactions and relationships. Because Japanese behavior is sensitive to situational variation, especially the boundary between, within, and without the intimate situation, a person is naturally cautious about his exposure to the outside world. The Japanese must control their behavior to conform to situationally prescribed codes of conduct. Inadvertent social exposure may subject one to embarrassment and loss of face (Lebra, 1976). By distinguishing between *Omote* (external or public) and *Ura* (internal or private), Japanese are known to behave differently according to the nature of the setting. Among interpersonal relationships of varying degrees of intimacy, that is, with complete strangers, with very intimate persons, and with intermediate intimate persons, the latter needs more delicate attention and careful judgment in making

appropriate interactions. It has been pointed out by Japanese psychiatrists that it is with the intermediate intimate persons that anthrophobic patients usually have difficulty in coping (Kimura, 1983). Thus, anthrophobia can be understood as a pathological amplification of culture-specific concerns about the social presentation of self and the impact of improper conduct on others (Kirmayer, 1991).

Based on such cultural contexts, anthrophobia was considered a culture-related specific disorder for the Japanese (Kasahara, 1987; Kimura, 1983; Tseng and McDermott, 1981). However, it is interesting to note that recently Korean psychiatrists (Lee, 1987) have claimed that such a disorder is also common among Korean patients. Chinese psychiatrists in mainland China have also reported that social phobia is not rare among Chinese patients who seek psychotherapy.

It has become more clear among psychiatrists that diagnostic patterns for psychiatric disorders vary among clinicians of different schools and locations (Cooper et al., 1969). This is more so for anxiety disorders and somatoform disorders (Tseng et al., 1986). To what extent is social phobia a culture-related psychopathology? To what extent is it the result of the influence of diagnostic patterns and styles? In order to explore these questions, the present investigation was undertaken.

METHODS

Four "Japanese" social phobic cases from Tokyo, clinically diagnosed by Japanese psychiatrists (at the Morita Therapy Institute of Jikei University) and considered typical anthrophobia cases, and two "Japanese-American" social phobic cases from Hawaii, clinically diagnosed and being treated by practicing American psychiatrists, were used as the study cases. (Only two cases of Japanese-American patients were included because there were only two cases available during the period of investigation.)

Clinical interviews of these patients were videotaped by the clinician-investigators (in Japanese by W.-S. T. for the Japanese cases and in English by H. K. for the Japanese-American cases) and consisted of a routine clinical assessment including the chief complaint, major symptoms, present history, and brief background history. The results of the clinical assessment were written up as case histories.

The clinicians who participated in the diagnostic exercise were staff/faculty psychiatrists (with clinical experience of more than 5 years) and residents (with clinical experience of 1 to 4 years). From the Keio University in Tokyo, 15 psychiatrists and 16 residents participated; from the University of Hawaii, 10 psychiatrists and 12 residents participated.

For the investigation of diagnostic patterns, 5-minute segments of the initial interview videotapes and (two-page) written case histories (in their respective languages) were presented to the clinicians. After viewing the videotape and reading the written history of each case, the clinicians at each site were asked to make a diagnosis for each case. In addition, they were asked to comment on how they arrived at the diagnosis and their reasons for making the diagnosis for each case.

The six cases used for this investigation were as follows.

Case 1

Mr. A. (Japanese case) was a 26-year-old single male college graduate and a company employee who had been taking excessive sick leave for 1 year. He presented with the chief complaint of feeling uneasy about maintaining eye contact with others and experiencing difficulty in relating to his colleagues and friends. His problems started at age 16 when he moved from his freshman to sophomore high school class. He found that most of his classmates had changed and he had difficulty talking to the teachers and his new classmates, particularly his female classmates. He was concerned about how others might feel about him. Someone had commented to him that he had a severe look in his eyes, and from then on he always looked into mirrors to check his eyes.

He managed to be accepted into college, but through his 4 years of college life he was always in seclusion and tended to avoid close contact with others. Three years ago, after graduation, he was employed by his present company. He worked for 1 year, although he was always concerned about other people's attitudes toward him.

One year prior to presentation, there was a rearrangement of the office where he worked and he was moved to a new and larger office. Here, he felt he had more difficulty relating with his colleagues, especially women. He was particularly uncomfortable with his newly assigned superior; therefore, he took sick leave from work and has stayed at home.

Case 2

Mrs. B. (Japanese case) was a 25-year-old housewife who had been married for 3 years. When she was 14 and a second-year student in junior high school, her closest friendship was severed due to a minor misunderstanding. During the disagreement, this special friend had made a cynical comment about the patient's "ugly face." Since then, she became seriously concerned about her "ugly face." Although she did not actually have any facial deformity, she was uncomfortable about facing her classmates in the classroom.

She managed to graduate from high school and worked at a factory. But she continued to feel uncomfortable about being stared at by others and had difficulty maintaining eye contact with others. She coped with the situation by wearing glasses. In spite of her difficulties, she met her present husband and married 3 years ago. Her condition did not improve much after her marriage.

Case 3

Ms. C. (Japanese case) a 26-year-old single woman and computer factory worker, came to the hospital with the complaint of being easily flushed when she interacted with people. She has suffered from this condition for almost 8 years. Her difficulties in relating to her co-workers, and particularly to her superiors, who were mostly men, affected her job performance.

Her problems started when she was 17 and a sophomore in a girl's high school. She was best friends with two of her classmates, with whom she went to school every day. Her two best friends became jealous of each other and had a quarrel. The patient tried to arbitrate the dispute, but one of her friends became angry at her. After that, the patient became overly concerned about this friend's eye contact toward her. Her concern soon extended to her surrounding classmates, who she feared might find out about her shortcomings and/or failures.

The patient described her father as a stubborn person with whom she had difficulty communicating. She felt that her father never understood her and that whenever she had a conversation with him it always ended up in an unpleasant argument. As a child, she recalled that occasionally there were quarrels between her father and mother, and her father would become violent toward her mother. The patient would try to stop her father's violent behavior toward her mother and was hit by her father on several occasions. This could possibly be the reason that even now she is fearful of relating to men.

Case 4

Mr. D. (Japanese case) was a 23-year-old single male sophomore at a dental school who had been taking excessive sick leave from school for 1 year. As early as when he entered grade school, he found himself becoming very nervous and speechless when he was asked to talk in class. This made him feel very embarrassed.

When he entered junior high school, it was very difficult for him to adjust to the school environment, and it was certainly more difficult for him to talk to female classmates. His problems became worse after entering high school. He lacked self-confidence, had difficulty talking in front of others, and could not relate to female classmates, although he wanted very much to do so. He was not successful in his college entrance examination and was not accepted into medical school as he had originally planned. Instead, he was accepted into a dental school, which he did not like at all.

He did not have problems walking by himself on the street, getting into the subway or elevator, or being surrounded by a crowd as long as he did not need to talk. However, he found it difficult to go to his dental school classes because he had to talk to his teachers and classmates. His absence from school became so frequent that he eventually had to take 1 year off.

Case 5

Mrs. E. (Japanese-American case) was a 35-year-old housewife who had been married for 16 years and who had a 15-year-old daughter. She visited the clinic with the chief complaint of "paranoia," with sensitivity to not being liked by others and a fear of criticism from others.

She had been sensitive to rejection from others since her early years. Being the middle child of seven children, she recalled that her siblings would receive attention and praise while she received a minimal amount. Even though her parents were not critical of her, she always believed that if she made a mistake, she was a failure. She described herself as a failure as a student, wife, mother, and worker.

Social situations were very difficult for her because she did not know what to say to others and did not know how to respond to others' questions. Therefore, she used alcohol to alleviate her anxiety before going out to social events.

She worked as a gift wrapper but left her job after a few months. She would become depressed for the rest of the day if fellow workers made comments about her.

Case 6

Mrs. E. (Japanese-American) was a 34-year-old married woman who worked as a stenographer. She presented with the chief problem of anxiety and anxiety attacks that occurred in social situations, especially staff meetings.

Her first anxiety attack, described as an upset stomach and tenseness, occurred the night before her wedding. Since then, she has had "panic attacks" from almost any social situation.

She describes herself as generally nervous, but especially uncomfortable in groups. She has felt anxious and afraid of possibly being looked upon, scrutinized, and thought of poorly in staff meetings when asked a question. Frequently, she could only manage a brief "yes" or "no" type answer. She would become tongue-tied and flushed in public situations with people from

work or in family gatherings with her in-laws, whom she described as disapproving and critical of her and her husband.

RESULTS

In order to examine whether there were any considerable differences between the psychiatrists and residents, the results were reviewed according to these two groups. Since all the clinicians were instructed to make a diagnosis in the way that they would do in their usual clinical practice, the diagnostic terms used were varied, without adherence to any particular diagnostic classification, although the American psychiatrists tended to use the diagnostic terms of DSM-III. The Japanese psychiatrists used diagnostic terms that recognized subtypes of anthrophobia such as erythrophobia, dysmorphophobia and eyesight phobia (*shisen-kyofu-sho*). In addition, the Japanese psychiatrists used the diagnosis of sensitive paranoia, originally defined by German psychiatrists as a condition in which a person is pathologically sensitive to his surroundings with ideas of reference, but without psychotic paranoid delusion.

The data were compared among the psychiatrists, the residents, and the total Tokyo clinician group. The results are summarized as follows.

Regarding Cases from Tokyo vs. from Hawaii

1. The Japanese psychiatrists, regardless of their years of experience as a total group, tended to make the diagnosis of social phobia congruently for the four Japanese cases (90.3% for case 1, 80.6% for case 2, 90.3% for case 3, and 64.5% for case 4). This is significantly different from American psychiatrists, who, as a total group, made fewer diagnoses of social phobia (only 31.8% for case 1, 40.9% for case 2, 27.3% for case 3, and 13.6% for case 4; $p < .0001$, $p = .0073$, $p < .0001$, and $p = .0007$ for cases 1, 2, 3, and 4, respectively). The Japanese psychiatrists, with relatively high agreement, made the diagnosis of social phobia with its subtype or a specific type of social phobia, such as anthrophobia (74.2% for case 1), dysmorphophobia (67.7% for case 2), and erythrophobia (51.6% for case 3).

2. However, regarding the Japanese-American cases from Hawaii, although they were considered social phobia cases by the practicing American psychiatrists in Hawaii, Japanese psychiatrists who participated in the investigation seldom made the diagnosis of social phobia (6.5% each for cases 5 and 6). The American psychiatrists who participated in the study also seldom did so (13.6% for case 5 and 19.2% for case 6). Thus, there was no significant difference between the Japanese psychiatrists and the American psychiatrists in diagnosing Japanese-American cases as social phobia. For the two Japanese-American cases

from Hawaii, Japanese psychiatrists tended to make a diagnosis other than social phobia, such as dysthymic disorder (48.4%) or sensitive paranoia (25.8%) for case 5 and anxiety disorder (71.0%) for case 6. American psychiatrists made the diagnoses of dysthymic disorder (40.9%), major depression (19.2%), or unspecified personality disorder (9.1%) for case 5, and panic disorder (22.7%) or unspecified anxiety disorder (13.6%) for case 6.

It is clear that Japanese psychiatrists would congruently make a diagnosis of social phobia if the cases were Japanese patients, but not for the Japanese-American patients. As for the American psychiatrists who participated in the assessment study, social phobia was not the primary diagnosis for most of the Japanese or the Japanese-American cases. Actually, some of them felt it was difficult to make a decision based only on the information given to them. Therefore, they were unable to make a diagnosis for some Japanese cases (18.2% for cases 1 and 2 and 13.6% for cases 3 and 4). Only one Japanese psychiatrist made no diagnostic interpretation in only one case.

Regarding Psychiatrists vs. Residents

1. While the Japanese group as a whole, in contrast to the American group, tended to make similar diagnoses, there was considerable difference in the diagnostic pattern between experienced psychiatrists and psychiatrists-in-training (residents). The experienced Japanese psychiatrists received training in the traditional Japanese classification system in the past. In contrast to this, the Japanese residents who were under training were less strictly adherent to the traditional Japanese classification system. Based on this different professional training background, the experienced psychiatrists tended to make the diagnosis of social phobia by specific subtype rather than generally as social phobia. For example, regarding case 1, 80.0% of the psychiatrists made the diagnosis of anthrophobia, whereas only 68.8% of residents made such a specific diagnosis. This tendency was noted for dysmorphophobia for case 2 and erythrophobia for case 3 also. (According to the Japanese classification system, dysmorphophobia is considered a subtype of social phobia.) Thus, it is illustrated that the professional background, either senior or junior, made a difference in the pattern of diagnosing social phobia.

2. As for the American psychiatrists, there was no clear pattern of difference observed between the psychiatrists who had clinical experience of more than 5 years and residents who were under training. Both psychiatrists and residents manifested similar patterns in that they tended to make diversified diagnoses.

DISCUSSION

There are several factors that deserve discussion regarding the diagnostic patterns observed between psychiatrists in different social settings. The following factors deserve elaboration:

1. Whether the patient *develops* any "particular," or "specified" psychopathology to be identified as a given diagnostic category;
2. Whether the patient *presents* his/her complaints/problems in a "unique" and "stylized" pattern to the clinician;
3. Whether clinicians are *familiar* with the clinical picture of the disorder "presented" by the patient; and
4. Whether clinicians *utilize* a given professional orientation and classification system to categorize the disorder encountered.

The Impact of Professional Orientation

From the present investigation, it is clear that Japanese psychiatrists and American psychiatrists share different sets of diagnostic classification. For whatever reason, it is apparent that, historically, Japanese psychiatrists have developed specific, elaborate and differentiated diagnostic categories relating to the disorder of social phobia. In addition to anthrophobia, the diagnoses of erythrophobia, dysmorphophobia, eye-sight phobia (*shisen-kyofu-sho*), and body smell phobia have been commonly utilized in their daily clinical practice. In contrast to this, for American psychiatrists, the diagnostic term of social phobia was included as an official diagnostic category only a decade ago (by DSM-III in 1980).

Clinician's Familiarity with the Disorder

Closely related to the professional orientation is the clinician's familiarity with the disorder, which would definitely influence the pattern of diagnosis. As a part of this investigation, the psychiatrists and residents were asked to what extent they had encountered patients who presented to them with the disorder of social phobia. Most of the Japanese psychiatrists and residents indicated that they experienced these kinds of patients "occasionally," whereas their American counterparts indicated "seldom." The majority of the Japanese group also indicated that approximately 10% of their patients in the clinical setting belong to the social phobia category, whereas their American counterparts estimated approximately less than 5%. These results indirectly illustrated that Japanese psychiatrists have more opportunity and experience working with social phobic patients and were more familiar with that kind of disorder.

The Patient's Style of Problem Presentation

From the clinical interview of patients from Tokyo and Hawaii, the impression obtained by the investigators was that the Japanese patients, in contrast to the Japanese-American patients, tended to present their problems in a specific and stylized way that could be relatively easier to perceive by the Japanese psychiatrists as anthrophobia (or social phobia). The patient would present their symptoms using medical terminology such as *shisen-kyofu* (eye to eye contact phobia), *sekimen* (erythrophobia), *shiukei-kyofu* (dysmorphophobia), or *taishiu-kyofu* (body smell phobia). In general, American patients would present their complaints as paranoia, anxiety, panic, or depression to their psychiatrists.

When the six patients' case histories were reviewed in detail by the investigators, the impression obtained was that the four Japanese patients tended to present their problems in the line of interpersonal difficulty and behavior problems associated with socialization, whereas the two Japanese-American patients, in addition to focusing on difficulty in socialization, tended to emphasize their emotional problems, including depression and anxiety. The difference in the patient's style of presenting to the clinician does affect the clinician's perception and formulation of the patient's disorder. This is coupled with the fact that the Japanese patients' style of presentation was familiar to the Japanese clinicians and this combination resulted in the Japanese clinicians making congruent diagnoses of social phobia for the Japanese patients, but not for the Japanese-American patients.

The Patient's Different Pattern of Psychopathology

There is one more fact that remains for discussion. Namely, even with the same group of disorders, the psychopathology may be manifested differently by the patients from different sociocultural backgrounds to such an extent that it may lead the clinician to make a different diagnosis.

In order to understand the cardinal clinical picture of the patients described as anthrophobic, Kitanishi and Tseng (1988) reviewed the major symptoms manifested by 152 social phobia cases treated at the Morita Therapy Institute in Tokyo. The results indicated that, when more than one symptom was permitted for calculation among the studied samples, the percentages of the major symptoms presented were: 51.3% for interpersonal anxiety, 27.0% for fear of how others looked at them, 15.8% for facial flushing, 13.8% for eye contact difficulty, 11.2% for ideas of reference, 9.2% for concern about one's body odor, and 5.9% for concern of others' expression. There were only a few cases who presented the symptoms of anxiety (2.7%) and depression (2.0%). The results tended to indicate that the clinical picture of the Japanese anthrophobic patient is uniquely different. To what extent the profile of symptoms of Japanese social phobia is similar to or different from that of the Japanese-American patients is not yet known. Such information will be useful to have in the future to explain to what extent the manifestation of psychopathology may affect the result of a diagnosis.

However, the present study does illustrate that the clinician's diagnostic orientation and the familiarity with the clinical picture of the disorder, coupled with the patient's style of presenting problems, do affect the diagnostic pattern of social phobia, at least for the situation in Tokyo and Hawaii.

REFERENCES

American Psychiatric Association (1968) *Diagnostic and statistical manual of mental disorders* (2nd ed). Washington, DC: Author.

American Psychiatric Association (1980) *Diagnostic and statistical manual of mental disorders* (3rd ed). Washington, DC: Author.

Cooper JE, Kendell RE, Garland BJ, Sartorius N, Farkas T (1969) Cross-national study of diagnosis of the mental disorders: Some results from the first comparative investigation. *Am J Psychiatry* 125(Suppl):21–29.

Good BJ, Kleinman AM (1985) Culture and anxiety: Cross-cultural evidence for the patterning of anxiety disorders. In AH Tuma, J Maser (Eds), *Anxiety and the anxiety disorders*. Hillsdale, NJ: Lawrence Erlbaum.

Iwai H (1982) *Shinkeisho* (neuroses). Tokyo: Nihonbunka Kagakusha.

Kasahara Y (1974) Fear of eye-to-eye confrontation among neurotic patients in Japan. In TS Lebra, PL Lebra (Eds), *Japanese culture and behavior*. Honolulu: University Press of Hawaii.

Kasahara Y (1975) *Taijin-kyofu-sho* (anthrophobia). In Kato M (Ed), *Seishin-Igaku-Jiten* (psychiatry dictionary). Tokyo: Kobunduo.

Kasahara Y (1987) Social phobia in Japan. In *Social phobia in Japan and Korea, Proceedings of the First Cultural Psychiatry Symposium between Japan and Korea*. Seoul: The East Asian Academy of Cultural Psychiatry.

Kimura S (1983) *Nihonjin to taijinkyofusho* (Japanese and anthrophobia). Tokyo: Keiso Shobo.

Kirmayer LJ (1991) The place of culture in psychiatric nosology: Taijin kyofusho and DSM-III-R. *J Nerv Ment Dis* 179:19–28.

Kitanishi K, Tseng WS (1988, December) *Social phobia among Japanese: Clinical, family, and cultural exploration*. Paper presented at the Fourth Scientific Meeting of the Pacific Rim College of Psychiatry, Hong Kong.

Kora M (1955) Taijin-kyofusho to nihonjin no rekishiteki shakaiteki kankyo (anthrophobia and Japanese historical and social environment). *Kyushiu Seishin-Igaku* (Kyushiu Psychiatry) 9:125.

Lebra TS (1976) *Japanese patterns of behavior*. Honolulu: University Press of Hawaii.

Lee SH (1987) Social phobia in Korea. In *Social phobia in Japan and Korea, Proceedings of the First Cultural Psychiatry Symposium between Japan and Korea.* Seoul: The East Asian Academy of Cultural Psychiatry.

Liebowitz MR, Gorman JM, Fyer AJ, Klein DF (1985) Social phobia: Review of a neglected anxiety disorder. *Arch Gen Psychiatry* 42:729–736.

Mori W, Kitanishi K (1984) Morita-shinkeishitsu to DSM-III (Morita nervous temperament disorders and DSM-III). *Rinsho-seishini-qaku* (Clin Psychiatry) 13:911–920.

Takano R (1977) Anthrophobia and Japanese performance. *Psychiatry* 40:259–269.

Tan ES (1988) Transcultural aspects of anxiety. In M Roth, R Noyes Jr, GD Burrows (Eds), *Handbook of anxiety:* Vol. 1. *Biological, clinical, and cultural perspectives.* Amsterdam: Elsevier.

Tseng WS, McDermott JF Jr (1981) *Culture, mind, and therapy: An introduction to cultural psychiatry.* New York: Brunner/Mazel.

Tseng WS, Xu D, Ebata K, Hsu J, Cui Y (1986) Diagnostic pattern for neuroses in China, Japan, and the United States. *Am J Psychiatry* 143:1010–1014.

World Health Organization (1978) *International classification of diseases, injuries, and causes of death* (rev 9). Geneva: Author.

CHAPTER THREE

Culture and Personality Development

The neural networks of the brain that control cognition, emotion, and behavior are structured through the brain's interaction with its environment, including the internalization of cultural schemas. A person learns a language, a belief system, roles of behavior, and so on to function successfully in a particular society. An individual cannot develop into a functioning member of society without internalizing cultural schemas in the neural networks of the brain. Assessing mental disorders without appreciation of this basic fact of personality development results in a skewed view. Culture, mental illness, and personality development are intimately related.

One of the most useful concepts for the study of personality development and mental illness coming from anthropology is the distinction between *sociocentric* and *egocentric* personality structures (Shweder & Bourne, 1984); in cross-cultural psychology this distinction is usually referred to as collectivism versus individualism (e.g., Triandis, 1995).

A sociocentric personality is, as the name implies, a personality with an identity centered in the group or society. This individual derives his or her primary identity from membership in a social group, usually the extended family. The family is typically seen as an immortal structure in which the individual constitutes only a temporary, subordinate part (Lewis-Fernandez & Kleinman, 1994). There are variations in sociocentrism across cultures, but what they have in common is that individual interests are subordinated to the good of the collectivity.

A sociocentric society has strict rules of interdependence. Social obligations are of paramount importance, and proper behavior is determined by the individual's position in the social structure. Thus, individuals are not perceived of as possessing a fully formed identity outside of group membership. In many ways, group membership provides personal identity. There is little or no attempt to distinguish the individual from the social position he or she occupies. The group is seen as a kind of organic whole, and the individual is a living cell within the organism. Life outside the group is usually not attempted and, if contemplated, would be seen as a kind of exile and loss of identity.

Modern western concepts, such as personal freedom and individual human rights, are foreign to sociocentric societies and have very little if any meaning. Rather than individual freedom, emphasis is placed on duties and social obligations. In sociocentric societies individuals are deeply dependent on others in their group for their own sense of self and personal well-being.

In contrast to sociocentric personalities, egocentric personalities have their personal identity centered in the self. They perceive themselves as autonomous individuals with personal choices, desires, and rights, and they see dependence as undesirable. In an egocentric society the "self" becomes the primary object of interest, and personal freedom and power are the supreme values.

In an egocentric society, social relationships are viewed as voluntary associations arising out of consent of the individuals involved, and individuals are free to terminate associations if they so choose. In this type of society, individuals are perceived as autonomous agents with the freedom to pursue their own personal goals, in some cases, even to the detriment or harm of others. "Look out for #1"

Another important sociocultural influence on personality development is the presence or absence of dominance hierarchies in a society's social structure. Of course, this is the central insight of Marxist theory, that persons always act as social individuals. Individuals are not actually autonomous, regardless of how independent they believe they are. Individual behavior is influenced to a large extent by social position (Bock, 1994).

In terms of personality development, in general, the presence of dominance hierarchies based on gender, class, race, age, ethnic group, or all of the above, promotes development of a *primary role identification* (Rohrer & Edmonson, 1960) that structures elements of individual personality development in relation to positions in the dominance hierarchy. Thus, an individual identifies with a particular primary role and the correlated behavior assigned to him or her by the society.

In an extremely hierarchical society such as India, an individual's primary role identification may be minutely delimited by factors such as caste, gender, age, language, region, village, and family. In this case, a particular role carries with it norms of behavior and patterns of thought that are appropriate for that particular primary role and only for the person(s) occupying that social position.

The presence of dominance hierarchies results in systems of discrimination that reify social distinctions, thus legitimating the status and privileges of the ruling groups. This is far different from an egalitarian society, which classifies people as a single group with similar status, role expectations, norms of behavior, and patterns of thought for everyone.

In a society with dominance hierarchies, individuals at the low end of the social scale have a stigma or impaired identity imposed upon them by the dominant group(s). The moral career of these stigmatized individuals is compromised in interpersonal relations. The term *moral career* refers simultaneously to the moral status of an individual and the morale of the individual. The moral status of individuals is an indication of their perceived value in society, that is, whether they are "good" or "bad" persons as judged by the cultural definitions of morality. Thus, someone in a stigmatized social group (e.g., racial, ethnic, gender, or class) can be a "bad" person by definition of the cultural meaning system. If an individual's moral status is compromised in this fashion, the individual's morale or sense of self-esteem can be negatively affected also (Goffman, 1963).

There are a number of ways that a person with a stigmatized moral career can adapt to the social environment, thus structuring personality development. One adaptation is to view victimization as being built into the system, and thus normal and expectable. The adaptative strategy is to victimize others before allowing themselves to be victimized.

The first article in this chapter is an ethnography by psychological anthropologist Cherry Lindholm. The author and her anthropologist husband Charles Lindholm lived for two years among the Swat Pukhtun, an Islamic tribal society in the mountains of Northern Pakistan. Pukhtun society is hierarchical, extremely egocentric, and premodern. The paper describes how children develop in this extremely violent society. The dominance hierarchies in this society, primarily based on gender and wealth, create a social environment in which there is much aggression and violence. The fact that this society is also egocentric means that the aggression and violence occurs mostly between individuals, although alliances of individuals can quickly form for purposes of conflict.

The Pukhtun social environment is harsh and competitive. The combination of dominance hierarchies and extreme egocentrism influence individuals to strive for personal power and prestige. In this society there are only two types of people—the weak and the strong. The strong take from the weak, dominate them, and thereby gain prestige. The weak are controlled, exploited, and dominated by the strong. The weak are then stigmatized because of their weakness.

Pukhtun individuals are completely ruthless in the pursuit of personal power and wealth, and these values are taught to children at a young age. Children are taught to fight, steal, lie, cheat, and be completely self-seeking. The primary values of this society are aggression, egotism, pride, fearlessness, and treachery. No one dares trust anyone else.

Because of the extreme egocentrism in this society, there is a great deal of violence within families. Husbands regularly beat their wives, and wives fight back. Pukhtun women display the scars incurred during fights with their husbands as signs of honor. Children are also regularly beaten by their parents, and this preoccupation with violence is manifest in the behavior of the children. Children constantly fight among themselves for dominance or over personal possessions, and they are frequently cruel to animals.

Pukhtun individuals experience no guilt for their many forms of exploitation and violence against others. Guilt or remorse appears to be an emotion that is missing from this society. However, they do experience shame when they are caught attempting to victimize someone and are prevented from completing the act. They are ashamed because they were not successful.

Among the Swat Pukhtun, the social environment emphasizing hierarchic egocentrism influences individual personality development in the direction of violence, aggression, treachery, egotism, and cruelty. The children (including girls) are taught to lie, steal, cheat, fight, and survive. Persons in Pukhtun society trust no one, especially their closest relatives. Moreover, they have no remorse for any of their treachery and believe that persons who are victimized deserve their plight because they are too weak or too stupid to defend themselves.

The extreme violence of the Swat Pukhtun is contrasted with the peacefulness of the Senoi Temiar in the second article in this chapter, an ethnographic study by psychological anthropologist Marina Roseman. This paper on the Senoi Temiar provides an illustration of personality development in a society that is highly egalitarian and sociocentric. The Temiar, a tribal society in the interior of Malaysia, are some of the most peaceful people in the world, with no reported internal violence of any kind. The absence of dominance hierarchies among the Temiar, combined with sociocentrism, influences the society to be extremely peaceful, without the exploitation and violence seen in Pukhtun society.

Because of their egalitarianism, the Senoi Temiar have only informal leaders who attempt to lead by influence and persuasion. If there is a dispute, the Temiar resort to four methods for resolving the problem: (1) mediation, (2) group discussion moving toward consensus, (3) harangue, and (4) fission. Physical violence of any form is not used within Temiar society. Nor is anger expressed in face-to-face interactions. Rather, anger is expressed in an indirect form, which Roseman refers to as "harangue." In a harangue, the angry person waits until the middle of the night and then addresses the person with whom he or she has a dispute, but always from a separate room or separate building, and often in the third person. The person is addressed as "he" or "she," rather than "you" to further distance the confrontation. Even then, this indirect form of address is considered to be a hyperdirect and aggressive form of interaction among the Temiar.

If disputes cannot be resolved using peaceful methods, the group will fission into two groups with one group moving to a new location. Thus, in Temiar society the cultural meaning system structuring a society that is egalitarian and sociocentric influences individual personalities to be peaceful. This paper, as well as the article by Lindholm have implications for many personality disorders listed in DSM-IV.

REFERENCES

Bock, P. K. (1994). Social structure and personality. In P. K. Bock (Ed.), *Psychological anthropology* (pp. 41–59). Westport, CT: Praeger.

Goffman, E. (1963). *Stigma*. Englewood Cliffs, NJ: Prentice-Hall.

Lewis-Fernandez, R., & Kleinman, A. (1994). Culture, personality, and psychopathology. *Journal of Abnormal Psychology, 103*, 67–71.

Rohrer, J., & Edmonson, M. (1960). *The eighth generation grows up*. New York: Harper & Row.

Shweder, R. A., & Bourne, E. J. (1984). Does the concept of person vary cross-culturally? In R. A. Shweder & R. A. LeVine (Eds.), *Culture theory: Essays on mind, self, and emotion* (pp. 158–199). Cambridge: Cambridge University Press.

Triandis, H. C. (1995). *Individualism and collectivism*. Boulder, CO: Westview Press.

CHERRY LINDHOLM

The Swat Pukhtun Family as a Political Training Ground

Nothing has been written about family life among the Swat Pukhtun of Northern Pakistan, perhaps because researchers have been more interested in the politics of the area (see Barth 1965; Ahmad 1962; Ahmed 1975), perhaps because no one has had the opportunity to observe the domestic sphere. The Pukhtun women of Swat keep a strict *purdah*, and the life that goes on behind the high stone walls of the private compounds is not for public viewing.

I was fortunate enough to be able to spend nine months within one of these households, and so had the unique chance to see the hidden lives of the Pukhtun, the side that is not visible from the *hujera* (men's house) where the village men lavish their proverbial hospitality and generosity on guests, sit about on the long verandah discussing politics, or else silently dream about their glorious pasts (if they are old) or their glorious futures (if they are young). As they are talking or dreaming, pots of tea and platters of food will miraculously appear, carried by a young boy or an older male servant, and the men will eat and drink. To the visitor, the tea and food provide the only evidence that women exist, for the women themselves remain invisible. Inside the *hujera* (as in the mosques, the cowsheds, the little one-room shops, and the narrow streets), it is strictly a man's world. That world is the realm of land and ownership, intrigues and power-plays, alliances and treacheries—in a word, politics.

There is, however, another world beside that of the *hujera*, and though effectively denied by the men, it is equally as powerful as the public political arena. In fact, the very structure of the Swat political system finds its roots in the home, in the manner in which children are raised, and in the ideology that first finds expression within the *purdah* compound. Pukhtun society, which operates primarily on the basis of political manipulation and the striving for power, possesses a hidden dimension where a complementary political system exists and where children are trained to survive within the harsh and competitive environment of their elders. This hidden dimension is the subject of this paper.

When a baby is born, it is the occasion for either congratulations or condolences—the former if the child is a boy, the latter if a girl. Sons rather than daughters are desired as the family land passes down through the male line only, and the political strength of the family depends on its men. A family with many sons will be more powerful than one with few. Although rivals

individually for their father's land, the sons will unite against others whenever necessary. This property of the segmentary lineage system is nicely described in the famous Middle Eastern saying: "I against my brothers; my brothers and I against our cousins; my brothers, cousins, and I against the world."

Women as well as men prefer boy children, for adult sons not only bring home wives as subservient helpers for their mothers but also tend to ally themselves with their mothers in their competitive struggles with their fathers over land. Because men and women alike are early instructed in the pride of their own patriline, there is an automatic hostility built into the marriage relationship (see Lindholm and Lindholm 1979), for each partner considers his own patriline superior to the other's. In the regular fights between husband and wife, the insults that fly back and forth are not restricted to the individuals alone. "Your ancestor was nothing, and mine was great!" the wife may scream, voicing her anger and family pride at the same time. As the long-time adversary of her husband, her loyalty rests not with him but with her own patriline. The wife is only too glad to find staunch allies in the personages of her grown sons who now have their own reasons for wanting to outwit their father. Although grown men, they are still living in their father's house and eating his food—a situation of dependency abhorred by any Pukhtun, and which he will struggle to change. It is not uncommon for an elderly Pukhtun (who is generally at least ten or fifteen years older than his wife) to retreat to the *hujera* to find some peace from his wife's constant nagging and the badgering of his sons for their share of his land. He is loath to distribute this land to his sons because his ownership of the land is the source of his power and sense of identity. In addition, he fears that were he to allow his sons control of the land he might eat considerably less well.

So while the husband is sitting in the *hujera* contemplating his vanished youth and weakening power, his sons are busy plotting against him inside the walls of the *purdah* compound their mother now rules like a real matriarch. Gone are the early days of her marriage when she was still somewhat shy and unsure of herself in her in-law's household, where her position was one of little prestige. In those days, she was under the heavy thumb of her own mother-in-law, and her husband used to beat her regularly in a vain attempt to render her docile and submissive. But now that she has produced sons to carry on the lineage and inherit the family land, her prestige is great. With her daughters-in-law to supervise and command, the allegiance of her grown sons, and her husband lacking his former energy and heart for fighting, the tables have turned, and she is able to wield an extraordinary amount of power. As the Pukhtun writer Ghani Khan once wrote: The Pukhtun "thinks he is as good as anyone and his father rolled into one, and is stupid enough to try this sort of thing even with his own wife. She pays for it in youth, he in old age" (1958:47). Nor is her influence restricted to the home; it can also have repercussions in the society at large. Men often seek the advice of their shrewd old mothers who have had many years' experience of political strategy and manipulation within their own family compounds.

The violence and strife characterizing the marriage relation is the result of the constant battle between two equally proud and determined opponents to achieve power over the other and avoid being dominated and controlled. Significantly, when a young girl marries (often before puberty), her mother will instruct her in ways to gain power over her husband and at the same time prevent him from having power over her. The girl will be advised, for example, always to sleep with her arm behind her husband's head, and to be the first to speak whenever the husband enters the compound, "even if you only manage to cough." The husband, too, of course, is well aware of the nature of the situation he is entering, and his primary concern is to keep his wife under control. The ideal wife is docile, quiet, and submissive, but this image is more a fantasy than a reality. The wife's main fear is that the husband may humiliate her and her lineage by bringing in a second wife; the husband's fear is that the wife, if not strictly controlled, will render him *begherata* ("man without honor") by taking lovers. Each partner fears the other's ability to dishonor and humiliate, and both must be constantly on guard in the inevitable struggle for domination.

Far from being a refuge from the rest of society, Pukhtun marriage is rather a reflection of it as Pukhtun life, whether public or private, is primarily concerned with politics in the very broadest sense—that is, in the pursuit of power. The politics of Swat is, in fact, pure power politics, and personal power and prestige is the main goal of every Pukhtun. In Pukhtun thought, there are only two types of individual—the weak and the strong. The strong survive, take power, and gain prestige; the weak are controlled and dominated by the strong. To survive within such a society, the individual cannot afford to be weak. The qualities the individual needs are aggression, egotism, pride and fearlessness. The Pukhtun male must be able to defend himself against others, be adept at the art of manipulation and intrigue, and above all trust no one. He must learn to be competitive, clever, and completely ruthless in pursuit of his own personal advantage. These are the hard facts of life among the Pukhtun, and children learn these facts at a very early age.

In the household the child enters at birth, hostilities and strife are likely to be the order of the day. Arguments and fights regularly flare up between the child's mother and father, between the mother and grandmother, between the mother and her sisters-in-law, and the children of the compound are continually squabbling. Adults make no attempt to prevent children from witnessing their fights or overhearing the streams of abuse that accompany these angry recriminations. This abuse is often sexual in content, such as "Hole-giver, I copulate with the vulva!" and children become quite skilled in such abuse even while their speech is still baby-talk. Though adults do not try to teach a child how to walk or talk, they will laughingly encourage a toddler to make funny faces and repeat sexual insults. When not arguing with one another, women complain bitterly in front of the children about their husbands' treatment and display the bruises and scars that result from their marital fights. There is, however, an element of pride involved, too, for the scars are marks of honor in domestic politics, and women will say of a man who rarely beats his wife that he is "a man with no penis."

Emotions tend to run high in the compound because there is always some cause for the women to be angry, irritated, jealous, or frustrated. Because there is no escape for them from the four walls, situations and feelings often escalate until a fight ensues to clear the air. In such an atmosphere, feeding times for infants are not necessarily occasions of tranquillity or tenderness. The child is breast-fed on demand, but the mother is usually engaged in doing something else at the same time and may or may not be in a good mood. A child is breast-fed until the next baby comes. A suckling infant may already have a set of sharp teeth, and the mother may cuff him smartly for biting her during feeding. "May God drown you!" she might angrily mutter as he greedily attacks the breast for the umpteenth time that day, and she will continue stirring the cooking pot while the baby essentially feeds himself on her lap.

Because a crying baby is immediately either given the breast by the mother or picked up and carried by an older sister, he or she soon becomes very demanding, screaming lustily whenever left unattended. One of the most persistent sounds of village life is that of wailing babies. When a new baby arrives, the older one is roughly banished from the breast without ceremony and must abruptly adjust to a new status. The child is no longer the recipient of immediate attention and must learn to take his or her place within the rough-and-tumble community of older brothers and sisters, competing with them for any interesting sticks or stones or bits of left-over material to play with, and for pieces of dry bread to snack on during the day. Within the household, as without, the strong take from the weak, and children soon learn that they must fight as well as scream for what they want. Young children are no match for older siblings who regularly take from them by force and laugh at their impotent tears, but later the child will be older and stronger and then too will be able to take from others. There is no notion of sharing or cooperation among children, and the dialogue in their arguments is typically: "That's not yours, that's mine!" "No, it's mine!" "No, mine!" It is also interesting to note that the child's first words are likely to be "ma la," meaning "for me."

Adults do not intervene in children's disputes, except perhaps to order the children to be quiet if they are making too much noise too close by. Nor do adults intervene in the child's relationship with his or her environment; small children are not forewarned about dangers or watched carefully at play. Accidents happen; toddlers may burn their fingers in the fire or lose their balance and fall down steps. While I was in the village, a small boy was rushed to the hospital with his head split open by another child wielding an axe. Learning occurs by personal experience in these matters. Very young children frequently get hurt one way or another, but older children have few accidents. They race across the flat rooftops and walk along the narrow tops of the compound walls, only rarely falling off.

It is believed that children are incapable of feeling or understanding anything until they are at least seven years of age. Therefore, it is considered a waste of time to explain things to a small child. Children are given orders by adults, and unquestioning obedience is expected. On the very rare occasion when a child would ask an adult "why?", the answer was invariably, "sakh" or "asai," meaning respectively, "it just is so" and "I know but I'm not about to tell you," accompanied by an irritated glance. The parents' job is to train children to respect their elders, obey them to the letter, and know the proper way to behave. Failure to comply with an adult order, whether the failure is due to willful naughtiness, forgetfulness, misunderstanding, or accidental mismanagement, is met with immediate anger and a variety of physical punishments ranging from a simple slap across the face to more elaborate procedures such as tying the child to the bedpost for the day or hanging the child upside-down from the ceiling for a while. Such punishments as these, which I had the opportunity to witness firsthand, are not considered at all extraordinary, and the parent may even exhibit considerable pleasure during their administration. In addition to disobedience, acts resulting from carelessness, such as walking into a wall or dropping a bowl of curd, are also severely punished. Although parents have favorites among their children and there is no pretense of "loving all equally," the favorites are also beaten when the occasion arises. Children do not cry during punishments, for they soon learn that crying only elicits further violence from the parent.

I was initially shocked at such violence, but I soon came to regard it, as did everyone else, the children included, as a perfectly normal everyday occurrence. Indeed, verbal and physical violence is so much a part of domestic life that it loses much of its emotional impact and becomes more of a divertissement than a subject for serious concern. The main amusement of village life is, in fact, a lively domestic fight. Women will rush onto the rooftops whenever a heated argument is in progress in an attempt to get a better view and not to miss a word, and they will send their young daughters over to the house in question as on-the-spot reporters. As well as learning to receive violence without fear and with stoic acceptance, children also learn to enjoy watching violence being offered to others and perpetuating acts of violence themselves. Whenever a child was being punished by a parent, the other children would watch with undisguised glee, and children would amuse themselves by killing small birds with stones or blithely torturing frogs or lizards.

Boys, of course, being the favored sex, tend to have a somewhat easier time of it in the home than girls. A girl will be punished for striking her brother, but a boy may hit his sister with impunity. One might think that the mother, out of a sense of solidarity with her own sex, might prevent her sons from beating her daughters. However, far from preventing such violence, she is more likely to encourage it. Not only does it prepare her daughter for the treatment she will receive from her future husband, but it also gives her son practice in handling his future wife who is, after all, the mother's future daughter-in-law. It is in the mother's personal interest that her sons should be able to control their wives properly.

Much more is expected of little girls than of little boys in terms of self-development and ability to work hard; after all, the girl must be trained within a fairly short span of time for her early marriage. Girls soon start helping their mothers with domestic chores and are expected to wash and dress themselves and take care of their younger siblings. Boys tend to remain babies for much longer, being washed and dressed by their mothers and older sisters and having no domestic jobs, which are strictly "women's work," thrust upon them. The little girl is expected to defecate outside the house at a young age, but her brother will still be having "accidents," which she will have to clean up for him. The girl is trained to wait on men, whereas the boy is trained to expect service; he is generally treated like a little prince, being given, along with his father, the best pieces of food, and always being dressed in clean, freshly-pressed clothes. One thing that is expected of a boy, however, is that he should learn to behave like a little man; hitting his sisters is permitted, but if he sticks his fingers in his mouth and assumes a dull or foolish expression, his father will disgustedly accuse him of being *bedagh* (passive homosexual) to shame him into more manly deportment and will give him a sound slap for good measure. When the boy is about eight or so years of age (around the same time as his sisters spontaneously begin wearing head-shawls and staying within the family compound), he will be expected to join a village gang where he will engage in fights and competitive struggles with other boys. His experience in these gangs develops his character and fighting ability, and should he come home crying after an unsuccessful bent with an older boy, he will receive no sympathy whatsoever.

The differential treatment of boys and girls prepares them for their different roles in life, but within these limits both sexes develop identical character traits, which are necessary for survival. All children learn to be tough and fearless, to accept violence as normal, and to be aggressive and self-seeking in their dealings with others. They learn to be demanding and to know the best ways of getting what they want. A male child will take a severe punishment without flinching, but he also knows the coercive value of the tearless tantrum. If he continues long and loud enough, the parent will often give in to his demands simply to shut him up. However, parents as well as others are notoriously unpredictable, and a parent will frequently promise a child something without the slightest intention of keeping the promise. In this way and others, the child learns that he cannot trust or rely on anyone. The mother is nurturant but may accompany a feed with a slap; other children will take from him by force if allowed and will laugh when he is punished. Trust is an unaffordable luxury in Pukhtun society, and the child learns early that trusting another is both foolish and dangerous. He learns to defend himself and be constantly on guard against the maliciousness and treachery of even (and especially) his closest kin.

In addition to aggression, the child also learns to be wily in his competitive dealings with others, for aggression alone is not sufficient as a means of either defense or attack. Children will hide objects they have found to prevent others from taking those objects by force and will sneak off secretly to the hiding place from time to time for a peek at their treasure and to reassure themselves that the hiding place has not been discovered. Children also learn the art of telling lies to avoid punishment and have no compunction whatsoever about passing the blame for the misdemeanor in question onto another child. Children rarely play together for long without an argument erupting because someone will soon try to cheat, and stealing is rampant in the household, preferably being accomplished by cleverness and sleight-of-hand rather than by open aggression as the perpetrator's guilt is then not provable. While I was there, a teapot, several spoons, a bracelet, some hairclips, a pen, some plates, a chicken, and a huge roll of electrical wiring (to mention only a few items) were all spirited out of the compound with great expertise, the thefts only being discovered after the fact. In all cases, it was known who had taken the article as its disappearance was noted directly after a visit from some female relative. A child was promptly dispatched to the relative's house, not to ask for the return of the item (the theft would only be denied) but to resteal it without being caught and bring it home again. In this way, children are actively encouraged by adults to develop cer-

tain skills, and a child may even be congratulated if he steals something worthwhile from a relative's house. A very young child will scream and fight in an attempt to gain something he wants, but the older child is more likely to rely on cleverness, subterfuge, and manipulation as the more successful methods for achieving his ends. The child learns that he must counter the aggression of others with an equal aggression, but he must also defend himself against others' treachery by becoming even more treacherous himself.

Lying, cheating, and stealing are considered perfectly legitimate ways of seeking personal advantage and do not evoke any sense of guilt among the Pukhtun, even though it is recognized that Islam does not condone such behavior. Guilt does not, in fact, form a part of the Pukhtun's emotional make-up, its place being taken instead by the acute shame that is felt when there is a loss of honor for whatever reason. As long as an individual's actions do not result in loss of honor or loss of face, those actions are acceptable. It is more dishonorable and shameful to be cheated than to cheat someone else successfully. In the latter case, one has proved one's superior ability and achieved one's objective, whereas in the former case one has simply been made to look a fool. The individual's main fear is that "people will laugh behind me." Lying, cheating, and stealing, therefore, are not punishable offenses, providing that the child knows from whom he may or may not steal. He should on no account steal from his father or a guest, for example, for *Pukhtunwali* (the Pukhtun code of honor) insists that the guest be treated with the utmost respect, and the father of a household is the "king of his castle" par excellence (at least theoretically) and will not take lightly any insult to his person or position (see Newman 1965). Even a man's grown sons (who may be trying to persuade him to hand over his land to them) would not show disrespect to their father by smoking a cigarette in his presence. Such an act would be totally against accepted etiquette, and the child is trained early as to what constitutes proper conduct and the correct attitude for a "true Pukhtun."

The "true Pukhtun" is proud and fearless, courageous in warfare (whether inside or outside the home), and generous to the guest. He (or she) prefers death to dishonoring, and though he might lie, cheat, and steal, he will never beg. He values his independence above all else and will never submit to the domination of others. He upholds the tenets of *Pukhtunwali* (whose three cornerstones are hospitality, refuge, and blood revenge) and firmly believes that his way of life is infinitely superior to all others.

The Pukhtun way of life is governed by a set of rules that are strict and all-encompassing. All members of the society are expected to follow these rules with the same unquestioning obedience as that with which they were expected, as children, to follow their elders' commands. To go against the rules is to go against the society, and the individual who tries it will find himself a dishonored outcast. As the Pukhtun say, "Nothing is stronger than custom." The Pukhtun who remains in his own society is therefore very much the conformist, for there is no leeway to be anything else. Children are trained to know the rules and conform to them and are actively discouraged from being creative and questioning; such activities constitute a threat both to the individual and to very fabric of the society. The children must be socialized into conforming adults, and these adults, although individualistic, are in a certain sense all the same. As the Pukhtun themselves say, "We are like rainsown wheat."

Within this framework, the individual is free to seek his own personal power and prestige, but only by acceptable means—any other way of progressing automatically spells disaster. The fabric of the society, therefore, remains intact. Power may oscillate from this side to that, from one individual to another, but the essential structure continues, as rigid and persistent as ever. This is the strength of the system and the reason that the Pukhtun have remained unconquered and relatively unchanged for so long.

Although many aspects of Pukhtun society may seem strangely contradictory to the Western observer, there is a very persuasive logic to its somewhat unexpected morality. Many aspects of family life and child-raising may seem excessively cruel and harsh, but that very harshness is a necessary component in the adequate preparation of the child for his adult life. Indeed, a less harsh upbringing would in the long run be much more cruel. In the realm of pure power politics, whether the arena is the *hujera* or the *purdah* compound, the proud Pukhtun is a formidable adversary, and for good reason—he begins his training as soon as he is born.

REFERENCES

Ahmad, M. 1962. *Social Organization of Yusufzai Swat*. Lahore: Punjab University.

Ahmed, A. 1976. *Millennium and Charisma among Pathans*. London: Routledge and Kegan Paul.

Barth, F. 1965. *Political Leadership among Swat Pathans*. London: Athalone.

Khan, G. 1958. *The Pathans—A Sketch*. Peshawar: University Book Agency.

Lindholm, C., and C. Lindholm. 1979. Marriage as Warfare. *Natural History*, 88(8): 11–21.

Newman, R. 1965. *Pathan Tribal Patterns: An "Interim" Study of Authoritarian Family Process and Structure*. Ridgewood: Foreign Studies Institute.

MARINA ROSEMAN*

Head, Heart, Odor, and Shadow

The Structure of the Self, the Emotional World, and Ritual Performance among Senoi Temiar

Moving through daily and ceremonial life, Temiar rain forest dwellers of Malaysia exhibit their concern with the permeable person, which they conceive of as a number of potentially detachable selves. When one Temiar passes around the back of another, he may softly recite, "Odor, odor, odor" to keep that person's odor soul from entering him. Another Temiar, angry at his son for not helping clear the swidden fields, chooses to express his anger from afar in a nighttime harangue uttered several cubicles away from his erring son, rather than risk causing his son's startled head soul to flee from a more direct confrontation. A Temiar woman, trance-dancing to the sound of bamboo tube stampers, feels the sounds pulse with her heart, pushing her heart soul aside and drawing her into contact with the spirits. These snippets of action, moments when Temiar negotiate the boundaries between self and other, human and superhuman, demonstrate the manner in which concepts about the structure of the self reverberate in social life, the emotional world, and ritual performance.

In this paper, I investigate how the Temiar sense of self, society, and cosmos impacts upon emotional and ritual realms.[1] I begin with an ethnography of Temiar socio-emotional concerns, then trace their ramifications for social life, on the one hand, and ceremonial performance on the other. I describe how Temiar praxis maintains the boundaries of Temiar "sociocentric selves," which by definition are permeable. Boundary maintenance is thus a major concern in Temiar social and ritual life. I examine the way the Temiar structure the self in relation to others, cushioning social interaction so as to avoid inappropriate intermingling or detachment of selves. I then outline the consequences of inappropriate social interactions in the pathogenicity of emo-

tions leading to illness, conceived of as a dislocation of self. Finally, I examine how the sounds and movements of healing rituals are structured to modulate affect, playing on emotions and boundaries to restore balance and integrity of self.

Since the category of the person was delineated as a domain of anthropological inquiry by Marcel Mauss (1960a, 1960b), the problem of the relationship between individual and society has been variously redefined. Building upon developments in phenomenology, questions regarding the subjective experience of self and the inter-subjective world of the social person have been productively recast in terms of the social construction of reality (Berger and Luckmann 1966; Schutz 1967). Consequently, recent research on symbolic systems and concepts of self and person increasingly emphasizes processes of social interaction and interpretation (Geertz 1973a; Lutz 1985; Marsella, De Vos, and Hsu 1985; White and Kirkpatrick 1985). In the Temiar case, the problem of constructing and maintaining relatedness is conceptualized through understandings of various components of selves and particular emotions, especially "longing" and (anxiety about) anger.

Studies of culture and affect show that notions of both the "person" in society and the more interior world of the "self" are intricately interconnected with the cultural construction of the emotional world (Shweder and LeVine 1984). Among Philippine Ilongot, for example, the relative capacity for knowledge and passion is related to the respective "height" of men's and women's hearts (Rosaldo 1980:99–136). Durkheim (1965 [1915]) suggested a relationship between ritual and emotion, noting how the emotional effervescence of collective ritual action subsumes the individual within the social order. Bateson showed how cultural knowledge and emotional valence coalesce in ceremonial performance when he identified the dimensions of ethos ("a culturally standardized system of organization of the instincts and emotions") and eidos ("a standardization of the

*Marina Roseman is Assistant Professor of Music and Anthropology at the University of Pennsylvania, Philadelphia.

cognitive aspects of the personality") in his prismatic analysis of New Guinea initiation rites (1956:118, 220).

Self and sentiment, illness and aesthetics articulate in the performance of healing. Constructs of self and other implicate concepts and actions surrounding mind and body; the cultural patterning of emotional constraint and expression extend into matters of illness and health (Scheper-Hughes and Lock 1987; Ito 1985; Kleinman and Good 1985). Healing rituals draw their transformative powers to move persons from illness to health from the symbolic properties of metaphor, which "move" meanings (Fernandez 1977); and dramaturgically, from the ritual reframing of reality in the manipulation of sounds, movements, roles, and other dimensions of performance (Kapferer 1979; Schieffelin 1985; Roseman 1988).

In my analysis, I examine how the structure of performance resonates with the structure of the self to intensify affect and resituate the boundaries of self and other, human and superhuman, thereby effecting a movement from illness to health.[2] This analysis rectifies a shortcoming of performance theory, which points toward the manipulation of ritual media but often fails to fully examine the texture of performance, to ask why forms of language, music, or dance are structured in a particular way. By failing to analyze the relationship between the structure of the self and the structure of performance, such studies are unable to determine how these symbolic forms effect the culturally constructed person. For Temiars, emotional excess can lead to loss of self and thereby to illness, while the aesthetics of socially organized sound (music) and movement (dance) modulate the emotions, reintegrate lost aspects of the self, and can lead back to health.

Temiars live in small, politically autonomous, relatively egalitarian settlements of 20–100 people along rivers in the rain forest running down the center of the Malay peninsula. The Temiar have become familiar to Western audiences through "Senoi dreaming" and its interpretations in American psychological circles (Domhoff 1985; Dentan 1983). The approximately 11,000 Temiar form one of the major groups within the Senoi ethnic division among the aboriginal peoples (Orang Asli, 'original people') in peninsular Malaysia. Temiars mix swidden agriculture with hunting, fishing, and gathering. They have a peculiarly intimate relationship to the land, the jungle, its flora and fauna, as they move through it daily, garnering cues as they travel from the sounds of various birds, insects, and animals that penetrate the dense jungle foliage.

THE STRUCTURE OF THE SELF

This closeness to the land comes out in the way they think about it. Temiars recognize multiple, detachable, and permeable selves in both human and nonhuman entities. These components include the head (upper), heart (lower/inner), shadow, and odor selves. Humans have head and heart selves or "souls," trees have leaf and root souls, mountains crest and cave souls. This homologous structure shared by all entities sets up a relationship of resemblance, of essential similarity between humans and what we would call "nonhumans." The various selves can detach, interact, and even intermingle as bound "soul" becomes unbound "spirit."

This is a very different world than that of the individuated self of the West, conceived of as an isolable unit fundamentally different from anything not human (Johnson 1985). Scheper-Hughes and Lock (1987) refer to the Temiar type of self, an interactive self that doesn't quite end at the boundaries of the individual, as a sociocentric self. They note that there are consequences in the domain of illness and health for societies who conceive of the self in sociocentric terms. Indeed, for Temiars, whose concept of self is both multiple and sociocentric, there are consequences. Improper social interaction or emotional excess—a word harshly uttered, a promise broken, a desire unfulfilled—can cause illness or misfortune. In turn, to treat illness, the community participates in singing and trance-dancing ceremonies, working together to bring spirits through mediums into the human realm. In order to diagnose and heal, then, Temiars create not only a sociocentric whole through community participation, but indeed a cosmological whole with spirits in attendance as well.

The multiple components or selves are bound inside their respective human bodies, trees, mountains, and rivers in everyday contexts, but can become unbound in the extraordinary contexts of dreams, ritual, and illness. Dreams and trance rituals are appropriate, temporary contexts for selves to become detached and mobile; however, detachment of these components outside of the momentary contexts of dream and trance precipitates illness and misfortune. Interpersonal interaction is cushioned from emotional excess in order to guard against triggering such inappropriate detachment of components of the self. And in the Temiar case, "interpersonal" must be read not only as referring to interactions between human persons, but to those among humans and all other entities. For all entities within the Temiar world are potentially *bə-sɛn'ɔɔy*, 'having person,' capable of becoming animated.

THE HEAD COMPONENT

The head or upper-portion component (*rəwaay*) is the vital, animating principle.[3] In humans, it is situated in the crown of the head or top of the forehead. Proper situation of the head component or "head soul" during everyday, waking life is essential to well-being and the continuance of life.

During dreams, the head soul of the dreamer detaches, in a tiny human form, and meets with the unbound souls of entities (e.g., trees, fruits, flowers) who are also detached and anthropomorphized. The head soul of an entity might express his or her desire to become the dreamer's spiritguide, and confirms the relationship by teaching the dreamer a song, often with concomitant dance steps, ceremonial ornaments, and other performance constraints. Later, during nighttime, housebound, singing and trance-dancing ceremonies, a person sings the song thus received in order to bring the spiritguide into the ceremonial realm. Patients are treated in this context, as mediums are filled with the vision and knowledge of their spiritguides. These ceremonies, like dreams, are temporally bounded contexts in which head souls are safely detached, anthropomorphized, and set in motion.

Prolonged absence of the head soul outside of the contexts of dreams and trance leads to the illness of soul loss (*rɛywaay* 'to lose one's head soul'). Soul loss is marked by weariness, excessive sleeping, and weeping, and may lead to coma, delirium, and death, while the patient's dislocated head soul takes up residence outside the body with spirits of the jungle. During ceremonies, mediums—with the help of their spiritguides—locate and return the lost head soul.

Abrupt occurrences and excessive behavior such as sudden, loud noises or voices raised in anger may cause one to "be startled" (*kəjɨd*, Malay: *kejut*) and thereby disembody the head soul. Many rules of Temiar emotional restraint, social appropriateness, and etiquette are predicated upon avoiding such occurrences. Objects are passed slowly and carefully between persons to avoid dropping the object, which might startle the recipient's head soul to detachment. In the moments between a flash of lightning and subsequent clap of thunder, adults and adolescents will cover the ears of babies and young children, whose head souls are considered more labile than those of adults, to protect their head souls from being startled and detached.[4]

In order to lessen the possibility of startling and soul loss, anger is rarely vented in face-to-face interaction, but rather is formalized in a relatively indirect harangue. Harangues are cloaked in the obscurity of nighttime or predawn darkness, when the angry person begins to vocalize from a sleeping compartment or building separate from the person being criticized. Harangues are often in the third person: the object is referred to as "he" or "she" rather than "you" to further distance the confrontation. Men and women both engage in intra- or interfamily arguments and monologue critiques in this fashion. The object of the harangue, or one of his/her kin, may respond with a counterargument; or, the object might listen in silence. Yet for all its indirect structuring (separate cubicles, third-person pronouns, nighttime darkness), Temiars still consider this a hyper-direct form of interaction capable of shocking the souls of participants or by-

standers into taking flight, resulting in the illness of soul loss. Thus, before resorting to a harangue, people prefer to express their problems to older kin, who then approach the opponent and attempt to dispassionately mediate.

The "true natures" (*kənɨɨh mɨn*) of people and other entities are intimately connected with their head souls or vital essence. Names that "fly above" the "true" name are employed so as not to startle and detach a person's head soul. To use a person's true name indicates anger. Temiars are known for their lack of physical violence toward one another; such drastic behavior is hardly necessary in a society in which the use of a person's true name, or an angry harangue, is considered able to cause serious illness and even death.[5] Abruptness, directness, and activation are thus juxtaposed to indirection, circumlocution, and suspended animation.

Even foods to be consumed are circumspectly designated. When hunted, gathered, or prepared for consumption, they must be referred to by names that "fly above" the true name; otherwise the upper-portion soul of the animal is startled and, when the food is eaten, it transforms into a small cat and bites the heart of the consumer, causing diarrhea, fever, and possibly death. Dentan (1967) and Diffloth (1981) discuss similar linguistic practices among the Senoi Semai; language praxis is thus closely aligned with ethnopsychological dynamics.

THE HEART COMPONENT

The lower-portion component in humans is localized in the heart (*hup*). It is also associated with the blood (*loot*) and breath (*hənum*). Heart and breath are here elided in an indigenous sense of body imagery, one that recognizes rhythmic continuity, and duple rhythm, of both heartbeat and breath—a point I return to later.

While the head soul is the vital or animating principle, the heart soul is the locus of thought, feeling, awareness, and memory. One "thinks" (*na-nim* 's/he thinks'), "becomes aware" or "recalls" (*na-bəlaak*), and feels (*na-sop*) in the heart. Internal debate and rumination are functions of the heart. Memory is heartbound; songs given by spiritguides are inserted into and retained in the heart. While internalized thought is a function of the heart, language, speech, and expression are associated with the head. Temiar distinctions differ from the traditional Western dichotomy between thought and feeling, and turn rather on the distinction between inner experience and vocalized expression.

Temiars have a rich vocabulary of what Diffloth (1976) terms "expressives" to describe emotions felt in the heart, especially longing, lovesickness, or nostalgic remembrance. The wind sways the leaves inside the heart (*ləlangooy*); there is quickened motion in the heart (*pəpəsooy*); the heart whirls and flutters (*sɛrsudɛɛr*). Expressives are formed by reduplicative play; the importance of this play with sound in matters of the heart will be raised again below.

A "well" heart or "true" heart (*hup mʉn*) is "hard" (*təgah*). In longing, trance, and illness, the heart is weak, shaky, and pliable (*bə-gə-ntah*, Malay *bergentar* 'quivering'). The heart soul, like the head soul, is a focal point of illness etiology and treatment. The heart in illness becomes shaky, hot (*bɛdbʉd*), and narrow (*'angɛd*). The heart soul can be startled into whirling and fluttering by the breaking of ceremonial restrictions or restrictions accompanying curative treatment.

Stored anger, like illness, compacts the heart. A heart narrowed by anger can be "opened" or "cleared" through invective or harangue. This is why, despite the risk of causing head-soul loss in the object of one's harangue, one might finally indulge in a harangue—one's heart needs to be cleared.[6] During the divorce of a recently married young couple, the female relatives of the groom were angered that the bride had rejected their male kin. On the ground in the moonlight, outside the house where male representatives of bride and groom were negotiating a divorce, the female relatives of the groom launched into stylized invective, graphically describing and exaggerating the body parts of the bride, who huddled in a darkened building several houses away. The intonation pattern of this stylized invective, like that of the harangue, consists of a suspended monotone leading into a plaintive downward curve.[7] Through their stylized invective, the groom's female kin "expanded" and "cleared" their hot, compacted, angry hearts until finally they were seized with laughter at the absurdity and ingenuity of their exaggerated descriptions. Yet, while the groom's kin are cooled and cleared, the head soul of the bride is endangered—startled by bearing the brunt of this angry invective and verbal assault.

What might such concepts of self and concomitant behaviors do demographically for the group? Temiars are a segmentary society, living in politically autonomous settlements with informal leaders who attempt to influence or persuade. When problems arise, Temiars may resort to (1) mediation, (2) group discussion moving toward consensus, (3) harangue, or (4) fission. Ecologically, Temiars need to keep enough people together in a settlement to provide for cooperative work efforts and to form a distributive base for generalized exchange. But too high a population would overtax land, game, and fish in the area.

Striking a balance between fusion and fission, between consolidating a community and overpopulating it, has its correlate in emotional restraint, a respectful recognition of the detachability and permeability of self and other, as opposed to the harangue, an intentional abuse that could lead to soul loss, a symbolic ejection of self from community. Indeed, the object of a harangue may choose to leave the community altogether, as eventually did the harangued bride. Significantly, the bride's kinship relations in the village were much weaker than those of the groom, who was associated with the sibling group at the core of the linkage of extended families constituting the village. Small-scale, segmentary Temiar villages comprise cognatic descent groups or "ramages" (membership is traced through both parents), which are agamous; inhabitants may marry within or outside the village group, with marriages contracted or terminated by bride and groom (see Firth 1966; Benjamin 1967). Yet the member of the couple that was ejected from the village by what amounts to a strategy of emotional abuse, the bride, was the one in a weaker position vis à vis the cognatic descent group. We thus find specific connections between social structural processes (such as village fission or procedures for handling interpersonal conflict) and ethnopsychological formations.

As village fusion must be balanced by fission, so too, in the Temiar pathogenicity of emotions, must the potential permeability of self be balanced by separation from the other. It is all too easy to typify the sociocentric self as a static state, to envision an idyllic scene of interconnected entities where separation and alienation are not an issue. But I contend that societies that posit sociocentric selves are exhibiting their very concern for the relationship between self and other when they elaborate the concepts and actions which formulate and continually reinstate the sociocentric self.

The behaviors surrounding the odor component are a prime example, for here the permeability of self and other must be balanced by separation, since absorbing someone else's odor causes illness.

ODOR

The odor component emanates from the lower back, and is a composite of a person's labors in obtaining and transporting food. Men exude the odor of game; women, primarily fish and tubers, reflecting the economic division of labor (Roseman 1991). These items are themselves linked with the ultimate source of odor, a potent tree species (Temiar *cəhɔɔŋ*; unidentified) located at the river's source.

When a person walks behind the lower back of another seated person, he or she recites, "Odor, odor, odor." If a person walks by silently without reciting, the odor becomes startled and confused, and is absorbed into the abdomen of the silent passerby, causing an illness characterized by a hard, swollen stomach; gas; vomiting; and belching. The recitation "odor, odor, odor" at once promotes social interaction *and erects a barrier*, halting the potential permeability of the other's odor into the self. Speaking obviates merging; naming the odor separates self from other.

In another illness complex, *pərɛnhǫǫd*, to deny someone's request causes illness or misfortune for the person denied. Here, the problem is that the flow of goods (from self to other, giver to recipient) has been halted. Temiar society is relatively egalitarian with an economic system of generalized exchange that limits the accumulation of individual surplus or wealth. The concepts and behaviors associated with illness help keep the goods flowing, keeping the Temiar egalitarian: good exchange is good health. Again, we find a connection between social structural processes and economic systems (such as the regulation of status and wealth in generalized exchange), and ethnopsychological formations.

Temiar interactions with one another and the cosmos are driven by a dynamic tension that celebrates the potential detachability of self while guarding the integrity of self. The cultural subscript of sociocentric interdependence, then, is the continual reinstatement of an independent, bounded self. Similarly, in societies commonly characterized as egocentric, such as contemporary mainstream United States, the emphasized cultural value on the independent, individuated self exists in tension with a cultural subscript that values interdependence in the family, in the community, in nationalism, in employer-employee relations, or within unions. And the seemingly indivisible self is variously divided into a multiplicity of selves or social roles (wife, mother, teacher, daughter, citizen) constituting the social person in sociological theory, or is analyzed psychologically in multiple terms such as Freud's ego, id, and superego or Jung's anima and animus. Building on a study of these and other sources, such as the imaginal beings of child's play, actors' dramatic personae, and religious visitations, Watkins (1986) proposes a contemporary Western psychotherapeutic technique that entertains a multiplicity of selves or "invisible guests."

Both egocentric and sociocentric societies, then, contain cultural subscripts that implicate their opposites. Behaviors surrounding the odor component provide a window into the Temiar concept of the sociocentric self, and are a prime example of how the permeability of self and other must be balanced by its inverse, separation. The tension is articulated in terms of illness and health: excess permeability leads to illness, maintenance of the integrity of self constitutes health. And just as issues of connection and separation, fusion and fission exist in dynamic tension in the Temiar constructions of self and society, so do issues of generosity and greed dog the path of distributive exchange. While the *pərɛnhǫǫd* complex employs ethnopsychological formations and illness concepts to *encourage* the flow of goods, techniques also abound for *reserving* enough materials for personal use. I was taught just how small a bit of tobacco to give to fulfill social etiquette and avoid causing *pərɛnhǫǫd*, while reserving some for myself (and my teachers, my immediate household members!). In a distributive economy, an overflow of generosity can be as problematic as undue greed.

Temiars, then, are constantly negotiating the sociocentric self. Balance involves maintaining the interactive flow between persons, while properly demarcating boundaries. This concern for the relation between self and other is also played out around the emotion of longing as it is modulated in ritual.

HEARTBEATS AND BAMBOO TUBES; PERFORMANCE AND AFFECT

The sentiment of longing is initially elaborated within dreams when Temiar mediums first meet their spiritguides. During dreams, the head or heart component of an entity such as a fruit tree detaches itself and emerges in humanized form, male or female. It speaks to the roaming head soul of the Temiar dreamer: "I come to you, I desire you. I want to be your teacher, I want to call you father." The acquaintance is thus begun in a mélange of desire, pedagogy, and kinship.[8] Male mediums often speak of their female spiritguides as "wives" in addition to their being "children." Bemoaning the fate of transitory dream encounters, they comment: "I sleep with her at night, but in the morning, my bed is empty."

The longings initiated and momentarily fulfilled during dreams are later recapitulated and intensified during ceremonial performances. The affective sensibility pervading the relationships of spiritguides with humans, the sentiment of longing, is aroused by the socially structured sounds and movements of ceremonial performance. Singing at first with his own voice, crouching on the floor with eyes closed and hand cupped over his ear, listening at once deep within himself and far away, the medium "causes [the spirit] to emerge." Continuing to sing, standing, beginning to dance, the medium becomes imbued with the voice, vision, and knowledge of the spiritguide. As the medium continues to sing, he is transformed; his simultaneous presence of body and absence of self is described as "one's heart being elsewhere, to the side" (*hup 'ɛh 'ɛn-tuuy 'əh*). The medium's voice becomes the spiritguide's vocalization; his heart is elsewhere, but the subsequent experience of emptiness or incompleteness, which gives rise to the emotion of longing, is completed by the presence of the emergent spiritguide.

Each phrase the medium sings is interactively responded to by a female chorus beating pairs of bamboo tubes against a log. Performance practice interweaves the male aspect (initial singer) and the female aspect (choral respondents) in a heterophonic overlap in order to generate spiritual power. This dynamic is reiterated in a cosmological theory that combines a male medium, free-ranging in everyday life but "stuck on the ground" when he sings, with a female spiritguide. Women are seen as relatively constrained to the settlement area during everyday life, but, in a symbolic inversion, have far-ranging vision when they arrive as spiritguides. (Roseman 1984, 1989). The interweaving of genders in performance is found again in the terminology used to refer to the pairs of bamboo tubes that members of the chorus beat in alternation to produce the duple rhythm of the percussive accompaniment: the longer, lower-pitched tube is termed "father" (*bəah*) and the shorter, higher-pitched tube, "mother" (*bo'*). Both genders are necessary to create the rhythm that helps evoke the sentiment of longing.

The term *hɛwhəyaaw* 'longing' is central to the complex of desire and remembrance as it crosscuts dimensions of spirit-mediumship, courtship, trancing, and curing. A Temiar medium comments:

> One hears it in one's ear, like wind: *"Yaaw-waaw-waaw."* If we sit, dream, we hear this in our ear, its uncomfortable. We must having a singing ceremony, it orders us to have a trance-dancing ceremony, only then are we relieved. Otherwise, after a while, we would go mad. [*Hɛwhəyaaw*] is like a hot, dry wind rustling the leaves when there is no rain; we must hold a ceremony.[9]

Female trance-dancers also describe their participation in singing ceremonies as an intensification and culmination of longing for male spirits, as this woman explains:

> *Bərenlii'*. It is just like *hɛwhəyaaw*. There is a male spirit of the fruits that desires to sleep with me. Even when I dream, he's there. After a while, one doesn't feel right, one's heart is shaky, one thinks only of him, one wants to go off into the jungle, one's spirit is drawn to the jungle. I must participate in a singing ceremony, only then can I stand it. We sing and dance, the male spirit of the fruit trees alights on the leaf ornaments, and I am transformed.[10]

The sentiment of longing is transformed into a momentarily satisfying communion between trancer and spirit-entity when properly channeled within the context of trance-dancing ceremonies. Unrequited longing, however, leads to the illness of soul loss. Here, the direction of the interaction is reversed. Instead of the movement from jungle to household exemplified by emergent spiritguides attracted during ceremonies, the soul of the ill person is drawn to the jungle, seduced by a spiritguide into residing far from that person's settlement. In one such case, a young woman was experiencing weariness, weeping, and general malaise.[11] The medium Abilem Lum dreamt that he found her head soul upriver living with a spirit that had taken a liking to her when he'd seen her traveling by during a recent river journey. They had set up house together, and were comfortably ensconced upriver. Abilem Lum arranged for a singing and trance-dancing ceremony to be held, so that with the help of his spiritguides he could bring her head soul back to her body.

Illnesses traced to excessive longing, such as soul loss, are treated in the context of singing and trance-dancing ceremonies accompanied by bamboo-tube percussion because the cere-monies play upon this emotion, focusing and momentarily satis-fying it. The sentiment of longing is intensified and modulated in the ceremonial setting through the agencies of sound and movement. Continuous pulsating sounds of certain birds (such as the golden-throated barbet, *Megalaima franklini*) and insects (such as the cicada *hərɲɔɔd*) that alternate high and low tones are said to beat in rhythm with one's heart (see Figures 1 and 2). Moving with the heart until it whirls and flutters, these sounds are said to move the heart to longing for a loved one or a deceased relative. Even the onomatopoetic replication of the barbet's song (howaaw-howaaw) and the cicada's call (laaw-laaw-laaw) recall the expressives denoting the sentiment of longing felt in the heart: *hɛwhəyaaw, bərenlii' bərolaaw*.

The bamboo tube percussion in singing/trance-dancing cere-monies is socially structured as a continuous, two-toned pul-sation alternating between higher and lower frequencies (see Figure 3). The continuous pulsation of the sound renders each successive tone familiar, cushioning the listener against startle. In performance, this pulsing sound is said to "move with one's heart," focusing and intensifying longing to effect the transfor-mation of trance. During the ritual, the trancer's subjective expe-rience of incompleteness is momentarily relieved by connecting with spiritguides; Temiars have developed an ingenious way of projecting their desires onto the spirits, who can then be brought into the ceremonial realm to effect momentary fulfillment. Trancers report feeling refreshed and physically "lighter" after the ceremonies.

The pulsing beat of the bamboo tubes is an iconic sign in that it gains its meaning through the association of similar forms: the continuous two-toned beating of hearts, certain bird and insect calls, and the percussive rhythm of the tubes. As an iconic sign, it brings together sounds of the rain forest and sounds of the body, and links these with a theory of selves and spirits that can be loosened and rebound through the modulation of feeling. An-choring themes of boundaries and interconnection in natural and physiological forms, the sounds of the bamboo tubes resemble Turner's dominant symbols (1968:28), which pack their affec-tive power through the simultaneous condensation of physiolog-ical and ideological poles. The Beckers (1981) suggest that a symbol gains legitimacy and authority to the extent that it is rooted in a culture's concept of the "natural" and thus the "true"; this rootedness through similar form they term "iconicity." The beating of Temiar tubes gains affective power through its rooted-ness in the rain forest and the body as these are culturally transformed into signs and symbols. Daniel highlights the poly-chromy or multimodality of the sign, reminding us that "iconic as well as indexical aspects may be concealed within the same sign" (1984:39). To the extent that the meaning of the bamboo tubes is rooted in the body and thus contiguous with that which it signs, it also has an indexical aspect.

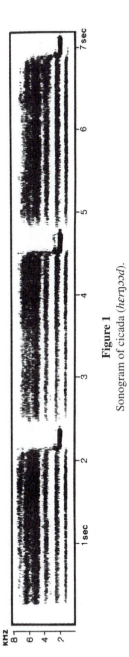

Figure 1
Sonogram of cicada (*hɛɳɔɔd*).

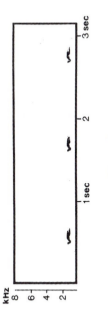

Figure 2
Sonogram of golden-throated barbet (*Megalaima franklini*).

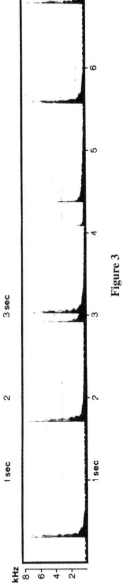

Figure 3
Sonogram of bamboo-tube stampers (one pair; alternation begins with higher-pitched tube).

THE AESTHETICS OF SWAY

The swaying movements of trance-dancers also link the human body and rain forest themes, especially the undulating movements of windswept jungle foliage, with the emotion of longing. The expressives *ləlaŋooy* and *loŋɛt-loŋat* are used to refer to women swaying as they walk to the river, palm fronds swaying in the breeze, and trance-dancers bending and swaying to the beat of the bamboo tubes. All these movements evoke the yearning of *hewheyaaw*, the undulation a visual correlate of the audio pulsation of bamboo tubes. The overtones of seduction are not to be lost here: in daily life, swaying bodily movements attract other humans; in ceremonies, they entice spirits to attend. As trancers progressively bend and sway more deeply to the accompaniment of pulsating tubes, their hearts begin to "beat with the tubes" and their longing is intensified until they begin to stumble and shake (*kɛnrook*) and their head souls disengage. While the dancers' bodies lie fainted on the dance floor, their unbound head souls meet with unbound spirits of the jungle—and in this fleeting encounter, longings, which have been projected onto spirits who can then be brought through ceremony into one's midst, are momentarily fulfilled.

When Temiars gather for a singing and trance-dancing ceremony, a time when healing can be performed, they simultaneously celebrate an intimacy with the spirits, and frame the potentially overwhelming power of such intimacy within the appropriate spatiotemporal bounds and paced sounds of ceremonial performance. The ceremony celebrates a momentary, balanced intimacy with the spirits; it is thus the appropriate context in which to treat a patient whose interactions with the spirits have exceeded proper bounds. The ceremonies are preventative in that they provide a forum for trancers to engage in longing, temporary detachment, and momentary completion; they are curative for those patients for whom longing has gone awry.

The themes of permeability and integrity of self, the two horns of the sociocentric dilemma, are choreographed into trance-dancing. Singing mediums, voicing the spiritguides, are in a state of "other-awareness" or "unconsciousness" (*bə-ralii'*) with their "hearts elsewhere" and their "eyes changed"; but they continue to control their trance and sing without fainting. Dancers, however, commence a cycle of changing or "transforming" (*lɛslɑɑs*) in which the head soul is "twisted off like a young plant shoot," leading through fainting and back to consciousness.

In one ceremonial genre received from the spirits of the annual fruits, dancers begin by dancing a slow, strolling-in-place movement, bending and swaying the torso as first one arm, then the other, swings in front of the body. The dancer begins to lose his or her balance, becoming unsteady and shuddering. When the chorus notices such a dancer, they begin to push the tempo of the bamboo tubes, subdivide the duple rhythm, sing more loudly, and if possible, push their vocal range up an octave. At a certain point, the dancer breaks step and begins a double-footed, low-level, rapid-paced jump. After about a minute of jumping, the dancer falls to the floor in a faint (*na-kəbʉs* 'he/she faints'). This term, used also for "death," describes simultaneous immobility and mobility: the physical body lies immobile, while the head soul is released into movement and dances with the visiting spirits, or travels above the forest canopy. Fallen dancers are laid together in the center of the dance floor, to prevent other dancers from tripping over them. Some dancers report a total lack of sensation while fainted; others tell of hearing the sounds of singing and percussion faintly, as if from a distance, while others describe visions of soaring above the forest canopy and circling the mountain tops.

Eventually, when the fallen dancers begin to stir, a medium sings over the fainted dancers, shaking his hand-held leaf whisk over them. Participants along the sidelines, often members of the opposite sex who are attracted to particular dancers, now enter the dance space. With help from others, they raise the dancers to a standing position and, support them around the waist (*cɛbcaab*), begin to dance them back to consciousness. A dancer, her head rolled to the side and down, limply waves her arms as she is gently lifted up and down, reminiscent of the bending and swaying in her original movements. Slowly she comes back to consciousness and begins to dance on her own, her helper retreating to the sidelines. After a few minutes of strolling in place, she too retreats to the sidelines and sits. Another spectator, perhaps her helper, often expressing his attraction, rolls her a cigarette. Sitting and smoking, she comes back to her "true heart" and "true eyes," and begins to "think" (*na-nim*) again.

The dance enacts the process of detachment of the head component and its interaction with the visiting spirits, creating a cosmocentric whole as humans and nonhumans cross boundaries and meet in the ritual realm. It also enacts themes of community support and interdependence, the sociocentric whole. For after having fainted and then begun to stir, the dancer is picked up by members of the community, who dance him or her back to consciousness by physically supporting the dancer's body. This kinetic and proxemic statement of interdependence is counterbalanced when community members offering support subsequently withdraw to the sidelines as the dancer shows she can now support her own weight. Yet even as the dancer dances on her own, she is surrounded by other dancers and singers who together co-create the event. The choreography recognizes the individual, permeable yet bounded, enmeshed within the web of connections constituting a sociocentric society.

CONCLUSIONS

For societies with sociocentric selves, the beauty of interconnectedness with community and nature is offset by concern for the integrity of self. Temiar concepts of permeable, multiple, detachable selves enable a special sense of comradery with the humans and nonhumans of their social universe, but this supportive network is also fraught with danger: benevolent spiritguides are there to be met, but so are illness agents. Temiars celebrate interactions with the animated spirits of the landscape in dreams and trance, but these contexts are temporally and spatially controlled to avoid excessive contact. To overstep the balance is to enter the realm of illness, of soul loss.

Temiars share their concern for the multiplicity and separability of components of the self with other Southeast Asian peoples: the Malays with their *semangat, angin,* and the more Islamic *nyawa, ruh,* and *napas* (Endicott 1970; Laderman 1987:297); the 32 *khwan* of the Thai (Rajadhon 1962; Inge-Heinze 1977), the Thai *chitaphud* and *phi* (Inge-Heinze 1977:338–340); the *leip-bya* of the Burmese; the *pralüng* of the Cambodians; and the *püng khamau* of the Mons (Rajadhon 1962:121). Emotional restraint is an issue in each of these societies; Geertz, for example, writes of the Javanese value placed on the smooth, emotionless response of *ikhlas* (1973b, 1983), while Phillips (1965:66) characterizes Thai politeness as a "social cosmetic" based on a fundamental concern with structuring one's behavior, irrespective of intentions, so as least to disturb others.

In these societies, where the boundaries between self, other, and cosmos are less distinct, where detachability of components of the self is a recognized dynamic and emotional restraint a concomitant strategy for social interaction, we find sudden or excessive emotions considered pathogenic. When a Thai child, whose *khwan* is more "tender," suffers a shock from some sudden fright and cries sharply and continuously, the child's *khwan* is said to have taken flight. An adult man experiencing a great fright may die of its effect. The ceremony of *tham khwan,* performed to strengthen or confirm the *khwan* after a fright, involves recalling the *khwan* and tying cotton threads around the wrists to keep it within bounds. To harm a person, or a person's animals or possessions, is to injure the *khwan,* requiring a *tham khwan* to restore the *khwan* to its normal state. *Tham khwan,* in everyday use, has thus come to mean compensation for an injury done (Rajadhon 1962:122–123). The coalescence of detachability, startle, illness, and matters of property and compensation recalls the Temiar predilection toward good health through good exchange. Temiars pass items carefully among themselves. To drop an item while passing it to someone else is to endanger that person's head soul through startle; to deny a person's request for an item is to place him or her in danger of unfulfilled, excessive longing. Social interaction and economic exchange are inextricably intertwined with concepts surrounding the structure of the self.

Given their susceptibility to fragmentation, Temiars are equally prone to celebrate its benefits in the pleasure of the connection with spiritguides within the appropriate ritual contexts, or to guard against unwanted permeability by cushioning interaction and erecting barriers when necessary. So Temiars maintain the separation of self from other by reciting the name "odor" as they pass behind another person, guarding against the affliction that results from absorbing the emanation of that person's odor. Similarly, Malays recite "locking charms" (*pengunci*) with verses such as "Oh, shut it and lock it, shut it and lock it, may enemies keep their distance" to erect barriers between themselves and human or supernatural harm (Laderman 1988). An angry word or sudden shock may startle a Temiar's head soul to disembody; for a Malay, a shock can cause a portion or all of the *semangat* to take flight, rendering a person vulnerable to spirit attack and illness. Yet while Temiars cushion social interaction out of concern for this fragile integrity of self, Malays take pleasure in startling hypersensitive individuals in order to provoke displays of *latah,* characterized by utterance of expletives, imitation of other people's words and actions, and indiscriminately following people's orders. *Latah* might best be understood in terms of the dissolution of boundaries of the self, a weakening of personal barriers that leaves the *latah* open to other people's speech, gestures, and selves (Yap 1952:561; Simons 1985:56; Laderman 1988).

Rituals speak to particular cultural sensibilities; the formalized speech and concerted action of Javanese funerary rituals, when properly performed, promote the smooth emotional detachment from grief of *ikhlas* and the communal harmony of *rukun.* On the other hand, the raucous animality of the Balinese cockfight, the tears of grief shed during a Balinese trance séance, and the stylized abandon of some genres of Balinese trance-dancing provide a symbolic inversion, a counterpoint to the emotional restraint of daily existence (Geertz 1973c; Connor, Asch, and Asch 1986; Bateson and Mead 1942; Babcock 1978). Temiar singing and trance-dancing ceremonies, whether held for entertainment and the pleasure of the spiritguide connection or for healing purposes, allow for a momentary loosening of restraint. Music and dance are structured to push upon the affective sensibility of longing so that healers, trancers, and patients can effectively cross (and reestablish) boundaries between self and other.

To comprehend the objectives of ritual and the techniques by which they are accomplished—such as the symbolic formations of music and dance—we would do well to begin by studying the cultural construct of the person. Temiars' iconic use of pulsing bamboo-tube percussion to "move with the heart" and set head souls in motion is rendered intelligible when viewed in relation to their structure of the self and the emotional world. Given a theory of self that relates vocalized expression to the disembodied head soul, we can see why vocalized sound is an especially potent medium for Temiars, and why song is the medium that spirits are said to choose when, unbound from their physical entities, they cross into the human realm. In the Southeast Asian area, where listeners are affected by the mere sound (*bunyi*) of a beautiful voice (Laderman, 1987:299; Errington 1975; Siegel 1979), the relationship between performance and affect has many levels. We need to examine not only the content of what is said, as meaning-centered approaches to the study of symbolism ask us to do, nor merely who is speaking in sociological terms of role, status, and gender, as sociolinguistics and the ethnography of speaking have taught us to do. We also need to ask how social interaction and ritual expression take shape, given specific local theories of the structure of the self and the emotional world.

NOTES

Acknowledgments. This paper is based on 20 months of field research conducted among the Temiar of Ulu Kelantan, Malaysia, 1981–1982. Research was funded by the Social Science Research Council, the National Science Foundation (BNS81-02784), and the Wenner-Gren Foundation for Anthropological Research (Grant No. 4064). The assistance of these institutions is gratefully acknowledged. The paper has benefited from comments by James Boon, Robert K. Dentan, Joseph de Rivera, A. Thomas Kirsch, Carol Laderman, Susan Ostrander, Steven Field, Karl Heider, Carol E. Robertson, Signe Howell, and Geoffrey M. White.

[1]The term "emotion" is sometimes used to distinguish a biological substratum from the culturally constructed response of "sentiment." I use both terms to refer to the culturally constructed affective experience.

[2]For further examples of the interrelation of culture, sentiment, and performance, see Feld (1982), Basso (1985), and Abu-Lughod (1986).

[3]Cognates of *rəwaay* refer to a "soul" principle among several Malaysian aboriginal (Orang Asli) groups. Blagden lists *ro-wai* as "soul" only among the Semang of Sungai Plus (Skeat and Blagden 1966 [1906]:II:720). Subsequent researchers, however, report cognates among other Aslian speakers. Howell (1984:127–141) interprets *ruwai* among the Chewong as a "vital principle," "consciousness," and "spiritguide." *Ruai* as "soul" among the Semai is located just behind the center of the forehead and is detachable in dreams (Dentan 1979:82). Jah Hut have seven types of *ruay* or "soul" (Couillard 1980:33).

[4]Thunderstorms themselves may result from displays of emotional excess.

[5]For comparable data on nonaggression among neighboring Orang Asli groups, see Robarchek (1979b) and Dentan (1979) on the Semai, and Howell (1986) on the Chewong.

[6]Robarchek (1979a) discusses the clearing of dissent or "desensitization of emotion" through lengthy, repetitive discussions (*bcaraa'*) among the Semai. For Temiars, longings in the heart can also be "cleared" or "opened" by playing solo instruments (flutes, jaws' harps) in the late afternoon, or singing late at night while lying on one's sleeping mat.

[7]These intonation patterns are called *jenhook*, a term also used to describe a song phrase characterized by a recitation tone evolving into a downward curve.

[8]Temiar terms for "desire" include the verbs *pət* ('*i-pət ma-* . . . 'I miss, long for . . .'), *cɛn* 'want,' *hǫǫd* 'desire,' and *hog* 'desire sexual in-

tercourse.' The second and third may be used to express both material desires and human passions. These two are also the words reportedly used by spirit-guides when expressing their intentions toward humans.

[9]For comparative purposes, I indicate where quotes are located in the field corpus. "AF" signifies "Author's Fieldnotes." Information includes name or initials of informant, informant's residence, date recorded, location in author's fieldnotes. AF: Abilem Lum, Belau, September 1981, FN 659.

[10]AF: LBK, Pulat, 24 July 1982, FN 1822.

[11]Approximately one month later, the young woman exhibited the full symptoms of malaria, including fever, shaking, and enlarged spleen, confirmed by blood test. The depressive syndrome may have been an early indication of this disease.

REFERENCES

Abu-Lughod, Lila. 1986. *Veiled Sentiments: Honor and Poetry in a Bedouin Society*. Berkeley: University of California Press.

Babcock, Barbara. 1978. *The Reversible World: Symbolic Inversion in Art and Society*. Ithaca: Cornell University Press.

Basso, Ellen B. 1985. *A Musical View of the Universe: Kalapalo Myth and Ritual Performances*. Philadelphia: University of Pennsylvania Press.

Bateson, Gregory. 1956. *Naven*. Stanford: Stanford University Press.

Bateson, Gregory, and Margaret Mead. 1942. *Balinese Character: A Photographic Analysis*. New York: New York Academy of Sciences.

Becker, Judith, and Alton Becker. 1981. A Musical Icon: Power and Meaning in Javanese Gamelan Music. *The Sign in Music and Literature* (Wendy Steiner, ed.), pp. 203–215. Austin. University of Texas Press.

Benjamin, Geoffrey. 1967. Temiar Kinship. *Federation Museums Journal* 12(n.s.):1–25.

Berger, Peter L., and T. Luckmann. 1966. *The Social Construction of Reality*. New York: Anchor Books.

Connor, Linda, Patsy Asch, and Timothy Asch. 1986. *Jero Tapakan: Balinese Healer*. Cambridge: Cambridge University Press.

Couillard, Marie Andre. 1980. *Tradition in Tension: Carvings in a Jah Hut Community*. Penang: Universiti Sains Malaysia.

Daniel, E. Valentine. 1984. *Fluid Signs: Being a Person the Tamil Way*. Berkeley: University of California Press.

Dentan, Robert Knox. 1967. The Mammalian Taxonomy of the Sen'oi Semai. *Malayan Nature Journal* 20:100–106.

_____. 1979. *The Semai*. Fieldwork edition. New York: Holt, Rinehart and Winston.

_____. 1983. *A Dream of Senoi*. Special Studies Series No. 150. Buffalo: State University of New York, Council on International Studies.

Diffloth, Gerard. 1976. Expressives in Semai. *Austroasiatic Studies, Part 1* (Phillip N. Jenner et al., eds.), pp. 249–264. Honolulu: University Press of Hawaii.

_____. 1981. To Taboo Everything at All Times. *Proceedings of the Berkeley Linguistic Society*, pp. 157–165.

Domhoff, G. William. 1985. *The Mystique of Dreams*. Berkeley: University of California Press.

Durkheim, Emile. 1965 [1915]. *The Elementary Forms of the Religious Life*. New York: Free Press.

Endicott, Kirk. 1970. *An Analysis of Malay Magic*. Oxford: Clarendon Press.

Errington, Shelly. 1975. A Study of Genre: Meaning and Form in the Malay *Hikayat Hang Tuah*. Ph.D. Dissertation. Department of Anthropology, Cornell University.

Feld, Steven. 1982. *Sound and Sentiment*. Philadelphia: University of Pennsylvania Press.

Fernandez, James. 1977. The Performance of Ritual Metaphors. *The Social Use of Metaphor* (J. D. Sapir and J. C. Crocker, eds.), pp. 100–131. Philadelphia: University of Pennsylvania Press.

Firth, Raymond. 1966. Bilateral Descent Groups: An Operational Viewpoint. *Royal Anthropological Institute Occasional Papers* 16:22–37.

Geertz, Clifford. 1973a. Person, Time and Conduct in Bali. *The Interpretation of Cultures*, pp. 360–411. New York: Basic Books.

_____. 1973b. Ritual and Social Change: A Javanese Example. *The Interpretation of Cultures*, pp. 142–169. New York: Basic Books.

_____. 1973c. Deep Play: Notes on a Balinese Cockfight. *The Interpretation of Cultures*, pp. 412–453. New York: Basic Books.

_____. 1983. "From the Native's Point of View": On the Nature of Anthropological Understanding. *Local Knowledge*, pp. 55–70. New York: Basic Books.

Howell, Signe. 1984. *Society and Cosmos: Chewong of Peninsular Malaysia*. New York: Oxford University Press.

_____. 1986. To Be Angry Is Not to Be Human, But to Be Fearful Is. Paper presented to the Conference on Peace, Action, and the Concept of Self. Edinburgh.

Inge-Heinze, Ruth. 1977. The Need for *Tham Khwan*: A Psychocultural Study of Animist Tenets in a Buddhist Society, The Case of Thailand. *Berkeley Working Papers on South and Southeast Asia*, Vol. 1: 1975–1976, pp. 321–428. Berkeley: Center for South and Southeast Asian Studies.

Ito, Karen L. 1985. Affective Bonds: Hawaiian Interrelationships of Self. *Person, Self, and Experience: Exploring Pacific Ethnopsychologies* (G. W. White and J. Kirkpatrick, eds.), pp. 301–327. Berkeley: University of California Press.

Johnson, Frank. 1985. The Western Concept of Self. *Culture and Self: Asian and Western Perspectives* (A. J. Marsella et al., eds.), pp. 91–137. New York: Tavistock.

Kapferer, Bruce. 1979. Mind, Self, and Other in Demonic Illness: The Negation and Reconstruction of Self. *American Ethnologist* 6:110–133.

Kleinman, Arthur, and Byron Good, eds. 1985. *Culture and Depression*. Berkeley: University of California Press.

Laderman, Carol. 1987. The Ambiguity of Symbols in the Structure of Healing. *Social Science and Medicine* 24:293–301.

_____. 1988. Discussant: Comments on the Panel, "Cultural Dimensions of Healing in Southeast Asia." 40th Annual Meetings of the Association for Asian Studies, San Francisco, 1988.

Lutz, Catherine. 1985. The Anthropology of Emotions. *Annual Review of Anthropology*. Palo Alto: Annual Reviews.

Marsella, Anthony J., George De Vos, and Francis L. K. Hsu, eds. 1985. *Culture and Self: Asian and Western Perspectives*. London: Tavistock.

Mauss, Marvel. 1960a. Une Catégorie de l'esprit humaine: La notion de personne, celle de "moi." *Sociologie et Anthropologie*, pp. 313–364. Paris: Press Universitaire de France.

_____. 1960b. Les techniques du corps. *Sociologie et Anthropologie*, pp. 365–388. Paris: Press Universitaire de France.

Phillips, Herbert. 1965. *Thai Peasant Personality*. Berkeley: University of California Press.

Rajadhon, Phya Anuman. 1962. The Khwan and Its Ceremonies. *Journal of the Siam Society* 50:119–164.

Robarchek, Clay. 1979a. Conflict, Emotion, and Abreaction: Resolution of Conflict among the Semai Senoi. *Ethos* 7:104–123.

_____. 1979b. Learning to Fear: A Case Study of Emotional Conditioning. *American Ethnologist* 6:555–567.

Rosaldo, Michelle Z. 1980. *Knowledge and Passion: Ilongot Notions of Self and Social Life*. Cambridge: Cambridge University Press.

Roseman, Marina. 1984. The Social Structuring of Sound: The Temiar Example. *Ethnomusicology* 28:441–445.

_____. 1988. The Pragmatics of Aesthetics: The Performance of Healing among Senoi Temiar. *Social Science and Medicine* 27:811–818.

_____. 1989. Inversion and Conjuncture: Male and Female in Temiar Performance. *Women and Music in Cross-Cultural Perspective* (Ellen Koskoff, ed.), pp. 131–149. Urbana: University of Illinois Press.

_____. 1991. *Healing Sounds form the Malaysian Rainforest: Temiar Music and Medicine*. Berkeley: University of California Press.

Scheper-Hughes, Nancy, and Margaret Lock. 1987. The Mindful Body: A prolegomenon to Future Work in Medical Anthropology. *Medical Anthropology Quarterly* 1(n.s.):6–41.

Schieffelin, Edward. 1985. Performance and the Cultural Construction of Reality. *American Ethnologist* 12:707–724.

Schutz, Alfred. 1967. *Collected Papers I: The Problem of Social Reality* (M. Natonson, ed.). The Hague: Nijhoff.

Shweder, R. A., and R. A. Levine. 1984. *Culture Theory: Essays on Mind, Self and Emotion*. Cambridge: Cambridge University Press.

Siegel, James. 1979. *Shadow and Sound: The Historical Thought of a Sumatran People*. Chicago: University of Chicago Press.

Simons, Ronald C. 1985. The Resolution of the Latah Paradox. *The Culture-Bound Syndromes* (R. C. Simons and C. C. Hughes, eds.), pp. 43–62. Boston: D. Reidel.

Skeat, Walter W., and Charles O. Blagden. 1966 [1906]. *Pagan Races of the Malay Peninsula*, Vols. 1 and 2. London: Frank Cass.

Turner, Victor. 1968. *The Forest of Symbols*. Ithaca: Cornell University Press.

Watkins, Mary. 1986. *Invisible Guests: The Development of Imaginal Dialogues*. Hillsdale, NJ: Analytic Press.

White, Geoffrey M., and John Kirkpatrick, eds. 1985. *Person, Self, and Experience: Exploring Pacific Ethnopsychologies*. Berkeley: University of California Press.

Yap, P. M. 1952. The *Latah* Reaction: Its Pathodynamics and Nosological Position. *Journal of Mental Science* 98:515–564.

CHAPTER FOUR

Sociocultural Assessment of Mental Illness

A large portion of what is considered mental illness is structured in emotional distress. Emotions are structured within sociocultural systems of meaning and interpersonal behaviors. Therefore, sociocultural assessment is essential for client-centered psychiatry.

Cultural psychologist Richard Shweder (1985) has devised a six-aspect procedure for the cultural assessment of emotions. When an anthropologist goes to a foreign culture to study the emotions of the people there, he or she first asks the question: What type of emotions does a particular cultural group experience? Some emotions that are found in western culture may not be present in the culture being studied, and other emotions not found in the West may be present. For example, guilt seems to be an emotion that is not found among the Swat Pukhtun (see Chapter 3). Similarly, other cultures have a number of emotions related to what westerners would call depression, but these emotions carry different meanings, most of them not related to mental illness (Kleinman & Good, 1985). Thus, we cannot assume that all cultural groups experience the same exact set of emotions.

The next question that needs to be asked is: Which emotions are elicited by which situations? The same situation cannot be presumed to elicit the same emotion across cultures, because similar situations can have different meanings cross-culturally. For example, a rape of a woman in American society can result in a rape trauma syndrome characterized by anxiety and depressive symptoms, while in a different cultural context rape may not be associated with such a trauma syndrome (Gregor, 1990).

The next question that needs to asked is: What do the emotions mean to indigenous observers? This is a crucial question when assessing pathological emotions. Should we assume a biomedical perspective that a client with disordered emotions is suffering from a brain disease? Emotional distress can be a reaction to social stress as well as a means of manipulating interpersonal relationships. Indigenous meanings can include biological, spiritual, economic, and interpersonal explanations for emotional distress. The meaning of emotional distress must be assessed in its sociocultural context.

The next question that needs to be asked is: What are the vehicles or means of expression for the communication of an emotion? This is also extremely important when assessing pathological emotions because emotional distress can have varying cultural forms of expression. These are known in medical anthropology as idioms of distress. For example, a Brazilian woman may express her anxiety and anger stemming from social stress in the form of physical illness (see Chapter 11). In another culture, spirit possession may be the vehicle of expression. And in another culture it could be suicidal gestures. Thus, it is very important to understand the cultural idioms of distress when assessing emotions.

The next question that needs to asked is: What emotions are proper or improper for a person of a particular social status? This is also very important when assessing emotional pathology because of the effects of dominance hierarchies on personality development (see Chapter 3). Social structures define the statuses of people in different ways with differing sets of emotions and behaviors that are considered proper or improper according to positions in dominance hierarchies (gender, racial, ethnic, and so on). For example, anger and aggressiveness in a woman is considered deviant and even pathological in some cultures, although the same behavior is considered normal in a man. Thus, the effects of dominance hierarchies in a particular culture need to be considered when assessing an individual's emotions.

The next question that needs to be asked is: How are unexpressed emotions handled? This is also very important when assessing emotional pathology. For many people, especially those in subservient positions, the open expression of emotional distress may be socially or politically difficult as this could imply dissatisfaction with the status quo (Kleinman, 1986). For these people, some alternative means of expression is found which does not reflect on them in a social or political way. One common avenue of expression is *somatization*, that is, the expression of emotional distress in somatic (bodily) symptoms (see Chapters 10 and 11). Another possibility is *dissociation*, in which the person assumes an alternative identity from the cultural repertoire through spirit possession and expresses negative emotions in a way that does not reflect on the person because he or she is considered to be possessed by a demon or spirit (see Chapter 13).

The need for sociocultural assessment of patients with mental disorders is recognized in DSM-IV (American Psychiatric Association, 1994) by the inclusion of an *Outline for Cultural Formulation* for use in cultural assessment. This cultural outline is the first attempt in the DSM to alert clinicians that an assessment of a mental disorder should be made within the cultural context of the patient and to judge the implications that has for clinical treatment. These five factors should be assessed:

DSM-IV Outline for Cultural Formulation
1. Cultural identity of the individual
2. Cultural explanations of the individual's illness
3. Cultural factors related to psychosocial environment and levels of functioning
4. Cultural elements of the relationship between the individual and the clinician
5. Overall cultural assessment for diagnosis and care

SOURCE: American Psychiatric Association, 1994

DSM-IV suggests that the clinician making an assessment of a patient provide a narrative summary for each of these categories. This is in essence a *brief clinical ethnography* as suggested by Kleinman (1988).

The first category in the cultural outline is the *cultural identity of the individual.* This refers to the collective mass of cognitive schemas of an individual's cultural or ethnic reference group. There may be typical forms of mental illness in different cultures. What is typical in one culture may be exotic in another. How this behavior is understood depends on the cognitive schemas of the observer.

Subcultural groups will also have differing forms of mental illness. Immigrants in North America may have varying degrees of involvement with the culture of their country of origin and the Anglo American culture in the United States. Therefore, they will behave with varying degrees of consistency to cultural norms of mental illness. The same situation is also true for ethnic minorities.

Conversely, in nonwestern societies westernized minority segments of the society possessing a more western cultural identity may present with westernized forms of mental illness. Therefore, in a client-centered psychiatry it is vital that the cultural identity of each patient be assessed individually.

To understand the cultural identity of the patient, the clinician must assess the individual's cultural schemas. This means that clinicians must study the cultures of the persons they are likely to see in their region's clinics and hospitals. However, knowing whether a particular patient fits a cultural generalization only comes from asking. Because cultural schemas vary by individual, each patient should be treated as a unique case. Each individual should be asked about cultural identity in an open-ended fashion, allowing the person to elaborate on his or her cultural schemas.

The second aspect of the DSM-IV cultural outline is the assessment of *cultural explanations of the patient's illness.* This is where the distinction between illness, the patient's subjective ex-

perience of being sick, and disease, the clinician's diagnosis, becomes crucial. If the clinician is not treating *illness* (client's subjective experience) but only *disease* (clinician's diagnosis), the course and outcome of the case is likely to be detrimentally affected. However, if the clinician can simultaneously treat illness and disease, the course and outcome of the case are more likely to be benefited.

Arthur Kleinman (1988, pp. 43–44) has defined what a clinician needs to do in assessing cultural schemas regarding an individual's illness. The clinician needs to discover what the patient thinks is the nature of the problem by asking:

1. Why has the problem affected you?
2. Why has the illness had its onset now, and what course do you think the illness will follow?
3. How does the illness affect you?
4. What treatment do you think is appropriate, and what treatment do you want?
5. What do you fear most about the illness and its treatment?

Disease-centered psychiatrists are not typically willing to give this much control to the patient in defining the nature of the problem and its treatment. Training programs in psychiatry usually teach clinicians to assess and diagnose on the basis of symptoms observed by the clinician, followed by appropriate treatment as defined by the disease-centered paradigm (e.g., medications). However, this disease-centered approach does not assess the illness experience of the patient. If this is ignored, the patient may not receive the treatment that will be most effective in alleviating the illness. Indeed, the treatment may even exacerbate or complicate the patient's condition.

The third aspect of the DSM-IV cultural outline is assessing *how culture is related to the psychosocial environment and levels of functioning.* This refers to culture-based sources of social and environmental stress on the patient, as well as social supports that have impact on functioning, impairment, recovery, and relapse. In client-centered psychiatry, clinicians need to assess the patient and his or her mental disorder within the total sociocultural context. This includes looking for unusual or severe stressors on the patient in the social environment as well as discovering how emotional distress manifests in the cultural context and illness experience of the patient. In assessing the cultural and psychosocial environment, clinicians need to inquire about social relationships, including dominance hierarchies within the social and family structure that may be sources of extreme stress.

Immigrants and others may also have severe emotional stress or trauma in their personal histories. For example, refugees may have endured tremendous hardships, including torture, beatings, starvation, rape, or imprisonment. Patients may have lost family members, homes, financial resources, careers, and so on. Clinicians need to assess possible traumatic experiences and losses in the personal histories of clients (Lu, Lim, & Mezzich, 1995).

The fourth aspect of the DSM-IV cultural outline is the *effect of culture on the clinician-client relationship*. This refers to differences in the construction of clinical reality caused by differing cultural schemas in the clinician and the client. This can be something as simple as a misunderstanding of the clinician's instructions based on class or language differences or something as serious as a misdiagnosis based on widely differing cultural backgrounds. Clinicians need to be aware that it is not just the patient who has cultural schemas. The clinician also has cultural schemas, and diagnostic ethnocentrism can lead to many problems in assessment and diagnosis.

Typically, clinicians understand a patient's problem according to the way they have been professionally trained. Thus, clinicians need to critically assess the effects of their own cultural schemas in relation to individual clinical cases (Hinton & Kleinman, 1993). To avoid diagnostic ethnocentrism, clinicians need to reflexively assess their own conceptions of a client's illness and attempt to see the situation from the client's perspective as much as possible.

This client-centered approach is essentially an ethnographic technique. Anthropologists in the field attempt to understand as clearly as possible the subjective experience of the people being studied, to "get things right" from the native's point of view. In the clinical situation, the "native" is the patient or client. This is the person with firsthand experience of the illness. Understanding his or her subjective experience is central to making an assessment of the differences between the clinician's and patient's conceptions of the problem. This can allow the clinician to critically assess what disease concepts are being appropriately or inappropriately projected onto the client and allow for assessment of diagnostic ethnocentrism.

The fifth aspect of the DSM-IV cultural outline is *overall cultural assessment*. This step is essentially a negotiation of clinical reality between the clinician, the client and, ideally, the client's family. A plan of treatment should be drawn up that is the result of a negotiated consensus of the problem and the appropriate treatment. In this way, all the parties concerned will be operating on the same set of assumptions and will understand and willingly agree to follow the course of treatment. This provides the best opportunity for creating a therapeutic alliance and obtaining optimal care and outcome.

The article in this chapter by well-known medical anthropologist Byron J. Good describes the culture-bound somatoform syndrome of "heart distress" in Iran. Heart distress is experienced as physical sensations in the chest, such as palpitations, that are assumed to be precursors of a heart attack and are linked with feelings of anxiety. Heart distress is common in Iran, especially among females in lower social classes. Good describes how heart distress is conceptually associated in the Iranian cultural meaning system with anxieties concerning miscarriage, menstruation, taking contraceptive pills, old age, and loss of fertility. In this article, Good also demonstrates the ethnographic technique of *semantic analysis* in which the researcher gains an understanding of the cognitive associations structuring and connecting emotions and symptoms. This ethnographic study has implications for cross-cultural definitions of anxiety disorders and the somatization of anxiety. To understand this ailment, clinicians need to see it and the individual within the total sociocultural environment. This requires assessment of the factors contained in the DSM-IV Outline for Cultural Formulation.

This article is an excellent example of the sociocultural complexity of mental disorders. So much of mental illness is based in emotional distress that understanding emotions in their cognitive, interpersonal, and cultural contexts is crucial to comprehensive assessment and optimal treatment. Good points out that categories of emotional distress are not natural entities but rather are embedded in the sociocultural environment. This article provides an illustration of ethnographic techniques in the assessment of emotional distress and its idioms of expression within a particular sociocultural context.

REFERENCES

American Psychiatric Association. (1994). *Diagnostic and statistical manual of mental disorders* (4th ed.). Washington, DC: American Psychiatric Association.

Gregor, T. (1990). Male dominance and social coercion. In J. W. Stigler, R. A. Shweder, & G. Herdt (Eds.), *Cultural psychology: Essays on comparative human development* (pp. 477–495). Cambridge: Cambridge University Press.

Hinton, L., & Kleinman, A. (1993). Cultural issues and international psychiatric diagnosis. In J. Costa de Silva & C. Nadelson (Eds.), *International review of psychiatry* (pp. 111–129). Washington, DC: American Psychiatric Press.

Kleinman, A. (1986). *Social origins of distress and disease: Depression, neurasthenia, and pain in modern China.* New Haven: Yale University Press.

Kleinman, A. (1988). *The illness narratives: Suffering, healing and the human condition.* New York: Basic Books.

Kleinman, A., & Good, B. (1985). *Culture and depression: Studies in the anthropology and cross-cultural psychiatry of affect and disorder.* Berkeley: University of California Press.

Lu, F. G., Lim, R. F., & Mezzich, J. E. (1995). Issues in the assessment and diagnosis of culturally diverse individuals. In J. M. Oldham & M. B. Riba (Eds.), *Review of psychiatry, volume 14* (pp. 477–510). Washington, DC: American Psychiatric Press.

Shweder, R. A. (1985). Menstrual pollution, soul loss, and the comparative study of emotions. In A. Kleinman & B. Good (Eds.), *Culture and depression: Studies in the anthropology and cross-cultural psychiatry of affect and disorder* (pp. 182–215). Berkeley: University of California Press.

BYRON J. GOOD

The Heart of What's the Matter

The Semantics of Illness in Iran[1]

ABSTRACT. Our understanding of the psychosocial and cultural dimensions of disease and illness is limited not merely by a lack of empirical knowledge but also by an inad quate medical semantics. The empiricist theories of medical language commonly employed both by comparative ethnosemantic studies and by medical theory are unable to account for the integration of illness and the language of high medical tradition into distinctive social and symbolic contexts. A semantic network analysis conceives the meaning of illness categories to be constituted not primarily as an ostensive relationship between signs and natural disease entities but as a 'syndrome' of symbols and experiences which typically 'run together' for members of a society. Such analysis directs our attention to the patterns of associations which provide meaning to elements of a medical lexicon and to the constitution of that meaning through the use of medical discourse to articulate distinctive configurations of social stress and to negotiate relief for the sufferer. This paper provides a critical discussion of medical semantics and develops a semantic network analysis of 'heart distress', a folk illness in Iran.

1. INTRODUCTION

Human disease has provided anthropologists with an important domain for the investigation of cultural relativity, that is the meaningful shaping of 'natural' reality. Such studies are not of academic import alone. Our understanding of the way in which psychosocial and cultural factors affect the incidence, course, experience and outcome of disease is crucial for clinical medicine, both in the determination of what data is clinically relevant and where the therapeutic intervention should occur. Our conception of disease and illness is thus basic to cross-cultural studies of medicine and to medical practice (Kleinman, Eisenberg and Good 1976).

There have been a variety of recent efforts to 'de-entify' disease theory, to explore the view that diseases are not constituted as natural entities but as *social and historical realities*. A philosopher of medicine contends that a new 'ontological' basis for disease theory and medical practice is required, which can incorporate our recognition that a person's suffering is both a 'medical fact' and a 'socio-historical fact' (Wartofsky 1975). Foucault's critical studies of medicine in Western history pose sharply the question of whether diseases are artifacts of historically-specific modes of treatment and theoretical constructs (Foucault 1965, 1973). On the other hand a variety of studies have assumed the view that disease is a dynamic product of a person's relationship to his social and cultural environment: disease may be a response to social stresses or life events (e.g., Heisel *et al.* 1973) and is shaped in part by the nature of the cultural label which is applied to a person's condition (e.g., Waxler 1974). Efforts to apply such a perspective clinically have found it necessary to reformulate disease theory in terms of 'open systems models' (Minuchin et al 1975). Notwithstanding these constructive efforts, the 'medical model', which conceives diseases as natural entities that are reducible to physiological terms and are essentially free of cultural context, continues to have great force. Ironically, this perspective is assumed by a great deal of recent cross-cultural research. Ethnoscientific studies have conceived comparative analysis as the examination of the way diseases are mapped onto culturally constructed classifactory schemata. It is the contention of this paper that such studies share with the medical model of disease certain basic (often unrecognized) assumptions about the relationship of language to medicine and about the nature of 'medical semantics'—the theory of how the meaning of medical language is constituted. These assumptions present obstacles to our understanding of the role of psychosocial and cultural factors in disease and therefore to an adequate cross-cultural research strategy.

The link between medicine and empiricist theories of language is a very old one in Western philosophy. Givner (1962) argues that Locke's theory of language was modeled on the medical experiments of his friend Sydenham. Locke believed the two primary functions of language to be *designation* and *classification*. (Givner 1962:346). This view predominates in ethnoscience. Meaning, it is held, is constituted as the relationship between classificatory categories and the diseases which they designate. Categories are defined by distinctive features which provide their boundaries. Such a theory of meaning is closely modeled on one mode of medical activity—*diagnosis*. Diagnosis is viewed as the linking of a patient's condition to a disease category through the interpretation of symptoms as distinctive features (e.g., Frake 1961). My criticism of this perspective is not that diagnosis is an unimportant mode of medical activity. Medical diagnosis, however, is an unsatisfactory model for the construction of new theories of disease, particularly when such theories are intended to redefine what data are relevant to diagnosis. And the ethnocentricity in the assumption in cross-cultural research that diagnosis is simply 'based on' physical symptomatology is exposed by, for example, Turner's analysis of Ndembu divination as the diagnosis of *pathology in a patient's social field* (1975).

It is my argument, then, that we need not simply new theories of disease, but a new understanding of the relationship between medical language and disease. We need to develop a theory of medical language that does not reify the conception of disease and reduce medical semantics to the ostensive or naming function of language. Such a theory should direct cross-cultural research away from simply examining how societies map classificatory categories onto disease to an analysis of the manner in which illness and disease are deeply integrated into the structure of a society.

It will be proposed here that we use an analysis of 'semantic networks' to understand the meaning of medical language as it is used in various communicative contexts. The meaning of a disease category cannot be understood simply as a set of defining symptoms. It is rather a 'syndrome' of typical experiences, a set of words, experiences, and feelings which typically 'run together' for the members of a society. Such a syndrome is not merely a reflection of symptoms linked with each other in a natural reality, but a set of experiences associated through networks of meaning and social interaction in a society. The conception of medical semantics directs our attention to the use of medical discourse to articulate the experience of distinctive patterns of social stress, to the use of illness language to negotiate relief for the sufferer, and thus to the constitution of the meaning of medical language in its use in a variety of communicative contexts.

In this paper, I will analyze 'heart distress', one category of illness in Iran, in terms of its semantic network. This analysis will be used as the basis for suggestions for further research. The data for this paper was gathered during two years of field research in Maragheh, a Turki-speaking town in the province of East Azerbaijan in northwest Iran.[2]

2. HEALTH CARE AND ILLNESS IN IRAN

This impediment in my speech produced grief in my heart, and at the same time my power to digest and assimilate food and drink was impaired; I could hardly swallow or digest a single mouthful of food. My powers became so weakened that the doctors gave up all hope of successful treatment. "This trouble arises from the heart", they said, "and from there it has spread through the constitution; the only method of treatment is that the anxiety which has come over the heart should be allayed.
   al-Ghazali

In his autobiography, the eleventh century Islamic scholar Ghazali described his experience of anxiety and personal crisis that was only resolved by his turning to mysticism. the people of Maragheh today would understand Ghazali's expression very well, for they too articulate certain experiences of crisis and distress as 'malaise of the heart' (*narahatiye qalb*). Women feeling trapped in the crowded homes behind the high walls along the winding alleyways of Maragheh, men feeling distress over a fight with their mother or wife, women who are taking the contraceptive pill or who have delivered a child—all frequently complain that their heart is pounding or beating irregularly. They complain that they are sick (*maris*) and go to the local physicians for treatment. What does it mean to have 'heart distress' in Maragheh? Can we gloss this illness complex simply as mild anxiety or depression with tachycardia, or is there a distinctly Iranian network of meaning which must be described if we are to understand heart distress? Why are seemingly diverse anxieties—contraception, pregnancy, old age, interpersonal problems, money worries—all associated with one illness? Before I explore this issue, a brief description of Maragheh and its systems of health care is necessary.

Maragheh is an old agricultural town and marketing center, today having a population of over 60,000 people. It was the capital of the Mongul empire briefly in the thirteenth century, a regional center and residence of a powerful tribal and landowning family in the thirteenth century, and more recently a modest provincial bureaucratic center known throughout Azerbaijan for its decadent landlords and religiously conservative population.

Its winding alleyways, old marketplace or bazaar, and vigorous religious life, particularly during the elaborately staged Moharram rituals, preserve a sense of community coherence and a style of life which is disappearing in much of urban Iran.

Maragheh has for many years been a prominent regional center of health care, to which villagers from the surrounding countryside would come for treatment by specialists of Galenic-Islamic, sacred, or more recently cosmopolitan medicine.[3] In 1920 approximately 13 *hakims* (traditional physicians) treated Maragheh's population of 18,000 people according to the herbal therapeutics of Galen and Abu Ali Sina (Avicenna). Sellers of herbal medicine, specialists in setting bones and treating dislocations, barbers who kept leeches and performed scarification or venesection, specialists in cupping, and midwives, all practiced in the bazaar and in the neighborhoods of Maragheh. Specialists in religious divination and the writing of curative prayers practiced in the mosques or in their homes. And a variety of popular medical treatments were carried out by family members, especially the older women. Dieting, treatment with dried and distilled herbal medicines, informal religious rites for the cure of illness caused by the evil eye or fright, small rites at local shrines, and other popular therapies were undertaken without assistance of specialists.

Cosmopolitan medicine began to seriously affect Maragheh in the beginning of the twentieth century, when the *hakims* began to import and dispense European drugs and when a few physicians trained in Russia or in missionary schools began to practice in the town. But major changes occurred only in the 1930s, when Reza Shah instituted a licensure, forcing all *hakims* to either pass an examination covering Western medicine or give up their legitimate practice. During the 1930s public health facilities were opened, medical paraprofessions developed, and the professionalization of medicine began. The modern health care sector has continued to grow in Maragheh, and now comprises two hospitals, two public clinics, approximately twenty-five physicians with private practices, eight drugstores, twenty-one injectors, and sixteen dentists. The past forty years has seen a continuous effort by Iranian physicians to professionalize and gain dominance over the whole field of health care. As a result the high practice of Galenic-Islamic medicine has been eliminated, and while traditional medicine continues to flourish in the popular sector, traditional health care specialists constantly fear suppression of their practice. There remain in Maragheh sellers of herbal medicine (ca. 3), traditional orthopedists (ca. 6 of wide reputation), neighborhood midwives (perhaps 25), and women in each neighborhood who specialize in cupping (perhaps 50 or more). Few of these persons are high specialists in the old tradition, but all are steeped in the popularized version of the high tradition and many are highly skilled technically.

While all *mullahs* (clerics) have a 'medical' role through their interpretation of ritual purity in terms of hygiene, the only religious specialists in curing are the writers of curative prayers (*du'a nevis*). Many *syyids* or *mullahs* write an occasional prayer, but perhaps ten have city-wide reputations in Maragheh. *Du'a nevis* practice a form of divination, using four strung die (*raml*), an astrolobe, the Qur'an, or a system of assigning numbers to the letters of one's name. In some parts of the country these men are highly trained, some having been apprentices in India, and use divination to practice a kind of folk psychiatry (Fischer 1973:288).

The prayer-writers in Maragheh play a less conscious 'psychiatric' role, but in treating problems believed to respond to curative prayers—infertility, some forms of madness, and illness caused by evil eye, fright, or intentional magic—they become involved in the emotional and interpersonal crises of their clients.

Three high traditions of medicine—Galenic-Islamic, sacred, and cosmopolitan—provide the underlying structure for the medical theories and therapeutic forms of both the health care specialists and lay persons in Iran. Classical humoral medicine, continuous through the Greeks, Arabs, and Persians, provides the basic structure for popular physiology, images of illness, and therapy.[4] In simple terms, illness is conceived as arising from an excess or deficiency of the humors or the basic qualities (hot-cold, wet-dry), and therapy is directed at restoring the equilibrium characteristic of an individual's nature (*tabe'e*). Sacred medicine is grounded in the cosmology of the Qur'an and the Tradition (*Hadith*) (Nasr 1968), from which are drawn the images of *jinns* (spirits) and evil eye as agents of disease, and the logic of healing through the power of the sacred words, the breath or touch of holy men, or the manipulation of impurity. Sacred medicine is also based on the Hermetic tradition of astrology, alchemy, letter magic, and divination (Nasr 1967). Both of these sources provide the basis for popular notions of illness caused by spiritual invasion or interpersonal harm and for the therapy of the prayer-writers.

The three high traditions of medicine provide the basic explanatory models and theories of disease causation and cure that make up popular medical culture in Maragheh today.[5] While including ideas and therapies elaborated in several different high theoretical traditions, popular medicine integrates these into a distinctive system of health care. This includes a popularly shared ethnophysiology, several 'folk illnesses' only partially recognized in the high traditions, a 'hierarchy of resort' for seeking care (Schwartz 1969), and forms of home care which vary from bed rest and diet to brief curing rites undertaken at home or in the neighborhood.

The popular system of medical care is above all medicine of the lay population and medicine of the home. It provides a language, passed on from generation to generation, in which people voice their experience of disease. And it provides a set of ideas, cognitive models, expectations, and norms that guide the responses to disease by a patient and by those persons in the patient's home, family and neighborhood who care for him. In this way the popular system of medicine socially and meaningfully constructs the experience of disease and the care of the ill.

A careful examination of popular medicine immediately poses a dilemma for understanding. On the one hand it appears to be made up of bits and pieces of ideas and therapeutic practices drawn from diverse sources, from medical traditions elaborated at a great remove—historically, geographically, culturally—from its present context in Maragheh. As in all complex societies, popular medicine in Iran includes a collection of ideas and practices, idiosyncratic and contradictory beliefs, mistaken metaphors (Percy 1975:64), and therapies followed cook-book style. It appears as a 'bricolage', a collection of elements "retained on the principle that 'they may always come in handy'" (Levi-Strauss 1966:18), a set of tools for constructing responses to disease. On the other hand this diverse collection seems somehow to be coherent and woven intimately into the structured fabric of social life behind the high courtyard walls and within the neighborhoods and the shops of Maragheh.

Popular medicine in many complex societies seems deeply integrated into the social life and symbolic structures of the community. From the products of diverse historical periods and high theoretical traditions, popular medicine constructs illness configurations which articulate conflicts and stresses peculiar to that community, and often provides therapies which reinforce integration and conservative values of the community. Currier (1966) describes how the hot-cold dichotomy, developed in ancient Greece and elaborated by Islamic science, provides a basic structuring principle of Mestizo culture and social interaction. Hildred Geertz shows how *latah,* a psychological disorder existing with similar symptomatology in several Asian societies, seems to be "tailor-made for Javanese" (1968:98). The same could be demonstrated for elements of popular medicine in Maragheh: the idiom of hot and cold, the humors (blood, dirty blood, bile), the extended meanings of the heart and liver, the use of the ritually polluted (*najes*) in curing, or folk illnesses caused by fright or the evil eye, each seem specially suited to Iranian social life.

Medical language, whatever its sources, acquires meaning specific to a particular social and cultural context and in turn integrates illness and cure deeply into that context. How does this occur, and what does it imply for our analysis of the meaning of medical language, for a theory of the relationship between language and disease? The description of 'heart distress' in Iran will allow us to address this issue in more detail.

3. DISTRESS OF THE HEART

Shortly after we arrived in Maragheh, a shopkeeper told me that he had been having heart problems and, knowing that I was asso-

ciated with the Health Office, wondered if I could help. He illustrated how his heart pounded (fist against his hand, "tak, tak, tak"), and replied to my query that he had already been to several doctors without success. At the same time, my wife, who regularly observed a family planning clinic, began to note that women constantly complained that the contraceptive pill caused them to be ill. The most common complaint was of 'heart distress' (*narahatiye qalb*); many women gave this as their reason for leaving the program, a problem which had serious consequences for the whole family planning effort. It was puzzling to us that people should complain so much about their hearts. Beginning with the simple hypothesis that people in Iran attend closely to their pulse and define heart palpitations as illness, we were compelled to pursue the question, "What does it *mean* when a person says '*qalbim narahatdi,* my heart is uncomfortable or upset'?"

Heart distress is a category of disease (*maraz*) in Maragheh. Its symptoms are described in very physical terms. 'My heart is pounding' (*qalbim vurur*); 'my heart is trembling' (*qalbim tittirir*), or 'fluttering' (*chirpinir*), or 'beating rapidly' (*dovinir,* or *tez tez vurur*); 'my heart feels pressed or squeezed, bored or lonely' (*qalbim sixilir, daruxir*). These statements are often illustrated graphically, fist pounding on the chest, or hand squeezing together to illustrate a 'pressed heart'. Each of these are members of a general class of sensations described as 'heart distress' (*qalbim narahatdi,* 'my heart is uncomfortable, upset, in distress, uneasy or in "dis-ease"').

Heart discomfort has several degrees of severity. According to one informant:

> If I come from the bazaar, for example, and you say my brother has come, my heart starts pounding (*vurur*), because I worry he may be in a fight, or someone is sick or something. But no, this isn't really an illness. However, if I don't go to the doctor and get something to cure the problem, it can get much worse. It may get so bad that my heart 'goes to sleep' (*qalbim yattar*). There are two meanings of this; either the person dies (*yol gider,* 'he goes on the road'), or he becomes unconscious (*behush, hesh özu bilmirir,* unconscious, 'doesn't even know himself').
>
> You know the heart is like a motor, the motor of the body. If the heart goes bad, then everything else may.

Thus heart distresses range along a continuum from mild excitation of the heart to chronic sensations of heart irregularities, to fainting and heart attack (*saxteye qalb*).

This statement also indicates a central characteristic of heart distress: it is a complex of physical sensations associated with particular feelings of anxiety. Not all occurrences of a rapid pulse are considered to be signs of illness. Some women in Maragheh told us that sexual intercourse can lead to or aggravate disease, because it makes one's heart beat rapidly. It should therefore be avoided if one has heart distress. But clearly not all persons consider a rapid pulse during intercourse as a symptom of illness. On the other hand 'the heart' often represents the subject of experience (e.g., 'my heart longs for you . . .'; see below), but saying 'my heart is uncomfortable' does not mean simply '*I* am uncomfortable'. Heart distress or discomfort is experienced as a physical sensation and as a stage of illness that may eventuate in a heart attack. It is when certain physical sensations are linked with certain feelings of anxiety that a person labels the sensations symptoms of illness. Examination of this illness complex must thus focus on those particular anxieties that are articulated in the idiom of heart discomfort. First, a general epidemiological profile of the illness will be given, two cases will be described, and the explanatory model of the heart which provides the cognitive framework for the illness will be discussed. These will then provide the data for an analysis of the meaning of heart distress in popular medicine in Maragheh and an examination of the particular cluster of social stresses that are experienced, communicated and dealt with as heart ailments.

Heart distress is a commonly experienced illness, in Maragheh, particularly amongst women of the lower social classes. In a survey we did of a stratified population of 750 persons in Maragheh and three surrounding villages, we asked respondents whether anyone in their family had been sick (*maris*) with heart distress in the past eight months; if so, who, what treatment was sought, and what was believed to have caused the illness. Nearly 40% of all households had had at least one person who suffered heart distress in eight months. Table I indicates the incidence by household as reported by men and women. The incidence is highest in bazaari and working class households, and is uniformly higher as reported by women in comparison with men.

Table I
Rate of heart distress by social class (Percent answering 'yes' to question: Has anyone in your household been sick with heart distress in the past eight months?)

		Social Class		
	*Professional**	*Bazaari**	*Worker*	*Villager*
% female respondents	35%	55%	62%	56%
% male respondents	20%	43%	25%	34%
Total respondents	112	147	138	146

* 'Lower Professionals' and 'Upper Bazaaris' have been deleted from these categories.

This is because, as Table II shows, heart distress is most commonly an illness of women, particularly women of childbearing age. Of all reported cases, 55% were women of fifteen to forty-four years of age, and 73% were women of more than fifteen years of age. But it is important to remember that the illness is not limited to women.

When respondents were asked what they believed to be the cause of the illness, almost 40% of the causes suggested were specifically emotional and interpersonal.[6] (The semantic network analysis below will explain in detail my system of grouping of reported causes.) *'Qus qam, fikr, xiyalet'* (sorrow, sadness, worry, anxiousness) were common responses. These were often specified: sorrow because of a death in the family; worry due to poverty; worry or anxiety because of a fight with a spouse or mother-in-law; or distress at having too many children crammed into a woman's narrow living space. One man reported that he had divorced two previous wives because they could not bear him children. His third wife had produced a child, but he now worried about the women he divorced. A related set of responses (6%) blamed nerve problems—upset nerves, weak or tired nerves—as the cause of heart distress. Weakness, tiredness, and problems of blood pressure (13%); the contraceptive pill, pregnancy, miscarriage, infertility (16%); and a variety of specific diseases, including pneumonia, diphtheria, rheumatism, liver disease, and hemorrhoids (10%), were all reported as the cause of the heart distress.

Nearly half (49%) of those ill with heart disease were taken to a physician—even more (69%) if the patients were elderly. Fewer persons were treated with herbal medicines (13%), given drugs of some kind (7%), or were given no treatment at all (17%). Virtually no patients (1 out of 266) were treated for this illness by a prayer-writer.

Heart distress is thus typically experienced as irregular heart sensations believed to be caused by emotional or interpersonal problems, by childbirth, pregnancy or contraception, or by a variety of diseases. It is most common in women and the elderly (but not restricted to them), and is regularly treated by a physician, often more than once. Two cases will more clearly illustrate the nature of heart distress.

Table II
Age breakdown of persons reported ill from heart distress

Age	0–14	15–44 Female	15–44 Male	45 plus Female	45 plus Male
Percentage of total cases of heart distress	*3%*	*55%*	*16%*	*18%*	*7%*

3.1 Case I

Mrs. Z. was 27 years old when we first met her. She has five children ranging in age from six months to twelve years, three girls and two boys. Mrs. Z. lives with her husband (a stove craftsman in the bazaar) and her five children in one room of her husband's father's house. The other room is occupied by her husband's mother, father, and two sisters. They all maintain a single kitchen. Their simple house is surrounded by a fifteen foot brick wall that encloses a small courtyard with a piped water supply. The house has electricity but no water. The family income averages about 100 dollars per month, plus a small income from Mrs. Z's sister-in-law who works as a seamstress. The family leads a simple life, their income providing for sufficient food but little in the way of extras.

Mrs. Z. has never attended school, is completely illiterate, and knows no Persian. She does not know how to count money and has to be accompanied by her husband or sister-in-law on those few occasions when she goes to the market to shop. She goes out to visit her parents, who are poorer than her husband's family, about once per week to clean their house for them. Other trips into the outside world are limited to rare wedding celebrations, a few religious mourning rituals, and an occasional trip to a doctor or a public health clinic. Thus Mrs. Z. passes nearly all of her days within the confines of her walled courtyard and home, surrounded by children and the women of her husband's family.

From the time we knew her Mrs. Z. complained about heart distress. She fretted continuously about her weak condition, her lack of strength and lack of blood, and the lack of meat on her bones. She complained of her heart pounding, her nerves being upset, and the sensation of her heart being squeezed (*darus*) and depressed. This continued for the 18 months that we knew her, without any significant change in her symptoms. She complained to anyone who would listen—her husband, others in the household, her neighbors, and the visiting anthropologist. On one occasion she told my wife that she always felt like screaming out. She blamed this on the fact that she was 27, already had 5 children, was stifled by narrow living quarters, and lived with her mother-in-law as the head of the household. She said, "I feel like screaming. But if you heard me you would be frightened I would scream so loudly." Her desire to scream out was released in a series of fights with her mother-in-law which occurred at least weekly, loud fights with shrill screaming and crying which sounded over the walls and into the street. The fact that these fights were heard was a source of great embarrassment, for a woman's voice should not be heard outside of her courtyard just as her face should not be seen beyond the intimacy of her home.

In an attempt to limit her family size, Mrs. Z. took birth control pills for a brief period (less than one month) at the urging of her more educated neighbors. But when she took the pill, she said, she had heart palpitations, shaking hands, and upset nerves, all symptoms that she had experienced before but believed were exacerbated by the pill. Previous to taking the pill for contraceptive purposes, Mrs. Z. had once taken a whole month's supply in an effort to abort her last child. (She thus associated the pill with abortion and with prevention of pregnancy.)

Mrs. Z. occasionally used herbal medicines for both her weakness and her heart distress. She also visited the doctor several times to complain of her weakness and her heart problems and was given a Vitamin B tonic. She never received any lasting relief. Mrs. Z. blamed her illness on having too many children, her cramped living conditions, the poverty of her parents and the chronic illness of her younger brother (who has a rheumatic heart condition), her past use of the contraceptive pill, and the conflict she feels over her desire to avoid pregnancy while still satisfying her husband. These conditions continue, and so does her heart distress.

3.2 Case II

Mrs. B. is a 34 year old woman with a university degree. When we first met she had a responsible position in a woman's organization. She is married to a civil servant with a university degree, who comes from a wealthy old merchant family from Maragheh (brothers include both wealthy bazaar merchants and professionals). She lives in an expensive, well-furnished house with her husband and two children. She works long hours at the office, does all the cooking for the family, and cares for the children with the aid of an old woman.

When we first met her, Mrs. B complained occasionally of heart distress and upset nerves. She treated herself primarily with teas brewed with herbs bought from the bazaar. She also complained of her husband's lifestyle. He spent a great deal of time with his friends, drinking, talking, and smoking opium, and at times stayed out quite late at night. While both of them pretended that she did not know that he smoked opium, she did know and worried that he would be addicted. (He was quite careful to avoid addiction.) Mrs. B. would make rather sharp joking comments about her husband being the cause of her heart distress. (He and his friend, in turn, joked that each was 'afraid' of his respective wife.)

In the spring of 1974, Mrs. B.'s husband's mother suffered a stroke, was eventually moved to a Tehran hospital, and died there. Mrs. B. was very involved in caring for the family members who came to Maragheh, then went with her mother-in-law to Tehran to help the family. While in Tehran, Mrs. B. was told one day that her children had been in a car accident. She was 'severely frightened' (*batar disjindim*), she said, and was able to learn only after several hours that her children were safe. After her mother-in-law's death, she returned to Maragheh to help stage the elaborate mourning ceremonies. A short time later she received another 'fright' when she saw her sister's husband in the hospital following a car accident. From this time she began to complain of depression (*darixma*), of the sensation of her heart being squeezed, of weak nerves, and of colitis pains. She went to local doctors to treat her abdominal pains, and continued to treat her heart problems with herbal teas (which are mild sedatives). She became more morose through the spring and began to avoid people.

In the summer of 1974 her husband came home very late one evening from a gathering of friends, when he had promised to return early. When he came in and had obviously been drinking and smoking, she flew into a rage. She began crying uncontrollably and continued through the night. In the following days her depression and crying went on. She went to local physicians, then physicians in Tabriz; she was given tranquilizers but felt no better and continued to cry uncontrollably. In the fall she went back to work but on a reduced schedule.

Finally, several months after her breakdown, her husband took her to Tehran. "We saw several nerve doctors", she remembers, "but without relief."

"Finally when I went to the last one, *he asked me what was wrong with me*. I began to cry and told him about my fears for my husband, about my anger, and about my youth. When I was a student I was both teaching and going to the university. My father died during this time, but I had to continue to work and go to the university. As I talked about my anger with my husband, I began to feel better."

The doctor prescribed tranquilizers for her, and her condition improved through the rest of the fall and winter. Her husband promised never to smoke opium again and stopped coming home late. (She says that even if he stays out late now, she no longer worries because she knows that he is not smoking opium.) By the summer of 1975 Mrs. B. felt nearly recovered.

These two cases illustrate the social and affective context of the experience of heart distress. The first case is very typical. Mrs. Z. is poor, has too many children, lives and fights with her mother-in-law, and fears both pregnancy and contraception. Her heart distress is accompanied by complaints of feeling weak, constricted and depressed. She occasionally goes to the doctor, but her condition is essentially unalterable and continues to be experienced in the idiom of heart distress. Mrs. B.'s case began in a typical manner, resulting from the dispute with her husband and the stress of her work. When treatment failed to deal with these issues and when additional stresses arose, her condition advanced to a new stage of 'nervous disorder' (*narahatiye asab*). In these and other cases of heart distress, the illness is perceived as a complex which includes and links together both physical sensations of abnormality in the heart beat and feelings of anxiety, sadness, or anger. Why is the heart the focus of concern in these cases? Why are certain feelings of anxiety experienced and expressed as abnormalities of the heart?

Explanatory models for the functioning and malfunctioning of the heart provide the cultural framework for focusing the attention of individuals on heart beat, for labeling some conditions as disease symptoms, and for establishing causal links between irregularities in heart beat and specified personal and social conditions. The explanatory models in popular medicine in Maragheh for the functioning of the heart are drawn primarily from the Galenic paradigm. The precise function of the heart was debated over the centuries by Greek physicians and anatomists, by Islamic scholars and doctors, and later by Europeans.[7] But while certain aspects of the model provoked debate, the general framework for understanding the heart was unchallenged: the heart is *at once* a central physiological organ (related to innate heat, nutrition, and distribution of the blood) and an organ of emotional functioning (or the seat of the vital soul) in man.

It would be inappropriate to fully describe the classical view here, but in both Greek and Islamic science the theory of the heart is based in cosmology. Man is a Microcosm of the greater Universe, which consists of an ontological hierarchy from the sublunary realm (of generation and decay), the cosmic spheres, and the intelligible world of pure form.[8] All levels of the ontological hierarchy are represented in man. The liver is the seat of the natural faculty and the baser human appetites; its primary physiological function is the transformation of (raw) food into (cooked) blood. The brain is the seat of the rational faculty, which enables man to relate to the intelligible order. The vital or animal faculty resides in the heart; it provides the 'innate heat' and 'vital breath' (*pneuma* or *nafs*) to the body and is the seat of the emotions, particularly fear and anger ("because they coincide with the expansion and contraction of breath"—Ibn Sina 1930:118). The primary physiological function of the heart is not circulation, of course, but the provision of heat necessary for life and the transformation of breath into the *pneuma,* which vitalizes the body. If the heart fails in these functions, particularly if it loses its strength as the source of innate heat, weakness and death may result. But for many diseases known in modern medicine to be heart diseases, Galen believed heart problems to be secondary rather than primary. Galen also believed that anger and grief may cause heart pain because they lead to excessive heat, and that fear and fright may cause the heart to leap and to register irregular pulse. But he does not (to my knowledge) describe the syndrome of mild palpitations and heart sensations which is called in Maragheh 'heart distress'.

The explanatory model of the heart in popular medicine in Maragheh is continuous with this long tradition: the heart is a pulsing physiological organ, but not responsible for the circulation of blood; and the heart articulates and is affected by the emotional state of the person. Blood is generally believed to travel around (*dolanir*, it 'strolls around') to provide nutrition to all parts of the body. Some believe this results from random movement of the body ("this is the reason your feet feel numb if you sit too long"). One man described a wind (*bad, yel*) which forces the blood through the veins, as blowing through a tube into a pot of water causes activity. The heart is not described as a lamp or furnace (Galen), as a reservoir for blood (Aristotle), nor as a pump, of course. It is sometimes called the 'clock' of the body, focusing attention on the regularity of its rhythm. It is more often described as the motor of the body: it is the central driving force of the body; it inhales and exhausts air; and if it fails the whole organism comes to a halt. Thus the physiological models of the heart only loosely link the heart to blood, instead emphasizing centrality of the heart to life and focusing attention on the regularity of pulse in normal heart function.

Popular medicine does not speculate on a vital soul abiding in the heart and controlling passions, but 'the heart' is used linguistically to express affect, and emotional problems are believed to cause heart disease. In a variety of expressions, many still having English correlates, 'the heart' is treated as the subject of emotional experience and a symbol of the true essence of the person: *urayim istir* ('my heart wants. . . .'); *urayimin dardin kimi diyim* ('whom can I tell of the pain in my heart'); *urayim kebab olur* ('my heart is broiled as a kebab' or 'my heart is scorched'—said when describing a tragic event); *qalbim xaber verir* ('my heart gives me news'—said of a premonition); *qalbidan qalba yol var* ('there is a way from heart to heart'—said to a person one loves); *zahremar urayivan bashina* ('snake's poison to the top of your heart!'—a curse). The phrase *qalbim narahatdi* ('my heart is upset, uncomfortable, distressed') is a member of this class of expression. The heart thus provides an idiom for expressing emotion. In addition to this, however, the functioning of the heart and its physical activity is believed to be directly and adversely affected by stress and dysphoric affect—sadness, fear, anger, and general anxiety. These lead to irregularities in the beat of the body's 'clock', threatening ultimately a temporary halt or a sudden attack and death.

The conception of the heart in the classical tradition and in popular medicine provides the explanatory model that links physical sensations of heart abnormality to affective states and the experience of social stress. It provides the theoretical framework for the expression of stresses peculiar to Iranian society and to Maragheh in the idiom of the heart. But why are certain particular stresses most commonly believed to cause heart distress? Why, for example, is the contraceptive pill so generally believed to cause heart distress? Why are certain social stresses believed to cause heart distress, others to cause fright, nervous distress, 'anger' (*asabanilix*) or depression? A proper semantic theory should allow us to explore the *meaning* of these disease categories in a fashion which answers such questions. It should direct our attention to the integration of these illness categories into their psychosocial context in Maragheh.

4. SEMANTICS OF THE HEART

An ethnosemantic (or ethnoscientific) analysis of disease categories in popular medicine in Maragheh would produce a hierarchically ordered taxonomy of categories, defined by their boundaries, whose meanings are essentially independent of their context of use. Methodologically, ethnoscience rigorously standardizes the context of elicitation, thus producing an analytic domain not necessarily congruent with the meaning of a category as used in typical communicative contexts (cf. Schneider 1965). Such analysis directs our attention away from the social and symbolic context which gives an illness category its distinctive semantic configuration. Heart distress is indeed one element of the more inclusive category *narahati*, 'distress', and ethnoscientific analysis can help elicit the formal, symptomatic distinctions between, for example, 'heart distress' and 'fright'. But an alternative semantic analysis is necessary if we are to explore the question, "What do Mrs. Z. and Mrs. B. mean when they say 'my heart is distressed'?", if we are to understand what it means to have heart distress in Maragheh (or a heart attack in Peoria).

The work of Turner, Izutsu, and Fox suggests a model of semantic analysis that is an important alternative to the ethnoscience model. Each contends that a system of discourse has certain symbols which gather their power and meaning by linking together a set or field of disparate symbols and condensing them into a simple image which can "invoke a nexus of symbolic associations" (Fox, 1975:119). [Turner calls these "dominant ritual symbols" (1967:30); Izutsu, "focus-words" (1964:29); Fox, "core terms" (1975:111).] These symbols attain their depth not through their taxonomic generality but through their quality of polysemy—"the property of a symbol to relate to a multiple range of other symbols" (Fox 1975:119). Such core symbols join together in a polysemic relationship a network of heterogeneous symbols that "cross-cut conventional grammatical categories" (Fox 1975:110). "Their very generality enables them to bracket together the most diverse ideas and phenomena" (Turner 1967:28). Understood subjectively, these symbols or images condense not merely a field of symbols, but a whole 'syndrome of experiences', as Lienhardt shows for the Dinka divinities (Lienhardt 1961:161). "As images, the Powers contract whole fields of direct experience and represent their fundamental nature each by a single term" (Lienhardt 1961:169). Methodologically, then, tracing out these networks of symbols and experiences should provide a "glimpse of the structuring of the cultural code . . ." (Fox 1975:111), yielding insight into the meaning of the most important elements in any semantic domain.

Turner goes on to show that these dense ritual symbols attain their meaning not merely as elements in a symbolic system, but as 'forces' in social interaction. They represent 'gross' social experience in the society, displaying at once the most basic normative or ideological principles of the society and a collection of "frankly, even flagrantly, physiological" *significata* (such as breast milk, breasts, blood, or male and female genitalia) (Turner 1967:28–29). Because they link basic social and motivational elements, manipulation of these symbols has the power to affect social action. These core symbols thus play a crucial role in forming a symbolic pathway which links the values and aspirations of purposive interation, the stresses, shames and disappointments of social contingencies, and the affective and ultimately physiological elements of the personal.

This model suggests a method for approaching not merely ritual symbols but the language and discourse of illness and healing as well. It suggests we seek out for analysis the potent elements in the idiom of social interaction and explore the associated words, situations and forms of experience which they condense. These patterns of associations or semantic networks, which give meaning to the elements in the vocabulary of illness and healing, should lead us phenomenologically to those typical stress situations in a society and in the personality of individuals. Through a kind of *social free association,* we may gain an entry into the 'inscape' of individuals, "the distinctive reality as it is apprehended" (Percy 1975:79), and into meaningful structuring of social reality.

The illness terms we have been discussing (heart distress, fright, weakness, nerves, etc.) should be amenable to such analysis. Following the model described above, illness categories can be understood as images which condense fields of experience, particularly of stressful experience. And they can be understood as the core symbols in a semantic network, a network of words, situations, symptoms, and feelings which are associated with an illness and give it meaning for the sufferer. The meaning of an illness term is generated socially as it is used by individuals to articulate their experiences of conflict and stress, thus becoming linked to typical syndromes of stresses in the society. Meanings of terms change as social conditions and the social context of their use are altered. The meaning of an illness term may decay or it may be newly constituted as it is linked to an altered network of symbols and stressful situations. Furthermore, if the

form of analysis suggested here is successful, it should reveal both the distinctive semantic configuration of each illness term and the overlapping associational patterns of different terms. Our data on heart distress provides an opportunity for such an analysis.

When we asked people in our survey the cause of each case of heart distress in their family, we received a long list of answers. Figure 1 shows these reported causes, arranged in general categories. Causes include feelings of sadness and anxiety (*qus o qam, fikr, xiyalet,* sadness and mourning, worry, anxiety) and the situational bases of these feelings (deaths, debts and poverty, quarrels, fights, family illness); old age; pregnancy, delivery, and miscarriage; contraception; feelings of weakness, blamed on lack of blood, high or low blood pressure, too few vitamins; problems of nerves; fright or the evil eye; dampness and foul cli-

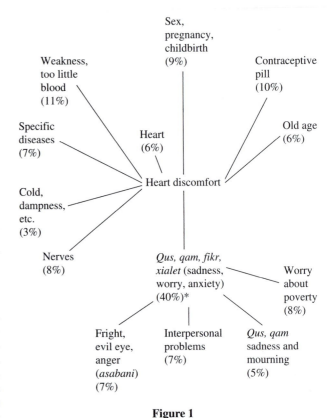

Figure 1

Listed causes of heart distress. (Percentages refer to the responses to the question: What was the cause of the heart discomfort?)

* The total 40% consists of the general answers 'sadness, worry, anxiety', in addition to members of the four subcategories listed

mate; and a variety of specifically named diseases. These causes clearly indicate a wide set of feelings and social situations associated with heart distress. By tracing the semantic links between the elements of this array, semantic fields that are associated with clusters of experience and with more basic structural elements of the society emerge from a long list of causes.

The two most important fields of symbols and experience which emerge may be called 'the problematics of female sexuality' and 'the oppression of daily life'. These two semantic fields are outlined in Figures 2 and 3 and are described in the following several pages. They were developed by noting first the semantic links between causes given for heart distress (Figure 1), then the common associations which extend the meaning of the linked terms. (For example, the *contraceptive pill* is said to make a woman appear *old,* and both are associated with *infertility.*) Such associative links are taken from informants' statements, complaints of symptoms, or explanatory models from popular medicine, and are joined together in the semantic networks outlined.

4.1 Female Sexuality: Potency and Pollution

Women in Maragheh often complain that taking the contraceptive pill causes a variety of distresses, most commonly that it causes heart palpitations and heart distress. Women also believe that it causes spotting between periods or reduced menstrual flow. They complain that the pill causes them to feel weak (*za'if*) and 'lacking blood' (*qansiz*), to have shaking hands, and to have problems of upset nerves. And they believe it causes a woman's milk to dry up (and so should be avoided during nursing), that it dries up the womb and reduces fertility.

It can be seen that the contraceptive pill is associated with several of the other causes given for heart distress, forming the following semantic links (see Figure 2). *Heart distress—contraceptive pill—menstrual blood—pollution:* All menstrual blood is ritually polluting (*najes*). The pill is sometimes used during the month of fasting (*Ramazan*) or during Pilgrimage (*Hajj*) to prevent menstruation and pollution, which could spoil the fast or the Pilgrimage. Spotting between periods is a serious side effect of the pill because it causes pollution, making prayer (*namaz*) or sexual intercourse impossible. *Contraceptive pill—weakness—menstruation:* Women complain that the pill makes them feel weak, which in vulgar Galenism is equated with insufficiency of blood.[9] Menstruation also causes weakness. "It is the nature of women to be weak", we were told, in part because they regularly lose blood through menstruation. *Childbirth—uterine blood—contraceptive pill—pollution:* Abortion and miscarriage, pregnancy and normal delivery are perceived causes of heart distress and are related to the pill because each involves polluting uterine blood. After delivery a woman is ritually un-

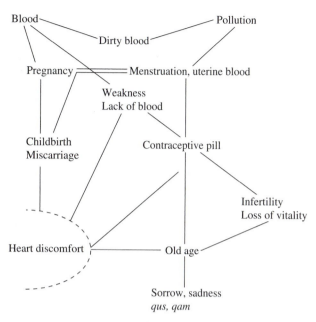

Figure 2
Female sexuality: Potency and pollution

clean (*najes*); she goes to the bath for her ritual washing (*ghosl*) on the tenth day, but is not ritually pure (nor allowed to have sexual intercourse) until after her ritual bath on the fortieth day. The blood of childbirth (or miscarriage) is one of the ten or twelve categories of *nejasat,* items which are ritually polluted or unclean, a set which includes feces, urine, and the sweat of sexual exertion.

Pregnancy—menstrual blood—dirty blood—contraceptive pill: Menstrual blood is believed to be 'dirty blood' (*kasif qan*), which produces darkness of the skin and aches of the body and which should be relieved through scarification or leeching. [Dirty blood is a popularization of the Galenic theory of morbid atrabilious humor, which, when present in the blood, should be expelled through venesection (Ibn Sina 1930:503).] The contraceptive pill may cause reduced menstrual flow and thus illness due to dirty blood. I inquired of one woman whether pregnant women, who have no menstrual bleeding, are ill from dirty blood. "For the first several months of pregnancy the mother often feels very uncomfortable", she pointed out to me. "But after that time the child in the womb grows large enough to begin drinking the blood. For this reason the mother often feels better during the later months of pregnancy." Another woman reported that she did cupping with bleeding (*hajamat*) during the seventh month of her pregnancies so that the children would not be so dark (*qara*). Light-skinned children are more beautiful, and dirty blood leads to darkness of the face. The conceptual model of the baby consuming the dirty blood also seems to be confirmed by the old tradition of bleeding a baby during the first several months after it is born. Tiny cuts were made on the top of the head and on the joints to rid the baby of dirty blood, presumably obtained from the mother's womb. (This tradition is remembered as common in the past, but seldom practiced today.) Thus pregnancy and childbirth, weakness, and the contraceptive pill are linked semantically and in the experience of women to dirty blood and illness and to menstrual blood and pollution.

Contraceptive pill—infertility—old age: Use of the contraceptive pill is also a threat to fertility and to the normal mothering function of producing milk. The contraceptive pill is used to prevent pregnancy and on occasion to attempt abortion. It is a general threat to fertility, and women believe that one should have her children before she risks taking the pill. The explanatory model of conception is relevant here, for uneducated women have no general notion of the production of ova that combine with the sperm to produce children, and of the pill preventing ovulation. While there is no single clear model, it is generally believed that the sperm lodges in the 'vessel' of the woman and grows to become the foetus. Contraception then may involve some harm to the womb, which makes it an inhospitable environment for the sperm to rest. As a threat to vitality and fertility the contraceptive pill is linked to old age, to menopause (when women lose their fertility and sexual potency), and to the stage of life when one's constitution grows cold and dry. This is the time of life when it is sometimes said women must fear loss of interest of their husbands and even divorce. One young university woman in Tabriz expressed several of these links explicitly: "Women here say it is very bad for a woman to have reduced bleeding during one's menstrual period [due to the contraceptive pill] because she will get old faster and her face and hands will become like a man's."

'Heart distress' thus has as one important nexus of *meaning* a complex of stresses common to the experience of Iranian women: she is sexually potent and attractive to men; her potency is dangerous and must be secluded; but her fertility and attractiveness are regularly disrupted by states of pollution and ultimately threatened by the coming of old age. The complex of female sexuality leads to a typical set of stresses which women experience and articulate as heart distress. But viewed sociologically these patterns of stress are more than a set of typical experiences; they are linked to central cultural and social structures of Iranian society. A brief outline of these structural characteristics will indicate the context for the complex which has been described.

Female sexuality is surrounded by great ambivalence in Iran. Women have almost magical potency to attract men, according to Persian folk ideology. Their hair has the power to stimulate and should be veiled to prevent random arousal [a characteristic described by Fischer as the " 'magical hair' component" (1975:24)]; their eyes may evoke male passion and should be averted from the faces of men outside of intimate relationships. On the one hand a woman's potency can attract a husband, arouse in him passionate and jealous love, and earn for her rewards of his devotion, faithfulness and gold. On the other hand this potency is dangerous and must be guarded. No man except a closest relative should enter another man's household when his wife is at home alone. Women who leave the household should be veiled and accompanied by their husband, children, or female relatives. This ambivalence is exemplified in the character of some men said to be 'black-hearted' (*qara qalbi*). Black-hearted men may keep their wives extremely secluded, suspecting any contact they have with other men, reacting constantly with jealousy (*hasud*). A civil servant friend of mine was known for being extremely black-hearted. When first married, he would lock his wife into the courtyard and go to the villages for days at a time on business, taking the only key with him. Such excesses are extremely confining for women, but black-heartedness is also a sign to a woman that her husband cares for her passionately, and may be a role played out with great romance.

Female sexuality is also a matter of basic cultural ambivalence in that women produce children—especially sons—for men, but the honor of men can be easily destroyed by the immodesty of women. Men can demonstrate their virility and maintain their blood line only through fertile women. (Proof of virginity before marriage and seclusion of a new bride are necessary to insure that offspring are the husband's. As a prayer writer told me, in explaining the use of the name of a person and his mother in divination, "you can never really know who the father is".) And if a man's virility can only be displayed through a fertile woman, his honor can only be protected by modest women. Immodesty in his wife, his daughter, sister, or brother's daughter (in that order) will cause a loss of face (*abir, aberuh*) and a more long-standing loss of honor (*sherafat*). Iranian women, especially in a conservative town such as Maragheh, are thus restricted by a relatively severe modesty code. Specifically, a woman should be '*heya ve esmati*'. She should be careful not to attract the attention of men, remaining veiled and circumspect.

An immodest (*biheya*, or *yaman*) woman is 'bold-faced' and 'unafraid of men'. Ideally, a woman's voice should not carry beyond her courtyard. if a child runs outside to the street and the mother has to chase him; if a woman has to shout something and men hear her; then other people will say "*heyavu hifs ele*", "(May God) protect your modesty."

The women in Maragheh are thus confined within the boundaries of modesty and purity regulations. Their sexual potency is a threat to their modesty and must be jealously guarded. And their menstrual pollution is a threat to their personal piety and to the purity of the entire household. In sermons to women during religious ceremonies and in women's conversations, my wife tells me, three topics are most frequent: wearing *chador* (veil), proper ritual bathing (*ghosl*), and proper ritual praying (*namaz*). Thus modesty, purity, and essential religion are linked as the pillars of a proper life for women.

These broad cultural and social structures provide the framework for the complex of stresses surrounding female sexuality, which are voiced in terms of distress of the heart. The framework is not monolithic but a flexible idiom through which enormous individual, class and situational variations are expressed.[10] It provides the structure within which the typical experiences of conflict and stress are generated, experiences we have outlined in the semantic network above. It is in this context that the complaints of heart distress and the desire to *scream out* by the woman in Case I can be understood as a protest at being segregated within the bounded confines of her courtyard and a desire to escape not merely the high walls surrounding her home but the even higher boundaries of modest behavior. A direct protest of norms of modesty and purity would of course be unthinkable, for they define membership in the social group. But the semantic network makes clear that an unspoken meaning of the woman's complaints of heart distress is the confinement entailed by social belonging to Maragheh.

4.2 The Oppression of Daily Life

The second major complex of meaning associated with heart distress includes sadness and grieving, worry about the general condition of life, and interpersonal conflict (see Figure 3). Both men and women attribute their heart distress to these causes.

Heart distress—grieving—loss—Moharram—old age: Heart distress is often said to be caused by sadness and grieving (*qus o qam*), by general feelings of melancholy, or by a specific loss or death. Excessive mourning, whether for a personal loss or as part of Moharram rituals, is dangerous to the heart.

The grieving complex and the sense of sadness is one which resonates deeply in Iranian culture. The central Shi'ite ritual during Moharram reenacts the martyrdom of Imam Hossein, beloved grandson of the Prophet, and his 72 followers on the dusty plain of Kerbala. The rites are structured specifically to make all participants and observers weep, teaching the true meaning of *qus* and *qam*. The twelve-day ritual portrays a long series of grief-filled partings, as one by one the family and followers of Imam Hossein bid farewell and go off to their martyrdom. The small

nephews, the children, and finally the brother of Imam Hossein bid farewell to their mothers, sisters and kin, tear themselves away and go to the battle. At the center of the drama stands Imam Hossein, "the lonely stranger of the place of disaster", "the one enmeshed in the pain and sadnes (*qam*) of the world", "wandering apart from homeland and kin, . . . to be martyred on the field of Kerbala" (from a text collected in 1974). This complex of feelings, elicited and shaped during these performances, provides the model for grieving and melancholy in other contexts.

Funerals with elaborate mourning and commemorative rites or 'black holidays' (*qara bayram*) are regular and vivid in Maragheh. Their ritual structure, meaning, and emotional tenor are patterned and experienced in the shadow of Moharram. The experience of sadness, of *qus* and *qam*, often associated with heart distress, is an intimate part of this broader pattern. Deaths of relatives—parent, a brother, a child—are given as the cause of heart distress. And the attendance of *mersias* (female religious mourning ceremonies), so common amongst older women, is believed harmful to one with heart problems. Thus the complex of meanings associated with *qus* and *qam* adds affective depth to the meaning of heart distress.

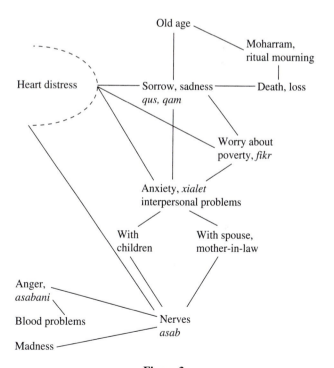

Figure 3
The oppression of everday life.

Qus o qam also has the meaning of general depression which is associated with interpersonal conflict and the anxieties accompanying poverty. *Heart distress—anxiety—interpersonal problems:* Interpersonal problems, quarrels, and fights are often perceived as the cause of heart distress. Fights between husband and wife (see Case II) and between a woman and her mother-in-law (see Case I) were commonly given as the cause of heart distress cases in the survey. Mother-in-law conflicts are deeply rooted. The marriage ceremony enacts a spiriting away of the bride to her father-in-law's house in the middle of the night and a display of her father's unreadiness to give her up. Traditionally the bride would move into the household of her husband's parents and live under the guardianship and tutelage of her mother-in-law for several years. When the husband was financially able or when the tension in the household became too great, the young couple would finally move out to establish a new household of their own. In old age the mother-in-law would often return with her son and daughter-in-law. While there are wide variations in this broad pattern, it still provides the framework for the stresses upon many married women. Of those in our survey, the husband's mother lived in 24% of the households, husband's father in 28%, and wife's mother or father in less than 2% of the households. The experience of the stress of these situations is often articulated (by men as well as women) both in terms of heart distress and of nervous problems.

Heart distress—interpersonal problems—nervous disorders—blood, madness: Heart distress in tense interpersonal situations is often closely associated to complaints of upset nerves or weak nerves. Nerve distress (*narahatiye asab*) is most often marked by irritability and weariness or lack of patience (*hurselisiz*) in personal relations. It is believed related to blood problems: "*asabin qatishir, qan qalxdi bashima fishar geler*" 'my nerves are mixed up, the blood has rushed up to my head, and I am getting [high] blood pressure.' A person with a more acute condition of nervousness is called *asabani* (*asab* = nerve, *asabani* = angry). A person who is *asabani* is quick to take offense, constantly and severely angered, and 'hot-headed'. Such a condition may eventuate madness. [A crazy person is *dali* (mad), *qizirmish* (heated up).]

Heart distress—worry about poverty: Heart distress, nerve distress, sadness, anxiety, anger—all of these can be caused or exacerbated by living in poverty. Concern about debts and worry (*fikr*) about money are often given as specific causes of heart distress. "We are poor, we don't have any money, we all have heart problems", a worker or a lower class woman will say rhetorically. And many of the conditions associated with heart distress are more common and more severe in lower class and poverty stricken families. More persons in such families live cramped in fewer rooms, which exerts particular stress on the women of the household. And anxiety about daily survival, increasing the strain of interpersonal relationships, is ever present.

This semantic network analysis is intended to define the meaning of heart distress as it is experienced by the people of Maragheh. It is not a neatly bounded 'category', defined primarily in distinction to other categories. 'Heart distress' is used sometimes to name an illness, sometimes as a symptom, sometimes as a cause of other illness. And it shares a great deal of the same meaning as several other forms of 'distress' (*narahati*), such as nervous distress or fright. But heart distress has a unique configuration of meaning, which we have outlined as a symbolic network which only partially overlaps those of other illnesses. An awareness of this semantic network should allow an observer (or a therapist) to quickly formulate hypotheses about the problems facing a patient who says "my heart is in distress". This semantic analysis also allows us to answer the question which first led us to investigate heart distress while we were in the field: Why does the contraceptive pill lead to heart palpitations? Why the *heart* more than the head, stomach or nerves? The answer is that the contraceptive pill is associated with a variety of concerns—menstruation, infertility, attractiveness, sexual intercourse—which are a part of the network of meaning of heart distress, linked semantically more closely to the heart than to the head, stomach, or nerves. The contraceptive pill raises certain anxieties which are most commonly articulated as heart distress. This may in turn focus the attention of the user on the sensation of the heart beat and increase her anxiety. But rather than voicing her anxiety over these specific concerns and the general stresses of female sexuality, she expresses her anxiety in somatic terms.

In conclusion, the meaning of 'heart distress' is not some disease entity in the 'real world' to which the term points, nor is it simply a set of discriminations along culturally specified dimensions that set it off from a set of other illness terms. Nor is the meaning of heart distress a particular strain at the level of social structure, although it is linked to complexes of social strains. Heart distress is an image which draws together a network of symbols, situations, motives, feelings, and stresses which are rooted in the structural setting in which people of Maragheh live. It is one element in a language or idiom of illness, in what Foucault calls 'an order of discourse' (1970). Heart distress is a public, collective project, a collective representation, with fields of meaning which extend beyond the consciousness of any individual at any given time. But while not explicitly recognized, these extended associations give meaning and depth to the experience for a man or woman who is possessed of a disturbed or unruly heart.

5. THE COMMUNICATIVE CONTEXT OF HEART DISTRESS: FAMILY AND THERAPY

I have been arguing that the meaning of an illness term is not constituted simply by its relationship to a 'disease', whether defined as a set of characteristic symptoms or as a physiological state. The meaning of an illness term is rather constituted by its linking together in a potent image a complex of symbols, feelings, and stresses, thus being deeply integrated into the structure of a community and its culture. And the meaning of an illness term is constituted as it is used in social interaction to articulate the experience of distress and to bring about action which will relieve that distress. It is in the purposive use of medical language in particular institutional and communicative contexts that semantic networks are generated and change. Careful analysis of the use of the language of the heart in social interaction could help us to understand how the articulation as 'heart distress' of those particular configurations of stress I have described is effective in bringing about relief to the sufferer. Here I can only make a few suggestions.

Heart distress is primarily a self-labeled illness, rather than one for which diagnosis is necessary. While a person with heart distress is not typically exempted from ordinary role obligations, certain privileges are extended to a person who is recognized as *legitimately* suffering from a heart ailment. First, the sufferer can expect expressions of sympathy and concern in response to his/her complaint. Many times this is the only privilege or treatment granted. (Twenty-one percent of the cases in our survey were reported as having received no treatment.) Secondly, if the illness is recognized as more severe, the patient may receive some form of medical treatment: first a herbal medicine, then a drug, and finally a trip to visit a physician. The most common treatment by physicians is the prescription of vitamins (especially a B vitamin injection) or some form of tranquilizer (commonly valium). Thirdly, a person suffering from heart distress may be able to make demands on members of the household for behavioral changes. These privileges will be granted, however, only if the complaints are recognized as legitimate. It is precisely in this reciprocal process of the labeling or legitimation of the person as ill and the granting of privileges to the patient that negotiations occur.

Our cases exemplify this process. Mrs. B. resented her husband's activities, which were symbolic of a traditional or backward life style. Smoking opium, drinking vodka, gambling large sums of money, and spending hours loafing with friends are all status symbols used to characterize the decadent style of life of the traditional landlords and merchants in Maragheh. Unlike her husband, who came from this class, Mrs. B. was upwardly mobile from the traditional to the modern middle class. She saw her husband's behavior not only as a threat to his health but as a

threat to the achievement of the status which she sought for herself and their children. Mrs. B.'s pointed jokes about her husband's laziness causing her heart aches were a direct expression of this feeling. And her early complaints of heart distress can be understood as efforts to negotiate changes in his behavior through the rhetorical use of illness language. Mrs. B. was given sympathy, medication, and visits to the doctor, but it was only when her illness became much more severe—a serious 'nerve disease' (*maraze asab*)—that she was able to negotiate changes in his style of life.

The first case, that of Mrs. Z., illustrates less dramatically the use of the idiom of heart distress to negotiate changes in a family's pattern of interaction. But it is also typical in this way, for many of the stresses underlying heart distress are unalterable, based in the broader structural context in which the whole family lives. Mrs. Z. and her children lived in two crowded rooms along with her husband and his parents because the family was poor. This basic cause they were powerless to change. Using somatic language, Mrs. Z. was able to voice her discontent and gain sympathy from her neighbors and the other women of the household, even from her mother-in-law with whom she constantly fought. Complaining of her condition to her mother-in-law and other women while her husband sat listening in the next room, she was able to ally the women, including her mother-in-law, as a means of influencing her husband. While there was little that he could do about the condition in which she lived, he was able to take her out to visit a doctor occasionally and buy her the prescribed tonics. In one case she was able to force her husband to make a more specific change. Mrs. Z. felt seriously conflicted between the fear of having more children and her anxiety about taking the contraceptive pill. When the pill caused her to become ill, she was able to coerce her husband to take responsibility for contraception himself.

Medical specialists play a minor role in this process. Physicians are most often consulted for heart distress, but being trained in cosmopolitan medicine they consider heart distress to be neurotic, as opposed to somatic, and thus not a *real* disease. Some young physicians in Maragheh recognize the need to allow a heart distress patient to talk about her problems. But the most common reaction is to listen to the patient's heart with a stethoscope, tell the patient "it is nothing, only your nerves", then prescribe a tonic or tranquilizer. This interaction, an example of the very limited patient-physician contract in Iran (Good 1976b), in no way begins to unpack the meaning of the complaint, to lead the patient and her family to a conscious understanding of the dynamics of the illness. The trip to the physician and the purchase of drugs do serve a therapeutic function: the patient is allowed a trip out of the house and is shown special concern. It also inadvertently serves to legitimize the patient's complaint. While the physician's pronouncement—"it is your nerves"—may simply be further mystification, his statement along with the prescription of drugs serves nonetheless to legitimize the patient's role and give her some additional support in her use of the illness to manipulate the social situation.

This perspective suggests questions for further research. For example, it is my impression that there is a general hierarchy of resort in the use of medical idiomata in Iran to manipulate social situations. Heart distress is a relatively passive mechanism. The condition of being *asabani* ('angry', a state of unusual irritability and quickness to fight with others) and the quarrels which it generates is a more active mechanism, directed more clearly at the objects of the distress. Threatened or attempted suicide is a third resort and may be consciously used to manipulate unbearable situations.[11] It is used, for example, by recently married girls who are being abused by their husband and in-laws in an attempt to force their parents to allow them to return home and ultimately to force a return of the bride price paid in the marriage. Thus the relationship outlined between medical language, its purposive use in culturally defined contexts, and the semantic networks that provide its meaning suggest hypotheses which may be pursued in further research.

6. THEORETICAL IMPLICATIONS

"Then you should say what you mean," the March Hare went on. "I do", Alice hastily replied; "at least—at least I mean what I say—that's the same thing, you know." "Not the same thing a bit", said the Hatter.
Lewis Carroll, *Alice's Adventures in Wonderland*

In this exchange, the Hatter points out to Alice that meaning resides not merely in words but in the intentionality of the user of language.[12] We *can* mean something different than what we say. Meaning is *not* constituted by a word-to-object link with empirical reality. It has been the argument of this paper that a good deal of talk about disease assumes what we might call the empiricist theory of medical language. I contend that for cross-cultural studies *and* for medical practice such a perspective is grounded both in an inappropriate theory of disease and an inadequate theory of meaning in medical language. And I claim the Mad Hatter a witness to this position.

This argument can be made more specific. Cross-cultural studies, ethno-scientific analyses in particular, are often based on the following implicit assumptions:

1. Diseases are discrete pathological conditions, which can be adequately described in biochemical and physiological terms.
2. These diseases are categorized differently in different societies, using various discriminating principles; and culturally varied causal explanations are attached to each category.

3. Because of the culturally constructed categorization and explanation of a particular disease, individuals experience the disease differently from one society to the next.

While this is a powerful model which can claim to account for the social and cultural construction of illness, two important implications should be noted. First, it implies that there exist discrete diseases in the natural order that can be ultimately reduced to a set of physiological or biochemical conditions. Secondly, it implies that various societies have a set of conventional disease labels that can be mapped onto the objective diseases. The *meaning* of the label is its *designatum,* the disease to which it points. Its meaning is thus essentially free of social context and free of the perspective of the user.

This general framework is parallel to that described by Harrison as "the empiricist theory of language" (1972).[13] Very briefly, this theory holds that language consists of basic and non-basic utterances, and that it is only through basic utterances that meaning enters a language. Meaning attaches to basic utterances through a *conventional* stipulation "that a given language element shall henceforth be associated with a given world element" (1972:33). Concatenation of basic utterances depends first then upon "how the world is, as a matter of empirical fact, constituted" (1972:33). Children learn language and the meaning of signs by inductively and ostensively learning which elements of language are conventionally associated with which elements of the world (semantic rules). They learn to combine or refrain from combining certain signs with each other by inductively learning syntactic rules, rules concerned solely with 'relationships between signs' (1972:33).

This theoretical perspective also provides the framework for much of American anthropology in the past several decades. Greenberg formulated this framework in an influential paper in 1964. He began with two sets of distinctions made by the semiotician Charles Morris: that between syntactics, semantics, and pragmatics; and that between the user of the sign, the sign itself, and the *designatum* (Greenberg 1964:27). Combining these, he suggested the bounds of anthropological and linguistic investigation.

> If we include reference to the users of the language we are in the field of pragmatics. If we abstract from the user of language and consider only expressions and their *designata,* we have an investigation in semantics. If we abstract also from the *designata* and study only the relations between the expressions themselves, we have syntax.
> Greenberg 1964:27

This formulation, as the empiricist theory of language, defines semantics as the study of the relationship between signs or linguistic categories and their *designata*. Semantic analysis is thus set off from the study of linguistic actors, the contexts of verbal behavior, and the pragmatics of communications, all of which belong to the domain of sociolinguists and the ethnography of communications. Ethnosemantics, including the ethnoscientific study of medical language, makes precisely these assumptions.

Several fine ethnosemantic analyses of disease categories, including those by Frake (1961) and Fabrega and Silver (1973), illustrate the cultural variability of the distinctive features used in disease categorization. They assume, however, that the association of symptoms with each other in a category should reflect simply their association in the objective world. Unexpected configurations are thus inexplicable (e.g., Fabrega and Silver 1973:101). Further, disease categories with the same set of dimensions are said to "seem to have equivalent meaning", and those sharing one common dimension are said to form "groups of illness", with no further evidence that they are associated semantically or in the experience of the members of the society (Fabrega and Silver 1973:106). These studies thus even have problems explaining what they claim as their particular domain—the grouping of symptom or illness terms into associated clusters in a particular society.

A theory of medical language should help us understand the process by which language and communication are effectively related to feelings and physiology, to understand what Kleinman calls the "symbolic pathway of words, feelings, values, expectations, beliefs and the like which connect cultural events and forms with affective and physiological processes" (1973:209). Only such a theory can provide a sound basis for cross-cultural research and for medical practice which takes into consideration the psychosocial aspects of illness. A theory of medical language should provide a framework for understanding the following aspects of medical language and communications:

1. *The pathways linking the symbolic with the affective and physiological;* Clearly, a 'copy model' of the type compared by Wittgenstein to a museum filled with exhibits, each with its own label, is inadequate. Physiological states do not have simple linguistic correlates, as studies of affect have shown (e.g., Schachter 1971; Valins 1970). The degree to which disease itself is shaped by symbolic and social experience is a matter for empirical research. But an adequate conceptual framework should *make problematic* precisely those symbolic links that might affect such variability, rather than assuming diseases to be like trees to which one can only append names.

2. *The role of language in linking social experience to diseases;* We know that many disorders are the result of maladaptive behavior and are directly linked to the typical stresses of the society through the experience of the patient. Illness thus must be understood to have its meaning in a social context, and analysis must make problematic the role of the experience of illness

(its meaning to the patient) as a link between typical stresses in the society and disease process.

3. *The strategic use of illness language;* Illness language is used strategically by individuals in a variety of interaction settings: in a home care setting in which a mother comforts a child; in a setting of conflict, e.g., when a wife uses illness to manipulate her husband; in a patient-practitioner interaction. In each of these settings the 'meaning' of illness terms is dependent upon the perspective and 'structure of relevance' of the various actors. An adequate semantics of medical language should focus our attention on the creation of meaning in the context of interaction and upon the problems of communication between actors who use words with differing structures of meaning.

4. *How change in medical language is generated in broader social change.* Change in cognitive systems understood as the placing of new tags on old meanings or as the application of an old classification scheme to new objects (Basso 1973) is clearly inadequate for understanding medical change. If illness terms are associated with typical experiences of stress in a society, changes in medical language will be intimately related to more basic changes in the society. As new medical terms become known in a society, they find their way into existing semantic networks. Thus, while new explanatory models may be introduced, it is clear why changes in medical rationality seldom follow quickly.

In conclusion, if we are to develop a framework for understanding the relationship between disease and language that will advance our knowledge of the way psychosocial and cultural factors affect disease, we need to develop both new theories of disease and a new medical semantics. Disease will have to be conceived, as Wartofsky claims, as "a socio-historical and cultural phenomenon" (1975:67), as "an intricate and many-layered network of social, personal and organic contexts—from society to cell, so to speak—in which the doctor intervenes at specific points, diagnostically and therapeutically . . ." (1975:79–80).[14] And a corresponding semantics is necessary that understands the meaning of medical language to be constituted in relation to disease as semantic networks, configurations of symbols and experiences mobilized in social interaction and deeply integrated into the social and cultural structure of a society.

NOTES

[1]An earlier form of this paper was delivered to the Harvard Research Seminar on the Implications for Health Care Delivery of the Cross-Cultural Study of Health, Illness and Healing, October 1975. The author wishes to acknowledge his indebtedness to members of that group.

[2]Research for this paper was carried out jointly with Mary-Jo DelVecchio Good from 1972 to 1974. Research was supported by a

USPHS Traineeship and a grant from the Pathfinder Fund. Ms. Good is responsible for much of the case material upon which this paper is based.

[3]Details of these three medical traditions and their practice in Maragheh today can be found in Good (1976a, 1976b). In the use of the term 'cosmopolitan' medicine rather than modern, scientific, or Western, I follow Leslie (1976:5).

[4]See, for example, Bürgel (1976), Levey (1967), and Nasr (1968).

[5]In use of the term 'explanatory models', I follow Engelhardt (1974) and Kleinman (1975).

[6]There was little significant variation by social class in the cause attributed to heart distress.

[7]This description is drawn from Galen (1968), May (1968), Shaw (1972), Siegel (1968), Wilson (1959), and Levey (1967). For a fuller discussion see Good (1976a:Ch. IV).

[8]For a fuller discussion see Good (1976a:Ch III) and Nasr (1968).

[9]"Some think that strength of body depends on abundance of blood; that weakness is associated with paucity of blood. But is is not so. It is rather this, that the state of the body determines whether the nutriment will be beneficial to it or not." (Ibn Sina 1930:87)

[10]It may be noted in passing that use of the idiom of the heart is common throughout the Middle East. For example, Waziri (1973:215) notes that many depressed patients in Afghanistan "described their feeling 'as if a strong hard hand was squeezing' their 'hearts' . . . This was the most stressed symptom from which the patient wanted relief." Analysis such as I have suggested would reveal similarities and differences in the Afghan and Iranian cases.

[11]The matter of suicide in Iran deserves extended research. In the internal medicine hospital in Maragheh, which usually handled emergency suicide attempt cases, 18% of all patients admitted (117 of 654 cases) in the year 1352 (1973–74) were attempted suicide cases.

[12]This passage from *Alice's Adventures in Wonderland* is quoted by Palmer (1976:4) to illustrate different uses of the term 'meaning'.

[13]The critique of the empiricist theory of meaning which I outline here is argued in great detail by Beeman (1976). Other recent critiques include Wagner (1975:145–151) who argues that the 'natural order' is an invention of culture, and that ethnosemanticists have taken "plants, animals, colors, kinship, skin diseases [as] in some way 'real' and self-evident *things*'; and Polanyi and Prosch (1975), who argue for the necessary role of the intentional subject in the constitution of all meaning and knowledge.

[14]Kleinman, Eisenberg and Good (1976) suggest clinical applications of such a broadened perspective on illness and disease phenomena.

REFERENCES

Basso, Keith H. (1972) Semantic Aspects of Linguistic Acculturation. *In* Culture and Cognition. J.P. Spradley, ed. San Francisco: Chandler; pp. 344–354.

Beeman, William O. (1976) The Meaning of Stylistic Variation in Iranian Verbal Interaction. Ph.D. Dissertation. University of Chicago: Department of Anthropology.

Bürgel, Christoph J. (1976) Secular and Religious Features of Medieval Arabic Medicine. *In* Asian Medical Systems: A Comparative Study. C. Leslie, ed. Berkeley: University of California Press; pp. 44–62.

Currier, Richard L. (1966) The Hot-Cold Syndrome and Symbolic Balance in Mexican and Spanish-American Folk Medicine. Ethnology 5:251–263.

Engelhardt, H. Tristram (1974) Explanatory Models in Medicine: Facts, Theories, and Values. Texas Reports on Biology and Medicine 32:225–239.

Fischer, Michael M.J. (1973) Zoroastrian Iran Between Myth and Praxis. Ph.D. Dissertation. University of Chicago: Department of Anthropology.

___. (1975) Complementary But Equal: On Changing the Concept and Position of Persian Women. Unpublished Ms.

Foucault, Michel (1965) Madness & Civilization: A History of Insanity in the Age of Reason. New York: Random House.

___. (1970) The Order of Things: An Archaeology of the Human Sciences. New York: Vintage Books.

___. (1973) The Birth of the Clinic: An Archaeology of Medical Perception. New York: Vintage Books.

Fox, James J. (1975) On Binary Categories and Primary Symbols: Some Rotinese Perspectives. *In* Interpretation of Symbolism. Roy Willis, ed. New York: Halstead; pp. 99–132.

Frake, C.O. (1961) The diagnosis of disease among the Subanum of Mindanao. American Anthropologist 63:113–132.

Galen (1968) On the Usefulness of the Parts of the Body (*De usu partium*). Margaret May Tallmadge, tr. Ithaca, New York: Cornell University Press.

Givner, David A. (1962) Scientific Preconceptions in Locke's Philosophy of Language. Journal of History of Ideas 23:340–354.

Good, Byron J. (1976a) The Heart of What's the Matter; The Structure of Medical Discourse in a Provincial Iranian Town. Ph.D. Dissertation. University of Chicago: Department of Anthropology.

___. (1976b) Medical Change and the Doctor-Patient Relationship in an Iranian Provincial Town. *In* The Social Sciences and Problems of Development. Khodadad Farmanfarmaian, ed. Princeton: Princeton University Programs in Near Eastern Studies.

Greenberg, Joseph H. (1964) Linguistics and Ethnology. *In* Language in Culture and Society. Del Hymes, ed. New York: Harper and Row; pp. 27–31.

Harrison, Bernard (1972) Meaning and Structure: An Essay in the Philosophy of Language. New York: Harper and Row.

Heisel, J.S. *et al.* (1973) The Significance of Life Events as Contributing Factors in the Disease of Children. Journal of Pediatrics 83:119–123.

Ibn Sina (1930) The Canon of Medicine. *In* A Treatise on The Canon of Medicine of Avicenna. O. Cameron Gruner, ed. London: Luzac & Co.

Izutsu, Toshihiko (1964) God and Man in the Koran: Semantics of the Koranic Weltanschauung. Tokyo: Keio Institute of Cultural and Linguistic Studies.

Kleinman, Arthur M. (1973) Medicine's Symbolic Reality: On a Central Problem in the Philosophy of Medicine. Inquiry 16:206–213.

___. (1975) Explanatory Models in Health Care Relationships: *In* National Council of International Health: Health of the Family. Washington, D.C.: National Council for International Health; pp. 159–172.

Kleinman, Arthur, Leon Eisenberg and Byron Good (1976) Culture, Illness and Care: Clinical Lessons from Anthropological and Cross-Cultural Research. Forthcoming in Annals of Internal Medicine.

Leslie, Charles, ed. (1976) Asian Medical Systems: A Comparative Study. Berkeley: University of California Press.

Levey, Martin (1967) Medical Ethics of Medieval Islam with Special Reference to Al-Ruhawi's 'Practical Ethics of the Physician'. Transactions of the American Philosophical Society 57: Part 3;1–100.

Levi-Strauss, Claude (1966) The Savage Mind. Chicago: University of Chicago Press.

Lienhardt, Godfrey (1961) Divinity and Experience: The Religion of the Dinka. Oxford: Clarendon Press.

May, Margaret Tallmadge (1968) Introduction to Galen, On the Usefulness of the Parts of the Body. Ithaca, New York: Cornell University Press; pp. 1–64.

Minuchin, Salvador, *et al.* (1975) A Conceptual Model of Psychosomatic Illness in Children. *Archives of General Psychiatry* 32:1031–1038.

Nasr, Seyyed Hossein (1967) Islamic Studies. Beirut: Librairie du Liban.

___. (1968) Science and Civilization in Islam. Cambridge, Massachusetts: Harvard University Press.

Palmer, F.R. (1976) Semantics: A New Outline. Cambridge: Cambridge University Press.

Percy, Walker (1975) The Message in the Bottle: How Queer Man is, How Queer Language is, and What One Has To Do with the Other. New York: Farrar, Straus and Giroux.

Polanyi, Michael and Harry Prosch (1975) Meaning. Chicago: University of Chicago Press.

Schachter, Stanley (1971) Emotion, Obesity, and Crime. New York: Academic Press.

Schneider, David M. (1969) American Kin Terms and Terms for Kinsmen: A Critique of Goodenough's Componential Analysis of Yankee Kinship Terminology. *In* Cognitive Anthropology. Stephen A. Tyler, ed. New York: Holt, Rinehart and Winston, Inc; pp. 288–310.

Schwartz, L.R. (1969) The Hierarchy of Resort in Curative Practices: The Admiralty Islands, Melanesia. Journal of Health and Social Behavior 10:201–209.

Shaw, James R. (1972) Models for Cardiac Structure and Function in Aristotle. Journal of the History of Biology. 5:355–388.

Siegel, Rudolph E. (1968) Galen's System of Physiology and Medicine. Basel: S. Karger.

Turner, Victor (1967) The Forest of Symbols: Aspects of Ndembu Ritual. Ithaca, New York: Cornell University Press.

___. (1975) Revelation and Divination in Ndembu Ritual. Ithaca, New York: Cornell University Press.

Valins, Stuart (1970) The Perception and Labeling of Bodily Changes as Determinants of Emotional Behavior. *In* Physiological Correlates of Emotion. Perry Black, ed. New York: Academic Press; pp. 229–243.

Wagner, Roy (1975) The Invention of Culture. Englewood Cliffs, New Jersey: Prentice-Hall, Inc.

Wartofsky, Marx W. (1975) Organs, Organisms and Disease: Human Ontology and Medical Practice. *In* Evaluation and Explanation in the Biomedical Sciences. H.T. Engelhardt, Jr. and S.F. Spicker, eds. Dordrecht: D. Reidel Publishing Co; pp. 67–83.

Watt, William Montgomery (1953) The Faith and Practice of al-Ghazali. London: G. Allen and Unwin.

Waxler, Nancy E. (1974) Culture and Mental Illness: A Social Labelling Perspective. Journal of Nervous and Mental Disease 159:379–395.

Waziri, Rafiq (1973) Symptomatology of Depressive Illness in Afghanistan. American Journal of Psychiatry 130:213–217.

Wilson, Leonard G. (1959) Erasistratus, Galen, and the *Pneuma*. Bulletin of the History of Medicine 33:293–314.

CHAPTER FIVE

Culture and Psychotherapy

Because clients' subjective experiences of mental illness are structured by cultural schemas, psychotherapy should be appropriate to the cultural identity and explanatory model of the client. Psychotherapy should be based on a negotiated construction of clinical reality (including diagnosis, prognosis, and treatment plan) between the clinician, the client, and the client's family. The reason for this negotiation is due to the need to treat illness (client's subjective experience) as well as disease (clinician's diagnosis).

The article in this chapter illustrates what is referred to in medical anthropology as symbolic healing. Symbolic healing refers to the use of transformational symbols in healing rituals for purposes of psychotherapeutically altering the client's illness experience, including meaning of life events, emotional experience, and mental disorders. This psychotherapeutic process can be analyzed according to a model of symbolic healing reformulated from earlier sources by Dow (1986). The four steps of symbolic healing are:

1. The experiences of clinicians and clients are structured in terms of specific symbols from a set of cultural schemas.
2. A suffering client comes to a clinician, who negotiates the construction of a clinical reality with the patient using symbols from the cultural schemas.
3. The clinician attaches the client's intellect and emotions to transformational symbols particularized from the cultural schemas.
4. The healer manipulates the transformational symbols to help the client therapeutically restructure his or her cognitive appraisal of events and emotions.

Through a negotiated diagnosis and prognosis, the clinician engaged in symbolic healing isolates the part of the client's set of cultural schemas relevant to the illness and interprets the problem in terms of this negotiated clinical reality. In the therapeutic process, transformational symbols are formed that become intellectually and emotionally charged for the patient.

Transformational symbols can be any ideas, objects, or actions performed by the healer that facilitate the client's transformation of emotions and subjectively experienced reality. Examples of transformational symbols can include medications,

herbs, massage, prayer, rituals of reconciliation, penance for sin, various "holy" objects, sacred words, incantations, proverbs, scriptures, and so on. If the client accepts the healer's explanation as a valid model of his or her illness, then by skillful manipulation of the transformational symbols the client's cognitive construction of emotions and lived experience of the illness can be therapeutically altered. Dow (1986), following Ehrenwald, refers to this alteration as the existential shift—that is, a change in the client's experienced reality creating new opportunities for psychological adaptation.

In the therapeutic process of symbolic healing the clinician and the client do not need to share the same set of cultural schemas. For example, a clinician may provide a placebo treatment that can have a highly therapeutic effect on the client based on the symbolic value of the placebo in the mind of the patient. However, the manipulation of symbols and placebos is greatly facilitated if both clinician and client understand the meaning of symbolic objects based on the same set of cultural schemas.

Medical anthropologist Thomas Csordas (1983) has described three types of folk healing used by some Charismatic Christians in the United States. These are *spiritual healing*, *healing of memories*, and *deliverance*. Spiritual healing is conceptualized by the Charismatic Christians as God healing a soul that has been injured by sin. Healing of memories is treatment for traumatic memories that may be troubling a person even after that person has received the Holy Spirit. Deliverance is treatment characterized by freeing a person from the adverse effects of demons or evil spirits. In this case, a distinction is made between oppression, in which the effect of a demon is experienced in some limited aspect of a person's life, and possession, in which a demon takes over complete control of a person. Oppression by a demon usually takes the form of sinful behavior, such as lust, masturbation, adultery, and so on. Possession by a demon is essentially the Charismatic Christian equivalent of the spirit possession illnesses found in many nonindustrialized societies. Deliverance can be described as the Charismatic Christian version of exorcism. The offending demon is contacted, addressed by name, and commanded to depart in the name of Jesus Christ.

The healing of memories ritual is somewhat different from deliverance and illustrates clearly the structure of folk healing.

In healing of memories the individual's entire life is prayed for in chronological stages from conception to the present. Special attention is paid to any events or relationships that caused the individual emotional pain or trauma. The individual is usually asked to visualize the painful incident and to alter the original memory by visualizing Jesus there at the person's side, more or less guiding the person through that painful event. The meaning of the event is thus altered. The individual now has the understanding that Jesus was there all the time and wanted the person to go through that difficult time to bring the person closer to Himself. Therefore, the event was actually a good thing, because it brought the individual closer to God. Thus, the meaning of the event is altered. This allows the negative emotions surrounding the painful incident to be released and replaced with feelings of gratitude toward Jesus. Simultaneously, any lingering effects of the stress or trauma will also be reduced. This process is done for all stressful events, in effect, "walking Jesus through" the person's life, thus altering the meaning of all those events and therapeutically altering the emotions associated with them.

The article in this chapter is by psychiatrist Eliezer Witztum and clinical psychologist Onno van der Hart. The paper is a description of two cases, one historical and one recent, in which western clients complaining of possession and persecution by demons were successfully treated by employing symbolic forms from the patient's own meaning system in conjunction with hypnotherapy. The paper provides an example of symbols taken from the client's cultural background and applied to psychotherapy. This paper also reintroduces the historical concept of hysterical psychosis, which may be relevant to cases of spirit possession syndromes in many contemporary nonwestern cultures.

REFERENCES

Csordas, T. (1983). The rhetoric of transformation in ritual healing. *Culture, Medicine and Psychiatry, 7,* 333–375.

Dow, J. (1986). Universal aspects of symbolic healing: A theoretical synthesis. *American Anthropologist, 88,* 56–69.

ELIEZER WITZTUM, M.D.
ONNO VAN DER HART, PH.D.

Possession and Persecution by Demons

Janet's Use of Hypnotic Techniques in Treating Hysterical Psychosis

When a person believes him- or herself to be possessed or persecuted by a demon, this can be described as a possession syndrome. Another description would be hysterical psychosis (HP). Some authors would even argue in favor of a diagnosis of multiple personality disorder (MPD). All three diagnostic categories are trauma induced and have dissociative features. It is possible that they are functionally equivalent, differing in their clinical picture according to types and patterns of trauma, cultural background of the patient, and explanatory models used by the clinician (Bourguignon 1979; Kenny 1981; Krippner 1987; Varma et al. 1981). The following cases focus on the diagnostic categories of HP and possession syndrome.

We will describe two patients who were diagnosed with HP by their clinicians: Achille, Pierre Janet's patient a century ago in France, who believed he was possessed by the devil, and Avraham, a patient we treated in Israel a few years ago. In both cases, HP could be seen as a posttraumatic stress response characterized by dissociative features.

In this chapter, we focus on the cultural, symbolic, and dissociative nature of trauma-induced HP and its treatment using hypnosis. We review the early and more recent literature on HP, emphasizing Janet's dissociation model, and we identify cultural factors influencing the patient's and clinician's choice between a diagnosis of HP or of possession syndrome. Given the dissociative nature of HP, we advocate psychotherapy using hypnosis as the treatment of choice rather than drug therapy. Both Janet's case study of a century ago and our case example demonstrate the efficacy of hypnosis.

HYSTERICAL PSYCHOSIS

The concept of hysterical psychosis (HP) has suffered a curious fate in the history of psychiatry. During the latter half of the nineteenth century, this disorder was well known and thoroughly studied, particularly in French psychiatry. In the early 20th century, the diagnoses of hysteria and of HP fell into disuse. Patients formerly thought to have HP were rediagnosed as having schizophrenia or as being malingerers. Clinicians have subsequently attempted to reintroduce the diagnostic category of HP, but it has not regained official recognition. The Index of the DSM-III-R (American Psychiatric Association 1987) contains HP, then refers readers to either Brief Reactive Psychosis or to Factitious Disorder with psychological symptoms. Brief Reactive Psychosis, first included in the DSM-II (American Psychiatric Association 1968), was considered a response to major stress, such as the loss of a loved one or the psychological trauma of combat.

Early Literature on Hysterical Psychosis

Moreau de Tours (1845/1973, 1855, 1865, 1869) distinguished two modes of mental life: life in the external world and life in dreams. The modes are separated from each other by sleep. The psychotic individual "dreams while awake." The psychosis is a continuation of a dream in the waking state (Moreau de Tours 1855). In chronic psychosis, patients are completely absorbed in their internally generated worlds. They have jumped into a dream state from which nothing can pull them out. According to Moreau de Tours (1865, 1869), HP was a brief and often intermittently recurring psychosis in patients with hysteria.

Hysteria was not well defined at that time, but one of its characteristics was thought to be somnambulism. Moreau de Tours (1865, 1869) and some of his contemporaries found four basic features of HP: 1) its similarity to dreams, 2) its curability (using psychotherapy), 3) its plasticity or polymorphism, and 4) its analogy with chemically induced (as by hashish) "artificial delirium."

Hysterical Psychosis in Janet's Dissociation Theory

Pierre Janet, the most important French authority on hysteria and HP, viewed HP in much the same way as Moreau de Tours (Janet 1894/1898a, 1911b). Janet emphasized that HP constitutes a kind of waking dream in which the subject gradually loses the ability to differentiate between dream elements and normal perceptions. In hysterical attacks, in ecstasies, and in somnambulism, patients play or speak out their dreams. These dreams usually take place in abnormal states or subconsciously, and they disturb the normal thought process by diminishing the disposable force of attention. Janet (1894–1895/1898b) said that a psychosis could be considered hysterical if its dissociative nature could be established. The criteria for that are as follows:

1. The psychosis is embedded in dissociative phenomena;
2. The psychosis itself can be seen as a dissociated mental state;
3. Splitting or doubling of the mind (dédoublement de la personalité) occurs;
4. Subconscious phenomena are present; and
5. Altered states of consciousness occur.

Janet (1889) defined dissociation as the splitting off, separation, and isolation of certain parts of the personality from the conscious awareness and control of one's habitual personality. These split-off parts of the personality remain unknown to waking consciousness and start to lead lives of their own. They alternate with the habitual personality in dominating the patient's behavior (Van der Hart and Horst 1989). Through clinical observation of many hysterical patients, Janet established that these dissociations were in many cases related to traumatic experiences (Janet 1889, 1898c, 1911b; van der Kolk and van der Hart 1989). The extreme emotions (e.g., anxiety and panic) experienced during the trauma trigger dissociative reactions.

The simplest and most basic forms of dissociated phenomena, memories of traumatic experiences, were labeled as "primary idées fixes" or primary emotional states (Janet 1894/1898a, 1898c). Dreams and fantasies based on these traumatic memories are "secondary idées fixes" or secondary emotional states. The most complex are the alter personalities of patients with MPD, each of which has its own identity and distinguishes itself from the habitual personality.

As we understand Janet, the subject experiences HP as a waking dream based on a traumatic experience (Janet 1894/1898a, 19898c). The subject presents as if in a delusional state that has no apparent connection to his or her current reality. Janet emphasized the fact that the dissociative nature of hysteria implies high hypnotizability. Hypnotherapy was the treatment of choice in these cases (van der Hart et al. 1989).

The early views of Breuer and Freud (1893–1895/1955a, 1893–1895/1955b) on hysteria and HP were strongly influenced by Janet, as Breuer testified. . . . They emphasized, among other things, the traumatic origins of these disorders. Breuer also pointed to the dreamlike nature of HP and to the often rapid alternation of such dreams with the normal waking state. He believed that patients dreaming these waking dreams were in a state of self-hypnosis—what the French termed "somnambulism." Unlike Freud, Breuer believed that such "psychotic states" could persist for a long time, as exemplified by the case of Anna O.

The Decline of Hysteria

At the beginning of the 20th century, interest in HP, hysteria, and hypnosis had vanished. The few attempts to establish the clinical validity of HP were not accepted. This led to regarding patients suffering from HP and MPD as malingerers or as following suggestions. Furthermore, Bleuler's introduction of the term "schizophrenia" (Bleuler 1911/1950) as a diagnostic entity encompassing widely divergent mental disorders may have led to the decline of diagnostic entities such as MPD or HP (Maleval 1981; Rosenbaum 1980). Bleuler opposed strongly the diagnosis of HP:

> I have never yet had any reason for making a diagnosis of "hysterical psychosis." All cases so diagnosed by others differed in no wise from other schizophrenics. When a supposed hysteric becomes psychotic or deteriorates, he is in my experience not a hysteric at all but a schizophrenic.
> (Bleuler 1911/1950, p. 289)

Bleuler's influence was so great that after 1911, the majority of psychiatrists, including Freud, no longer used the diagnosis of HP (Maleval 1981).

The careful clinical studies of Janet and others, which proved that hysteria and HP are distinct clinical entities with dissociation as the essential feature, were overlooked. Both syndromes required a special treatment approach—namely, psychotherapy using hypnosis, which was used by very few clinicians (Breukink 1923, 1924, 1925). Most clinicians struggled with treating cases of hysteria or HP that were formally diagnosed as "schizophrenia" but that did not neatly fit the diagnostic criteria of schizophrenia.

Dissociation Rediscovered

After World War II, several attempts were made to revive the concept of HP. In line with Janet's dissociation model, the Dutch psychiatrist Hugenholz (1946) stated that HP can develop in individuals with hysterical characteristics who are exposed to traumatic events. These events evoke and reactivate dissociated earlier painful experiences with their associated affect, such as resentment and hate. Patients with HP exhibit a lowering of consciousness, dreaming, fantasizing, staring, inattentiveness, and abulia (loss of will power); the disorder can be complicated by other hysterical symptoms such as abasia (inability to walk), astasia (incoordination with inability to stand), and aphonia.

In America, the work of Hollender and Hirsch during the 1960s became influential. To these researchers, HP is characterized by a sudden and dramatic onset temporally related to a profoundly upsetting event or circumstance and by a short duration (less than 3 weeks). Its manifestations include hallucinations, delusions, depersonalization, and grossly unusual behavior (Hirsch and Hollender 1969; Hollender and Hirsch 1964).

Janet's dissociation model reappeared in the work of Pringuet (1977), who underscored the dissociative aspects of HP, including the doubling of the personality, conversion symptoms, and suggestibility. Spiegel and Fink (1979) stated that HP usually involves brief and intense periods of psychotic behavior, generally with graphic decompensation, severe environmental stress, and rapid recompensation in individuals with other hysterical features. They found that these patients have a poor response to antipsychotic medication but will respond to individual and family therapy. Steingard and Frankel (1985) explicitly stated that dissociation underlies the phenomenon and that certain highly hypnotizable people are prone to experience transient but severe psychotic states while in spontaneously occurring trance. The researchers believed hypnotherapy to be the treatment of choice.

Hysterical Psychosis and Possession Syndrome

Many individuals with HP, including the two patients described in this chapter, experience hallucinations in which possession or persecution by a devil or demon plays a dominant role (Aikins 1929; Spiegel and Fink 1979). In other words, they are in possession states. Similarly, students of possession emphasize its dissociative nature (Zusane and Jones 1989). Comparing HP and possession syndrome, Langness (1976) concluded that they are functionally equivalent. He observed that in cultures where such cases are diagnosed as HP, the diagnosis of possession state is absent, and vice versa.

The important cultural differentiator in this dichotomy is whether the culture is characterized by religious beliefs in spirits. Belief in possession and religious tradition have always gone together. Thus, in Christianity, the Roman Catholic church has always recognized possession by the devil, and exorcists have existed since the third century to treat such cases. In Judaism, the soul of a dead person may enter someone's body during the course of his or her life, not just at conception or birth (Bilu 1985). In Jewish mystical communities adhering to this doctrine, *dybbuk* possession was a well-known phenomenon. In India

today, belief in supernatural entities and transmigration of souls is still an important part of the Hindu and Buddhist traditions. In a recent survey of dissociative disorders, records of 2,631 patients seen in adult outpatient services in India were screened for dissociative symptoms (Saxena and Prasad 1989). In 62 cases, a DSM-III (American Psychiatric Association 1980) diagnosis of dissociative disorder could be given; 9.7% of these patients had a possession syndrome (with MPD being conspicuously absent). Clinical observations indicate that possession syndrome is also common in other South Asian countries (Adityanjee et al. 1989).

Not all possession cases are culturally regarded as pathological or demonic. It is important to distinguish between "normative" ritual possession, which serves social functions, and "peripheral possession" (Ward 1980). The latter represents the long-term, pathological reactions with control by malevolent or immature spirits (Krippner 1987; Ward 1980; Zusane and Jones 1989). It is often the patient's local community or sect that interprets his or her behavior as pathological (i.e., as a possession syndrome; Langness 1976).

In conclusion, where possession states are a recognized part of a culture, the community and local clinicians tend to speak of possession syndrome in pathological cases. In dominant Western culture, HP or a related diagnosis (such as MPD) will be used. As Kenny (1981) has shown us, William James (Taylor 1982) was probably the first to recognize this when he ironically remarked, "If there are real demons they might possess only hysterics."

Treatment

Our discussion of the literature on the traumatic origins, dissociative nature, and cultural mode of HP, sometimes characterized as possession state, points to at least three principles that should guide clinicians in their assessment and treatment of patients with this trauma-induced disorder:

1. The dissociative nature of the disorder should be established and treatment should be based on its recognition. This implies psychotherapy using hypnosis as the treatment of choice, with medication having an auxiliary function (Breukink 1923, 1924, 1925; Hoek 1868; Janet 1898c; Spiegel and Fink 1979; Steingard and Frankel 1985; van der Hart and van der Velden 1987). Hypnosis is the most powerful medium for transforming the patient's pathological imagery.
2. The traumatic origins of the disorder should be traced and become the focus at the appropriate stage of treatment (Brown and Fromm 1986; van der Hart et al. 1989).
3. When Western-oriented clinicians treat these patients, they should treat them within the context of cross-cultural therapy. They should allow these patients to articulate and resolve their dissociative symptoms in the mode of the prevailing idiom

and metaphors of their unique cultural background (Crapan-zano 1975; Good and Good 1986; Witztum et al. 1990).

In the two following case studies, similarities are striking despite vast differences in time and cultural background, which demonstrates how these treatment principles are relevant in widely different contexts.

CASE STUDY 1:
ACHILLE—POSSESSION BY THE "DEVIL"

Janet (1894–1895/1898b) reports that Achille, 33—elsewhere called Daill (Janet 1893/1911a)—was admitted to the Salpêtrière in a state of HP. He presented with unintelligible speech and actions, reporting that he saw the devil, black and horned, sneering at him. He heard one demon whispering menaces, damnation, and pernicious advice and felt another in his chest forcing him to utter blasphemies.

Achille, though somewhat fearful, had been a cheerful, happily married family man. Although both his parents had been alcoholic and his father had also been very superstitious, Janet pronounced Achille as having had a rather normal childhood. Achille had been a sensitive and assiduous boy who read a great deal. He was highly impressionable, taking everything seriously "as if it all really happened like that." After a punishment or small insult, he could be upset for days. He was unable to make friends, and at school he was often the butt of ridicule. However, his marriage, at age 22, proved developmentally fortunate; his wife was a dedicated woman able to keep him in touch with reality and make a happy man of him. They had a daughter, who developed quite normally. For 12 years, everything went smoothly.

At the end of the winter of 1890, a year before his admission, Achille returned home from a business trip in a sour mood, became extremely uncommunicative, and avoided contact with his wife and daughter. Shortly thereafter, he lost his power of speech. When he regained it, he was extremely anxious and felt he was being choked. Several doctors were consulted who made varying diagnoses of somatic illnesses. Achille stopped eating, became immobile, barely spoke, and avoided all contact with his wife and daughter. One morning, he laughed satanically for hours, terrifying everyone present. Afterwards, he saw and heard demons, felt them within himself, and behaved quite oddly.

Janet viewed this as the exterior (symptomatic) aspect of Achille's illness. He believed there was another state, dissociated from this one, in which the patient could explain his illness clearly. Janet was able to evoke this state by using hypnosis. Direct attempts to hypnotize the wildly gesticulating, ranting man were unsuccessful, preventing a traditional induction. However, while Achille was in the midst of hallucinating, Janet slipped a pencil into his hand, carefully guiding the hand to write the name "Achille." The writing spontaneously turned into automatic writing, which Janet interpreted as originating from a dissociated state. Janet then tried verbal commands. While Achille was still distracted, Janet seated himself behind him and softly suggested that he would make certain movements. The movements were not made, but to Janet's surprise the hand rapidly wrote:

"I don't want to."

"And why don't you want to?" Janet responded softly.

"Because I am stronger than you are."

"Who are you then?"

"I am the devil."

"Oh, very well, then we can talk to each other."

To subject the "devil" to his control, Janet appealed to his weak point, his vanity.

"I don't believe in your power and I won't believe in it unless you give me proof."

"What proof?" asked the "devil."

Janet instructed him to allow the left arm of the patient to rise without the patient knowing it. This was done, and Janet gave a series of instructions of the same sort, all of which were performed by the "devil."

Then Janet demanded a final proof: The "devil" was to hypnotize Achille without his noticing it. This, too, was done. The patient slumped over in a deep trance state. Once hypnotized, Janet addressed Achille and elicited the cause of his present condition: During the business trip at the end of the winter in 1890, he had a brief extramarital affair. Afterwards he was tormented by remorse and by the idea of having caught a contagious disease; this was why he had avoided contact with his wife and daughter. Following the doctors' diagnoses of physical illnesses, he dreamt that he died from illness; it was after this that he became immobile.

Janet remarked, "When one has dreamt that one has died, what is there left to dream about? After death, hell." Thus the dreams about demons who came to torture him in hell. To Janet, it was at this point that the subconscious dream amplified, intruding on the patient's normal consciousness in the form of hallucinations. Achille's belief that he was indeed in hell and possessed by the devil determined the content of his delusional ideas.

Achille's remorse about his sexual misdeed was so intense that he experienced it as traumatizing. This emotional flooding in connection with his immoral behavior was the traumatic root of his disorder. Janet's treatment plan was to detraumatize the emotionally overwhelming event and discharge Achille's remorse. He accomplished this by using his hypnotic substitution technique. "An idea, a memory can be seen as a system of images which one can destroy, by separating its elements, by changing these isolated elements, by substituting in this compound one partial image or another for existing ones" (p. 404). Janet did not go into detail but remarked that "the memory of his [Achille's] misdoing was transformed in all respects because of suggested hallucinations. Finally Achille's wife herself, evoked by hallucination at the suitable moment, completely forgave this more unfortunate than guilty husband" (p. 404).

Once out of hypnosis, Achille felt very much relieved and liberated. He regained all his memories and began to use critical judgment on his delusions. Within a couple of days he was able to laugh about his devil, explaining the delusion to himself as a result of having read too many novels.

However, the delusion continued to haunt him in his sleep, during nightmares in which devils were torturing him. Traces of the delusion were also discernible in automatic writing. Janet therefore applied his substitution technique again, and these dreams also disappeared. Janet concluded that the "devil" was beaten and had disappeared forever. It became difficult to evoke automatic writing or to induce the deep hypnotic state which Achille had attained in previous stages of treatment. The unity of the mind was reestablished. For Janet, the disappearance of the pathological dream (symbolic reliving of the highly charged emotional experience)—which he called an idée fixe—indicated the resolution of the traumatically induced dissociation. The hysterical psychosis remitted completely.

Follow-up at 3 and 7 years indicated that Achille was doing well in all respects.

CASE STUDY 2: AVRAHAM—PERSECUTED BY A "DEMON"

On October 16, 1986, terrorists threw three hand grenades into a crowd near the Western Wall in the Old City of Jerusalem, killing one person and wounding 69. Two months later, Avraham, 35, an ultraorthodox Israeli Jew, was brought to a mental health outpatient clinic by his wife. During the intake session, Avraham frequently cried and moaned as if in physical pain. His affect was depressed. He was oriented to place and time but not to current events. His cooperation with the therapists was so poor that is was impossible to evaluate him accurately for a thought disorder. He denied suicidal tendencies. A tentative diagnosis of Major Depressive Episode was made, and treatment with an antidepressant medication was initiated.

Avraham, accompanied by his wife, attended therapy weekly. During the first 3 sessions, the following background information was gathered from Avraham's wife, as the subject himself hardly spoke. His father, Avraham's first Torah teacher, was, in his time, a well-known Orthodox rabbi and Kabalist. The father was killed in a car accident when Avraham was 8 years old. His

mother never recovered from her grief and was incapable of caring for Avraham and his 8 siblings. At the age of 12, he was placed in an orphanage. He studied in a series of Orthodox yeshivas (religious schools that emphasize Jewish studies to the exclusion of secular subjects). At 20, he married and subsequently had 5 children.

As an observant Jew, Avraham frequently went to the Western Wall, the last remains of the Second Temple, the most sacred site in Judaism. Praying there was a continuation of his father's religious habits. Avraham was thus engaged during the evening when the hand grenades were thrown. He was not hit, but the force of the explosions threw him into the air. As far as he remembered, he had not been unconscious. According to his wife, he immediately returned home.

Over the next 2 weeks, Avraham's wife noted a marked change from his normal behavior. He began talking to himself in fragmentary sentences, speaking constantly of bombs and people dying. He was easily startled and distracted. He paid little attention to the family. During the third week, he began to consume huge quantities of food, even compulsively taking food from his children's plates. Over the next month, he gained more than 15 kilograms, developing peripheral edema and episodes of cellulitis that required medical attention. During the fifth week he withdrew further, had extensive crying spells and was obviously depressed. He experienced severe sleep disturbances, including insomnia and periods of shouting and crying during apparent sleep. He refused to bathe, shave, or change his clothes, completely neglecting personal hygiene and appearance. Because of poor attendance and his inability to concentrate on his studies, Avraham was dismissed from the yeshiva, and the family lost its sole source of income. Apart from his deranged behavior, which led his wife to bring him to the clinic, the family's deteriorating economic situation became a stressful factor of increasing magnitude.

Despite the patient's initial presentation as psychotic, he was not responsive to antipsychotics, which were withdrawn along with antidepressants after 1 month. Because the precipitating event was traumatic and followed by rapid deterioration, Brief Reactive Psychosis was the logical diagnosis. However, Avraham was not responsive to medication, and his symptoms persisted for several weeks. We as therapists began considering another possibility. We noticed severe regressive characteristics: Avraham's behavior resembled that of a frightened child—terrified affect rather than detached or remote behavior. He showed no aggressive tendencies. The content of his "hallucinations" was polymorphic, bizarre, and colorful, but also ambiguous and vague. These features were seen as congruent with diagnosis of posttraumatic stress response with strong dissociative features. As more evidence emerged to support this position, we initiated a treatment plan accordingly.

Avraham's Treatment

Whenever the traumatic event at the Western Wall was mentioned in session, the therapists observed that Avraham made agitated arm movements: first upward and then back and forth horizontally. Following Janet, the therapists regarded these movements as expressions of flashback phenomena, iconic representations of overwhelming experiences during the attack: the explosions and people falling and running into each other in panic. When they inquired about this, the patient, who until then had barely spoken in sessions, cried and moaned and began haltingly to explain what had happened.

During the following sessions, Avraham and his wife explained that his frequent prayers at the Western Wall had a dual nature: both to pray and to show respect for the memory of his late father. The attack shattered Avraham's defenses against the unresolved traumatic grief following his father's untimely death. His subsequent compulsive eating was his effort to fill the deep emptiness he felt at the loss of his father.

The therapists made this unresolved grief the focus of treatment. They asked Avraham to write a leave-taking letter to his father in which he could tell his father everything he wanted and needed to tell him (van der Hart 1983). Avraham's wife assisted him in this task. The letter he brought to the next session began with the words, "Father, father, father, why did you leave me? Why didn't you come when I was married?" The handwriting in the first sentence was appropriate for a 35-year-old man, but it quickly degenerated into a disorganized pattern, with large letters typical of the handwriting of a young child, and by the end it had become a scribble. Avraham was asked to read the letter aloud, and the same regression was noted. Although he began in a composed manner, he soon alternated between episodes of screaming and hitting himself vigorously on the chest, and episodes of sinking into a state of masticatory movements of sucking and rocking back and forth. The traumatized child part of his personality reexperienced the intense grief of the loss of his beloved and powerful father. With deep emotion, he expressed the feeling that he would "forever be alone, that life would never be the same, and that forever there would only be a cloud of emptiness."

After this session, the frequency of his nocturnal persecutory attacks increased and persisted into the day as well. He began to eat even more. The continuing weight gain caused additional medical complications, which often prevented him from attending scheduled therapeutic sessions.

The therapists realized they had to explore the nature of these intrusive nocturnal episodes. These experiences occurred mainly during sleep, in the transition state from sleeping to waking, and finally, during the waking state itself. In them, Avraham was threatened by a bizarre figure whom he initially described as "the Black." Additional information from him and his wife, who kept a diary on these attacks, revealed that this ugly creature was nonhuman and had red eyes and the legs of a chicken, the stereotypical description of a demon in traditional Jewish folk religion. When this vision occurred, Avraham would run around the room shouting for help and hitting his head against the wall, trying vainly to shake off the frightening images. During this period he refused to leave the house and kept all windows and curtains closed, because he believed that people were trying to kill him.

The therapists decided to use hypnosis as a means of entering and controlling these frightening dissociative experiences. The hypnotic state was very easily induced. Avraham was directed to see the black figure who was mocking and threatening him: "I killed your father and now I will kill you like I killed him." Avraham also reported seeing his father standing in the shadows looking at him sadly. He cried to his father for help, but his father could not help him. He tried to escape from the black figure but was unable to do so. He could admit that the figure was a "demon," a courageous admission in light of the cultural taboo against naming demons or discussing them.

In the next sessions, the therapists assisted Avraham in gaining some control over this demon. Under hypnosis he was given the traditional instructions for exorcising a demon. Whenever he saw the black figure, he was to incant loudly and clearly: "Go, go, go away, because you do not belong to our world." He used this incantation in hypnosis during the session and saw "the Black" running away. At home in the presence of his wife this incantation was effective, but when Avraham tried to utter it alone it was not.

In order to promote Avraham's ability to cope with the dream when alone, the therapists instructed him to demand forcefully that the "demon" tell him its name. This derived from traditional beliefs that knowing and identifying a demon by name is a prerequisite for overpowering it. Avraham rehearsed this during the session, but the "demon" refused to disclose its identity and ran away. To generate a greater sense of self-control, the therapists taught Avraham self-hypnotic relaxation techniques to practice at home with his wife's assistance.

During the next session, Avraham reported some improvement after using these techniques. When he, in the company of his wife, demanded that "the Black" reveal its name, the "demon" again became frightened. "The Black" now enlisted two aides, and this demonic triad tried, almost successfully, to drown Avraham when he was in the Miqveh (ritual bath).

Therapy reached a stalemate, as Avraham could not engage the "demon." In order to break through the stalemate in the next session, Avraham was asked to visualize the setting where he had last seen the "demon" and its aides. "A desolate place in the desert," was his reply. The therapists interpreted this as a metaphoric kernel statement (Fernandez 1977) expressing his problematic life situation. The "demon" and its two aides were hidden behind nearby boulders. The therapists urged Avraham to search for signs indicating the direction he should take in order to find protection. At first he saw nothing; then, when encouraged to scan the horizon, he found a distant, small spot of green.

It was suggested that this green spot might be an oasis where he could find shelter, water, food, and the company he was looking for—the latter being an indirect suggestion of symbolically meeting his father. When the therapists suggested that Avraham walk in that direction, the "demon" and its aides immediately appeared, trying to distract him from going his own way. (This symbolized the conflict about separating and becoming independent.) He was asked to demand their names and to lure them toward him, holding them captive until they gave their names. The fact that they were still too afraid to approach him restored some of Avraham's self-confidence. At the end of the session, he was asked how old he felt. "Twelve," he answered; older than before.

Avraham continued his imagery process at home with his wife's assistance. During the next session he was encouraged to advance toward the "green," despite the obstacles and recurrent attacks of the "Black" triad. Avraham and his wife reported that at home, the number of episodes involving the "demon" was greatly reduced. Avraham felt more confident in his ability to control the "demon."

During one therapy session, a demonic aide suddenly appeared, in the form of a black dog, and Avraham repelled it by throwing an imaginary stone. Afterwards, he reported his age as 14.

The "Secret Weapon" and the Regaining of the "Lost Paradise"

During the next session, Avraham reported having found a new and powerful ally in his struggle with the demons: The very famous Tsaddik (righteous man) Rabbi Chaim Ben Attar (1696–1743). Avraham had visited the grave of the Rabbi on the anniversary of his death earlier that week. It is believed that a request made on such a pilgrimage to the grave of a Tsaddik will be granted (Bilu and Abramovich 1985). Avraham visited the grave on the Mount of Olives with many others, but afterwards he remained there alone. He cried, asked for help, and prayed for many hours.

Finally, Avraham felt that his prayers were answered. After that, he felt supported by this Tsaddik and experienced himself as more powerful. This event signified an important shift in the development of an internal locus of control. Without direct instructions from us as therapists, Avraham had initiated action to solve his problem. He began assuming responsibility for his situation and enlisted the help of a wise and powerful father figure, which he internalized.

At home, Avraham worked with his wife to come closer to the green area, determined to reach it during the next session with our help and encouragement.

In the 18th session, Avraham described the green area as a beautiful garden surrounded by a high wall. He circled it and found a gate. Suddenly, "the Black" and its aides tried to grab him and throw him in a pit, but with the power of the Tsaddik and with our encouragement, he showed that the balance of power had definitely changed. He actually shouted to the "demons": "In the name of Rabbi Chaim Ben Attar, I tell you, go away! I am not afraid of you! I am not afraid of you! Go away!" He invoked verses from the Psalms: "He that dwells in the secret place of the Most High shall abide under the shadow of the Almighty . . ." (Psalm 91:1). He stood in the center of the therapy room, actually fighting with his arms and legs, until at last he overcame the "demons" and they withdrew, defeated.

Next, Avraham approached the guardian at the gate, explained that he had to enter the garden, and asked permission to enter. From outside, he saw many beneficent, white-bearded Tsaddikim. Suddenly he saw his father among them, called to him, and asked him to instruct the guardian to let him in. Avraham's affect changed remarkably and his depressed expression completely disappeared as he informed his wife and us that he was entering the Lower Paradise. He said that the air smelled like perfume and that he saw two springs of water. (Avraham's experience of the Lower Paradise was consistent with traditional descriptions of this well-known place in Jewish mysticism.) Encouraged to drink and satisfy his thirst, he described the water as sweet and fresh. He himself appeared completely revitalized.

Then he saw his father again and ran to him, embracing him and talking to him joyfully. He saw his admired grandfather, for whom he was named, and embraced him also. Next he met his own Rabbi who had died in a traffic accident when Avraham was 18. He described these experiences with wonder, excitement, and joy, using Biblical verses to express his feelings. At the end of the session, we suggested that from then on Avraham would have the power of Rabbi Chaim Ben Attar with him, plus the additional protective power of the Tsaddikim and his father, grandfather, and former Rabbi. Internalizing their positive qualities would enable him to be a more functional husband and father. Closing suggestions were given for a comfortable, uninterrupted sleep.

In the next and final session, Avraham's wife brought no notes from home. For the first time in 6 months, there was nothing to report. Avraham was sleeping well at night, and apparently all hallucinations and delusions had disappeared. He felt very good, albeit a bit weak. He had spent considerable time in healthy interaction with his children. Both he and his wife felt that his visit to the Lower Paradise had been a mystic miracle, a great privilege that, traditionally, is granted to only a few very righteous men. Avraham did not want to undergo hypnosis again, as the experience in the Lower Paradise felt completed. During the preceding week, on the anniversary of his father's death, he had visited his father's grave and cried intensely. Afterwards, he felt greatly relieved. (This completed the mourning seen as therapeutically necessary to release the dissociated affect of the first traumatizing event.)

Follow-Up

More than 5 years after the terrorist incident, Avraham functions relatively well. He experiences mild sleep problems and is a bit phobic of cars, but evidences no psychotic or paranoid ideation or signs of depression. He goes every day to study at the synagogue and yeshiva.

DISCUSSION

Hysterical Psychosis as a Posttraumatic Stress Response

The immediate cause of HP is usually a traumatic or stressful life event. In addition to environmental stressors, subjective factors can be sufficiently traumatizing to produce a posttraumatic stress response. In the case of Avraham, the environmental stressors, the terrorist attack, and the sudden death of his father at age 8 are widely recognized as extremely upsetting. Avraham's enduring belief that his father abandoned him exemplifies the subjective aspects of his traumatic reaction. An amorous affair, as was the case with Achille, hardly fits the criterion of an event that would be markedly stressful to almost anyone in similar circumstances in that person's culture. With Achille, the conviction of having caught a contagious disease and intense feelings of remorse indicate that sometimes the subjective aspects of such an event are most important.

With Avraham, the trauma of the terrorist attack triggered and activated previous traumatic memories regarding the sudden death of his father and its disturbing aftermath. According to Janet (1903), this gives rise to the phenomenon of "double emotion." The traumatic reaction, characterized by "vehement emotions," relates to both the current trauma and the previous traumatic memories. The person is therefore even more overwhelmed and even less able to make sense of his or her experiences. He or she is more at risk, we believe, to develop a more severe posttraumatic disorder such as HP rather than simple posttraumatic stress disorder (PTSD).

Trauma, Dissociation, and Hysterical Psychosis

Dissociating the experience from normal consciousness is the primary defense against trauma (Janet 1889, 1894/1898b,

1911b; Putnam 1989; Spiegel 1984). Dissociation leads to the formation of mental systems outside the experiencing ego (dédoublement de la personnalité), in Janet's terms. In the cases presented in this chapter, the dissociated traumatic experiences—called primary idées fixes or primary emotional states by Janet—evoked dreams and fantasies—secondary idées fixes or secondary emotional states in which certain highly charged thoughts dominated, giving rise to the supernatural, demonic figures. These contents were borrowed from the internalized cultural-symbolical world of these patients.

Achille was a highly impressionable man living at the end of the 19th century in the French countryside where occasionally possession epidemics still occurred (e.g., in 1860 the village of Morzine and in 1880 in Verzegnies). His remorse about his amorous affair and his belief in having caught a contagious disease with which he could contaminate his wife and daughter led to his dream and hallucinations in which he died, went to hell as a sinner, and became possessed. Avraham as a child felt abandoned by his revered father, who, in his imagination, could only be killed by a demon. The childhood dream about this demon was reactivated as a posttraumatic reaction to the terrorist attack—first as a nightmare, then a "waking dream" or hallucinations in which he himself had become the target of this demon.

Duration of Hysterical Psychosis

Although it is recognized that PTSD may become chronic, in HP a short duration is regarded as a necessary condition. According to Hollender and Hirsh (1964), HP lasts no longer than 3 weeks; DSM-III-R allows for a duration of 1 month for Brief Reactive Psychosis. The cases of Achille and Avraham, which we consider examples of HPT, and other cases (Breukink 1923, 1924, 1925; Hugenholz 1946; van der Hart and van der Velden 1987) support the possibility of a longer duration.

The disturbance resulting from trauma-induced dissociation does not impair the organization of thought processes as does "true" psychotic disorder. As the examples illustrate, even when the patients' behavioral responses do not seem appropriate to the present reality, the patient can narrate the delusional (symbolic) content, comment on it as an observer, and recall and refer to it after experiencing it—all functions that are impaired in psychosis. When their posttraumatic HP episodes are resolved, patients return to their former levels of functioning and thought processing.

Some authors emphasize high hypnotizability in these patients (Breukink 1923, 1924, 1925; Spiegel and Fink 1979; Steingard and Frankel 1985). Both patients described in this chapter showed high trance capacity, although Achille was not easy to hypnotize.

We propose that for a "psychosis" to be HP, it's dissociative nature—not its short duration—must be established. According to Janet (1894/1898b), this is apparent in the alteration of different states of consciousness, the presence of subconscious phenomena, and high hypnotizability. This alteration of states of consciousness is referred to in modern literature as the intrusion of traumatic memories, flashbacks, and nightmares. The rapid and persistent intrusion of these traumatic phenomena into daily life creates an alternative reality in which subjects experience themselves. At best, the intrusion is minimal; at worst, traumatic imagery alternates increasingly with current reality until it dominates. It is the subjective experience of this dual reality that defines the psychotic features of HP.

The Role of Hypnosis and Culture-Sensitive Techniques in Treatment

Patients with HP usually respond poorly to antipsychotic medication and have a high degree of hypnotizability. Although systematic research validating these impressions is needed, for the time being they suggest that psychotherapy, particularly with the use of hypnosis, is the treatment of choice.

Hypnosis can be used to diagnose and identify the traumatic experiences that produced this extreme reaction. Thus, Janet identified the nature of Achille's dissociated material and the cause of his psychosis. Using a hypnotic substitution technique, he changed the hallucinations into more positive images, as with Achille's imagined confession of the affair to his wife and her forgiveness of him. Although in this case Janet describes his substitution technique only briefly, contemporary works (Janet 1889, 1894/1898a) show that he used it widely (van der Hart and Horst 1989; van der Hart et al. 1989).

In Avraham's case, relevant information was collected without hypnosis about the traumatic loss of his father and his bizarre behavior after the terrorist incident. The nonhypnotic technique of writing a leave-taking letter (van der Hart 1983, 1988) was used to address the unresolved mourning and caused regression with an intensification of demonic hallucinations. Hypnosis was used, first to explore the nature of the patient's subjective experience of the demon, and subsequently as a means to help the patient defend himself against "the Black." We as therapists introduced traditional counterdemonic measures, such as magic incantations, investigations of the nature of "the Black" and its aides, and demands that it reveal its name and identity.

We then used the hypnotic technique of guided imagery to transform Avraham's metaphoric kernel statement of desolation into a more positive one (van der Hart 1986; Witztum et al. 1988). In this metaphoric imagery, the patient's arduous journey from the desert to the green spot ended in a joyful reunion with his father in the Lower Paradise. This event within the domain of metaphoric imagery, coupled with his visit in real life to the grave of the Tsaddik and the visit to his father's grave, constituted the resolution of his chronic, traumatic grief (Bilu et al. 1990).

Thus, both in hypnosis and in the waking state, we joined and utilized the patient's own language and metaphors, as illustrated in his use of blessings, prayers, and Biblical verses, in order to enter his experiential world and facilitate the healing of his trauma (Good and Good 1986). Instead of trying to convince Avraham of the irrational nature of his hallucinations, we used culture-sensitive therapeutic techniques based on the patient's explanatory model that consisted of traditional religious and mystical sources congruent with his belief system and cultural background.

CONCLUSION

In this chapter, we have stressed the importance of accurately diagnosing HP or possession syndrome. A recent traumatic event can trigger and combine with past traumata in forming the representational nature of the symptomatology. Hypnotic procedures help therapists enter the patient's world and join and utilize the patient's cultural explanatory model and idiosyncratic symbols to transform this inner world.

We suggest that when a delusional presentation or hallucination follows a traumatic event, the proposed model would prevent the precipitous diagnosis of psychosis and provide an effective treatment approach. This approach is based on our clinical experience and on anecdotal evidence from both historical and recent sources, but more systematic studies are needed.

REFERENCES

Adityanjee M, Raju G, Khandelwal S: Current status of Multiple Personality Disorder in India. Am J Psychiatry 146:1607–1610, 1989

Aikins H: Casting out a "stuttering devil," in An Outline of Abnormal Psychology. Edited by Murphy G. New York, Modern Library, 1929, pp 175–192

American Psychiatric Association: Diagnostic and Statistical Manual of Mental Disorders, 2nd Edition. Washington, DC, American Psychiatric Association, 1968

American Psychiatric Association: Diagnostic and Statistical Manual of Mental Disorders, 3rd Edition. Washington, DC, American Psychiatric Association, 1980

American Psychiatric Association: Diagnostic and Statistical Manual of Mental Disorders, 3rd Edition, Revised. Washington, DC, American Psychiatric Association, 1987

Bilu Y: The taming of deviants and beyond: an analysis of dybbuk possession and exorcism in Judaism. The Psychoanalytic Study of Society 11:1–32, 1985

Bilu Y, Abramovich H: In search of the Saddiq: visitational dreams among Moroccan Jews in Israel. Psychiatry 38:145–159, 1985

Bilu Y, Witztum E, van der Hart O: Paradise regained: miraculous healing in an Israeli psychiatric clinic. Cult Med Psychiatry 14:105–127, 1990

Bleuler E: Dementia Praecox or the Groups of Schizophrenias (1911). New York, International Universities Press, 1950

Bourguignon E: Psychological Anthropology. New York, Holt Rinehart & Wilson, 1979

Breuer J, Freud S: Studies on Hysteria (1893–1895), in The Standard Edition of Complete Psychological Works of Sigmund Freud, Vol 2. Translated and edited by Strachey J. London, Hogarth Press, 1955a, pp 1–18, 183–252

Breuer J, Freud S: On the psychical mechanism of hysterical phenomena: a preliminary communication (1893–1895), in The Standard Edition of the Complete Psychological Works of Sigmund Freud, Vol 3. Translated and edited by Strachey J. London, Hogarth Press, 1955b, pp 25–42

Breukink H: Over de behandeling van sommige psychosen door middel van een bijzondere vorm der kathartisch-hypnotische methode. New Tijdschr Geneeskd 67:1321–1328, 1923

Breukink H: Nadere mededeelingen over de hypnotische behandeling bij sommige geesteszieken. Ned Tijdschr Geneeskd 68:911–918, 1924

Breukink H: Nadere mededeelingen over de behandeling door hypnose bij zenuw-en geesteszieken. Ned Tijdschr Geneeskd 69:1877–1887, 1925

Brown D, Fromm E: Hypnotherapy and Hypnoanalysis. Hillsdale, NJ, Lawrence Erlbaum, 1986

Crapanzano V: Saints, jnun and dreams: an essay in Moroccan ethnopsychology. Psychiatry 38:145–159, 1975

Fernandez JW: The performance of ritual metaphors, in The Social Use of Metaphor: Essays on the Anthropology of Rhetoric. Edited by Sapir J. Crocker J. Philadelphia, PA, University of Pennsylvania Press, 1977, pp 100–131

Good B, Good M: The cultural context of diagnosis and therapy: a view from medical anthropology, in Mental Health Research and Practice in Minority Communities: Development of Culturally Sensitive Training Programs. Edited by Miranda M, Kitano H. Rockville MD, National Institute of Mental Health, 1986, pp 1–27

Hirsch S, Hollender M: Hysterical psychosis: clarification of a concept. Am J Psychiatry 125:81–87, 1969

Hoek A: Eenvoudige mededelingen aangaande de genezing van eene krankzinnige door het levens-magnetisme. Gravenhage, De Gebroeders van Cleef, 1868

Hollender M, Hirsch S: Hysterical psychosis. Am J Psychiatry 120:1066–1074, 1964

Hugenholz P: Kliniek der psychogene psychosen, in Antrhopologische psychiatrie. Deel II: Randpsychosen. Edited by van der Horst L. Amsterdam, Van Holkema and Warendorf, 1946, pp 415–478

Janet P: L'Automatisme psychologique. Paris, Félix Alcan, 1889

Janet P: Histoire d'une idée fixe. Revue Philosophique 37:121–168, 1894. Also in Janet P: Névroses et idées fixes, Vol 1. Paris, Félix Alcan, 1898a

Janet P: Un cas de possession et l'exorcisme moderne. Bulletin de l'Université de Lyon, Dec. 1894–Jan. 1895, pp 41–57. Also in Janet P: Névroses et idées fixes, Vol 1. Paris, Félix Alcan, 1898b

Janet P: Névroses et idées fixes, Vol 1. Paris, Félix Alcan, 1898c

Janet P: Les obsessions et la psychasthénie, Vols 1, 2. Paris, Félix Alcan, 1903

Janet P: Contribution à l'étude des accidents mentaux chez les hystériques. Thêse médicale. Paris, Rueff and Cie, 1893. Also in Janet P: L'État mental des hystériques, 2nd Edition. Paris, Félix Alcan, 1911a

Janet P: L'État mental des hystériques, 2nd Edition. Paris, Félix Alcan, 1911b

Kenny MG: Multiple personality and spirit possession. Psychiatry 44:337–358, 1981

Krippner S: Cross-cultural approaches to multiple personality disorder: practices in Brazilian spiritism. Ethos 15:273–295, 1987

Langness I: Hysterical psychoses and possessions, in Culture-Bound Syndromes, Ethnopsychiatry, and Alternate Therapies. Edited by Lebra W. Honolulu, HI, University Press of Hawaii, 1976, pp 56–67

Maleval J: Folies hystériques et psychoses dissociatives. Paris, Payot, 1981

Moreau de Tours J: Du hachisch et de l'aliénation mentale (1845). Paris, Librairie de Fortin, Masson et Cie. English edition: Hashish and Mental Illness. New York, Raven, 1973

Moreau do Tours J: De l'identité de l'état de rêve et de la folie. Annales Médico-Psychologiques (3e serie) I:361–408, 1855

Moreau de Tours J: De la folie hysterique et de quelques phénomènes nerveux propres à l'hystérie convulsive, à l'hystéro-épilepsie et à l'épilepsie. Paris, Masson, 1865

Moreau de Tours J: Traité pratique de la folie névropathique (vulgo hystérique). Paris, Germer Baillière, 1869

Pringuet G: A propos d'un cas de psychose hystérique. La Nouvelle Presse Médicale 6:441–443, 1977

Putnam F: Pierre Janet and modern views of dissociation. Journal of Traumatic Stress 2:413–429, 1989

Rosenbaum M: The role of the term schizophrenia in the decline of diagnosis of multiple personality. Arch Gen Psychiatry 37:1383–1385, 1980

Saxena S, Prasad K: DMS-III subclassification of dissociative disorders applied to psychiatric outpatients in India. Am J Psychiatry 146:261–262, 1989

Spiegel D: Multiple personality as a post-traumatic stress disorder. Psychiatr Clin North Am 7:101–110, 1984

Spiegel D, Fink R: Hysterical psychosis and hypnotizability. Am J Psychiatry 136:777–781, 1979

Steingard S, Frankel F: Dissociation and psychotic symptoms. Am J Psychiatry 142:953–955, 1985

Taylor E: William James on Exceptional Mental States. The 1896 Lowell Lectures. New York, Scribner's, 1982, pp 93–112

van der Hart O: Ritual in Psychotherapy. New York, Irvington, 1983

van der Hart O: Metaphoric and symbolic imagery in the hypnotic treatment of an urge to wander. Aust J Clin Exp Hypn 13:83–95, 1986

van der Hart O: Coping With Loss: The Therapeutic Use of Leave-Taking Rituals. New York, Irvington, 1988

van der Hart O, Horst R: The dissociation theory of Pierre Janet. Journal of Traumatic Stress 2:397–412, 1989

van der Hart O, van der Velden K: The hypnotherapy of Dr. Andries Hoek: uncovering hypnotherapy before Janet, Breuer, and Freud. Am J Clin Hypn 29:264–271, 1987

van der Hart O, Brown P, van der Kolk B: Pierre Janet's treatment of posttraumatic stress. Journal of Traumatic Stress 2:379–395, 1989 van der Kolk B, van der Hart O: Pierre Janet and the breakdown of adaptation in psychological trauma. Am J Psychiatry 146:1530–1539, 1989

Varma V, Bouri M, Wig N: Multiple Personality in India: comparison with hysterical possession state. Am J Psychother 35:113–120, 1981

Ward C: Spirit possession and mental health: a psycho-anthropological perspective. Human Relations 33:149–163, 1980

Witztum E, van der Hart O, Friedman B: The use of metaphor in psychotherapy. Journal of Contemporary Psychotherapy 18:270–290, 1988

Witztum E, Buchbinder J, van der Hart O: Summoning a punishing angel: treatment of a depressed patient with dissociative features. Bull Menninger Clin 54:524–537, 1990

Zusane L, Jones WH: Anomalistic Psychology: A Study of Magical Thinking. Hillsdale, NJ, Lawrence Erlbaum, 1989, pp 94–96

CHAPTER SIX

Culture and Personality Disorders

One aspect of modern societies related to personality development is the concept of adolescence. In all societies adolescence is the period between the onset of puberty and the attainment of adulthood. This period of development seems very much like a "natural" stage directly related to human biological development and, therefore, a universal stage of personality development in all societies. However, cultural factors play an important role in defining adolescence, particularly in the behavior expected of the adolescent and in the length of time spent in this period. In modern societies like the United States, the onset of puberty frequently occurs sooner than in premodern societies. In America, puberty commonly occurs around age 10–12, whereas in nonindustrialized societies it is more common for puberty to occur later, around age 13–15. Thus, in America, adolescence usually covers a period of six to eight years. However, in nonindustrialized societies the period is much shorter, usually lasting only several days, weeks, or months. Individuals in nonindustrialized societies enter adulthood shortly after the onset of puberty.

The transitory period between childhood and adulthood is a period of *liminality*. Liminality refers to the period "betwixt and between" two social categories and states of being (Turner, 1962). In nonindustrialized societies, once a child has reached sexual maturity that individual ceases to be socially recognized as a child. However, the child is not an adult until he or she is formally initiated into adulthood. That period in between is the nonindustrialized society's equivalance of adolescence.

In modern societies, this clear break with the child identity and the public creation of the adult self does not usually occur. Rather than a brief period of liminality between childhood and adulthood, ending with a definite creation of an adult self, modern societies have the long period of liminality we call adolescence. This period is in effect a culturally mandated extension of childhood, in that the individuals are still considered "boys" and "girls" and denied adult roles, even though they are sexually mature. This cultural practice keeps alive the child self and behav-

ior well past the onset of biological adulthood, and it keeps individuals psychologically and socially immature.

This cultural extension of childhood for several years into the period of biological maturity can create confusion in identity in that the person is biologically mature yet is socially defined as immature and is denied access to adult roles and behaviors. This has an impact on self-identity. The individual may be forming an adult self-identity but is given conflicting messages by society. Thus, adolescence is probably as much cultural as it is natural.

It has been suggested that the symptoms of borderline personality disorder are far more common in the adolescents and young adults of modern societies than in nonindustrialized ones (Paris, 1991, 1996). This is probably related to the long period of liminality between childhood and adulthood that is forced on individuals in modern societies. In the following article, medical anthropologist Larry G. Peters hypothesizes that the absence in modern societies of initiation ceremonies that mark the transition from childhood to adulthood, which help to solidify the new self-identity, has led to the disruptions in personality development that are associated with borderline personality disorder. Individuals in modern societies, especially in the highly egocentric United States, are left to more or less form their own adult self-identity several years after reaching biological maturity and with little help and support from the community.

REFERENCES

Paris, J. (1991). Personality disorders, parasuicide, and culture. *Transcultural Psychiatric Research Review, 28*, 189–197.

Paris, J. (1996). Cultural factors in the emergence of borderline pathology. *Psychiatry, 59*, 185–192.

Turner, V. W. (1962). Three symbols of passage in Ndembu circumcision ritual: An interpretation. In M. Gluckman (Ed.), *Essays on the ritual of social relations*. Manchester: Manchester University Press.

LARRY G. PETERS

Rites of Passage and the Borderline Syndrome
Perspectives in Transpersonal Anthropology

The purpose of this study is to compare and contrast certain prevalent contemporary pathological symptoms—parasuicide (especially impulsive "self-cutting" or wrist cutting and other forms of self mutilation), anorexia/bulimia, substance abuse, and a predisposition to frequent transient psychotic episodes, all of which, as a constellation, combination, or in some cases individually, are identified by clinicians as presumptive signs of "borderline personality disorder" (BPD)—with those same behaviors in tribal societies. The focus is anthropological and cross-cultural; it is a study of rites of passage, many of which involve food deprivations (fasting and purgations), body mutilations (circumcision, scarification), accompanied by episodes of altered or nonordinary states of consciousness (visions, loss of boundaries). It is argued that there is a relationship between BPD and the failure of Western culture to provide context and myth for meaningful rites of passage. The typical symptoms of borderline disorder have neither an appropriate cultural channel nor symbol system to provide direction and consequently are not fully appreciated by clinicians. However, these "symptoms" may actually be attempts at self-healing gone astray in a culture bereft of an integrative spiritual and ritualistic context, and therefore without an education for transcendent states of consciousness.

"How, but in custom and ceremony, are innocence and beauty born?"
(W. B. Yeats)

CULTURAL BOUND SYNDROMES (CBSs)

Every culture provides a model for the expression of psychopathology. Linton (1956) speaks of "patterns of misconduct," Devereux (1956) of the "ethnic psychoses," Yap (1969) of "cultural bound reactive syndromes." Over 150 have been iden-

tified in the ethnographic literature (Hughes 1985). Tseng and McDermott (1981) define a "culture-related specific psychiatric disorder" as having three aspects: (1) a specific set of symptoms not seen in other mental illnesses; (2) commonly observed in some cultural areas but not in others; and (3) manifested in a manner closely related to culture. CBS as a concept is descriptive and not explanatory (Prince 1985). Thus, in this paper I will not focus on theories regarding the etiology of mental disorders, whether these be biomedical, infantile trauma, or by level of personality development. Rather, my focus is on observable behaviors within socio-cultural context. Classic examples of CBSs include koro (impotence panic) in China and Malaysia (Yap 1965), *latah* (startle reaction) in Indonesia (Kenny 1985; Simons 1985), *susto* (fright, soul loss) in Central America and Mexico (Rubel et al. 1985), *wiitiko* (cannibalistic frenzy) among Native Americans in Central and Northeast Canada (Parker 1960), and "possession-trance" found in numerous cultural areas. The type of possession identified as a CBS is anthropologically referred to as "negative possession-trance" which is an involuntary, dissociative, uncontrolled, spontaneous experience and is contrasted with voluntary, controlled, ceremonial, shamanic, non-disordered "positive possession-trance" (Bourguignon 1968; 1976; Lewis 1989; Oesterreich 1966; Peters and Price-Williams 1980).

The West also has cultural bound syndromes, as Littlewood and Lipsedge (1986; 1987) attest. CBSs represent tensions basic to a society, whether traditional or modern. Many of the non-Western CBSs have been equated to Western pathological syndromes. For example, negative possession-trance has often been thought of as a cultural variant to multiple personality disorder (MPD), the latter being a Western CBS (Kenny 1992) shaped by Western cultural and psychiatric beliefs (Hacking 1992) but psychologically similar to negative possession because both involve alterations of identity, parallel types of dissociative amnesia, and splitting of consciousness (Ellenberger 1970; Kenny 1986; Spanos 1986). While there is a certain plausibility to this argument, there are also differences between the two categories. Possession, a less precise traditional category which may include any number of heterogeneous Western psychiatric conditions (Bourguignon 1992), is nevertheless considered by most ethnological researchers to be a less severe neurotic disorder, a "pseudopsychotic hysterical reaction" (Yap 1960) or "hysterical psychosis" (Langness 1976), the symptoms of which are amenable to short-term therapy (Kennedy 1967; Kiev 1964; Peters 1978; Wallace 1966). MPD, on the other hand, is a severely damaging chronic dissociative disorder in which each personality is complexly integrated with enduring patterns of behavior in a wide range of personal and social contexts, giving it a distinct clinical picture from possession which is much less global and pervasive to the personality (Cardeña 1992; DSM III; DSM III-R).

The hysterical psychosis is marked by the inability to deal effectively with psychosocial stress. Symptoms include brief psychotic episodes with hallucinations, delusions, depersonalization, derealization, and grossly unusual behavior. These symptoms may last a few hours to a few weeks (at most) and recede as dramatically as they appeared, leaving no residual psychotic deficiency. It is not a schizophrenia. The episodes may include suicidal gestures. Second or third episodes are likely to occur. There may be amnesia but not necessarily. The hysterical psychosis is the end point of severity on a continuum of hysterical disorders. Psychoanalytically speaking, the transient episodes are interpreted as an overwhelming of the ego by the id, a temporary ego annihilation (Hirsch and Hollender 1969; Hollender and Hirsch 1964; Langness 1967). The likelihood of experiencing periodic but reversible psychotic episodes are also a primary feature of BPD (Easser and Lesser 1965; Millon 1981) and are sometimes referred to as "borderline states" (Knight 1953). As will soon be discussed, this and many other of the disordered hysterical psychosis characteristics overlap with the DSM III-R criteria for BPD, albeit BPD is a chronic disorder and not treatable in short term therapy as is the hysterical psychosis.

In the Western CBSs, as well as non-Western CBSs, there is projection of accountability for acting-out behavior onto agencies that are beyond the patient's control (mystical symbols in traditional societies, psychiatric and bio-medical in contemporary cultures). This explains why CBSs are seen in the West as "disorders" (Littlewood and Lipsedge 1986; 1987). However, in non-Western contexts, there have been many investigations that indicate that the hysterical psychosis may actually be beneficial to adaptation, and therapeutic. Among the Bena Bena of New Guinea, for example, "wildman behavior," an episode of antisocial violent behavior which is explained as being due to a spirit possession, is quickly forgotten and leaves no social stigma (Langness 1967;

1976; Salisbury 1968). A brief episode or two occurs in adults who have delayed assuming full, mature, culturally-defined responsibilities. This apparently psychotic behavior, however, leads to psychosocial reintegration and is accepted indigenously to be a prelude to the necessary transition to adult life (Langness 1965:267). In another New Guinea group, observed by Newman (1964), such wild-man behavior leads to a permanent loss of status, chronic reoccurring episodes, and the person is not allowed and/or expected to fulfill normal adult obligations. It is not valued as transitional behavior. This ethnographic distinction is important because it demonstrates how differently the same behavior is responded to in two similarly "primitive" cultures, and the psychosocial consequences for the individual because of cultural beliefs and values.

Nonetheless, in almost all of the examples of the non-Western CBSs, the behavior is a culturally prescriptive means to communicate distress. In Haiti, for example, negative possession-trance is considered a disorder by Western researchers. However, Haitian "negative" possession is the precondition for admission into the possession cult. Initiation into the cult is concomitant with ceremonial control of the possession state. Negative possession-trance is thereby transformed into positive or ceremonial possession-trance. This process is described by Bourguignon (1965:55) as a "dissociation in the service of the self" that "enhances the field of action for the self." In other words, the appearance of "symptoms" begins a process of initiation leading to psychosocial transformation. Thus, ". . . negatively valued trances," Leavitt (1993:54) writes, "are just as religious, just as culturally defined, as positively valued ones . . ." He contends that it seems arbitrary to separate out the negatively valued aspect of a total process, in which both positive and negatively valued trances are the different parts of one experience, and label only one part non-pathological. It was from a similarly erroneous perspective that the initial "calling" experiences of shamans often reported as due to a negative (unsolicited) possession became inaccurately labeled by Western psychiatrists as schizophrenia (Silverman 1967).

Thus it is enthocentric bias to interpret many of the non-Western CBSs according to our categories of illness outside of their socio-cultural context. In the West, however, behavior such as seen in the hysterical psychosis is not initiatory and instead leads to labeling, social stigma, and intrapsychic guilt and shame. Symptoms of the hysterical psychosis as documented in Western contexts include chronic "impulsive" acting-out such as self-cutting episodes in which patients are dissociated from feeling any physical pain (Pao 1969; Siomopoulos 1971; 1983:100ff). Similar chronic impulsive behavior is considered a "presumptive sign" of

BPD (Grunebaum and Klerman 1967; Kernberg 1975; 1977; Tupin 1984).

The discussion of CBSs began by defining them as belonging to specific cultures. They are more prevalent in tribal and third-world cultures in their non-chronic form. They are distinct from Multiple Personality Disorder. It was also suggested that it might be unwarranted to equate many of the non-Western CBSs with our mental disorders in that they initiate cultural processes that further adaptation, and may be a means of resolving conflict, acquiring social support, and are part of a religious initiatory system (Boddy 1992). Although the non-Western CBSs are considered to be illnesses by Western observers, the supposed illness becomes a means of reducing social inequalities (Peters 1978), becoming a member of a new social organization (e.g. a culturally sanctioned possession cult) (Kennedy 1967), is a means of transitioning to new social responsibilities, is a "calling" to a new vocation as in shamanism (Lewis 1989) and consequently, as discussed above, "an enhancement to the self." More than this, these so-called and misidentified "illnesses" carry relatively little social stigma. Thus it is important to keep in mind that the psychiatric terms utilized in much of the cross-cultural research belie a cultural prejudice for equating our categories of mental disorder with the relatively non-stigmatizing "idioms of distress" of other cultures (Nichter 1981; Obeyesekeye 1969).

Consider the *ataques de nervios* among Puerto Ricans and other Latin Americans, also known as the "Puerto Rican Syndrome" by Western psychiatric researchers. First of all, the attack of nerves is not natively considered to be a mental illness and thereby avoids the consequent stigma. It is believed to have "material" (medical) or "spiritual" causes. Symptoms include a transient altered state of consciousness, and possibly convulsive movements, hyperventilation, moaning and groaning, profuse salivation, aggression toward self and others, impulsive suicidal acts, hallucinations and delusions, derealizations and depersonalizations, i.e. psychotic manifestations according to Western prejudice. There is a sudden onset and termination lasting a few minutes to a few days (Fernandez-Marina 1961; Rubio et al. 1955; Trautman 1961); in other words, a transient psychosis. When medical problems are not found, the attack is natively attributed to a spirit, possibly through malevolent witchcraft. 76% of the cases reporting to an *espiritista* in New York City for treatment were diagnosed as being spiritually caused and, in a majority of cases, especially among adolescents and young adults, the episodes were interpreted as spiritual evidence (i.e., a "calling") to develop one's transic faculties for mediumship (Garrison 1977). Thus, in most cases, the attack is initiatory and, while seen as critical by the culture, is a prelude to initiation into a new social organization and the development of a socially honored profession. Still, even in the cases that were not seen as evidence to begin training for mediumship, they are

indigenously understood as socially acceptable means of alleviating stress, pent-up anger, and frustration (Rothenberg 1964). It is cathartic and therefore psychotherapeutic according to Garrison (1977), a "regression in the service of the ego" according to Fernandez-Marina (1961), and a culturally honored means for asking and getting care and support from others who are demanded by the norms of good behavior to rally to the aid of the victim (Garrison 1977). Thus, as Leavitt (1993) suggests, what may be involved in such non-Western cases, is the misappropriation of psychiatric nosology.

THE WESTERN BORDERLINE SYNDROME

According to Vaillant and Perry (1980), personality disorders fall on a continuum between neurosis and psychosis. They are distinct from neurotic disorders in that they are ego syntonic. They are pervasive and much more like maladaptive life patterns than the isolated symptoms of a neurosis. Personality disorders affect the individual's long term functioning by creating social impairment and distress. One of the crucial concerns of transcultural psychiatry is to illuminate the role of cultural factors in the etiology, expression, course, outcome, and epidemiology of mental disorders (Marsella 1984). Cultural bound disorders are culture bound because culture both shapes their manifestations or symptoms and influences their course, outcome, and severity. For example, there are numerous significant studies that indicate that extreme and chronic forms of mental illness, including schizophrenia, depression, as well as MPD, are much more prevalent and/or chronic in the West than in third world or tribal communities (Coons et al., 1991; Fabrega 1989; Kennedy 1973; Marsella 1980; Murphy 1968; Prince 1968; Ross 1991; Sartorius 1973; Sartorius et al., 1978; Torry 1980). Similarly, it is my hypothesis that BPD is an insidious CBS found specifically in the West or in cultures undergoing Westernization (see Peters 1988; Tseng and McDermott 1981).

On an individual symptom and syndrome level, there are many similarities between hysterical psychosis and BPD including impulsivity, physically self-damaging acts (such as suicidal gestures and physical fights), lack of control of anger, identity disturbances, lack of goals and values, affective instability, and brief psychotic episodes without residual damage (see DSM III-R). However, borderline disorders are a chronic personality disorder (a "stable instability" [Schmideberg 1947]) unlike the acute short-term non-Western CBSs.

For many years, borderline has been a "magic word" for Western psychiatrists (Havens 1972) and BPD is highly prevalent in our society making up about 2% of the population (Swarz et al., 1990). Millon (1987), the social learning theorist, proposes that BPD is a response to cultural changes in the West, including the breakdown of social cohesion, norms, values, and families. Paris (1991), a transcultural psychiatrist, believes BPD may be a universal reaction to social disintegration and it has indeed been reported in non-Western developed and developing cultures like Kuwait (Suleiman et al., 1989), Chile (Cardenas 1985), Korea (Lee and Lee 1982), and Egypt (Okasha and Lotaif 1979). However, this severe and chronic disorder is much less prevalent in non-Western contexts (Paris 1991).

BPD is a mixture of psychotic, neurotic and characteralogical disturbances combined with healthy personality aspects. There is a weak ego that creates an unstable clinical picture in that patients under stressful conditions may experience a "temporary psychosis" (Grinker 1977; Grinker et al., 1968). Gunderson and Kolb (1978) and Gunderson and Singer (1975) identify as criteria for BPD: lowered achievement or work capacity; impulsivity, especially in areas of drug abuse; manipulative suicidal gestures like wrist slashing (see Graff and Mallin 1967); brief psychotic episodes; rapid shifting identifications; disturbances in interpersonal relations. Carpenter et al. (1977) emphasizes the borderline's intense affects, frequent dissociated states, and lack of stable interpersonal relationships.

However, BPD is not "borderline schizophrenia," although patients may describe psychotic experiences that appear like "acute schizophrenia" (see DSM III-R). The overall symptom pattern more resembles anxious and irritable depression. It is an affective, rather than "thinking disorder" (Spitzer and Endicott 1979). Borderline patients, unlike schizophrenics, do not deteriorate over time; there is no residual damage of cognitive disorganization. After episodes, the individual rapidly returns to usual levels of functioning but remains vulnerable, easily agitated, and prone to rapid mood swings and recurrent psychotic episodes (see Carpenter et al., 1977; Grinker 1977; Gunderson and Kolb 1978).

BPD is considered a self disorder (Kohut 1971; Rinsley 1982) characterized by a developmental failure to achieve a coherent self structure or identity, i.e., an "identity diffusion" (Kernberg 1975). Grinker (1977) separates those individuals closer to the "psychotic border" from those with a better prognosis and a less brittle ego who are closer to the "neurotic border." Yet the susceptibility to be overwhelmed by unconscious material (i.e. borderline states) and the absence of a consistent self-identity are clinical factors in both borderline groups, while a greater capacity for positive affect with less withdrawing and distancing defenses, i.e. an "anaclitic depression," predominates at the neurotic border (Grinker et al., 1968).

Psychoanalysts call attention to the role of "splitting" in BPD, in which contradicting "ego states," i.e. constellations of perceptions, thoughts, and feelings, vacillate between extremes of good and bad, and idealization and devaluation (Kernberg

1967:667–670). That is, BPD patients are split and their attitudes may shift between remorse about acting out, at other times rationalizing the same behavior, making it ego syntonic (Kernberg 1967:648). Searles (1977) speaks of "multiple identities" supported by splitting defenses. Fairbairn (1952) states that splitting is a manifestation of "separate dissociated subpersonalities." The characteristics of splitting in BPD include conflicting feelings and identities, and acting-out episodes where the individual is dominated by uncontrollable impulses. The latter may involve dangerous self-destructive behavior and may reach psychotic proportions. Given the overwhelming nature of the borderline's autonomous split-off complexes or "internal objects," it is not surprising that psychoanalytic investigators draw a parallel between BPD and "possession" states (Grotstein 1979; 1981; Taylor 1978).

In an earlier paper (Peters 1988), I proposed that the "possession" state identified by these Western analysts is a more severe, chronic, and pervasive variety of the "possession syndrome" than is prevalent in most third world and indigenous cultures. Yap (1960) reached a similar conclusion regarding chronicity, and epidemiology of the severe-pervasive type in his comparison of the possession syndrome in Chinese and French contexts.

Of interest are the variations and reversals in male vs. female epidemiology for BPD cross-culturally which may parallel distinct social tensions (Paris 1991). In the West, for example, there is a prevalence of women over men diagnosed as BPD (DSM III-R), a ratio as large as 3:1 in one study (Stone 1980). This may be due in part to cultural bound factors such as the stress for women to be thin, leading to high rates in women with anorexia/bulimia (Newman and Halvorson 1982), considered by numerous clinicians to be a borderline-associated condition (Grotstein 1981; Masterson 1977; Stone 1980; 1983). Another factor may be the overwhelming ratio of male over female suicide completion: 70% vs. 30% (Schneidman and Faberow 1983), as compared to suicide attempts ("parasuicide") (Wekstein 1979). Further, as some scholars of Western psychiatric history for the last few hundred years have pointed out, women make up the preponderance of mental patients, including diagnosis of such disorders as demonical possession, hysteria, schizophrenia (Chesler 1972). They especially call our attention to "dependency" personality disorders, like BPD and the hysterical personality disorder, and the recent craze over "codependency," all of which, in many ways, are a reflection of Western feminine social reality (Nuckolls 1992; Ussher 1991). As Chesler (1972) indicates, madness in our culture functions as a mirror image of the feminine social experience and the penalty for being feminine.

Unlike the non-Western CBSs discussed above, the borderline syndrome, although primarily affecting young individuals who are having difficulty making the transition to adult responsibilities, goals, identity, values, and career choices (see DSM

III-R), does not initiate a cultural rite of passage and is instead a severe form of mental illness with chronic reoccurring psychotic episodes and impulsiveness lasting for years, even decades, until they eventually "burn out" with age (Paris 1988). The borderline state, unlike the *ataques de nervios* or negative-possession states in tribal cultures, is not a culturally legitimate means of coping with overwhelming stress nor is it a "calling" to initiation. Rather it is a socially isolating mental illness.

RITES OF PASSAGE AND SPIRITUAL EMERGENCIES

In small scale societies, labeling someone ill is a precondition for effective social action (Edgerton 1980). The penalties which one might accrue are not significant in the light of the care and support offered (Westermeyer and Winthrob 1979). The New Guinea example and the Puerto Rican Syndrome cited above can best be understood as "transitional" experiences. In New Guinea, the hysterical psychosis (wild-man behavior) was occasioned by a failure to assume normal adult roles and, in the Bena Bena example, as a means for making that transition. The *ataques de nervios* was typically treated as a "calling" to develop spiritist-mediumistic faculties. This is a transition to a spiritual vocation and is similar to becoming a shaman (Hastings 1991; Kalweit 1988; Lewis 1989; Peters and Price-Williams 1980; 1983). They form an initiatory scenario.

There is, of course, a distinction between transitional experiences and a pathological syndrome. But, in the West, labeling and consequent stigma have been implicated in the chronicity of mental disorders (Foucalt 1965; Scheff 1966; Szasz 1961; Waxler 1974; 1979). Cross-culturally, there are distinct ways in which unusual states of consciousness are labeled and treated. As mentioned above, many of the non-Western CBSs are not indigenously considered to be "mental disorders." In Western societies, practically any radical alteration in consciousness is considered a sign of "craziness" and "so usually induce great fear in people when they begin to experience them" (Tart 1971:119). In non-Western cultures, CBSs are generally recognized as spiritual crises, analogous to "spiritual emergencies," a concept of significance to transpersonal anthropology and psychology, as well as to the current-day psychiatric nosology, treatment, and conceptualization of spiritual experiences (see Grof and Grof 1989; 1990; Lukoff 1985).

Cultural rites of passage occur during crisis situations in the life cycle of an individual. They are periods of transition in cultural expectations, in social roles and status, in interpersonal relations, in psychological state and way of being-in-the-world (Chapple and Coon 1942; Turner 1967; van Gennep 1960; Wil-

son 1967; Young 1965). The typical rites of passage relevant to this study are male and female tribal or puberty rites and initiations into sacred vocations (e.g. shamanism). Rites of passage have three phases: separation, transition (liminal), and worldly return. Separation is from one's familiar surroundings, life style and identity. Australian aborigine children are taken to sacred huts or clearings away from their homes by initiation masters masked and clad like the eternal ancestors of the dream time, to make contact with the sacred (Eliade 1958). Native American youths traditionally make contact with the sacred through fasting and "vision quests" in the wilderness (Foster and Little 1987). Shamans seclude themselves during their "calling" (Rasmussen 1929) or are chosen due to near fatal illnesses (Myerhoff 1974), or near-death experiences (Ring 1988), in some cultures running off naked into the forest for days (Peters 1981), in others immersing themselves in icy water for long periods (Blacker 1986), or cutting themselves with knives (Crapanzano 1977), or quite commonly having visions of body dismemberment ("skeletonization") (see Eliade 1964), all of which result in spiritual awakening (Harner 1990; Kalweit 1988; Peters 1989; 1990). On the other hand, Western psychiatrists note that dreams of body fragmentation, dismemberment, and mutilation occur frequently to individuals with BPD and are often indicative of the borderline disorder (Stone 1979).

The second phase, transition or liminality, is "betwixt" and "between" social categories and states of being. The novices are "travelers in a transitional area" (Turner 1962). The individual, now separated, is no longer what she/he was before, but not yet what will be once passage is achieved. The process is comparable to gestation; the old dies and gives way to the new (death and rebirth). Herein the candidate acquires sacred knowledge; the new life is explained through the means of sacred myth and object (*sacra*) or received through a vision. The neophytes are typically referred to as "dead: or "being in the womb," symbolic of "dying" and "resurrection," the completed passage (Campbell 1968). In puberty rites, a sacred operation is performed by the initiation masters, typically a form of body mutilation like circumcision, scarification, symbolizing the transition to a new form and way of being.

Once the new state of being is imprinted, the novice is reintegrated into the community, expected to fulfill the new role of adult or shaman, etc. There is a resumption of ordinary reality, but now others are treated in a new way and new types of interactive patterns emerge, as when the aborigine mother performs a bereavement ritual for her child when he returns to the ordinary world as a man (see Eliade 1958). The person has been reborn, transformed as the chrysalis becomes the butterfly, the child the adult, the adult a shaman. The cognitive function of rites of passage is the "transformation of the model of reality" (McManus 1979).

The period of transition is paradoxical; within it the symbols of life and death both dominate. Eliade (1958:21ff, 72) considers the existential state of consciousness created during initiations to be one of "dread," "awe," and of a "belief in impending death." Everything is done to cause a "disintegration of the personality." In other words, there is a nonordinary state of consciousness created, typically through fasting, ingestion of psychoactive drugs, and physical deprivations and mutilations, all to aid the process of passage: disintegration, transformation, and psychosocial reintegration.

The Latin term *transitio* means "the act of going across," the passage from one state to another. *Initio* is to go back to the beginning, to reconnect with the origin of life, the eternal and sacred, i.e. to transition by "regressing" to initial conditions (Eliade 1954). Such are the goals of rites of passage and, in my opinion, the symptomatic acts of the borderline patient. Because transition involves a death and rebirth, the initiate's food and blood, necessities for life and the integrity of the body, are challenged. These procedures bring the individual, contemporary and tribal, to the "threshold" of transformation.

As documented earlier, fasting, body mutilation, and/or the use of psychoactive drugs are often parts of rites of passage. Yet these same behaviors, albeit from a distinct psychiatric and pathological perspective, are all highly implicated in BPD. As regards anorexia, it is now generally accepted to be a Western CBS and has not been reported in small scale societies (DiNicola 1990; Prince 1979, 1983) while fasting, as stated above, is a typical part of a rite of passage in tribal societies. Likewise, the borderline traits of addiction and substance abuse are uncommon in small scale tribal societies (Fabrega 1984). In these societies, the use of intoxicating substances are part of the sacred ritual context and quite commonly part of rites of passage into adulthood (Grob and Dobkin de Rios 1992). In such context intoxicants seldom produce disruptive behavior (Marshall 1979). Such is also the case with body mutilations in "primitive" cultures (see Favazza 1987).

It is my contention that the parasuicidality and other life-threatening borderline symptoms are "ritualistic" attempts to provoke an encounter with death. As the Jungian analyst, James Hillman (1965), believes, the underlying meaning of suicidal behavior is that the psyche needs the "death experience" in order to undergo radical change. These self-destructive symptoms are thus actually attempts at self-transformation or "rites of passage," as Reeves and Tugend (1987) say, that have "gone wrong." Similarly, Bateson (1961) has argued that the psychotic episodes, which he sees as an attack upon the self, have the function of "endogenous rites of passage," but without exogenous social support and validating belief system and are therefore failures at healing. In other words, these regressions to the potentially transformational "prima materia" (to use Jung's [1969]

term) become stigmatizing and culturally isolating. And, seeing that the person is in crisis, this influences the course of the experience and predisposes the person to a chronic mental illness.

Rites of passage in traditional societies are culturally sanctioned "spiritual emergencies" (Grof and Grof 1989; 1990). Spiritual emergencies can be triggered by physical factors (disease, accident, lack of sleep or food, the birth experience in women). They may be started by psychosocial stress or loss such as a death or divorce. They can be the result of "hitting bottom" due to alcohol or drug addiction. In essence, these are all "peak" and "nadir" type transpersonal and transformational experiences (Grof and Grof 1989; 1990; Maslow 1962). Spiritual emergencies follow a trajectory of death and rebirth, the paradigmatic scenario of a "rite of passage." As Grof and Grof (1990) write, "Ego death," that is, being reduced to nothing but one's "essential core," is the precondition for a "spiritual emergence." The nearness to death experience is a prerequisite part of the transformational experience, and is recognized in nearly all the great mystical traditions of humankind including alchemy, shamanism, and the mystery religions (Metzner 1986). The transitional and sacred symbols of the ritual process help negotiate the major psychological transformations—and deaths and rebirths—life demands. If handled with understanding, these become unique moments of growth and restructuring of consciousness (also see Grof 1985; Grof and Grof 1980).

CLINICAL IMPLICATIONS

Borderline patients, as has been discussed, have a propensity to anorexia, addictions, and suicidality; i.e., to a cycle of self-destructive behaviors. Further, these are "framed" as psychiatric disorders and therefore stripped of spiritual purpose. It is highly prevalent in contemporary society. However, in traditional cultures where "hysterical psychosis" or borderline states are treated in the context of the sacred, they are typically acute and transitory. It may well be that social stigma and rejection consequent upon labeling is one of the causal factors, as is our lack of viewing these experiences from the context of the sacred. In others words, CBSs are successfully treated in traditional communities whereas the Western individual is more dependent on his or her own resources in order to successfully complete a spontaneous endogenous rite of passage. Thus the lack of sacred community rites of passage that aid individuals in critical and transitional life phases is an important implicating factor in BPD.

During rites of passage, according to Turner (1969), "*communitas*," an existential state of oneness with others and the sacred, is established in the novice. *Communitas* is "antistructure," an ecstatic feeling of unity beyond all categories and hierarchies. Occurring during the transitional or threshold period, it is a relatively undifferentiated "living together." It is the precondition of community and social structure. From it, the differentiations of status and role which is society emerges. Anti-structure or *communitas* is the existential base of society that transcends all psychosocial boundaries. *Communitas* is the feeling of our "common humanity" stripped of all differentiating qualities. The social function of ritual, according to Durkheim (1957) is to create such social solidarity, i.e. to bring people together in an "effervescent" state of consciousness to celebrate and commemorate their unity. This communal social experience is, in many ways, analogous to Wilber's (1979:134) description of "no-boundary" transpersonal and therapeutic experiences in which we learn through ego transcendence to care for others, not because they respect, love, secure, support, or reflect us, but because they *are us.*"

These transpersonal experiences of community and oneness are, in my opinion, what borderline patients are attempting to achieve through drug use and abuse, mutilations, and other self-destructive behavior but which, however, become isolating and labeled. Like rites of passage and spiritual emergencies, borderline states may be ego annihilating crises in which acts and symbols of life and death are evoked. But they, unlike traditional rites of passage, are bereft of cultural value, spiritual context, and an education for transcendence, which hinders their transpersonal potentiality.

In the Western contemporary world, we separate psychology from religion. Emotional problems have to do with personal trauma in the family or in childhood, and not with the cultural loss of spirituality or our sense of interconnectedness to each other and to the whole. We don't diagnose the absence of personal and/or cultural spiritual sensibility or deep meaningful myth and rite. Through ritual, we access the spirit and move closer to what our souls aspire (Some 1993). Yet, when culture does not fulfill a human "need for myth, ritual and a spiritual life," a person is deprived, suffers and, according to Moore (1992:203), becomes symptomatic. The symptoms of BPD are, in themselves, impulsively ritualistic and, while not culturally sanctioned, replete with cultural meaning. As Moore (1992: 205) writes, persons who are starving themselves anorexically evoke in their ascetic ". . . food rituals, vestigial forms of religious practice . . . [and] as [our] society's symptom, anorexia could be trying to teach us that we need a more genuine spiritual life . . ." (parentheses mine). Thus we are starving ourselves spiritually rather than fasting in a sacred way for a vision or a transcendent experience.

Paris (1991) has suggested that borderline disorders are rapidly increasing in Western societies. As indication of this, he asserts that suicide attempts (parasuicide) have more than doubled in the United States, Australia, and Great Britain in the last ten years. High suicide rates among youths are found in cultures undergoing rapid change, loss of traditional and spiritual mores and values, and other situations of cultural disruption (see Jilek-Aall 1988). Although suicide attempts are not exclusively part of BPD, appearing in other diagnostic categories, especially depression, they are also quite prevalent during the depressive swing in BPD and are worthy of mention in this regard.

May (1991) believes that suicide and major personality disorders like BPD stem from a lack of meaningful sacred myths. In our age of "ruthlessness," "narcissism," "individuation," and "scientific rationalism," he contends, the divine is absent to many. Without myth, we are without soul. Myths and the rituals they explain guide the formation of cultural identity. As Geertz (1973) writes, they are models "of" and "for" identity and reality. Models *of* in that they provide a blueprint of what culture maps as real and valuable; a model *for* in that they form charters with which individuals identify and are thereby guides for behavior, identity, and reality.

According to Eliade (1954), reality and identity are established for "primitive" peoples through "participation" and "repetitions" of the mythological paradigms. In other words, an action, event or person acquires meaning only to the extent that there is an identification with what was revealed in the sacred mythos. Through myth and rite, we learn of our identity and bring value to the world. The lack of sacred myth and rites in our culture has led to an erosion of meaning for both sexes (Bly 1987; Woodman 1987). In the extreme, this "identity diffusion," i.e. the lack of the goals and values that form personality and community solidarity, is a principal feature in BPD (Kernberg 1975).

In a seminal article on the !Kung Zhu/twasi of South Africa, Katz (1973) writes about their "education for transcendence." The transcendent state of consciousness described as *!kia* involves a "death" to normal identity and leads to the activation of a powerful and mysterious energy (*n/um*) that is used by half of the adult males and one-third of adult females for religious and healing functions in rituals in which the entire band, including children, participate and learn about transcendental experiences. Katz (1973) believes that, analogous to the !Kung youths, Western young people are looking for the experience of transcendence and transformation, but many are instead left in a state of "identity diffusion." According to Katz (1973), "education for transcendence" is a principal factor that distinguishes !Kung trancers from their contemporary counterparts who have little sense of place in the universe. That is, there is no identity forming spiritual base or mythological system to support the psychological death experience necessary for transformation and spiritual rebirth, nor rituals that create *communitas*. Unlike the !Kung, we do not have meaningful myths and rites of passage to aid in the formation, transformation, and, on a higher transpersonal level, the reformation of identity.

From the perspective of cultural psychology, rituals heal because their purpose is to create social support and thereby decrease alienation, encouraging hope and faith which, in turn, reduces depression and anxiety (Frank 1979). Achterberg (1992:158, 162) suggests that rituals are "the foundation for transpersonal medicine" in that they increase well being because, "through ritual one can gain access to the transpersonal forces of community and spirit . . . a sense of knowing that we are intimately connected to all that is." Charlene Spretnak (1991:22) asks, how can we expect to achieve a fundamental deepening of our modes of being without ". . . cultural practices that encourage us to grow in awareness, to come to realize we live in a participatory universe."

Borderline "psychotic" episodes are attempts to achieve identity, transition, and rebirth through ego death. The borderline is fixated in transition—betwixt and between, repetitively reinvoking symptomatic concrete "ritualistic" acts of self-destruction unacceptable in contemporary culture, yet at the same time symbolic of the necessity to psychologically die to the old before worldly return and reintegration to complete the cycle of transformation. All too often, therapists fail to appreciate the initiatory nature of many borderline addictive and impulsive behaviors as ecstatic and agonizing attempts to achieve healing and transformation through a "dark night of the soul," which may become, in a milieu of sacred myth and rite, a healing experience (Bragdon 1988; S. Grof 1987; Grof and Grof 1989; 1990; Small 1991).

BPD and borderline self-destructive "acting-out" behavior has been investigated extensively by psychoanalysts and described as being akin to "trance" and "dream states" and, while seen by many as pathological (Greenson 1966; Grinberg 1968; Stein 1969), there are other psychoanalytical clinicians who interpret acting out episodes as providing "relief of tension" (Rexford 1978:323), as "experimental recollection," and a "necessary detour" that is potentially therapeutic (Ekstein and Friedman 1957; Kan 1964). Limentani (1966) believes that acting-out is a cry for help and an indication of hope which therefore should not be censured in therapy unless the patient's vital needs must be safeguarded. Acting-out is therefore not necessarily a disturbance, but may be a means of gaining insight and integration (Kanzer 1957). Angel (1965:79) maintains that the borderline patient's acting-out is an attempt to separate and achieve identity. Blos (1978:166–167) posits that acting-out during the "second separation-individuation process" in adolescence is adaptive, "in the service of progressive development," and that the individual could not go forward without first regressing temporarily. Thus acting-out is potentially "transitional phenomenon," a necessary temporary regression which aids passage from one developmental level to another. As Limentani (1966:280) says, it should be expected in therapy with the borderline patient

and is part of the process of "working through" feelings of envy and hatred. Milner (1952) maintains that such temporary regressive experiences of "merging," "fusion," and "loss of boundaries" are necessary for psychological change and should be fostered in therapy (see Kris 1952). In these studies, there is an underlying recognition of transitional processes; that destructuring precedes restructuring, and that the destructuring symptoms are part and parcel of the total healing experience, as fever is the body's curative reaction to infection.

The psychological value of such critical processes has of course been recognized in humanistic and transpersonal literature for many years (Jung 1969; Laing 1967; Maslow 1962). Still, in our culture, the patient is thrown upon his/her own resources again because of our lack of sanctioned sacred rites of passage (Bernstein 1987). As Achterberg (1985) suggests, the symbols and rituals that hold power culturally appear to be necessary with many patients to open the healing mechanisms. Myth and ritual are pathways to the transformative and the transpersonal. The term "ritual" stems from the Indo-European root which means "to fit together" for the purpose of creating order (Combs and Holland 1990). The ritual process represents a movement from "chaos to cosmos" (Eliade 1954; Turner 1969). In tribal cultures, there is ritual support for change and life transitions, i.e. to help fit things together anew, ordered and balanced socially and psychospiritually. As Arrien (1993:6) affirms, our loss of myth and rite contribute to mental illness by making it necessary for individuals to accomplish their transitions alone and with private symbols (see also Kimball 1960).

In a previous article, I reported a clinical example of a case I anthropologically followed of a borderline patient whose acting-out episodes of self-cutting and deep depression oscillated with periods of high functioning as a licensed psychotherapist (Peters 1988). This patient's mental condition was rejected by her psychiatrists and by society. She was advised not to continue her work as a therapist. Indeed, it seems appropriate to us that a disturbed individual should not be employed in treating other disturbed individuals. Yet it was only after nearly a decade of parasuicidal behaviors and intermittent hospitalizations that the patient decided to leave her native state and resume her profession in another (against psychiatric advice). Today, she is a therapist of adolescents and youths, married and a functioning mother without episodes for nearly four years. One is reminded of the archetypal theme of the "wounded healer" who returns from near-death, after skeletonization and dismemberment, transformed with new purpose, value and way of being (Halifax 1982). The patient described her transformation retrospectively as having been catalyzed by the realization that, contrary to what her doctors said, she felt she was better qualified to be a therapist because of her own inner journey. Her encounter with madness had made her able to understand others who had embarked upon a similar course; that is to say to find empathetic *communitas* with them. Thus she came to believe in the inherent value in her "illness" which set her on a renewed path of service.

In traditional societies, such experiences typically lead to initiation. Shamans, for example, are thought to be "healed madmen" (Ackerknecht 1943). Their so-called "psychotic episodes" are indigenously framed as a "calling" from which recovery is expected and a signal to begin an apprenticeship (Peters and Price-Williams 1980; Walsh 1990). They are "creative illnesses" (Ellenberger 1970). Such experiences are a socially acknowledged stage of a spiritual discipline (Peters 1989; 1990) and are analogous to the cross-cultural experiences discussed earlier.

Clinically, it seems necessary to learn from the past and become more sensitive to the potentially progressive function of many hysterically psychotic or borderline experiences.

While such states of consciousness may be uncomfortable to both patient and therapist, as the transpersonal psychology literature indicates, loss of identity boundaries possesses value and may be healing. From this perspective, the role of a psychotherapist is possibly closer to that of initiation master, a creator of *communitas*, than to a medical doctor (see van der Hart 1983). Such a temporary regression might be *initio* for psychology and psychiatry—a going back to our shamanic medicine and healing roots, a reincorporation of spirit and community into psychiatric ritual. In tribal cultures, the weight of a whole society and its belief in myth, ritual, and united community spirit (*communitas*) enters into the healings. The power of such rites far overshadows modern psychiatric methods. Tranquilization and insight oriented psychotherapies pale in comparison to the emotionally evocative community healing rites of shamans. Thus the job of even the best neo-shaman therapist is more difficult in our heterogeneous community which has no relation to myth, ritual, and *communitas*. Likewise difficult is the task of present-day psychiatric patients who must navigate a virtual Sea of Dragons of psychotropics, hospitalizations, stigmatization, isolation, and discomfirmation, in contrast to our tribal brothers and sisters who receive education in transcendence and transformation through sacred myth and ritual.

In tribal societies, "soul loss," "spirit possession," and other typical CBSs are not considered individual problems per se. Rather they are seen as problems involving the whole social network, and the balance and relationship to the spiritual forces of the cosmos. That is, because "illnesses" are considered transpersonal and sacred crises, they involve the intense participation of deity, family, and social network. Thus treatment is simultaneously psychosocial and spiritual.

Spiritual and religious experiences are all too often considered negative by psychiatry. Yet there is a significant and positive relationship between religiosity, spirituality, and psychological well being. For example, consider the superior efficiency

of the 12-Step programs (all modeled after Alcoholics Anonymous) and other treatments for addiction which involve relationship to a transpersonal "power greater than ourselves" (Lukoff et al. 1992), as well as strong supporting social network of other members. There are also analogies to "rites of passage" through emotionally cathartic "testimonies," and to the mentor-initiate type relationship with the "sponsor." As Lukoff et al. (1992:5) write, "The founders of AA did not ponder whether religion or spiritual factors are important in recovery, but rather if it is possible for alcoholics to recover without the help of a higher power." In another study, Christian psychiatrists reported that, in cases which included such borderline traits as "suicidal intent" and addictions, the Bible and prayer scored as the most effective modality of treatment (see Lukoff et al., 1992:53). Spiritual, religious, and *communitas* experiences may also explain such cases as the one reported by the psychoanalyst, Rinsley (1982) of a long-term hospitalized borderline patient who improved markedly following a "possession" by the Holy Spirit, which the patient experienced when she began attending services at a charismatic church. Or the possibly borderline patient discussed by Waldman (1992) who explained her own experience of "healing" as being due to her new found faith and church membership.

Engler (1986:34, 39) believes that there is a special attraction for individuals with self pathologies (borderline and narcissistic characters) to meditation practice and Buddhist doctrines such as *anatta* (or no-self), basically because the doctrine legitimizes and rationalizes their lack of self-structure and integration. He warns of the dangers and contraindications, and basically cautions against the practice of meditation or any unconscious uncovering psychotherapies by the borderline patient because of their lack of stable self structure. In other words, one needs an ego or non-diffuse identity before beginning the process of discarding it (Epstein 1990; Wilber 1986a; 1986b; 1986c). However, it may also be that, in our society with its high prevalence of self pathology, that a spiritual discipline or education for transcendence is needed to help such individuals find identity, wholeness, and healing. It is not that the borderline patient is without ego. Rather, the borderline condition is a mixture of healthy and pathological characteristics. And, it may be that the borderline person is drawn to meditation and other spiritual practices because he/she is seeking transitional experiences, to transcend in order to reform the ego. Culturally sanctioned rites of passage typically elicit unconscious dynamics and altered experiences of consciousness that are at variance with the ego structuring therapies suggested for unstable self pathologies. These rites, however, are the very means of achieving identity and acquiring community in traditional cultures and are, in my opinion, fundamental psychotherapeutic goals in any society.

If people need a strong or stable ego in order to undergo healthy transformation, then there couldn't be any psychological development in the first place. Children and adolescents do not have, nor do they seem to need, a stable ego identity to undergo radical change. Consider the writings of Erik Erikson (1980:143–144), the psychoanalyst who developed the concept of "identity diffusion" and who, in discussing therapy with dangerous regressed acting-out borderline characters, speaks of a mechanism which he calls the "rock-bottom attitude" that consists of a tremendous pull toward ". . . both the ultimate limit of regression (which is at the same time) the only firm foundation for a renewed progress" [parenthesis mine]. Thus, an extreme regression in the service of the self may lead to a recovery that often coincides with the discovery of previously hidden creative gifts.

Chronic borderline states are attempts to achieve healing change, but failures in that they haven't completed this progressive function. It is in this area that culture, with all its multifaceted complexity, either supports the transition or contributes to the problem, by failing to provide meaningful transpersonal symbol systems for identity reformation or education for transcendence, and thereby fosters chronic transitional illnesses like BPD.

The healing power of rites of passage foster an awareness of the presence of the transpersonal, however this is understood cross-culturally, and this, in my opinion, is the missing element in our psychiatric understanding and treatment of the borderline patient. The loss of rites of passage and their sacred context could be one of the principal factors in the West's transformation of an endogenous healing mechanism—which, in tribal societies, is a culturally sanctioned, sacred, transitional process—into the chronic and insidious medical/secular/profane/unfit for spiritual practice borderline disorder that has become an endemic public health problem. In other words, the borderline syndrome, as mentioned above, like most other chronic and severe psychiatric disorders (e.g., schizophrenia and depression), is less prevalent in cultural contexts with meaningful rites of passage that aid individuals, by evoking *communitas* and other transpersonal experiences, to successfully traverse life's critical transitional periods. It is not the borderline state itself that is the problem, but cultural and psychiatric phenomenology if it views such radical alterations of consciousness with fear and trepidation, and labels as crazy what may well be endogenous attempts at healing and transformation in need of exogenous social, familial, and psychiatric support, validation, and guidance.

The psychotic episodes of BPD do not have a channel or cultural "container" that is provided by indigenous rites of passage in which chaotic feelings are shaped and thereby become manageable (Plaut 1975). It is this cultural channel, illuminated by the myths and symbols of initiation, that help form identity by providing a transpersonal meaning and context to critical life periods. Without such cultural practices that educate for transcendence, it is difficult to build the self structure that can utilize and integrate experiences of non-ordinary consciousness. Thus, even the natural healing mechanism of the best "psychotic experience," which Bateson (1961) calls an endogenously orchestrated rite of passage that, in all too many cases, is insufficient to catalyze transition and reintegration.

REFERENCES

Achterberg, J. (1985) Imagery and Healing. Boston: New Science Library.
___. (1992) Ritual: The Foundation for Transpersonal Medicine. ReVision: Journal of Consciousness and Transformation 14(3):158–164.
Ackerknecht, E. (1943) Psychopathology, Primitive Medicine and Primitive Culture. Bulletin of the History of Medicine 14:30–67.
Angel, K. (1965) Loss of Identity and Acting-out. Journal of the American Psychiatric Association 13:79–84.
Arrien, A. (1993) The Four-Fold Way. San Francisco: Harper San Francisco.
Bateson, G. (1961) Introduction. In Perceval's Narrative. G. Bateson, ed. New York: William Morrow.
Bernstein, J. (1987) The Decline of Rites of Passage in Our Culture: The Impact on Masculine Individuation. In Betwixt & Between: Patterns of Masculine and Feminine Initiation. L. C. Mahdi, S. Foster, and M. Little, eds. LaSalle, IL: Open Court Publishing.
Blacker, C. (1986) The Catalpa Bow. London: Allen & Unwin.
Blos, P. (1978) The Concept of Acting-Out in Relation to the Adolescent Process. In A Developmental Approach to Problems of Acting-Out (revised), E. Rexford, ed. New York: International Universities Press.
Bly, R. (1987) The Erosion of Male Confidence. In Betwixt & Between: Patterns of Masculine and Feminine Initiation. L. C. Mahdi, S. Foster, and M. Little, eds. LaSalle, IL: Open Court Publishing.
Boddy, J. (1992) Comment on the Proposed DSM-IV: Criteria for Trance and Possession Disorder. Transcultural Psychiatric Research Review 29(4):323–330.
Bourguignon, E. (1965) The Self, the Behavioral Environment and the Theory of Spirit Possession. In Context and Meaning in Cultural Anthropology. M. E. Spiro, ed. New York: The Free Press.
___. (1968) World Distribution and Patterns of Possession States. In Trance and Possession States. R. H. Prince, ed. Montreal: R. M. Bucke Memorial Society.
___. (1976) Possession. San Francisco: Chandler and Sharp.
___. (1992) The DSM-IV and Cultural Diversity. Transcultural Psychiatric Research Review 24(4):330–332.
Bragdon, E. (1988) A Source Book for Helping People in Spiritual Emergency. Los Altos, CA: Lightening Up Press.
Campbell, J. (1968) The Hero with a Thousand Faces, Second Edition. Princeton, NJ: Bollingen Series/Princeton University Press.
Cardeña, E. (1992) Trance and Possession as Dissociative Disorders in Transcultural Psychiatry. Transcultural Psychiatric Research Review 29(4):287–300.
Cardenas, R. (1985) Estudio Descriptivo del Intents de Suicidio en Pacientes Atennudos. Revista Chilena de Neuro-Psychiatrica 23:97–110.

Carpenter, W. T., J. G. Gunderson, and J. S. Strauss (1977) Considerations of the Borderline Syndrome. *In* Borderline Personality Disorders. P. Hartocollis, ed. New York: International Universities Press.

Chapple, E. D., and C. S. Coon (1942) Principles of Anthropology. New York: Henry Holt.

Chesler, P. (1972) Women and Madness. New York: Avon Books.

Combs, A., and M. Holland (1990) Synchronicity: Science, Myth, and the Trickster. New York: Paragon.

Coons, P., E. Bowman, R. Kluft, and V. Milstein (1991) The Cross-Cultural Occurrence of MPD: Additional Cases from a Recent Survey. Dissociation, 4(3):124–128.

Crapanzano, V. (1977) Mohammed and Dawia: Possession in Morocco. *In* Case Studies in Spirit Possession. V. Crapanzano and V. Garrison, eds. New York: Wiley & Sons.

Devereux, G. (1956) Normal and Abnormal. *In* Some Uses of Anthropology, Theoretical and Applied. J. Casagrande and T. Galwin, eds. Washington, DC: The Anthropological Society of Washington.

DiNicola, V. F. (1990) Anorexia multiforme: Self Starvation in Historical and Cultural Context, Parts I and II. Transcultural Psychiatric Research Review 27(3):165–196, 27(4):245–286.

DSM III (1987) Diagnostic and Statistical Manual of Mental Disorders, Third Edition. Appendix C: Annotated Comprehensive Listing of DSM-II and DSM-III. Washington, DC: American Psychiatric Association 3:371–395.

DSM III-R (1987) Diagnostic and Statistical Manual of Mental Disorders, Third Edition-Revised. Washington, DC: American Psychiatric Association.

Durkheim, E. (1957) The Elementary Forms of the Religious Life, 4th Edition. London: Allen & Unwin.

Easser, B. R., and S. W. Lesser (1965) Hysterical Personality: A Reevaluation. Psychoanalytic Quarterly 34:390–405.

Edgerton, R. (1980) Traditional Treatment for Mental Illness in Africa: A Review. Culture, Medicine, & Psychiatry, 4:164–189.

Ekstein, R., and S. W. Friedman (1957) Acting-Out, Play Action, and Play Acting. Journal of the American Psychoanalytic Association 5:581–629.

Eliade, M. (1954) The Myth of the Eternal Return or Cosmos and History. W. R. Trask, trans. Princeton, NJ: Princeton University Press.

———. (1958) Rites and Symbols of Initiation. W. R. Trask, trans. New York: Harper & Row.

———. (1964) Shamanism: Archaic Techniques of Ecstasy. W. R. Trask, trans. Princeton: Princeton University Press.

Ellenberger, H. (1970) The Discovery of the Unconscious. New York: Basic Books.

Engler, J. (1986) Therapeutic Aims in Psychotherapy and Meditation. *In* Transformations of Consciousness. K. Wilber, J. Engler & D. Brown, eds. Boston: New Science Library.

Epstein, M. (1990) Psychodynamics of Meditation: Pitfalls on the Spiritual Path. Journal of Transpersonal Psychology, 22(1):17–34.

Erikson, E. (1980) Identity and the Life Cycle: A Reissue. New York: W. W. Norton.

Fabrega, H. (1984) Culture and Psychiatric Illness: Biomedical and Ethnomedical Aspects. *In* Cultural Conceptions of Mental Health & Therapy. A. J. Marsella and B. M. White, eds. Boston: D. Reidel.

Fabrega, H. (1989) On the Significance of an Anthropological Approach to Schizophrenia. Psychiatry 52(1):45–65.

Fairbairn, W. (1952) Schizoid Factors in the Personality. *In* Psychoanalytic Studies of the Personality. W. Fairbairn, ed. London: Tavistock Press.

Favazza, A. (1987) Bodies Under Siege: Self-Mutilation in Culture and Psychiatry. Baltimore: Johns Hopkins University Press.

Fernandez-Marina, R. (1961) The Puerto Rican Syndrome: Its Dynamics and Cultural Determinates. Psychiatry 24:79–82.

Foster, S., and M. Little (1987) The Vision Quest: Passing from Childhood to Adulthood. *In* Betwixt and Between: Patterns of Masculine and Feminine Initiation. L. C. Mahdi, S. Foster, and M. Little, eds. LaSalle, IL: Open Court Publishing.

Foucault, M. (1965) Madness and Civilization. R. Harvard, trans. New York: Random House.

Frank, J. (1979) Persuasion and Healing (revised edition). New York: Schocken Books.

Garrison, V. (1977) The "Puerto Rican Syndrome" in Psychiatry and *Espiritismo*. *In* Case Studies in Spirit Possession. V. Crapanzano and V. Garrison, eds. New York: Wiley & Sons.

Geertz, C. (1973) Religion as a Cultural System. *In* The Interpretation of Culture. C. Geertz, ed. New York: Basic Books.

Graff, H., and B. S. Mallin (1967) The Syndrome of the Wrist Cutter. American Journal of Psychiatry 124:74–79.

Greenson, R. R. (1966) Comment on Dr. Limentani's Paper. International Journal of Psychoanalysis 49:171–178.

Grinberg, L. (1968) On Acting-Out and Its Role in the Psychoanalytic Process. International Journal of Psychoanalysis 49:171–178.

Grinker, R. S. (1977) Borderline Personality Disorders. New York: International Universities Press.

Grinker, R. S., S. Werble, and R. C. Drye (1968) The Borderline Syndrome: A Behavioral Study of Ego Functions. New York: Basic Books.

Grob, D., and M. Dobkin de Rios (1992) Adolescent Drug Use in Cross-Cultural Perspective. The Journal of Drug Issues 22(1):121–138.

Grof, C., and S. Grof, eds. (1989) Spiritual Emergency: When Personal Transformation Becomes a Crisis. Los Angeles: Jeremy Tarcher.

———. (1990) The Stormy Search for the Self. Los Angeles: Jeremy Tarcher.

Grof, S. (1985) Beyond the Brain: Birth, Death, and Transcendence in Psychiatry. Albany, NY: SUNY Press.

———. (1987) The Adventure of Self-Discovery. Albany, NY: SUNY Press.

Grof, S., and C. Grof (1980) Beyond Death: The Gates of Consciousness. London: Thames and Hudson.

Grotstein, J. (1979) Demonical Possession, Splitting, and the Torments of Joy. Contemporary Psychoanalysis 15:407–457.

Grotstein, J. (1981) Splitting & Projective Identification. New York: Aronson Press.

Grunebaum, H. U., and G. L. Klerman (1967) Wrist Slashing. American Journal of Psychiatry 124:113–120.

Gunderson, J. G., and J. E. Kolb (1978) Discriminating Features of Borderline Patients. American Journal of Psychiatry 135:792–796.

Gunderson, J. G., and M. T. Singer (1975) Defining Borderline Patients: An overview. American Journal of Psychiatry 132:1–10.

Hacking, I. (1992) Multiple Personality and Its Hosts. History of the Human Sciences 5(2):3–31.

Halifax, J. (1982) Shaman: The Wounded Healer. London: Thames and Hudson.

Harner, M. (1990) Commentary. Shamanism: The Transpersonal Dimension. ReVision: Journal of Consciousness and Change 13(2):101–102.

Hastings, A. (1991) With the Tongues of Men and Angels. San Francisco: Holt, Rinehart, Winston.

Havens, L. L. (1972) Approaches to the Mind. Boston: Little, Brown.

Hillman, J. (1965) Suicide and the Soul. New York: Harper & Row.

Hirsch, S. J., and M. H. Hollender (1969) Hysterical Psychosis: Clarification of the Concept. American Journal of Psychiatry 125:909–915.

Hollender, M. H., and S. J. Hirsch (1964) Hysterical Psychosis. American Journal of Psychiatry 120:1066–1074.

Hughes, C. C. (1985) Glossary of "Culture-Bound" or Folk Psychiatric Syndromes. *In* The Culture Bound Syndromes. R. C. Simmons and C. C. Hughes, ed. Boston: D. Reidel.

Jilek-Aall, L. (1988) Suicidal Behaviors Among Youth: A Cross-Cultural Comparison. Transcultural Psychiatric Research Review 25(2):87–105.

Jung, C. G. (1969) Psychology and Religion. *In* The Collected Works of C. G. Jung, Vol. 11. R. F. C. Hull, trans. Princeton, NJ: Princeton University Press.

Kalweit, H. (1988) Dream Time and Inner Space: The World of the Shaman. Boston: Shambala Books.

Kanzer, M. (1957) Acting Out, Sublimation, and Reality Testing. Journal of the American Psychoanalytic Association 3:663–683.

Katz, R. (1973) Education for Transcendence: Lessons from the !Kung Zhu/twasi. Journal for Transpersonal Psychology 5(2):136–155.

Kennedy, J. (1967) Nubian Zar Ceremonies as Psychotherapy. Human Organization 26:185–194.

___. (1973) Cultural psychiatry. *In* Handbook of Social and Cultural Anthropology. J. J. Honigmann, ed. Chicago: Rand McNally.

Kenny, M. G. (1985) Paradox Lost: The Latah Problem Revisited. *In* The Culture Bound Syndromes. R. C. Simmons and C. C. Hughes, eds. Boston: D. Reidel.

___. (1986) The Passion of Ansel Bourne: Multiple Personality in American Culture. Washington: Smithsonian Institution.

___. (1992) Notes on Proposed Revisions of the Dissociative Disorders Section of DSM III-R. Transcultural Psychiatric Research Review, 29(14):337–341.

Kernberg, O. (1975) Borderline Conditions and Pathological Narcissism. New York: Aronson Press.

___. (1977) The Structural Diagnosis of Borderline Personality Disorder. *In* Borderline Personality Disorder. P. Hartocollis, ed. New York: International Universities Press.

___. (1980) Neurosis, Psychosis, and the Borderline States. *In* Textbook of Psychiatry III, 3rd ed., Volume 1. H. I. Kaplan, A. M. Freedman, and B. J. Sadock, eds. Baltimore, MD: Williams & Wilkins.

Khan, M. M. R. (1964) Ego Distortion, Cumulative Trauma, and the Role of Reconstruction in the Analytic Situation. International Journal of Psychoanalysis 45:279–281.

Kiev, A. (1964) The Study of Folk Psychiatry. *In* Magic, Faith, and Healing. A. Kiev, ed. New York: The Free Press.

___. (1972) Transcultural Psychiatry. New York: The Free Press.

Kimball, S. T. (1960) Introduction. *In* The Rites of Passage. A. van Gennep. Chicago: University of Chicago Press.

Knight, R. P. (1953) Borderline States. Bulletin of the Menninger Clinic 17:1–12.

Kohut, H. (1971) The Analysis of the Self. New York: International Universities Press.

Kris, E. (1952) Psychoanalytic Exploitations in Art. New York: International Universities Press.

Laing, R. D. (1967) The Politics of Experience. London: Penguin Books.

Langness, L. L. (1965) Hysterical Psychosis in the New Guinea Highlands. Psychiatry. 28:258–277.

___. (1967) Hysterical Psychosis: the Cross-Cultural Evidence. American Journal of Psychiatry 124:143–152.

___. (1976) Hysterical Psychosis and Possession. *In* Culture-bound Syndromes, Ethnopsychiatry, and Alternative Therapies. W. P. Lebra, ed. Honolulu: University Press of Hawaii.

Leavitt, J. (1993) Are Trance and Possession Disorders? Transcultural Psychiatric Research Review 30(1):51–57.

Lee., S. H., and M. H. Lee (1982) A Social Psychiatric Study on Suicide Attempts in Some Areas of Kangwon District in Korea. Journal of Korean Neuro-Psychiatric Association 21:462–470.

Lewis, I. M. (1989) Ecstatic Religion, second edition. Harmondsworth, England: Penguin Books.

Limentani, A. (1966) A Re-Evaluation of Acting-Out in Relation to Working Through. International Journal of Psychoanalysis 47:274–282.

Linton, R. (1956) Cultural and Mental Disorders. Springfield: C. C. Thomas Publishers.

Littlewood, R., and M. Lipsedge (1986) The "Culture-Bound Syndromes" of the Dominant Cultures. *In* Transcultural Psychiatry. J. Cox, ed. London: Croom Helm.

___. (1987) The Butterfly and the Serpent: Culture, Psychopathology, and Biomedicine. Culture, Medicine and Psychiatry 2:289–335.

Lukoff, D., and H. Everest (1985) Myths in Mental Illness. Journal of Transpersonal Psychology 17(2):123–153.

Lukoff, D., R. Turner, and F. Lu (1992) Transpersonal Psychiatric Research Review: Psychoreligious Dimensions of Healing. Journal of Transpersonal Psychology 24(1):41–60.

Marsella, A. J. (1980) Depressive Experience and Disorder across Cultures. *In* Handbook of Cross-Cultural Psychology, Volume 6: Psychopathology. J. G. Draguns, and H. R. Triandis, eds. Boston: Allyn & Bacon.

___. (1984) Culture and Mental Health: An Overview. *In* Cultural Conceptions of Mental Health and Therapy. A. J. Marsella and G. M. White, eds., Boston: D. Reidel.

Marshall, M. (1979) Beliefs, Behaviors, and Alcoholic Beverages: A Cross-Cultural Study. Ann Arbor: University of Michigan Press.

Maslow, A. (1962) Toward a Psychology of Being. Princeton, NJ: Van Nostrand.

Masterson, J. (1977) Primary Anorexia Nervosa in the Borderline Adolescent: An Object-Relations View. *In* Borderline Personality Disorder. P. Hartocollis, ed. New York: International Universities Press.

May, R. (1991) The Cry for Myth: New York: Bantam.

McManus, J. (1979) Ritual and Human Social Cognition. *In* The Spectrum of Ritual. E. G. D'Aguila, C. D. Laughlin, Jr., and J. McManus, eds. New York: Columbia University Press.

Metzner, R. (1986) Opening to Inner Light. Los Angeles: Jeremy Tarcher.

Millon, T. (1981) Disorders of the Personality, DSM III: Axis II. New York: Wiley Interscience.

___. (1987) On Genesis and Prevalence of Borderline Personality Disorder: A Social Learning Theory. Journal of Personality Disorders 1:354–372.

Milner, M. (1952.) Aspects of Symbolism in Comprehension of the Not-Self. International Journal of Psychoanalysis. 33:191–195.

Moore, T. (1992.) Care of the Soul. New York: Harper-Collins.

Murphy, H. B. M. (1968) Sociocultural Factors in Schizophrenia. *In* Social Psychiatry. J. Zubin and F. Freyhan, eds. New York: Grune & Stratton.

Myerhoff, B. (1974) Peyote Hunt. Ithaca, NY: Cornell University Press.

Newman, P. (1964) Wild Man Behavior in a New Guinea Highland Community. American Anthropologist 66:1019–1028.

Newman, P., and P. A. Halvorson (1982) Anorexia Nervosa and Bulimia. New York: Nostrand Reinhold.

Nichter, M. (1981) Idioms of Distress. Culture, Medicine, and Psychiatry 5:5–24.

Nuckolls, C. (1992) Toward a Cultural History of Personality Disorders. Social Science and Medicine 35:37–47.

Obeyesekeye, G. (1969) The Ritual Drama of the Sanni Demons: Collective Representations of Disease in Ceylon. Comparative Studies in Society and History 2:174–216.

Oesterreich, T. K. (1966) Possession: Demonical and Other Among Primitive Races, in Antiquity, the Middle Ages, and Modern Times. Secaucus, NJ: Citadel Press.

Okasha, A., and F. Lotaif (1979) Attempted Suicide: An Egyptian Investigation. Acta Psychiatrica Scandinavica. 60:69–75.

Pao, P. N. (1969) The Syndrome of Delicate Self-Cutting. British Journal of Medical Psychology 42:195–210.

Paris, J. (1988) Follow-up Studies of Borderline Personality: A Critical Review. Journal of Personality Disorders 2:189–197.

___. (1991) Personality Disorders, Parasuicide, and Culture. Transpersonal Psychiatric Research Review 28(1):25–39.

Parker, S. (1960) The *Wiitiko* Psychosis in the Context of Ojibwa Personality and Culture. American Anthropologist 62:603–623.

Peters, L. G. (1978) Psychotherapy in Tamang Shamanism. Ethos 6(2):63–91.

___. (1981) An Experiential Study of Nepalese Shamanism. Journal of Transpersonal Psychology 13(1):1–26.

___. (1988) Borderline Personality Disorder and the Possession Syndrome: An Ethno-Psychoanalytic Perspective. Transcultural Psychiatric Research Review 26(1):5–45.

___. (1989) Shamanism: Phenomenology of a Spiritual Discipline. Journal of Transpersonal Psychology 21(2)115–137.

___. (1990) Mystical Experience in Tamang Shamanism. ReVision: Journal of Consciousness and Change 13(2):71–85.

Peters, L. G., and D. Price-Williams (1980) Towards an Experiential Analysis of Shamanism. American Ethnologist 7:397–418.

___. (1983) A Phenomenological Overview of Trance. Transcultural Psychiatric Research Review 20(1): 5–39.

Plaut, A. (1975) Where Have All the Rituals Gone? Observations on the Transforming Function of Rituals and the Proliferation of Psychotherapies. Journal of Analytical Psychology 20:13–17.

Prince, R. (1968) The Changing Picture of Depressive Syndromes in Africa: Is It Fact or Diagnostic Fashion? Canadian Journal of African Studies 1:177–192.

___. (1979) Anorexia Nervosa in Developing Countries. Transcultural Psychiatric Research Review 16: 114–115.

___. (1983) Is Anorexia Nervosa a Culture Bound Syndrome? Transcultural Psychiatric Research Review 20: 299–300.

___. (1985) The Concept of Culture-bound Syndromes: Anorexia Nervosa and Brain-fag. Social Science & Medicine 21:197–203.

Rasmussen, K. (1929) Intellectual Culture of the Iglulik Eskimos. Copenhagen: Gyldendalske Boghanel, Nordisk Forlag.

Reeves, M. S., and A. Tugend (1987) Suicide's Unanswerable Logic. *In* Betwixt & Between: Patterns of Masculine and Feminine Initiation. L. C. Mahdi, S. Foster, and M. Little, eds. LaSalle, IL: Open Court Publishing.

Rexford, E. A. (1978) A Selective Review of the Literature. *In* A Developmental Approach to Problems of Acting Out. E. A. Rexford, ed. New York: International Universities Press.

Ring, K. (1988) Near-death and UFO Encounters as Shamanic Initiations. ReVision: Journal of Consciousness and Change 11(13):14–22.

Rinsley, D. (1982) Borderline and Other Self Disorders. New York: Aronson Press.

Ross, C. (1991) The Dissociated Executive Self and the Cultural Dissociation Barrier. Dissociation 4(1):55–61.

Rothenberg, A. (1964) Puerto Rico and Aggression. American Journal of Psychiatry 120(10):962–970.

Rubel, A. J., C. W. O'Nell, and R. Collado (1985) The Folk Illness Called *Susto*. *In* The Culture Bound Syndromes. R. C. Simons and C. C. Hughes, eds. Boston: Reidel Publishing Company.

Rubio, M., M. Urdanetta, and J. L. Doyle (1955) Psychopathological Reaction Patterns in the Antilles Command. U.S. Armed Forces Medical Journal 6:1767–1772.

Salisbury, R. (1968) Possession in the New Guinea Highlands: A review of the Literature. International Journal of Social Psychiatry 14:89–94.

Sartorius, N. (1973) Culture and the Epidemiology of Depression. Psychiatria Neurologie et Neurochirugia 76, 479–487.

Sartorius, N., A. Jablensky, and R. Shapiro (1978) Cross-Cultural Differences in the Short-Term Prognosis of Schizophrenia Psychosis. Schizophrenia Bulletin 4:102–113.

Scheff, T. (1966) Being Mentally Ill: A Sociological Theory. Chicago: Aldine Publishing.

Schmideberg, M. (1947) The Treatment of Psychopaths and Borderline Patients. American Journal of Psychotherapy 1:45–55.

Schneidman, E. S., and N. L. Faberow (1983) Attempted and Committed Suicide. *In* The Psychology of Suicide. E. S. Schneidman and N. L. Gaberow, eds. New York: Aronson Press.

Searles, H. F. (1977) Dual and Multiple-Personality Processes in Borderline Ego Functioning. *In* Borderline Personality Disorders. P. Hartocollis, ed. New York: International Universities Press.

Silverman, J. (1967) Shamans and Acute Schizophrenia. American Anthropologist 69:21–31.

Simons, R. C. (1985) The Reinvention of the *Latah* Paradox. *In* The Culture Bound Syndrome. R. C. Simons and C. C. Hughes, eds. Boston: D. Reidel Publishing.

Siomopoulos, V. (1971) Hysterical Psychosis: Psychopathological Aspects. British Journal of Medical Psychology. 44:95–100.

___. (1983) The Structure of Psychopathological Experience. New York: Bruner Mazel.

Small, J. (1991) Awakening in Time: The Journey from Co-dependence to Co-creation. New York: Bantam Books.

Some, M. (1993) Ritual. Portland, OR: Swan, Raven & Company.

Spanos, N. (1986) Hypnosis, Demonic Possession, and Multiple Personality. *In* Altered States of Consciousness and Mental Health: A Cross-Cultural Perspective. C. Ward, ed. Newbury Park, CA: Sage.

Spitzer, R. L., and J. Endicott (1979) Justification for Separating Schizotypal and Borderline Personality Disorders. Schizophrenia Bulletin 5:95–100.

Spretnak, C. (1991) States of Grace: The Recovery of Meaning in the Postmodern Age. San Francisco: Harper San Francisco.

Stein, M. (1969) States of Consciousness in Acting-out. Paper presented at the meeting of the American Psychoanalytic Association, Panel on Action and Acting-out and the Symptomatic Act.

Stone, M. (1979) Dreams of Fragmentation and of the Death of the Dreamer: A Manifestation of Vulnerability to Psychosis. Psychopharmacology Bulletin 15:12–14.

___. (1980) The Borderline Syndromes. New York: McGraw-Hill.

___. (1983) Borderline Personality Disorder. *In* New Psychiatric Syndromes. S. Akhtar, ed. New York: Aronson Press.

Suleiman, M. A., A. A. Nashef, M. M. A. Moussa, and M. F. El-Islam (1989) The Profile of Parasuicide Repeating in Kuwait. International Journal of Social Psychiatry 85:146–155.

Swarz, M., D. Blazer, L. George, and J. Winfield (1990) Estimating the Prevalence of Borderline Personality Disorder in the Community. Journal of Personality Disorders 4:257–273.

Szasz, T. (1961) The Myth of Mental Illness. New York: Harper & Row.

Tart, C. (1971) Scientific Foundations for the Study of Altered States of Consciousness. Journal of Transpersonal Psychology 3(2):93–124.

Taylor, G. (1978) Demonical Possession and Psychoanalytic Theory. British Journal of Medical Psychology 51:53–60.

Torry, E. F. (1980) Schizophrenia and Civilization. New York: Aronson Press.

Trautman, E. C. (1961) The Suicidal Fit: A Psychobiolgic Study on Puerto Rican Immigrants. Archives of General Psychiatry 5:96–105.

Tseng, W. S., and J. F. McDermott (1981) Culture, Mind, and Therapy. New York: Bruner/Mazel.

Tupin, J. P. (1984) Introduction. *In* Transient Psychosis: Diagnosis, Management and Evaluation. J. P. Tupin, V. Halbreich, and J. J. Pena, eds. New York: Bruner/Mazel.

Turner, V. (1962) Three Symbols of Passage in Ndembo Circumcision Ritual. *In* Essays on the Ritual of Social Relations. M. Gluckman, ed. Manchester: Manchester University Press.

___. (1967) Forest of Symbols. Ithaca: Cornell University Press.

___. (1969) The Ritual Process. Chicago: Aldine Press.

Ussher, J. (1991) Women's Madness: Misogyny or Mental Illness. Amherst, MA: University of Massachusetts.

Vaillant, G. E., and J. C. Perry (1980) Personality Disorders. *In* Comprehensive Textbook of Psychiatry/III, 3rd ed., Volume 2. H. I. Kaplan, A. M. Freedman, and B. J. Sadock, eds. Baltimore: Williams & Wilkins.

van Gennep, A. (1960) The Rites of Passage. M. B. Vizedon and G. L. Caffee, trans. Chicago: University of Chicago Press.

Van der Hart, O. (1983) Rituals in Psychotherapy. New York: Irvington.

Waldman, M. (1992) The Therapeutic Alliance, *Kundalini*, and Spiritual/Religious Issues in Counseling: The Case of Julia. Journal of Transpersonal Psychology 24(2):115–149.

Wallace, A. F. C. (1966) Culture and Personality, 2nd ed. New York: Random House

Walsh, R. (1990) The Spirit of Shamanism. Los Angeles: Jeremy Tarcher.

Waxler, N. E. (1974) Culture and Mental Illness: A Social Labeling Perspective. The Journal of Nervous and Mental Disease 159:379–395.

___. (1979) Is Outcome for Schizophrenia Better in Traditional Societies? The Case of Sri Lanka. Journal of Nervous and Mental Disease 167:144–158.

Wekstein, L. (1979) Handbook of Suicidology. New York: Bruner/Mazel.

Westermeyer, J., and R. Winthrob (1979) "Folk" Criteria in the Diagnosis of Mental Illness in Rural Laos: On Being Insane in Some Places. American Journal of Psychiatry 136:755–761.

Wilber, K. (1979) No-boundary: Eastern and Western Approaches to Personal Growth. Boston: Shambala Books.

___. (1986a) The Spectrum of Psychopathology. *In* Transformation of Consciousness. K. Wilber, J. Engler, and D. Brown, eds. Boston: New Science Library.

___. (1986b) The Spectrum of Development. *In* Transformation of Consciousness. K. Wilber, J. Engler, and D. Brown, eds. Boston: New Science Library.

___. (1986c) Treatment Modalities. *In* Transformation of Consciousness. K. Wilber, J. Engler, and D. Brown, eds. Boston: New Science Library.

Wilson, P. J. (1967) Status Ambiguity and Spirit Possession. Man 2:366–378.

Woodman, M. (1987) From Concrete to Consciousness: The Emergence of the Feminine. *In* Betwixt and Between: Patterns of Masculine and Feminine Initiation. L. C. Mahdi, S. Foster, and M. Little, eds. LaSalle, IL: Open Court Publishing.

Yap, P. M. (1960) The Possession Syndrome: A Comparison of Hong Kong and French Findings. Journal of Mental Science 106:114–137.

___. (1965) *Koro*—A Culture-bound Depersonalization Syndrome. British Journal of Psychiatry 111:43–50.

___. (1969) The Culture Bound Reactive Syndromes. *In* Mental Health Research in Asia and the Pacific. W. Caudill and T. Lin, eds. Honolulu: East-West Center Press.

Young, F. W. (1965) Initiation Ceremonies: A Cross-Cultural Study of Status Dramatization. Indianapolis: Bobbs-Merrill.

CHAPTER SEVEN

Culture, Social Organization, and Sexuality

The sexual disorders are among the most culturally sensitive of all the disorders in DSM-IV. This is true of the sexual dysfunctions as well as the paraphilias and gender identity disorder. Cultural factors play a central role in that many of these disorders are, in fact, *cultural entities*. That is, the disorders exist because of the collective intentionality of a cultural group, in this case, primarily western culture. Because of the thoroughly cultural nature of sexual disorders, it is necessary to appreciate the effects of culture on sexual development and behavior in order to put the sexual disorders within a proper sociocultural context.

MALE DOMINANCE AND FEMALE SEXUALITY

In general, female sexuality is highly controlled in most human societies. This high degree of control is illustrated by comparing human societies with other primate societies. Generally speaking, the higher the degree of male dominance existing in a society, the more complete will be control over female sexuality. Conversely, the more freedom females have from male dominance, the less will be the control over female sexuality.

Male dominance is defined by a social condition in which the lives of females are by and large controlled by males. In contrast, female dominance is defined by a social condition in which the lives of males are by and large controlled by females.

This relationship between dominance hierarchies and sexual behavior can be illustrated by categorizing the social organization of primate societies into five general types (Castillo, 1997, p. 115):

1. Competitive male dominance
2 Semicooperative male dominance
3. Cooperative male dominance
4. Cooperative female dominance
5. Cooperative egalitarianism

These five types of social organization are ideal types intended for heuristic purposes. In reality there is much more variation and overlap between the categories. However, the categories are useful for illustrating differences in the effects of social organization on sexual behavior.

Competitive Male Dominance

The first type of primate social organization is competitive male dominance. Competitive male dominance is typified among primates by gorillas (Stewart & Harcourt, 1987; Watts, 1991). This social organization is characterized by males competing with each other through combat or other means for the exclusive sexual rights to a group of females. One dominant male controls a harem of females.

This is an extreme form of male dominance. The social group is small, usually only several individuals, and all of them are controlled by the physical force and threats of the alpha (dominant) male. The females are generally limited to sexual relations only with the alpha male, although there are a few exceptions.

Semicooperative Male Dominance

Chimpanzees show somewhat more cooperation between males than do gorillas. They have larger social groups and more sharing of sexual partners. This type of social organization can be categorized as semicooperative male dominance. Chimpanzee females tend to have relatively few sexual partners compared to species without male dominance, and sexual behavior is associated with competition, aggression, and violence among the males and toward the females.

Cooperative Male Dominance

Cooperative male dominance is characterized by high levels of cooperation among males to dominate females and control female sexuality. Competition between males is controlled through typically elaborate systems of rules and rituals, and sharing the sexuality of females is generally compulsory.

Only one primate species has highly developed cooperative male dominance, and that is *Homo sapiens*. By cooperating with each other, males assure their control over females and access to female sexuality by sharing the females in social systems designed to provide exclusive sexual access to usually one female for every one male. This is the system of controlling sexual behavior known as *marriage.*

Almost all known human societies have some form of cooperative male dominance. More extreme forms tend to look somewhat like semicooperative male dominant societies in which one male can control a small harem of females in the practice of polygyny. Human societies with a lower level of male dominance tend to look more like a cooperative egalitarian society in which females have control over their own sexuality. However, almost all human societies have some degree of cooperative male dominance, and female sexuality is placed under at least nominal male control.

The systems of rules and rituals established by males in cooperative male dominant human societies are known as religions and systems of laws. Females have largely been excluded from the governing bodies that create the rules that control sexuality. For example, in almost all human societies there are organizations of religious leaders, political leaders, police forces, military forces, secret clubs, and so on that exclude females to some degree, depending on the level of male dominance in that society. These powerful male organizations control female sexuality through either political force or religious belief, or some combination of both.

In the United States, control of female sexuality is accomplished through a combination of religious beliefs and political force. Christianity has been the most important religious influence in American society. Traditional Christianity for the most part is antisex. The Fathers of the Church who formed the theology of Christianity between the 2nd and 6th centuries were mostly monastics dedicated to asceticism and celibacy. These values have pervaded Christianity for centuries. However, in the last several decades more liberal forms of Christianity in the United States as well as secularized segments of the population have supported more freedom in sexual behavior for women and men. Nevertheless, for millions of people the older, fundamentalist Christian view of sexuality is still their cultural reality.

The theology of fundamentalist Christianity is an expression of cooperative male dominance. Cooperative male dominance was developed by men to facilitate control of female sexuality and to provide structures for large scale male cooperation such as armies, police forces, priesthoods, legislative bodies, trading and economic systems, military and political alliances, and so on.

Fundamentalist Christian cultural schemas of female sexuality have even found their way into the scientific study of sexuality in the late 20th century. For example, *sociobiology* views females as naturally reluctant to have sex (Symons, 1987; Wilson, 1975). In sociobiology it is presumed that all individuals want to maximize their chances of successfully passing on their genetic material. Supposedly, this makes females choosy about sex partners because they have only a few eggs. The reasoning is that if these eggs get fertilized and develop the females face a long period of childrearing. Thus, females are thought to be reluctant about sex, postponing sexual intercourse until they are sure they have the best possible partner. The best partner is defined in sociobiology as the one with the best genes, or the one best able to help with childrearing. Sex for the female is thought to be controlled primarily by factors affecting procreation and childrearing. Thus, it is thought that women are not as interested in sexual pleasure as are men. In contrast, men are thought to be naturally promiscuous because they produce millions of sperm. Men increase the chances of their genetic material being passed on by "spreading" their sperm to as many females as possible.

These ideas in sociobiology fit very well with fundamentalist Christian ideas about female sexuality and seem like common sense to many Americans. However, the evolutionary theory in sociobiology concerning sexuality was devised without actually looking at the sexual behavior of most primate species, our closest animal relatives. It was simply assumed that because most human females traditionally have only one sexual partner (the husband) that this was the natural pattern of sexual behavior for female primates. It was also assumed that female primates are very choosy, generally only having sex with the father of their offspring.

However, during the past two decades many more studies of primate behavior covering more species have been done. The findings do not support the view of sociobiology. Most primate species do not have male dominance, either competitive like gorillas, semicooperative like chimpanzees, or fully cooperative like humans. Most primate species have cooperative female dominance or are egalitarian. As a result of not having male dominance, female sexual behavior in these societies is radically different (Small, 1993).

Cooperative Female Dominance

In societies with cooperative female dominance, females cooperate to control the lives of males. For example, Rhesus macaque societies are formed around large female family groups. A female macaque is born into a particular family group and stays in that group for her entire life, focused on intense relationships with her close female relatives (Rawlins & Kessler, 1986; Small, 1993).

Males are forced out of the family group at adolescence and must attempt to join another family group by behaving subserviently and by attracting the sexual attentions of one or more females in the new group. Thus, males move in and out of family groups by being accepted and rejected by the females. Males stay in groups only temporarily until the females no longer find them sexually attractive. They are forced to move to a different group if they are going to have any chance for sexual relations. Thus, the lives of the males are controlled by the females (Small, 1993).

Also, in macaque society it is the females who are sexually aggressive, in many cases pursuing males and initiating copulation. Macaque females have sex only during their estrus cycles, but during this time they have sex with as many males as possible. Macaque females only have sex when they want to, and only with males they have selected. No male macaque can force a female to have sex, and rape does not occur in primate societies without male dominance. Most primate species have social organizations and patterns of sexual behavior similar to those of the Rhesus macaques (Small, 1993).

Cooperative Egalitarianism

In cooperative egalitarianism, the two genders are roughly equal and there is no gender dominance hierarchy. As a result, female sexuality is not controlled at all by male dominance, or by a female dominance hierarchy. Bonobos (or "pygmy chimps") typify a primate cooperative egalitarian society (de Waal, 1987, 1995; Small, 1993). In bonobo society there is little or no violence, and bisexuality is normative. There is a female-centered family structure without male dominance, and all individuals are highly sexual, engaging in sex several times a day with various partners for purposes unrelated to reproduction.

The social organization and sexual behavior of bonobos is radically different from that of chimps and humans. In bonobo society, females band together to form close lifelong friendship bonds with other females. These female homosexual relationships form the primary social bonds and family structure of bonobo society. However, bonobos are not homosexual per se. They are pansexual, meaning that they have sexual relations with all of the other members of their social group, including females, males, and juveniles.

Small (1993) calls bonobos "the most sexual animals on earth" (p. 175). Bonobos appear to have sex mostly for the purposes of creating and maintaining close friendship bonds, defusing disputes, and for sheer pleasure. Unlike chimpanzee females who only have sex during their estrus cycles, bonobo females have sex every day. And as far as reproduction goes, bonobo females are not at all choosy about their male sex partners, unless you could call "choosing" every male she meets being choosy (Small, 1993).

In the egalitarian bonobo society, individuals have sex more often and in more variations than in any human society. Males have sex with males. Females have sex with females. Even juveniles participate by rubbing their genitals against those of adults, although adult males never actually insert their penises into juvenile females (Small, 1993).

Juvenile males are also very fond of performing oral sex on each other. Bonobos also love to kiss, including inserting their tongues into each other's mouths. Bonobos frequently have sexual intercourse face-to-face like humans, which is rare for chimps or gorillas. This is probably also related to the absence of male dominance; the face-to-face position seems to be preferred by females as it allows more direct clitoral stimulation.

Female bonobos have sex with each other by rubbing their genitals together and kissing and embracing. Female bonobos have large clitorises and are highly orgasmic. Group sex is also very common for bonobos. When two individuals initiate sex, others are free to join in by sticking their fingers into the genital area, or they may wait in line for copulation (Small, 1993).

What we see from looking at sexual behavior across primate species is that in the majority of species, females are not subject to male dominance. Contrary to the thinking of sociobiologists, in those societies where females control their own sexuality, they are highly "promiscuous." That is, they are highly orgasmic, enjoy sex with a great many different partners, and are not at all "choosy" or reluctant to have sex. In the few primate societies that have male dominance (e.g., chimpanzees, gorillas, humans), females are allowed a smaller number of sexual partners consistent with the level of male dominance, and female orgasm may be less common or absent. Thus, we see that it is not "natural" but sociocultural for primate females to mate with only a limited number of male sexual partners. When primate females are allowed to express their sexual desires free from male dominance, they have many sexual partners (male and female) and are highly orgasmic.

HUMAN CULTURAL VARIATIONS

When we examine the relationship of social organization to sexuality in human societies, it is seen that male dominance is created and maintained not only by political force, as it is in other primate societies, but also by complex symbolic systems reflecting humans' larger brain and greater cognitive ability. Nevertheless, the net effect of male dominance is the same. It limits females to a minimum number of male sexual partners.

Although almost all human societies have at least some degree of cooperative male dominance, there is much variation. In those societies with less male dominance and control on female sexuality, women typically have more sexual partners and are more likely to be orgasmic. In contrast, in human societies with greater male dominance and control on female sexuality, females have fewer sexual partners and are less likely to be orgasmic. The contrast in sexual behavior resulting from social organization can be illustrated by looking at different human societies.

Sexuality in Inis Beag

The first article in this chapter is by anthropologist John C. Messenger. Inis Beag is a small island off the coast of Ireland studied by Messenger in the 1950s and '60s. The society is a peasant community of devout Roman Catholics. When studied by Messenger, it was thought that the Catholicism of the islanders embodied a religious ideal unmatched in Ireland. It was a particularly ascetic style of religion with strong influences of Irish Catholic monasticism, Augustinianism, Jansenism, and probably some English Puritan influences.

In this society, sexual renunciation was identified with moral and religious virtue. Moreover, male solidarity was idealized in the form of the "loveless Irishman" whose loyalty was directed toward his comrades. Women were relegated to serfdom. A "good" woman was one who did not like sex, and a "bad" woman was one who enjoyed sex. "Bad" women were thought to disrupt social relations between a man and his male comrades, distracting him from his purpose in life. Likewise, men were supposed to be socially active in the community, but women were restricted to visiting other women and to church-related activities. Some women left their homes only to attend mass, wakes, and funerals.

In Inis Beag, virtually anything related to sex was highly controlled and socially suppressed. Courtship was almost non-existent, and late marriage and celibacy were prevalent. However, after marriage contraception was prohibited, and the women were under pressure from the local priests to produce as many offspring as possible. The women resented this because they felt it increased their work, restricted their freedom, and perpetuated their poverty. Moreover, they were resentful of the social freedom held by men.

Ignorance of sexual practices was profound in this society, along with a lack of sexual variation found in other societies. Sexuality was almost never openly discussed, and mothers rarely gave advice to daughters about sex, assuming that "after marriage nature takes its course." As a result, French kissing, kissing breasts, female hand stimulation of the male genitals, cunnilingus, fellatio, anal intercourse, premarital sex, extramarital sex, open homosexuality, and sadomasochism were either unknown, not performed, or so highly suppressed as to be not discussable.

In Inis Beag, men were believed to be more interested in sex than women were. Like other highly traditional Christians, the islanders believed that sex was a "duty" that a wife must "endure." Therefore, the husband reached orgasm as quickly as possible, not wanting to make his wife "endure" intercourse any longer than necessary. Sexual foreplay was limited to kissing and rough fondling of the buttocks. The man on top was viewed as the only proper position to be used in coitus, and underclothes were worn during sex. The husband fell asleep immediately after orgasm, and female orgasm was either unknown, doubted to exist, or at least considered deviant.

Sexuality in Mangaia

The second article in this chapter is by anthropologist Donald S. Marshall. In contrast to Inis Beag, the island of Mangaia in the South Pacific is a society in which females have achieved a great degree of sexual freedom. This traditional Polynesian society was studied by Marshall during the 1950s and '60s.

The Mangaians of that time lived in single room huts housing 5 to 15 family members. From puberty on, all family members including daughters were free to copulate at night in this same room, with the rest of the family sleeping. Postpubescent daughters especially could receive and make love to varied suitors nightly. For the Mangaians, sex for pleasure was a major concern.

Mangaian boys began to masturbate at about age seven or eight. Around age 13 or 14, boys underwent an initiation ceremony marking their transition to adulthood. The ceremony involved superincision of the penis, "beautifying" the organ, marking them as adult males and suitable sexual partners. After this, boys no longer masturbated but began regular sexual intercourse with postpubescent females.

The man who performed the superincision also served as an instructor in sex, educating the young initiate in how to please a woman. The young male was taught how to perform cunnilingus, how to kiss and fondle breasts, and how to stimulate a woman to multiple orgasms before his own climax. Also, about two weeks after the initiation, he recieved formal "hands on" training from an older experienced woman who taught him various sexual positions and techniques in giving pleasure to a woman.

After this, the initiated Mangaian male would have sexual intercourse every night with various young females. A young male could have ten or more female sex partners. Multiple partners were preferred, as the Mangaians believed that avoiding sex with the same partner prevented pregnancy.

The young Mangaian male developed a good reputation with the postpubescent females of the community if he proved he could continue with the vigorous in-and-out motion of coitus for extended periods of time. By the age of 18, the average Mangaian male had three orgasms per night, seven nights per week.

After their first menstruation, Mangaian females began regular sexual intercourse with the initiated males of the community. The average postpubescent female could have three or four regular sexual partners. The Mangaians believed that a female learned to be orgasmic by sexual experience with a "good" man. The females learned to be orgasmic almost immediately after beginning regular coitus. Apparently all females in Mangaia had orgasms every time they had sex, with most having multiple orgasms.

In Mangaia, females were also sexually aggressive. If they perceived that a man was not copulating often enough, they would tell him insultingly that he was lazy, letting his penis go to waste, and letting it "get rusty." They often made sexual remarks to men that in Anglo American society would be considered sexual harassment. Moreover, coitus was the only possible end of any sexual encounter. There was no equivalent of "dating" or "necking" in the American sense. Phrases such as "I love you" were understood as invitations to copulate. Also, sexual intercourse was not achieved after demonstrating personal affection as it is in western societies. Rather, sexual intimacy was used to create and maintain bonds of personal affection. In addition, adult women frequently performed fellatio on small boys in the family.

Thus, we see that normative sexual practices vary widely around the globe and are related to social organization and levels of male dominance. In all cases, prevailing cultural schemas create and maintain normative patterns of behavior and profoundly affect individual sexual development. This has important implications for all of the sexual disorders including the paraphilias and sexual dysfunctions.

REFERENCES

Castillo, R. J. (1997). *Culture and mental illness: A client-centered approach.* Pacific Grove, CA: Brooks/Cole.

de Waal, F. B. M. (1987). Tension regulation and nonreproductive functions in captive bonobos (Pan paniscus). *National Geographic Research, 3*, 318–335.

de Waal, F. B. M. (1995, March). Bonobo sex and society. *Scientific American, 272*, 82–88.

Rawlins, R. G., & Kessler, M. J. (1986). *The Cayo Santiago macaques: History, behavior, and biology.* Albany: State University of New York Press.

Small, M. F. (1993). *Female choices: Sexual behavior of female primates.* Ithaca: Cornell University Press.

Stewart, K. J., & Harcourt, A. H. (1987). Gorillas: Variation in female relationships. In B. B. Smuts, D. L. Cheney, R. M. Seyfarth, R. Wrangham, & T. T. Strusaker (Eds.), *Primate societies* (pp. 155–164). Chicago: University of Chicago Press.

Symons, D. (1987). An evolutionary approach: Can Darwin's view of life shed light on human sexuality? In J. H. Geer & W. T. O'Donohue (Eds.), *Theories of human sexuality* (pp. 91–126). New York: Plenum.

Watts, D. P. (1991). Mountain gorilla reproduction and sexual behavior. *American Journal of Primatology, 24*, 211–255.

Wilson, E. O. (1975). *Sociobiology: The new synthesis.* Cambridge: Harvard University Press.

JOHN C. MESSENGER*

Sex and Repression in an Irish Folk Community

In this chapter I will discuss sexual repression—its manifestations in behavior and beliefs, its causes, its inculcation, and its broader historical and cultural implications—in a small island community of the Gaeltacht that I will call Inis Beag.[1] My wife and I conducted enthographic research there for nineteen months, between 1958 and 1966, which included a one-year stay and eight other visits of from one to seven weeks—at Christmas or during the summer. Ours is the only holistic enthographic study of this community, although archeologists, linguists, philologists, folklorists, geographers, anthropometricians, and other scientists have undertaken research there for over a century. We collected a large body of culture and personality data on three other Irish islands for the purposes of making comparisons and testing hypotheses concerning culture and personality concomitants of island living. Ins Beag is ideally suited to ethnographic and folklore research in that its population possesses a tradition which is less acculturated than that of any other local Irish group.

According to anthropological definition (Lewis 1960: 1–2), the islanders qualify as folk people in almost every respect. The community has maintained its stability for at least 200 years; there is a strong bond between the peasants and their land, and agriculture provides them with the major source of their livelihood; production is mainly for subsistence and is carried on with a simple technology, using the digging stick, spade, and scythe as primary implements; the island folk participate in a money economy, but barter still persists; a low standard of living prevails, and the birth rate is high; the family is of central importance, and marriage figures prominently as a provision of economic welfare; the island is integrated into the country and national governments and is subject to their laws; the people have long been exposed to urban influences and have borrowed cultural forms from other rural areas on the mainland, integrating them into a relatively stable system; and, finally, the experience of living under English rule for centuries has created in islanders an attitude of dependence on—yet hostility toward—government which continues to this day. The only conditions in Inis Beag which run counter to those found in most other peasant communities are low death and illiteracy rates and bilateral, rather than unilineal, descent (although inheritance is patrilineal).

Inis Beag culture also characterizes people of nearby islands, and the traditions of the several together might be regarded as forming a subculture of the total Irish system. Many island customs are shared with rural peasants on the mainland (where numerous regional subcultures exist), and some are part of a broader European matrix. The island has experienced considerable cultural change since the establishment of the Congested Districts Board (forerunner of the Gaeltacht) in 1891 and the growth of tourism in this century. But conditions there still approximate those which must have prevailed two generations ago, throughout this region of peasant Ireland.

Inis Beag has a population of approximately 350 persons living in seventy-one "cottages" distributed among four settlements, called "villages." Bordering a "strand" and a large tract of common land on the northeastern side of the island are a series of limestone terraces, separated by water-bearing shales and faced by small cliffs, on which the villages are situated. Most of the arable land is found on this side, where the shales have been broken down by weathering and alien soils deposited by wind and by ice of the Weichsel glacier. Over many generations, the islanders have deepened these soils and created new soils on rock surfaces by adding seaweed, sand, and human manure. On the southwestern side of Inis Beag, known as the "back of the island," limestone pavements slope rather evenly, almost as the gentle dip of the strata, from the crest of the highest terrace to the sea, a mile away. The bared surfaces are intersected in all directions by crevices, which contain a large portion of the natural flora—herbs and shrubs—of the island. Stone fences delimit many hundreds of plots which compose most of the two-square-mile land surface of Inis Beag.

*A grant from the Indiana University Ford International Program enabled me to write this chapter.

[1] For other reports on Inis Beag, consult Messenger 1962, 1968, and 1969.

The island boasts a post office with radio-telephone facilities, a "national school" in which three teachers instruct ninety pupils in the seven "standards," two provision shops with attached "pubs," a former coast guard station now housing the nurse and a knitting industry which employs local girls, a lighthouse, and a chapel served by a curate who resides nearby. Inis Beag lacks electricity and running water, and the only vehicles are several ass-drawn carts which are able to travel the narrow, fence-bordered trails. A small "steamer" carrying supplies, passengers, and mail to and from a mainland port visits the island at least once each week. That Inis Beag has experienced far less cultural change than other island communities of Ireland is largely due to the fact that, in the absence of a deep water quay, the steamer has had to stand off the strand and be met by "canoes." Most of the tourists who come to the island stay only for the hours that the steamer is anchored and go ashore mainly for the thrill of riding in the canoes, which the island men row with consummate skill. Insofar as I can discover, the inhabitants of Inis Beag are less prone to visit the mainland than are the peoples of other Irish islands.

INIS BEAG HISTORY AND CULTURE[2]

The prehistory and history of Inis Beag are recorded dramatically in a multitude of monuments and artifacts of stone and metal, including Neolithic axe-heads and kitchen middens, Copper-Bronze Age gallery grave tombs and burial mounds of earth and stone, an Iron Age promontory fort, and medieval Christian monasteries, churches, cemeteries, stone houses, and a sacred well, as well as a three-story tower house built by the political overlords of the island. Irish nativists claim that the contemporary folk are lineal descendants of ancient, once civilized Celts. But local legend, historical evidence, and genealogical data collected by my wife and me indicate that the present population is descended from immigrants who came to the island from many parts of Ireland following the Cromwellian incursion of the seventeenth century. The islanders still express bitterness over conditions of poverty and servitude experienced by their ancestors during the 300 years that they lived under absentee Anglo-Irish landlords. All of the excesses of foreign domination suffered by mainland peasants were suffered by the inhabitants of Inis Beag, but were aggravated by the ordinary hardships of island living. Little was known about events in

---

[2]The culture described herein is that of 1959–1960 and excludes important changes which have occurred since then, such as those resulting from the introduction of television, a summer language school for pupils from the mainland, and free secondary education.

Inis Beag during the eighteenth and early nineteenth centuries until the island was visited by archeologists and publicized in their scientific writings. The surrounding area of the mainland was very much isolated and seldom visited at that time, although trading between Inis Beag and nearby communities was carried on, and passing ships sometimes called at the island.

Agricultural pursuits have always dominated the subsistence economy of Inis Beag. Most householders own land on which they grow potatoes and other vegetables, grass, and sometimes rye and sally rods and where they pasture cattle, sheep, goats, asses, and horses. The back of the island, behind the communities, is divided into four strips, and each landowner possesses numerous plots located along the "quarter" on which his village fronts. The average combined holding is sixteen acres, and almost 50 percent of the land is composed of arable indigenous and manufactured soils. Potatoes are the staple crop, and they are supplemented by various other vegetables, milk from cattle and goats, meat from island sheep, fish, eggs, and other foods, many of which are imported and sold in the shops. Rye is grown for thatching, and sally rods are used to weave several types of containers. Other subsistence activities (which also provide income for some folk) are knitting, weaving, crocheting, tailoring, and sandal making.

A slowly expanding cash economy features the export of cattle and sheep fattened on the island and of surplus potatoes and fish, the collection of seaweed for extraction of iodine at a mainland factory, the keeping of tourists in private homes, and the manufacturing of craft objects for sale to visitors and for export. At the turn of the century, fishing from canoes—with nets and lines often many miles out in the ocean—was an important subsistence and income activity. A few islanders who owned little or no land lived primarily by fishing and kelp-making. But over the past few decades, fish have become less plentiful and the weather more inclement, especially during winter months; less than a dozen crews now fish regularly, and most fish are consumed locally rather than exported. Government subsidies of many sorts and remittances from relatives who have emigrated supplement the cash economy. The government further aids the islanders by not collecting "rates" and by setting low rents on land. Income information is as difficult to come by as data on sex, disputes, and pagan religious retentions; since the people do not wish to jeopardize their unemployment benefits (most of them receive the "dole") and old age pensions and fear taxation in the future, they are secretive about sources and amounts of income.

More important than the formal political structure of Inis Beag are the local informal system and social control techniques of gossip, ridicule, satire, and the like. Crime is rare in Inis Beag, and there are no "guards" stationed there. The island is seldom visited by politicians, and many inhabitants are either apathetic or antagonistic toward the county and national governments. Those asked to account for their antigovernment attitude cite widespread nepotism and corruption among officials, the slight differences between the platforms of the two major parties, and "foolish" government schemes in Inis Beag—usually instituted without consulting the islanders. Government aid is sought and even expected as a "right," but it is seldom considered adequate. Taxation in any form, especially of tobacco and stout, is bitterly opposed.

The informal political system is dominated by the curate, the "headmaster" of the national school, and a self-appointed local "king." In the past, the amount of influence exerted by curates has varied; some have been concerned mostly with fulfilling spiritual responsibilities, while others have attacked by sermon, threat, and even physical action such activities as courting, dancing, visiting, gossiping, and drinking spirits. Anticlerical sentiment (seldom manifested in overt acts) is as strong as, or stronger than, its antigovernment counterpart. The clergy are said to interfere too much in secular affairs, to live too "comfortably," to be absent from the island too often, and to act overly aloof and supercilious. The most outspoken anticlerics assert that curates have employed informers, allocated indulgences, withheld the sacraments, and placed curses ("reading the Bible at") in their efforts to regulate the secular life of Inis Beag. The headmaster, appointed and rigidly supervised by the parish priest and curate, presides over social events and serves as an adviser to the islanders in many matters, in addition to carrying out his official duties.

Inis Beag lacks a class system, and the status symbols which affect human relationships are few. There is, in fact, little difference in the style of life between the most and the least prosperous of the islanders. The web of kinship rather than the possession of status attributes, for the most part, determines who will interact with whom and in what manner. Land and money are the principal symbols, with formal education and influential relatives (particularly priests, nuns, and teachers), on the mainland and abroad, becoming more important. Two generations ago, strength, courage, economic skills, and musical and storytelling abilities were highly regarded as well, but acculturation has lessened their significance.

Although there are fifty-nine nuclear families, only thirteen surnames exist today. There is much inbreeding, as might be expected, and the church carefully checks the genealogies of prospective spouses to ascertain their degree of consanguinity. Courtship is almost nonexistent, and most marriages are arranged with little concern for the desires of the young people involved. Late marriage and celibacy are as prevalent in Inis Beag as elsewhere in Ireland. The average marriage age for men is thirty-six and for women twenty-five, and 29 percent of those

persons eligible for marriage are single.[3] The functions of the family are mainly economic and reproductive, and conjugal love is extremely rare. A sharp dichotomy exists between the sexes; both before and after marriage men interact mostly with men and women with women. The average family has seven offspring, and many women are unhappy about being forced by the unauthorized decree of local priests to produce as many children as possible. They feel that the constant bearing and rearing of offspring increase their work, restrict their freedom, and perpetuate the poverty of their families. Jealousy of the greater freedom of men is commonly expressed by women who have many young children. Mothers bestow a considerable amount of attention and affection on their offspring, especially on their sons. However, tensions between fathers and sons which develop in childhood often flare into scarcely repressed hostility later on, particularly in those families where competition for the inheritance of property is engendered among siblings by the fathers' attempts to ensure favored treatment in old age.

Men are far more active socially than are women. The latter are restricted by custom mostly to visiting, attending parties during the winter, and participating in church-associated activities. Many women leave their cottages only to attend mass, wakes, and funerals or to make infrequent calls on relatives; my wife and I talked with some elderly women who had not visited other villages or walked to the back of the island for thirty or more years. Men not only attend parties with their womenfolk but go to dances during the summer, frequent the pubs, play cards almost nightly during November and December (the period when once people congregated to hear storytellers), visit the homes of kin and friends or meet along the trails at night, and range the entire island and the sea about it in their economic pursuits. Before the age of benevolent government, women shared many

[3]Twenty-nine percent of those islanders of marriageable age are single. This rises to a high of 37 percent among first and second generation Inis Beag emigrants, indicating the actions of more than just economic causes. Irish scholars, for obvious reasons, tend to stress economic and other (climate, race, English oppression, the famine, loss of the Irish tongue, etc.) monistic causes in their analyses of culture and personality phenomena. Inadequate statistics for second and third generation migrants from Inis Beag suggest that the celibacy rate lowers markedly only when descendants of immigrants dissociate themselves from Irish ethnic communities and Irish-American priests. Ethnographic research is sorely needed among Irish of several generations in the countries to which they have migrated to probe this and other phenomena.

economic tasks with men, such as collecting seaweed, baiting lines, and gutting fish. But now they tend to household chores and only milk cows and perform some of the lighter farming jobs with their fathers and husbands.

The island folk are devout Catholics, despite the fact that they are critical of their priests and hold pagan religious beliefs. Youth of Inis Beag overtly disallow the existence of other than church-approved supernatural entities. However, their elders cling to traditional pagan beliefs and practices (many of which are Druidic in origin) about which they are extremely secretive for fear of being ridiculed by outsiders and their more skeptical neighbors. The non-Christian array of spiritual beings includes various spirits and demons, ghosts, witches, phantom ships, and animals and material objects possessing human attributes and volitions. Prominent among the spirits thought to inhabit Inis Beag are the trooping and solitary fairies, sea creatures, mermaids, and the banshee. The most formidable of the demons is a pooka which lives in a Bronze Age burial mound and roams the strand and common land at night altering its shape and size at will; during the day it will twist the limbs of unwary persons who choose the hill for a resting place. Ghosts, called "shades," are frequently seen after dark performing economic tasks. They are thought to be doing penance in purgatory, which embraces the earth as well as a spiritual locus; this is one example of the many reinterpretations of Christian and pagan belief effected by the islanders. The only form of witchcraft practiced together is the casting of the evil eye. At least three persons, suitably ostracized, are believed to be able to perpetrate evil by the act of complimenting their victims. Other religious retentions found in Inis Beag are a multitude of taboos, divination through the seeking of omens, magical charms and incantations of a protective nature, and an emphasis on "natural" foods, folk medicines, and other products impinging on the human body.

It is believed by many people in Ireland that the Catholicism of the islanders embodies an ideal unattained on the mainland, where the faith is thought to set an example for the world. In fact, the worship of the folk is obsessively oriented toward salvation in the next world, with a corresponding preoccupation with sin in this world; there is a resemblance to polytheism in the manner in which they relate to the Blessed Virgin and Irish saints; Christian as well as pagan rituals and religious artifacts are often employed to serve magical ends; and many beliefs that they hold to be orthodox Catholic are in reality idiosyncratic to Inis Beag or Ireland. Christian morality in its "outward" manifestation is realized to a remarkable degree. This can be attributed, in part, to the emphasis placed on good works as a means of gaining salvation; but, more importantly, it results from the already-mentioned techniques of so-cial control exercised by the clergy, based on an overwhelming fear of damnation.

RESEARCH PROCEDURES

The most active researchers in Inis Beag have been folklorists. Although ethnology as a discipline is not represented in the national universities and elsewhere in the Republic, folklore in the European humanistic tradition is strongly developed. The deliberate recording of the immense body of Irish folklore, folk beliefs, and folk customs began in the early part of the last century, was spurred by nativism—of which the Gaelic Revival was the main strand, and was institutionalized in the Republic with the formation of, first, the Folklore of Ireland Society in 1926, then the Irish Folklore Institute in 1930, and, finally, the Irish Folklore Commission in 1936 (Delargy 1957). For many years, commission collectors have visited Inis Beag, recording mostly the verbal art and material traits—with their associated behavior—of the island folk. They have not attempted to describe and analyze functionally and dynamically the total culture of the island; their visits have been brief and intermittent; they have depended on a limited sample of respondents; and most of their queries have been guided by Sean O'Suillaebhain's *A Handbook of Irish Folklore*, which does not contain numerous categories of significance to anthropologists.

My wife and I devoted most of our research to documenting the contemporary culture of Inis Beag: its economic, political, social, religious, esthetic, and recreational aspects. We also described formal and informal education and the personality traits formed by it, reconstructed Inis Beag history of the past century by examining historical materials of many types and probing the memories of aged island respondents, and recorded cultural change in process over an eight-year period. The standard ethnographic research techniques that we employed included guided and open-ended interviews, external and participant observation, collection of life histories, cross-checking, photography, and phonography. The sample for much of our data was the total universe of 350 inhabitants.

It is extremely difficult to obtain information in Inis Beag about such matters as amounts and sources of income, disputes, pagan religious retentions and reinterpretations, and sex. This brief list might be increased by at least threefold and gives rise to a consideration of the problems associated with obtaining reliable data from the Irish in general and the islanders in particular. Honor Tracy, in the first chapter (aptly entitled "Forebodings") of her book, *Mind You I've Said Nothing*, humorously presents one of the shortest, yet most discerning analyses of Irish national character yet written by a novelist and predicts the various reactions that her volume will evoke in Irish readers.[4] She concludes with the following remarks about the difficulties surrounding fact finding in Ireland:

> This question of fact was another of the spectres hovering in my path. In every book there should be a fact here and there or the writer is charged with aimless frivolity. But facts in Ireland are very peculiar things. They are rarely allowed to spoil the sweep and low of conversation: the crabbing effect they have on good talk is eliminated almost entirely. I do not believe myself that the Irishman conveniently ignores their existence, as sometimes is said, so much as that he is blithely unaware of it. He soars above their uninviting surfaces on the wing of his fancy. Who then would answer my questions truthfully, who would supply me with that modicum of sober and accurate information required to give my book a serious air? No one, as far as I know. And if facts are elusive and shadowy things in Ireland, opinions are more so. An Irishman, sober, will say not what he thinks but what he believes you would like him to think; he is a man of honeyed words, anxious to flatter and soothe, cajole and caress. When he has taken a jar or two . . . he will say whatever he judges will give the greatest offence. In neither case does he reveal his own true thoughts if, to be sure, he has any. He would be in dread lest you quoted him and the story went round and he got the name of a bold outspoken fellow, which might be bad for business. And then again so many Irishmen find an innocent glee in misleading and deceiving for its own sake. Obfuscation is the rule, and while it may seem a little foolish at times, there is no doubt that it makes for a great deal of fun. It cultivates too a sharpness of ear, a feeling for half-tones and shades and subtleties, and a wary alertness that would be worth its weight in gold should one ever be lost in a jungle (Tracy 1953: 20–21).

I will not concern myself with the various cultural and psychological causes accounting for this state of affairs, which would require an essay equal in length to this one. Suffice it to say, the quotation in considerable measure applies to interviewing in Inis Beag, where my wife and I took great pains to disentangle real from ideal culture by substantiating interview data with observation, wherever possible. The existence of the conditions depicted by Tracy, as well as the numerous cultural practices shrouded in secrecy, led us to return to the island several times after 1960 before attempting an ethnography, to emphasize various modes of participant observation in order to gain added rapport, to devise ad hoc research methods of an unorthodox nature,[5] to "hone" our orthodox tools and employ cross-checking techniques at every stage of our research, and to cultivate that "sharpness of ear . . . feeling for half-tones and shades and subtleties, and . . . wary alertness" which characterize ethnographic endeavor as an art as well as an epistemology.

The use by the folk of "wings of fancy," "honeyed words," and "obfuscations"—popularly known as "blarney"—reflects a long tradition of verbal skill. It is a vital component of Irish and Inis Beag "charm," which often is a product of a delicately poised set of defense mechanisms; beneath it can lie feelings of inferiority and dislike, envy, and jealousy of others. Blarney can very effectively serve to shield genuine thoughts and feelings and thus protect the ego. Irish folklore and literature also reflect this tradition of verbal skill, and it is probably expressed most formidably in James Joyce's *Ulysses* and *Finnegan's Wake*. (At least one folklorist has collected "Joycean utterances" from Irish peasants.)

Most of our information came from observation and unguided interviews. It proved impossible to take field notes openly, except when collecting innocuous data–such as the number of livestock owned by each householder—from a few particular persons. Thus, we were forced to limit our visits to less than two hours, after which we immediately transcribed what our combined memories could resuscitate. Despite frequent explanations of our presence in Inis Beag, which were candid and truthful, it was thought by the islanders that I was interested only in archeological sites and oral literature, and that my wife was not a trained and experienced co-worker; this, obviously, reflects their previous experiences with scientists and their conception of

---

[4]These reactions appear to be institutionalized, as my writings and conversational remarks have also evoked them. Two additional responses that I have encountered are: my conclusions are invalidated because I failed to consult certain "source materials" written in Gaelic, and my inferior writing style precludes serious consideration of my findings. I take pains to explain, usually in vain, the many methods of fieldwork utilized by ethnographers to Irish persons who are critical of my data and who invariably use the phrase, "You can't trust what an Irishman tells you." On a rare occasion, one listener to my lengthy explanation said, "Ah, you're cuter than we are"—a compliment indeed!

[5]Departures from methodological orthodoxy were our use, as projective devices, of literary works and a ballad that I composed. Islanders read at our request books about Inis Beag, and we recorded and analyzed their responses. The ballad that I wrote, now embedded in the local verbal art tradition, is based on a shipwreck and rescue that we witnessed, and a series of fascinating events which ensued during the following months. The manner of its composition, the alteration of it by Inis Beag singers after it was written, and the circumstances surrounding its public presentation by various balladeers before differing audiences gave us invaluable ethnographic insights.

the position of women in society. Their inability to evaluate adequately our intentions proved to be a research boon. For once "accepted" (a relative term, since no outsider is ever accepted) after many months in the island, we were allowed to listen to and participate in conversations and activities from which we would otherwise have been excluded.

Our data on sex came from my involvement as a participant-observer in personal and often intimate conversations with men and my wife's counseling of women who were bothered by such matters as explaining and coping with menstruation, menopause, mental illness, the sexual curiosity of their children, and "excessive" sexual demands of their spouses. Our sexual knowledge and sympathy coupled with their needs and inquisitiveness gave rise to a "counselor-client" relationship between many of the folk and ourselves. They came to speak freely, albeit indirectly at times, with each of us about this sphere of behavior which arouses so much anxiety and fear. I must mention that the relationship arose partly out of our desire to alleviate distress and not solely to collect information. We had performed the same role seven years earlier among primitive Nigerians, and for similar reasons. However, the Africans were uninhibited, talked freely with us about sex, and were not offended by what we subsequently wrote.

Another important source of information on sex was the island nurses, who supplied us with accounts of their own observations over an eight-year period and gave us access to pertinent medical records. My wife and I believe that our information is, for the most part, reliable, but that some of it may well be erroneous. This report will, we are afraid, offend and alienate some of our Inis Beag friends, for whom we hold deep affection; they do not comprehend the aims and values of anthropology and may regard our reporting of sexual beliefs and behavior as a breach of friendship and trust. Certainly our findings will be denied by many Irish readers.

More than any other type of research, culture and personality investigations are needed in Ireland today. Social and cultural anthropologists, rural sociologists, folklorists, and geographers in small numbers have managed to describe and analyze the major sociocultural forms of the Irish folk, but personality generalizations, by and large, have been the by-products of research into other areas and have tended to be impressionistic. Some of the most penetrating studies of Irish character have been made "at a distance" and through the analysis of projective systems and narrow units of culture, such as drinking patterns (Bales 1962). Some Irish writers—"intuitive anthropologists" I call them—also have had insightful things to say about Irish character (usually at a distance too, from church and state). What is sorely needed is a holistic community study done by a culture and personality specialist—a person skilled not only in ethnography, social psychology, and psychiatry (and able to administer

projective tests), but well versed in Irish history, literature, and contemporary affairs as well.

SEXUAL REPRESSION: ITS MANIFESTATIONS

Both lack of sexual knowledge and misconceptions about sex among adults combine to brand Inis Beag as one of the most sexually naive of the world's societies. Sex never is discussed in the home when children are about; only three mothers admitted giving advice, briefly and incompletely, to their daughters. We were told that boys are better advised than girls, but that the former learn about sex informally from older boys and men and from observing animals. Most respondents who were questioned about sexual instructions given to youths expressed the belief that "after marriage nature takes its course," thus negating the need for anxiety-creating and embarrassing personal confrontation of parents and offspring. We were unable to discover any cases of childlessness based on sexual ignorance of spouses, as reported from other regions of peasant Ireland. Also, we were unable to discover knowledge of the sexual categories utilized by researchers in sex: insertion of tongue while kissing, male mouth on female breast, female hand on penis, cunnilingus, fellatio, fem-oral coitus, anal coitus, extramarital coitus, manifest homosexuality, sexual contact with animals, fetishism, and sado-masochistic behavior. Some of these activities may be practiced by particular individuals and couples; however, without a doubt they are deviant forms in Inis Beag, about which information is difficult to come by.

Menstruation and menopause arouse profound misgivings among women of the island, because few of them comprehend their physiological significance. My wife was called on to explain these processes more than any other phenomena related to sex. When they reach puberty, most girls are unprepared for the first menstrual flow and find the experience a traumatic one—especially when their mothers are unable to provide a satisfactory explanation for it. And it is commonly believed that the menopause can induce "madness"; in order to ward off this condition, some women have retired from life in their mid-forties and, in a few cases, have confined themselves to bed until death, years later. Others have so retired as a result of depressive and masochistic states. Yet the harbingers of "insanity" are simply the physical symptoms announcing the onset of menopause. In Inis Beag, these include severe headaches, hot flashes, faintness in crowds and enclosed places, and severe anxiety. Mental illness is also held to be inherited or caused by inbreeding (or by the Devil, by God punishing a sinner, or by malignant pagan beings) and stigmatizes the family of the afflicted. One old man came close to revealing what is probably the major cause of neuroses and psychoses in Ireland, when he explained the incarceration of an Inis Beag curate in a mental institution for clerics as caused by his constant association with a pretty housekeeper, who "drove him mad from frustration." This elder advocated that only plain-appearing older women (who would not "gab" to "our man") be chosen for the task. Earlier, according to island opinion, the same priest had caused to be committed to the "madhouse" a local man who publicly challenged certain of his actions. The unfortunate man was released six months later, as per law, since he was not mentally ill.

Sexual misconceptions are myriad in Inis Beag. The islanders share with most Western peoples the belief that men by nature are far more libidinous than women. The latter have been taught by some curates and in the home that sexual relations with their husbands are a "duty" which must be "endured," for to refuse coitus is a mortal sin. A frequently encountered assertion affixes the guilt for male sexual strivings on the enormous intake of potatoes of the Inis Beag male. (In Nigeria, among the people whom my wife and I studied, women are thought to be more sexually disposed than men and are the repositories of sexual knowledge; it is they who initiate coitus and so pose a threat to their spouses. Nigerian men place the blame on clitoridectomy performed just prior to marriage.) Asked to compare the sexual proclivities of Inis Beag men and women, one mother of nine said, "Men can wait a long time before wanting 'it,' but we can wait a lot longer." There is much evidence to indicate that the female orgasm is unknown—or at least doubted, or considered a deviant response. One middle-aged bachelor, who considers himself wise in the ways of the outside world and has a reputation for making love to willing tourists, described one girl's violent bodily reactions to his fondling and asked for an explanation; when told the "facts of life" of what obviously was an orgasm, he admitted not realizing that women also could achieve a climax, although he was aware that some of them apparently enjoyed kissing and being handled.

Inis Beag men feel that sexual intercourse is debilitating, a common belief in primitive and folk societies. They will desist from sex the night before they are to perform a job which will require the expenditure of great energy. Women are not approached sexually during menstruation or for months after childbirth, since they are considered "dangerous" to the male at these times. Returned "Yanks" have been denounced from the pulpit for describing American sexual practices to island youths, and such "pornographic" magazines as *Time* and *Life*, mailed by kin from abroad, have aroused curates to spirited sermon and instruction.

The separation of the sexes, started within the family, is augmented by separation in almost all segments of adolescent and adult activity. Boys and girls are separated to some extent in classrooms, and completely in recess play and movement to and from school. During church services, there is a further separation of adult men and women, as well as boys and girls, and each of the four groups leaves the chapel in its turn. The pubs are frequented only by men or by women tourists and female teachers who have spent several years on the mainland while training and thus are "set apart" (and, of course, by inquisitive female ethnographers). Women occasionally visit the shops to procure groceries, but it is more common for them to send their children to do so, since supplies and drinks are proffered across the same counter, and men are usually to be found on the premises. Even on the strand during summer months, male tourists tend to bathe at one end and women at the other. Some swimmers "daringly" change into bathing suits there, under towels and dresses—a custom practiced elsewhere in Ireland which has overtones of sexual catharsis.

It is often asserted that the major "escape value" of sexual frustration among single persons in Ireland is masturbation; frustration-aggression theorists, however, would stress the ubiquity of drinking, alcoholism, disputes, and pugnacity as alternative outlets. Pugnacity can also be linked to the widespread problem of male identity. Our study revealed that male masturbation in Inis Beag seems to be common, premarital coitus unknown, and marital copulation limited as to foreplay and the manner of consummation. My wife and I never witnessed courting—"walking out"—in the island. Elders proudly insist that it does not occur, but male youths admit to it in rumor. The claims of young men focus on "petting" with tourists and a few local girls, whom the "bolder" of them kiss and fondle outside of their clothing. Island girls, it is held by their "lovers," do not confess these sins because they fail to experience pleasure from the contact. The male perpetrators also shun the confessional because of their fear of the priest.

We were unable to determine the frequency of marital coitus. A considerable amount of evidence indicates that privacy in the act is stressed and that foreplay is limited to kissing and rough fondling of the lower body, especially the buttocks. Sexual activity invariably is initiated by the husband. Only the male superior position is employed; intercourse takes place with underclothes not removed; and orgasm, for the man, is achieved quickly, almost immediately after which he falls asleep. (I must stress the provisional nature of these data, for they are based on a limited sample of respondents and relate to that area of sexual behavior least freely discussed.)

Many kinds of behavior disassociated from sex in other societies, such as nudity and physiological evacuation, are considered sexual in Inis Beag. Nudity is abhorred by the islanders, and the consequences of this attitude are numerous and significant for health and survival. Only infants have their entire bodies sponged once a week, on Saturday night; children, adolescents, and adults, on the same night, wash only their faces, necks, lower arms, hands, lower legs, and feet. Several times my wife and I created intense embarrassment by entering a room in which a man had just finished his weekly ablutions and was barefooted; once when this occurred, the man hurriedly pulled on his stockings and said with obvious relief, "Sure, it's good to get your clothes on again." Clothing always is changed in private, sometimes within the secrecy of the bedcovers, and it is usual for the islanders to sleep in their underclothes.

Despite the fact that Inis Beag men spend much of their time at sea in their canoes, as far as we could determine none of them can swim. Four rationales are given for this deficiency: the men are confident that nothing will happen to them, because they are excellent seamen and weather forecasters; a man who cannot swim will be more careful; it is best to drown immediately when a canoe capsizes far out in the ocean rather than swim futilely for minutes or even hours, thus prolonging the agony; and, finally, "When death is on a man, he can't be saved." The truth of the matter is that they have never dared to bare their bodies in order to learn the skill. Some women claim to have "bathed" at the back of the island during the heat of summer, but this means wading in small pools with skirts held knee-high, in complete privacy. Even the nudity of household pets can arouse anxiety, particularly when they are sexually aroused during time of heat. In some homes, dogs are whipped for licking their genitals and soon learn to indulge in this practice outdoors. My wife, who can perform Irish step-dances and sing many of the popular folk songs, was once requested to sing a seldom-heard American Western ballad; she chose "The Lavender Cowboy," who "had only two hairs on his chest." The audience response was perfunctory and, needless to say, she never again was "called out" to sing that particular song.

The drowning of seamen, who might have saved themselves had they been able to swim, is not the only result of the sexual symbolism of nudity; men who were unwilling to face the nurse when ill, because it might have meant baring their bodies to her, were beyond help when finally treated. While my wife and I were on the island, a nurse was assaulted by the mother of a young man for diagnosing his illness and bathing his chest in the mother's absence. (In this case, Oedipal and sexual attitudes probably were at work in tandem.)

It must be pointed out that nudity is also shunned for "health" reasons, for another obtrusive Inis Beag character trait is hypochondria. In some cases, however, it is hard to determine whether concern with modesty or health is dominant in a particular behavioral response. Fear of colds and influenza is foremost among health concerns; rheumatism and related muscular joint ailments, migraine headaches and other psychosomatic dis-

orders, tooth decay, indigestion ("nervous stomach"), and hypermetropia are other widespread pathologies which cause worry among the folk—not to mention those of supernatural origin.

Secrecy surrounds the acts of urination and defecation. The evacuation of infants before siblings and strangers is discouraged, and animals that discharge in the house are driven out. Chickens that habitually "dirty" their nests while setting are soon killed and eaten. Although some women drink spirits privately, they seldom do so at parties. In part this is because of the embarrassment involved in visiting the outside toilet with men in the "street" looking on. One of the most carefully guarded secrets of Inis Beag, unreported in the many works describing island culture, is the use of human manure mixed with sand as a fertilizer. We were on the island eight months before we discovered that compost is not "street drippings" and "scraw," but decomposed feces. With "turf" becoming more difficult to procure from the mainland, some islanders have taken to importing coal and processed peat and burning cattle dung. The dung is prepared for use in difficult-to-reach plots at the back of the island when tourists are few in number; it is burned covertly because of the overtones of sex and poverty. Another custom that my wife and I learned of late in our research, due to the secrecy surrounding it, concerns the thickening of wool; men are required to urinate in a container and tread the wool therein with their bare feet.

Other major manifestations of sexual repression in Inis Beag are the lack of a "dirty joke" tradition (at least as the term is understood by ethnologists and folklorists) and the style of dancing, which allows little bodily contact among participants. I have heard men use various verbal devices—innuendoes, puns, and asides—that they believed bore sexual connotations; relatively speaking, they were pallid. In the song that I composed, one line of a verse refers to an island bachelor arising late in the day after "dreaming perhaps of a beautiful mate"; this is regarded as a highly suggestive phrase, and I have seen it redden cheeks and lower glances in a pub. Both step- and set-dancing are practiced in Inis Beag, although the former type is dying out. This rigid-body dancing, from which sex is removed by shifting attention below the hips, appears to have originated in Ireland during the early nineteenth century. The set patterns keep partners separated most of the time; but, even so, some girls refuse to dance, because it involves touching a boy. Inis Beag men, while watching a woman step-dance, stare fixedly at her feet, and they take pains to appear indifferent when crowding at a party necessitates holding women on their laps and rubbing against them when moving from room to room. But they are extremely sensitive, nevertheless, to the entire body of the dancer and to these casual contacts, as are the women. Their covert emotional reactions (which become overt as much drink is taken) are a form of catharsis.

SEXUAL REPRESSION: ITS HISTORICAL CAUSES

Analysts of Irish character have put forth various hypotheses to account for sexual repression, ranging from the sophisticated to the absurd. The former can be classified under three rubrics: historical (e.g., the influence of ascetic monasticism, Augustinianism, and Jansenism), sociocultural (e.g., the Oedipus complex in the Irish family and male solidarity), and psychological (e.g., masochism). Beyond serious scientific consideration are such hypotheses as the loss of the Irish tongue, lack of a Catholic aristocracy, fear of Protestant libertinism, and the ever-appealed-to factors of race, climate, and the famine. In the following paragraphs, I will quote excerpts from Irish authors and from critical observers of the Irish scene, including social scientists, rather than dissect their views myself.

Paul Blanshard, in his polemical but insightful (and, in my estimation, often understated) work, *The Irish and Catholic Power*, says that "whatever the explanation, the total sexual expression of the Irish people is much less than it is in other countries, and that the Catholic crusade against normal sexual life has actually created a nation of men and women who try to drown their fundamental instincts." In attempting to account for sexual repression on such a scale, he writes:

> Ireland was . . . one of the world's most ascetic countries, and the monastic ideal has undoubtedly left a deep mark on the Irish mind. Although Irish priests were permitted to have wives as late as the eighth century, sexual renunciation came to be identified with virtue and distinction in the community, and thousands of the best men and women lived apart from each other. Kevin Devlin in his Christus Rex article on "Single and Selfish" . . . says of the ancient Irish that "when they 'fell in love with Christianity' . . . they took to the ideal of virginity with a Pauline enthusiasm unknown elsewhere. St. Patrick himself noted this with an inflection of surprise in the *Confessions* . . ." (Blanshard 1954: 160–161).

Several Irish scholars since 1955 have expressed the opinion in personal conversations that the rapidity of Irish conversion to monasticism in the early medieval period can be attributed, in large measure, to masochism. This ancient character trait is most evident in the projective system of early Irish verbal art, if one discounts the possibility of widespread distortion through the actions of Celtic defense mechanisms and later revisionists.

In a recent book, the impact of Augustinianism at this time and in the centuries to come is examined by Fr. Alexander Humphreys. He says in *New Dubliners*:

> The specific doctrinal tradition to which Ireland and the Irish countryman in particular has fallen heir is the Augustinian.

. . . [It] lays relatively greater emphasis on the weakness and evil to which human nature is prone as the result of original sin. By the same token, it attributes relatively less efficacy to natural knowledge and human action and relatively more validity to God's revelation and more power to the action of God's grace. . . . [The] Irish countryman has acquired a more than average distrust of native human reason. As a Catholic he cannot and does not deny the validity of rational thought, but he tends to be quite suspicious of the pride of the mind and so wary of ultimate rationalism that he shies away from reasoned discussions of high truths. . . . The tradition he inherits tends toward a certain historical and theological positivism in regard to the major truths and values of life, and, together with other historical factors, has led him to an intensified reliance upon the teaching power of the Church as voiced by the clergy. At the same time, while appreciating the need for positive good works, he is inclined to place relatively greater emphasis on those which are directly concerned with obtaining grace and relatively lesser store by simple ethical behaviour. And finally, although he is certain that man's bodily nature with its emotions is at root good, he is rather more suspicious of it and deals with it somewhat more severely. As a result he inclines to a jaundiced view of sex and a generally ascetic outlook which places a high premium upon continence, penance and, in most spheres of life, on abstemiousness (Humphreys 1966: 25–26).

Humphreys further points out that "the effects of the religious tradition of the Irish, let alone of the countryman, upon the social behavior and attitudes of the people has never been systematically studied from a sociological point of view." He notes that the classic study, *Family and Community in Ireland*, by Conrad Arensberg and Solon Kimball, based on research done over thirty years ago, "leaves the matter virtually untouched," and "attributes the countryman's attitude towards sex almost exclusively to the structure of life in the rural community."

> Granted the profound influence social structure has on such a basic matter, a purely structural-functional analysis is hard put to explain adequately the quite ascetic sexual morality of the Irish countryside. . . . [An] attitude similar to that of the countryman is far from uncommon in a city such as Dublin—and among new Dubliners and Old Dubliners to boot—whose social structure differs so radically from that of the countryside. Structural-functional explanations of attitudes do hold up to a point. But world-views and their ethical consequences also have their special effect (Humphreys 1966: 24–27).

Monasticism and Augustinianism certainly "set the stage" for later Jansenism, although all three probably are connected with basic Irish culture and personality traits of long standing.

Jansenism is succinctly placed in its historical context in Ireland by Joe McCarthy.

Like most everything in Ireland, the severe strictness of the old-time Catholic clergymen was rooted in historical events of the country's past. During the dark era of the anti-Catholic Penal Laws in the 18th Century, young Irishmen had to study for the priesthood on the Continent. In the early 1790's, the British Government became alarmed by the rise of Theobald Wolfe Tone's Irish Protestant revolutionary movement and made hurried bids of appeasement to Irish Catholics in an effort to win their loyalty. One of these conciliatory moves was the establishment of the Catholic theological seminary at Maynooth in 1795. Perhaps not entirely by accident, the faculty of the new college was staffed by refugees from the French Revolution, promonarchy theologians who hated Tone's republican ideas. Most of these theologians had been influenced by Jansenism—the rigid and gloomy doctrine, denounced as Calvinistic by the Jesuits, that man is a helplessly doomed being who must endure punishing soul-searching and rigorous penances to prove his love of God. Mere faith and constant church-going . . . are not enough to win salvation. . . . Thanks to the influence of the French theologians at Maynooth, most of the Irish Catholic hierarchy sided with the British against Tone in the rebellion of 1798, and supported Prime Minister William Pitt's Act of Union. Their forbidding and stern Jansenist theory strongly flavored Irish Catholicism until it was finally officially discouraged in the middle of the 19th Century. The last vestiges of the doctrine have long since disappeared from Irish Catholicism, but the unusual devotion of the Irish people today to physically punishing religious pilgrimages possibly could be traced in part back to the old teaching of Maynooth that love of God must be demonstrated by harder acts than receiving the sacraments and going to daily Mass (McCarthy 1964: 78).

Our research reveals that in some areas of Ireland "the last vestiges of the doctrine" are still associated with Irish Catholicism. In fact, one Dublin social scientist with whom I correspond asserts that Jansenism as manifested in sexual repression probably reached its zenith in the 1930s and has gradually been dying out since then. However, it is still very apparent, even among "emancipated" Dubliners of the middle and upper classes.

A much harsher evaluation of Jansenism, again in an historical context, is found in Bryan McMahon's chapter in *The Vanishing Irish*, edited by Fr. John O'Brien, a collection which also includes pertinent essays by Arland Ussher and the editor himself. McMahon says:

Associated with the heresy of Jansenism were the principles of an exaggerated moral and disciplinary rigorism under the

pretext of a return to the primitive Church. The Celtic spirit, despite or rather because of its essential volatility . . . would appear to me to provide an ideal field for the culture of Jansenism. The penances of the early Celtic monks were severity itself. . . . Today, when the idea of physical penance would appear to be repugnant to the entire world, such laudable manifestations of physical denial as the exercises of Lough Derg and Croagh Patrick are beacons amid the darkness. But the danger is that by a flaw in the Celtic nature we are apt to be led by overcompensation into penitential excesses; then it is that the traits of Jansenism are there to fill lacunae in our nature. Significant in this context is the presence of four refugee doctors of the Sorbonne on the staff of Maynooth College in its early and formative years. [Their] teachings . . . cannot but have in some measure colored . . . the whole course of Irish seminary life and consequently the whole body of Irish lay thought (O'Brien 1953: 215–216).

Might not the "volatile nature" of the "Celtic spirit" and the "flaw in the Celtic nature" whose "lacunae" Jansenism fills be persistent masochism? Ussher addresses his remarks more directly to the sexual implications of Jansenism.

Certainly the puritanic bias of the Church in Ireland surprises visitors from other Catholic communities. It is often said that Irish schools and seminaries in the last century were infected with the remnants of Jansenism. . . . The dismal fact remains that Irishmen tend to regard procreation as a shameful necessity, and Irish girls grow up to think of sex as something dark, cold, and forbidding. Statistics are scarcely available, but it seems to me that the word "dirty" is used in modern Ireland in one sense only, namely, to cover every manifestation, even the most natural, of sex passion. . . . Irish married couples seldom give the impression of being biologically satisfied or even awakened; and if they are not, it may partly account for the slovenly, listless, don't care rather than devil-may-care quality of Irish life—the "spit" but never the "polish" (O'Brien 1953: 161–162).

It is interesting to note that Ussher, an Irishman, uses the word "puritanic." I have been severely criticized by Irish readers for using it in this and previous works, since it refers to an English religious movement as well as Cromwell's party.

The editor presents an equally down-to-earth pronouncement of the effects of Jansenism.

Here Father Murphy has singled out a factor of enormous importance in explaining the grotesque proportion of bachelors and spinsters among the Irish: the typical Irish attitude toward marriage, which, as he and many other priests have suggested, would seem to have an underlying touch of

Jansenism. That attitude looks upon marriage and sex as rather regrettable necessities in the propagation of the race: it would have been much better if God had arranged for offspring in some other way. Irish parents shy away from the distasteful task of lifting the veil upon this earthy, unappetizing, and somewhat unclean subject (O'Brien 1953: 105).

The plea for a less "distasteful" manner of reproduction was actually voiced by several Inis Beag women; and most island parents do not lift the "veil," in part because of their own ignorance of sexual matters.

The impact of the Oedipus complex on Irish character has been explored by cultural analysts and writers almost from the time Freud first conceptualized the phenomenon. Indeed, Freud might have been describing Ireland rather than a particular class in Austria at the turn of the century (just as Marx might have had Ireland in mind when positing religion as the opiate of the oppressed masses). Two recent controversial novels use the Oedipus complex as a focus. *Michael Joe*, by William Murray, examines the role of the emasculating Irish mother, and John McGahern, in *The Dark*, probes the conflict between father and son so characteristic of Irish society.

One of the most penetrating studies of this sociocultural configuration, which has such momentous psychological consequences, is that of Marvin Opler and Jerome Singer, conducted among first, second, and third generation Irish male schizophrenic patients in New York hospitals. The intent of these social scientists was to determine how psychotic syndromes are culturally patterned. For a year they observed their respondents to obtain total psychiatric, anthropological, and psychological profiles. Their observations included ward scrutiny, interviews, the collection of life histories and case histories, and the administration of thirteen tests, among them the Rorschach, Thematic Apperception, Sentence Completion, and Porteus Maze. The investigators conclude that there is a continuity of Irish (and Italian) culture and personality forms among immigrants for at least three generations; their psychological findings are buttressed by research data collected in Irish and English mental institutions. My wife and I visited one of these hospitals and interviewed several Irish psychiatrists both there and in America. Our own conclusions support many of those reported by Opler, Singer, and the psychiatrists interviewed.[6] Opler and Singer have the following to say about the Oedipus complex in Ireland:

[6]Irish psychiatrists in that country, England, and America are often reticent about discussing sex. Psychiatric theory in Ireland is modified by Catholic dogma, and specialists are influenced in writings, therapy, and discussions by subtle religious and political forces, as well as by their own character structure shaped by the Irish milieu. One psychologist, well acquainted with psychiatry in Ireland, dubbed much of it "Freud with clothes on."

Normative cultural standards led to the hypothesis that the central female figure in the Irish family, the mother, could instill primary anxiety and fear toward female figures. . . . This hypothesis grew out of anthropological observations that the central figure in Irish families is more likely to be a controlling figure on the distaff side, while fathers, especially in straitened economic circumstances, are frequently by contrast shadowy and evanescent. . . . An Irish male patient beset with anxiety and fear of female figures early in life, and lacking possibilities of firm male identification with a father, would later experience the sexual repressions and socio-religious definitions of marriage and sexuality for which his culture, with its high celibacy rates, protracted engagements, and sin-guilt emphases, is justly famous. . . . All this spells a final anxious and fearful lack of positive sexual identification, varying in a continuum from repressed and latent homosexual balances through to added displacements and distortions that are either pallid asexuality or fearful and bizarre misidentifications. Since the culture does not condone sexual expression or postpones and then rigidly defines it in marriage . . . latent homosexual balances [were hypothesized] for this group, no overtly sought interpersonal manifestations, and a facade of asexual misogyny varied only by the most personalized and bizarre female identifications. . . . [The] basic personality has stamped into it such feelings as male inadequacy, the masculine protest, hostility toward females, and the kind of latent homosexual feelings which produce a further sense of sin and guilt (Opler and Singer 1956: 15–18).

Among the seven diagnostic variables utilized by the researchers, the Irish patients ranked highest in the "Sin, Sex, and Guilt Ideology" (93 percent of the sample) and "Homosexuality Types" (90 percent of the sample latent, none overt) categories.

Complementing the Oedipus complex in the etiology of sexual puritanism is male solidarity. It has a long history in Ireland—revealed in legend and modern literature alike—and is instrumental in delaying marriage and making for marital maladjustment. Freudian psychologists see it as one of the many possible by-products of the "universal" Oedipus complex—"male inadequacy, the masculine protest, hostility toward females, and . . . latent homosexual feelings"; but many anthropologists (especially structural-functionalists) analyze it as a sociocultural phenomenon, for it is found in societies in which the Oedipal configuration appears not to exist. Elizabeth Coxhead, in discussing Lady Gregory's play, *Grania*, alludes to the tragic plight of most Irish women, past and present.

Grania is . . . a play in which a woman is ousted from an emotional relationship between two men. The "love" is that of man for man, of brother for brother; it is loyalty to the warrior band, and a corresponding resentment of the woman who takes away the warrior's freedom, makes trouble with his comrades, distracts him from his purpose in life. It is an attitude which filters through the play as light filters through crystal; which runs through the heroic Irish sagas. . . . Its continuing validity was borne out by all Lady Gregory had observed in the world around her, the world of the "loveless Irishman," the peasant society which relegated women to serfdom, the middle-class intellectual society which left them only donkey-work. . . . Such a view of the Irish-woman's role, of her relegation to insignificance and her resentment under it, is not exclusively feminine. It is abundantly confirmed by Synge. His heroines . . . are creatures caged and raging, given no scope for their powers, condemned to love men who are poor things beside them and do not really care for them at all. O'Casey's Juno offers further positive support, and on the negative side, so to speak, are the quantities of second-rate Irish plays and stories that have for their mainspring a panic dislike of women, invariably represented as shrews, hussies, and Aunt Sallies at whom anything can be thrown. A woman has only to put her nose into a saloon bar . . . to realise that Almhuin is with us still (Coxhead 1961: 145–146).

In concluding this section, I would like to mention briefly an ingenious hypothesis of the cause of sexual repression in Ireland, presented by Sean de Freine in *The Great Silence*. His book is the most "convincing" expression to date of what linguists (outside of Ireland) term "language determinism," a monism still popular in that country a century after the advent of the Irish nativistic movement. Displaying a lack of knowledge both of contemporary linguistic theory and of sexual ethics in the "heart of the Gaeltacht," de Freine says:

The Irish are often accused of a Jansenist approach to sex, which is supposed to date from the French influence in the Irish Church in and just after the penal times. But this attitude did not exist in Irish Ireland and does not exist in the Gaeltacht today. It would seem as though, when English spread through the country, it was English Puritanism and not French Jansenism, which brought about the change. For example, certain English words with prudish connotations were accepted, with their connotations, by the Irish, while their equivalents in Irish have no such nuances. In its English setting Puritanism was kept in reasonable check by the other native traditions: in Ireland, as the old culture died, there were no such natural checks to contain it (de Freine 1965: 164).

Space does not permit me to consider other causal factors listed earlier which are equally untenable.

SEXUAL REPRESSION: ITS INCULCATION

The inculcation of sexual puritanism in Inis Beag must be examined in four contexts: the role of the curate, the influence of visiting missions, enculturation in the home, and what I will term "secular social control"—the behavioral regulations imposed on themselves by Inis Beag adolescents and adults. It is through these agencies that Jansenism, masochism, the Oedipus complex, male solidarity, and other inextricably linked factors shape the severe sexual repression which gives rise to the cultural manifestations discussed in the last section of the chapter.

Priests of Jansenist persuasion have had subtle means of repressing the sexual instincts of the islanders in addition to the more extreme methods of controlling behavior—"clerical social control," such as employing informers, allocating indulgences, and refusing the sacraments to, and placing curses on, miscreants. Through sermons and informal classroom talks, the pulpit and the national school have served as effective vehicles of church discipline. The talks are especially telling, since they take advantage of the personality malleability of the formative years. The adult Irish person is rare who, although anticlerical, and even agnostic or atheistic, can transcend these early enculturative experiences, particularly in times of social crisis or personality disorganization. Erring islanders have often been sought out by priests and talked to privately after their ways have become known through gossip, informers, or the confessional. Some curates have suppressed courting, dancing, visiting, and other behavior either directly or "indirectly" (widely interpreted in Ireland) sexual in nature by physical action: that is, roaming the trails and fields at night seeking out young lovers and halting dancing by their threatening presence. This outward form of intrusion into island affairs is resented by most folk, as is the inward intrusion through priestly remonstrances; they question the right of the young, virginal, inexperienced, and sexually unknowledgeable curates to give advice in this sphere.

Church influence is also exerted through missions which visit Inis Beag every three to five years. On these occasions, two Redemptorist priests (occasionally Franciscans, Dominicans, or Passionists) spend a week on the island, where they conduct mass each morning and deliver long sermons in the chapel every afternoon or early evening. Everyone, even old people and mothers with young infants, is urged to attend to receive the "blessings of the mission." To some, this means shortening the time in purgatory for themselves or a deceased relative (an indulgence used to enforce church discipline). To others, absence carries with it the penalty of damnation, just as viewing an eel or small fish in the sacred well, appropriated from the Druids, promises salvation in an equally magical fashion. A mission usually has a theme, the variations of which are explored with high emotion and eloquence by the visiting clerics in their exhortations. The most common theme is "controlling one's passions," but two others have often been addressed in the missionizing effort: abstaining from intoxicating drink and maintaining the faith as an emigrant. Collections are made by children to support the endeavor, and a list of contributors and their respective donations is displayed publicly. This technique of social control is also used by the curate at the several yearly offerings. A mission creates an emotionally charged atmosphere on the island, which continues for weeks after the departure of the clerics.

The seeds of repression are planted early in childhood by parents and kin through instruction supplemented by rewards and punishments, conscious imitation, and unconscious internalization. Although mothers bestow considerable affection and attention on their offspring, especially on their sons, physical love as manifested in intimate handling and kissing is rare in Inis Beag. Even breast feeding is uncommon because of its sexual connotation, and verbal affection comes to replace contact affection by late infancy. Any form of direct or indirect sexual expression—such as masturbation, mutual exploration of bodies, use of either standard or slang words relating to sex, and open urination and defecation—is severely punished by word or deed. Care is taken to cover the bodies of infants in the presence of siblings and outsiders, and sex is never discussed before children. Several times my wife inadvertently inquired as to whether particular women were pregnant, using that word before youths, only to be "hushed" or to have the conversation postponed until the young people could be herded outside. The adults were so embarrassed by the term that they found it difficult to communicate with her after the children had departed. She once aroused stupefaction among men on the strand when she attempted unsuccessfully to identify the gender of a bullock about to be shipped off.

It is in the home that the separation of sexes, so characteristic of Inis Beag life, is inaugurated among siblings in early childhood. Boys and girls in the family remain apart not only when interacting with the parent of the same sex at work, but when playing in and near the cottage and traveling to and from school. Parents and their older offspring read popular religious journals, found in most homes, many of the articles in which deal with sexual morality of the Irish Catholic variety.

One sociologist (Berger 1963: 66–92) classifies social control methods as those which involve physical violence or its threat (e.g., political and legal sanctions), those which result in economic pressures (e.g., occupation and market place relations), and, finally, those which govern our "morality, custom, and manners" (e.g., persuasion, ridicule, and gossip). I will not consider political and economic manipulation; more significant are other techniques that I have labelled secular social control. Inis Beag, as much as any human community, is characterized by gossip, ridicule, and opprobrium. Influenced by nativism, primitivism, and structural-functional theory, writers and social

scientists have painted a distorted picture of culture and personality equilibrium among Irish peasants. Actually, the folk are neither glorified Celts nor "noble savages," and dysfunctional sociocultural forms, mental aberrations (neuroses, psychoses, and psychosomatic disorders), and exaggerated defense postures abound.

Inis Beag people are ambivalent about gossip; they welcome every opportunity to engage in it, yet detest the practice when they are its victims. When asked to cite the major deficiencies of their way of life, islanders usually place the prevalence of malicious gossiping near the top of their list. Boys and men hide themselves in the darkness or behind fences to overhear the conversations of passersby; they maintain close scrutiny of visitors during the summer, both day and night, in order to discover them in "compromising" situations. Parties are organized at the last moment and persons will leave the island without any previous announcement—often to emigrate or enter the hospital or join a religious order—in order to circumvent gossip. Rumors run rife in Inis Beag, especially when they concern, for example, the "nude" sun bathing of a visiting actress (bared shoulders and lower thighs) or the "attack" on a Dublin girl late at night by an island youth (an effort to hold her hand while under the influence of stout). Over a dozen efforts on our part to determine the truth behind the most pernicious rumors of this genre revealed sexual fantasy at their core in every case.

The force most responsible for limiting the potential social activities of women—which would make their lot much easier and possibly stem the tide of emigration—is the fear of gossip: "If I went for a walk, they'd wonder why I wasn't home tending my chores." Even couples who might otherwise disregard religious teachings and the wrath of the priest do not court, because it might be observed and reported through gossip to the entire population.[7] An islander must carefully regulate his own words and actions in the presence of others so that the fires of factionalism are not ignited. Equally feared are informers of the curate and relatives or close friends of persons in an audience who might be offended by a heedless remark brought to their attention by the listeners.

It is sometimes heard in Ireland, from those aware of, and willing to admit, the fact, that the inability of most Irish to "share themselves" with one another, even husbands and wives, is a heritage of the fear of gossip—a fear that one's intimate revela-

---

[7]The fear of being observed, as well as repression, may account for the apparent lack of sexual contact with animals. This practice may be common among mainland peasants, if one is willing to accept as evidence the existence of a genre of dirty jokes popular there, and hearsay among certain scholars concerning confessional materials.

tions will become common knowledge and lead to censure and "loss of face." A more likely explanation, according to those of Freudian bent, is the Oedipus configuration, which numbers among its many effects the following: the prevalence of romantic attachments and the rarity of conjugal love; the lack of sexual foreplay, marked by little or no concern with the female breast; the brevity of the coital act and the frequent spurning of the woman following it; the need to degrade the woman in the sexual encounter and the belief that the "good" woman does not like sex, and, conversely, that the sexually disposed woman is by virtue of the fact "bad." All of these widely reported phenomena bespeak the overwhelming influence of the mother image.

Ridicule and opprobrium, as well as satire in song and tale, are effective control mechanisms in light of the emphasis placed by Inis Beag folk on saving face. Most islanders could not believe that I was the author of the ballad referred to in footnote 5 because several stanzas attack my character: they find it difficult to conceive of anyone publicly proclaiming their own faults, under any circumstances. Opinions, once formed, are clung to tenaciously, even in light of obviating circumstances, since to alter them would be an admittance that they were ill advised in the first instance. The folk pride themselves on being able to judge a stranger's character immediately on meeting him, and this initial impression is rarely modified no matter how long their interaction continues. A seldom revealed tradition of satirical balladry exists in Inis Beag, but its employment is infrequent and then calculated according to singer and audience so as not to offend directly. Apprehensiveness and anxiety about real and imagined ego assaults by others are dominant personality traits of the islanders.

HISTORICAL AND CULTURAL IMPLICATIONS

I have already touched tangentially on some of the historical and broad cultural implications of sexual puritanism, in Ireland as well as Inis Beag. In this final section I will examine the perennially addressed phenomena of late marriage, celibacy, and emigration, in their island setting, with special reference to the factor of sexual repression.

In a population of 350, 116 persons are married, 13 are widows, 3 are widowers, and 33 males over twenty-three years of age and 21 females over seventeen are single. Since marriage occurs between twenty-four and forty-five for men and eighteen and thirty-two for women, on the basis of past statistics, only 18 men and 9 women are eligible for marriage. As mentioned earlier, the average marriage age for males is thirty-six and for females twenty-five. My wife and I isolated almost two dozen interrelated causes of late marriage and the prevalence of bache-

lor and spinsterhood. The most emphasized cause in Ireland is the pattern of inheritance: one son, usually the eldest, must wait until the father is ready to pass on his patrimony and his own siblings have married or emigrated. In an attempt to alleviate the situation somewhat, a law today requires that to receive the "old-age" (pension) a man at seventy must will his property to a son, or other appropriate person. This cause is important in Inis Beag, although primogeniture is not so well defined (of those sons inheriting property, 47 percent are first born, 42 percent second, 8 percent third, and 3 percent fourth and later). Inis Beag fathers are loath to surrender their land and control of the household to their sons and will often play off the sons, one against another, in order to achieve favored treatment for their wives and themselves in their waning years. Occasionally this procedure "backfires": the sons, acting in concert, emigrate together, and an increasing amount of land lies idle because of this.

Equally loath to disturb the family status quo, island mothers will resist incoming daughters-in-law, who threaten not only their commanding position but the loss of their sons' affection. Mothers whom we have interviewed in Inis Beag and elsewhere in Ireland display the extreme of Oedipal attachment when they rejoice in their sons' decision to join the priesthood; not only are spiritual blessings and prestige brought to the family as a result, but their sons are at last removed from potential wives. Yet the Inis Beag man who wants to marry and is prevented from doing so by domineering and jealous parents is the subject of much gossip. Outwardly, at least, his plight is considered a "shame."

To the man in his late twenties and thirties who is secure in his home and has established regularized patterns of conduct (and has a mother who acts in most ways as a wife surrogate), the general responsibilities of marriage, and specifically its sexual responsibility, are factors militating against his seeking a spouse. Some men who have land, the consent of their parents, and willing "sweethearts" will balk at a match because they are too happy "running with the lads," and if persuaded to marry, they will try to retain as much of their bachelor role as possible within marriage. It was hinted to my wife and me on several occasions that particular island celibates almost married several times in succession, only to find the sexual commitment too difficult to make at the last moment.

Three other causes of late marriage and the single estate in Inis Beag must be mentioned. Girls are more dissatisfied with their future lot than are boys and men and are emigrating at ever younger ages, thus sharply reducing the number of eligible females. During the 1950–1959 period, the average age at which girls emigrate dropped below twenty-one years. Each year more of them attend schools on the mainland and thus are more exposed to stimuli which promote emigration. Mothers are puzzled at the increasing exodus of their daughters, since women today have a far easier time than they did a generation or two ago; but some are glad to see them escape the drudgery and boredom of island existence. Since late marriage has been a persistent phenomenon in Ireland since the great famine, it has become institutionalized and serves as an expectation for young people. We heard Inis Beag adults assert that marriage should be postponed to conform to island mores; this usually was buttressed by a rationale of males not having "enough sense" to marry until they are nearly forty years of age. Reflected in this rationale is the male age-grading conceptualized by the folk: a man is a "boy" or "lad" until forty, an adult until sixty, middle-aged until eighty, and aged after that (exhilarating to the American anthropologist approaching forty who comes from a society obsessed with the "cult of youth"). A final cause, often articulated by the islanders,

is the fact that divorce is impossible in Ireland, therefore the choice of a spouse must be well considered. It appears, however, that this argument is usually used as a rationalization for late marriage, when other causal factors are, in reality, responsible—certainly when "considering" covers two or more decades!

The population of Inis Beag has dropped from a high of 532 persons in 1861 (up 76 from the prefamine census a decade earlier) to 497 in 1881, 483 in 1901, 409 in 1926, 376 in 1956, and 350 when my wife and I were there two years later. Today, there is grave concern over the future of the island, and some folk hold that within another generation or two Inis Beag will have gone the way of the Blasket Islands.

DONALD S. MARSHALL

Sexual Aspects of the Life Cycle

The Mangaian is born, as he lives and loves and dies, in the midst of his clustered kinsmen. The woman in labor is surrounded by family members; assistance is given to her by the grandmother and the husband or father—and by the midwife. More powerful than the physical presence of these kinfolk is the social warmth and approval that envelop a newborn child. For the new member is additional insurance of the continued existence of the family. He is an added source of strength and power, an increment to their means of subsistence. In fact, he is the foundation of the marriage bond itself—which his conception may have caused to be formalized. Far from serving as a potential wedge between parents, as can occur in other societies—including our own—the birth of the child serves both to strengthen ties of sexual affection between mother and father and to extend the web of kinship; the child's conception has made more attractive, rather than less so, the sexual relations between the couple.

The Mangaian couple copulates regularly, up until the onset of labor pains. Some Mangaian men prefer intercourse with their wives during this period of pregnancy to that during any other time, for the woman's privates are believed to become "wetter, softer, fatter, and larger"; natural secretions provide the lubrication that Mangaian lovers prefer. Some slight adjustments in coital position are made, with the rear approach (*pāto'e*) being used more frequently than otherwise. There is a belief shared by some Mangaians that frequent copulation up until the time of delivery eases the path of the child (though some differ, and abstain from coitus with their wives—out of jokingly expressed fear that "the baby will bite"). Copulation between the couple may be resumed within a few days after delivery, although the cultural ideal is to wait for three months or so.

Boys and girls may play together until they are three or four years of age. But between ages four and five, they separate into those sex-age groups that will distinguish them socially for the rest of their lives. Brothers and sisters, sweethearts and lovers, husband and wife, mother and father, old man and old woman—such pairs rarely mix together socially in public, despite their intense private relationships. A six-year old Mangaian brother and his three-year-old sister would no more walk together hand in hand along the main street of the town than would the dignified Mangaian deacon think of walking down the same street with his wife on his way to church. Seeing such behavior by my children, my principal informant expressed this "don't" of the cultural system thus: "No Māori brother and sister allowed to go together like that!"

The bare bottom and penis of the preschool Mangaian boy are only covered when going to church or on other formal occasions. Mothers attempt to justify this undress to the European visitor by saying that it's "hard to teach them to wear trousers." But there is no real shame associated with seeing a child's penis before he has been superincised, at about age twelve (or in seeing a little girl's genitals—up until she has reached age four or five). However, if the boy child has been circumcised in the European fashion at birth, he must then keep his organ covered. For it is the glans of the penis that must not be seen. Normally, this is covered up by the foreskin of the nonsuperincised male youth; but when this skin is cut, the penis then has "no hat," as the Mangaian expression goes, and must no longer be viewed by anyone.

Young children imitate the work and activities of their elders as a basis of play. In the course of this, according to some informants, they are thought to play at copulation. But this activity is never seen in public. In a somewhat different sense, the adult act itself is never socially acknowledged in public. For the Mangaian enjoys an extraordinary sense of "public privacy." He may copulate, at any age, in the single room of a hut that contains from five to fifteen family members of all ages—as have his ancestors before him. His daughter may receive and make love with each of her varied nightly suitors in that same room. Clothes are changed and accidents, such as public loss of a menstrual pad, may happen. But under most conditions, all of this takes place without social notice; everyone seems to be looking in another direction.

Despite varied sexual activities that occur continuously within the one-room houses, it is outside of the home that the child learns more intimate details of sex and their results—such as "where the babies come from." This knowledge is achieved at about age eight or nine. For just as brother and sister are not seen together in public, so they do not discuss sexual matters together, nor do they joke together. Brothers do not advise brothers, nor do closely related age-mates joke with one another. Mothers and daughters or fathers and sons do not discuss sexual matters with one another—or even with the older persons among whom they work.

These "do's" and "don'ts" of what is permissible at home and what must be discussed elsewhere produce odd contrasts. Offsetting the lack of discussion of sexual matters within the family are actual sexual acts that regularly take place in the home and the lingual manipulation of the penis of small children by women of the family. Just as anomalous is the cultural atmosphere of the Mangaian community itself. Despite lack of public social contact between sexes of all ages, there is a continual public evocation of sex. The slightest attention of an unrelated boy to a girl will raise the buzz of gossip, whether based upon a public compliment or a casual touch or smile. And a very common technique of active leadership is to introduce a sexual joking element into the public situation. The district chief, the territorial governor, the church elder, the proud storekeeper—each knows that a risqué remark, a suggestive comment, or a timeworn sexual proverb provides the element of public amusement that is required to keep things moving. As my pastor-friend and host noted, proverbs are *not* religious in this community, although local activities are geared to a religious calendar cycle. Such proverbs would, he explained, "only make the deacons and a pastor happy"—one needs a sexual story to "make all the people happy and work fast." The Mangaian proverb or story must have a biological, a scatological, or a sexual basis if it is to be used to get people in the mood for group work. The work leader must have a strong voice and a "good sense of humor"—that is, a good store of sexual proverbs and stories—or the work "never gets done." Hence, one may find oneself sitting in the village pastorate, listening to the local minister tell the anthropologist and visiting pastors a ribald story of how the island of Manihiki became renowned as a "finger work" island; while, from the next room, comes the sound of his daughter reading her Bible aloud. Or one may watch, over and over again, as the *Ekalesia* of the church increase their work efforts threefold in response to the ribald implication of a deacon's publicly told story.

Further compounding this apparent ambivalence in social attitudes is a typical Polynesian concern with the sexual genitalia and lack of concern with the rest of human anatomy. The Mangaian is completely flabbergasted at the American and European male's interest in the female breast, for the Polynesian considers this organ to be of interest only to a hungry baby. Yet, the Mangaian male is as fully concerned with the size, shape, and consistency of the mons Veneris as is the American male with the size, shape, and consistency of the female bust. Moreover, the Mangaian concern with sex is supplemented by considerable knowledge of the genital organs; the average Mangaian youth has fully as detailed a knowledge—perhaps more—of the gross anatomy

of the penis and the vagina as does a European physician. In fact, the Mangaian vocabulary contains terms for features of the genitalia that users of English have not found necessary to specifically name or classify; for example, *tipipā*, the ridge of the glans of the penis, *ngutupako*, the exposed area of the glans of the non-superincised penis; *keo* and *keokeo*, modifying terms for the shape of the clitoris. For the clitoris itself there are several synonyms (*kaka'i, nini'i, tore, teo*, etc.), as there are for the cunnus (*kāwawa, mete kōpapa, 'ika*). One indication of the significance attached to sexual organs is found in the fact that the clitoris, which is said to be some three-quarters of an inch long, is classified as either one or another degree of "sharpness" or is considered to be "blunt"; alternate terms describe it as "projecting," "erecting," or "protruding." (This fact may be functionally and physiologically related both to the deliberate manipulation of children's sexual organs by older people in an attempt to change their size and to the activity rate to which they are subjected.)

The principal sexual factor in the development of the Mangaian personality is, thus, the early and constant exposure to patterned ambivalence. There is an emphatic social division of the sexes, in an atmosphere redolent with cultural emphasis on sexual organs and sexual intercourse; unique modesty as to exposure of adult organs (Polynesian men are horrified at European casualness in exposing the penis in urination) is contrasted with extreme sensuousness in local dance and explicitly detailed accounts of sexual acts and organs in folktales; the utmost lack of interest in modern European-style clothing is offset by lavish use of perfumed scents and flowers; perhaps most importantly, intricate incest prohibitions are contrasted with the restriction of most social contacts to those that take place only between kinsmen.

A Mangaian boy supposedly first hears about masturbation (*tītoi, kurukuru*, or *pa'ore*; sometimes referred to in the village of Oneroa as "Ivirua poetry"—Ivirua being a neighboring village) sometime between the ages of seven and ten. He discusses it with his friends and, eventually, he experiments with himself while off feeding the pigs or fishing. Boys are often stimulated to do this by hearing the young men (*māpū*) talk about sex. Boys may masturbate themselves an average of two or three times a week; excessive masturbation is thought to expose the glans of the penis (*ngutupakō*) prior to superincision. Mangaians believe that boys with few friends tend to masturbate more than those who spend more time with other children. After erection, even without masturbation, the boy is said to notice the "pressure of fluid" on the penis. (This is different from the "morning erection," which goes down without trace after urination.) Boys also begin to experience nocturnal emissions ("wet dreams") at this age, although they tend to blame these upon the visits of variously described, but always sexually avaricious, "ghost women." The emission in wet dreams and the subsequent walking up always occur, however, before the penetration is made.

Nocturnal emissions are much more frequent when the men are denied free access to women, as on the labor island of Makatea. Later, the Mangaian boy will frequently be brought to erection by sexual talk or even by sight of a girl.

Girls also masturbate (*tirau*) by thigh pressure or by rocking on their heel. This female masturbation is known to have been practiced from life history data, and it has been witnessed in public by Europeans, in contrast to the privacy of the boy's behavior. But I have too few data available to discuss it more fully. And I have never seen, or known anyone who actually claims ever to have seen, boys masturbating publicly. Although parents may try to stop children from masturbating, once they know of it, their efforts are not very heavy nor their punishment severe. And, if without a girl, the older boy or traveling husband may masturbate. Only the hand is used, without elaborate devices. There is accompanying imagery of girls or thinking about the orgasm.

It is important to note that, up until recent years, very small children were taught who their kinsmen (*taeake*) were and learned their genealogy ('*akapapa 'anga*) in great detail. This practice has now fallen away, leading to unfortunate results that will be discussed later in this chapter.

SUPERINCISION

Some Mangaian boys experiment with sexual intercourse prior to superincision. But such "new boys" must content themselves with sexually knowledgeable and promiscuous older women and widows of the village, rather than copulate with either the younger girls or with what are referred to as the "good girls." Most boys wait until age thirteen or fourteen to commence their sexual adventures (*kitenākenga*), following the act of superincision. The Mangaian girls' personal knowledge of, and appetite for, sex also begins at this age, about the time that they have begun to menstruate. (Some girls experience very severe menstrual cramps, sufficient to require bed care.)

Mangaians recognize the arrival of male puberty by two signs: the growth of pubic hair and (they say) an ability to "retract the foreskin of the penis." These signs presage the approach of the most traumatic, most clear-cut, and most meaningful of the Mangaian males' varied "rites of passage": the superincision, which marks the transition from boy to man. There are, of course, several subphases of boyhood and adulthood, but the critical transition is that of the youth with an uncut smegma-sullied penis to the adult with a clean and virile male organ.

At the same age that girls are experiencing the onset of menstruation and are beginning to have their initial sexual experience, the Mangaian boy is subject to aggressive social pressure from his male age mates and the jeers of village females. He may be accused of a lack of courage and of having a stinking penis (*ure piapia*). It is not long before he himself, or his father or uncle, decides that he must undergo the superincision operation (*te'e*). If he waits too long, he may be forcibly knocked out and operated on by his age mates. But most boys succumb at an early age to the pressures of society and custom. Typically, the sequence today is as follows. When a father notes his son coming of age, perhaps because of the social stigma of his son's non-superincision, he starts "feeding a pig" for the boy and has a word with a cousin or an older brother of the son, who will "give the idea" to the boy. The father then brings in an expert from outside the immediate family to take care of the actual details and to carry out the operation; two experts may, in fact, be required: one to make the cut, another to tie the bandages. There are several of these superincision experts (*ta'unga te'e*) in the villages today. (Once these were special "priests" called *waikea*.)

The expert approaches the boy and lets him know that the father has actually initiated arrangements for the operation. It is he who makes the cut who is the most important source of the boy's information about sexual behavior, of "what to do with women," and who may actually arrange for the woman who will remove the superincision scab and provide more practical instruction in sexual matters. This was, say my informants, "like a law before" (that is, it was once a publicly acknowledged, explicit cultural pattern). Variant forms of the custom are found elsewhere in central Polynesia, such as the Society and Austral Islands (Marshall 1961, n.d.).

The superincision operation itself, which may be performed upon one boy or upon a group of age mates, takes place in a secluded spot. Preferably, this is by the sea; alternatively, it may be by a mountain stream. The cut was formerly made with a flake of a semi-flintlike local stone (*ruarangi*); in a few cases this stone is still used. But most modern "experts" prefer an imported straight razor; although they recognize that there is more danger of infection, the cut is more easily made. In addition, a superincision anvil is required. Formerly, this anvil is said to have been made of stone; now, it is whittled from coconut shell to about the size and shape of the bowl of a tablespoon. The shell anvil serves to protect the glans of the penis and to provide a firm surface upon which to make the cut. Many experts carefully study the organ and lay out a line on the surface of the skin in order to avoid cutting veins; others are less careful. In any event, severe hemorrhaging may take place, during and after the operation. The foreskin is retracted, and the anvil inserted; then the skin of the penis is pulled tightly over it and slit down the medial dorsal line through the white cartilaginous underlayer—statedly, right up to the stomach, in most cases. The more carefully done and the more lengthy the incision, the neater is said to be the final result. Mangaian men are quite concerned over the appearance of the superincised organ. An insult of major social magnitude, only slightly less severe than reference to a man's smegma, is to imply that a man has a "dog-eared" penis, with pendulous skin below the shaft.

Severe pain characterizes the superincision operation, and the youth runs directly into the sea or the stream for relief—at the same time exultantly proclaiming, "Now I am really a man."

After the cut has been cleansed with water, the superincised organ is soothed with a poultice of coconut oil, sandalwood powder, and succulent leaves that have been chewed to release their juice. Then a leaf that has had a hole cut in it is wrapped around the organ, the expert being careful to lay open the cut at the same time so that the contractions of healing will expose the glans. The organ is wrapped with cloth, now purchased specifically for the operation, and then tucked up under the belt of a loincloth that also has been made up from specially purchased cloth. Then the boy returns home, meeting with apparent indifference his family's lack of notice of his condition.

During the first day following the operation, any foods may be eaten. But for two weeks following this first day, the boy must carefully avoid those foods characterized by Mangaians as "hot" (meat, coconut sauce, salt, tea) and eat only "cold" foods (taro and taro leaf greens). His mother, who supposedly does not know what has happened, cooks special "nonhot" foods, which she puts in a "special place" for him; usually, however, the boy is not particularly interested in eating, owing to the pain of the cut area. Twice a day the superincised youth must bathe his cut in the sea, no matter what the weather or what his other problems, and then have the wound redressed by the expert. A yellow powder found on the base of the coconut frond or on the leaves of the mountain fern is sprinkled on the wound at this time, in order to produce the proper scab (*tōpā*). Blisters, which may have been caused by urine coming in contact with the cut, are reduced and treated with the use of heated stones (*māinaina*); infections may be treated with wads of spider web.

But more important than physiological treatment (from the sociocultural standpoint) is the knowledge of sexual matters and the training in sexual behavior given to the youth by the circumcision expert. Not only does this detailed information concern techniques of coitus but it is also said to include the means of locating a "good girl." The expert teaches the youth (as the elderly woman instructs the young female) about such techniques as cunnilingus, the kissing and sucking of breasts, and a means of achieving simultaneous mutual climax, as well as how to bring the woman to climax several times before the male partner permits himself to achieve the goal. Some of this instruction is by straightforward precept, some by the use of figurative stories. Among lore taught is that related to the use of raw eggs, believed by Mangaians to make men more virile and to aid women in speeding up their orgasms.

This period of formal instruction is followed some two weeks after the operation, by a "practical exercise" in copulation, the purpose of which is to have the superincision scab removed by actual sexual intercourse. The intercourse, often arranged by the expert, must be with an experienced woman; formerly she was an appropriately related kinswoman, but now she may be any mature and experienced female, including the village trollop. There is said to be a special thrill involved for the woman, although there are also some indications that many women object to the role. Of significance to the youth is the coaching he receives in the techniques that he has learned about from the expert. The woman teaches him to hold back until he can achieve orgasm in unison with his partner; she teaches him the techniques involved in carrying out various acts and positions about which the expert has advised him—especially the matter of timing (*kite i te tā'ei*). A touch of the old ceremony is often preserved in that the woman may insist upon carrying out this practical instruction on the beach, at a place where water seeps through the sands. Here the mistress and the pupil, these Polynesian "children of the sea," are in contact with the mother waters.

The newly cut male organ itself provides other rewards. Socially, perhaps more than biologically, it provides the youth with the mandatory cleanliness for acceptability as a sexual partner. Psychologically, the youth believes that it enables him to better thrill his partner, to permit him to make the sexual act more vigorous, and to enable him to bring his partner to orgasm three times as compared to his once. And, if the cut has been properly made and the scab properly removed by an experienced partner, the organ in itself is thought to be beautiful.

In modern times, the last day that the expert takes care of the boy is marked by a feast given for both the boy and his mentor. The father acknowledges the help given to his son and sends part of the pig to the expert's home. (When the pig is killed and cooked, the superincision expert receives the head–the part of honor—and one of the thighs; the bandager receives another of the thighs.) This feast is the signal for the boy to be called a man by the people.

Not all individuals experience the ideal pattern as generalized above. Although at least 95 percent of Mangaian men are said to be cut, a very few are able to resist for their entire life the social shame and scorn and mockery heaped upon unsuperincised males; some few others may resist it until they have become fathers. (The most successful and sought after young girl-chaser during my last visit to Mangaia had not yet been circumcised.) Now that there are European-trained medical practitioners on the island with modern drugs and techniques, some infants are being circumcised at birth rather than superincised at puberty. And there is a tendency to cut the penis at an ever more youthful age; some Mangaian youths of ten years are now undergoing the ordeal, to the despair of the old men. (One of the governors attributes a supposed decline in local physique and athletic prowess to the earlier age of superincision.) In "the old days," they say, the act awaited a boy's training as a warrior and was carried out "in secrecy," at anywhere from fifteen on up to thirty-six years. And warriors abstained from sex for from three to seven days before battle, lest they lose their physical power. Now the superincision is "announced" to the village by the killing of a pig; a practitioner may use a local anesthetic rather than go off to a lonely place by the sea; and he may make the Jewish cut. With these "new medicines" the youth can "eat any food." Methylate may be used instead of the chewed medicines of leaves and powder; and some boys no longer lose their scab in actual sexual intercourse. Some boys now make the cut upon one another, rather than have an expert assist them.

Once he is made acceptable by superincision, a boy leaves off masturbation in favor of girls; he aggressively seeks them out or is sought out by them. Soon copulation becomes an every-night affair.

SEXUAL ATTITUDES

Copulation is a principal concern of the Mangaian of either sex. This concern is evident in the number of words for coitus, for the sexual parts of the body, and for sexual activities and other intimate matters in the Mangaian insults. To tell a man *maumau 'ua te ure i āau'* is to tell him, insultingly, that he's lazy and that he's letting his penis go to waste, letting it "get rusty." For the act of coitus or copulation itself there is a formal specific word, *ai*, that is related only to the human act. *Oni* is the formal word for animal copulation, although this word may be used for human intercourse in a joking sense. There are innumerable synonyms including some that are similar to English usage. "To sleep" (*moe*) and "to lie down" (*takoto*) also mean "to copulate" and are often used as socially acceptable or "polite" terms. And the terms for "male" (*tāne*) and "female" (*wahine*), when used by a member of the opposite sex, may also infer copulation. The twenty-seventh night of the lunar month (also called *tāne*) is considered "an especially good night for searching out women," as well as for net fishing.

The Mangaians' approach to sex must be as indirect as the final proposition is direct. There is no dating whatsoever (in the American sense) between youths of the two sexes. In this day of public elementary school and general knowledge of writing, a note carried by an intermediary or left in a hidden location may ask the direct question; rarely would it be handed directly from writer to receiver. The slight pressure of a finger or arm in danc-

ing, the raising of an eyebrow, the showing of a seed pod or flower cupped in the hand so as to provide a sexually suggestive sign are all that is required to raise the question in this society where boy is not seen with girl in public. Or (as will be seen later in the discussion of *motoro*) the boy (or girl) may simply go at night to the house and bed of the sought-after partner. Today the phrases "I love you" or "I want you" play a role in the note or the go-between's message, for "sweet talk" is recognized as a necessary social lubricant. But such phrases mean only "I want to copulate with you."

Whatever the indirect approach or whoever the social go-between, the proposition raised is direct and unmistakable. There is no contact between the sexes, no rendezvous, no equivalent of our "necking" that does not culminate directly and immediately in copulation. Coitus is the only imaginable end for any kind of sexual contact among Mangaians. Less than one out of a hundred girls, and even fewer boys—if, indeed, there are any exceptions in either sex—have *not* had substantial sexual experience prior to marriage. Although the sexual act is understood to be related to childbirth, Mangaians believe that if one spreads the relationship between varied partners and avoids continuous or regular intercourse with the same partner, pregnancy will not result. They also maintain that although sexual intercourse is one of the prerequisites between partners in formal marriage or in mating, it in itself bears no implication of love or connotation of marriage.

COITUS

Little stimulation is required to prepare the Mangaian male for sexual intercourse; custom and habit seem sufficient. However, the Mangaian does admit to increased sexual excitement and desire upon hearing music. Somewhat more exciting is the sight of the nude female body—a knowledge used by Mangaian females to arouse flagging interest in their partners. Perfume, the sight of a woman's well-rounded hips, and the actions of the Polynesian dance also incite the male Mangaian to thoughts of copulation, as does the sight of female genitalia—particularly a prominent mons Veneris. The rotating motion of his partner's hips in the actual sex act is what then spurs the Mangaian male on to greater sexual achievements; female passiveness dampens the male's abilities. Most particularly, the Mangaian is sexually excited by the sound of moist genitalia coming together (*'ikawaiwai*).

With the exception of copulation between married partners or *motoro* partners, which takes place in the home, sexual connection between young Mangaians takes place in out-of-the-way places: on the beach, in the woods, out of the village in "the bush," and in empty houses. Most of it occurs at night, but some takes place during the day—if other circumstances are right. The act may take only minutes to complete, or the session can be prolonged over several hours and (successively) be carried on all through the night. As the male youth has been instructed by the older male, the young female by the older women, and the male youths have been schooled in practice as well as theory at the period of their *te'e*, little time need be devoted to self-discovery.

There is seldom any kissing or affectionate foreplay and demonstration prior to coitus. (Polynesians did have the *'ongi* [*PPN *hongi*]*—improperly called "nose rubbing," actually a kind of sniffing of the scent of one another—but it was more a demonstration of kinship affinity and formal emotion than of sexual intent.) Although the concept of lip kissing has recently begun to be used with approval on Mangaia, stimulated by the moving pictures and/or by experience overseas or with European partners on the other Cook Islands, the older Mangaian female still cannot understand why her youthful partner attempts to kiss her just prior to climax; kissing appears to be restricted to the present younger generation. Sexual intimacy is *not* achieved by first demonstrating personal affection; the reverse is true. The Mangaian, or Polynesian girl takes an immediate demonstration of sexual virility and masculinity as the first test of her partner's desire for her and as the reflection of her own desirability. (In fact, the Cook Island female may test the male's desire rather severely, as did the Aitutaki girl who went for several days without washing her privates and then insisted that her would-be lover perform cunnilingus upon her before admitting him to more intimate acts of coitus.) One virility test used by Mangaian women is to require a lover to have successful intercourse without making contact with any part of the partner's body other than the genitalia. Personal affection may or may not result from acts of sexual intimacy, but the latter are requisite to the former—exactly the reverse of the ideals of western society.

The foregoing is not to be construed as meaning there is no Mangaian sexual foreplay; it indicates that the component of affection is separate from the coital act, at least as far as the young Mangaian is concerned. In fact, there is a considerable technique involved in Mangaian coital foreplay, even though the preliminary period may be brief. Such foreplay, directed toward achieving a heightened erotic interest and bringing about the full arousal of passion before actual copulation, includes the manual and lingual caressing of each other's nipples by the partners of either sex and manipulation of the genitalia of one another by both partners. Not only is erection of the nipples desired, but some of the sexual foreplay is aimed at moistening the sexual parts to make it easier to come together. For this same reason there is penilingual and cunnilingual foreplay, although some in-

formants said these later may be used to achieve climax—"if the two partners like each other very much." In addition, the young Mangaian male may use erotic words and "dirty talk" to excite his partner and to make her "hotter." But, in the main, the Mangaian (and the Polynesian) rejects the use of very much sexual foreplay, as this would take away from the pleasures of actual copulation; it takes place largely after the first act and is a prelude to the next. One informant noted, "Fooling around would cut down the time that we could actually go in and out." The man who incites a girl to sex and then "wastes her time" with too much preliminary fooling is likely to be pushed away and called *ure paruparu*, "limp penis," by the disappointed girl, as she runs away. This insult is his penalty for not having immediately "got on with the work." The "good man," as the term is used by informants, can go and stop, play and go, continuing each act for fifteen minutes or a half hour. But even between married partners the first foreplay is likely to be only for a five-minute period—"enough to warm her up."

Setting aside experimental sessions of the very young and the just-mated, Mangaians are not very concerned with the use of a variety of positions for the coital act. The use of the more elaborate positional variations and a desire to watch the partner's nude body are related to the newly mated, as is copulation in the daytime. After the first five years or so of partnership, these aesthetic devices are dispensed with. Conversely, coitus between two youthful partners who are not well acquainted will not be in the nude; any of their small talk or caressing will follow the first penetration and orgasm.

The Mangaian prefers sexual intercourse without the inconvenience of clothing, but he is also concerned lest he be seen. "Be careful—much talk around the island if you are seen." Hence, this social pressure serves to restrict most mature marital coitus to the night-time hours and often to "under-the-cover" of bedclothes. Again, there is little real desire to actually watch one's partner during the act; the principal interest is in "making every part of the body move." The principal requirement of the female (and the reason that the Mangaian male dislikes coitus with a European female) is that the woman "must move"—there must be plenty of pelvic action to satisfy her lover. Without question, the essential and principal component of Mangaian sexual ability and interest is not the foreplay or between-play, not the nakedness, not the scene or the props, and certainly not the position. Rather, it is the ability to continue the in-and-out position of coitus over long periods of time.

All of the principal varieties of coital position are practiced by the Mangaians: the partners facing each other or in the same direction while lying on their side (*aikaukau*); the male lying prone on top of the woman while facing one another (the most common position) or vice versa (*aitīra'a*); both partners standing, facing one another (*aitū*); the woman bending over and the

*PPN = proto-Polynesian; * = reconstructed word.

male mounting from behind (*ai'aka'oro*); penilingus (*kaiure*); cunnilingus (*kai'ika*); soixante-neuf. There is no recorded term for the latter, despite informant statements that the act is performed; however, the Mangaian fighting words (used as an insult on other islands), "*Mangaia Kai Kiore*," though ostensibly translated as "Mangaians eat rats," are a not-too-well-veiled allusion to genital-lingual practices. Anal intercourse, axillary intercourse with the penis held between breasts, thighs, feet, or in armpits, and other noncunnal means of sexual relief, including mutual genital manipulation to climax and masturbation, are used during the menstrual period—despite the older generations' horror at the concept of sexual contact during menstruation. (Mangaian grandfathers indicate that they were advised by their sexual mentors that copulation during menstruation was the cause of venereal disease.) The manual techniques are said to be used less frequently than in the northern Cook Islands. Europeanized Mangaians dislike discussing these variant positions.

The Mangaian desires a well-lubricated sexual path and may use his own saliva or a concoction of the viscous chewed bark or stalk of the hibiscus tree to assist him. Mangaians also say that a youthful or small female may require lubrication of her privates with soap, prior to intercourse.

Once penetration has been made, the male realizes that his action must be continuously kept up in order to bring his partner to climax (as has been pointed out by Kinsey). He may deliberately "think of other things" to avoid premature ejaculation; he may also fantasy to more rapidly bring on the climax. During copulation there is talk, the passing of compliments, and a good deal of moaning and sighing. Biting, or more particularly a strong sucking on the flesh of the body, may also accompany the sexual act. (The latter produces a red welt "bee sting," which provides evidence of one's sexual activities—to the annoyance of the church members when these occur on the elder members of the community.) Biting of the partner's body is a common expression of passionate involvement in the sexual act, as is oral-genital intercourse. My principal Mangaian informant (with whom I had previously been working on setting up an electric generator and voltmeter for my field equipment) expressed himself metaphorically as follows. When you "play" between the sexual acts, as in the oral-genital contact, your "voltage goes high," and "high voltage stops the smell" and the partners "do anything." But once the climax arrives, "the voltage drops down." However, when the "voltage is high," a "good man" will be able to continue his actions for fifteen to thirty minutes or more, and in the middle of this "a woman thinks she's urinating—but that's not urine." (But it is *not* the orgasm, according to Mangaians—it is "another type" of sensation.) Above all, the man's goal is to continue the coital action—"the longer you go, the more the pleasure"; "the man who goes only a short time does not 'love' (that is, want to please) his woman." Young cou-

ples may carry this act to climax three to five times in an evening. But marriage and the concomitant presence of children, and the increasing need for continuous physical exertion of work, reduce the number of climactic acts. There is also a decrease in the talk, stroking, and (for today's younger couples) the kissing between partners.

There is no indication of group intercourse on Mangaia other than the gang rapes, which will be discussed later in the chapter.

Currently, the most favored coital position on Mangaia is that of the couple prone, facing one another; most frequently the male assumes the superior role, although the female commonly assumes it also. The second most frequently practiced position is that of the woman bending over from the standing position, the man approaching her from the rear. Third most frequent (practiced, for the most part, when the woman is pregnant) is the position of the couple lying on their side with both partners facing in the same direction, the male approaching his partner from the rear (*păto'e*; this is *not* anal penetration). Very much less frequently practiced is the variant of the side position, in which partners face one another. Fourth most common of the positions (but very infrequently practiced) is that of the female facing down, prone, with the male approaching from the rear. Today, although the sitting or the "oceanic" position is "tried" among the newly mated, it is rarely practiced. But it is important to note that it is specifically acknowledged by informants that, "the older people, they 'know' (i.e., 'believe') that this is the best."

THE ORGASM

Despite the fact that the Mangaian male and female realize that orgasm is a culminating peak of the sexual act, it is not the sole goal to be achieved. As indicated above, the interplay of copulation and the prolongation of this interplay are the focus of the act. The Mangaian says that the orgasm "feels good" and "we enjoy it"; but he has not built up the elaborate concern with it that characterizes the American folklore of sex. This is, perhaps, due to the fact that it is so universally achieved among Polynesians of both sexes. It is stated that the orgasm must be "learned" by a woman and that this learning process is achieved through the efforts of "the good man." Formerly, it was the older woman who taught the young girls to achieve orgasm. Now, if one man is not successful in teaching this to her when she is young, then another man will soon take his place and provide more adequate tutelage.

The Mangaian male is not known to achieve the so-called extended orgasm, the effects of which in of itself—separately from the coital buildup—supposedly last from half an hour to one hour. (It has been reported for the premodern period by one worker on another Polynesian island on the basis of informant statements.) However, Mangaian men indicate that this extended orgasm—which they translate by the English term "knock-out"—has been observed among their womenfolk. In any event, the Mangaian male lover aims to have his partner achieve orgasm (*nene*) two or three times to his once. But the ultimate and invariable goal of two lovers is to so match their reactions that when the male finally does permit himself to reach climax it is achieved simultaneously with the peak of his partner's pleasure. The older males indicate that even though the young *māpū* has not yet learned to care much for his partner's pleasure, he will still concern himself with bringing her to climax, in order to "hold" her and to preserve his own reputation. Men say that they are always careful of "women's talk," in order that the female will "pass on the good name" of the male. For the Mangaian believes that once he gives his girl the climactic pleasure, she "cannot keep away from him"—unless someone else deliberately "holds her back" by bettering the other male's performance. But it was generally agreed among my several informants that the really important aspect of sexual intercourse for either the married man or the more experienced unwed male is to give pleasure to his wife or woman or girl—the pleasure of the orgasm; supposedly this is what gives the male partner his own pleasure and a special thrill that itself is set apart from his own orgasm. In this connection, it appears to be an accepted cultural fact that following an argument between the couple, Mangaian (and central Polynesian) women in general must have intercourse with their partners before they can "make up." For, the women say, this copulation is proof that the male is still "in love" (desires her).

A consensus of the formal Mangaian sexual discussion group, in analyzing the phenomenon of orgasm, was that the "average" number per night or week was as set forth [in Table 1]. Individual informant data and other sources of information, not only from Mangaia but from elsewhere in central Polynesia, indicate that these estimates are probably reasonably valid. However, I would, myself, tend to reduce slightly the younger male figures on frequency per week, because of situational factors that preclude continual night after night copulation. But I would tend also to raise slightly the frequency figures for the older males, because of the apparent strong demands of older Polynesian females. Further, one must keep in mind the variability between individuals. Some men may come to orgasm four times a night, every night; others, only once a night, two or three times a week. These data should be borne in mind during the discussion of impotency and sterility.

It is significant to note that the Mangaian males very definitely believe that men tend to want sexual activity more frequently than do their women but that women tend to "hold them back" from full sexual indulgence. Some husbands, however, may "beat the wife into submission." And, in contrast to western sexual folklore, Mangaians believe that it is the female who becomes thin from sexual exertion; males boast, *Me ū ana i a tāua, 'ua topa te to'e*—"If we two thump together (I will go so many times that) her rectum will fall out." And, again in contrast to western sexual folklore, the Mangaian emphasis is not upon the number of times a night that a male can achieve climax; rather, he sets his sights on the number of nights in the week that he is capable of coitus. In his teens and twenties, he aims at an every night capability; it is in the thirties and forties that he starts to "miss" nights. He also judges potency by his ability (or that of others) to get the same woman pregnant twice in one year, as well as to "make a girl grow thin."

Table 1

Approximate Male Age	Average Number of Orgasms per Night	Average Number of Nights per Week
18	3	7
28	2	5–6
38	1	3–4
48	1	2–3

REFERENCES

Marshall, D. S. 1961. *Ra'ivavae: An Expedition to the Most Fascinating and Mysterious Island in Polynesia.* New York: Doubleday.
n.d. "Polynesian Sexual Behavior." Manuscript
n.d. "The Village of God: An Ethnography of Mangaia." Manuscript.

CHAPTER EIGHT

Culture and Eating Disorders

Both anorexia and bulimia occur far more commonly in modern, industrialized societies where there is an abundance of food and female beauty is associated with thinness. Females usually comprise 90% to 95% of the cases. These disorders are most common in the United States, Canada, Europe, Australia, Japan, New Zealand, and among the white population of South Africa. However, a few cases have recently been identified in at least some nonindustrialized populations (Ritenbaugh, Shisslak, & Prince, 1992).

There has been an increase in the incidence of eating disorders in recent decades. This increase is very likely associated with changing cultural tastes regarding standards of female beauty in western society, which haved changed notably over the past 100 years. During the late 19th century, the ideal of female beauty consisted of a very "full figured" woman with large hips and breasts, far heavier than today's standards. Later, during the 1920s, the slim "flapper" style became the standard of female beauty. However, beginning in the mid-1930s, during the Great Depression era when food was scarce for many people, a more rounded figure for women began to return as the ideal, possibly indicating that the person was well fed. This trend culminated in the 1950s, with the ideal of female beauty exemplified by "full-figured" actresses Marilyn Monroe and Jayne Mansfield.

However, since the 1960s, the ideal of female beauty in the United States and other western nations has become increasingly thin. This cultural trend toward thinness as the ideal of female beauty continues to the present day, and women are under increasing pressure to lose weight to consider themselves physically attractive.

Overall, the risk for eating disorders among nonwesterners appears to rise with exposure to western culture (Rittenbaugh, Shisslak, & Prince, 1992). Individuals from groups without a history of eating disorders, upon assimilating western values and patterns of thought, come to fear fatness in a similar fashion to westerners (Mumford, Whitehouse, & Choudry, 1992; Nasser, 1986). For example, in a study of female Egyptian university students in Cairo and London, the Cairo sample showed no evidence of eating disorders, but the Egyptian students in London showed 12% positive for eating disorders (Nasser, 1986).

In studying body aesthetics in Fiji, Becker (1995) found that the sociocentric Fijians largely concerned themselves with culti-vation of social relationships through food exchange and had important interests in eating and sharing food for social reasons. Rejecting food for purposes of remaining thin was simply not a meaningful concern in Fijian culture. Becker argues that cultivation of thinness for purposes of personal beauty is directly related to western egocentrism and the autonomous self. If this is true, eating disorders will be directly related to the degree of western acculturation in any given population. As the influence of western culture continues to spread throughout the world, eating disorders will become increasingly common.

In the past, eating disorders in the United States have been found primarily in white women of the upper socioeconomic classes. This is still generally the case, although the situation is changing as more ethnic minorities become assimilated into Anglo American culture. The article in this chapter is by psychologists Kay K. Abrams, La Rue Allen, and James J. Gray. This is an epidemiological study of eating disorders among female college students in the United States. This study provides further evidence that most eating disorders are directly related to western cultural values. The authors found a lower prevalence of eating disorders in black females than in white females. They also found that the level of eating disorders among black females was related to their level of assimilation into Anglo American culture.

REFERENCES

Becker, A. E. (1995). *Body, self, and society: The view from Fiji.* Philadelphia: University of Pennsylvania Press.

Mumford, D. B., Whitehouse, A. M., & Choudry, I. Y. (1992). Survey of eating disorders in English-medium schools in Lahore, Pakistan. *International Journal of Eating Disorders, 11,* 173–184.

Nasser, M. (1986). Comparative study of the prevalence of abnormal eating attitudes among Arab female students of both London and Cairo universities. *Psychological Medicine, 16,* 621–625.

Ritenbaugh, C., Shisslak, C., & Prince, R. (1992). Eating disorders: A cross-cultural review in regard to DSM-IV. In J. E. Mezzich, A. Kleinman, H. Fabrega, B. Good, G. Johnson-Powell, K. M. Lin, S. Manson, & D. Parron (Eds.), *Cultural Proposals for DSM-IV* (pp. 158–165). Submitted to the DSM-IV Task Force by the NIMH Group on Culture and Diagnosis. Pittsburgh: University of Pittsburgh.

KAY KOSAK ABRAMS,[1] LA RUE ALLEN,[2] JAMES J. GRAY[3]

Disordered Eating Attitudes and Behaviors, Psychological Adjustment, and Ethnic Identity

A Comparison of Black and White Female College Students

The low prevalence of restrictive eating disorders among black women has been attributed primarily to cultural differences in the definition of beauty. Utilizing self-report measures, this study examined differences in the nature of disordered eating behaviors for black and for white female college students. Analyses of covariance and correlational tests revealed that white females demonstrated significantly greater disordered eating attitudes and behaviors than black females. Additionally, the data indicated that although disordered eating behaviors and attitudes are related to actual weight problems for black females, this is not the case for white females. Furthermore, this study is the first to provide evidence that restrictive eating disorders among black women are related to the degree to which they assimilate to mainstream culture. Finally disordered eating behaviors and attitudes were related to depression, anxiety, and low self-esteem in both groups.

Women representing ethnic minorities are reportedly less susceptible to developing eating disorders compared to white women in Western industrialized society (Dolan, 1991; Gordon, 1988; Schwartz, Thompson, & Johnson, 1982). The prevalence of anorexia nervosa and bulimia nervosa is reportedly rare among young black females in the United States (Andersen & Hay, 1985; Dolan, 1991; Gray, Ford, & Kelly, 1987; Hsu, 1987; Pumariega, Edwards, & Mitchell, 1984).

Among black female college students at a private university, Gray et al. (1987) found that the prevalence of bulimia nervosa was rare although dieting and binge behaviors were frequent. The prevalence rate of anorexia nervosa among nonwhite females has been estimated to be 0.42 per 100,000 between 1970 and 1976, as compared to 3.26 for white females (Jones, Fox, Babigan, & Hutton, 1980).

Although the frequency of obesity is greater among black women than white women in the United States, and while black women do report body-image dissatisfaction, black women are less driven to achieve thinness than white women (Rand & Kaldau, 1990; Thomas & James, 1988). Additionally, although black women may binge eat and may diet to manage their weight (Gray et al., 1987), they are not likely to engage in the extreme weight-loss behaviors that constitute an eating disorder, such as anorexia nervosa or bulimia nervosa.

The etiology of anorexia nervosa and bulimia nervosa is, in part, attributable to the internalization of particular cultural values and standards concerning the importance of thinness and beauty as central in the formation of self-concept for females (Boskind-White & White, 1983; Chernin, 1981, 1985; Garner & Garfinkel, 1980; Garner, Garfinkel, Schwartz, & Thompson, 1980; Rodin, Silberstein, & Striegel-Moore, 1984). A few researchers have suggested that as black females gain greater socioeconomic status and as they acculturate into mainstream society, they will be more at risk for developing anorexia nervosa and bulimia nervosa (Bulik, 1987; Gordon, 1988; Hsu, 1987; Theander, 1970; White, Hudson, & Campbell, 1985).

Although studies reveal a low prevalence of eating disorders among black women and differences in dietary behaviors

[1] Kay Kosak Abrams, Ph.D., is in private practice specializing in eating disorders in Silver Spring, Maryland. This article reports the results of her doctoral dissertation at the University of Maryland.

[2] La Rue Allen, Ph.D., is Professor at Michigan State University.

[3] James J. Gray, Ph.D., is Professor and Director of Clinical Training at American University.

Correspondence should be addressed to Dr. Abrams at 12115 Sweet Clover Drive, Silver Spring, MD 20904.

SOURCE: From the *International Journal of Eating Disorders, 14,* 49–57. Copyright © 1993 John Wiley & Sons, Inc. Reprinted by permission of John Wiley & Sons, Inc.

between white and black female populations, no study has examined whether disordered eating behaviors among black women are related to the maladaptive attitudes or negative psychological correlates that have been identified for young white women who have eating disorders. Additionally, this study examined whether black women who identify to a greater extent with being white in American society than with being black, are more likely to develop disordered eating behaviors and attitudes.

METHODS

Subjects

A total of 100 black females and 100 white females were recruited from the psychology department at a middle Atlantic state university. The students at this university are predominantly from middle and upper-middle socioeconomic groups. Participation required that black females identify themselves and both parents as black and from the United States and that white females identify themselves and both parents as white and also from the United States.

The mean age was 20.5 for white females and 19.3 for black females. White and black females were of equal mean heights, 64.93 inches (SD = 2.46) and 64.91 (SD = 3.15) inches, respectively, whereas weight varied significantly between groups [t (1,195) = −2.31, p < .05], with a mean of 128.8 for white females (SD = 16.3) and a mean of 136.2 for black females (SD = 26.79). There was no significant group difference in social class distinction (t, 195) = 1.95, p > .05 as measured by the Hollingshead scale (Hollingshead & Redlich, 1964).

MEASURES

Disordered Eating Behaviors

The Hawkins' and Clement's Binge Scale (1980) was used to identify subjects along a continuum of severity of binge eating. The Restraint Scale (Herman & Mack, 1975) was used to assess group differences in degree of dietary restraint.

Disordered Eating Attitudes

Drive for Thinness and Body Dissatisfaction were measured using the subscales of the Eating Disorder Inventory (EDI; Garner, Olmsted, & Polivy, 1983). Additionally, five items taken from Johnson's (1984) Diagnostic Survey of Eating Disorders were added to further measure body dissatisfaction. The Goldfarb

Fear of Fat Scale (GFFS; Goldfarb, Dykens, & Gerard, 1985) was utilized to measure attitudes about fatness.

Psychological Correlates

Psychological correlates measured included self-esteem, depression, and anxiety using the Rosenberg (1979) Self-Esteem Inventory, the Beck Depression Inventory-21 (BDI; Beck, Ward, Mendelson, Mock, & Erbaugh, 1961), and the State-Trait Anxiety Inventory (STAI, Form Y-2; Spielberger, Gorush, Lushene, Vagg, & Jacobs, 1983), respectively.

Assimilation

To identify cultural assimilation among blacks, the Racial Identity Attitude Scale for Blacks (RIAS-B; Helms, 1990) was administered. The RIAS-B allows identification of four conceptually independent stages of racial identity consciousness for blacks (Helms, 1990). In this study it was expected that for black females, disordered eating attitudes and behaviors would be significantly positively related to the Preencounter stage that reflects idealization of values and beliefs associated with white identity and rejection of values and beliefs associated with black identity.

Procedure

Questionnaires were administered to students in groups of three to six, and took approximately 30 minutes to complete. The order of the presentation of the measures was randomized to minimize error due to order effects.

RESULTS

All scales used in this study were found to have adequate reliability separately calculated for each racial group (Cronbach's alpha ranged from .56–.84). t Tests demonstrated a significant group difference for weight, t (1, 165) = −2.31, p < .05, but not for socioeconomic status, t (1, 165) = 1.95, p > .05. Analyses included analyses of covariance with weight as the covariate or correlational tests with weight partialled out. Alpha levels for significance were adjusted using Bonferroni's adjustment.

Disordered Eating Behaviors and Attitudes

Regarding disordered eating behaviors, white women demonstrated significantly greater dietary restraint than black women

$F (1, 195) = 60.14$, $p < .0001$. Although there were no significant group differences in severity of binge eating for those women who endorsed binge eating behavior, $F (1, 108) = 1.73$, $p > .10$, significantly fewer black women (35%) than white women (65%) reported binge eating behavior, $\chi^2 (1, 200) = 11.82$, $p < .001$ (Table 1).

Regarding purge behavior, chi-square analysis did not demonstrate a significant group difference in the proportion of blacks compared to whites who did or did not purge, using either self-induced vomiting, $\chi^2 (1, 199) = 3.27$, $p > .05$, or laxatives, $\chi^2 (1, 199) = 2.16$, $p > .10$. Although there was no significant difference between the groups, more than twice as many (12%) white female college students as black female students (5%) reported using self-induced vomiting for weight control.

White female students endorsed significantly greater Fear of Fat $F (1, 197) = 16.64$, $p < .001$, Drive for Thinness, $F (1, 195) = 22.14$, $p < .0001$, and significantly greater Body Dissatisfaction, $F (1, 195) = 50.67$, $p < .0001$ than black female students (Table 1).

Additional Group Differences Regarding Body Image and Weight Control

A different profile emerges between black and white subjects when responses from the test battery are compared. Although both white and black female students often feel that becoming fat would be displeasing, and both often engage in dieting, fasting, and exercise, approximately twice as many white than black female students binge or vomit once a week or more; would be negatively affected by a small upward weight fluctuation; and are preoccupied with the desire to be thin. Despite being heavier

Table 1
Means and standard deviations of measures of behaviors and attitudes toward food and thinness for white and for black females

Dependent Variable	White Women M	White Women SD	Black Women M	Black Women SD
Restraint	16.20[a]	6.10	10.97[b]	6.02
Binge	7.50[a]	4.65	6.25[a]	4.18
Fear of Fat	22.99[a]	7.02	18.81[b]	6.26
Drive for Thinness	7.12[a]	6.89	3.50[b]	4.96
Body Dissatisfaction	28.49[a]	11.86	20.26[b]	11.40

Note: Dissimilar superscripts indicate significant differences between means $p < .0001$, with alpha level set at .01 using Bonferroni's adjustment.

Table 2
Selected item frequencies for whites and blacks on binge scale, restraint scale, purge behavior questionnaire, drive for thinness scale, body dissatisfaction scale, and fear of fat

Item	Percentages of Yes Responses Whites	Percentages of Yes Responses Blacks
Subjects who binge	68	42
Subjects who binge once a week or more	21	11
Vomit after binge	12	7
Diet—sometimes often or always	57	40
Effect of 5 pound weight fluctuation on way you live your life—moderate and very much	49	21
Vomit to get rid of food—occasionally/often	12	5
Vomited once a week or more	5	1
Exercise once a day or more	28	24
Fasting once a week or more	13	15
Terrified of gaining weight—always, usually, often	55	30
Preoccupied with the desire to be thinner—always, usually, often	42	20
Satisfied with the shape of my body—always, usually, often	28	60
Two pounds weight gain negatively affect feelings about self—moderately, very much, extremely	52	26
Becoming fat would be the worst thing that could happen to me—somewhat true, very true	52	41

overall as a group, twice as many black than white female students are satisfied with the shape of their body as it is (Table 2).

Disordered Eating Behaviors and Attitudes as Related to Actual Weight

For black college females but not for white female students, the correlations between weight and three of the disordered behaviors and attitudes measured (e.g., Restraint, Body Dissatisfaction, and Drive for Thinness) were significant (Table 3).

Disordered Eating Behaviors and Attitudes as Related to Assimilation

As predicted, for black female students, the Preencounter stage of the RIAS (reflecting assimilation to white racial identity) was

Table 3
Intercorrelations between disordered eating behaviors and restrictive attitudes
about body image and weight for whites and blacks

	Weight	*Restraint*	*Binge*	*Body Dissatisfaction*	*Drive for Thinness*
Whites					
Restraint	.27				
n	100				
p	.006				
Binge	−.02	.70*			
n	68	68			
p	.872	.000			
Body Dissatisfaction	.28	.60*	.39*		
n	100	100	68		
p	.004	.000	.001		
Drive for Thinness	.04	.76*	.57*	.70*	
n	100	100	68	100	
p	.696	.000	.000	.000	
Fear of Fat	−.03	.70*	.54*	.65*	.87*
n	99	99	68	99	99
p	.808	.000	.000	.000	.000
Blacks					
Restraint	.55*				
n	.98				
p	.000				
Binge	.26	.66*			
n	40	41			
p	.101	.000			
Body Dissatisfaction	.70*	.74*	.52*		
n	98	99	41		
p	.000	.000	.000		
Drive for Thinness	.36*	.73*	.70*	.67*	
n	98	99	41	99	
p	.000	.000	.000	.000	
Fear of Fat	.16	.61*	.56*	.58*	.77*
n	98	99	42	99	99
p	.127	.000	.000	.000	.000

*$p < .003$, set using Bonferroni's adjustment.

significantly positively related to dietary Restraint, Fear of Fat, and Drive for Thinness (Table 4).

Disordered Eating Behaviors and Attitudes as Related to Psychological Correlates

For both groups, Restraint, Fear of Fat, and Drive for Thinness were significantly positively related to depression, anxiety, and low self-esteem (Table 5). For the white female college students, binge eating was significantly positively related to depression but not to anxiety or low self-esteem. For black females, binge eating was not significantly positively related to any of the psychological correlates measured (Table 5).

Although there were no significant group differences in the level of correlational relationships obtained between the psychological correlates and the dependent variables, the correlation

Table 4
Correlations of racial identity substages for blacks with
Restraint, Drive for Thinness, and Fear of Fat

	Restraint	Drive for Thinness	Fear of Fat
Substage			
Preencounter	.28*	.37*	.38*
(*N* = 95)	(*p* = .003)	(*p* < .0001)	(*p* < .0001)
Encounter	.01	.11	.09
(*N* = 94)			
Immersion	–.07	.01	.03
(*N* = 95)			
Internal	–.06	.01	–.07
(*N* = 95)			

*p < .02 (alpha set with Bonferroni's adjustment).

between anxiety and each of the disordered eating attitudes—Body Dissatisfaction, Fear of Fat, and Drive for Thinness—showed a stronger tendency toward a significant relationship for white women than for black women. Lack of a significant difference was due to the stringent alpha level required for the multiple correlational tests.

DISCUSSION

Results of the current study support previous findings that behaviors and attitudes related to eating disorders are culture bound. Black women were less concerned about weight loss and made less effort to achieve a thin body than white women as also found by Gray et al. (1987), Rand & Kaldau (1990), and Thomas and James (1988). Although the black female college students were heavier overall than the white female college students, they were less likely to engage in behaviors that characterize anorexia nervosa or bulimia nervosa, that is, severe restrictive dieting, binging, and purging.

Within the black culture, there is apparently greater acceptance for a range of normal body weights that are heavier than what most white women deem acceptable. This greater acceptance is likely based on a different standard of beauty.

Furthermore, the findings of this study indicate that weight-loss efforts and body dissatisfaction for the black female students were significantly positively related to weight. In contrast, white female students were likely to adopt disordered eating attitudes and behaviors regardless of actual weight problems. These findings together provide clarity for our understanding about why black women are less afflicted with restrictive eating disorders. There is less drive to achieve thinness among young adult black women and efforts to lose weight tend to be more realistic and less extreme. Weight-loss concern and efforts for white college women are seldom about actual weight problems; rather, the concern and efforts are about perceived weight problems.

This study further demonstrates that black women who endorse attitudes reflecting rejection of their black identity and idealization of white identity are more likely to also endorse attitudes about body image and related dietary behaviors that are associated with eating disorders, that is, Fear of Fat, Drive for Thinness, dietary Restraint.

Table 5
Correlations between psychological variables and
disordered eating behavior and attitudes about body image

	Depression White : Black		Anxiety White : Black		Low Self-Esteem White : Black	
	r		*r*		*r*	
Binge	.38*	.28	.31	.12	.29	.28
Restraint	.46**	.34**	.53**	.28**	.46**	.41**
Body Dissatisfaction	.48**	.41**	.55**	.38**	.48**	.55**
Fear of Fat	.48**	.42**	.56**	.37**	.43**	.52**
Drive for Thinness	.39**	.58**	.52**	.31**	.45**	.48**

Note: Alpha set at .003 by Bonferroni's adjustment.
*p < .003.
**p < .0001.

Blacks in the United States can be thought of as belonging more or less to two cultures (Helms, 1990), the African-American culture and the larger dominant white culture, each culture having a different band of acceptability in regard to weight and attractiveness. Thus, individuals within the black culture can be seen as differentially influenced by the two cultures. Several of the variables in this study—Restraint, Fear of Fat, and Drive for Thinness—were found to be significantly positively correlated with scores on the Preencounter subscale of the RIAS-B and not on the other three subscales of the RIAS-B (Table 4). It was confirmed that black women who adhere more to attitudes and beliefs reflecting a relative rejection of their own black identity, with idealization of white identity, are more likely to demonstrate dietary Restraint, as well as Fear of Fat, and Drive for Thinness, all of which already place white women at risk to develop eating disorders.

All measures of disordered eating in this study except binging were found to be related to three measures of pathology (low self-esteem, anxiety, and depression) in both the white and black groups. It is likely that a young woman who is dissatisfied with her appearance and engaging in severe dietary behaviors is also troubled by low self-esteem, anxiety, and depression or conversely if she had low self-esteem, anxiety, and depression, she might focus on dissatisfaction with her appearance. The association between disordered eating and other pathology has been found before in white college samples (Orleans & Barnett, 1984) but has been found for the first time in this study for a sample of black female college students.

The findings of the present study regarding restrictive dietary behavior and attitudes about body image as related to negative psychological dispositions (anxiety, depression, and low self-esteem) may be understood in terms of theories linking the development of eating disorders to traditional female socialization and recent sex-role changes in society (Bruch, 1985; Boskind-White & White, 1983; Timko, Striegel-Moore, Silberstein, & Rodin, 1987). According to feminist theorists, restrictive dietary practices and binge-purge behaviors may reflect a means of coping with conflict and subsequent anxiety about achieving independence. This study indicates a stronger relationship between anxiety and dieting attitudes/behaviors for young white women. Additionally, eating disorder attitudes and behaviors were found to be less likely linked to actual weight problems for whites than for blacks. Therefore, for black college women, efforts to be thin may not develop into an eating disorder because such efforts are not linked to the conflicts that white college women might have with respect to dependency issues. For example, establishing independence, i.e., a comfortable sense of autonomy, may be less conflictual for black female college students. Such an explanation, along with the greater acceptance of body weight within the black culture, would further explain why young adult black women are significantly less at risk for eating disorders.

REFERENCES

Andersen, A. E. & Hay, A. (1985). Racial and socioeconomic influences in anorexia nervosa and bulimia nervosa. *International Journal of Eating Disorders, 4,* 479–487.

Beck, A. T., Ward, C. H., Mendelson, M., Mock, J., & Erbaugh, J. (1961). An inventory for measuring depression. *Archives of General Psychiatry, 4,* 561–571.

Boskind-White, M., & White, W. C., Jr. (1983). *Bulimarexia: The binge/purge cycle.* New York: W. W. Norton.

Bruch, H. (1985). Four decades of eating disorders. In D. M. Garner & P. E. Garfinkel (Eds.), *Handbook of psychotherapy for anorexia nervosa and bulimia.* New York: The Guilford Press.

Bulik, C. M. (1987). Eating disorders in immigrants: Two case reports. *International Journal of Eating Disorders, 6,* 133–141.

Chernin, K. (1981). *The obsession: Reflections on the tyranny of slenderness.* New York: Harper Colophon Books.

Chernin, K. (1985). *The hungry self: Women, eating and identity.* New York: Time's Books.

Dolan, B. (1991). Cross-cultural aspects of anorexia nervosa and bulimia: A review. *International Journal of Eating Disorders, 10,* 67–78.

Garner, D. M., & Garfinkel, P. E. (1980). Socio-cultural factors in the development of anorexia nervosa. *Psychological Medicine, 10,* 656–657.

Garner, D. M., Garfinkel, P. E., Schwartz, E., & Thompson, M. G. (1980). Cultural expectations of thinness in women. *Psychological Reports, 47,* 483–491.

Garner, D. M., Olmsted, M. P., & Polivy, J. (1983). Development and validation of a multidimensional eating disorder inventory for anorexia nervosa and bulimia. *International Journal of Eating Disorders, 2,* 15–35.

Goldfarb, L. A., Dykens, E. M., & Gerard, M. (1985) The Goldfarb Fear of Fat Scale. *Journal of Personality Assessment, 49,* 329–332.

Gordon, R. A. (1988). A socio-cultural interpretation of the current epidemic of eating disorders. In B. J. Blinder, B. F. Chaiting, and R. Goldstein (Eds.), *The eating disorders* (pp. 151–163). New York: PMA Publishing Corp.

Gray, J. J., Ford, K., & Kelly, L. M. (1987). The prevalence of bulimia in a black college population. *International Journal of Eating Disorders, 6,* 733–740.

Hawkins, R. C., & Clement, P. F. (1980). Development and construct validation of a self-report measure of binge eating tendencies. *Addictive Behaviors, 5,* 219–226.

Helms, J. E. (1990). *Black and white racial identity: Theory, research and practice.* New York: Greenwood Press.

Herman, C., & Mack, D. (1975). Restrained and unrestrained eating. *Journal of Personality, 43,* 647–660.

Hollingshead, A. G., & Redlich, F. C. (1964). *Social class and mental illness.* New York: Wiley & Sons, Inc.

Hsu, L. K. (1987). Are eating disorders becoming more common among blacks? *International Journal of Eating Disorders, 6,* 113–124.

Johnson, C. (1984). Initial consultation for patients with bulimia and anorexia nervosa. In D. M. Garner & P. E. Garfinkel (Eds.), *Anorexia nervosa and bulimia* (pp. 19–55). New York: The Guilford Press.

Jones, D. J., Fox, M. M., Babigan, H. M., & Hutton, H. E. (1980). Epidemiology of anorexia nervosa in Monroe County, New York: 1960–1976. *Psychosomatic Medicine, 42,* 551–558.

Orleans, T. C., & Barnett, L. R. (1984). Bulimarexia: Guidelines for behavioral assessment and treatment. In R. C. Hawkins, W. J. Frmoun, & P. C. Clement (Eds.), *The binge-purge syndrome* (pp. 144–183). New York: Springer Publishing Company.

Pumariega, A. J., Edwards, P., & Mitchell, C. B. (1984). Anorexia nervosa in black adolescents. *Journal of the American Academy of Child Psychiatry, 23,* 111–114.

Rand, C. S. W., & Kaldau, J. M. (1990). The epidemiology of obesity and self-defined weight problems in the general population: Gender, race, age, and social class. *International Journal of Eating Disorders, 9,* 329–343.

Rodin, J., Silberstein, L., & Striegel-Moore, R. (1984). Women and weight: A normative discontent. In T. B. Sonderegger (Ed.), *Nebraska symposium on motivation: Vol. 32. Psychology and gender* (pp. 267–307). Lincoln: University of Nebraska Press.

Rosenberg, M. (1979). *Conceiving the self.* New York: Basic Books.

Schwartz, D. M., Thompson, M. G., & Johnson, C. L. (1982). Anorexia nervosa and bulimia: The socio-cultural context. *International Journal of Eating Disorders, 1,* 20–35.

Spielberger, C. D., Gorush, R. L., Lushene, R. E., Vagg, P. R., and Jacobs, G. A. (1983). *Manual for the State-Trait Anxiety Inventory (Form Y) (Self-Evaluation Questionnaire).* Palo Alto, CA: Consulting Psychologists Press.

Theander, S. (1970). Anorexia nervosa: A psychiatric investigation of 94 female patients. *Acta Psychiatrica Scandinavica (Supplement), 214,* 1–194.

Thomas, V. G., & James, M. D. (1988). Body-image, dieting tendencies, and sex role traits in urban black women. *Sex Roles, 18,* 523–529.

Timko, C., Striegel-Moore, R. H., Silberstein, L. R., & Rodin, J. (1987). Femininity/masculinity and disordered eating in women: How are they related? *International Journal of Eating Disorders, 66,* 701–712.

White, W. C., Hudson, L., & Campbell, S. N. (1985). Bulimarexia and black women: A brief report. *Psychotherapy: Theory Research Practice Training, 22,* 449–450.

CHAPTER NINE

Culture and Substance-Related Disorders

Each society has its own values, beliefs, and customs regarding the use of mood altering substances, as well as differences in the availability of various substances. Therefore, when considering the topic of substance abuse, it is very important to view any individual's substance taking behavior from within his or her own set of cultural schemas.

In DSM-IV substance abuse is defined as "repeated negative consequences resulting from a maladaptive pattern of substance use" (American Psychiatric Association, 1994, p. 182). The negative consequences can include legal, social, and occupational problems. However, negative consequences resulting from substance use can vary dramatically by sociocultural context. For example, what is socially considered to be "alcohol abuse" differs across cultures. Laws regarding alcohol use, social standards of drinking, and standards regarding alcohol use while working differ in different societies. For instance, the United States and Saudi Arabia have radically different cultural standards for alcohol use and abuse. Drinking alcohol is normal and normative in the United States, but it is immoral, illegal, and punishable in Saudi Arabia.

Even in societies where drinking alcohol is normative, attitudes toward alcohol use may differ from U.S. norms. For example, in Puerto Rico, a large percentage of heavy drinking males do not meet the DSM-IV criteria for alcohol abuse, mostly because they are not indigenously considered to be impaired in their social or occupational functioning. This is due to a great extent to the highly male dominant social structure that allows a permissive attitude toward heavy drinking in males (Canino, Burnam, & Caetano, 1992). Thus, these heavy drinking males do not face the kind of negative social and legal consequences that heavy drinkers in another society might encounter. A similar situation is also found in Korea and Japan. In these societies, heavy alcohol use is expected and, to some extent, required by cultural custom for normal social interaction among males. Not engaging in heavy alcohol use would have negative social and occupational consequences for males in these societies. Using the DSM-IV definition of alcohol abuse, which is based on the presence of negative social consequences, means that the characteristics of alcohol abuse will vary by cultural context. This point needs to be appreciated by clinicians.

The behavioral response of any given individual to a specific drug is highly variable and is dependent on three factors. First are the psychopharmacological effects of the drug. This is complicated by the type of substance used, the dose taken, the method of dosing, the duration of dosing, the individual's physiological tolerance for the drug, and time since the last dose. Second are the psychocultural characteristics of the individual. This refers to the person's cultural identity, personality traits, cultural beliefs about the behavioral effects of the drug, and the cultural meaning of taking the drug. Third is the sociocultural setting in which the drug is taken. This includes the people who are present and their beliefs, moods, and behaviors. All of these have an impact on the behavioral response of the individual to a drug.

Increasingly, theorists are viewing addictive behavior as a single concept encompassing all types of mood altering substances such as alcohol, drugs, food, and tobacco (Donovan, 1988; Doweiko, 1996; Franklin, 1987). Although theories about the etiology of addictions are still controversial, the tendency in recent years has been to view persons with addictions as possessing an *addictive personality*. This means that persons are not necessarily addicted to any particular mood altering substance but generally feel the need to alter their moods with substances. Thus, they will have substances of choice based on substance effects, availability, and so on, but they will use whatever mood altering substance is available if the substance of choice is not readily obtainable.

For example, Schmitz et al. (1991) found that 50% of persons seeking treatment for alcoholism were also regularly using other mood altering drugs. Doweiko (1996) has also noted that addiction to a single mood altering substance is becoming increasingly rare. If addicts can switch so easily between drugs, it implies that their problem is not an addiction to a particular substance but an addictive personality.

Furthermore, it is increasingly being found that persons with other mental disorders are comorbid with substance-related disorders. Recent estimates of mentally ill persons comorbid for substance-related disorders range from 50% to 74% (Khalsa, Shaner, Anglin, & Wang, 1991; Leshner, 1991; Millman, 1991; Polcin, 1992; Robertson, 1992). Mentally ill persons who are also substance abusers tend to have low social functioning, low educational achievement, increased poverty and homelessness, increased medical problems, and increased arrests compared to mentally ill persons who are not substance abusers (Bartels et al., 1993; Kutcher et al., 1992; O'Hare, 1992). Whether these characteristics are a cause or an effect of substance abuse is unclear. They are probably both. However, it does seem clear that these people are trying to alter their moods with the substances, in effect, attempting to self-medicate for their psychological problems.

It appears likely that environmental stress is an important factor in the etiology of substance-related disorders. Stress may be implicated in two ways. First, substance abuse may be a response to stress presently occurring in a person's life. An example of this would be using drugs to escape the emotional pain of some stressful life event such as the death of a loved one or an unexpected loss of employment. This can trigger a downward spiral in which substance abuse leads to further social or occupational impairment, which increases environmental stress, which leads to further susbstance abuse, and so on.

Second, stress that occurred earlier in a person's life during a critical period of personality development may cause that person to be more susceptible to subsequent stress. Some evidence suggests that hypersensitivity to environmental stress can become structured into the neural networks of the brain as a result of emotional trauma early in life. For example, rhesus monkeys separated from their mothers for 2 six-day periods during infancy, later as adults exhibited pathological behavior such as aggression, signs of depression, increased alcohol consumption when allowed to self-administer alcohol and, in females, neglect or abuse of offspring. In addition, these monkeys showed elevated levels of stress hormones (Suomi, 1991). Thus, the emotional trauma of early separation produced pathological changes in personality in the monkeys and hypersensitivity to further stress.

The traditional intoxicating substance in western culture is alcohol. The intoxicating effects of alcohol are variable. Some individuals are capable of developing tremendous physical tolerance to alcohol. They are able to drink amounts of alcohol that would be toxic for other persons and still fulfill all of their social and occupational obligations.

Patterns of drinking also differ by culture. For example, in France, alcohol consumption for an individual is typically spread out over the course of the day, with 3 to 5 glasses of wine being consumed with meals on a daily basis. Thus, a considerable amount of alcohol is consumed during a one-week period, but the individual does not experience significant intoxication or impairment. In contrast, alcohol consumption in the United States is usually reserved for the end of the workday, weekends, or holidays. At these times, alcohol consumption can be heavy. This type of "partying" consumption can result in extreme intoxication because drinking is confined to a short period of time.

The overall amount of alcohol consumed over a one-week period is usually less than in France, but it is more intoxicating because it is consumed all at once.

Similarly, the psychocultural effects of alcohol intoxication differ by culture. For example, there is a pervasive belief in the United States that alcohol intoxication instigates aggressive conduct or violence (Critchlow, 1986). And, in fact, alcohol has been implicated in violent crime in both offenders and victims in the United States (Bartol, 1995). However, the alcohol-violence connection appears to be strongest in the United States. In many countries, including France, Germany, Italy, Portugal, and Spain, more alcohol is consumed per capita than in the United States, but there is far less violence and crime. This is also probably related to the differences in patterns of drinking behavior in which people in the United States experience more intoxication even though their overall consumption is less.

The psychological effects of alcohol intoxication can also vary by culture. For example, in Japan alcohol intoxication does not make people violent but rather brings out affectionate childishness (DeVos, 1984). The propensity toward violence during alcohol intoxication in the United States is probably related to the same factors that promote aggression and violence in overall personality development (Chapter 3). Thus, the negative behavioral effects of alcohol intoxication are influenced by the person's cultural identity, personality traits, cultural beliefs about the behavioral effects of alcohol, cultural patterns of drinking, and the sociocultural setting. Alcohol-related behavior becomes pathological by DSM-IV standards only when a combination of factors is present.

In the United States people generally adhere strictly to the Alcoholics Anonymous (AA) definition of alcoholism. According to AA, alcoholism is viewed as a progressive physical disease for which there is no cure, and the only successful treatment strategy is complete abstinence. This AA definition of alcoholism is a cultural construct. Like other cultural constructs, it has the ability to affect subjective experience of illness, idioms of distress, culture-based diagnosis, culture-based treatment, and culture-based outcome.

For example, if persons who abuse alcohol but are not physically dependent on alcohol enter an AA program, they are very likely to be classified as "alcoholics." If those persons accept this definition, their subjective experience of the problem will be affected. They are likely to view themselves as "diseased" and powerless over their condition. This can be detrimental to their confidence and self-esteem, promoting anxiety about drinking. They may become obsessed with either drinking too much or not at all. Similarly, their idioms of distress—the way they express themselves and interact with others—will be affected. They may publicly present themselves as "recovering alcoholics" or "alcoholics" even though they have never been physically dependent on alcohol and may have been abstaining for months or even years.

The culture-based treatment in the AA model is commonly "detoxification," consisting of inpatient stays of one month in a substance abuse treatment center. This is combined with indoctrination in the AA model in which individuals are repeatedly instructed to admit that they are powerless over their "disease" and are asked to turn their will over to God or some higher power. The culture-based outcome of this treatment can result in abstinence from drinking. However, some people become more convinced of their powerlessness and give in to their "disease," drinking even more and fulfilling the prophecy of a progressive course for their disorder. This progressive course can also be considered a culture-based outcome if their drinking habits were adversely affected by the AA treatment. More recently, treatment programs that teach alcohol abusers how to drink in moderation have been established and have shown some success (Kishline, 1996).

The article in this chapter is by cross-cultural psychiatrist Wolfgang G. Jilek. Jilek reviews folk healing methods in nonwestern societies and points out the inadequacies of the AA 12-step method across cultural groups. Other more culturally appropriate types of treatment are often more successful. For example, traditional Alcoholics Anonymous groups have not generally been successful among Native American populations (Heath, 1983) because the cultural schemas underlying the AA healing ceremonies are not consistent with Native American culture. Healing systems consistent with Native American culture have more symbolic healing power (see Chapter 5). Therefore, in recent decades, many Indian groups have revived the traditional Sweat Lodge ceremony for treating alcoholism (Hall, 1986).

In the Sweat Lodge, hot rocks are placed in the center of the lodge and are sprinkled with water to release steam. In the small enclosed space this produces profuse sweating in the small group who sit in a circle facing the center. Beyond the direct therapeutic effects of the sweating, the ceremony utilizes symbolic objects manipulated by a spiritual leader to alter the cognitions and emotions of the participants. The ceremony itself and the objects used within it are symbols of the revival of the Native American culture and the removal of the harmful effects of the dominant white culture. The ceremony is experienced as a purification from the pollution of white culture and the effects of alcohol, which are seen as a manifestation of white cultural pollution. The ceremonies are designed to help individuals strengthen their Indian personal and group identity; relieve depression related to cultural alienation, relative deprivation, and cultural identity confusion; and create a new healthy way of life for the individual and the group.

This transformation is achieved in a ritualized symbolic death of the old polluted self and rebirth of a new, strong, purified Indian self. The sociocentric bonds of traditional Native American culture are renewed and strengthened in the ceremony. Individuals receive the emotional support of group identity and escape the alienation of the egocentric white culture. This creates new social networks, alters negative social relationships, and allows healed individuals to take on new social roles. The sick role of the alcoholic is exchanged for the prestigious role of the supernaturally purified traditional Indian identity.

This use of culturally validated symbolic healing and group reinforcement of the new healthy identity is more effective in this sociocultural context for the treatment of alcoholism than the traditional Alcoholic Anonymous healing method. Thus, treatment for alcohol and drug dependence should always be conducted in a way that is consistent with the cultural identity of the individual for optimal outcome. In this article, Jilek highlights the use of culturally appropriate symbolic healing methods in the treatment of substance-related disorders in various nonwestern societies.

REFERENCES

American Psychiatric Association. (1994). *Diagnostic and statistical manual of mental disorders* (4th ed.). Washington, DC: American Psychiatric Association.

Bartels, S., Teague, G., Drake, R., Clark, R., Bush, P., & Noordsy, D. (1993). Substance abuse in schizophrenia: Service utilization and costs. *Journal of Nervous and Mental Disease, 181*, 227–232.

Bartol, C. R. (1995). *Criminal behavior: A psychosocial approach* (4th ed.). Englewood Cliffs, NJ: Prentice Hall.

Canino, G., Burnam, A., & Caetano, R. (1992). The prevalence of alcohol abuse/dependence in two Hispanic communities. In J. Helzer & G. Canino (Eds.), *Alcoholism in North America, Europe and Asia* (pp. 131–155). New York: Oxford University Press.

Critchlow, B. (1986). The powers of John Barleycorn: Beliefs about the effects of alcohol on social behavior. *American Psychologist, 41*, 751–764.

DeVos, G. (1984). *Heritage of endurance*. Berkeley: University of California Press.

Donovan, D. M. (1988). Assessment of addictive behaviors: Implications of an emerging biopsychosocial model. In D. M. Donovan & G. A. Marlatt (Eds.), *Assessment of addictive behaviors*. New York: Guilford Press.

Doweiko, H. E. (1996). *Concepts of chemical dependency* (3rd ed.). Pacific Grove, CA: Brooks/Cole.

Franklin, J. (1987). *Molecules of the mind*. New York: Dell.

Hall, R. (1986). Alcohol treatment in American Indian populations: An indigenous treatment modality compared with traditional approaches. *Annals of the New York Academy of Science, 472*, 168–178.

Heath, D. B. (1983). Alcohol use among North American Indians: A cross-cultural survey of patterns and problems. In R. G. Smart, F. B. Glaser, Y. Israel, H. Kalant, R. E. Popham, & W. Schmidt (Eds.),

Research advances in alcohol and drug problems (Vol. 7, pp. 343–396). New York: Plenum Press.

Khalsa, H., Shaner, A., Anglin, M., & Wang, J. (1991). Prevalence of substance abuse in a psychiatric evaluation unit. *Drug and Alcohol Dependence, 28,* 215–223.

Kishline, A. (1996). A toast to moderation. *Psychology Today, 29*(1), 53–56.

Kutcher, S., Kachur, E., Marton, P., Szalai, J., et al. (1992). Substance abuse among adolescents with chronic mental illnesses: A pilot study of descriptive and differentiating features. *Canadian Journal of Psychiatry, 37,* 428–431.

Leshner, A. (1991). Treatment. *National conference on drug abuse research and practice: Conference highlights.* Rockville, MD: NIDA.

Millman, R. (1991). Indentification of dual diagnosis in drug abusers. *National conference on drug abuse research and practice: Conference highlights.* Rockville, MD: NIDA.

O'Hare, T. (1992). The substance-abusing chronically mentally ill client: Prevalence, assessment, treatment and policy concerns. *Social Work, 37,* 185–187.

Polcin, D. (1992). Issues in the treatment of dual diagnosis clients who have chronic mental illness. *Professional Psychology: Research and Practice, 23,* 30–37.

Robertson, E. (1992). The challenge of dual diagnosis. *Journal of Health Care for the Poor and Underserved, 3,* 198–207.

Schmitz, J., DeJong, J., Roy, A., Garnett, D., Moore, V., Lamparski, D., Waxman, R., & Linnoila, M. (1991). Substance abuse among subjects seeking treatment for alcoholism. *Archives of General Psychiatry, 48,* 182–183.

Suomi, J. (1991). Uptight and laid-back monkeys: Individual differences in the response to social challenges. In S. Branch, W. Hall, & E. Dooling (Eds.), *Plasticity of development* (pp. 27–55). Cambridge, MA: MIT Press.

WOLFGANG G. JILEK

Traditional Healing in the Prevention and Treatment of Alcohol and Drug Abuse [1]

This article reviews traditional non-Western approaches to the treatment and prevention of substance abuse and dependence. Therapeutic practices reported here are based on Buddhist, Taoist, Hindu, Islamic and shamanic traditions as well as on syncretistic Christianized folk beliefs. Traditional practitioners operate outside the official health care system but in some areas in collaboration with it. Analysis of these practices reveals general principles of traditional healing, and permits hypotheses on the advantages and disadvantages of traditional approaches.

INTRODUCTION

The joint declaration on primary health care made in 1978 by the World Health Organization and UNICEF at Alma Ata, Kazakhstan, for the first time internationally recognized the positive role of traditional indigenous practitioners (World Health Organization, 1978). By that time, the portrait of the traditional healer of non-Western cultures, as depicted in psychiatric and ethnologic literature, had changed from that of a mentally abnormal individual permitted by his/her culture to act out personal psychopathology in a prestigious role, to that of a skilled practitioner, potentially useful to modern health care schemes as an inexpensive therapeutic resource. This reversal in the Western perception of traditional healers in other cultures reflects the profound changes that took place in the Western zeitgeist in the historical context of global decolonization: the abandonment of a eurocentric world view and of Western superiority claims, leading to an upgrading of the Western view of non-Western cultures and their exponents (Jilek, 1971).

Meanwhile, most developing countries, encouraged by the World Health Organization, have included traditional healing resources in their national health plans and have at least made some moves towards systematic collaboration with traditional practitioners in primary health care. Initially, such collaboration was thought to be necessary only during an interim phase until there was sufficient professional manpower available for an all-encompassing modern health care system. However, the general expectation that with the establishment of universal modern health care traditional healing practices would disappear, has failed to materialize. Even in populations to whom modern health care is freely available, such as to the great majority of North American Native peoples, traditional therapeutic resources are often preferentially utilized, especially in conditions with important psychosomatic and psychosocial aspects (Jilek, 1978).

A recent review of substance use research by Oyefeso (1994) confirms the significant relationship between sociocultural factors and substance use and misuse, and in its conclusions notes that intervention must be relevant to the sociocultural context of substance use and misuse. It would appear plausible, then, that intervention by the culture-congenial practices of indigenous traditional healing is most relevant to the sociocultural context of substance problems.

While the role of traditional healing resources in primary health and mental health care is now generally acknowledged, the important contribution of traditional indigenous therapeutic resources to the management of substance abuse and dependence among non-Western populations is not as well known.

To document this contribution, I have over many years collected pertinent data through personal observation among non-Western populations in North and South America, Asia and Africa whenever I had the opportunity, as well as through correspondence and search of the scientific literature whereby I relied mainly on authors whose work had already become known to me in the field.

The uneven geographical distribution of the observations and investigations presented in this overview is explained by my considering only populations on whose sociocultural situation I have first-hand knowledge, and by my giving priority to the contributions of researchers and professionals on whom I have work-related information.[2]

The term "traditional healing" as used here refers to non-orthodox therapeutic practices based on indigenous cultural

SOURCE: From *Transcultural Psychiatric Research Review, 31* (3), 219–256. Copyright © 1994. Reprinted with permission.

traditions and operating outside official health care systems. Although often validated by experience, these practices are not founded on a positivist system of logico-experimental science.

Included in the present review are therapeutic ventures based on Islamic, Buddhist, Taoist, shamanic and Hindu religious traditions, syncretistic amalgamations of traditional non-Western indigenous practices with Christian faith healing as well as originally Western-inspired mutual aid groups which have been reinterpreted and repatterned according to local cultural traditions so as to now be essentially different culture-specific approaches. Not defined as traditional healing, and therefore not included here, are "alternative therapies" which are demonstrably offshoots of Western schools of medicine—whether as idiosyncratic interpretations or oppositional variations (e.g., homeopathy, naturopathy, etc.). Likewise, not included here is acupuncture; although derived from Chinese traditional medicine, it is now practised on a global scale.

OUTLINE

In accordance with the above stated limitations, this paper presents a selective geographical overview of traditional indigenous therapeutic approaches to substance use problems among populations in Asia, North, Central and South America, and in southern Africa, with descriptions and, whenever available, information on utilization and outcome.

The first part of the paper contains reports on the following therapeutic ventures that are serving the prevention and treatment of substance use and abuse:

1. in Asia: Thai Buddhist treatment centres; Lao folk treatment; Hmong shamanic rituals; therapeutic approaches based on Malay Islamic traditions, on Chinese medicine and Taoist traditions, on Hindu traditions, on Japanese Buddhist traditions, and on Arab Islamic traditions.
2. in North America: Alaska Eskimo "Spirit Movement"; Amerindian "AA" groups; revived traditional Amerindian ceremonials (Sweat Lodge ceremony, Sun Dance, Winter Spirit Dance, Gourd Dance); syncretistic religious Amerindian cults (Native American Church, *Gaiwiio*, Indian Shaker Church).
3. in Central and South America: *Espiritismo*, Mexican, Ecuadorian and Peruvian folk healing.
4. in southern Africa: syncretistic Afro-Christian cults in the Republic of South Africa, Namibia and Malawi.

The second part of the paper discusses the conceptual basis and efficacy of traditional healing, the relevant principles operant in traditional healing and some of the advantages and disadvantages of traditional as compared to modern treatment approaches, as well as implications for the clinician. An appendix summarizes legal regulations pertaining to the practice of traditional medicine.

ASIA

Buddhist Treatment Centres in Thailand

Detoxification and rehabilitation treatment for substance dependence is performed at five Buddhist monasteries in Thailand (Anonymous, no date; Jilek, unpublished notes, 1988/89; Jilek-Aall & Jilek, 1985; Poshyachinda 1980; 1982; 1985; Westermeyer, 1979, 1980). In four of these the focus is on opiate dependence although cannabis, solvent and *kratom* (*Mitragyna speciosa*) addicts are also admitted. At one monastery (Wat Ta Shee) the majority of the clientele are alcoholics. The duration of obligatory inpatient treatment is short, ranging from a few days to a few weeks according to centre but patients are invited to stay longer and some join the monastic community and become co-therapists. Each centre has its own procedures but common principles can be identified. The treatment requires total commitment and utilizes the culture-congenial death and rebirth myth and the symbolism of religious initiation. The patient is shedding the vestiges of his evil addict-self—in some centres by taking a solemn public vow to forever abstain, in others by participating in the mock funeral of his old self. In most centres, mixtures of various herbal medicines (not identified) are orally administered during the initial treatment phase with the stated purpose of eliminating chemical and spiritual pollution. At Wat Tam Krabok, the patient has to go through a truly nauseating ordeal in a group therapeutic setting reminiscent of Pavlovian deconditioning although the addicting drug is only talked about. The herbal medicine, said to consist of "100 plant ingredients," is administered daily for five days with copious amounts of water and has a strong emetic effect which is intensified by the visual, auditory and olfactory stimulus of collective retching and vomiting, accompanied by the loud rhythmic drumming of already detoxified fellow patients and by the exhortations of the monk-therapists. The herbal medicines employed at Wat Pa Pang, Wat Tam Talu and Wat Ta Shee induce a brief period of semi-comatose sleep or unconsciousness followed by a delirium-like state which may counteract physical withdrawal symptoms. The effects of both herbal treatments—physical exhaustion after prolonged vomiting and loss of consciousness—emphasize death-rebirth symbolism suggesting to the patient the start of a new life. This intensive and dramatic treatment is followed by a period of recuperation, assisted by physiotherapeutic measures such as herbal steam baths. During the rest and recreation phase, religious teaching and therapeutic counselling are intensified. These are mostly conducted in groups but if needed also individually, with rehabilitated addicts playing an important role. There is also an opportunity for musical and other entertainment, and at some centres for helping in temple and facility construction and at religious art works in a kind of voluntary ergotherapy. The treatment is free as Thai temple communities rely on donations by pious people. A subsistence contribution is often minimal and may be waived. Maintaining contact with family is encouraged and, in some centres, family members are accommodated.

From 1963 to 1977 slightly more than 40,000 cases were treated at Wat Tam Krabok according to Poshyachinda (1980), and certainly many more since then. Thousands must have been treated at other centres which started in the 1970s.

Patients come from Thailand but also from other countries of South East and South Asia, and a few Westerners can always be found among clientele and monk-therapists. In spite of the initial treatment ordeal the patients' dignity is always safeguarded and there is no stigma attached to having been a drug addict as many therapists share the same history.

The larger community participates by funding through donation, sponsorship and volunteer activity. The work of the Buddhist treatment centres has found recognition by government authorities such as the Narcotics Control Board, and has led to some grant support. The centres have found positive publicity in national and international media, especially Wat Tam Krabok. The attitude of the official health care system appears favourable and Thai experts on drug addiction treatment are completely open-minded *vis-à-vis* this approach.

Enquiries on long-term results are made by the centres in an unsystematic way, e.g., in reunions of former patients organized by the monk therapists, through contact persons and community key informants. In pamphlets issued by the centres, results are quoted in round figures such as "70% success, 25% relapse" without specifying time limits. Scientific follow-up studies conducted by the Drug Dependence Research Centre, Institute of Health Research, Chulalongkorn University in the late 1970s, indicated that the rate of success as measured in six-months post-discharge abstinence rates was not inferior to that achieved by modern drug dependence treatment in medical institutions (Poshyachinda, 1980; 1982; 1985). A similar conclusion has been reached by Westermeyer (1979; 1980) who in 1972/73 compared treatment outcome in Laotian narcotic addicts treated at Wat Tam Krabok with that attained in an official drug treatment program in Laos. In terms of public cost-effectiveness, the Buddhist centres are admittedly far superior to official treatment programs. In terms of safety for the patient there may be some concern regarding possible toxic effects of the unknown herbal

agents inducing either emesis, which sometimes may result in collapse, or impairment/loss of consciousness. A higher mortality than in medical facilities was in the past reported among aged opium addicts; however, the number of admissions of such patients has been steadily decreasing.

Folk Treatment in Laos

In Laos, opium addicts are treated by Buddhist monks in religious and quasi-religious settings, often after making a solemn vow to abstain (Jilek, unpublished notes, 1989; Westermeyer, 1973; 1982). Withdrawal symptoms are treated by massage, induced sweating, special diet and herbal remedies some of which have sedative effects. Addicts may stay at a temple for an individually determined period, receive counselling and participate in religious ceremonies. Herb doctors operating outside religious settings also treat opium addicts and may add tapering doses of opium or alcohol to the herbal remedies they administer during the withdrawal period; some may also apply massage, acupuncture and moxibustion.

Due to the traditional therapeutic role and the high prestige of the Buddhist clergy, treatment in religious settings is very well accepted by the community and by motivated addicts. Government attitude toward the Buddhist clergy is tolerant and sympathetic in general and this also extends to healing activities.

Hmong shamanic rituals in a refugee camp.   In consultation with the author, the International Rescue committee integrated shamanic rituals, traditionally used in Laotian Hmong villages to free opium addicts from their dependence, in a modern opium detoxification and rehabilitation programme for drug addicts in a hill tribes refugee camp in northern Thailand (Jilek, videos, 1988/89; Jilek & Jilek-Aall, 1990a, 1990b). Each new patient group entering the programme is initiated by a ceremony performed by prestigious Hmong shamans, intended to entice the opium goddess to leave the addicts for a new residence in a miniature palace built and symbolically provisioned for her needs. Opium smoking utensils are surrendered by the addicts and choice specimens are put in the "palace." In front of the "palace" the addicts take a sacred vow never to use drugs again, while the senior shaman invokes supernatural powers for confirmation. The patient group is exorcised in a ritual in which they are joined by a rope tied to a sacrificed pig which acts as spirit messenger while the officiating shaman symbolically travels to the other world to free the addicts' souls from their captivity under the power of the opium spirits. Finally, the new abode of the opium goddess and the surrendered opium utensils are burnt in a great bonfire. As the smoke ascends, it is declared that the opium goddess has definitely left the addicts and has returned to the other world with their opium utensils. The ceremony is concluded by a communal meal shared by patients, shamans, and staff. Throughout the three weeks of inpatient treatment, the shamans render spiritual support to clientele of the IRC Detox Centre.

Although participation in the shamanic rituals is absolutely voluntary most patients take part. The ceremonial appeals to the great majority of hill tribes refugees of various ethnic groups more than unadapted medical programmes or those with Christian religious input. Most hill tribes patients belonging to the Christian minority also participate in the ceremonial. Catholic religious functionaries are tolerant and supportive.

The main effectiveness of this shamanic input is in motivating hill tribes addicts to remain compliant and cooperative with the modern therapeutic programme. In marked contrast to the previous experience of having many patients drop out while under treatment (which is also the experience of programs for voluntary patients in other camps) the new program with shamanic input achieved unexpectedly high treatment course completion rates of 80–90% and a significantly increased half-year abstinence rate of around 70% in 1988/89.

Traditional Treatment in Malaysia

In Malaysia, traditional treatment of substance dependence (mostly opiate addiction but also alcohol abuse) is performed by Malay traditional therapists, Chinese-Taoist practitioners and Hindu-Ayurvedic healers (Heggenhougen, 1984; Heggenhougen & Navaratnam, 1979a; Jilek, unpublished notes, 1989; Johnson, 1983; Lee, 1985; McGovern, 1982; Spencer, Heggenhougen & Navaratnam, 1980; Teo Hui Khian, 1983; Werner, 1979). The clientele of those healers who have built a reputation in drug rehabilitation is not limited to co-religionists and adaptations of ritual procedures may be made in a remarkably tolerant manner to accommodate patients of other religious persuasions. In recent years, treatment centres based on Malay-Islamic and on Chinese-Taoist traditions specializing in the detoxification and rehabilitation of substance dependent patients have become operational. These centres treat groups of clients in inpatient programmes of one to several weeks duration that are more standardized than the widely varying approaches of individually operating practitioners.

Traditional treatment approaches to substance dependence appear well accepted by motivated addicts and by the community in Malaysia. They also meet with a generally supportive attitude of government health authorities which are well informed on the activities of traditional treatment centres. Surveys have shown that traditional resources are extensively used for the management of substance abuse problems and are often the

treatment of first resort (Heggenhougen & Navaratnam, 1979a; Teo Hui Khian, 1983; Werner, 1979).

Treatment based on Malay Islamic traditions. In spite of considerable variety in procedures, most treatments follow the general principle of initial internal purgation and external cleansing from chemical and spiritual pollution combined with sedative alleviation of withdrawal symptoms, followed by spiritual-didactic counselling. The drug is assumed to remain in the body and is commonly conceived of as a kind of evil poison. Internal purgation of the drug is achieved by inducing emesis and/or diuresis and bowel movements through herbal medicine, salt water and pushing fluids, often using water treated by religious and magical ritual (e.g., mixed with the ashes of holy scriptures). External cleansing is part of an exorcistic ritual of highly suggestive symbolism intended to release the addict from drug-possession or the effects of black magic wrought by drug manufacturers or dealers. As a result of such exorcistic procedures the addict feels unburdened of guilt and free to restore a healthy lifestyle under the guidance of spiritual-religious counselling. Techniques employed include writing on the body with Islamic verses, magical or Hindu symbols according to the client's religion; rubbing the whole body with the ashes of sacred items; face washing and cooling baths in blessed water (scented rose or flower water or water with added lemon or lime juice). The latter has physiologic as well as psychologic effects and usually terminates the phase of intensive treatment. Ritual acts are accompanied by religious-magical formulae. The patient may enter an altered state of consciousness by repetitious changing of the divine appellation and thereby become especially receptive to preventative didactic counselling. The treatment is often concluded with a sacred oath or other religiously buttressed commitment by the client to remain abstinent of substances, to embrace a healthy lifestyle and to avoid the company of drug users. Frequently, clients are fortified against relapse through protective charms and/or talismans.

Among the identified herbal remedies which are administered as medicinal teas are the following: with antiphlogistic action: *Limacea oblongata, Erythrina subumbrans, Gomphandra*; with diuretic action: *Moringa olifera, leaves of white hibiscus*; with purgative action: *Cassia alata*; with sedative action: *Mimosa pudica, Acanthus ebracteatus*; with tonic action: *Aquilaria malaccensis*; with antispasmodic/anticolic action: *Mesua ferrea, Randia, Turmeric, Zingiber officinale*.

Experimental pharmacological studies at the School of Pharmaceutical Sciences, Universiti Sains Malaysia in Penang, have shown that certain herbal medicines administered in traditional treatment of opiate addicts have the effect of suppressing withdrawal symptoms in mice and a similar effect in humans appears likely (Heggenhougen & Navaratnam, 1979b). One follow-up investigation of addicts treated by Malay traditional methods was conducted under strict scientific criteria (rating non-traceable patients as therapy failures) and found one-year post-therapy abstinence rates ranging from 8% to 35% in the total clientele of five different healers (Spencer, Heggenhougen & Navaratnam, 1980).

Treatments based on Chinese medicine and Taoist traditions. Chinese practitioners use herbal remedies according to *yin-yang* principles and magical rituals founded in Taoist tradition. In Malaysia, the intended objectives and some of the methods used in traditional Chinese drug dependence treatment are similar to those employed in Malay Islamic therapy. Sometimes there is an initial purging of the body from the drug-poison by inducing vomiting, diuresis and defecation. Treatment always involves sedation, and often sleep-induction, by herbal medicines. This is followed by baths, usually in flavoured or spiced rain water which is often magically treated to counteract the addiction-provoking supernatural forces that are generally assumed to have been instilled in the drugs by the manufacturers.

Chinese herbal remedies have traditionally been used to alleviate withdrawal symptoms in opium addicts. For example, the "anti-opium leaf" *Combretium sundaicum* was used by Chinese opium smokers around the turn of the century (McBride, 1910). Today, the main tradition-derived therapy of drug addiction among Chinese populations everywhere consists of acupuncture, often combined with physiotherapy (especially acupressure massage) and sometimes also with administration of herbal remedies. Commonly used are extracts of mixed herbs such as *qiang huo, gou teng, chuan xion, fu zi,* and *yan hu suo,* which were shown to have a suppressive effect on the morphine withdrawal syndrome in addicted laboratory rats in experiments conducted at the University of Hong Kong (Yang & Kwok, 1986). Encouraged by the example of Chinese traditional medicine, administration of herbal tea blends and other plant remedies and nutrients is today incorporated in many drug treatment programmes of the industrialized world, not only in China and Malaysia, in addition to other therapeutic modalities and is often claimed to be highly beneficial (cf. Nebelkopf, 1987).

Treatments derived from Hindu traditions. In Malaysia, Hindu-derived therapies focusing on the treatment of drug addicts appear to be more common than in India. These treatments include Ayurvedic herbal remedies, yogic practices, transcendental meditation and ritual practices involving altered states of consciousness.

In the treatment of substance dependence, herbal remedies may be prescribed according to the rules of Ayurvedic medicine to counteract withdrawal symptoms and provide relaxation, usually in combination with soothing lime or lemon water baths. Ayurvedic medicine has official status as an indigenous health care system in India and Nepal. Drug dependence treatment based on Ayurvedic and other Hindu traditions enjoys the same government support in Malaysia as do treatments based on Islamic or Chinese traditions. Acceptance and cross-utilization of traditional therapies by adherents of other religions is not uncommon in Malaysia and on the Indian subcontinent.

Some classical texts of Ayurveda refer to a precursor of severe mental disorder which is brought on by alcohol abuse but do not describe a specific treatment (M. Weiss, personal communication, 1990). Somatic consequences of chronic alcohol abuse such as gastrointestinal and hepatic complications were already described by C'araka (First century AD) who recommended herbal remedies with thirst-reducing, appetite-enhancing, generally roborant, digestion-stimulating, muscle-relaxing and tranquillizing properties. These herbal remedies are still used today in Ayurvedic treatments of alcohol abuse in India and Malaysia. They are administered only in the form of an *asavam,* a weak (1–2%) alcoholic preparation of mixed herbal remedies obtained by fermentation of an aqueous solution with added sugar-containing nutrients.

SKV, an Ayurvedic formula employed to curb alcohol abuse, produced by fermentation of cane sugar, raisins and a solution of 12 identified herbal ingredients was tested at the University of Madras for its effectiveness in controlling ethanol addiction and reversing ethanol-induced pathological changes in rats (Shanmugasundaram & Shanmugasundaram, 1986a; Shanmugasundaram, Umarani Subramaniam Santhini & Radha Shanmugasundaram, 1986b). The observed marked reduction in ethanol intake was attributed to inhibition of craving for alcohol. Other findings were increased food intake, reversal of ethanol-induced ECG and EEG abnormalities and reduction of the elevated gamma-GT levels indicative of alcoholic liver damage. The hepatic and cerebral lesions seen in ethanol addicted rats were not apparent in alcoholic rats treated by SKV which had no adverse effect on the test animals.

Yogic techniques are commonly employed for the physical and spiritual strengthening of the recovering client during and after traditional detoxification. Yoga therapy has a crucial role in the rehabilitation of drug dependent patients at the Nav-Chetna Drug De-addiction and Rehabilitation Centre, Varanasi, India which provides a package of systematic yoga exercises in the pre- and post-detoxification phase (Sharma & Shukla, 1988). The exercises relating to body postures, breathing, and "purification" appear especially suited to counteract withdrawal symptoms. A pre-detoxification yoga programme was developed which reduced drug craving and engendered positive attitudinal changes so that the addicts were well motivated. In the post-detoxification period, yoga furthered the process of physical recovery and psychosocial reintegration. No follow-up data on outcome are available.

Transcendental Meditation (TM) originated in ancient Vedic traditions of India but has, in recent decades, spread around the globe. In the management and prevention of drug dependence it appears to be employed today more often in western countries and has lost much of its traditional Hindu connotation. TM organizations and teachers are to be found in over 100 countries and in many of these special programmes have been designed to combat drug abuse (Clements, Krenner & Moelk, 1988). These operate largely outside the official health care system. TM technique is said to be acquired by most adepts in four to five instructional sessions and then supposed to be practised by the individual twice a day for periods of 15 to 20 minutes, without further supervision, counselling or advice.

TM is offered as a program for personal development and not as a specific treatment of substance dependence, it may therefore be more acceptable to those young people who basically condone drug use. It is claimed that alleviation of drug abuse occurs as an "automatic side effect" in the context of overall personality development under TM, irrespective of reasons given for substance use and of the particular substance used.

In one questionnaire study of 1,862 mostly young people practising TM, which was conducted in the USA in 1972 (Benson & Wallace, 1984), results indicated that in the great majority of subjects who had been using cannabis, hallucinogens, narcotics, amphetamines, barbiturates, and/or high-percentage alcohol prior to starting the TM program, there was a significant decrease in the amount or discontinuance of drug use as well as a decrease or cessation of drug trafficking activity and attitudinal changes in the direction of discouraging others from abusing drugs. A recent review of research studies states that the TM program was found to be associated with significant decreases in the use of a variety of substances (Clements *et al.*, 1988).

Hindu healers often enter a trance state in order to contact spirits and divine entities and perform ritual acts of suggestive symbolic connotation (Jilek, unpublished observations in Singapore, 1985; Malaysia, 1989; India, 1992). Sacred vows taken by worshippers of Lord Murugan to undergo the ordeal of piercing the body with miniature spears and with hooks to bear sacred objects or help pull religious vehicles during the Hindu *thaipusam* festival celebrated annually in Hindu communities of Malaysia and, to a lesser extent, in South India, may include a commitment of total and ongoing abstinence from alcohol and drug use in continuation of the obligatory period of fasting and abstinence prior to the celebrations. These vows are made in supplication of some act of divine mercy and are taken very seriously indeed as they carry supernatural sanction and are associated with an intense experience of ecstatic trance which affords the suppli-

cant relative analgesia (Jilek, unpublished notes & videos, 1989; Simons, Ervin & Prince, 1988).

Approaches Based on Japanese Buddhist Traditions

While Alcoholics Anonymous (AA) in Japan, as generally in Asia, has only a limited appeal and mainly attracts westernized persons and western expatriates, the Danshukai Alcohol Abstinence Society, founded in 1958, has been a notable success with 25,000 members attending meetings by 1977, the majority abstinent for more than one year (Suwaki, 1979; 1980; Takemoto, Usukine & Otsu, 1979). Based on traditional Japanese values, Danshukai encourages positive dependence and reliance on family members. It invites the active cooperation of spouses and children who are asked to participate in the meetings so that the family as a whole makes a joint effort to overcome alcohol abuse in one of its members. Unlike AA, Danshukai is not anonymous; names and addresses of members are not confidential and outside persons, also non-alcoholics, are welcome to join meetings and talk freely in the group. It may be noted here that Danshukai has these features in common with the culture-congenial North American Indian "AA" groups described below.

Naikan therapy is derived from the *mishirabe* self-examination practice of Shinshu Buddhism (Reynolds, 1983). It utilizes the self-disciplinary tendencies in Japanese culture and the repetitive ritual methods of Zen training to achieve concentrated and critical self-observation by focused solitary meditation on a specific theme, namely the client's past and present relationship with a significant family member, beginning with the mother, under the guidance of a therapist who poses relevant questions at regular intervals but who is not present all the time. Naikan aims at a critical self-assessment of the alcoholic's past conduct, which causes realization of dishonoured obligations toward significant others. This instills a feeling of shame together with a strong motivation to further abstain, and a new appreciation for the love of the family whose cooperative support is emphasized. Naikan therapy courses of all-day concentrated self-scrutiny for one week are mainly practised in institutional settings, followed by shorter daily sessions and after discharge involvement in the Danshukai movement. One follow-up study of 129 alcoholics treated by Naikan therapy found that 53% were totally abstinent six months after discharge, 49% were abstinent after one year (Takemoto *et al.*, 1979).

Therapeutic Approaches Based on Arab Islamic Traditions

The integration of Islamic spiritual approaches in the therapy of drug addiction has been pioneered in Egypt (Baasher & Abu El

Azayem, 1980; Abu El Azayem, 1987) and Saudi Arabia (Al Radi, 1990). In 1977, a treatment unit for drug addicts was established at Abu El Azayem Mosque in Cairo, in which the religious leader (*sheikh*) assumed special functions on the therapeutic team by holding group meetings, providing religious teaching with emphases on Islamic injunctions regarding dependence-producing substance use, strengthening social ties and encouraging mosque-centred activities, counselling on personal matters and organizing social support. Propagation of anti-drug messages through religious media and during Friday mass prayers served preventative purposes and promoted the rehabilitation of drug addicts in the community.

In subsequent years, the number of new cases reporting to the mosque clinic and the compliance rate was found to be significantly higher than at other city clinics without religious component, while treatment at the mosque clinic was more cost-effective (Baasher & Abu El Azayem, 1980). A comparative double-bind study showed that substance addicts treated at the mosque clinic realized a significantly higher rate of therapeutic objectives than equivalent patients at a regular public treatment centre (cited by Abu El Azayem, 1987). According to information provided by WHO/EMRO in 1991, spiritual counselling based on Islamic traditions was provided in several mosques in Cairo where drug addicts, after chemical detoxification, are helped by religious leaders to unburden their feelings of guilt and restore a healthy lifestyle. In Saudi Arabia, the addiction unit at Shahar Hospital, Taif, has for several years now integrated a programme of religious therapy in which the mosque is the centre of therapeutic activity. Behavioural changes are engendered in group therapy following prayer sessions with joint worship and recitation of the Koran.

The importance of fostering a religious motivation compared to other motivations for attaining abstinence in Saudi drug addicts was shown in a follow-up study comparing relapse rates in patients of the Shahar Hospital Addiction Unit: 75% of subjects motivated by "inner religious considerations" maintained abstinence over two years, as compared to 33% of subjects motivated by other considerations (cited by Al Radi, 1990).

NORTH AMERICA

Alaska Eskimo Spirit Movement

The *Inupiaq Ilitqsat*, "Eskimo Spirit Movement," was initiated in the early 1980s by the Northwest Alaska Native Association as a response from within Eskimo society to increasing rates of alcohol abuse and related psychosocial problems facing Alaska Native communities, out of a sense of frustration that Eskimos were losing control of their lives by leaving the responsibility

for solving these problems to outside agencies (Jilek, unpublished notes on the Comprehensive Alcohol Program in northwestern Alaska, 1982; Mala, 1985). The movement is based on traditional Eskimo values that include sharing, caring for others, responsibility for one's own people, knowledge of language and customs, pride in one's cultural heritage, respect for the elders and their inclusion in family life. The main rehabilitative and preventive instrument of the Eskimo Spirit Movement is the "Spirit Camp" which provides a cultural learning and therapy experience for young Eskimos involved in, or at risk of, substance abuse. Without modern conveniences, young people in the Spirit Camp acquire from the elders knowledge of Eskimo heritage and traditional survival skills and thus regain a lost cultural identity. Traditional methods of healing are employed in the rehabilitation programme, such as body manipulation and massage, hydrotherapy, herbal remedies and group rituals.

The Eskimo Spirit Movement has the active support of the new Commissioner for Health of the State of Alaska, Dr. Theodore Mala (himself Eskimo and a physician), who encourages close collaboration of health and social service officers and professionals with indigenous therapeutic and preventive resources. He has likened the impact of the Eskimo Spirit Movement on indigenous alcoholism problems to that of Alcoholics Anonymous in western societies. The Eskimo Spirit Movement is widely popular among Native leaders in Northwest Alaska as a culture-congenial approach to the substance abuse issue that addresses the need for positive cultural identification and meaningful activity among the young. Inupiaq and Inuit (Eskimo) representatives in other parts of the arctic who come to know about the Eskimo Spirit Movement see it as an inspiring example.

North American Indian "AA" Groups

Western-type Alcoholics Anonymous has in general not been successful among North American Indian populations for various reasons (Heath, 1983). However, where North American Indian alcoholics have been inspired by AA to organize self-help groups which incorporate important indigenous cultural elements and omit certain western features of philosophy and practice, such transformed "AA" groups have been quite successful in attracting and rehabilitating alcohol-abusing persons among native populations (e.g., in British Columbia, cf. Jilek-Aall, 1978; 1981). Amerindian "AA" groups first came into being among the Coast Salish Indians in the 1960s and developed the following features: The concept of anonymity is rejected in favour of open identification of participants and open meetings to which family members, including children, are invited. Western-type formality in conducting meetings with a defined membership according to set rules of procedure and time frame is abandoned in favour of more traditional ways of congregating,

without predetermined times of arrival or departure of the participants including extended family and community members. Indian "AA" meetings are often not unlike spiritual ceremonies in
which the "higher power" as understood in AA philosophy becomes identified with the personal spirit power as understood in
the traditional guardian spirit complex. Meetings may also assume the pattern of traditional exchange feasts (*potlatch*) whenever there is an occasion to commemorate anniversaries of
sobriety, with solemn speeches echoing the traditional mythological theme of death and rebirth into a new and healthier existence. The Indian-White conflict, intimately associated with the
history of Amerindian alcohol use and abuse, is resolved in
Amerindian "AA" groups by emphasizing cultural identity and
self-respect, while extending friendship to white members of the
general AA who, as invited guests, have an opportunity to give
up stereotyped notions about the "drunken Indian."

The success of the culturally transformed Amerindian "AA"
movement is shown by the fact that there are now such groups
not only in most Coast Salish communities but also among other
Amerindian populations of British Columbia and neighbouring
areas.

Revived Traditional Ceremonials of North American Indians

Under the socio-political impact of global decolonization in the
1960s, some ancient North American Indian ceremonials have
been revived. Examples relevant to the combat against substance
abuse are the revived cult dance ceremonials and the Sweat
Lodge ceremony. The Sweat Lodge ceremony is widely practised today throughout indigenous communities in North America, offering participation on a regular basis without seasonal
restriction both on and off reservations—even to Amerindian inmates in federal prisons of Canada and the United States (Hall,
1986). Sweat lodges can be easily erected; they are small circu-
lar dome-shaped structures made of arched willow poles which
are tied together and tightly covered by blankets. Hot rocks are
placed in the centre of the lodge on which water is sprinkled to
release steam which, in the enclosed space, produces intense
sweating in the small group of users who sit in a circle facing the
centre. Beyond the physiotherapeutic effects of intense sweats
and the ensuing feeling of energetic serenity, it is the religious
ritual imbued with elements of Aboriginal beliefs, in which the
lodge represents archetypal symbols, and the group therapeutic
interaction under the guidance of a spiritual leader, that creates a
powerful somato-psycho-social experience. The revived Sweat
Lodge ceremony has become a pan-Amerindian symbol for the
resurgence of indigenous culture and a focus for Native peoples'
strivings to regain an Amerindian identity and way of life free
from the harmful influences of "White" majority society, no-

tably from alcohol and drug abuse. Among Amerindians, the
Sweat Lodge is considered an antidote for alcohol which likewise produces strong physical and mental effects. Many Sweat
Lodge ritual leaders are rehabilitated alcoholics who rely on involvement in this and other revived Amerindian ceremonials for
their sobriety and provide role models especially for young
Amerindian people at risk. Participation in the Sweat Lodge ceremony combined with involvement in other revived Amerindian
ceremonials such as the cult dances, in Amerindian "AA" and in
indigenous sport activities, creates for some Amerindian alcohol
and drug abusers a year-round rehabilitation program and protection against relapse.

The Sun Dance of Amerindian tribes in Alberta, Wyoming,
Idaho, Utah, Colorado and the Dakotas (Jilek, 1978; 1989; Jorgensen, 1972), the Winter Spirit Dance of the Coast Salish of
British Columbia and Washington (Jilek, 1974; 1981; 1982a;
1982b), and the Plains Indian Gourd Dance which now has a
pan-Indian connotation (Howard, 1976), were adapted to current
psychosocial needs. They were given a therapeutic emphasis
geared to the management and prevention of culture-change related personality problems, particularly alcohol and drug abuse
among younger Amerindians which is typically associated with
"anomic depression" related to anomie, relative deprivation and
cultural identity confusion (cf. Jilek, 1974). Initiation to the
Winter Spirit Dance and Sun Dance ceremonials involves the
utilization of altered states of consciousness under the guidance
of experienced ritualists by culture-congenial physiological and
psychological techniques. The initiation process is designed to
help the novices build up their personal and cultural identity to
establish a healthy new existence. This is achieved in a symbolic
process of ritualized depth and rebirth through traditional means
of personality depatterning and subsequent resynthesis and re-
orientation.

The therapeutic effects of traditional group ceremonials involving ritualized altered states of consciousness are due, on the
psychological level, to cathartic abreaction, deflection of feelings of guilt and shame, gratification of frustrated emotional
needs in the supportive group milieu and symbolic expression of
otherwise hidden feelings in front of an empathetic audience.
Some initiates in the Winter Spirit Dance ceremonial have
likened their ecstatic experience to the transient "high" previously felt under the influence of mind-changing drugs but without the drug withdrawal effects (Jilek, 1982b, p. 73). On the
social level, participation in a ceremonial group helps in the resolution of interpersonal, intergenerational and interfamily problems by altering social relationships, creating a new social
network, and providing the opportunity to graduate to the prestigious role of ritual leader through converting the initial sick role
of a powerless substance dependent individual into that of a supernaturally sanctioned helper imbued with spirit power. Ritual

leaders exert therapeutic influence through example and advice and, most importantly, through the manipulation of culturally validated symbols in a setting conducive to collective suggestion and social learning.

The message of leading ritualists in the revived Amerindian cult dance ceremonials is that alcohol (still by far the most important abuse substance among Amerindians) is a poison historically introduced into Amerindian societies by outsiders frequently with pernicious motivations, that drinking and drug use, therefore, are "non-Indian" and a sign of alienation from Aboriginal culture. Leading ritualists and prominent participants in the ceremonials are total abstainers. New dancers must abstain during the time of preparation, initiation, and training; active dancers abstain or restrict their alcohol intake during the dancing season. The contemporary Sun Dance is usually conducted throughout three days and nights in summer but requires of active participants months of preparation under total abstinence. To show their commitment, participants often take a sacred vow to "dance with pierced flesh," hooked to the centre pole, in consecutive annual ceremonies. The Winter Spirit dancing season in the Coast Salish region lasts about five months from late fall to spring. Persons under the influence of alcohol are not supposed to attend ceremonials even as mere spectators. This has a discouraging effect on alcohol consumption in the area where ceremonials are held, as moderate intake without intoxication in general appears unattractive while major ceremonial occasions draw many spectators and conflict with weekend drinking parties. Alcohol-related problems have significantly decreased in some Coast Salish reservations where community leaders promoted the revival of ceremonial activity and the creation of Indian "AA" groups, and where educated younger persons participate actively in ceremonials to demonstrate their "Indianness." In a follow-up study of 24 young Coast Salish Indian persons with alcohol and/or drug abuse problems who were initiated into the Winter Spirit Dance from 1967 to 1972, ten were fully rehabilitated and abstinent in 1973 for one or more years after their initiation; 11 showed significant improvement, two showed no change and one deteriorated (Jilek, 1982b). In the Upper Stalo population surveyed by the author, there were about 50 active spirit dancers among ca. 2000 Amerindian people in 1972, five years after revival of the ceremonial had been started. Since then, new initiates have been entering the ceremonial every year in Coast Salish communities of southern British Columbia and northern Washington. The revival of the Winter Spirit Dance has created an annual therapeutic programme in which not only the initiated dancers but also their relatives and friends participate in a group enterprise which provides mutual support, acceptance and stimulation. The effectiveness of the Winter Spirit Dance ceremonial in moving substance abusers to sobriety was confirmed independently by two investigators (Anderson, 1986).

The Sun Dance ceremonial has been growing steadily since the 1960s. It involves teams of singer-drummers in addition to the active dancers, and crowds of spectators that comfort and encourage the dancers. The "pan-Indian" Gourd Dance is today practised on many festive occasions by Amerindians throughout North America and has been credited with rehabilitating alcoholics (Howard, 1976), although its impact is limited due to the absence of a rigorous and formal initiation process comparable to the other two cult dances.

The cult dance ceremonials appeal to those among the younger generation who are accessible to the pan-Amerindian culture propaganda which emerged in the 1960s and which emphasizes the reattainment of an Aboriginal identity in opposition to the overwhelming influence of majority society. The ceremonials are opposed by those in majority society and among the Amerindians who perceive them as outdated, "primitive" or "pagan"—whether for reasons of Christian fundamentalism, modern western views on young individuals' right to choose any lifestyle irrespective of group concerns and traditions, or concern about the risks involved in arduous training and practices that may cause pain and injury. In majority society there have been calls for legal measures instituting public supervision of the ceremonials and official screening of candidates for initiation. It is to the credit of today's government authorities in North America that they have categorically refused any legal infringement that would suppress these revived ceremonials which have a valuable psychohygienic and sociotherapeutic function. One of the most important aspects of all revived traditional Amerindian ceremonials is that they turn participants from egocentric and hedonistic preoccupations to constructive community concerns.

Syncretistic Religious Cults of North American Indians

Native American Church ("Peyote Cult"). The original pre-Columbian worship of the divine cactus called *peyotl* by the Aztecs survives among the Mexican Huichol Indians (Benzi, 1972) but the Peyote Cult spread northward toward the end of the 19th century and through syncretic amalgamation of Christian forms with the religious symbolism of many Amerindian tribes became the Native American Church, today one of the most important pan-Amerindian religious movements between the Rocky Mountains and the Mississippi, with a membership of many thousands (Jilek, 1978; LaBarre, 1969). The avowed purpose of participation in the Peyote Cult is to allay physical and mental distress and to combat alcoholism by enhancing health and strength through communication with supernatural powers made accessible in an arduous ritual. Collective goals are to create positive feelings among fellow peyotists, their relatives and friends, and in general to promote pan-Amerindian ideals by "walking the peyote road" in strict adherence to the principles of temperance ("alcohol and peyote do not mix"), honesty and social reliability (Aberle, 1966). Most active members of the Native American Church are total abstainers from alcohol and from other chemical substances. The success of the Native American Church in rehabilitating Amerindians from alcohol and opiate dependence and the safety of ritual peyote use have been attested to by experienced clinicians including Karl Menninger (Albaugh & Anderson, 1974; Bergman, 1971; Roy, 1973). Therapeutic efficacy is sometimes attributed to the bio- and psychoactive ingredients of the ritually consumed "peyote buttons" of the cactus *Lophophora williamsi Lemaire*, strychnine-like and hallucinogenic alkaloids (notably mescaline) as well as neuroactive isoquinolines (Blum, Futterman & Pascarosa, 1977). However, there is evidence that the therapeutically important altered state of consciousness experienced during the night-long cult sessions may be induced by exposure to continuous rhythmic drumming and chanting alone, without any ingestion of peyote buttons. The altered state of consciousness facilitates the often cathartic expression of personal problems and pent-up emotions before an empathetic audience. The ritual leader's message of sobriety and responsibility for one's own health and the welfare of one's people, repeatedly perceived in a suggestible state, has a good chance to become incorporated in the person's lifestyle (Pascarosa & Futterman, 1976; Pascarosa, Futterman & Halsweig, 1976).

Gaiwiio (Handsome Lake Movement). The "new" Iroquois religion of Handsome Lake, a native prophet of the early 1800s, is still a vital force among the "Six Nations" Amerindians of New York and Ontario (Heath, 1983; Jilek-Aall, 1978; Wallace, 1972). Handsome Lake's revelation depicted gruesome eternal punishments for those drinking "fire-water." The Handsome Lake movement became established as an Amerindian church after his death, combining elements of pre-contact Iroquois culture with the prophet's original version and Christian principles. The prophet's demand for temperance led to the first Aboriginal anti-alcohol movement and was enshrined in the *Code of Handsome Lake* in the 1840s. It is still the doctrine of the followers of *Gaiwiio* who combine a desire for personal spiritual salvation with identification as "true Iroquois," in opposition to vices introduced by majority society, such as alcohol and drug abuse, in this way affirming "Indianness" as do Amerindians who now practice the revived indigenous ceremonials on the plains and on the Pacific coast.

Indian Shaker Church. Founded by the ex-alcoholic John Slocum in 1881, this nativistic and messianic cult with Catholic

form and Amerindian content found followers on many Indian reservations in the Pacific Northwest and reached its peak in the 1920s (Barnett, 1957; Collins, 1950; Gunther, 1949; Jilek-Aall, 1978). Slocum taught that those who had received the Shaker spirit ("shake") thereby obtained the power to heal others and to lead a wholesome life themselves, but would die if they resumed alcohol, even if tasting only one drop. The Shaker Church has been consistent in its insistence on the total sobriety of its members. In recent decades, some Shakers have merged with "white" fundamentalist Christian groups. Those more conscious of Indianness are now actively participating in the revived Winter Spirit Dance ceremonial and in the Amerindian "AA" groups so that today there is no strict delimitation between these indigenous movements in the Pacific Northwest which all emphasize freedom from alcohol and drug use as part of traditional values. They also share the archetypal birth and rebirth myth: the prophets Handsome Lake and John Slocum both "died" of alcohol abuse and were reborn to a new life, just as the faulty old self "dies" in the Spirit Dance initiation ordeal and the alcoholic has "nearly died" before reaching sobriety through Amerindian "AA."

FOLK HEALING IN CENTRAL AND SOUTH AMERICA

Latin American folk healing is influenced by Aboriginal Amerindian beliefs and traditional medicine, by populist Catholicism, and by modern spiritism (cf. Jilek-Aall & Jilek, 1983). For the campaign against alcohol abuse in Latin America, it is unfortunate that the possession-trance cults—which derived from West African religions through syncretic amalgamation with folk Catholicism and modern spiritism and have developed into religious-therapeutic enterprises with millions of participants in the Caribbean (Vodun, Santeria, Shango) and in Brazil (Umbanda, absorbing Candomble and Macumba)—never acquired an anti-alcoholic emphasis. Indeed, Vodun ritual leaders sometimes resort to the ceremonial use of rum (Jilek, film documentation, 1964). However, the example of *espiritismo*, a healing religion which developed from amalgamation of the Afro-Caribbean possession cult *Santeria* with Christian and spiritist elements, demonstrate that group therapeutic movements involving altered states of consciousness have considerable potential for the rehabilitation of alcohol and drug dependents among Latin Americans. This is exemplified by Puerto Rican *espiritismo* centres in the eastern USA (Singer & Borrero, 1984). In such *centro*, spiritual consultations are provided by *espiritistas*, usually themselves rehabilitated substance abusers. They interpret problem causation within the magico-religious and sociocultural belief system of their patients and employ individual and family counselling techniques of confrontation, suggestion and manipulation, as well as "spiritual treatment" involving symbolic rituals of cleansing with herbal baths, prayer sessions, exorcism and magical protection. Spiritual treatment is designed to "break the grip" of malevolent spirits causing the patient's alcoholism, thus relieving his guilt and changing the family's often rejecting attitude.

In one typical *centro*, over one thousand problem drinkers were treated in a three year period. Although complete abstinence was the declared therapeutic goal, only reduced consumption and improved personal and family function could be achieved in the majority of cases (Singer & Borrero, 1984). Costs, however, were minimal.

In Mexican folk medicine, alcoholics are treated by counselling (which always involves the family) by religious exercises, magical rituals and symbolic acts aimed at removing supernatural causes, as well as through the social engineering of charismatic *curanderos* (Arredondo, Weddige, Justice & Fitz, 1987; Trotter & Chavira, 1978; Trotter, 1979). Sedative herbal teas are administered to control nervous symptoms after cessation of drinking. Nausea-inducing substances such as powderized old eggs or rat urine may be put into the alcoholic's drink surreptitiously to diminish his desire to imbibe. Of interest is the Antabuse-like aversion therapy employed by some Mexican healers and herbalists using toasted and ground seeds of *haba de San Ignacio* (*Hura polyandra* L. and *Hura crepitans* L.), containing toxalbumines that induce nausea and vomiting in conjunction with the subsequent intake of alcohol (Trotter, 1979).

A similar example in Ecuador is the Pavlovian-type deconditioning with emetic herbal teas prepared from the *nepe* root, to be taken by the alcoholic together with beer, in a healing compound of the Colorados Indians which is frequently used by urban patients (Jilek-Aall & Jilek, 1983).

In Peruvian folk healing, especially in the northern Coast area, chronic alcoholics are treated by *curanderos* (Chiappe Costa, 1970; Chiappe Costa, Campos Fuentes & Dragunsky, 1972; Chiappe Costa, Lemlij & Millones, 1985; Seguin, 1974). The folk-etiological theory of causation of alcoholism and other afflictions by a *daño*, a harmful magical substance slipped into the patient's drink or food by a malevolent person, is utilized by the *curandero* to turn the status of the alcoholic from that of a social offender into that of a victim who can count on the sympathy of family and friends to facilitate his rehabilitation. In a diagnostic session, the healer enters an altered state of consciousness induced by ingesting the sacred "San Pedro" cactus (*Trichocereus pachanoi*) containing mescaline and other psychoactive substances. In this state, the healer signals with supernaturally sanctioned authority the person(s) responsible for the *daño*. Through the naming process, the divining healer is able to modify the patient's and the family's attitude and to manipulate social relationships, for example, by making the patient avoid

undesirable drinking companions. In order to qualify for the actual treatment, the patient must submit to severe restrictions of his alcohol consumption for about one month while a fortifying diet and herbal tonics are prescribed for physical strengthening. The subsequent treatment starts with common curing rites of Peruvian folk medicine. The patient then undergoes an intensive aversion therapy in which vomiting and diarrhea are induced by herbal emetics and laxatives while at the same time he is offered alcoholic drinks. For this arduous treatment, the patient is often admitted to the healing compound of the *curandero*, usually together with his mother or spouse, sometimes with his entire family. After discharge, the patient is given a protective charm and is supposed to make regular visits to the healer for several months.

In one follow-up study by the Instituto de Psiquiatria Social, Universidad Nacional Mayor de San Marco, 39 of 57 chronic alcoholics treated by *curanderos* were found to be fully rehabilitated (Chiappe Costa, Campos Fuentes & Dragunsky, 1972). Of these, 77% had post-therapy abstinence periods of over one year, and 44% over six years; 18 of the 57 subjects had relapsed since receiving treatment, 56% of these had relapsed within eight months, 78% within sixteen months, and 89% within two years.

For their curing ceremonies, Amerindian shamans of the Amazon region have traditionally prepared so-called *ayahuasca*, *caapi*, or *yaje* drinks from the bark of *Banisteriopsis spp.* which contains hallucinogenic dymethyltryptamines. In recent decades, syncretistic healers in the Peruvian Amazon have been sharing *ayahuasca* extracts in group therapeutic sessions with a clientele that consists mainly of neurotic and psychosomatic patients but also includes alcohol and cocaine dependents with good results according to anecdotal reports (Chiappe Costa, 1979; Dobkin de Rios, 1990; 1992; Jilek-Aall & Jilek, 1983).

SYNCRETISTIC RELIGIOUS CULTS IN SOUTHERN AFRICA

The independent Black-African churches of southern Africa, sometimes named "Zionist," "Ethiopian" or "Apostolic," combine messianic Christianity and pan-African consciousness with traditional elements of Bantu culture and a mandate to heal spiritually, mentally and physically (Benz, 1965; Peltzer, 1987; Sundkler, 1961). In the Republic of South Africa, Malawi and Namibia, these churches, often led by charismatic prophet-healers, have a very numerous though rapidly changing membership and considerable socio-political influence. Members are subject to proscriptions which usually include injunctions against the consumption of alcoholic beverages and, in many cases, also against the use of other drugs. This religious prohibition is associated with a readiness to rehabilitate the repentant substance user as a patient in the context of the church's healing mandate, usually without charge beyond general tithing. The patient is expected to confess with a free admission of personal problems. In many congregations, this is combined with purification rites for the "elimination of all evil," both spiritual and material, by ritual vomiting and body cleansing. Counselling is conducted by faith healers and ex-alcoholic church members. Often there is also dream interpretation by authorized leaders. In Malawi, the alcohol and drug (cannabis) rehabilitation of "Zionist" church groups is divided into spiritual therapy (purification by sprinkling with blessed water, songs and prayers, spiritual rebirth through river baptism), a common practice in most congregations, and body therapy. The latter is seen as a kind of detoxification treatment of withdrawal symptoms and consists of: (1) the oral administration of exactly dosed fluids (concentrated salt solution, tea, lake water, milk, coffee, oil) distributed over a course of 28 days; and (2) body stimulation at specific asymmetric points of head, trunk and extremities, performed at 70 points with a wooden stick and at 60 different points with a needle. Some of these points appear identical to acupuncture points also used in the treatment of alcoholics but there is no known historical or contemporary connection.

A study conducted in Malawi indicated that the average time of alcohol abstinence after joining a healing church was 2.8 years (Peltzer, 1987). A follow-up investigation of 11 men with alcohol and cannabis related disorders treated in a "Zionist" church showed that after six months, five were regular church attenders and abstinent, two were drinking again, one had died after relapse, three could not be followed, i.e., the therapy can be considered relatively successful. In the alcohol rehabilitation program of another church which does not feature physical treatment (body therapy), the results were less successful: after six months, only one of five men remained abstinent, two had relapsed, two could not be found.

DISCUSSION:
THE CONCEPTUAL BASIS AND EFFICACY
OF TRADITIONAL HEALING

The traditional non-Western treatment approaches described in this overview are essentially psychotherapeutic modalities applied more often to groups than to individuals. The main features held in common by these traditional approaches are the ritual use of culturally validated symbolic words, acts, and objects, associated with implicit and explicit suggestion. Common additional features in the traditional therapeutic management of substance use problems are the client's public admission of harmful behaviour combined with a solemn pledge of correction, and specific procedures intended to eliminate the addicting substance by various methods of internal and external "purification."

Scientific evaluation of the effectiveness of traditional healing in the treatment and prevention of substance abuse and dependence is frequently limited by the inherent constraints of scientific research in this field. These constraints are due to the following: (1) the sacred or arcane character of the ceremonies; (2) the healer's practices and prescriptions are often considered private or clan property; (3) the healer's reluctance to divulge information because of negative experience with enquiring authorities interested in illicit drug use; (4) the undeniable interference effects of experimental research with the conduct of traditional ceremonies; (5) the difficulty of evaluating the merits of a single therapeutic method when several are often combined in case management; and (6) the practical difficulties in conducting outcome studies by case follow-up, due to the lack of reliable records, the problems of finding and accessing former clients and verifying their statements, which are especially great under the conditions obtaining in many developing countries.

Statements on the results of traditional management are, therefore, mostly based on the referenced authors' observations and information rather than on hard scientific evidence. In fairness to the traditional non-Western psychotherapeutic approaches described in this overview it should be acknowledged that most of the claims to effectiveness which are made for modern Western psychotherapies are likewise not based on evidence that would satisfy the criteria of experimental science.

The many general observations and the few investigations reported by scientific observers and summarized in the above geographical overview allow the following conclusions. In the rehabilitation and prevention of chemical substance dependence, therapeutic modalities based on indigenous cultural and religious traditions have been found to be generally as successful, and in some instances more successful, than "official" treatment and rehabilitation programs, as attested by many authors.[3]

Some general principles of traditional and folk healing can be extracted that are operational in many different traditions and are of relevance to the therapeutic and preventive management of substance abuse. Traditional therapy is usually conducted in the context of a ceremonial composed of ritual-symbolic procedures involving the use of culturally validated sacred or arcane symbols by traditional practitioners. These symbols include meaningful words uttered in incantation and invocation, recitations of stories, parables and similes; skillful manipulation of images and objects. Patients, and often also the audience, actively participate in the therapeutic ceremonial. Implicit and explicit suggestions based on collective beliefs are employed in the ritual-symbolic procedures of treatment and prevention. The effects of suggestion are intensified through the relatively common utilization of altered states of consciousness in traditional therapies.

Various procedures are intended by the traditional practitioner and understood by the patient as purifying measures to eliminate the addicting and "polluting" substances and sometimes also as a general cleansing of body and mind. This is accomplished through herbal emetics and laxatives, intake of holy or healthy fluids, ablutions, washings, dousings, sweat baths, steam baths, fumigation with incense or smoke, brushing with twigs, or rubbing with oils. Some of these procedures have hydro- and physiotherapeutic as well as suggestive-symbolic aspects.

The confession or admission of harmful behaviour associated with substance use as a transgression against divine rules and a neglect of obligations to kinspeople or community members, is combined with a solemn pledge or sacred vow in front of healer and audience to correct one's behaviour in the future. This pledge is usually associated with the commitment to make a personal sacrifice for rehabilitation and/or compensation. These actions, intended to appease and reconcile supernatural agencies and/or significant others, have a marked anxiety alleviating and guilt relieving effect on the patient. They may also lead to re-acceptance by kin group and community.

In a culture-congenial situation that facilitates psychodramatic abreaction, affective release may be achieved through catharsis triggered by adequate sensory stimulation, or in an altered state of consciousness induced by psychological, physiological or phytochemical means. Therapeutic effects are increased through the experience of empathy shown by an understanding and accepting audience of kinsmen and community members.

Compared to the treatment approaches of cosmopolitan medicine, traditional healing practices have several advantages:

A. *Culture-congeniality.* Traditional healers and ritualists share the sociocultural value system of their clientele which cannot be said of many modern health staff.
B. *Use of the personality of the healer.* Traditional healing recognizes the importance of the personality characteristics of the therapist who has to achieve and maintain a confidence-inspiring charisma. In modern medicine, the therapeutic technique rather than the person of the therapist is assumed to be the most important variable. While technical skills are obviously of paramount importance in some medical specialties, such as in surgery, the personality of the therapist plays a significant role in any therapeutic relationship in which the patient must accept the therapist as a person in order to develop trust and confidence, such as is often the case in general medical practice and always important in psychotherapy.
C. *Holistic approach.* Traditional healing practices usually integrate physical, psychological, spiritual and social methods, while modern medicine is becoming increasingly fragmented due to over-specialization and technology.
D. *Accessibility and availability.* Traditional healers are the first resort in most developing areas which, apart from their ther-apeutic merits, is due to their geographical permanence and accessibility. Modern health staff tends to be urban located, highly mobile and changing.
E. *Use of affect and altered states of consciousness.* Traditional healing utilizes suggestive methods and the manipulation of cultural validated images and symbols, working on the patient's affectivity to achieve the therapeutic goal, rather than relying on rational understanding and "insight" to correct faulty behaviour. The effective use of altered states of consciousness, induced by physiological and psychological means in the ritual therapy of substance dependence, is of special interest in view of the hypothesized relationship of such states to alterations in the endogenous neuroendocrine opioid system (cf. Lex & Schor, 1977; Prince, 1982).
F. *Collective therapy management and social engineering.* Traditional healing in most cases also involves the patient's kinspeople and other community members who may join forces with healer and patient to help define the underlying problem and the remedial actions to be taken. Traditional therapies, therefore, tend to be relational; they tend to foster kinship and community cohesion and facilitate the patient's re-integration. The traditional healer's advice carries weight due to his or her prestige and charisma and may, in some cases, also be sanctioned by supernatural authority. The healer is, therefore, in a position to directly or indirectly manipulate the patient's immediate human environment in favour of achieving the therapeutic goal.
G. *Cost effectiveness.* There is no doubt that utilization of traditional therapeutic resources is considerably more cost-effective for the public than utilization of the official health service, as public funds need not be invested beyond occasional grants to deserving non-profit treatment operations. Consumer costs of utilizing traditional healing vary and are usually individualized; often there is no obligatory fee but an expectation of donations which may be in kind. It is worth noting here that cost considerations have not impeded utilization of traditional healing resources in many countries where health care services, including substance abuse rehabilitation, are free or covered by state insurance schemes.

At the same time, it must be acknowledged that traditional healing approaches have their own potential disadvantages. The secrecy surrounding some traditional procedures and the religious aspects of many healing ceremonials make effective supervision by health authorities difficult. Attempts to impose controls would have a discouraging effect due to the known unsympathetic attitude of many health professionals. However, it has been the experience of this and of other authors that traditional healers respond positively to professionals who seek their collaboration with an attitude of respect and genuine understanding; they are willing to share information and to take advice in a collaborative relationship that entails mutual referrals of patients.

Certain procedures and remedies used by traditional healers, usually with imprecise dosage, may cause physical harm, either due to toxic effects of the administered medicines, especially when "purgation" or aversion therapies are applied, or when the patient's reduced physical condition places him/her at special risk, e.g. due to alcohol or drug-induced organic damage. However, it must be considered that many medications used in modern medical treatments may also have unintended harmful effects (such as habituation) and that the risk of ongoing substance abuse in most cases outweighs the risk of even drastic intervention.

CONCLUSION: IMPLICATIONS FOR THE CLINICIAN

Clinicians concerned with the preventative and therapeutic management of substance abuse and dependence in non-Western populations, should inform themselves about culture-specific concepts of health and disease, attitudes toward substance use and abuse, and the views on prevention and treatment prevailing in this population. In general, the clinician can assume that practitioners of traditional healing exist in any sizable non-Western population, including immigrant groups, and that such practitioners are commonly consulted in parallel with modern health care providers. The clinician should make an effort to contact any traditional healer involved in the care of his/her patients and display and open-minded, unbiased attitude in order to learn of culture-congenial therapeutic approaches practised in the patients' ethnocultural or religious group.

On the interpersonal level, the clinician would serve the patients' interest well by seeking collaboration with their traditional practitioners, including mutual information exchange and referral practices in appropriate cases.

On the organizational level, health professionals' associations, treatment facilities and training institutions should advocate the implementation of a general policy of promoting close collaboration between modern cosmopolitan health care systems and traditional non-Western treatment resources. Such a policy would be in line with recommendations repeatedly made by the World Health Organization since the historic declaration on primary health care of Alma Ata (WHO, 1978; cf. Akerele, 1987).

Laws authorizing health care provision affect the legal status of traditional medicine and healing, and such regulations vary greatly from country to country (see Appendix). If the legal framework governing health care in the clinician's country is not in line with the recommendations of the World Health Organization advocating collaboration with traditional therapeutic re-sources (despite the fact that the country is a member state of the United Nations and therefore signatory to the Alma Ata declaration), the clinician should promote appropriate changes in legislation through the action of professional and political organizations.

NOTES

[1] An abbreviated version of this paper was presented at the XIII World Congress of Social Psychiatry, New Delhi, India, November 9–13, 1992.

[2] Most of the data presented in this overview were included in a report I composed in 1991 for the project on mapping the treatment response to alcohol and drug abuse, undertaken by the Programme on Substance Abuse, World Health Organization.

[3] See for example: Abu El Azayem, 1987; Albaugh & Anderson, 1974; Al Radi, 1990; Anderson, 1986; Baasher & Abu El Azayem, 1980; Bergman, 1971; Blum, Futterman & Pascarosa, 1977; Chiappe Costa, 1970; Chiappe Costa, Campos Fuentes & Dragunsky, 1972; Hall, 1986; Heath, 1983; Heggenhougen, 1984; Howard, 1976; Jilek, 1981; 1982b; Jilek & Jilek-Aall, 1990a; Jilek-Aall, 1978; Jilek-Aall & Jilek, 1985; Lee, 1985; Mala, 1985; McGovern, 1982; Pascarosa, Futterman & Halsweig, 1976; Peltzer, 1987; Poshyachinda, 1980; 1982; Roy, 1973; Seguin, 1974; Singer & Borrero, 1984; Spencer, Heggenhougen & Navaratnam, 1980; Suwaki, 1979; 1980; Trotter, 1979; Trotter & Chavira, 1978; Werner, 1979; Westermeyer, 1973; 1979.

REFERENCES

Aberle, D. F. (1966). *The Peyote religion among the Navaho*. Chicago: Aldine Publishing Company.

Abu El Azayem, G. M. (1987). A psycho-socio-religious approach to contain substance abuse in Egypt. In Congress Proceedings, World Islamic Association for Mental Health, Lahore, Pakistan, pp. 409–415.

Akerele, O. (1987). The best of both worlds: Bringing traditional medicine up to date. *Social Science and Medicine, 24*, 177–181.

Albaugh, B. & Anderson, P. (1974). Peyote in the treatment of alcoholism among American Indians. *American Journal of Psychiatry, 131*, 1247–1250.

Al Radi, O. (1990). *Islamic approach to treatment of addiction*. Typescript 8 pp.

Anderson, E. N. (December 29, 1986). Two modes of treating alcoholism: The Kakawis program and Salish Spirit Dancing. Revised version. pp. 1–24.

Anonymous. (no date). Tham Krabok Monastery. d offprint 8 pp., Wat Tam Krabok: Saraburi, Thailand.

Arredondo, R., Weddige, R. L., Justice, C. L. & Fitz, J. (1987). Alcoholism in Mexican-American: Intervention and treatment. *Hospital and Community Psychiatry, 38*(2), 180–183.

Baasher, T. A. & Abu El Azayem, G. M. (1980). Egypt (2): The role of the Mosque in treatment. In G. Edwards & A. Arif (Eds.) *Drug problems in the sociocultural context: A basis for policies and programme planning. Public Health Papers No. 73* (pp. 131–134). Geneva: World Health Organization.

Barnett, H. G. (1957). *Indian shakers: A messianic cult of the Pacific northwest.* Carbondale: Southern Illinois University Press.

Benson, H. & Wallace, R. K. (1984) Decreased drug abuse with transcendental meditation: A study of 1,862 subjects. In D. H. Shapiro & R. N. Walsh (Eds.) *Meditation: Classic and contradictory perspectives* (97–104). New York: Aldine.

Benz, E. (1965). *Messianische Kirchen, Sekten und Bewegungen im heutigen Africa.* Leiden: E. J. Brill.

Benzi, M. (1972). *Les derniers adorateurs du peyotl.* Paris: Gallimard.

Bergman, R. (1971). Navaho peyote use: Its apparent safety. *American Journal of Psychiatry, 128,* 695–699.

Blum, K., Futterman, S. & Pascarosa, P. (1977). Peyote, a potential ethopharmacologic agent for alcoholism and other drug dependencies: Possible biochemical rationale. *Clinical Toxicology, 11,* 459–472.

C'araka, S. (1976). *Suthrasthana* (First century A.D. English translation. P. K. Sharma & V. B. Dash) Varanasi, India: Chowkhamba Sanskrit Series.

Chiappe Costa, M. (1970). El tratamiento curanderil del alcoholismo en la Costa Norte del Peru. In A. Roselli (Ed.) *Psiquiatria en la America Latina* (pp. 542–548). Bogota.

Chiappe Costa, M. (1979). El empleo de alucinogenas en la psiquitria folklorica. In Carlos A. Seguin (Ed.), *Psiquitria folklorica* (pp. 99–108). Lima, Peru: Ediciones Ermar.

Chiappe Costa, M., Campos Fuentes, J. & Dragunsky, L. (1972). Psiquiatria folklorica peruana: Tratamiento del alcoholismo. *Acta psiquiatrica y psicologica de America Latina (Argentina), 18,* 385–394.

Chiappe Costa, M., Lemlij, M. & Millones, L. (1985). *Alucinogenos y shamanismo en el Peru contemporaneo.* Lima, Peru: El Virrey.

Collins, J. McC. (1950). The Indian Shaker Church. *Southwestern Journal of Anthropology, 6,* 399–411.

Clements, G., Krenner, L. & Moelk, W. (1988). The use of the Transcendental Meditation programme in the prevention of drug abuse in the treatment of drug-addicted persons. *Bulletin on Narcotics* (UN Division of Narcotic Drugs), *40*(1), 51–55.

Dobkin de Rios, M. (1990). *Hallucinogens: Cross-cultural perspectives.* Bridport, Dorset, UK: Prism Press.

Dobkin de Rios, M. (1992). *Amazon healer: The life and times of an urban shaman.* Bridport, Dorset, UK: Prism Press.

Gunther, E. (1949). The Shaker religion of the northwest. In Marian W. Smith (Ed.), *Indians of the urban northwest* (pp. 37–76). New York: Columbia University Press.

Hall, R. (1986). Alcohol treatment in American Indian populations; an indigenous treatment modality compared with traditional approaches. *Annals of the New York Academy of Science, 472,* 168–178.

Heath, D. B. (1983). Alcohol use among North American Indians. A cross-cultural survey of patterns and problems. In R. G. Smart, F. B. Glasser, Y. Israel, H. Kalant, R. E. Popham & W. Schmidt (Eds.) *Research advances in alcohol and drug problems. Volume 7.* (pp. 343–396). New York: Plenum Press.

Heggenhougen, H. K. (1984). Traditional medicine and the treatment of drug addicts: Three examples from Southeast Asia. *Medical Anthropology Quarterly, 16*(1), 3–7.

Heggenhougen, H. K. & Navaratnam, V. (1979a). *A general overview on the practices relating to the traditional treatment of drug dependents in Malaysia.* Minden, Penang: National Drug Dependence Research Centre, University of Science, Malaysia.

Heggenhougen, H. K. & Navaratnam, V. (1979b). *Traditional therapies in drug dependence management.* Article prepared for UNESCO, 16 pp.

Howard, J. H. (1976). The plains gourd dance as a revitalization movement. *American Ethnologist, 3,* 243–259.

Jilek, W. (1971). From crazy witch doctor to auxiliary psychotherapist: The changing image of the medicine man. *Psychiatria Clinica, 4,* 200–220.

Jilek, W. (1974). *Salish Indian mental health and culture change.* Toronto: Holt, Rinehart & Winston.

Jilek, W. (1978). Native renaissance: The survival and revival of indigenous therapeutic ceremonials among North American Indians. *Transcultural Psychiatric Research Review, 15,* 117–147.

Jilek, W. (1981). Anomic depression, alcoholism and a culture-congenial Indian response. *Journal of Studies on Alcohol, Supplement No. 9,* 159–170.

Jilek, W. (1982a). Altered states of consciousness in North American Indian ceremonials. *Ethos, 10,* 326–343.

Jilek, W. (1982b). *Indian healing: Shamanic ceremonialism in the Pacific Northwest today.* Surrey, BC, Canada: Hancock House.

Jilek, W. (1989). Therapeutic use of altered states of consciousness in contemporary North American Indian dance ceremonials. In C. A. Ward (Ed.) *Altered states of consciousness and mental health* (pp. 167–185). Newbury Park, CA: Sage Publications.

Jilek, W. & Jilek-Aall, L. (1990a) Culture, mental health and traditional medicine in Indochinese refugee camps. In C. N. Stefanis, C. R. Soldatos, A. D. Rabavilas (Eds.) *Psychiatry: A World Perspective, Volume 4.* (pp. 217–221). (Proceedings of the VIII World Congress of Psychiatry, Athens, 12–19 October 1989). Amsterdam/New York: Excerpta Medica.

Jilek, W. & Jilek-Aall, L. (1990b). The mental health relevance of traditional medicine and shamanism in refugee camps of northern Thailand. *Curare, 13*(4), 217–224.

Jilek-Aall, L. (1978). Alcohol and the Indian-White relationship. *Confinia Psychiatrica, 21*(4), 195–233.

Jilek-Aall, L. (1981). Acculturation, alcoholism and Indian-style Alcoholics Anonymous. *Journal of Studies on Alcohol, Supplement No. 9,* 143–158.

Jilek-Aall, L. & Jilek, W. (1983). Therapeutischer synkretismus in Latein-Amerikanischen Heilkulten. In J. Sterly (Ed.), *Ethnomedizin und Medizingeschichte:* Contributions to ethnomedicine, ethnobotany and ethnozoology. *Arbeitskreis Ethnomedizin Hamburg, 8,* 297–310.

Jilek-Aall, L. & Jilek, W. (1985). Buddhist Temple treatment of narcotic addiction and neurotic-psychosomatic disorders in Thailand. In P. Pichot (Ed.) *Psychiatry: The state of the art* (pp. 673–677). New York: Plenum Press.

Johnson, S. H. (1983). Treatment of drug abusers in Malaysia: A comparison. *The International Journal of the Addictions, 18*(7), 951–958.

Jorgensen, J. G. (1972). *The sun dance religion.* Chicago: University of Chicago Press.

LaBarre, W. (1969). *The Peyote cult.* New York: Schocken Books.

Lee, R. L. M. (1985). Alternative systems in Malaysian drug rehabilitation: Organization and control in comparative perspective. *Social Science and Medicine, 21*(11), 1289–1296.

Lex, B. W. & Schor, N. (1977). A proposed bioanthropological approach linking ritual and opiate addiction. *Addictive Diseases: An International Journal, 3*(2), 287–303.

Mala, T. (1984). Alcoholism and mental health treatment in circumpolar areas: Traditional and non-traditional approaches. In R. Fortuine (Ed.) *Circumpolar health '84* (pp. 332–334). (Proceedings of the Sixth International Symposium on Circumpolar Health, Anchorage, Alaska). Seattle, Washington: University of Washington Press.

Mala, T. (1985). Alaska Native "Grass Roots" Movement: Problem solving utilizing indigenous values. *Arctic Medical Research, 40*, 84–91.

McBride, C. A. (1910). *The modern treatment of alcoholic and drug narcotism.* New York: Rebman Co.

McGovern, M. P. (1982). Alcoholism in Southeast Asia: Prevention and treatment. *International Journal of Social Psychiatry, 28*(1), 36–44.

Nebelkopf, E. (1987). Herbal therapy in the treatment of drug use. *The International Journal of the Addictions, 22*(8), 695–717.

Oyefeso, A. (1994). Sociocultural aspects of substance use and misuse. *Current Opinion in Psychiatry, 7*, 273–277.

Pascarosa, P. & Futterman, S. (1976). Ethnopsychedelic therapy for alcoholics: Observations in the peyote ritual of the Native American Church. *Journal of Psychedelic Drugs, 8*(3), 215–221.

Pascarosa, P., Futterman, S. & Halsweig, M. (1976).Observations of alcoholics in the peyote ritual: A pilot study. In F. Seixas & S. Eggleston's "Work in progress on alcoholism." *Annals of the New York Academy of Sciences, 273*, 518–524.

Peltzer, K. (1987). *Some contributions of traditional healing practices towards psychosocial health care in Malawi.* Frankfurt/M.: Fachbuchhandlung fuer Psychologie Verlag.

Poshyachinda, V. (1980). Thailand: Treatment at the Tam Kraborg Temple. In G. Edwards & A. Arif (Eds.) *Drug problems in the sociocultural context: A basis for policies and programme planning.* Public Health Papers No. 73. (pp. 121–125). Geneva: World Health Organization.

Poshyachinda, V. (1982). *Indigenous drug dependence treatment in Thailand.* Bangkok: Drug Dependence Research Centre, Institute of Health Research, Chulalongkorn University.

Poshyachinda, V. (1985). Medecine traditionelle et traitement de la toxicomanie en Thailande. *Psychotropes, 2*(3), 63–72.

Prince, R. (Ed.) (Winter 1982). Shamans and endorphines. *Ethos (Special Issue), 10*(4).

Reynolds, D. K. (1983). *Naikan psychotherapy: Meditation for self-development.* Chicago: University of Chicago Press.

Roy, C. (1973). Indian peyotists and alcohol. *American Journal of Psychiatry, 130*, 329–330.

Seguin, C. A. (1974) What folklore psychotherapy can teach us. (Proceedings of the 9th International Congress of Psychotherapy, Oslo 1973). *Psychotherapy and Psychosomatics, 24*, 293–302.

Shanmugasundaram, E. R. B. & Shanmugasundaram, K. R. (1986a). An Indian herbal formula (SKV) for controlling voluntary ethanol intake in rats with chronic alcoholism. *Journal of Ethnopharmacology, 17*, 171–182.

Shanmugasundaram, E. R. B., Umarani Subramaniam Santhini, R. & Radha Shanmugasundaram, K. (1986b). Studies on brain structure and neurological function in alcoholic rats controlled by an Indian medicinal formula (SKV). *Journal of Ethnopharmacology, 17*, 225–245.

Sharma, K. & Shukla, V. (1988). Rehabilitation of drug-addicted persons: The experience of the Nav-Chetna Centre in India. *Bulletin of Narcotics, 40*(1), 43–49.

Simons, R. C., Ervin, F. R. & Prince, R. H. (1988). The psychobiology of trance: I: Training for Thaipusam. *Transcultural Psychiatric Research Review, 25*(4), 249–266.

Singer, M. & Borrero, M. (1984). Indigenous treatment of alcoholism: The case of Puerto Rican spiritism. *Medical Anthropology, 8*, 246–273.

Spencer, C. P., Heggenhougen, H. K. & Navaratnam, V. (1980). Traditional therapies and the treatment of drug dependence in Southeast Asia. *American Journal of Chinese Medicine, 8*, 230–238.

Stepan, J. (1983). Patterns of legislation concerning traditional medicine. In R. H. Bannerman, J. Burton, C. Wen-Chieh (Eds.) *Traditional medicine and health care coverage* (pp. 290–313). Geneva: World Health Organization.

Sundkler, B. G. M. (1961). *Bantu prophets in South Africa.* London: Oxford University Press.

Suwaki, H. (1979). Naikan and Danshukai for the treatment of Japanese alcoholic patients. *British Journal of Addiction, 74*, 15–20.

Suwaki, H. (1980). Culturally based treatment of alcoholism. In G. Edwards & A. Arif (Eds.) *Drug problems in the sociocultural context: A basis for policies and programme planning. Public Health Papers No. 73.* (pp. 139–143). Geneva: World Health Organization.

Takemoto, T., Usukine, K. & Otsu, M. (1979). A follow-up study of alcoholic patients treated by Naikan therapy. Communication to 2nd Annual Meeting on Kaikan, Kyoto, 1979. (cit. Suwaki, 1980).

Teo Hui Khian (1983). Traditional healing: Some observations on its use in drug addiction in West Malaysia. In R. Kusumanto Setyonegoro & W. M. Roan (Eds.) *Traditional healing practices.* (pp. 105–109). Jakarta: Directorate of Mental Health, Ministry of Health, Republic of Indonesia.

Trotter, R. T. & Chavira, J. A. (1978). Discovering new models for alcohol counseling in minority groups. In B. Velimirovic (Ed.) *Modern medicine and medical anthropology in the United States: Mexico border population. Scientific Publication No. 359.* (pp. 164–171). Washington, DC: Pan American Health Organization, Regional Office of the WHO.

Trotter, R. (1979). Evidence of an ethnomedical form of aversion therapy on the United States-Mexico border. *Journal of Ethnopharmacology, 1*, 279–284.

Wallace, A. F. C. (1972). *The death and rebirth of the Seneca.* New York: Vintage Books, A Division of Random House.

Westermeyer, J. (1973). Folk treatment for opium addiction in Laos. *British Journal of Addiction, 68*, 345–349.

Westermeyer, J. (1979). Medical and nonmedical treatment for narcotic addicts: A comparative study from Asia. *Journal of Nervous and Mental Disease, 167*, 205–210.

Westermeyer, J. (1980). Treatment for narcotic addiction in Buddhist Monastery. *Journal of Drug Issues, 10*(2), 221–228.

Westermeyer, J. (1982). *Poppies, pipes, and people.* Berkeley: University of California Press.

Werner, R. (1979). Die behandlung von malaysischen drogenabhaenigigen mit den methoden der traditionallen medizin. *Oeffentliches Gesundheitswesen, 41*, 332–343.

World Health Organization (1978). *Alma Ata 1978: Primary health care.* Report of the International Conference on primary health care, Alma-Ata, USSR, 6–12 September 1978. Geneva: World Health Organization ("Health for All" Series, no. 1).

Yang, M. M. P. & Kwok, J. S. L. (1986). Evaluation on the treatment of morphine addiction by acupuncture, Chinese herbs and opioid peptides. *American Journal of Chinese Medicine, 14*(1–2), 46–50.

CHAPTER TEN

Culture and Anxiety

Anxiety is essentially future-oriented fear. Barlow (1988) and Barlow, Brown, and Craske (1994) have analyzed the relationship between anxiety and fear. Their analyses conclude that anxiety is the emotion of fear linked to the anticipation of future danger or misfortune. In contrast, ordinary fear is linked to present-oriented danger or misfortune. Anxiety or future-oriented fear also seems to be connected to the cognition of uncontrollability (Barlow, 1988; Mineka, 1985a, b). Uncontrollability here means the cognition that one is not able to control upcoming stressful events. Anxiety is thus related to cognitive patterns constructing self-concept, and ideas about personal competence, self-confidence, and one's ability to deal effectively with events in one's life. Anxiety is clearly connected to a specific cognitive process related to sociocultural factors that influence overall personality development.

Vulnerability to anxiety can be either genetically inherited or acquired through traumatic experience and manifests simultaneously biologically and psychologically in the form of a hypersensitive nervous system. Biologically, the person is hypersensitive to environmental stress due to abnormalities in his or her stress hormone system. Psychologically, hypersensitivity to environmental stress is structured into the neural networks of the brain as a result of emotional trauma. These neural networks structure cognitive schemas that promote anxiety-producing cognitions. These cognitions appear to produce the symptoms of anxiety disorders.

The basis for the formation of anxiety-producing cognitive schemas appears to be stressful life events. Similarly, the triggers for subsequent activation of anxiety schemas also appears to be stressful events. Most of these events are related to interpersonal relationships, for example, interactions with family, peers, superiors, and so on. Other types of stressful life events, such as illness or injury, financial problems, or death of a loved one, can also be involved in producing or triggering anxiety schemas. Once these schemas are activated, they can produce negative misinterpretations in cognition, thus structuring a normal or less serious situation as something catastrophic, life-threatening, or seriously embarrassing. Because anxiety is so closely related to cognitive schemas, anxiety symptoms and syndromes differ significantly by cultural context and cultural identity of the individual.

The first article in this chapter is by Laurence J. Kirmayer, Allan Young, and Barbara C. Hayton. These authors point out that anxiety disorders are not simply biological disturbances but are based in cognitive interpretations structured by cultural schemas. A variety of culture-related syndromes and idioms of distress may mislead clinicians to the point of misdiagnosis. The authors discuss some of these syndromes and their cultural contexts.

The second article in this chapter is by James K. Boehnlein and J. David Kinzie. These authors discuss how the symptoms of posttraumatic stress disorder have been found to be very common in Southeast Asian refugees who experienced high levels of traumatic stress due to war-related events either as soldiers or as civilians. The traumatic events experienced by these people can include bombing of one's village or home, witnessing deaths of family members, recovering bodies of dead family members, beatings, starvation, forced labor, rapes, combat, and so on. Because of cultural schemas regarding shame and a fatalistic view of life, many Southeast Asians may be uncomfortable volunteering information about these traumatic life events unless specifically asked. Also, because of cultural schemas regarding the shamefulness of emotional illness that is common to many Asians, these patients are more likely to report somatic rather than emotional symptoms. Thus, clinicians should specifically inquire about personal trauma when assessing refugees. This article provides the latest information and specific recommendations on assessment and treatment.

REFERENCES

Barlow, D. H. (1988). *Anxiety and its disorders: The nature and treatment of anxiety and panic.* New York: Guilford Press.

Barlow, D. H., Brown, T. A., & Craske, M. G. (1994). Definitions of panic attacks and panic disorder in DSM-IV: Implications for research. *Journal of Abnormal Psychology, 103*, 553–554.

Mineka, S. (1985a). Animal models of anxiety based disorders: Their usefulness and limitations. In A. H. Tuma & J. D. Maser (Eds.), *Anxiety and the anxiety disorders* (pp. 199–244). Hillsdale, NJ: Lawrence Erlbaum.

Mineka, S. (1985b). The frightful complexity of the origins of fears. In F. R. Bruch & J. B. Overmier (Eds.), *Affect, conditioning, and cognition: Essays on the determinants of behavior* (pp. 55–74). Hillsdale, NJ: Lawrence Erlbaum.

LAURENCE J. KIRMAYER, ALLAN YOUNG, AND BARBARA C. HAYTON*

The Cultural Context of Anxiety Disorders

We are threatened with suffering from three directions: from our own body, which is doomed to decay and dissolution and which cannot even do without pain and anxiety as warning signals; from the external world, which may rage against us with overwhelming and merciless forces of destruction; and finally from our relations to other men. The suffering which comes from this last source is perhaps more painful than any other (p 24).[28]

The experience of fear in response to the threat of injury, and the surge of adrenaline that accompanies the fight-or-flight response, are human universals.[12] Since the time of William James, however, it has been well recognized that processes of cognitive appraisal and coping play a role in anxiety as with other emotional responses.[39, 49] Recent cognitive theory makes it clear that clinical anxiety disorders are not simply biologic perturbations, but reflect vicious cycles of bodily arousal, cognitive interpretation, and ineffective coping in a runaway feedback loop.[16] Cognitive interventions can be effective in the management of a range of anxiety disorders.[15] Indeed, cognitive factors play a role in the success of pharmacologic treatment of anxiety disorders; patients who attribute their recovery exclusively to anxiolytic medication are more likely to relapse.[3]

Cognitive-interpretive processes provide a natural locus for understanding the effect of cultural beliefs directly on the cognitive schemas that interpret events as threatening and specify coping or avoidant responses. Cultural practices may have other effects on anxiety disorders as well, acting through child-rearing practices and forms of social life that alter bodily experiences of secure attachment, separation, comfort, and danger in ways that subvert conscious efforts at explanation or reassurance. Usually, there is some degree of fit between cultural ideology and such practices so that their impact on the individual may be obscured.

Whereas anxiety may be a universal emotion, the contexts in which it is experienced, the interpretations of its meaning, and

*From the Division of Social and Transcultural Psychiatry, McGill University (LJK, AY); and the Department of Psychiatry, Sir Mortimer B. Davis–Jewish General Hospital (LJK, BCH), Montreal, Quebec, Canada.

the responses to it are, like those of other emotions, strongly influenced by cultural beliefs and practices.[58, 69] Indeed, whereas a few emotion terms name relatively simple patterns of motivational response or preparedness to act (e.g., anger or fear as fight or flight[12, 23]), most emotion terms name more complex sequences of thought, feeling, action, and social response and hence, are irreducibly social in nature.[41, 84] Translations of emotion terms cross-culturally often only can be achieved by stripping words of many of their important connotations. The cultural determinants of anxiety symptoms and syndromes mean that anxiety must be understood not just in terms of cognitive or physiologic mechanisms, but also in terms of its social meanings and the roles, situations, and cultural practices that may engender anxiety and influence its intrapsychic and interpersonal management.

In this article, we summarize what is known about social and ethnocultural variations in the prevalence of anxiety disorders as well as in symptomatology and course. We then consider the relationship of anxiety to specific cultural beliefs and practices. Finally, through the case study of a woman with post-traumatic stress disorder, we consider the social embedding and cultural meaning of anxiety disorders in clinical practice with a view to outlining culturally responsive strategies for diagnosis and treatment.

CROSS-CULTURAL PREVALENCE OF ANXIETY DISORDERS

Anxiety disorders are the single most common psychiatric conditions. Despite the impression that they are often mild disorders or simply part of the human condition, there is evidence that they contribute to a significant morbidity and mortality rates.[6, 20, 82]

Current nosology recognizes several distinct forms of anxiety including generalized anxiety disorder (GAD), panic disorder, obsessive-compulsive disorder (OCD), post-traumatic stress disorder (PTSD), agoraphobia, and other more specific phobias.[1] Whereas GAD and specific phobias long have been recognized to have a high prevalence rate, recent studies have shown panic, OCD, and PTSD are also very common.[67] Various forms of mixed-anxiety depression are also common in primary care.[43, 88]

Although most of these forms of anxiety are closely related and commonly co-occur, there is some evidence for different underlying mechanisms. For example, blood-injury phobia is the only anxiety disorder in which the usual physiologic concomitant is a drop in blood pressure rather than a rise; consequently, it is more likely to precipitate fainting.[77] There is some evidence for specific neurophysiologic mechanisms in OCD and panic disorder. Clearly, however, anxiety also constitutes a dimension of distress, ranging from mild to severe, and debate continues as to whether the range of anxiety-related problems is best understood in terms of severity or as discrete categories.

Although earlier studies examined cultural differences on self-report measures of anxiety symptoms, and established significant differences in prevalence,[33] accurate cross-cultural and cross-national data on the prevalence of discrete anxiety disorders are just recently being established with the use of standardized diagnostic interviews in epidemiologic surveys. In the Epidemiologic Catchment Area (ECA) study, significant differences in rates of anxiety disorders were found among ethnocultural groups.[20] At the Lost Angeles ECA site, whereas similar rates were found for panic disorder, social phobia, and OCD among Mexican Americans and non-Hispanic whites, differences were found for GAD, agoraphobia, and simple phobia.[42] Rates of simple phobia were higher among Mexican Americans, particularly those born in the United States. Mexican Americans born in Mexico, however, had lower overall rates of anxiety disorders (and other diagnoses) than did Mexican Americans born in the United States, perhaps owing to a selective migration. At the Baltimore and St. Louis ECA sites, African Americans were found to have higher rates of phobias than did whites even when sociodemographic characteristics were controlled.[9] This was attributed to greater numbers of stressful life events and the effect of racism and minority group status on African Americans.

There are, as yet, few data to help interpret these findings. A comparison of a small clinical sample of African-American and white patients with panic disorder and agoraphobia found similar symptom profiles but more frequent experiences of separation from parents and traumatic childhood events in the African-American group.[30] Although, as noted previously, African Americans reported higher rates of phobia in the ECA studies, a study of African-American school children found similar fears compared with white children; 8 of the 11 most common fears were the same for both groups.[63] A factor analysis found 5 factors for whites and 3 for African Americans; the major difference was the lack of a factor related to school fears. Although this may reflect differences in attitudes toward schooling, it may also be accounted for by an age difference between the groups (the African Americans were 1 year younger than the whites on average [8 years 8 months versus 9 years 3 months]).

A cross-national study involving surveys in the United States, Canada, Puerto Rico, Germany, Taiwan, Korea, and New Zealand found comparable annual rates of OCD across sites ranging from 1.1% in Korea to 1.8% in Puerto Rico, with the exception of Taiwan (0.4%).[81] This low rate in rural Taiwan is consistent with lower rates found for other disorders. Subjects fulfilling criteria for OCD in most countries reported only obsessions, except for in Taiwan and Germany where equal amounts of obsessions and compulsions were reported and in Korea, where compulsions were more common than obsessions.

Post-traumatic stress disorder (PTSD) is classified as an anxiety disorder in DSM-IV because anxiety symptoms are among its most prominent manifestations. PTSD can be understood, in part, as a form of conditioned emotional response. It is clear, however, that depressive, dissociative, and somatic symptoms commonly accompany the anxiety symptoms of PTSD and form part of the same complex response to severe stress, fear, and loss.[13, 37, 83]

Symptoms of PTSD are common in many refugee groups.[7, 44, 59, 60] Because such refugees must endure a continuing situation of threat and loss, however, it is a gross oversimplification to view their problem as a discrete disorder such as PTSD. It has been suggested that the plight and affliction of refugees can, in some respects, be better understood as one of cultural bereavement; particularly when, as in the case of Cambodian refugees, they not only escape horrors but must face the continuing loss of family, community, and tradition.[22]

There is evidence both from prospective studies of people exposed to a traumatic event and from longitudinal studies of symptomatology during treatment, that the recollection of traumatic events depends on the level of distress. Thus, more distressed individuals are more likely to recall traumatic events, compared with individuals exposed to the same events who do not experience as much subsequent distress.[55] Similarly, individuals who report traumatic events may no longer recollect them when they feel less anxious. These effects may reflect a sort of state-dependent memory with retrieval of traumatic memory tied to anxious mood. The influence of anxiety on memory also may reflect the well-established reconstructive nature of memory in which events are assembled and interpreted in a manner consistent with current beliefs and feelings. In either case, the feedback loop between memory and anxiety makes time move in two directions—from traumatic event to memory and anxiety, and from anxiety through memory to the recollection (reconstruction) of fearsome events.

Although many anxiety disorders show comparable prevalence among major ethnocultural groups in the general population, substantial differences in rates are found in clinical epidemiologic studies, probably owing to differential patterns of help-seeking. This may be due to both socioeconomic factors influencing access to health care and cultural interpretations of symptomatology and corresponding patterns of resort to care. For example, one study found African Americans with OCD and other anxiety disorders to be common among patients in dermatology clinics where they presented with pruritus or other skin complaints caused by compulsive washing with irritating cleansing agents.[29] Similarly, whereas agoraphobia is common in US samples of phobic patients, in Qatar only 8% of women with phobias reported agoraphobia. This may reflect the fact that it is unusual for women to leave the home unaccompanied by at least one adult male; their lives are contained within the household. Wrote El-Islam, "Being bound to the home, which is a sign of severe agoraphobia in the West, is a sign of virtue in a Muslim housewife."[24] This cultural difference could result in normal social behavior being misinterpreted as agoraphobia by a clinician unfamiliar with local mores. Such restriction of activity could, however, also mask agoraphobia or even contribute to avoidance behavior and so exacerbate an anxiety disorder.

Similarly, in societies where ritual plays an important role in religious life, repetitive behavior and anxious preoccupation with avoiding "pollution" and with doing things correctly may be misdiagnosed as OCD; on the other hand, such societies may predispose individuals to obsessive-compulsive symptoms and mask the disorder when present. Fears of contamination, which often are interpreted as symptoms of OCD, are common among peoples where much religious emphasis is placed on purity and many rituals and practices exist to avoid pollution and cleanse the self. Here, again, it may be very difficult to judge where zealous religious practice shades into obsessive preoccupation. As with all such judgments, information from family, peers, and other religious practitioners is crucial. In every case, though, the clinician must consider where this information comes from and whether there are reasons in family or social dynamics why the judgment of others might be biased. A culture broker, trained interpreter, or other cultural consultant can ensure that these biases are avoided.

Finally, most cross-cultural clinical and epidemiologic studies have not used culturally adapted questionnaires that tap culture-specific symptoms of anxiety. As a result, comparisons are limited by the imposition of definitions of anxiety disorders and distress that may themselves be culture-specific to unknown degrees. Clinical assessment of anxiety must canvas the range of culturally prevalent symptoms.

CULTURAL VARIATIONS IN THE SYMPTOMATOLOGY OF ANXIETY DISORDERS

Cross-cultural studies have found substantial differences in the symptomatology of anxiety. These include differences in the prominence and type of specific fears as well as associated somatic, dissociative, and affective symptoms and syndromes. A variety of culture-related forms of anxiety disorder also have been identified including *koro* in South and East Asia, semen-loss anxiety (*dhat* and *jiryan* in India, *sukra praneha* in Sri Lanka, *shen-k'uei* in China) syndrome, *taijin kyofusho* in Japan, as well as various "nervous fatigue" syndromes, including ordinary *shinkeishitsu* in Japan, "brain fag" in Nigeria, and neurasthenia in China.

Cultural influences are apparent in the content and focus of anxiety disorders. A study of patients referred to the only psychiatric outpatient clinic in Qatar found that panic disorder typically involved fear of after-death rather than of dying per se. Islamic religion teaches that a person may be tortured in his or her grave and after death if his or her wrongdoings outnumber his or her good deeds. Obsessional fears concern inability to control one's own harmful impulses. These were "invariably attributed to the devil (Shaitin), who is thought to force them on individuals whose faith is not strong enough to counter the evil."[24] Similarly, in studies of OCD patients seen in outpatient psychiatry clinics in Saudi Arabia and Egypt, the most common themes of obsessions and compulsions were religious.[53, 64]

Muslim upbringing puts an emphasis on religious rituals, including ritual cleansing before prayer five times a day as well as warding off blasphemous thoughts through repetition of phrases such as "I seek refuge with the Lord from the accused satan."[64] The symptomatology of OCD, here as elsewhere, then involves repetition and internal struggle with forbidden thoughts, as these engender the greatest anxiety for the individual and are most liable to become part of vicious cycles of effort and failure to control. The congruence between religious belief and practice and OC symptoms also probably contributes to relatively low rates of insight into the irrationality of the symptoms: in the context of orthodox Muslim religion moderate repetitions of protective thoughts and actions appear normal, at least to the afflicted person, although others may well recognize that the levels of religious preoccupation, scrupulosity, and anxiety are abnormal.

As another example of the effect of religious belief on anxiety, consider the widespread belief in reincarnation across the Middle East and Asia. Among the Druze, for example, "often a person who remembers a previous incarnation can point to a scar on the body as the place where the previous body was injured, and in some cases memories continue to influence children until adulthood. Some children suffer from phobias conceptualized by them as related to events in their previous incarnation. For example, a child who fears water will claim that in an earlier incarnation he drowned in a stream."[17]

When anxiety is described as excessive worry and apprehension about future events it appears to be pre-eminently a disorder of emotional or psychological distress. Somatic symptoms, however, usually accompany anxiety (e.g., restlessness, tachycardia, palpitations, piloerection, dry mouth, urinary urgency, insomnia, muscle tension, and so on) and for many patients predominate, leading to primarily somatic clinical presentations and medical diagnoses of a range of disorders from angina, mitral valve prolapse, atypical chest pain, and other cardiac-related disorders to irritable bowel, fibromyalgia, and other functional somatic syndromes, aggravated by anxiety or hyperventilation.[56, 72, 73] It is well known that many patients with panic attacks consult medical practitioners because their symptoms may closely mimic angina or myocardial infarction,[4] but patients with GAD seek evaluation for cardiac symptoms just as frequently.[52] Somatic symptoms are important features of anxiety disorders across most cultures studied but may take differing forms depending on local ethnophysiologic ideas and idioms of distress. Various cultural idioms referring to "heart distress," "nerves," and other organ systems may be used to convey physical sensations, emotional distress, and personal or social concerns.[32] Teasing apart the relative contributions of social, personal, and physiologic processes in such complaints requires careful assessment drawing on both biomedical and cultural expertise.

Cultural beliefs may make unusual symptoms salient and clinicians unfamiliar with local idioms of distress may be misled, at times to the extent of considering such patients psychotic. This is particularly likely when cultural differences make dissociative symptoms more prevalent. Hypnotic susceptibility has been posited to play a role in the development and persistence of some anxiety disorders.[27] In effect, hypnotically susceptible individuals may become absorbed in their fears in a way that amplifies their intensity; alternatively, they may dissociate frightening events from subsequent behavior and reassurance and so fail to extinguish the conditioned emotional response of acquired fear. When cultures sanction or reinforce dissociative experience, through religious or healing rituals and other aspects of communal life or illness models and idioms of distress, individuals may be more prone to exhibit dissociative symptoms in conjunction with anxiety, giving rise to a great range of symptoms viewed as "atypical" in the DSM and prompting the unwary clinician to think of psychotic disorders.

The Nigerian culture-related syndrome of *ode-ori* is marked by prominent somatic symptoms including such culture-specific symptoms as feelings of heat in the head or sensations of parasites crawling in the head.[54] Sensations of worms crawling in the head are common nonspecific somatic symptoms in equatorial Africa that may be prominent symptoms of panic disorder or GAD as well as other psychiatric disorders.[2, 21, 54, 61] Although these symptoms also might accompany psychosis, they are not in themselves, indicative of severe psychopathology.[24]

Ode-ori also may be associated with paranoid fears of malevolent attack by witchcraft. Such fears are common in societies where witchcraft is practiced or is a part of local belief. Fears of malign magic, bewitchment, or spirit attack may be misdiag-

nosed as symptoms of psychosis by the uninformed clinician. Where magic is part of shared belief, dramatic forms of epidemic anxiety may be precipitated by witchcraft accusations. For example, several Nigerian cities recently witnessed epidemics of magical penis loss.[38] Afflicted individuals were made apprehensive by previous reports. When bumped by a stranger on the city street they became alarmed and checked their genitals to discover they had shrunk or disappeared. Sounding the alarm, they quickly attracted a crowd who might attack the passerby accused of the magical theft. Professional thieves soon hit on this fear as a useful method to create a diversion while pick-pocketing and the brief epidemics may be attributed to this criminal activity. Nevertheless, the very peculiarity of the symptom points to the malleability of anxiety symptoms, so long as they fit with widely held beliefs.

Ataques de nervios is a culture-related syndrome found among Puerto Ricans and other Hispanic Caribbean peoples, with symptoms that may resemble those of panic disorder but which prominently feature uncontrollable shouting and attacks of crying.[34] *Ataques* usually follow immediately on a stressful event, to which they are attributed. In the Puerto Rican disaster study, *ataques* was a common reaction to a natural catastrophe.[35] Like other folk categories, it cuts across conventional psychiatric disorders, being associated with affective, somatoform, and dissociative disorders, as well as anxiety disorders.

The culture-related syndrome of *koro* involves the intense acute fear that the penis is shrinking into the body and, when involution is complete, the sufferer will die.[5] *Koro* most commonly occurs in epidemics, which also may affect a lesser proportion of women, who typically suffer from the fear that their nipples are retracting and their breasts shrinking.[14, 40] *Koro* affects individuals who are vulnerable due to pre-existing anxiety, sexual, reproductive and relationship concerns, recent stressful life events, and, perhaps, suggestibility.[79,80] *Koro* fits with cultural beliefs about the vulnerability of male sexual potency.[46] It has been suggested that, at a social level, *koro* affects cultural minority groups whose survival is threatened.[62] The symbolic loss of fertility then expresses the large group's concern about extinction.

A Japanese form of social phobia, *taijin kyofusho* (TKS), provides an instructive example of the interaction of cultural beliefs and practices with anxiety.[45, 74] In DSM-IV, the core symptoms of social phobia involve the fear and avoidance of social situations where one might be the object of scrutiny, humiliation, or embarrassment. In contrast, a core symptom of TKS is the fear that one will offend or make others uncomfortable through inappropriate social behavior and self-presentation including staring, blushing, emitting an offensive odor, or having a physical blemish or misshapen features. This fits with Japanese preoccupations with the proper public presentation of self in a society.[70] Japanese cultural values put an emphasis on harmonious relationships within a complex status hierarchy that demands skill and vigilance on the part of social actors to successfully negotiate. Takano[75] has suggested that this social context makes Japanese more aware of themselves as social actors. It may, thus, foster public self-consciousness, which has been shown to contribute to social anxiety.[11, 71] Indeed, Shoma Morita[66a] developed an indigenous form of psychotherapy based on the notion that the underlying psychological mechanism in TKS and related forms of *shinkeishitsu* (neurasthenia), was a vicious cycle of excessive self-awareness. Morita's theory is entirely consistent with contemporary cognitive models of social and performance anxiety.

A study of Japanese-American students and a community sample of adults in Hawaii found that symptoms of TKS were substantially correlated with those of social phobia (SP).[48] Although there were no differences between Asian and Western students in mean levels of TKS symptoms, higher levels of TKS symptoms (but not other SP symptoms) were found among less acculturated individuals, lending some support to the notion that the distinctive features of TKS are associated with the Japanese culture. Although women reported higher levels of SP, there was no gender difference on TKS. One interesting finding from this study is that TKS-like symptoms are not uncommon among US students. This suggests that culture not only influences the production of symptoms but also which symptoms are considered salient by patients and clinicians. The point of studying cultural differences then, is not just to understand how other cultures differ from the implicit norms and prototypes of North American psychiatry but to decenter those same prototypes to consider a broader range of symptoms.

The fears of TKS patients may be profoundly disabling and may reach delusional proportions. Patients with TKS may fit DSM-IV diagnoses of SP, body dysmorphic disorder, avoidant personality disorder or delusional disorders. Whatever the severity, however, some Japanese psychiatrists group all variants of TKS together on the grounds that the fundamental problem is similar.[76, 78] Clinical reports suggest that cognitive, group, and indigenous Morita therapy may be effective even for delusional cases.[86]

The roots of TKS can be found in Japanese patterns of child-rearing, which emphasize close attachment between mother and child.[45] Unlike American parents who encourage independent behavior in their child, Japanese encourage dependence, viewing it as a positive aspect of human behavior that binds people together in mutually satisfying hierarchical relationships.[19] Children may sometimes be punished, not by being confined to their rooms, but by being locked outside the house for a time, cut off from the secure nest of the family.[36] This emphasis on dependency and the effort to protect interpersonal bonds that begin in the family is extended to larger social circles over the course of maturation. Older children are expected to become highly con-

scious of and anticipate the needs of others, and enjoined to maintain good behavior by being warned that the neighbors are watching. These processes carry over into adulthood, not just as conscious values and collectively shared ideologies or concepts of personhood, but in the habitus and bodily responses of adults to social situations.[50] Cultural beliefs and practices then interact with individual variations in temperament and specific beliefs derived from personal history, to give rise to the runaway feedback loop of self-consciousness and social anxiety that characterizes TKS.

Sporadic cases of these culture-related anxiety syndromes have been described outside their cultures-of-origin, but without the specific cultural beliefs to shape the thinking of anxiety patients they remain rare.[37] The cultural fit with specific anxiety beliefs means several things: (1) they may occur at lower levels of stress or individual psychopathology, shading into subclinical or nonpathologic uses of symptoms and terms as cultural idioms of distress; (2) they may be less stigmatized, or at least have well worked out sociocultural meanings, which may contribute to a better prognosis even for seemingly severe cases; and (3) on the other hand, at times, they may be harder to treat precisely because of this fit with socially normative beliefs and practices. Thus, certain fears may not seem "excessive or unreasonable" to the sufferer because they are consonant with cultural values. This may lend delusional rigidity to anxieties.

In addition to these culture-related forms of anxiety, many ethnocultural groups use fear or fright as a part of an explanation for a great range of illnesses including infectious and other physical diseases as well as psychiatric disorders. Notions of "evil eye" are common in circum-Mediterranean societies as well as Latin America, and commonly convey feelings of interpersonal rivalry and jealousy. Many African Americans and Caribbean peoples, as well as Europeans ascribe illness and misfortune to hexing, "root-work," witchcraft, sorcery, or other evil influences of another person. In many cases, there is no elaborate cultural theory about how such evil influences work, they are experienced directly by affected individuals and families as a "force" or visceral feeling of the uncanny.

In Central and South America, many people attribute illness to an acute fright (*susto, espanto, pasmo*).[68] Similar ideas are found in Asia and Africa.[85] An intense fright leads to a sudden flight of the soul from the body. This soul loss is the underlying cause of illness. Despite its explicit link to fright, *susto* may be associated more closely with depression than with anxiety disorders. As Shweder[72a] has argued, "soul loss" metaphorically captures much of the experience of depression in North American folk psychology and psychiatric description. Here again, the culture-specific terms are not so much labels of syndromes but folk explanations, which, nevertheless, convey expectations about the symptomatology, course, appropriate treatment, and prognosis. Most importantly, all of these folk terms serve to direct attention to specific life events, apportion blame for misfortune and responsibility for illness management, and direct the search for effective help.

SOCIAL CAUSES AND MEANINGS OF ANXIETY

Case Study

Mrs. J, a 40-year-old Haitian immigrant mother of two children, was referred by a community health clinic psychologist to the psychiatric crisis service with symptoms of indecisiveness; trouble concentrating; compulsive rituals (eating boxes of cornstarch, repetitive hand-washing, bathing herself and her children in bleach); fear of knives, guns and dogs; insomnia; loss of appetite; palpitations; loss of interest in life; and suicidal ideation.

Her symptoms dated from an automobile accident 1 year earlier. She was returning from a trip to a neighboring city with her children in a car driven by a friend. She recalls being angry during the ride home because her common-law husband had spent the weekend flirting with another woman and was, in fact, driving with her in the car ahead of them on the way home. She also recalls thinking they were traveling too fast and being aware that her son in the front seat had taken his seat belt off, but she did not say anything about this at the time.

The driver of the car lost control, the car went off the road and both children were thrown from the car. Her daughter was quickly found and had suffered facial injuries. She recalls wandering around in the woods looking for her son thinking she heard him calling her. When the ambulance crew arrived they found him a great distance from the car, comatose.

Mrs. J and her children were hospitalized. The son remained in a coma for several months and has been left with brain damage and behavioral disinhibition. The daughter has facial scars. Mrs. J has chronic low back pain.

Mrs. J immigrated from Haiti 20 years ago. She describes her family of origin as having been privileged compared with the neighbors, financially stable, and placing a high value on education. One brother is a health professional and she herself was pursuing a degree in health sciences at the time of the accident. She has twice attempted to return to her studies but finds she is unable to concentrate adequately. Prior to the accident, Mrs. J had hopes her son would become a physician in a fulfillment of her own and her parents' dreams. Through his success he would become a leader in the black community of his generation; she states that this would be proof to

society at large that blacks could succeed. It has been extremely difficult for her to accept that her son will no longer be able to play this role. She finds that the various "helpers" in the hospital subsequently have shown racially prejudiced reactions to her and her family. During her son's long hospitalization he was often left unchanged and unwashed, which Mrs. J attributed to the nurses' assumption that he was "big, black, and dirty anyway." In school for remedial education, a teacher told her that her son had "a good vocabulary considering he's black."

Although she is eloquent in recounting these examples of racism, Mrs. J does not recognize her own help-rejecting behavior. She interprets every slight or inattention by care providers as a racially motivated attack or evidence of complete lack of concern. She neglects to call to make appointments with her son's physicians and interprets the fact that they do not call her as evidence of their unconcern.

Mrs. J has been troubled by "flashbacks" of the accident triggered by thoughts or by seeing her daughter's facial scars. She is fearful of nighttime when she often hears her son's voice calling her as she did at the time of the accident. Occasionally, she has visual hallucinations of a dog prowling her apartment at night. She relates her fear of dogs to a childhood experience when the family dog was left dead and genitally mutilated on her front step as a "voodou" retaliation against her father. She has fears of a stranger attacking her in her apartment and takes the children with her to the bathroom and sleeps with them in the same bedroom at night.

Mrs. J's symptoms fit a variety of DSM-IV diagnoses and have shifted over time. She initially presented with a major depression. Her paranoid suspicions were interpreted as evidence of psychosis but are more likely reflective of personality and sociocultural factors. Her flashbacks, rumination, visual hallucinations, nightmares, hyperarousal, irritability, sleep disturbance, hypervigilance, and avoidant behavior all fit with PTSD. Her obsessive fears and compulsive rituals fit OCD; they waxed and waned in conjunction with her depressive symptoms in response to medication. She also had persistent gastrointestinal complaints with cramps and nausea as well as headaches and intermittent low back pain. Her pattern of help-seeking and help-rejecting over a 3-year period of treatment prompted consideration of a personality disorder diagnosis.

Fears and suspicions that may be mistaken for paranoia are common among Haitian immigrants. Widespread beliefs in the harmful effects of envy or jealousy, whether through malign magic or physical efforts at poisoning or other injury, make people cautious about revealing hostile thoughts.[10, 18] Indeed, the suspicion of such envy-motivated injury itself often must be hidden lest it provoke further attacks. Disturbances in the blood are the mediating process between both physical and spiritual attack.[8, 25] Mental illness, in particular, often is attributed to the physiologic and spiritual consequences of such interpersonal hostility.

Haitians' status as a visible minority in North America subjects them to racial discrimination. This has been compounded by cultural differences from other African Americans. In the United States, some Haitians have dealt with this double alienation by attributing some of the prejudice they experience to their lack of proficiency with English. In Québec, however, despite the fact that French is the dominant language (although still different from Creole), racism and discrimination persist. For Haitians, racism has been compounded by spurious association with the threat of AIDS.[26, 31]

In this social context, a lack of trust toward authorities, including health care providers, bordering on paranoid suspicion, is not surprising. Such "paranoia" could be understood as an aspect of fear and anger rather than as indicating either psychosis or personality disorder in itself. It may, nonetheless, be difficult to resolve, as it reflects social structural problems and deeply rooted cultural beliefs that are not easily put aside.

Further, in an attempt to avoid both the North American race hierarchy and the Haitian class system, Haitian immigrants may construct a transnational identity in which they remain active in social settings of both country of origin and host society.[31] The meaning of the actions and events must then be understood in this transnational context. Mrs. J's emphasis on the academic achievement of her son must be seen not just as the average middle class Canadian parents' concern for their children's success but as part of creating an identity for herself and her family that will surpass and transcend the dominant societies' fixing of the position of Haitians in Canada.

Mrs. J's visual hallucinations were variously interpreted as "flashbacks" or intrusive imagery associated with PTSD, or as evidence of psychotic depression. The image of the threatening dog roaming her apartment at night is reminiscent of the *lougarou* (werewolf) of childhood tales,[66] although she herself did not make that connection. The "flashbacks" of PTSD have been interpreted as a replaying of the memory of traumatic events forcefully engraved on the nervous system but this metaphor has little empirical support. Flashbacks, like all memories, probably are in large measure imaginative reconstructions. Their vivid and intrusive quality may reflect processes of obsessing[51] or of absorption.

Haitians may be more prone to dissociative symptoms as a result of cultural beliefs and practices that support a concept of the person as made of easily dissociable parts. Pervasive beliefs in the supernatural in Haitian culture and specific facets of the cultural concept of the person may increase the prevalence of dissociative experiences.[10] In Haitian ethnopsychology, as influenced by both Vodou and Catholic religions, the person comprises three components: the body, the *gwo-bon-anj*, and the *ti-bon-anj*.[8, 18, 65] The *gwo-bon-anj* (literally, the big-good-angel) is akin to the source of the vital force and life of the person, embodied in blood of the body and giving rise to both mental and physical power. The *ti-bon-anj* (little-good-angel) is the personal ego, with its individual characteristics, "personality," and moral emotions. In health, these three components exist in a harmonious interplay but in illness they can be affected differentially and dissociated. To the extent that dissociation can result from specific body practices and culturally prescribed narratives of the self,[47] these beliefs and practices, shared to varying degrees by Haitians of different religious and educational background, may contribute to a tendency to experience dissociative phenomena.[47] One cluster of somatic and dissociative symptoms commonly reported among Haitians is indisposition.[65] Women, teenagers, and elderly people most commonly experience this syndrome characterized by sensations of emptiness in the chest, dizziness, and extreme weakness. Indisposition can be caused by either by bad blood (physiologic disturbance) or magico-religious (social/spiritual) manipulations.

Clinicians are faced with problems both of translation and position: of understanding the meaning of symptoms in a socio-cultural context and of understanding the power dynamics in society at large that get replayed in the therapeutic encounter. In this case, it is the power dynamics that are especially important and difficult for Mrs. J and her therapist. The clinician who would like to see him- or herself as benevolent is forced to play the role of the racist oppressor who cannot be trusted. This points to the need for a therapeutic approach that explicitly takes into account issues of race, gender, and power to clarify the forms of oppression outside and within the consulting room in order to rebuild a degree of trust and an alliance around collaborative problem solving. This in turn, however, requires attention to cultural norms and expectations, lest the clinician misinterpret the patient's erratic behavior as an unwillingness or inability to engage.

This is not to deny the obvious destructive elements in Mrs. J's behavior—immediately after the accident she broke up her stable relationship and sold her home and all her possessions. These actions make sense as responses to her sense of guilt and culpability for the accident ("I'm not entitled to any happiness.") as well as her feelings of betrayal by her husband. They also speak to her need for a sort of purging or cleansing of her life, focusing on material possessions as evidence of debasement. This destruction or death of her old life, however, was not followed by any subsequent rebirth.

Mrs. J was viewed as oppositional and uncooperative with treatment and this was attributed to a personality disorder. It also can be understood in terms of her fear and conviction that nothing that can be offered will be of help in mending her fractured life. Mrs. J's disorder was not simply a breakdown in biobehavioral adaptation brought on by trauma, but a continuing protest against the loss of a future for herself and her family. Acknowledging this protest, and helping her to find new and more powerful outlets for it, may allow the other modalities of treatment to take effect.

SUMMARY

About a century ago, George Crile, a surgeon and experimental physiologist, suggested that the meaning of pain could be discovered in the context of evolution.[87] Pain is a signal of a physical injury that would be otherwise ignored by the individual, a form of ignorance that would ultimately have mortal consequences. Crile believed that pain has a second purpose, that has important implications for how psychiatry now understands the emotions, specifically fear and anxiety. In essence, he suggested that fear is the memory of pain, and its adaptive advantage is that it enables individuals to anticipate and avoid injury. Fear-as-memory could be acquired either through individual experience (learned fear) or through species experience (instinctive fear). Among other things, this conception of pain and fear explained why surgical shock (from physical injury) and nervous shock (induced by fear or fright) appeared, at times, to provoke a similar physiologic response—a phenomenon first commented on by the British surgeon, Herbert Page. With this simple grammar, injury-pain-fear, Page and Crile laid the foundations for the modern concept of psychogenic trauma, extending the old idea of "trauma," meaning a wound or physical injury, to include psychological experiences and processes. The modern conception was completed by Freud, by connecting one more emotional state, anxiety. If fear is not simply a memory of pain but a memory that is bound to stimuli in the here-and-now, then anxiety is memory set loose. Put in other words, anxiety is the capacity to imagine pain and not merely to recollect pain.

From the time of *Beyond the Pleasure Principle* (1919), anxiety took on a life of its own, so to speak, no longer part of the constellation of emotions and experiences identified by Page and Crile. Without an external object toward which to direct itself, fear becomes anxiety—a state of nervous anticipation of the unknown, of what is hidden in the shadows or penumbra of awareness. Anxiety is not a vector directed toward a threatening object or event in the environment but is situated in the person's own bodily experience, the workings of the mind, the Cartesian theater of self-representation. As an experience and event located entirely within the psyche, to be mastered by asserting a strong ego, reflections on anxiety became one of the self-constituting experiences of the Western concept of the person.

In contemporary psychiatry, the constellation of injury, pain, fear, anxiety, memory, and imagination would seem to live on mainly in the context of traumatogenic anxiety and PTSD. "Traumatogenic," however, may be an overly restrictive term for describing this clinical phenomenon, for it assumes that the patient's memories and distress are inevitably products of a feedforward mechanism in which traumatic experience leads to traumatic memory, which, in turn, leads to anxiety. But anxiety, in the sense of memory set loose, can produce these same effects through a feedback mechanism, in which the contents of distressful events are appropriated by a pre-existing disorder. Clinical phenomena rarely conform to either of these two models, but rather conjoin imagination, memory, fear, anxiety, and pain in a self-perpetuating system.

To talk of the cultural context of anxiety disorder is to examine this system and its connections to the life worlds and socioeconomic realities of different groups and classes of people. This is reflected in patients' own use of cultural idioms of distress, which either accompany anxiety disorders or use references to fear, fright, and anxiety as means of exploring and communicating the larger ramifications of their personal and social predicaments.

Everyday talk about anxiety, or anxiety-related idioms of distress, is a way to draw attention to problems—it serves as a signal to others just as it serves as a signal to the individual. Locating the source of anxiety in the social world, the spirit world, or the existential predicament of the individual are all cultural strategies for constructing and living with a coherent world. The distortion of memory by current experience and imagination, although a nuisance for researchers trying to identify causal pathways, is a boon to clinicians. It reflects the self-healing properties of the psyche, which can be harnessed in useful clinical strategies based on working with cognitive interpretations, self-narratives, and dissociation.

The levels of economic deprivation, uncertainty, violence, and trauma in many war-torn parts of the world, as well as in inner city neighborhoods, may make anxiety endemic. Against this backdrop, it may be difficult for both patients and clinicians to judge when anxiety is excessive. People may become consciously habituated or oblivious to anxiety-provoking situations while continuing to suffer deleterious consequences. This is one possible interpretation of the experimental literature on repression and sensitization, which finds that individuals who say they are not distressed by potentially frightening movies of ritual mutilation, may nonetheless show prolonged periods of physiologic arousal, indicating physical stress. Cultures that encourage people to suppress or control emotional responses because these are viewed as potentially harmful to self and others, may nonetheless exact a toll. This possible tension between cultural styles and health consequences is in urgent need of further research.

There are special forms of uncertainty experienced by many patients that go beyond simple characterizations as stressors or sources of fear. For example, refugees face the predicament of enduring a prolonged period of waiting to find out their immigrant status, on which hinges not only their personal safety and ability to begin to imagine a future but, often, the safety of loved ones still caught in dangerous situations in the country of origin. Different fears, and different perceptions of risk and danger, are experienced by people who live in conditions of constant police surveillance or organized state violence and oppression or who must endure uncertainty about the well-being of family members who have disappeared. We might begin to think in terms of a typology of forms of uncertainty—the unknown without a face, impersonal and capricious, versus the terror that wears a familiar mask and may become routine and even insidiously banal. This, in turn, could encourage clinicians to think of innovative ways of approaching anxiety in social and cultural context.

REFERENCES

1. American Psychiatric Association: Diagnostic and Statistical Manual, ed 4. Washington, American Psychiatric Press, 1994
2. Awaritefe A: Clinical anxiety in Nigeria. Acta Psychiatr Scand 77:729, 1988
3. Basoglu M, Marks IM, Kilic C, et al: Alprazolam and exposure for panic disorder with agoraphobia: Attribution of improvement to medication predicts subsequent relapse. Br J Psychiatry 164:652, 1994
4. Beitman BD, Mukerji V, Flaker G, et al: Panic disorder, cardiology patients, and atypical chest pain. Psychiatr Clin North Am 11:387, 1988
5. Bernstein RL, Gaw AC: Koro: Proposed classification for DSM-IV. Am J Psychiatry 147:1670, 1990
6. Blazer DG, Hughes D, George LK, et al: Generalized anxiety disorder. In Robins LN, Reiger DA (eds): Psychiatric Disorders in America. New York, Free Press, 1991, p 180
7. Boehnlein JK, Kinzie JD, Leung PK, et al: The natural history of medical and psychiatric disorders in an American Indian community. Cult Med Psychiatry 16:543, 1993
8. Brodwin PE: Guardian angels and dirty spirits: The moral basis of healing power in rural Haiti. In Nichter M (ed): Anthropological Approaches to the Study of Ethnomedicine. Langhorne, PA, Gordon & Breach, 1992
9. Brown DA, Eaton WW, Sussman L: Racial differences in prevalence of phobic disorders. J Nerv Ment Dis 178:434, 1990
10. Brown KM: Mama Lola: A Vodou Priestess in Brooklyn. Berkeley, University of California Press, 1991
11. Buss AH: Self-Consciousness and Social Anxiety. San Francisco, WH Freeman, 1980
12. Cannon WB: Bodily Changes in Pain, Hunger, Fear and Rage (1929). New York, Harper & Row, 1963
13. Carlson EB, Rosser-Hogan R: Trauma experiences, posttraumatic stress, dissociation, and depression in Cambodian refugees. Am J Psychiatry 148:1548, 1991
14. Chowdury A: Koro in females. Transcultural Psychiatric Research Review 31:369, 1994
15. Clark DM: Cognitive therapy for panic disorder. In NIH Consensus Development Conference on Treatment of Panic Disorder. Bethesda, MD, National Institutes of Health, 1991
16. Clark DM, Salkovskis PM, Gelder M, et al: Tests of a cognitive theory of panic. In Hand I, Witthcen HU (eds): Panic and Phobias. Berlin, Springer-Verlag, 1988, p 149
17. Daie N, Witztum E, Mark M, et al: The belief in the transmigration of souls: Psychotherapy of a Druze patient with severe anxiety reaction. Br J Med Psychol 65:119, 1992
18. Desmangles LG: The Faces of the Gods: Vodou and Roman Catholicism in Haiti. Chapel Hill, University of North Carolina Press, 1992
19. Doi T: The Anatomy of Dependence. Tokyo, Kodansha International, 1973
20. Eaton WW, Dryman A, Weissman MM: Panic and phobia. In Robins LN, Regier DA (eds): Psychiatric Disorders in America. New York, Free Press, 1991, p 155
21. Ebigbo PO: A cross-sectional study of somatic complaints of Nigerian females using the Enugu somatization scale. Cult Med Psychiatry 10:167, 1986
22. Eisenbruch M: From posttraumatic stress disorder to cultural bereavement: Diagnosis of Southeast Asian refugees. Soc Sci Med 33:673, 1991
23. Ekman P: An argument for basic emotions. Cognition and Emotion 6:169, 1992
24. El-Islam MF: Cultural aspects of morbid fears in Qatari women. Soc Psychiatry Psychiatr Epidemiol 29:137, 1994
25. Farmer P: Bad blood, spoiled milk: Bodily fluids as moral barometers in rural Haiti. American Ethnologist 15:62, 1988
26. Farmer P, Good BJ: Illness representations in medical anthropolgy: A critical review and a case study of the representation of AIDS in Haiti. In Skelton JA, Croyle RT (eds): New York, Springer-Verlag, 1990, pp 132–162
27. Frankel FH, Orne MT: Hypnotizability and phobic behavior. Arch Gen Psychiatry 33:1259, 1976
28. Freud S: Civilization and Its Discontents (1930). New York, WW Norton, 1962
29. Friedman S, Hatch M, Paradis CM, et al: Obsessive compulsive disorder in two Black ethnic groups: Incidence in an urban dermatology clinic. Journal of Anxiety Disorders 7:343, 1993
30. Friedman S, Paradis C: African-American patients with panic disorder and agoraphobia. Journal of Anxiety Disorders 5:35, 1991
31. Glick-Schiller N, Fouron G: "Everywhere we go, we are in danger": Ti Manno and the emergence of a Haitian transnational identity. American Ethnologist 17:329, 1990
32. Good BJ: The heart of what's the matter: The semantics of illness in Iran. Cult Med Psychiatry 1:25, 1977
33. Good BJ, Kleinman AM: Culture and anxiety: Cross-cultural evidence for the patterning of anxiety disorders. In Tuma AH, Maser J

(eds): Anxiety and the Anxiety Disorders. Hillsdale, NJ, Erlbaum, 1985, p 297

34. Guarnaccia PJ: Ataques de nervios in Puerto Rico: Culture-bound syndrome or popular illness? Med Anthropol 15:157, 1993

35. Guarnaccia PJ, Canino G, Rubio-Stipec M, et al: The prevalence of ataques de nervios in the Puerto Rico disaster study: The role of culture in psychiatric epidemiology. J Nerv Ment Dis 181:157, 1993

36. Hendry J: Becoming Japanese: The World of the Preschool Child. Honolulu, University of Hawaii Press, 1986

37. Hinton WL, Chen Y-CJ, Du N, et al: DSM-III-R Disorders in Vietnamese refugees: Prevalence and correlates. J Nerv Ment Dis 181:113, 1992

38. Ilechukwu STC: Magic penis loss in Nigeria: Report of a recent epidemic of a Koro-like syndrome. Transcultural Psychiatric Research Review 29:91, 1992

39. James W: What is an emotion? Mind 9:188, 1884

40. Jilek W: Epidemics of "genital shrinking" (koro): Historical review and report of a recent outbreak in south China. Curare 9:269, 1986

41. Johnson-Laird PN, Oatley K: Basic emotions, rationality, and folk theory. Cognition and Emotion 6:201, 1992

42. Karno M, Golding JM, Burnam MA, et al: Anxiety disorders among Mexican Americans and Non-Hispanic Whites in Los Angeles. J Nerv Ment Dis 177:202, 1989

43. Katon W, Roy-Byrne PP: Mixed anxiety and depression. J Abnorm Psychol 100:337, 1991

44. Kinzie JD, Boehnlein JK, Leung PK, et al: The prevalence of post-traumatic stress disorder and its clinical significance among Southeast Asian refugees. Am J Psychiatry 147:913, 1990

45. Kirmayer LJ: The place of culture in psychiatric nosology: Taijin kyofusho and DSM-III-R. J Nerv Ment Dis 179:19, 1991

46. Kirmayer LJ: From the Witches' Hammer to the Oedipus complex: Castration anxiety in Western society. Transcultural Psychiatric Research Review 29:133, 1992

47. Kirmayer LJ: Pacing the void: Social and cultural dimensions of dissociation. *In* Spiegel D (ed): Dissociation: Culture, Mind and Body. Washington, American Psychiatric Press, 1994, p 91

48. Kleinknecht RA, Dinnel DL, Tanouye-Wilson S, et al: Cultural variations in social anxiety and phobia: A study in taijin kyofusho. The Behavior Therapist 17:175, 1994

49. Lazarus RD: Emotion and Adaptation. New York, Oxford University Press, 1991

50. Lebra TS: Japanese Patterns of Behavior. Honolulu, University of Hawaii Press, 1976

51. Lipinski JF Jr, Pope HG Jr: Do "flashbacks" represent obsessional imagery? Compr Psychiatry 35:245, 1994

52. Logue MB, Thomas AM, Barbee JG, et al: Generalized anxiety disorder patients seek evaluation for cardiological symptoms at the same frequency as patients with panic disorder. J Psychiatr Res 27:55, 1993

53. Mahgoub OM, Abdelhafeiz HB: Pattern of obsessive-compulsive disorder in Eastern Saudi Arabia. Br J Psychiatry 158:840, 1991

54. Makanjuola ROA: "Ode Ori": A culture-bound disorder with prominent somatic features in Yoruba Nigerian patients. Acta Psychiatr Scand 75:231, 1987

55. McFarlane AC: PTSD: Synthesis of research and clinical studies: The Australia bushfire disaster. *In* Wilson JP, Raphael B (eds): International Handbook of Traumatic Stress Syndromes. New York, Plenum, 1993, p 421

56. McLeod DR, Hoehn-Saric R, Stefan RL: Somatic symptoms of anxiety: Comparison of self-report and physiological measures. Biol Psychiatry 21:301, 1986

57. McNally RJ, Cassiday RL, Calamari JE: Taijin-kyofu-sho in a black American woman: Behavioral treatment of a "culture-bound" anxiety disorder. Journal of Anxiety Disorders 4:83, 1990

58. Mesquita B, Frijda NH: Cultural variations in emotions: A review. Psychol Bull 112:179, 1992

59. Mollica RF, Wyshak G, Lavelle J: The psychosocial impact of war trauma and torture on Southeast Asia refugees. Am J Psychiatry 144:1567, 1987

60. Mollica RF, Wyshak G, Lavelle J, et al: Assessing symptom change in Southeast Asia refugee survivors of mass violence and torture. Am J Psychiarty 147:83, 1990

61. Morakinyo O: Phobic states presenting as somatic complaints syndromes in Nigeria: Socio-cultural factors associated with diagnosis and psychotherapy. Acta Psychiatr Scand 71:356, 1985

62. Murphy HBM: Comparative Psychiatry: The International and Intercultural Distribution of Mental Illness. New York, Springer-Verlag, 1982

63. Neal AM, Lilly RS, Zakis S: What are African American children afraid of? Journal of Anxiety Disorders 7:129, 1993

64. Okasha A, Saad A, Khalil AH, et al: Phenomenology of obsessive-compulsive disorder: A transcultural study. Compr Psychiatry 35:191, 1994

65. Philippe J, Romain JB: Indisposition in Haiti. Soc Sci Med 13B:129, 1979

66. Reyes MB, Routh DK, Jean-Gilles MM: Ethnic differences in parenting children in fearful situations. J Pediatr Psychol 16:717, 1991

66a. Reynolds DK: Morita Psychotherapy. Berkeley, University of California Press, 1976

67. Robins LN, Regier D: Psychiatric Disorders in America: The Epidemiologic Catchment Area Study. New York, Free Press, 1984

68. Rubel AJ, O'Nell CW, Collado-Ardón R: Susto: A Folk Illness. Berkeley, University of California Press, 1984

69. Russell JA: Culture and the categorization of emotions. Psychol Bull 110:426, 1991

70. Russell JG: Anxiety disorders in Japan: A review of the Japanese literature on shinkeishitsu and taijinkyofusho. Cult Med Psychiatry 13:391, 1989

71. Schlenker BR, Leary MR: Social anxiety and self-presentation: A conceptualization and model. Psychol Bull 92:641, 1982

72. Sharpe M, Bass C: Pathophysiological mechanisms in somatization. Int Rev Psychiatry 4:81, 1992

72a. Shweder RA: Menstrual pollution, soul loss, and the comparative study of emotions. *In* Kleinman A, Good B (eds): Culture and Depression. Berkeley, University of California Press, 1985, p 182

73. Swinson RP, Cox BJ, Woszczyna CB: Use of medical services and treatment for panic disorder with agoraphobia and for social phobia. Can Med Assoc J 147:878, 1992

74. Takahashi T: Social phobia syndrome in Japan. Compr Psychiatry 30:45, 1989

75. Takano R: Anthropophobia and Japanese performance. Psychiatry 40:259, 1977

76. Tanaka-Matsumi J: Taijin Kyofusho: Diagnostic and cultural issues in Japanese psychiatry. Cult Med Psychiatry 3:231, 1979

77. Thyer BA, Himle J, Curtis GC: Blood-injury-illness phobia: A review. J Clin Psychol 41:451, 1985

78. Tseng W-S, Asai M, Kitanishi K, et al: Diagnostic patterns of social phobia: Comparison in Tokyo and Hawaii. J Nerv Ment Dis 180:380, 1992

79. Tseng W-S, Kan-Ming M, Li-Shuen L, et al: Koro epidemics in Guangdong China: A questionnaire survey. J Nerv Ment Dis 180:117, 1992

80. Tseng W-S, Kan-Ming M, Hsu J, et al: A sociocultural study of koro epidemics in Guangdong China. Am J Psychiatry 145:1538, 1988

81. Weissman MM, Bland RC, Canino GJ, et al: The cross-national epidemiology of obsessive compulsive disorder. J Clin Psychiatry 55:5, 1994

82. Weissman MM, Klerman GL, Markowitz JS, et al: Suicidal ideation and suicide attempts in panic disorder and attacks. New Engl J Med 321:1209, 1989

83. Westermeyer J, Bouafuely M, Neider J, et al: Somatization among refugees: An epidemiologic study. Psychosomatics 30:34, 1989

84. Wierzbicka A: Talking about emotions: Semantics, culture, and cognition. Cognition and Emotion 6:285, 1992

85. Wikan U: Illness from fright or soul loss: A North Balinese culture-bound syndrome? Cult Med Psychiat 13:25, 1989

86. Yamashita I: Taijin-Kyofu or Delusional Social Phobia. Sapporo, Hokkaido University Press, 1993

87. Young A: Harmony of Illusions. Princeton, NJ, Princeton University Press, 1995

88. Zimbarg RE, Barlow DH, Liebowitz M, et al: The DSM-IV field trial for mixed anxiety-depressive depression. Am J Psychiatry 151:1153, 1994

JAMES K. BOEHNLEIN AND J. DAVID KINZIE

Refugee Trauma

Epidemiological studies and theoretical models of refugee trauma based on ethnographic, biomedical and sociopolitical perspectives have focused on a variety of cultural and ethnic groups since World War II. Subjective distress and problems in psychosocial functioning are influenced by individual, family, cultural and social variables. Refugees are at risk for developing psychiatric illness resulting from pre-migration, migration and post-migration experiences. This paper reviews biological, psychological and sociocultural models for recognizing, conceptualizing and treating the psychiatric problems of traumatized refugees. The treatment approach of the Oregon Indochinese Psychiatric Program is summarized.

INTRODUCTION

Judah has gone into exile with suffering and hard servitude;
she lives now among the nations, and finds no resting place;
her pursuers have all overtaken her in the midst of her distress.
—*Lamentations 1:3*

Refugee trauma has been described in a wide variety of conditions and in a large number of displaced populations throughout the world. Refugees face acculturative pressures in resettlement countries such as financial and employment stressors, dissonance between traditional sociocultural values and those of the host country, intergenerational conflict and change, and social isolation. Following extraordinary trauma from war or concentration camp experiences, some refugees experience insomnia, nightmares, emotional numbing, startle reactions, and memory impairment.

This paper will emphasize a biopsychosocial perspective on refugee trauma, including the effect of culture on diagnosis, treatment, and the interpretation of traumatic experiences within cultural belief systems. Any discussion of trauma cross-culturally requires an examination of the sociocultural framework of affected populations, such as family and social structure, religious beliefs, and political environment. At the group level, previous patterns of authority and civility often no longer operate, and at the individual level uncertainty and identity confusion may arise after migration (Williams & Berry, 1991).

Epidemiological studies and the development of theoretical models of refugee trauma have occurred predominantly in Europe and North America since World War II, although the focus of these studies has been on a wide variety of cultural and ethnic groups in a variety of historical settings. Studies of the traumatic refugee experience have encompassed ethnographic, biomedical, and sociopolitical points of view. The formal study of refugee trauma began with published reports of the acute and long term psychosocial adjustment of Jewish refugees from Nazi Germany. Follow-up studies have been done in Europe, Israel, and the Americas on the long term adjustment of these Holocaust survivors. The Vietnam War was another major turning point in the developing science of refugee research with the mass migration of refugees from Southeast Asia after the war. These studies, in turn, have influenced the study of trauma among other refugees from wars in Central America, Africa and the Middle East in the 1980s and 1990s.

In discussing the various theoretical perspectives from which refugee studies have been conducted, it is important to consider the concept of post-traumatic stress disorder (PTSD), since the developing science of refugee studies historically has closely paralleled changing theoretical perspectives of the complex and controversial concept known as PTSD. The understanding of PTSD as a clinical phenomenon and a diagnostic entity within society and within the scientific community itself has been influenced by cultural factors over time. There has been a long-standing debate concerning the validity of the PTSD diagnosis; points of controversy include the definition of life event contexts and their influence on the development of this disorder, as well as the influence of pre-trauma personal characteristics on post-traumatic symptomatology and functioning (Horowitz, Weiss & Marmar, 1987). As late as the mid 1980's, some argued that there was little empirical research on the validity of the PTSD diagnosis or the distinctive nature of subsequent psychopathology (Breslau & Davis, 1987). Others have noted that different individuals, faced with the difficulties of cognitively and emotionally processing traumatic events, will behave in quite different ways, giving a different form to the total psychopathological picture. This individual variability does not mean that a distinct core PTSD psychopathology does not exist (Lindy, Green & Grace, 1987). Controversy remains regarding the cross-cultural validity of the PTSD concept, as we will discuss in later sections of this review.

TRAUMATIC STRESS IN HISTORICAL CONTEXT

A brief historical overview of the psychological concept of trauma will help to place the examination of cross-cultural refugee trauma studies in context.

Since recorded history there have been descriptions of societies' and individuals' reactions to traumatic events. Over 4,000 years ago the Sumerians described profound psychological reactions to the destruction of Ur (Kramer, 1969). Similar reactions attributed to Jeremiah are told in Lamentations (Holy Bible, Newly Revised Standard Version) of the destruction of Jerusalem in the Fifth Century B.C. At around the same time, Thucydides described the social breakdown of Athens in reaction to a devastating plague (Findley, 1959). In the last 150 years, similar reactions to traumatic events and disasters have been described in diverse cultures.

For example, in mid-nineteenth century England, Erichsen (1866) described the "railroad spine syndrome," with symptoms attributed to damage to the spinal cord due to the motion of trains. The primary symptoms included anxiety, memory and concentration problems, irritability, disturbed sleep, distressing dreams, and multiple somatic symptoms that were thought to have an organic etiology (Fischer-Homberger, 1970; Trimble, 1991). Railroad spine syndrome could be considered the beginning of the scientific description of traumatic neuroses. In 1869, Beard coined the term "neurasthenia" or nervous exhaustion to cover non-specific emotional disorders such as insomnia, headaches and melancholia, also recognized to occur after traumatic events (Gosling, 1987). Stierlin (1911) described similar reactions by survivors of different types of disasters, including earthquakes, a volcanic eruption, mine disasters, and a train accident. He noted that, after an earthquake in Italy, 25% of survivors suffered from sleep disorders of one to three months duration and many had vivid dreams of the event. Mott (1919) described traumatic reactions within the context of two of the major psychiatric diagnoses of the time: hysteria (paralysis, disorders of gait, tremors) and neurasthenia (fatigue, headaches). The major symptom he described was vivid and terrifying dreams of war experiences, causing the person to awaken in a cold sweat.

Between the two World Wars much was written about traumatic neurosis, but in the context of industrial and occupational medicine. During this period, a great debate raged as to what constituted a trauma, what types of syndromes could follow trauma, and which post-traumatic reactions were organic and which were neurotic. Larer (1933) noted the similarities among symptoms that occurred following war experiences, railroad accidents and automobile accidents.

Concurrent with this early to mid-twentieth century research was the publication of Sigmund Freud's pioneer work on the human psyche (Freud, 1919). Throughout the 1940's and 1950's, as Freud's theories became increasingly influential in Europe and North America, many of the post-traumatic symptoms observed in Holocaust survivors and war veterans were explained largely with reference to psychoanalytic principles, and treatment approaches were reflective of this theoretical model of causality (Archibald & Tuddenham, 1965; Dewind, 1971; Grauer, 1969; Niederland, 1964). Psychoanalytic theory may have been useful in studying mild trauma such as industrial accidents, but it was not comprehensive enough to conceptualize massive trauma such as occurred among World War II combatants, concentration camp survivors, or refugee groups.

Despite the accumulated evidence of traumatic responses to war among combatants and civilians in World Wars I and II, the American Psychiatric Association diagnostic classification in 1952 (DSM-I) only mentioned the concept of gross stress reaction under the category of transient situational personality disorder (American Psychiatric Association, 1952). Even with the publication of DSM-II in 1968, the only comparable diagnosis listed was adjustment reaction of adult life (American Psychiatric Association, 1968).

With the publication of DSM-III in 1980, a new term, *post-traumatic stress disorder*, was recognized as a diagnostic entity. This was due to a number of social and historical factors in the 1960's and 1970's. Traumatic responses were observed in Vietnam veterans returning to civilian life, and studies of Holocaust survivors and Southeast Asian refugees were beginning to be published. The understanding of human responses to trauma was further enhanced by significant advances in neurophysiology, psychopharmacology, and cognitive and social psychology that had occurred in the prior decades (Boehnlein, 1989). Investigators also were considering experimental laboratory models that focused primarily on human and animal physiological responses to stress. Horowitz and colleagues (Horowitz, 1974, 1975, 1976, 1986; Horowitz & Becker, 1971; Horowitz, Wilner, Kaltreider & Alvarez, 1980) began to show the important parallels that exist between human responses to traumatic war experiences and a wide variety of other stressors including bereavement, assault and accidents. A comprehensive model for understanding human responses to stress began to emerge that included physiological, cognitive, social, and cultural perspectives drawn from diverse theoretical points of view (Boehnlein, 1989).

At this point, it would be germane to focus on studies of specific refugee groups in order to more fully explore universal and particular refugee responses to trauma, migration, and resettlement. An historical approach to these refugee studies helps to maintain a social and political perspective on complex events without sacrificing a humanistic appreciation of the refugee experience.

EARLY REFUGEE STUDIES: JEWISH SURVIVORS OF THE NAZI HOLOCAUST

The modern era of refugee mental health research really began with the study of Jewish refugees from Nazi Germany after World War II. The brutal long-term effects of Nazi concentration camps began to be studied in the 1950's and reached a critical mass of information in the 1960's. The conditions experienced by these survivors included mass executions, torture, forced labor, and starvation. Despite a wide variety of methodologies used in these studies, the various countries in which these studies were conducted, and the time of follow-up, a consistent series of symptoms were described. Chronic effects of the trauma included fear and paranoia (Bensheim, 1960), mistrust (Mattusek, 1975), along with chronic personality changes (Venzlaff, 1967). Depression, anxiety and multiple somatic symptoms were described in long term follow-up studies of concentration camp survivors (Eitinger, 1961; Ostwald & Bittner, 1968; Klein, 1974; Eaton, Sigal & Weinfeld, 1982; Arthur, 1982). These symptoms often directly impaired survivors' social adjustment and resulted in a passive fatalistic personality style, hopelessness and loss of previously enjoyed activities (Chodoff, 1975). Again, distrust and hostility were common sequelae (Niederland, 1964).

In 1959, Eitinger reported on the 10-year hospitalization rates of post-World War II refugees in Norway and found that the incidence of schizophrenia was five times higher than the comparable Norwegian population. He also reported (1960) that paranoid and persecutory reactions were common. A 1973 report about refugees in Australia (Krupinski, Stoller & Wallace, 1973) showed that while the Jewish population had the most pre-migration trauma, their rates of schizophrenia were lower than among Polish, Russian, or Ukrainian refugees. However, the Jewish refugees had a higher rate of what was then recognized as the "concentration camp syndrome," characterized by insomnia, fatigue, irritability, restlessness, anxiety, and depression.

During the 1950s, organic factors were considered to be the major factor in the concentration camp syndrome (Hoppe, 1972). Although Eitinger (1961) initially thought that organic factors such as trauma, starvation, and infection caused some brain damage, he later modified his views (Eitinger, 1980) by describing both physical and psychological factors as being implicated in the etiology of the syndrome. As early as the early 1960s, Von Bayer (1961) argued for a psychophysiological reaction as the etiology of the trauma syndrome.

In the philosophical and political climate following World War II, and in the context of political chaos, some of the first writing concerning existential factors in the etiology of traumatic responses occurred (e.g., Frankl, 1969). Those who survived concentration camps were faced with the task of explaining to themselves or to others why the seemingly meaningless events occurred. Meaning in all cultures is influenced primarily by secular and religious values; therefore, what constitutes meaning in any society will be highly culturally determined. For example, Frankl (1969), in his work with concentration camp survivors, noted that it was important to encourage survivors to realize that their lives still had meaning and the future still was expecting something from them. These early writings related to existential and moral issues also influenced later studies of Vietnam veterans and Southeast Asian refugees (Boehnlein, 1989). It is conceivable that certain human responses to trauma (e.g., avoidance of thoughts or feelings associated with the trauma, a feeling of detachment from others, a sense of a foreshortened future) that are observed across a wide spectrum of clinical populations and cultures may represent a universal human response to the cognitive disruption of a sense of order and meaning that derive from a stable system of culturally specific beliefs and values.

LATER REFUGEE STUDIES: THE AFTERMATH OF THE VIETNAM WAR

Many Southeast Asian refugees who left their native lands after 1975 carried with them memories of brutal war, escape, or concentration camp experiences. Cambodians brought memories of the Khmer Rouge era between 1975 and 1979, during which over one million Cambodians died of disease, starvation, or execution. Vietnamese refugees described seeing family members killed, possessions confiscated and their villages destroyed. Ethnic Laotians, Mien and Hmong also had irreparable damage done to their cultures and societies. As data have accumulated on the mental health of Southeast Asian refugees, this population has been recognized to be at great risk for developing psychiatric illness.

Early epidemiological survey data of Vietnamese refugees in the United States by Gong-Guy (1987) and Lin, and Tazuma and

Masuda (1979), revealed high levels of distress and psychiatric needs. Initial descriptive studies of Southeast Asian refugees showed that depression was the most prevalent clinical problem that impaired psychosocial functioning (Kinzie, Tran, Breckenridge & Bloom, 1980; Kinzie & Manson, 1983; Westermeyer, 1985a) and depression is still noted to be a very common problem among Southeast Asian refugees (Kroll, Habenicht, MacKenzie, Yang, Chan, Vang, Nguyen, Ly, Phammasouvanh, Nguyen, Vang, Souvannasoth & Cabugao, 1989).

Among Southeast Asian refugee groups, post-traumatic stress disorder was described initially among Cambodian concentration camp survivors (Kinzie, Fredrickson, Rath & Fleck, 1984; Boehnlein, Kinzie, Rath & Fleck, 1985; Kinzie, 1986). Other clinical reports have continued to describe the debilitating effects of trauma on all Southeast Asian refugee groups (Kleinman, 1987; Mollica, Wyshak & Lavelle, 1987; Goldfeld, Mollica, Pesavento & Faraone, 1988; Mollica, 1988; Kinzie, 1989; Mollica, Wyshak, Lavell, Truong, Tor & Yang, 1990). Mollica, Wyshak and Lavelle (1987) reported a PTSD prevalence of 50% among a Southeast Asian patient population of multiple ethnic groups. A PTSD prevalence of 50% also was found in a non-patient community sample of Cambodian adolescents (Kinzie, Sack, Angell & Manson, 1986) and a PTSD prevalence of about 20% persisted over time among these young refugees (Kinzie, Sack, Angell & Clarke, 1989; Sack, Clarke, Him, Dickason, Goff, Lanham & Kinzie, 1993; Clarke, Sack & Goff, 1993). In a community sample of adult Cambodian refugees, 86% of subjects met criteria for PTSD (Carlson & Rosser-Hogan, 1991). A study in New Zealand with 223 adult Cambodian refugees found that most had experienced multiple severe traumas, and there was a prevalence rate of PTSD of 12.1% (Cheung, 1994).

Studies of acculturation and longitudinal psychosocial functioning among these refugee groups have been limited, but those studies that have been done have shown dysfunction related to trauma to be persistent and relatively treatment resistant. Westermeyer, Neider and Callies (1989) found that while some psychiatric symptoms such as depression and somatization became less evident with time and acculturation, other symptoms such as anxiety, hostility, and paranoia changed little. Others have noted that among Southeast Asian refugees depression often improves with treatment, but many PTSD symptoms are persistent and debilitating (Boehnlein, Kinzie, Rath & Fleck, 1985; Moore & Boehnlein, 1991a, 1991b). A recent epidemiologic study of two generations of nonpatient Cambodian refugees in two Western U.S. cities (Sack, McSharry, Clarke, Kinney, Seeley & Lewinsohn, 1994; Sack, Clarke, Kinney, Belestos, Him & Seeley, 1995) has added to the growing literature that PTSD endures over time in youth and adults, while depression is less chronic and more episodic. For example, in this adolescent sample, point (18.2%) and lifetime (21.5%) prevalence of PTSD did not greatly differ. However, the authors point out important generational differences in functioning. The adolescents' overall functional status (work, leisure, family relationships) appeared to be as good as the status of those adolescents with no diagnosis; adults, however, did not fare as well.

Factors correlated with the severity of PTSD have been identified in traumatized Southeast Asian refugees from a number of ethnic groups. Data are mixed in relation to the differential effects of pre-migration, migration, and post-migration trauma on subsequent psychological distress. A recent book describes a number of complex factors in the dislocation of refugees, dividing dislocation into pre-flight, flight, and reception periods (Desjarlais, Eisenberg, Good & Kleinman, 1995). Some studies have noted the primacy of pre-migration traumatic experiences (Carlson & Rosser-Hogan, 1991, 1994; Chung & Kagawa-Singer, 1993; Hauff & Vaglum, 1993, 1994). Factors in the host country can contribute to the reactivation of traumatic responses, such as accidents observed or experienced, exposure to crime, or anniversary reactions to traumatic events. In a very recent follow-up study of Vietnamese refugees in Norway, Hauff and Vaglum (1995) found that the level of distress did not decrease during the first years after resettlement. Some of the traumatic events experienced in Vietnam that were significantly associated with emotional distress on arrival did not show such an association three years later, but the most severe experiences (danger during flight, long captivity, being wounded) were still associated with mental health problems. The authors suggest that stress prior to, or subsequent to forced migration appears to have an independent impact on mental health in addition to other predictors of mental health well established in social psychiatry (gender, life events, social support). They further note that each refugee movement should be examined in its own context and that predictions concerning improvement, or lack thereof, of refugee mental health over time in a specific social or cultural setting cannot be absolutely generalized.

In some early resettlement studies among Vietnamese refugees before the advent of research studies of specific disorders, higher socioeconomic status in Vietnam (Vignes & Hall, 1979) and being a single female head of a household (Lin, Tazuma & Masuda, 1979) were correlated with more distress. Advanced age, female gender and the co-morbid diagnosis of depression have been correlated with a higher prevalence of PTSD in Southeast Asian refugee groups (Kinzie, Boehnlein, Leung, Moore, Riley & Smith, 1990; Sack, McSharry, Clarke, Kinney, Seeley & Lewinsohn, 1994). Psychosis either as a co-morbid diagnosis or as part of the post-traumatic syndrome has also been noted among Cambodian refugees (Kinzie & Boehnlein, 1989).

In recent years, family and network studies have become more prominent, and represent the next wave of studies of longitudinal and cross-generational refugee adjustment. The development of cross-cultural history can be advanced only by joining the search for biological and psychological patterning with attention to the social response to distress (Kirmayer, 1989). As the primary social unit of refugee cultures, the family is charged with the task of feeding, clothing, nurturing, educating, and supporting its members. During and after any type of migration, these family tasks are difficult enough, but after traumatic war experiences, these tasks may become even more formidable.

The lack of a complete nuclear family, the frequent lack of extended family support, and extensive change in, or loss of traditional cultural values frequently leads to confusion among parents and adolescents regarding the proper behaviour expected of each generation in the resettlement country. Among Vietnamese, for example, parents have been found to strongly endorse their traditional family value orientation regardless of their time in the U.S., and have considerable ambivalence toward the rights and privileges of their adolescent children (Nguyen & Williams, 1989). Intergenerational conflict is often marked between adolescent refugees and their families because adolescents tend to have more contact with the majority culture and are more likely to try out new roles (Williams & Westermeyer, 1983). Intergenerational conflicts due to differential rates of acculturation result in strained relations within the entire family (Stein, 1986). For adults, a nostalgic orientation to the country of origin is more correlated with distress after resettlement (Beiser, 1987; Beiser, Turner & Ganesan, 1989). For parents, traditional expectations of respect from their children and deference to authority can conflict with the imposed reality of a more passive position due to illness or poor English language skills. Women in single parent families who have lost their husbands during war or migration are required to function as both father and mother. Normal developmental struggles of adolescence are heightened by the mother's diminished authoritative role. Traditional expectations for parental authority can conflict with the less hierarchical relationships that children frequently observe among parents and adolescents in North America. Likewise, the resettlement society's expectations for increasing independence among adolescents can conflict with traditional cultural expectations to provide financial support for elderly parents, or supportive care for ill or disabled parents. Regarding family adjustment, the first empirical study of a refugee population that used DSM-III-R diagnostic criteria to examine rates of PTSD and major depression across two generations experiencing the same war trauma found that PTSD, but not major depression, occurred significantly more often in the same refugee family (Sack, Clarke & Seeley, 1995). Family PTSD concordance was not affected by socioeconomic status, a greater amount of reported war trauma, or a greater reporting of loss during or after the war.

OTHER REFUGEE POPULATIONS

As the world refugee population grows in the 1990's, reports are beginning to appear that describe refugee experiences among other ethnic groups.

Central American countries have seen much violence, and refugees from civil war in El Salvador have experienced much trauma from both domestic and state organized violence (Jenkins, 1991). Salvadoran refugee survivors have described multiple traumas, and their subsequent reactions have often been described as *nervios* ("nerves"). Men have described problems with fears, nightmares, alcohol abuse, and a sense of losing control, while women have described more angry feelings, headaches, somatic pain, and crying, often related to family and social problems (Farias, 1991). In a study of children in Los Angeles traumatized by Central American warfare, 10 of 30 subjects were diagnosed with PTSD (Arroyo & Eth, 1985).

The reactions of a group of Ethiopian Jews who migrated to Israel in 1984–85 were described by Arieli, Aril and Aycheh (1992). During their long trek, the Ethiopians endured starvation, physical abuse, life-threatening situations, and loss of family members. They had difficulty adjusting to the secular lifestyle prevalent in Israel and learning Hebrew. Moderate to severe symptoms were found in 27% of 87 people. Major problems included sleep disorders and nightmares (29%), depression (28%) and anxiety (37%). As with studies of other refugee groups, the more traumatic the events, the more difficult the subsequent adjustment. In a recent study of 38 young Afghan refugees in the United States, 59% reported one or more experiences of being close to death and multiple other traumas (Mghir, Freed, Raskin & Katon, 1995). There as a positive correlation between the number of traumatic events and a psychiatric diagnosis. Five had PTSD, 11 had major depression, and 13 had symptoms of either or both.

In summary, the literature over the past 50 years on refugee trauma has revealed that refugees are at great risk for developing psychiatric illness resulting from pre-migration, migration, and post-migration experiences. The more severe the trauma, the more difficult the adjustment. There are additional difficulties in attempting to overcome language and cultural barriers during the process of acculturation (Westermeyer, 1986). All of these factors often interact to produce a downward spiral of illness and social withdrawal. Accordingly, a model for understanding the adjustment of refugees after trauma includes biological, psychological and social factors. It is possible that neurochemical changes that occur during intense trauma may give rise to behavioural attempts by the individual (e.g., withdrawal from others) to minimize external environmental stimuli in order to decrease chances of an adverse emotional response. This withdrawal, in turn, reduces social interactions and opportunities for support relationships and may result in social isolation (Boehnlein, 1989). Coexisting with this response may be a cognitive set that, as a result of the trauma, looks upon the world as a hostile and dangerous place. In this unpredictable world, which has been turned upside down by the experienced trauma, one's previous acculturation, social values, or religious beliefs may appear useless in guiding one's subsequent adjustment in the world (Boehnlein, 1987b).

CLINICAL ASSESSMENT OF REFUGEE TRAUMA

The complexity of traumatic responses and challenges of understanding them in a cultural context can be difficult for even experienced clinicians. The clinical assessment of refugees who have undergone severe trauma is a process, since much of the traumatic material and many of the symptoms may be revealed only after years of treatment. One of the historical problems in diagnosis and assessment has been the lack of an adequate nomenclature. Without a diagnostic category which explicitly mentions the possibility of symptoms of intrusive thoughts, images and feelings, and avoidance behaviour following severe traumatic events, a clinician may not search for the traumatic event or inquire about specific symptoms. This neglect was seen in early refugee studies which searched for schizophrenia, depression, or anxiety among refugees, but paid less attention to cognitive and behavioral symptoms outside these categories. The delineation of the post-traumatic stress disorder criteria in 1980 has been helpful to clinicians working with traumatized refugees. It is important to recognize, however, that while in some cases the impact of traumatic exposure may lead to PTSD, in other cases such exposure may lead to a traumatic stress syndrome that overlaps with PTSD but that also features symptoms that are idiosyncratic to individuals from specific ethnocultural traditions (Friedman & Jaranson, 1994). Moreover, it is possible that arbitrarily applied thresholds for the number of intrusive or avoidant symptoms needed to make a PTSD diagnosis may have differing consequences for diagnostic frequency in different cultural groups and following different traumas; PTSD is not a uniform syndrome and some groups may have a differential threshold of intrusive or avoidant symptoms related to cultural factors (Ramsey, Gorst-Unsworth & Turner, 1993).

PTSD may have an avoidance or numbing phase and patients may be amnesic for the specific trauma. Variability in the recall of traumatic events at different points in time makes it imperative that clinicians be aware that the severity of symptoms itself may influence memory or the recall of traumatic events (Wyshak, 1994). Additionally, there is often co-morbidity with depression, the symptoms of which may predominate at the presenting interview.

There may be culture-specific problems in the diagnostic assessment of refugees. For example, it has been noted that certain Latino health behaviours, such as frequent somatization and the reluctance to discuss prior traumatic events because of respect or shame, may complicate the cross-cultural diagnosis of PTSD among individuals from Central or South America (Lopez, Boccellari & Hall, 1988). The meaning and interpretation of post-traumatic dreams may be problematic unless the health professional has knowledge of culturally specific beliefs and symbols (Rechtman, 1993).

There have been many attempts to use self-rating scales to determine cross-cultural psychopathology. These have included translations of standard tests and the development of culturally specific tests such as the Vietnamese Depression Scale (Kinzie, Manson, Vinh, Tolan, Anh & Pho, 1982). These scales are easy to administer, but pose problems for many traumatized refugees. Many refugees (80% of Cambodians in our clinic) cannot read their native language, making it necessary for an interviewer to administer the scale. Even those who can read have little experience with formal psychological testing. The history of the trauma itself presents the most important challenge to the validity of self-report scales. As a practical matter, the full history of the trauma often is not revealed until trust has been established over several interviews. The therapist must come to terms with his or her own difficulty hearing trauma stories which may be disturbing, and yet the therapist must not force patients to reveal more than they can handle. Many patients will have an activation of intrusive symptoms following a diagnostic interview. When the interview is part of an ongoing treatment plan, these clinical and ethical difficulties can be justified. Researchers continue to develop new methods to attempt to accurately assess refugee mental health, such as the Harvard Trauma Questionnaire (Mollica, Caspi-Yavin, Bollini, Truong, Tor & Lavelle, 1992).

In addition to obtaining a history of the trauma and symptom development, it is important to understand the pre-trauma life and culture. A very useful approach also is to ask about relationships with everyone in the extended family (or those all living in the same household) before the trauma and then ask what happened to each of these people after the trauma. This has often resulted in the recovery of memories of previously "forgotten" relatives and close friends.

TREATMENT

Treatment of traumatized refugees is not the major focus of this review, but some general guidelines will be suggested based on 16 years experience with over 1000 patients treated at the Oregon Indochinese Psychiatric Program. Ours is but one approach to the treatment process. Other programs may place less emphasis on the process of diagnosis and assessment, and still others may not use medications or use them minimally. Nevertheless, our treatment suggestions are based upon ongoing responses to patient needs and requests in the treatment setting of a comprehensive university medical center.

Treatment personnel must recognize that the effects of trauma and the experiences of being a refugee are both chronic conditions. There is no quick or short-term fix. Treatment must be considered as long-term and supportive. The course of the trauma syndrome waxes and wanes, and even when patients seem symptomatically improved, they remain extremely vulnerable. Further stresses such as automobile accidents, being victims of a robbery or legal problems with children can cause a complete reactivation of the entire syndrome. Offering patients a long-term relationship provides security and support which helps them ride through the ups and downs of an often difficult life.

The specific elements of our treatment approach include:

1. *Education*. Teaching patients about the somatic effects of trauma and the fact that the majority of those who undergo severe trauma will have symptoms helps patients feel more normal and accepted. Such a psychoeducational approach often helps to reduce patients' self-perceived stigma of being "crazy."
2. *Symptomatic relief of comorbid conditions*. Depression is often present with PTSD (schizophrenia is less common) and deserves to be treated. We have had good experience with tricyclic antidepressants and serotonin reuptake inhibitors. With the reduction of depression, nightmares and sleep disorders often improve.
3. *Reduction of intrusive symptoms*. We have found that clonidine greatly reduces irritability, startle reactions and nightmares. Clonidine usually is given in conjunction with an antidepressant, but many patients take it alone. About half of our Cambodian patients are on clonidine and acceptance is high. The mechanism of action in decreasing nightmares is unknown. In a recent pilot study, clonidine greatly reduced REM sleep (although nightmares occurred in all stages of sleep) (Kinzie, Sack & Riley, 1994).
4. *Reduction of other stresses*. Having the resources and staff to insure adequate finances, housing and medical care gives great security to patients and reduces realistic concerns refugees often face.
5. *Supportive psychotherapy*. Predictable, empathetic, reality-based ongoing psychotherapy with an American psychiatrist is a central element of our treatment model. Continued contact and appreciation of the refugee's experience and discussion of current issues and stresses is very affirming and comforting. Treatment sessions often include spouses and other family members. Modification of, and education about

medication is done in these sessions. Helping the refugee patient process current and past experiences, dream content and difficulties in interpersonal relationships often reduces symptoms and enhances perceived control and self-confidence.
6. *Socialization groups*. Group activities (led by an ethnic mental health counselor) have been very useful in providing a sense of community and shared experiences. These usually are bi-cultural, including activities from the culture of origin, such as a New Year's celebration, and sharing in American events such as Christmas and Halloween. Practical matters of transportation, insurance, housing, and learning English are often discussed. Group therapy with a more process orientation has been done with Cambodian groups. the earliest themes that emerged—and that persisted up to two years— were related to the Pol Pot trauma and losses. Other important themes have included the problems of raising children in America, issues of aging and death and the provision of appropriate ceremonies to ensure a good afterlife. With children less willing to follow traditional ways, patients feel that the necessary rituals will not be done. An important task may be to help each generation to understand and accept each other's new beliefs and roles as the family evolves through the life cycle. The clinician must approach the family with respect for the strengths that allowed its members to survive individually and as a unit.
7. *Indochinese Socialization Center*. At a separate location, a socialization center has been developed to provide increased social activities and an expanded experience with American volunteers. This has been a popular activity with sharing of cultural traditions, and now has expanded to include vocational rehabilitation and job training.
8. *Refugee opportunities to give back and participate*. Throughout the treatment program, the refugees contribute in many ways. All the groups offer ethnic meals to the hospital staff at times of their culture's New Year or other celebrations. Several groups (particularly the Mien) make craft items, such as embroidery, that represent their culture to the community. An advisory board for the Socialization Center includes many refugee members. The activities by the refugee patients are greatly appreciated by the staff and undoubtedly increase the self-esteem of the patients.

Dealing with traumatized refugee patients has been difficult and psychiatric staff have been greatly changed by the experience. The countertransference feelings are complicated and challenging (Kinzie & Boehnlein, 1993). Overall, assessment and treatment must always be offered within a broad context that integrates ethnocultural factors, problems of language, metaphors and symbols, and awareness of adaptational and acculturation pressures (Friedman & Jaranson, 1994).

CURRENT CONTROVERSIES
AND FUTURE DIRECTIONS

The diagnosis and treatment of psychiatric disorders cross-culturally remains an area of great opportunity and considerable controversy. As Westermeyer (1985b) has noted, cross-cultural diagnosis can have different meanings: it can refer to differing diagnostic schemata across cultures or it can refer to the ability of a clinician from one culture to make a diagnosis for a patient from another culture. As he also notes, not only must techniques, skills and conceptual frameworks be available for evaluating a patient who may not share the same culture as the clinician, but diagnostic classification is a key step in pursuing social and cultural factors related to epidemiology, etiology, prognosis, and treatment. Understanding the large sociocultural milieu in which the patient functions is crucial in distinguishing psychopathology from culture-bound beliefs or behaviour (Westermeyer, 1987). Moreover, cultural attitudes toward suffering play an important role in help-seeking and treatment response. For example, beliefs that suffering is inevitable or that one's life is predetermined, may cause some Southeast Asians not to seek health care (Uba, 1992).

Although cultural belief systems influence an individual's interpretation of events and also influence cognition and behaviour (Levy, 1984), after trauma the latter also are influenced by a persistent dysphoria and pervasive neurophysiological arousal that have been observed across many cultural groups. Addressing the physiological symptoms only addresses part of the problem (Rechtman, 1992). The refugee patient is left with other chronic and debilitating sequelae of trauma (social withdrawal, emotional numbing, nihilism) that are—in the patient's subjective experience and in the objective observation of his or her behaviour both inside and outside the cultural group—strongly influenced by social and cultural variables.

There are differences of opinion in the literature about the validity or appropriateness of the PTSD diagnosis cross-culturally. McFarland (1985) questions whether the symptoms experienced by trauma victims are indicative of a psychiatric disorder or are no more than signs of generalized emotional distress. Others note that some degree of intrusive imagery and increased arousal are common following any significant trauma; in their view, the relationship between this common reaction and the more extreme states seen in PTSD requires further evaluation (Ramsey, Gorst-Unsworth & Turner, 1993).

Eisenbruch (1991, 1992) argues that the DSM-III PTSD criteria are based on an ethnocentric view of health that prescribes how refugees should express stress and how their distress should be ameliorated. He suggests that the post-traumatic reaction should be termed cultural bereavement rather than PTSD, and that this bereavement may be a normal and constructive existential response rather than a psychiatric illness. He further asserts that the PTSD diagnosis labels people as mentally ill and pre-

scribes Western treatment for which efficacy is lacking. Others agree that reconstructing meaning and purpose in life after trauma through bereavement is highly culturally determined, but contend that the search for meaning itself and the struggle with grief (which includes the reconstitution of self-concept and comfort in interpersonal relationships) are experienced by many other groups besides refugees (Boehnlein, 1987a, 1987b; Kinzie & Fleck, 1987; Boehnlein & Kinzie, 1992; Kinzie & Boehnlein, 1993). For example. American veterans of the Vietnam War with chronic PTSD, although they returned to their country of origin, also have struggled with issues that are analogous to bereavement in refugee groups including a loss of social structures, cultural values and identity. Culturally constituted symbols, communication patterns, and healing approaches vary tremendously within the process of post-traumatic recovery, but cognitive disruption and existential pain remain a universal human response to traumatc events. Lifton (1967) described the culturally specific symbols and cognitive structures among survivors of Hiroshima, but also described guilt, psychic numbing, and the cognitive and emotional imprint of the death encounter that now have been described in many other cultural groups following trauma.

Kleinman and Kleinman (1991) contend that when misery that results from political calamity is transformed into the diagnoses of major depressive disorder or post-traumatic stress disorder, psychiatry delegitimates the patient's suffering as moral commentary. Some would go even further, stating that, in many cases, mental health treatment itself invalidates refugee patients' cultural understanding of their lives because they are taken through a medical acculturation process that moves from the particular and cultural to the framework of American science (Ong, 1995).

It is certainly imperative that any psychiatric taxonomy allow for variations in cultural background and, in the case of refugee trauma, this should include sensitivity to cultural values, religious beliefs and social structure in conceptualizing and treating symptoms and restoring the patient to health. The complex existential questions that center around loss and meaning are some of the major challenges for traumatized refugees. It is imperative, therefore, that the clinician understand the belief system of his or her patients that includes not only secular cultural attitudes and beliefs but also religious background. The traumatized refugee does not have to be religious in a formal sense; how the person was socialized to reconcile loss and deal with bereavement is important (Eisenbruch, 1984). The assessment of traumatized refugees from this perspective, regardless of cultural background, takes into account the impact of philosophy, values and social attitudes upon illness (Fabrega, 1975). No one theory can adequately encompass the phenomenon of refugee trauma. In assessment and treatment, excessive reliance on models of cultural determinism would be as unproductive as totally disregarding cultural factors (Morris & Silove, 1992).

The rituals that enable individuals or groups to deal with trauma, loss and death very often entail elements of both majority and folk religions, along with secular culture. The treatment of a broad spectrum of veterans in Vet Center treatment groups or groups for ex-POW's (Boehnlein & Sparr, 1993), the treatment of American Indian veterans with indigenous healing approaches (Silver, 1994), or the treatment of Southeast Asian refugees in socialization group settings (Kinzie, Leung, Bui, Keopraseuth, Ben, Riley, Fleck & Ades, 1988) all have a great deal in common through their focus on group healing in a social context. These group treatment approaches enable survivors to gradually come to a realization that life must go on for them and encourage them to reintegrate with the rest of society (Rosenblatt, Walsh & Jackson, 1976). Group interventions with patients from a variety of cultural backgrounds closely follow the therapeutic model of Frank (1961) by providing hope and relief from suffering, an explanatory model of healing, and therapeutic relationships to enhance healing. In fact, the use of ritual—which can take many forms not only in formal psychiatric treatment but in culturally specific modes of healing—attempts to reinforce central cultural beliefs which reestablish the concept that there is some order in the universe (Wallace, 1966; Leach, 1970; Lévi-Strauss, 1979).

As long as it is done in the proper cultural context, we feel that biomedical interventions have the potential to diminish PTSD symptoms cross-culturally and can enhance and complement the sociocultural interventions previously described. For example, the treatment of insomnia and nightmares with antidepressant medication or clonidine (Kinzie & Leung, 1989) can enhance daily functioning and improve subjective wellbeing, thus optimizing role functioning as spouse, parent, student, or employee. Reducing intrusive PTSD symptoms can allow the patient to benefit more fully from psychotherapy, tolerate interpersonal intimacy in their social environment, and participate in culturally sanctioned activities that enhance the grieving and recovery process.

Certain questions remain unanswered in regard to the prevalence of specific PTSD symptoms in different cultural groups. Despite the frequent mention of substance abuse, explosiveness and antisocial behaviour among American veterans of the Vietnam War, these characteristics have been found to be virtually absent in the refugee studies previously noted. These associated characteristics of PTSD among some American veteran populations may be instead reflective of the social milieu rather than specific characteristics of the core PTSD syndrome. Future research studies must take into account possible gender differences in post-traumatic responses, and also ascertain what developmental, personality, or social network characteristics contribute to, or prevent the development of acute and chronic PTSD and associated depression among refugees. A cross-national investigation of PTSD similar to the WHO study of depression using standardized instruments would be valuable (Mollica, Caspi-Yavin, Bollini, Truong, Tor & Lavelle, 1992). Since refugees represent the human capacity to survive despite great losses and assaults on human identity and dignity, future research with resettled refugees could help to further illuminate the processes and meanings of human change (Muecke, 1992). This must be done in a environment that does not dichotomize the PTSD concept into psyche or soma, but instead views trauma responses interactively and comprehensively (Andreasen, 1995).

Working with refugees who have experienced intense trauma can greatly change the clinician. One must be aware of differing concepts of personal identity and meaning that are influenced by cultural values, while at the same time remaining cognizant of the sociocultural values that one is influenced by not only in professional training but also in ongoing clinical practice. A clinician's store of cultural knowledge should serve as a general template against which an individual or family is assessed; knowledge of basic cultural norms, values and ideas are important, but there is a danger of ethnic stereotyping if the clinician does not recognize the immense intracultural variability of behaviour (Ishisaka, Nguyen & Okimoto, 1985).

Regardless of culture, patients often seek treatment after having gone through years of suffering. Although the DSM diagnostic criteria are severely limited in placing illness or suffering in a sociocultural context, they should not be limiting to the astute clinician. The DSM taxonomy is merely a scaffolding upon which the clinician constructs a multilayered picture of the biological, psychological and sociological effects of severe trauma upon the individual, family and the culture at large. A therapeutic relationship within a biopsychosocial framework can serve as an important catalyst in assisting the traumatized refugee.

REFERENCES

American Psychiatric Association. (1952). *Diagnostic and statistical manual of mental disorders* (First Ed.). Washington, D.C.: American Psychiatric Association.

American Psychiatric Association. (1968). *Diagnostic and statistical manual of mental disorders* (Second Ed.). Washington, D.C.: American Psychiatric Press.

American Psychiatric Association. (1980). *Diagnostic and statistical manual of mental disorders* (Third Ed.). Washington, D.C.: American Psychiatric Press.

Andreasen, N.C. (1995). Post-traumatic stress disorder: Psychology, biology, and the Manichaean warfare between false dichotomies. *American Journal of Psychiatry, 152*, 963–965.

Archibald, H.D. & Tuddenham, R.D. (1965). Persistent stress reaction after combat: A twenty year follow-up. *Archives of General Psychiatry, 12*, 475–481.

Arieli, Aril & Aycheh, S. (1992). Psychopathology among Jewish Ethiopian immigrants to Israel. *Journal of Nervous and Mental Disease, 180*, 465–466.

Arroyo, W. & Eth, S. (1985). Children traumatized by Central American warfare. In S. Eth & R.S. Pynoos (Eds.), *Post-traumatic stress disorders in children* (pp. 101–120). Washington, D.C.: American Psychiatric Association Press.

Arthur, R.J. (1982). Psychiatric syndromes in prisoners of war and concentration camp survivors. In C.T. Fiemann & R.A. Faguet (Eds.), *Extraordinary disorders of human behaviour* (pp. 47–63). New York, NY: Plenum.

Beiser, M. (1987). Changing time perspective and mental health among Southeast Asian refugees. *Culture, Medicine, and Psychiatry, 11,* 437–464.

Beiser, M., Turner, R.H. & Ganesan, S. (1989). Catastrophic stress and factors affecting its consequences among Southeast Asian refugees. *Social Science and Medicine, 28,* 183–195.

Bensheim, H. (1960). Die K.Z. Neurose rassische Verfolgter: Ein Beitrag zur Psycholpathologie der Neurosen. *Der Nervenarzt, 31,* 462–469.

Boehnlein, J.K. (1987a). Clinical relevance of grief and mourning among Cambodian refugees. *Social Science and Medicine, 25,* 765–772.

Boehnlein, J.K. (1987b). Culture and society in post-traumatic stress disorder: Implications for psychotherapy. *American Journal of Psychotherapy, 41,* 519–530.

Boehnlein, J.K. (1989). The process of research in post-traumatic stress disorder. *Perspectives in Biology and Medicine, 32,* 455–465.

Boehnlein, J.K. & Kinzie, J.D. (1992). DSM diagnosis of post-traumatic stress disorder and cultural sensitivity: A response. *Journal of Nervous and Mental Disease, 180,* 597–599.

Boehnlein, J.K., Kinzie, J.D., Rath, B. & Fleck, J. (1985). One year follow-up study of post-traumatic stress disorder among survivors of Cambodian concentration camps. *American Journal of Psychiatry, 142,* 956–959.

Boehnlein, J.D. & Sparr, L.F. (1993). Group therapy for WWII ex-POW's: Long-term post-traumatic adjustment in a geriatric population. *American Journal of Psychotherapy, 47,* 273–282.

Breslau, N. & Davis, G.C. (1987). Post-traumatic stress disorder—The stressor criterion. *Journal of Nervous and Mental Disease, 175,* 255–264.

Carlson, E.B. & Rosser-Hogan, R. (1991). Trauma experiences, post-traumatic stress, dissociation, and depression in Cambodian refugees. *American Journal of Psychiatry, 148,* 1548–1551.

Carlson, E.B. & Rosser-Hogan, R. (1994). Cross-cultural response to trauma: A study of traumatic experiences and post-traumatic symptoms in Cambodian refugees. *Journal of Traumatic Stress, 7,* 43–58.

Cheung, P. (1994). Post-traumatic Stress disorder among Cambodian refugees in New Zealand. *International Journal of Social Psychiatry, 40,* 17–26.

Chodoff, P. (1975). Psychiatric aspects of the Nazi persecution. In S. Arieti (Ed.), *American handbook of psychiatry* (Second Ed., pp. 932–946). New York, NY: Basic Books.

Chung, R.C. & Kagawa-Singer, M. (1993). Predictors of psychological distress among Southeast Asian refugees. *Social Science and Medicine, 36,* 631–639.

Clarke, G., Sack, W.H. & Goff, B. (1993). Three forms of stress in Cambodian adolescent refugees. *Journal of Abnormal Psychology, 21,* 65–77.

Desjarlais, R., Eisenberg, L., Good, B. & Kleinman, A. (1995). *World mental health: Problems and priorities in low income countries.* New York, NY: Oxford University Press.

Dewind, E. (1971). Psychotherapy after traumatization caused by persecution. *International Psychiatry Clinics, 8,* 93–114.

Eaton, W.W., Sigal, J.J. & Weinfeld, M. (1982). Impairment in Holocaust survivors after 33 years: Data from an unbiased community sample. *American Journal of Psychiatry, 139,* 773–777.

Eisenbruch, M. (1984). Cross-cultural aspects of bereavement, I: A conceptual framework for comparative analysis. *Culture, Medicine, and Psychiatry, 8,* 283–309.

Eisenbruch, M. (1991). From post-traumatic stress disorder to cultural bereavement: Diagnosis of Southeast Asian refugees. *Social Science and Medicine, 33,* 673–680.

Eisenbruch, M. (1992). Toward a culturally sensitive DSM: Cultural bereavement in Cambodian refugees and traditional healer as taxonomist. *Journal of Nervous and Mental Disease, 180,* 8–10.

Eitinger, L. (1959). The incidence of mental disorders among refugees in Norway. *Journal of Mental Science, 105,* 326–338.

Eitinger, L. (1960). The symptomatology of mental disease among refugees in Norway. *Journal of Mental Science, 106,* 947–966.

Eitinger, L. (1961). Pathology of the concentration camp syndrome. *Archives of General Psychiatry, 5,* 371–379.

Eitinger, L. (1980). The concentration camp syndrome and its late sequellae. In J.E. Dimsdale (Ed.), *Survivors, victims and perpetrators: Essays on the Nazi Holocaust* (pp. 127–160). Washington, D.C., Hemisphere.

Erichsen, J.E. (1866). *On railway spine and other injuries of the nervous system.* London: Walton and Moberly.

Fabrega, H. (1975). The need for ethnomedical science. *Science, 189,* 969–975.

Farias, P.J. (1991). Emotional distress and its socio-political correlates in Salvadoran refugees: Analysis of a clinical sample. *Culture, Medicine, and Psychiatry, 15,* 167–192.

Findley, M.I. (Ed.). (1959). *The portable Greek historians: The essence of Herodotus, Thucydides, Xenophon, and Polybius.* New York, NY: Viking Press.

Fischer-Homberger, E. (1970). Railway spine und traumatische neuroseseele und reuckenmark. *Desnerus, 27,* 96–111.

Frank, J.D. (1961). *Persuasion and healing.* Baltimore, MD: Johns Hopkins University Press.

Frankl, V.E. (1969). *Man's search for meaning.* New York, NY: Washington Square Press.

Freud, S. (1955). *The standard edition of the complete psychological works of Sigmund Freud* (vol. 17). London: Hogarth Press. (Original work published 1919).

Friedman, M. & Jaranson, J. (1994). The applicability of the post-traumatic stress disorder concept to refugees. In A.J. Marsella, T. Bornemann, S. Eckblad and J. Orley (Eds.), *Amidst peril and pain: The mental health and wellbeing of the world's refugees* (pp. 207–227). Washington, D.C.: American Psychological Association.

Goldfeld, A.E., Mollica, R.F., Pesavento, B.H. & Farone, S.V. (1988). The physical and psychological sequelae of torture. *Journal of the American Medical Association, 259,* 2725–2729.

Gong-Guy, E. (1987). *California Southeast Asian mental health needs assessment.* Oakland, CA: Asian Community Mental Health Services, California State Department of Mental Health.

Gosling, F.G. (1987). *Before Freud: Neurasthenia and the American medical community 1870–1918.* Urbana, IL: University of Chicago Press.

Grauer, H. (1969). Psychodynamics of the survivor syndrome. *Canadian Psychiatry Association Journal, 14,* 617–622.

Hauff, E. & Vaglum, P. (1993). Vietnamese boat refugees: The influence of war and flight traumatization on mental health on arrival in the country of resettlement. *Acta Psychiatrica Scandinavica, 88,* 162–168.

Hauff, E. & Vaglum, P. (1994). Chronic post-traumatic stress disorder in Vietnamese refugees. *Journal of Nervous and Mental Disease, 182,* 85–90.

Hauff, E. & Vaglum, P. (1995). Organized violence and the stress of exile: Predictors of mental health in a community cohort of Vietnamese refugees three years after resettlement. *British Journal of Psychiatry, 166,* 360–367.

Hoppe, K.D. (1972). The aftermath of Nazi persecution reflected in recent psychiatric literature. *International Psychiatry Clinics, 8,* 169–204.

Horowitz, M.J. (1974). Stress response syndromes: Character style and dynamic psychotherapy. *Archives of General Psychiatry, 31,* 768–781.

Horowitz, M.J. (1975). Intrusive and repetitive thoughts after experimental stress. *Archives of General Psychiatry, 32,* 1457–1463.

Horowitz, M.J. (1976) *Stress response syndromes.* New York, NY: Aronson.

Horowitz, M.J. (1986). Stress response syndromes: A review of post-traumatic and adjustment disorders. *Hospital and Community Psychiatry, 37,* 241–249.

Horowitz, M.J. & Becker, S.S. (1971). Cognitive response to stressful stimuli. *Archives of General Psychiatry, 25,* 419–428.

Horowitz, M.J., Wilner, N., Kaltreider, N. & Alvarez, W. (1980). Signs and symptoms of post-traumatic stress disorder. *Archives of General Psychiatry, 37,* 85–92.

Horowitz, M.J., Weiss, D.S. & Marmar, C. (1987). Diagnosis of post-traumatic stress disorder. *Journal of Nervous and Mental Disease, 175,* 267–268.

Ishisaka, H.S., Nguyen, Q.T. & Okimoto, J.T. (1985). The role of culture in the mental health treatment of Indochinese refugees. In T.C. Owan (Ed.), *Southeast Asian mental health: Treatment, prevention, services, training and research* (pp. 41–63). Washington, D.C.: National Institute of Mental Health.

Jenkins, J.H. (1991). A state construction of affect: Political ethos and mental health among Salvadoran refugees. *Culture, Medicine, and Psychiatry, 15,* 139–165.

Kinzie, J.D. (1986). Severe post-traumatic stress syndrome among Cambodian refugees: Symptoms, clinical course, and treatment. In J.H. Shore (Ed.), *Disaster stress studies: New methods and findings* (pp. 123–140). Washington, D.C.: American Psychiatric Press.

Kinzie, J.D. (1989). Therapeutic approaches to traumatized Cambodian refugees. *Journal of Traumatic Stress, 2,* 75–91.

Kinzie, J.D. & Boehnlein, J.K. (1989). Post-traumatic psychosis among Cambodian refugees. *Journal of Traumatic Stress, 2,* 185–198.

Kinzie, J.D. & Boehnlein, J.K. (1993). Psychotherapy of the victims of massive violence: Counter-transference and ethical issues. *American Journal of Psychotherapy, 47,* 90–102.

Kinzie, J.D., Boehnlein, J.K., Leung, P., Moore, L., Riley, C. & Smith, D. (1990). The high prevalence rate of PTSD and its clinical signifi-

cance among Southeast Asian refugees. *American Journal of Psychiatry, 147,* 913–917.

Kinzie, J.D. & Fleck, J. (1987). Psychotherapy with severely traumatized refugees. *American Journal of Psychotherapy, 41,* 82–94.

Kinzie, J.D., Fredrickson, R.H., Rath, B. & Fleck, J. (1984). Post-traumatic stress disorder among survivors of Cambodian concentration camps. *American Journal of Psychiatry, 141,* 645–650.

Kinzie, J.D., & Leung, P.K. (1989). Clonidine in Cambodian patients with post-traumatic stress disorder. *Journal of Nervous Mental Disease, 177,* 546–550.

Kinzie, J.D., Leung, P.K., Bui, A., Keopraseuth, K.O., Rath, B., Riley, C., Fleck, J. & Ades, M. (1988). Group therapy with Southeast Asian refugees. *Community Mental Health Journal, 24,* 157–166.

Kinzie, J.D. & Manson, S. (1983). Five-years' experience with Indochinese refugee psychiatric patients. *Journal of Operational Psychiatry, 14,* 105–111.

Kinzie, J.D., Manson, S.M., Vinh, D.T., Tolan, N.T., Anh, B. & Pho, T.N. (1982). The development and validation of a Vietnamese-language depression rating scale. *American Journal of Psychiatry, 139,* 1276–1281.

Kinzie, J.D., Sack, W.H., Angell, R.H. & Clarke, G. (1989). A three-year follow-up of Cambodian young people traumatized as children. *Journal of the American Academy of Child and Adolescent Psychiatry, 28,* 501–504.

Kinzie, J.D., Sack, W.H., Angell, R.H. & Manson, S. (1986). The psychiatric effects of massive trauma on Cambodian children: I. The children. *Journal of the American Academy of Child Psychiatry, 25,* 370–376.

Kinzie, J.D., Sack, R.L. & Riley, C.M. (1994). The polysomnographic effects of clonidine on sleep disorders in post-traumatic stress disorder: A pilot study with Cambodian patients. *Journal of Nervous and Mental Disease, 182,* 585–587.

Kinzie, J.D., Tran, K.A., Breckenridge, A. & Bloom, J.D. (1980). An Indochinese refugee psychiatric clinic: Culturally accepted treatment approaches. *American Journal of Psychiatry, 137,* 1429–1432.

Kirmayer, L.J. (1989). Cultural variations in the response to psychiatric disorders and emotional distress. *Social Science and Medicine, 29,* 327–339.

Klein, H. (1974). Delayed effects and after-effects of severe traumatization. *Israel Annals of Psychiatry, 12,* 293–303.

Kleinman, A. & Kleinman, J. (1991). Suffering and its professional transformation: Toward an ethnography of interpersonal experience. *Culture, Medicine, and Psychiatry, 15,* 275–301.

Kleinman, S. (1987). Trauma and its ramifications in Vietnamese victims of piracy. *Jefferson Journal of Psychiatry, 5,* 3–15.

Kramer, S.N. (1969). Lamentation over the destruction of Ur. In J.B. Pritchard (Ed.), *Ancient Near Eastern texts relating to the Old Testament* (Third Ed., pp. 259–276). Princeton, NJ: Princeton University Press.

Kroll, J., Habenicht, M., MacKenzie, T., Yang, M., Chan, S., Vang, T., Nguyen, T., Ly, M., Phommasouvanh, B., Nguyen, H., Vang, Y., Souvannasoth, L. & Cabugao, R. (1989). Depression and post-traumatic stress disorder in Southeast Asian refugees. *American Journal of Psychiatry, 146,* 1592–1597.

Krupinski, J., Stoller, A. & Wallace, L. (1973). Psychiatric disorders in East European refugees now in Australia. *Social Science and Medicine, 7,* 331–349.

Larer, R. (1933). Psychic trauma. *Physiotherapy Review, 13,* 229–232.

Leach, E. (1970). *Lévi-Strauss*. London: Fontana-Collins.

Lévi-Strauss, C. (1979). *Myth and meaning*. New York, NY: Schocken Books.

Levy, R.I. (1984). Emotion, knowing, and culture. In R.A. Shweder & R.A. Levine (Eds.), *Culture theory* (pp. 214–237). Cambridge, England: Cambridge University Press.

Lifton, R.J. (1967). *Death in life: Survivors of Hiroshima*. New York, NY: Basic Books.

Lin, K.M., Tazuma, L. & Masuda, M. (1979). Adaptational problems of Vietnamese refugees, part I: Health and mental health status. *Archives of General Psychiatry, 36,* 955–961.

Lindy, J.D., Green, B.L. & Grace, M.C. (1987). The stressor criterion and post-traumatic stress disorder. *Journal of Nervous and Mental Disease, 175,* 269–272.

Lopez, A., Boccellari, A. & Hall, K. (1988). Post-traumatic stress disorder in a Central American refugee. *Hospital and Community Psychiatry, 39,* 1309–1311.

Mattusek, P. (1975). *Internment in concentration camps and their consequences*. New York, NY: Springer.

McFarlane, A.C. (1985). The effects of stressful life events and disasters: Research and theoretical issues. *Australian and New Zealand Journal of Psychiatry, 19,* 409–421.

Mghir, R., Freed, W., Raskin, L. & Katon, W. (1995). Depression and post-traumatic stress disorder among a community sample of adolescent and young Afghan refugees. *Journal of Nervous and Mental Disease, 183,* 24–30.

Mollica, R.F. (1988). The trauma story: The psychiatric care of refugee survivors of violence and torture. In F.M. Ochberg (Ed.), *Post-traumatic therapy and victims of violence* (pp. 295–314). New York, NY: Brunner/Mazel.

Mollica, R.F., Caspi-Yavin, Y., Bollini, P., Truong, T., Tor, S. & Lavelle, J. (1992). The Harvard Trauma Questionnaire. *Journal of Nervous and Mental Disease, 180,* 111–116.

Mollica, R.F., Wyshak, G. & Lavelle, J. (1987). The psychosocial impact of war trauma and torture on Southeast Asian refugees. *American Journal of Psychiatry, 144,* 1567–1572.

Mollica, R.F., Wyshak, G., Lavelle, J., Truong, T., Tor, S. & Yang, T. (1990). Assessing symptom change in Southeast Asian refugee survivors of mass violence and torture. *American Journal of Psychiatry, 147,* 83–88.

Moore, L.J. & Boehnlein, J.K. (1991a). Post-traumatic stress disorder, depression, and somatic symptoms in U.S. Mien patients. *Journal of Nervous and Mental Disease, 179,* 728–733.

Moore, L.J. & Boehnlein, J.K. (1991b). Treating psychiatric disorders among Mien refugees from highland Laos. *Social Science and Medicine, 32,* 1029–1036.

Morris, P. & Silove, D. (1992). Cultural influences in psychotherapy with refugee survivors of torture and trauma. *Hospital and Community Psychiatry, 43,* 820–824.

Mott, F.W. (1919). *War neurosis and shell shock*. London: Oxford University Press.

Muecke, M. (1992). New paradigms for refugee health problems. *Social Science and Medicine, 35,* 515–523.

Nguyen, N.A. & Williams, H.L. (1989). Transition from East to West: Vietnamese adolescents and their parents. *Journal of the American Academy of Child and Adolescent Psychiatry, 28,* 505–515.

Niederland, W.G. (1964). Psychiatric disorders among persecution victims. *Journal of Nervous and Mental Disease, 139,* 458–474.

Ong, A. (1995). Making the biopolitical subject: Cambodian immigrants, refugee medicine and cultural citizenship in California. *Social Science and Medicine, 40,* 1243–1257.

Ostwald, P. & Bittner, E. (1968). Life adjustment after severe persecution. *American Journal of Psychiatry, 124,* 1393–1400.

Ramsay, R., Gorst-Unsworth, C. & Turner, S. (1993). Psychiatric morbidity in survivors of organized state violence including torture. *British Journal of Psychiatry, 162,* 55–59.

Rechtman, R. (1992). The appearance of ancestors and the deceased in traumatic experiences: Introduction of clinical ethnography in Cambodian refugees in Paris. *Cahiers d'anthropologie et biométrie humaine, 10,* 1–19.

Rechtman, R. (1993). Dreams, reality and traumatic experiences in Cambodian refugees. *Cahiers d'anthropologie et biométrie humaine, 11,* 259–279.

Rosenblatt, P.C., Walsh, R.P. & Jackson, D.A. (1976). *Grief and mourning in cross-cultural perspective*. New Haven, CT: HRAF Press.

Sack, W.H., Clarke, G., Him, C., Dickason, D., Goff, B., Lanham, K. & Kinzie, J.D. (1993). A 6-year follow-up study of Cambodian refugee adolescents traumatized as children. *Journal of the American Academy of Child and Adolescent Psychiatry, 32,* 431–437.

Sack, W.H., Clarke, G.N., Kinney, R., Belestos, G., Him, C. & Seeley, J. (1995). The Khmer adolescent project: II. Functional capacities in two generations of Cambodian refugees. *Journal of Nervous and Mental Disease, 183,* 177–181.

Sack, W.H., Clarke, G.N. & Seeley, J. (1995). Post-traumatic stress disorder across two generations of Cambodian refugees. *Journal of the American Academy of Child and Adolescent Psychiatry, 34,* 1160–1166.

Sack, W.H., McSharry, S., Clarke, G.N., Kinney, R., Seeley, J. & Lewinsohn, P. (1994). The Khmer adolescent project: I. Epidemiologic findings in two generations of Cambodian refugees. *Journal of Nervous and Mental Disease, 182,* 387–395.

Silver, S. (1994). Lessons from child of water. *Journal of the National Center of American Indian and Alaska Native Mental Health Research, 6,* 4–17.

Stein, B.N. (1986). The experience of being a refugee: Insights from the research literature. In C.L. Williams & J. Westermeyer (Eds.), *Refugee mental health in resettlement countries* (pp. 5–23). Washington, D.C.: Hemisphere.

Stierlin, E. (1911). Nervöse und psychische Störungen nach Katastrophen. *Deutsche Medizinische Wochenschrift, 37,* 2028–2035.

Trimble, M.R. (1991). *Post-traumatic neurosis from railway spine to whiplash*. Westchester: John Wiley & Sons.

Uba, L. (1992). Cultural barriers to health care for Southeast Asian refugees. *Public Health Reports, 107,* 544–548.

Venzlaff, V. (1967). *Die Psychoreaktiven Störungen nach Entschädigungspflichtigen Ereignissen* (Die Sogenanten Unfallneurosen). Berlin: Springer Verlag.

Vignes, A.J. & Hall, R.C.W. (1979). Adjustment of a group of Vietnamese people to the United States. *American Journal of Psychiatry, 136,* 442–444.

CHAPTER ELEVEN

Culture and Somatization

Somatization is the manifestation of emotional distress in the form of somatic (bodily) symptoms. Somatic symptoms appear to be directly related to anxiety. Cross-cultural studies indicate that somatic symptoms are the most common clinical manifestation of anxiety disorders worldwide (Kirmayer, 1984; Kirmayer & Weiss, 1994). As we know, anxiety is based in a cognitive process. Recurrent or generalized anxiety is based in deep-seated anxiety-producing cognitive schemas. This widespread expression of anxiety in the form of somatic symptoms challenges the classification system in DSM-IV (American Psychiatric Association, 1994), which places syndromes with prominent somatic symptoms in a separate category distinct from the anxiety disorders. There is no etiological basis for this distinction, nor does there seem to be much clinical utility in this grouping. Looking at mental illnesses from a cross-cultural perspective, the separation of mental disorders expressing emotional distress into distinct anxiety, somatoform, and mood groupings appears to be questionable.

An example of somatization is neurasthenia in China, a syndrome characterized by insomnia, weakness, headaches, difficulty concentrating, poor memory, irritability, nervousness, and some depression.

Mood disorders are relatively rare in China due to the Chinese use of bodily symptoms as cultural idioms expressing emotional distress. Because depressive symptoms are not important in the Chinese cultural schemas, little attention is paid to them in either subjective experience or interpersonal expressions of distress. Somatic symptoms have far more importance in the Chinese schemas. Therefore, the patient primarily notices and reports somatic symptoms. Likewise, clinicians trained in their own set of professional schemas pay attention to the symptoms they are trained to consider significant. A western-trained clinician would likely diagnose a mood disorder. However, a Chinese-trained clinician would have no trouble diagnosing neurasthenia, a diagnosis that does not exist in western medicine. This illustrates the effects of culture on both subjective experience of illness and professional diagnosis. The obvious common factor is patterns of cognition. Cultural schemas construct emotional distress as depressive symptoms in western patients and clinicians and as neurasthenia in Chinese patients and clinicians.

Neurasthenia in China illustrates the close relationship of mood, anxiety, and somatic symptoms and the effects of culture on the construction of a mental disorder. By having a subjective experience of illness validated by a professional diagnosis, the disorder neurasthenia becomes reified in the Chinese cultural context. It is a disorder that is both subjectively experienced and medically validated. This is not to say that neurasthenia is a fictitious disorder. Neurasthenia in China is certainly real and people definitely suffer from it. However, the constellation of subjective experience and professional diagnosis is a cultural entity, a reification.

In all likelihood, most of the diagnostic categories in DSM-IV probably have a similar level validity as neurasthenia in China. The cultural schemas in western culture have identified certain symptoms as signifying a particular disorder. These symptoms, in turn, are subjectively attended to because of their cultural significance and are then reported to a clinician, who validates a particular disorder from the professional schemas with his or her diagnosis. This reifies the cultural entity and creates a recognized category of mental disorder. Because cultural schemas differ, varying disorders may be constructed and reified from mostly the same basic symptoms of human suffering and emotional distress.

Another possibility in the somatization of emotional distress is *dissociation*. An example of this is conversion disorder. Conversion disorder is characterized by pseudoneurological (dissociative) symptoms such as amnesia, paralysis, impaired coordination or balance, localized anesthesia, blindness, deafness, double vision, hallucinations, tremors, or seizures without medical explanation.

The pseudoneurological symptoms of conversion disorder are dissociative somatic symptoms. In fact, ICD-10 lists conversion disorder symptoms as dissociative disorders such as dissociative motor disorders, dissociative convulsions, and dissociative anesthesia and sensory loss. Thus, conversion disorder is actually a manifestation of dissociation in somatic symptoms (Escobar, 1995). Dissociation is a splitting of consciousness based on trance (Chapter 13). Trance is a narrow focusing of attention. In the case of conversion symptoms, the sensory information (sight, hearing, touch, pain, and so on) or motor ability (in the case of paralysis) is placed outside of a narrow focus of attention and therefore outside of conscious awareness.

The contents of consciousness are determined by attention. Thus, sensory or motor modalities can be temporarily "forgotten" or "lost" to conscious awareness. Likewise, dissociative hallucinations are the product of attention narrowly placed on memory or imagination, shutting out external reality. Similarly, dissociative amnesia is attention focused away from memory or some aspect of memory. Dissociative seizures are actually pseudoseizures that are not related to brain pathology. Dissociative seizures result from narrowly focusing attention away from the bodily functions that normally maintain balance, muscle tone, posture, and overall body movement.

Conversion symptoms are the product of spontaneous trances resulting from emotional stress or trauma. Because of their emotional distress, some people enter a spontaneous trance and temporarily "lose" a sensory or motor modality, or experience dissociative hallucinations or seizures to avoid or escape some extremely stressful or traumatic situation

The article in this chapter is by medical anthropologist L. A. Rebhun. In this article Rebhun highlights the sociocultural factors affecting the construction of mental illness, particularly focusing on gender issues. In the male dominated society of Brazil, working-class women can use somatization in the form of the folk ailment *nervos* (nerves) to change others' behavior in social situations in which they would otherwise have very little control. In the highly male-dominant Northeast Brazilian cultural context, women are profoundly dependent on men. In this

situation, men are allowed to have concubines as well as their legitimate wives. Unlike a man, an adulterous woman would be severely beaten, abandoned, and possibly murdered by her husband. A woman is obligated to nurture, forgive, and love. Her job is to take care of her husband and children. Anger is not an emotion women are allowed to express openly. Instead, women experience *nervos*, a culture-bound somatoform syndrome characterized by trembling, dizziness, tiredness, chest pains, numbness, and physical weakness. This syndrome is used by women to control their husbands in the absence of more direct power. As this article points out, *nervos* is not a natural disease entity but an illness embedded in its sociocultural context.

REFERENCES

American Psychiatric Association. (1994). *Diagnostic and statistical manual of mental disorders* (4th ed.). Washington, DC: American Psychiatric Association.
Escobar, J. I. (1995). Transcultural aspects of dissociative and somatoform disorders. *Psychiatric Clinics of North America, 18,* 555–569.
Kirmayer, L. J. (1984). Culture, affect and somatization. *Transcultural Psychiatric Research Review, 21,* 159–188, 237–262.
Kirmayer, L. J., & Weiss, M. (1994). On cultural considerations for somatoform disorders. In J. E. Mezzich, A. Kleinman, H. Fabrega, D. Perron, B. J. Good, K. M. Lin, & S. Manson (Eds.), *Cultural issues and DSM-IV: Support papers* (pp. 137–147). Submitted for the DSM-IV Sourcebook by the NIMH Group on Culture and Diagnosis. Pittsburgh: University of Pittsburgh.

L. A. REBHUN

Nerves and Emotional Play in Northeast Brazil

Current theory on emotion posits that different cultures' emotional vocabularies constitute sets of glosses for negotiated understandings of interpersonal interaction. Folk illness terms can overlap emotion glosses, as in the case of the Northeast Brazilian folk ailment *nervos* ("nerves"), associated with anxiety and anger. Working-class women in Northeast Brazil can use their *nervos* to change others' behavior in social situations in which they otherwise would have limited control. Rather than passively feel emotion or submissively suffer illness, women actively play with emotion and illness roles. A woman's manipulations are more or less successful, depending on her skill at orchestrating perceptions of her situation. ["nerves," emotion, women, Brazil]

Emotion is a broad and varied phenomenon. It can be a set of glosses, an aspect of role, a role in itself, a body state, an ideology, a moral obligation, a performance, an individual experience, or any combination of these (Averill 1982; Ekman 1984; Kleinman and Good 1985; Lutz 1988; Lutz and White 1986; M. Rosaldo 1984). Taking form in the course of interpersonal interactions (Hochschild 1983), it can be played with for social gain. Emotion can also be part of sickness, and particular emotional states can be sickness in themselves. While both folk and scientific models portray emotion as an irrational force overwhelming passive consciousness, in fact, individuals can control their emotional experience and, through emotion, control others.

In this article, I use a case history approach to examine the Brazilian folk ailment[1] *nervos* as an emotional phenomenon. Similar to "nerves" or *nervios* described in other parts of the world (Barnett 1989; Camino 1989; Clark 1989; Davis 1983; Davis and Guarnaccia 1989; Davis and Low 1989; Finerman 1989; Guarnaccia, DeLaCancela, and Carrillo 1989; Kay and Portillo 1989; Lock 1990; Low 1985, 1989; Slutka 1989), Brazilian *nervos* is a folk diagnosis associated, in part, with anxiety, although it is more complex than simple tension (cf. Duarte 1986; Scheper-Hughes 1988, 1992). Seeing *nervos* as an emo-

tional state, as well as a folk ailment, allows a broader context for examination.

EMOTION: NEGOTIATIONS OF UNDERSTANDING AND SITUATION

The voluminous literature on emotion stretches back to the ancient Greeks, but despite generations of theories, the heart remains unknown country. In the 1980s and 1990s, interest in emotion has exploded in an "affect revolution" (Tomkins 1981), and theories have proliferated, influenced by anti-empirical approaches to human behavior (Harré 1986:vii) and by cross-cultural research.

Historically, theorists have seen emotion in terms of opposition between private and public, body and mind, irrational and rational, feminine and masculine (Lutz 1988:3), associating it with the first of each pair. However, ethnographic inquiry reveals the difficulty of seeing these pairs as polar opposites and brings out emotion's deeply interpersonal nature. The personal experience of any named emotion is embedded in culturally defined scenarios that include perceptions of propriety, etiology, and expected courses of response (Hochschild 1983:56–60; White 1990:47). Social actors perform according to the expectations of the sociomoral discourses encapsulated in emotion glosses (Abu-Lughod 1986; Hochschild 1983; Lutz 1988; Myers 1979; M. Rosaldo 1980; R. Rosaldo 1983; Sarbin 1986). Emotion is more a negotiation than an event; it constitutes a vocabulary that is "manipulated, misunderstood, reconstrued, and played with" (Lutz 1988:10) as social actors attempt to understand and control both themselves and others.

Each language glosses emotions differently. There is no one-to-one correspondence of definitions for all languages (Hiatt 1978:185; Leff 1977:322; R. Rosaldo 1980; Wierzbicka 1986:584). Emotion labeling, like illness labeling, can be a community statement about individuals who present themselves as experiencing a particular emotion in an attempt to manipulate community opinion.

In Brazilian Portuguese, *nervos* is an emotion gloss. *Nervosola* (nervousness) is the adjective describing a person who suffers from *nervos*, and *nervosismo* (nervous-ism) or *nervosidade* is the label for the sickness of being especially susceptible to attacks of *nervos*.[2] The multiple connotations of *nervos* can be played with, as they can for other emotions.

METHODOLOGY AND FIELD SITE

From December 1988 to December 1990, I conducted research in the Northeast Brazilian city of Caruaru (population 200,000) and neighboring villages in the Northeast Brazilian state of Pernambuco. My research focused on family relations in the context of Brazil's shifting economy; my data are drawn from a combination of direct and participant observation and 120 tape-recorded interviews.

Three types of questions were used in the interviews. The first type addressed demographic issues, such as birthplace and marital status. The second type dealt with emotional vocabulary, not only with words informants classed as dealing with what they call *sentimento* (sentiment), but also with words they used to describe body states they saw as part of *sentimento*. A third and open-ended type, intended for thematic analysis, was designed to elicit stories of life events and informant opinions. I also interviewed religious healers and their patients about emotion-related folk medical complaints, such as evil eye sickness, *nervosismo*, and shock sickness (*susto*).

Historically an area of plantation slavery, the Brazilian Northeast remains sharply divided between the powerful wealthy and the largely disenfranchised poor. The harsh economic climate is exacerbated by an arid physical climate subject to periodic droughts that force people to become *retirantes* or dust-bowl refugees moving toward less thirsty coastal areas. Caruaru is located in the transition between the fertile *Agreste* region and the semiarid *Sertão*, and many Caruaruenses descend from *retirantes*. They describe themselves as involved in a *luta*, a struggle for life against a hostile physical and social environment. They are a suffering people who survive by a combination of wit, fortitude, and sheer endurance. Caruaru is major market center, and there is constant traffic between local villages and the city, as part of the weekly market cycle. There are a umber of blue jeans factories in the area, and female pieceworkers also stitch jeans at home. My lower working-class informants included housewives, seamstresses, bakers, and vendors, and their factory-worker, painter, or mechanic husbands, boyfriends, and sons.

In the last 30 years, Northeast Brazil has undergone a mass migration into cities, accompanied by a sharp increase in population. The introduction of a cash economy and the substitution of industry for agriculture has had a dramatic effect on family relations, eroding both parents' authority over children and men's power over women. Nevertheless, the Northeast remains profoundly conservative. Both men and women live with their parents until marriage,[3] which is their ticket to independence.

Married women use extensive social networks to bring resources into the household. They work for gain, and they do what they can to manage their husbands, trying to get them to work hard and spend their earnings on the family rather than alcohol, gambling, or other women. In the cities, economic pressures increasingly fragment families, and men frequently float among several female-centered households. Despite their increasing marginality, men remain an important source of status and protection for women, and competition among women for men is fierce. Men find themselves pursued on the one hand by women willing to be *concubinas*[4] (a kind of illegitimate or secondary wife) in return for being provided with a house and children and, on the other hand, by their legitimate wives trying desperately to keep them home.

THE CASE OF IMACULADA

While I collected many case histories of *nervosismo*, I will concentrate on one particular case here. The micropolitics of interpersonal interaction are complex and often lost in multicase presentations. The case of a 41-year-old informant I shall call Imaculada[5] is typical in many respects and serves as an especially good example of the tangle of relations among family structure, gender role, illness, emotion, and economy that impacts *nervosismo*. Imaculada had made a traditional marriage with her first cousin and was the mother of two teenage daughters. She did piecework at home in a small town near Caruaru, stitching blue jeans, while her husband traveled the local market circuit, buying precut denim and selling the finished jeans for a profit of about US$0.10 per pair. He spent weekdays on the road, returning home only on weekends.

Imaculada complained of trembling, dizziness, tiredness, chest pains, and numbness, tingling, weakness, and partial paralysis of her hands. Her first *ataque de nervos* (attack of "nerves") occurred when her father died, and the *ataques* became more frequent after her husband had a car accident. During an especially severe *ataque de nervos*, she lost much of the use of her left hand. That *ataque* left her in a state of permanent *nervosismo*. She said that her most severe *ataque* was sparked by a single traumatic event. The details of Imaculada's case were typical of case histories I have collected in which women presented themselves as helpless victims of difficult circumstances and their own innate weakness; their weak or frayed nerves made them unable to bear tension, anger, or worry. But often their fortitude in surviving harsh conditions belied their self-description as weak, and their passive acquiescence in *nervos* covered deliberate action.

An Anonymous Letter

Imaculada told me that the trouble began with the arrival one Saturday of an anonymous letter detailing her husband's infidelity. Anonymous letters are a staple of the popular evening soap operas (*telenovelas*) that dominate Brazilian television, and they also appear occasionally in everyday life. Imaculada and her daughters had just returned from church (they are Seventh-Day Adventists) when the letter arrived. Because Imaculada is illiterate, her oldest daughter Lindinalva (age 18) read the letter to her. Imaculada described the dramatic scene when the letter was read:

> My girls cried a lot, we were all upset . . . Lindinalva, Virgin Mary! Lindinalva didn't even want to look at him, because she is very *nervosa* . . . she read the letter, she was trembling like this, with the letter in her hand, reading to him . . . I stayed crying, *ataque de nervos,* I fell down.[6]

When both mother and daughter begin to scream and cry, female neighbors came running, and by the time Imaculada's guilty husband came home from a bar where he had been socializing with male friends,[7] an angry crowd was waiting to greet him.

> My husband arrived, saw [the people], and asked: "Who died?" Lindinalva said: "It was your shame (*a vergonha do senhor*), that died a long time ago!" . . . So Laura [the younger daughter], when this happened, Laura is very artless, she spoke really very simply, so simply that it really touched his heart. My neighbor heard her talking, and cried.

Imaculada collapsed in the excitement, and there ensued frantic attempts to arrange a car to transport her to Caruaru (about a 45-minute drive) for medical treatment.

There she was diagnosed with high blood pressure, weak nerves, and a mild stroke. The doctor advised her husband to end his affair, asking him whether his sexual satisfaction was worth killing his wife and dishonoring his daughters. The husband cut off the affair and, to Imaculada's knowledge, has not entered into any other serious affairs since.

On the surface, this story seemed like so many others I heard in which women described themselves as suffering passively at the hands of their callously misbehaving men, but the interview took another turn when I asked if Imaculada knew who had written the letter.

It wasn't a secret, everyone knew about the *concubina*. Because people told me that he had another woman . . . but when I asked him, he resisted. He said that I believed everyone else and not him, that if I loved him I would believe him. It was the biggest mess, so I dropped it.

The "news" revealed by the anonymous letter was not in fact news at all. Neighbors had gossiped that her husband was living with a woman in one of the small towns on his weekly market circuit. During Carnaval, Imaculada had told her daughters she was going to visit a cousin who lived in that town. Actually, her visit had another purpose.

> I was following him. . . . I arrived directly there, and I saw what was happening with my own eyes. . . . He was really living there with her, sleeping with her . . . and then the anonymous letter arrived.

As I questioned further, she made an admission that changed the entire tone of her story:

> I knew, thank God, I knew about it and . . . with the powers of God I dismantled it all. I was clever (*esperta*). Really clever! . . . He thought it was an anonymous letter, but . . . it was I who ordered the letter written.

This admission shattered Imaculada's pose as a stereotypical Brazilian wife, passively suffering at her husband's callous hands. Instead, she had assertively acted to try to manipulate her daughters, her neighbors, and the doctor, in her attempt to control her husband. I asked why she used the letter instead of confronting her husband directly.

> It was in order for him not to say that [the story of the mistress] was just me lying. Also I didn't want to say who told me about the woman, so I ordered a letter written and then he couldn't keep saying that he hadn't gone out with her if it was the letter saying everything, rather than me.

Despite her orchestration of the letter, she insisted her *nervos* attack was not faked:

> It was a real *nervos* attack because it really hurt me very, very much. And since that time I can't use my left hand anymore because of the numbness of the nerves. It was the shock. . . . When Lindinalva read the letter, it was when it all descended on my head and I stayed with numbness in my hands.

Interviewing more women, I heard more stories in which they actively tried to manipulate others while posing as passive, although none of the stories was quite as dramatic as Imaculada's. Women carry a terrible emotional burden as they worry about, grieve over, and suppress their anger toward loved ones.

This emotional burden translates into folk illness like "open chest," evil eye sickness, *nervos*, and blood-boiling bruises (Rebhun 1993). Women suffer through exhausting daily labor, arduous economic straits, and an unjust gender hierarchy that places superhuman demands on both psyche and soma. In addition to the difficulties of their actual circumstances, the image of the sorrowful mother colors women's experience (Stevens 1973). In cases like that of Imaculada, women can play with both their actual circumstances and the moral image of the suffering woman to gain a measure of influence in a system that denies them power.

Understanding the full extent of Imaculada's cleverness in sending herself the "anonymous" letter requires comprehension of both the cultural context of her actions and tension between passivity and activity that characterizes not only her particular case, but also how emotion in general is played out in social interactions.

PAIXÃO AND SENTIMENTO: CONSTRUING THE PASSIVE

Brazilians, like other Westerners, tend to describe sentiment as passive, something that happens to a person rather than something that a person actively does. Brazilian Portuguese, like English, distinguishes between passions that engulf a passive consciousness (*paixão*) and actively experienced emotions (*sentimento*) (cf. Averill 1982:3[8]). Feelings are most likely to be judged as passions when they are experienced as submersion in a stream of impulses that "burst" like pride, "sweep away" like infatuation, or cause consciousness to "fall in" like love (Averill 1982:13–17).

Seeing passions as passively acquiesced to means seeing them as irrational, unthought-out experiences that can lead people to behave in untoward ways. In general, my informants characterized their *paixões* as irrational, describing them as *doido* (nutty) or *louco* (crazy). This contrast between the irrational emotional and rational cognitive also characterized anthropological thinking until the 1980s. According to current theory, however, emotion's image as irrational masks its nature as a cognitive judgment (Franks 1987; Lutz 1982; Myers 1979, 1986; R. Rosaldo 1983; Solomon 1976), and its relation to cognition belies its passivity. Anthropological attention has been captivated by the great variety of emotion definitions in different languages, differing vocabularies that often cannot be directly translated (Hiatt 1978:185; Leff 1977:322; Wierzbicka 1986:584) and can be a rich source of cultural information (cf. Morsbach and Tyler 1986; M. Rosaldo 1980).

People understand their feelings by construing their experience in terms of the emotion idioms given in their languages. To understand what they feel, they compare their own experience with culturally given descriptions of emotion and then construe that experience in terms of those linguistic descriptions (Roberts 1988:192). By thinking in the words their languages assign to feelings, people's inchoate, unconscious feelings become conscious and sensible within cultural expectations (Hochschild 1983:220–222). Not only is emotion a cognitive process, but cognition itself is "infused with value, affect, and direction"; the two are inseparable (Lutz and White 1986).

Hochschild characterizes emotion as "deep acting," in which individuals convince not only others, but also themselves, that they feel some named emotion mandated by cultural "feeling rules" that tell people which emotions are proper in which situations and what to expect in the course and consequences of glossed emotions (1983:38–55). She adopts Goffman's presentation of self, which sees society as a great stage on which actors work to direct others' impressions of them, concealing some aspects of behavior in a "backstage" while presenting others for public scrutiny (Goffman 1959). In Goffman's terms, by concealing the authorship of the "anonymous" letter, Imaculada was able to manage her husband's impression of her as a helpless victim, while hiding the self-sufficient action of researching and writing the letter in the backstage of her drama.

Sarbin distinguishes between dramaturgic and dramatistic role playing. In dramaturgic action, social actors use "deception, disguise, feigning, plotting, and other strategic devices to achieve their ends" (Sarbin 1986:89). Dramatistic actions are based on the acting out of traditional stories in the form of folktales, legends, and myths (Sarbin 1986:90). Imaculada's pose as a passive woman was dramaturgic in that it was a studied deception and dramatistic in that it conformed to cultural stories of women's passivity.

In the United States, we tend to believe that sentiment is genuine only if it is spontaneous; required, conventional, or manipulated sentiment seems false (Abu-Lughod 1986; Trawick 1990:153) and its falseness morally reprehensible. But deliberation, rehearsal, and requirement are as integral to emotion as spontaneity and do not render it any less "true." Lutz has shown how social actors "play with" sentiments as part of social manipulation (1988:10). Emotion is playful both in the sense of spontaneity and in the sense that it is full of play. Play can mean "manipulate" as in "play with," "imitate" as when children "play cowboys and Indians," "perform" as in "playing Hamlet," "moving freely within a confined space" as machine parts do, or "use in a game" as when we "play a card." All these aspects of play are part of sentiment and equally genuine. Emotion's ambiguity is not just a problem for theorists; folk models of emotion are ambiguous as well. Ambiguity is part of emotion's playfulness, allowing for negotiation of social meaning (Crespo 1986:213).

For example, Imaculada first construed her reaction to her husband's affair as personal anger. That definition did not persuade her husband to drop his affair. To change her husband's behavior, Imaculada had to try another construction, that of the more socially appropriate shocked and betrayed wife. This construction proved more effective, in part, because it was a more acceptable pose for a wife and because the device of the letter shifted the origin of the accusation of infidelity from her personally and, in part, because it allowed her to take on the role of the *nervosa*. Lost in the excitement was her knowledge of the affair before the letter and her prior history of *ataques de nervos*.

By her *esperta* playing with gender requirements, the sick role and the moral properties of emotion, Imaculada showed herself a powerful woman. Her imitation of passivity allowed her to play in the limited emotional space allotted to women. Playing the card of passivity trumped her husband's supposed dominance of the family, forcing him to give up his sexual liberty and accede to her construal of the situation.

In Hochschild's terms, Imaculada's shock at hearing the letter read out loud was a successful deep acting of the emotion expected of an unsuspecting wife at hearing such news. Her shock was neither feigned nor false. It was simply delayed until the appropriate situation allowed her to release her conscious control over it and experience it passively.

Delay is not unusual in the experience of emotion. People evoke or suppress emotion by attempts to control both behavior and physiological reactions. They may behave as though they were experiencing an emotion in order to work it up (Roberts 1988:204) or quell emotional excitement by relaxing muscles, slowing breathing, or distracting themselves. Often, they must complete a series of tasks before they allow themselves the luxury of releasing their control. For example, one of Imaculada's neighbors described how she delayed grief at a relative's death:

> Let's suppose if someone of my family dies, I do everything at that time, I buy flowers, and put [the body] in the coffin, do the burial, I do everything, you know, but that done, then afterwards I can stay five, six days in bed, crying without stopping.

Just as the neighbor's grief is no less true for being delayed until she finishes her funeral obligations, Imaculada's emotional reaction was no less real for being delayed until she engineered the dramatic letter reading. The reading of the letter allowed her to feel her shock fully with all its experiential and physiological consequences.

NERVOS, NERVOSISMO, AND NERVOSO

When Imaculada described her problem as *nervos*, she was referring to a multicausal, multimeaning, multicultural folk ailment, which anthropologists call "nerves." Although there are cross-cultural differences in the description of "nerves," there are also so many cross-cultural similarities that it can no longer be considered a culture-bound phenomenon, but rather a widespread cultural label for similar experiences (Finkler 1989, Low 1989). "Nerves" usually involves headache, dizziness, fatigue, weakness, and stomachache and is generally associated with sadness, anger, fear, and worry (Davis and Guarnaccia 1989:7), although symptoms and etiology vary cross-culturally. While some theorists discuss "nerves" among men (Duarte 1986; Koss-Chioino 1989; Low 1985, 1989), others see it as either a specifically female disorder (Barnett 1989; Davis 1983, 1989; Finerman 1989; Kay and Portillo 1989; Low 1989; Slutka 1989) or the female presentation of stresses expressed differently by men (Camino 1989; Davis and Low 1989; Slutka 1989).

Anthropologists have put forth several interpretations of "nerves," seeing it as a folk illness of strong emotion (Low 1989) or of menopause (Barnett 1989), a reaction to stressful family problems (Guarnaccia, DeLaCancela, and Carrillo 1989; Low 1981) or gender-based overresponsibility (Finerman 1989), an interpersonal manipulation (Krieger 1989), an idiom of women's social relationships (Davis 1983), a manifestation of hunger (Scheper-Hughes 1988, 1992) or of economic deprivation (Dunk 1989), a means of expressing socially unacceptable emotions (Clark 1989; Lock 1990), and a folk model of anxiety or depression (Koss-Chioino 1989; Kay and Portillo 1989). "Nerves" may well include all of the above and more; it is a very broad term. Scheper-Hughes aptly describes *nervos* in Northeast Brazil as "polysemic" (1992:169); a "large and expansive folk diagnostic category of distress," which is "seething with meaning" (1992:172).

Northeast Brazilians say that both men and women can be *nervoso*, although it is generally seem as more of a feminine problem, partly because *nervosismo* is a state of victimization, which is seen as feminine. Also, it may involve irritability and combativeness considered normal in men, but unacceptable in women (cf. Dunk 1989:38). A *nervoso* person cannot handle stress—crying, trembling, or flying into rages at minor provocation—whereas women are expected to be patient and self-effacing.

People say that *nervosismo* is caused either by sudden emotional shock or the frazzling of the nerves through repeated stress. For example, Imaculada's neighbor Fátima's *nervos* started with her shock at the murder of her brother-in-law:

> We were already sleeping when my niece arrived saying that they had murdered her father, so that news took me by surprise. I stayed cold for five minutes without being able to speak; I lost myself. I felt my chins trembling, isn't it? Now I stay trembling, *nervosa*. . . . It's horrible! Whatever little

thing, I start soon [crying], uncontrolled; I am very in-secure now.

Nervos also may be caused by a series of shocks or prolonged stressful period. This was Fátima's mother-in-law's theory:

> I've been a long time with my nerves trembling; you know from what? Worry. Because we get angry at something, then we get upset with something, get upset with something else, work too much, stay with the nerves drained, isn't it? . . . We get tired of everything. . . . We have lots of worries, we strug-gle a lot, we get suffering in the nerves. . . . It's already too much, we already can't stand it at all anymore.

Often the prolonged stress is caused by accumulated, un-expressed anger. One housewife explained: "Sometimes I have a big anger that I can't avenge; it's crying with anger, locked inside of me. We get revolted. Any little thing I'm upset. It's *nervos*."

Women are likely to suffer from suppressed anger because their obligation to nurture, forgive, and love requires them to avoid openly expressing emotions that assert the self or cause conflict. The emotional stress of suppressing conflict combines with the strains of poverty to create an unbearable ferment of barely contained furious frustration.

Brazilian folk metaphors describe anger as a dangerous force that can accumulate inside the body or even leap out through the eyes and enter others' chests (Rebhun 1993). They describe emotion as building up pressure inside the body in a classical hy-draulic conception (cf. Solomon 1984). *Nervosismo* is the result of erosion of the nerves, seen as little wires running through the skin and muscles, carrying emotional charges. Once a person's nerves have been frazzled, they can no longer carry even mild emotional strains.

Allen and Cooke, in a critique of theories that attribute fe-male alcoholism to stressful life events, point out that neither memory nor self-report are dispassionate. They propose that U.S. female alcoholics may attribute their problems to stressful life events more than male alcoholics because alcoholism is so stigmatized for women that they must invent sympathetic rea-sons for their failings (1988:149). A similar caution can be ap-plied to Northeast Brazilian women's tales about their *nervos*. The gloss of *nervos* contains an analysis of stressful events as emotionally destructive, so that individuals generally expect to lose control under stress. And in some cases, like that of Imacu-lada, individuals may manage situations to create the proper stressful events so that they can become *nervosa* if it suits their purposes. As with female alcoholism, female anger is a disap-proved condition in Northeast Brazil. Subsuming it under *nervos* marks it as both weakness and disease, and removes much of its accusatory power if the angry woman does not handle it as clev-erly as did Imaculada.

NERVES AND THE BODY: HUNGER, SCARCITY, AND WEAKNESS

Saying that emotion is a social phenomenon does not mean that it is not also a physical one; however, the body's role in emotion is more complex than the correspondence among metabolic states, facial expressions, and internal experiences often postu-lated. Some sentiments are accompanied by body states—the blush of embarrassment, the throbbing temple of anger, the shiver of fear, the pounding heart of anxiety. But neither body states nor facial expressions correspond one-to-one with named emotions (Averill 1982:11), and not all emotions produce bodily excitation (Franks 1987:224). Nor is bodily excitation a simple physical process.

The human body is not only an object, but also part of a sym-bol system functioning both in the microcosm of self and in the macrocosm of social world. Body discourse reveals attitudes on a myriad of issues, including gender relations, illness, and con-cepts of self (Bourdieu 1977; Cowan 1990; Foucault 1978; Scheper-Hughes and Lock 1987). Distress is embodied as physi-cal disorder (Kirmeyer 1984; Kleinman 1977; Low 1985; Scheper-Hughes and Lock 1987) in which somatization is not merely metaphorical expression of distress but the constitution of its embodiment (Finkler 1989:82).

Scheper-Hughes shows how in the desperately poor *favelas* (shantytowns) near Pernambuco's coast, *nervos* can gloss both physical symptoms of hunger and anxiety engendered by scarcity (1988, 1992). She argues that medicalization of *nervos* hides the social and economic roots of distress. Instead of blam-ing the grotesque unfairness of Brazil's class system for their problems, *nervoso* people blame themselves for being weak and spend money on pharmaceuticals instead of urgently needed food (1992:199).

Most of my informants were neither as impoverished nor as malnourished as *favelados* (squatters), but they were surrounded by brutal poverty above which they were only barely holding themselves. With hyperinflation rates upward of 2% per day and conditions of endemic underemployment, maintenance of any level of survival takes hard work and constant worry. And while they may not have been engaged in the daily battle for food waged by Scheper-Hughes's informants,[9] my informants faced daily battle with shortages, long lines, bureaucratic indifference, exploitative bosses, demanding children, abusive husbands, and a thousand other barriers to well-being. Like Scheper-Hughes's *favelados*, they saw themselves as hungry in the broader sense of general deprivation and insecure survival and as weak in com-parison to the wealthy and politically powerful who control the Northeast; that view was, in the main, accurate.

Foster, in a controversial study of Mexican peasants, said that their world view was characterized by an Image of Limited

Good in which all desired good things are seen as existing in limited quantities, and the good fortune of one person or group is believed necessarily to diminish the prosperity of others (1965, 1972). Scheper-Hughes relates this to *nordestinos'* (northeasterners) view of themselves as poor, hungry, weak, nervous people (1992:169).

While "nervous hunger" is clearly one kind of situation defined as *nervos* by *nordestinos*, it does not constitute the whole category of the gloss (nor does Scheper-Hughes argue that it does). It is not necessary for a *nordestino* to be clinically malnourished in order to be labeled *nervoso*, although simple hunger may be sufficient in combination with female gender and irritability.[10] *Nervos* is, however, generally categorized by a feeling of being on the edge of disaster, the desperation of not having enough strength to cope. It is this desperation that distinguishes *nervos* from simple anger. The *nervosa* woman has lost the ability to control or suppress her anger; she is passive, *fraca* (weak), and *falta força* (lacks strength).

Foster's Image of Limited Good also includes fatalism—the feeling of powerlessness over the decrees of fate—which Scheper-Hughes calls "existential insecurity" (1992:169). Here, secondary meanings of *nervos* are important. The word also refers to energy and to courage, much like the meaning of the English word "nervy." To say that one's *nervos* have been destroyed or eroded by shock, hard work, or suppressed anger is to say that one's courage and energy have been dissipated. Many informants said that after becoming *nervoso*, their *nervos* attacks were brought on by *qualquer coisinha* (any little thing), *qualquer raivinha* (any irritation [literally "little anger"]), *bobagems* (nonsense), *besterinhas* (foolishness), or other unimportant things. They lacked courage (*falta coragem*) to face the burdens of life.

Nervosismo, then, is a condition of having lost control. The *nervosa* individual reacts too strongly to minor stimuli; her personal weakness is expressed by her passive acquiescence in the passion of *nervos*. This is the cultural stereotype; Imaculada's story shows that, in fact, there is a dynamic between activity and passivity in *nervos* as there is in emotion in general. A *nervosa* individual may truly feel out of emotional control or she may be playing with ambiguities of control. The tensions among love, anger, worry, *nervos*, and control are nowhere stronger than in the family.

EMOTION, NERVOS, AND FAMILY STRUCTURE

In Northeast Brazil, women's emotional role is defined largely by the obligation to love and not to express anger verbally. A married woman is the center of her nuclear family, and her job is

to take care of her husband and children. Like Dona Davis's Newfoundland fisher-wives, a major way of taking care of loved ones for Northeast Brazilian women consists of worrying about them (cf. Davis 1983, 1989). Compassion for, worry about, and suffering on behalf of others is as much a part of women's work as providing physical comfort through cooking, cleaning, and sexual services.

Historically, Northeastern Brazilians have placed more emotional emphasis on the parent-child bond than the husband-wife dyad. In the 19th century, marriages were arranged either by parents or followed customary patterns, such as the marriage of first cousins, although young people could rebel through elopement. In the 20th century, young people's increased economic independence has enhanced their ability to choose their own mates. The modern romantic love complex with its fusion of the excitement traditionally associated with extramarital affairs and the calm interdependence of traditional marriage has charged marriages with a new, emotional tone.

But traditional patterns remain. Neither Imaculada's marriage nor her husband's affair were at base about romantic love. Both involved cousins, for example. According to Imaculada:

> I didn't want to marry him, but my sister arranged it so he wanted to court me. . . . I thought it was ugly to court your cousin. . . . I didn't like the idea, but he did . . . but later I created a little friendship in my heart for him, and we married. . . . Then my husband went to the house of my father's brother's son, his cousin too . . . he used to work there a little bit for them, and they wanted him to leave me and stay living there, working for them . . . so they arranged a little house for my husband to live in so he would stay near them . . . they gave him a bed, and arranged a woman to lie in it with him.

Imaculada's husband's affair was not only his personal betrayal of their marriage vows, but also her betrayal by treacherous cousins plotting to break up her marriage because of their economic interest in her husband. The *concubina*'s interest was probably economic as well. It is not hard to "arrange" (*arrumar*) a woman to provide both household and sexual services; the tradition of forcing sex with houseservants goes back to slavery. Also, sexual mores make it hard for either sex to live alone. A man cannot be publicly known to perform household chores without injury to his masculine reputation; he needs a woman to cook and clean for him. A woman alone is seen as sexually uncontrolled; she needs a man to obtain her own house, independent of her parents or siblings. There is fierce competition among women for men, and many women are willing to settle for the position of *concubina* of a married man to get a house of their own.

This competition means that no woman can afford to be complacent if she wants her husband to remain faithful to her. Not only do men feel pressure to prove their masculine independence from their women's control through extramarital affairs, but they are also pursued actively by women seeking a man with whom to set up housekeeping. While sexual relations are discussed in the idiom of the gloss love (*amor*), they take place under intense economic pressure. Many women, like Imaculada, "create friendship" in their hearts for the lovers they are given by circumstance rather than choosing those lovers freely on emotional grounds.

Women may feel emotionally wounded by their husbands' infidelities; they are also hurt economically. Imaculada's husband might eventually have moved over to the "other woman's" house permanently. Imaculada would have had to arrange with another man to sell her jeans and bring her the denim pieces, a man who might have cheated her or placed sexual demands on her. Abandonment by her husband would have put both her and her daughters at risk of being sexually harassed because they would have been without a man to protect them, and the daughters would have been in a less favorable position to make a legitimate marriage because their virginity could not be assured without a father to protect them.

Extramarital affairs are emotionally painful for both the wives and the daughters of men who cheat. Often, daughters react with more anguish to their fathers' affairs than wives. Sometimes their reaction includes sympathy with their mistreated mother. Also, daughters tend to idolize their fathers, enjoying the status of "daddy's little princess." Whereas custom puts limits on public expression of affection between husband and wife, fathers may cuddle daughters, dress them up in flirtatious, frilly costumes, and indulge them. A father's infidelity is not only a personal failing in an otherwise idealized figure, but it may be seen as a rejection of the daughter as well as of the mother.

This is why it was important for Imaculada to reveal the affair to her daughters. Their hurt, pain, and *ataques de nervos* could be added to hers to put greater emotional pressure on her husband to drop his affair. The device of the letter deflected responsibility for informing them from her. It is a parent's, and especially a father's, responsibility to keep his daughters sexually ignorant until marriage. Not only should good girls be virgins, they should behave as if they have no knowledge of sexuality before marriage. Revealing his sexual misbehavior to the daughters meant acknowledging it in their presence, violating the father's responsibility to protect them from sexual knowledge. This is what Lindinalva meant by saying that it was her father's shame that had died. He had conducted the affair without concern for its effect on the honor of his family.

Imaculada emphasizes how "artless" (*simples*) her younger daughter Laura is; the word also means naive. Laura was virtu-

ously *simples* until her father's shameless behavior destroyed her innocence. Revealing the infidelity to the daughters via the letter brought out the shocked betrayal they were freer to express than their mother, and impressed on the husband how his sexual misbehavior endangered not only his wife's health but his daughters', and by extension his own, honor.

Imaculada's *nervos* was also a response to gender politics within a marriage. Let us imagine for a moment that the situation were reversed and Imaculada had been caught in adultery by her husband. He would have been able to respond in a number of ways.

He could murder her. The mores of *machismo* demand a violent response to any insult to a man's honor. During one week in March of 1990 in Pernambuco's state capital of Recife, the Women's Police Station (*Delegacia da Mulher*)[11] received depositions in the murders of eight Pernambuco women suspected of infidelity, as well as the deaths of a couple dragged from their home and burned to death by the woman's outraged ex-husband (Jornal de Comércio March 18, 1990). The week was not unusually violent. Brazil's legal system has long permitted such actions by men (Corréa 1981:15). Most cases of wife-murder never go to trial, and wife-murderers continue to be acquitted by juries sympathetic to their *machista* motivations despite a 1991 Supreme Court ruling against such acquittals (New York Times March 29, 1991).

He could beat her severely. During August of 1989, the Hospital Pronto Socorro of Caruaru treated 13 women whose husbands had wounded them with fish knives and broken bottles. By September 15 of that year, another 13 women had been treated for similar injuries. In most cases, violence begins when a husband or boyfriend returns home drunk and accuses his wife or girlfriend of infidelity. Police do not prosecute such cases because they consider them a "routine occurrence" (Vanguarda September 15–31, 1989).[12]

He could leave her. Such an action is the least that is expected of a betrayed husband. Whereas a woman who stays with an adulterous husband is praised for her long-suffering loyalty, a man who stays with his adulterous wife is considered a weak fool. A man who leaves his wife can easily arrange for (*arrumar*) another woman, but is very difficult for a woman who has been identified publicly as unchaste to find a new husband or boyfriend because he would be forever in doubt about her honor.

None of these actions was open to Imaculada.[13] An intelligent, determined woman can gain a great deal of influence over her husband's behavior, but it is not a power as raw or as strong as that of the fist. *Nervosismo* is not only a passive emotional state related to feelings of weakness, but it is a tactic used by the weak to control in the absence of more direct power. That is another reason it is mostly a female malady.

WHEN A WOMAN IS NOT SKILLED AT IMPRESSION MANAGEMENT

Playing with images of *nervos* does not occur in a vacuum. While the *nervosa* woman tries to manage others' impressions of the meaning and legitimacy of her condition, others try to put their own spin on the situation. And *nervos* is so complex a gloss that many different interpretations are possible. Social actors judge cases of *nervos* according to the details of the situations in which they arise, the particular sympotomatology they exhibit, and preexisting judgments of the sufferer's character. Different factions may take different points of view.

For example, one day my neighbor Maria da Paz's husband returned home late and drunk. Furious, she chased him out of the house letting loose with a remarkable string of profanity, summarizing not only his dubious genealogy but also his personal resemblance to a number of virulent diseases, not to mention horrible things from another planet. While the neighbors peered out of their doors, her brother, who lived nearby, commented loudly: "My sister always was a big mouth, a really *nervosa* woman. Take a tranquilizer, my darling, and resign yourself *(se conformar)* to your fate."

In so doing, he effectively transformed Maria de Paz's anger from a justified comment on her husband's misbehavior into a personal failing on her part, best treated with medication. There were a number of differences between her case and Imaculada's, including community opinions about the precipitating shock causing *nervosismo*, the extremity of the situation setting off the *ataque de nervos*, and the symptoms of *nervosismo* displayed.

Imaculada was *nervosa* before the "anonymous" letter, attributing her condition to the death of her father and the near death of her husband, but with the arrival of the letter, she was able to wipe out the previous precipitating events, substituting her husband's behavior as the shock. That made his behavior the problem; thus, from then on, any sign of her *nervosismo* could be defined as his fault. Maria da Paz had a different precipitating shock. She was the only daughter in a family with 12 sons. Her mother said that she had been *nervosa* since childhood because of the stress of having so many big brothers to tease her. In addition, she had been involved in a serious car accident, requiring surgery on her badly broken legs and months of hospitalization.

The accident occurred when she was driving and failed to yield the right of way to a male driver at a busy intersection. Officially, she had the legal right-of-way, but in the informal system that actually determines how people drive in the Northeast, men take the right-of-way over women, and she failed to accommodate this. Driving is a rare opportunity for women of her class. As far as her family was concerned, the accident was caused by her inappropriate gender behavior, insisting on driv-

ing like a man and then being insufficiently deferent to the male driver.

The street on which we lived was inhabited mostly by Maria da Paz's parents, brothers- and sisters-in-law, and cousins, with only a few unrelated neighbors. They generally considered her husband to be a good man because he was very hard working and maintained her and their children in a very nice house that boasted all the luxury features like extra plumbing, tile floors, and expensive furniture. Their standard of living was above that of the neighbors, who generally thought that Maria de Paz had little to complain about in her industrious, generous, and unusually handsome husband.

On occasion, however, he would go out with her brothers and drink, returning home smelling of rum and staggering slightly but able to walk. To the neighbors whose husbands were regularly carried home unconscious from drink or jailed on drunk-and-disorderly charges, this was a minor infraction. Maria da Paz's husband was also widely believed to be faithful to her because he never spent a night away form home and was visibly working most of the time. Maria da Paz told me that she was terribly afraid that her brothers would corrupt her husband and that he would become accustomed to drinking with them and become like them. Whenever he returned home tipsy, she reacted as if he were deeply drunk because of that fear, which most regarded as inappropriate and yet another proof of her inability to handle men. In the community's opinion, her *nervosismo* was a sign of her incompetence and thus was used to further trivialize her anger, which was already designated as inappropriate by the community.

In contrast, Imaculada did not attribute her *nervosismo* to anger but rather to shock *(susto)*, which is much more appropriate for women. Her husband was actually misbehaving, and his misbehavior was in fact a threat to her family's well-being, whereas Maria da Paz's husband was not endangering his family with his behavior. Imaculada's *nervosismo* may have been a ploy, but it was an appropriate ploy, socially defined as her husband's fault. Maria da Paz's *nervosismo* was not defined by neighbors as appropriate or justified. Some saw it as amusing, recounting with pleasure the imaginativeness of her curses or the funny time when she dumped the beans on her husband and her 5-year-old went around crying "Mommy dumped the dinner on Daddy and there's nothing to eat in the house!" Others saw it as irritating, speaking of their fear of having to dodge thrown dishes when walking past her door. By overreacting to her husband's small infractions, she undermined any power she might have had to control any future major misbehavior on his part. Her *nervoso* strategy was less effective than Imaculada's.

We can now see just how clever Imaculada was. By having the "anonymous" letter sent, she shifted her husband's affair from a whispered-about speculation to a public certainty, exposing him to direct comment from neighbors. She shifted the origin of the accusation of infidelity from herself to society at large, revealed the affair to her daughters, and manufactured the single stressful event she needed to precipitate a *nervosismo* that would be her husband's fault, giving herself not only a guilt-producing crisis, but a continuing source of guilt manipulation.

As she stated, when she herself accused her husband, he was able to cast her charges as disloyalty to himself, saying she believed her gossip-mongering friends more than she believed him. The letter, however, demonstrated that his affair was general knowledge. There was no specific accuser to refute, and her reputation as a properly passive woman remained intact. The letter revealed her husband's infidelity to their daughters, blaming him for exposing them to the dishonoring knowledge. Through the device of the letter, Imaculada was able to play with family emotional dynamics in order to change her husband's behavior, forcing him to address his family's interest in his fidelity. Imaculada's *nervos* graphically demonstrated that his infidelity was dangerous to his family. More than a verbal statement could have, it demonstrated the cry, "I hurt" and pointed the finger of guilt at him. Because her *ataque de nervos* was accompanied by a mild stroke, she was able to enlist her doctor to help change her husband's behavior. As in other groups, Brazilian women use medicalization to legitimize their suffering (cf. Lock 1990:250). While medicalization can be harmful (cf. Scheper-Hughes 1992), it can also be manipulated by the clever. Imaculada used her *nervos* and its accompanying stroke as biological proof of her image as passive, victimized woman. Her manipulation of emotion does not obviate the legitimacy of her feelings. It reflects, rather, emotion's capricious, playful nature and her personal skill at managing not only others' but her own impressions of herself.

In their orchestration of events, women are not in complete control. Imaculada could not, for example, have known in advance that she would suffer a stroke when the letter was read. But once the stroke had happened, she was able to weave it into the ongoing improvisation that constitutes social drama. Like children's play, adult social play is characterized by flow in which actors are both immersed in, and acting to try to affect, perceptions and events. Attempts at manipulation are forays, which if effective, bring forth further attempts on the new situation created, and if not effective, require regrouping to reconsider new tactics. The actual social situation constructed is a fluid result of multiple, competing attempts at construal as well as competing points of view.

Emotions have interacting cultural, psychological, and biological aspects, and are experiential, interpretive, and interpersonal. Patterns of sentiment vary among cultures and among roles within a single culture. They are capricious, playful, and

essential to the micropolitics of power. Their definition as irrational passions forms part of calculated strategies of interpersonal manipulation. Using *nervos* to examine emotion theories, and emotion theories to interpret *nervos* provides an opportunity to unify different theoretical approaches to both emotion and folk ailments.

NOTES

Acknowledgments. The research upon which this article is based was supported by grants from the Fulbright Foundation-International Institute of Education, the Lowie Foundation, the Tinker Foundation, the Social Science Research Council, the National Science Foundation, and the National Institutes of Mental Health, and a Hannum-Warner Travel Fellowship from Mount Holyoke College, and was facilitated by affiliation with the Universidade Federál de Pernambuco, Departamento de Antropologia. This article benefited from comments by Stanley Brandes and Maria Massolo and could not have been written without the support of my parents, Mildred and Lionel Rebhun.

Correspondence may be addressed to the author at Prevention Research Center, Pacific Institute, 2532 Durant Avenue, Berkeley, CA 94704.

[1] I am using "folk ailment" to describe named illnesses found primarily among one or several related cultural group[s]. "Nerves" has been called a culture-bound syndrome, although Setha Low has called for the term "culturally interpreted syndrome," arguing that symptoms are culturally received and labeled expressions of distress responding to culturally defined theories of disease and etiology (1985:188–189). I prefer the term "folk ailment" because all syndromes and sicknesses are culturally interpreted. What distinguishes "nerves" form other forms of sickness is that it belongs to folk illness systems that coexist with official medical diagnoses.

[2] These are the grammatically correct terms. The most common of these words in ordinary usage are *nervos, ataque de nervos,* and *nervoso*.

[3] I am using "marriage" here in the sense my informants applied. They used *casamento* (marriage) and the verb *casar* (to marry) to refer both to legal marriage and to stable cohabitation unblessed by either law or church.

[4] A *concubina* can be distinguished from a mistress or extramarital girlfriend because she lives in a house either provided or supported by the man, while a mistress or girlfriend has a dating relationship with the man but does not share a residence with him.

[5] All names are pseudonyms.

[6] Quotations have been edited. Ellipses indicate where repetition and asides have been omitted.

[7] Maria Imaculada's husband had not converted to Seventh-Day Adventism, which advocates abstinence from alcohol and tobacco.

[8] Averill's original analysis contrasts the English "emotion" to "passion." The word "emotion" derives from the Latin *movere* "to move," also the root of "movement." An overwhelming sentiment or one with an origin invisible to consciousness is called a passion (Averill 1982) from the Latin *patí*, or *passus* "to suffer," the same root as "passive," "patient," and "pathology." The word *emoção* in Portuguese refers primarily

to excitement, similar to English meanings of "emotion" prior to the early 1700s. "Sentiment" and *sentimento* derive from the Latin *sent* meaning "to head for" or "to go." *Sentire* meant "to go mentally." *Paixão* is most commonly used to describe infatuation or sexual excitement, but it can be applied to any very strong feeling to which a person surrenders.

[9]Scheper-Hughes conducted her research in the Zona da Mata, an area characterized by monoculture of sugar cane. The Mata's inhabitants in general are likely to suffer chronic undernutrition, whereas those who live in the Agreste and Sertão grow their own beans, meat, and vegetables and generally eat better until droughts disrupt their food supply and they suffer periods of acute malnutrition (Levine 1978:6).

[10]The most common folk treatment I observed for *ataques de nervos* is a drink of water with sugar in it. The use of sugar-water as a folk treatment supports Scheper-Hughes' association of hunger symptoms with *nervos* symptoms, especially if "hunger" can be used to mean transient bouts of appetite, as well as chronic or acute malnutrition.

[11]These are special police stations that are staffed by and take depositions from women. They deal mainly with cases of domestic violence and rape.

[12]*Vanguarda* is Caruaru's newspaper.

[13]Some women kill their husbands or hire others to do it for them. A woman may also kick her man out of the house, and an occasional woman will strike her husband. There are men who manipulate their wives with *nervoso*, but the bulk of the cases go the other way. A man who beats or murders his wife when he suspects adultery is normal, whereas a woman who arranges the murder of her husband for adultery is deviant.

REFERENCES CITED

Abu-Lughod, Lila (1986) Veiled Sentiments: Honor and Poetry in a Bedouin Society. Berkeley, CA: University of California Press.

Allen, Carole A., and D. J. Cooke (1988) Stressful Life Events and Alcohol Misuse in Women: A Critical Review. Journal of Studies on Alcohol 16(2):147–152.

Averill, James R. (1982) Anger and Aggression: An Essay on Emotion. New York: Springer-Verlag.

Barnett, Elyse Ann (1989) Notes on *Nervios*: A disorder of Menopause. *In* Gender, Health, and Illness: The Case of Nerves. Dona L. Davis and Setha M. Low, eds. Pp. 67–78. New York: Hemisphere Publications.

Bourdieu, Pierre (1977) Outline of a Theory of Practice. Richard Nice, trans. Cambridge: Cambridge University Press.

Camino, Linda (1989) Nerves, Worriation, and Black Women: A Community Study in the American South. *In* Gender, Health, and Illness: The Case of Nerves. Dona L. Davis and Setha M. Low, eds. Pp. 203–222. New York: Hemisphere Publications.

Clark, Mari H. (1989) *Nevra* in a Greek Village: Idiom, Metaphor, Symptom, or Disorder? *In* Gender, Health, and Illness: The Case of Nerves. Dona L. Davis and Setha M. Low, eds. Pp. 103–126. New York: Hemisphere Publications.

Corréa, Mariza (1981) Os Crimes da Paixão. São Paulo: Editora Brasiliense, Serie Tudo é História.

Cowan, Jane (1990) Dance and the Body Politic in Northern Greece. Princeton, NJ: Princeton University Press.

Crespo, Eduardo (1986) A Regional Variation: Emotions in Spain. *In* The Social Construction of Emotions. Rom Harré, ed. Pp. 209–217. Oxford: Basil Blackwell.

Davis, Dona Lee (1983) Woman the Worrier: Confronting Feminist and Biomedical Archetypes of Stress. Women's Studies 10:135–146.

___. (1989) The Variable Character of Nerves in a Newfoundland Fishing Village. Medical Anthropology 2:63–78.

Davis, Dona Lee, and Peter J. Guarnaccia (1989) Health, Culture, and the Nature of Nerves: Introduction. Medical Anthropology 2:1–13.

Davis, Dona Lee, and Setha M. Low, eds. (1989) Gender, Health, and Illness: The Case of Nerves. New York: Hemisphere Publications.

Duarte, Luiz Fernando D. (1986) Da Vida Nervosa Nas Classes Trabalhadores Urbanas. Rio de Janeiro: Jorge Zahar Editor/CNPq.

Dunk, Pamela (1989) Greek Women and Broken Nerves in Montreal. Medical Anthropology 2:29–45.

Ekman, P. (1984) Expression and the Nature of Emotion. *In* Approaches to Emotion. K. Scherer and E.K. Man, eds. Pp. 319–343. Hillsdale, NJ: Erlbaum.

Finerman, Ruthbeth (1989) The Burden of Responsibility: Duty, Depression and *Nervios* in Andean Ecuador. *In* Gender, Health, and Illness: The Case of Nerves. Dona L. Davis and Setha M. Low, eds. Pp. 49–66. New York: Hemisphere Publications.

Finkler, Kaja (1989) The Universality of Nerves. *In* Gender, Health, and Illness: The Case of Nerves. Dona L. Davis and Setha M. Low, eds. Pp. 79–87. New York: Hemisphere Publications.

Foster, George (1965) Peasant Society and the Image of Limited good. American Anthropologist 67:293–315.

___. (1972) The Anatomy of Envy: A Study in Symbolic Behavior. Current Anthropology 13:165–202.

Foucault, Michel (1978) The History of Sexuality: Volume I, An Introduction. New York: Random House.

Franks, David D. (1987) Notes on the Bodily Aspect of Emotion: A Controversial Issue in Symbolic Interaction. Studies in Symbolic Interaction 8:219–233.

Goffman, Erving (1959) Presentation of Self in Everyday Life. Garden City, NY: Doubleday.

Guarnaccia, Peter, V. DeLaCancela, and Emilio Carrillo (1989) The Multiple Meanings of *Ataques de Nervios* in the Latino Community. Medical Anthropology 2:47–62.

Harré, Rom, ed. (1986) The Social Construction of Emotions. Oxford: Basil Blackwell.

Hiatt, L.R. (1978) Classification of the Emotions. *In* Australian Aboriginal Concepts. L.R. Hiatt, ed. Pp. 182–187. Canberra: Australian Institute of Aboriginal Studies.

Hochschild, Arlie R. (1983) The Managed Heart: Commercialization of Human Feeling. Berkeley, CA: University of California Press.

Kay, Margarita, and Carmen Portillo (1989) *Nervios* and Dysphoria in Mexican American Widows. *In* Gender, Health, and Illness: The Case of Nerves. Dona L. Davis and Setha M. Low, eds. Pp. 181–202. New York: Hemisphere Publications.

Kirmeyer, Laurence (1984) Culture, Affect, and Somatization, Parts 1 and 2. Transcultural Psychiatric Research Review 21:159–188, 237–262.

Kleinman, Arthur (1977) Depression, Somatization, and the New "Cross-Cultural Psychiatry." Social Science and Medicine 11:3–10.

Kleinman, Arthur, and Byron Good (1985) Culture and Depression: Studies in the Anthropology and Cross-Cultural Psychiatry of Affect and Disorder. Berkeley, CA: University of California Press.

Koss-Chioino, Joan D. (1989) Experience of Nervousness and Anxiety Disorders in Puerto Rican Women: Psychiatric and Ethnopsychological Perspectives. *In* Gender, Health, and Illness: The Case of Nerves. Dona L. Davis and Setha M. Low, eds. Pp. 153–180. New York: Hemisphere Publications.

Krieger, Laurie (1989) Nerves and Psychosomatic Illness: The Case of Um Ramadan. *In* Gender, Health, and Illness: The Case of Nerves. Dona L. Davis and Setha M. Low, eds. Pp. 89–102. New York: Hemisphere Publications.

Leff, Julian (1977) The Cross-Cultural Study of Emotions. Culture, Medicine and Psychiatry 1:317–350.

Levine, Robert M. (1978) Pernambuco in the Brazilian Federation 1889–1937. Stanford, CA: Stanford University Press.

Lock, Margaret (1990) On Being Ethnic: The Politics of Identity Breaking and Making in Canada or *Nevra* on Sunday. Culture, Medicine and Psychiatry 14:237–254.

Low, Setha (1985) Culturally Interpreted Symptoms or Culture-Bound Syndromes: A Cross-Cultural Review of "Nerves." Social Science & Medicine 21:187–196.

___. (1989) Health, Culture, and the Nature of Nerves: Critique. Medical Anthropology 2:91–95.

Lutz, Catherine (1982) The Domain of Emotion Words on Ifaluk. American Ethnologist 9:113–128.

___. (1988) Unnatural Emotions, Everyday Sentiments on a Micronesian Atoll and their Challenge to Western Theory. Chicago: University of Chicago Press.

Lutz, Catherine, and Geoffrey M. White (1986) The Anthropology of Emotions. Annual Review of Anthropology 15:405–436.

Morsbach, H., and W. J. Tyler (1986) A Japanese Emotion: *Amae. In* The Social Construction of Emotions. Rom Harré, ed. Pp. 289–307. Oxford: Basil Blackwell.

Myers, Fred R. (1979) Emotions and the Self: A Theory of Personhood and Political Order Among Pintupi Aborigines. Ethos 7:343–370.

___. (1986) Pintupi Country, Pintupi Self: Sentiment, Place, and Politics Among Western Desert Aborigines. Washington, DC: Smithsonian Institution Press.

Rebhun, L. A. (1993) A Heart Too Full: The Weight of Love In Northeast Brazil. Journal of American Folklore. (In press.)

Roberts, Robert C. (1988) What An Emotion Is: A Sketch. The Philosophical Review XCVH (2):183–209.

Rosaldo, Michelle (1980) Knowledge and Passion: Ilongot Notions of Self and Social Life. Cambridge: Cambridge University Press.

___. (1984) Toward an Anthropology of Self and Feeling. *In* Culture Theory: Essays on Mind, Self, and Emotion. Richard Shweder and Robert LeVine, eds. Pp. 137–157. New York: Cambridge University Press.

Rosaldo, Renato (1980) Ilongot Headhunting. Stanford, CA: Stanford University Press.

___. (1983) Grief and the Headhunters' Rage. *In* Play, Text, and Story. Edward Bruner, ed. Pp. 178–195. Washington, DC: American Ethnological Society.

Sarbin, Theodore R. (1986) Emotion and Act: Roles and Rhetoric. *In* The Social Construction of Emotions. Rom Harré, ed. Pp. 83–97. Oxford: Basil Blackwell.

Scheper-Hughes, Nancy, and Margaret Lock (1987) The Mindful Body: A Prolegomenon to Future Work in Medical Anthropology. Medical Anthropology Quarterly (n.s.) 1:1–36.

Scheper-Hughes, Nancy (1988) The Madness of Hunger: Sickness, Delirium, and Human Needs. Culture, Medicine and Psychiatry 12:429–458.

___. (1992) Death Without Weeping: The Violence of Everyday Life in Brazil. Berkeley, CA: University of California Press.

Slutka, Jeffrey A. (1989) Living on Their Nerves: Nervous Debility in Northern Ireland. *In* Gender, Health, and Illness: The Case of Nerves. Dona L. Davis and Setha M. Low, eds. Pp. 127–152. New York: Hemisphere Publications.

Solomon, R.C. (1976) The Passions. New York: Anchor Doubleday.

___. (1984) Getting Angry: The Jamesian Theory of Emotion in Anthropology. *In* Culture Theory: Essays on Mind, Self, and Emotion. Richard A. Schweder and Robert A. LeVine, eds. Pp. 238–254. Cambridge: Cambridge University Press.

Stevens, Evelyn P. (1973) Marianismo: The Other Face of Machismo in Latin America. *In* Female and Male in Latin America. Ann Pescatello, ed. Pp. 89–101. Pittsburgh, PA: University of Pittsburgh Press.

Tomkins, Silvan S. (1981) The Quest for Primary Motives: Biography and Autobiography of an Idea. Journal of Personality and Social Psychology 42(2):306–329.

Trawick, Margaret (1990) Notes on Love in a Tamil Family. Berkeley, CA: University of California Press.

White, Geoffrey M. (1990) Moral Discourse and the Rhetoric of Emotions. *In* Language and the Politics of Emotion. Catherine Lutz and Lila Abu-Lughod, eds. Pp. 46–68. Cambridge: Cambridge University Press.

Wierzbicka, Anna (1986) Human Emotions: Universal or Culture-Specific? American Anthropologist 88(3):584–594.

CHAPTER TWELVE

Culture and Depression

Emotions are essentially cognitive and are, therefore, associated with meanings. The differential meanings of situations and events are expressed in differing symptoms of emotional distress. The cognitive relationship between anxiety and depression appears to be especially strong. It is now clear that almost everyone who is depressed is also anxious. However, not everyone who is anxious is depressed (Barlow, 1988; DiNardo & Barlow, 1990; Sanderson, DiNardo, Rapee, & Barlow, 1990).

The key to the relationship between anxiety and depression as a chronic problem appears to be cognition. Depression is especially likely in persons with a stigmatized moral career or self-identity (see Chapter 3). A stigmatized person is more likely to view the cause of stressful events as internal, stable, and general. This kind of cognitive relationship will add the emotional symptoms of major depression onto those of anxiety. For example, in a hierarchical society a person with a stigmatized moral career could have very low self-esteem and a hypersensitive nervous system resulting from emotionally traumatic experiences of discrimination, humiliation, exploitation, or rejection. It is clear that in hierarchical societies there can be very real conditions of economic exploitation, degradation, extreme poverty, illness, and political domination associated with the symptoms of anxiety, somatoform, and mood disorders (Kleinman, 1986; Kleinman & Kleinman, 1995).

Stigmatized persons in hierarchical societies can be of the "wrong" race, gender, religion, ethnic group, social class, sexual orientation, and so on. These social causes of emotional distress can be internalized in the form of cultural schemas. Cultural schemas can construct an experience of social distress as having an internal cause. For example, cultural schemas stigmatizing certain groups can be internalized to the point where individuals subjectively experience that they really are the "wrong" race, gender, religion, and so on. They experience the problem as being internal to themselves rather than a sociocultural construction.

Moreover, because the problem may be something that is not easily changed, like race, gender, religion, or social class, these persons view the problem as stable. On top of this, because their stigmatized status affects many areas of social interaction, they view their situation as being a general problem affecting most aspects of their lives. Thus, stigmatized persons are more likely

to develop a sense of hopelessness and helplessness and, therefore, depression in addition to anxiety.

In the United States almost 70% of the persons with major depression and dysthymia are women (Nolen-Hoeksema, 1987; Weissman et al., 1991). These sex ratios are probably at least partially related to a social organization with male dominance where females are raised to be dependent and passive and males are raised to be independent and aggressive. Women in the United States are more likely to experience increased stress in the form of discrimination, poverty, and harassment. Similar kinds of situations are found in all hierarchical societies, but the cognitive construction of the situation, and therefore the meanings and emotions associated with them, will vary.

Depresssive emotions can also have different meanings and be based in different sociocultural contexts. In some societies, a depressive syndrome is not recognized as an illness (Lutz, 1985; Marsella, Sartorius, Jablensky, & Fenton, 1985; Schieffelin, 1985; Tanaka-Matsumi & Marsella, 1976; Terminsen & Ryan, 1970; Tseng & Hsu, 1969). Many studies have also found a reduced frequency or absence of reports of the typical western psychological components of major depression in nonwestern societies. This is especially true for the emotions of guilt, existential despair, self-denigration, and suicidal ideation (Beiser, 1985; Ebigbo, 1982; Furnham & Malik, 1994; Katon, Kleinman, & Rosen, 1982; Kleinman, 1982, 1986; Ohara, 1973; Rao, 1973; Shinfuku et al., 1973). In these societies, somatic symptoms may be more meaningful and therefore primarily experienced by individuals and diagnosed by local clinicians (Crittenden et al., 1992; Ebert & Martus, 1994; Ulusahin, Basoglu, & Paykel, 1994).

This does not mean that a western-trained clinician could not find depressive symptoms that would be labeled major depression in the West. However, these depressive symptoms would be structured by nonwestern cultural schemas, and the subjective experience would be different from the concept of major depressive disorder developed in the West (Bebbington, 1993; Schieffelin, 1985).

Guilt is one emotion associated with major depression in western countries that is less likely to be found in nonwestern societies. The World Health Organization Collaborative Study on Depression represents one of the most extensive cross-cultural comparisons of depressive symtomatology (Sartorius et al., 1983; Thornicroft & Sartorius, 1993). Depressed patients from five countries (Canada, India, Iran, Japan, and Switzerland) were interviewed concerning their subjective experience of depression. Guilt feelings were found in 68% of the Swiss sample, but only in 32% of the Iranian sample. Highly significant cultural differences were found even though all the patients from the various countries were highly educated and westernized. It may be that guilt is a more culturally salient concept in western societies. In contrast, somatization was present in 57% of the Iranian sample, but in only 27% of the Canadian sample.

From a cross-cultural perspective, it appears that differing sets of cultural schemas are shaping cognition and the experience of anxiety or emotional distress. This is probably the reason depressive symptoms like guilt seem to be more common in western societies and somatic symptoms appear to be more common in many nonwestern societies. Anxiety symptoms appear to be widespread in all parts of the world, and it appears that anxiety can be either somaticized or psychologized. That is, anxiety resulting from stressful life events can further manifest in the form of somatic symptoms or depressive symptoms, or both. The differences will depend on the cultural schemas of the persons involved. Westerners tend to psychologize, but many nonwesterners tend to somaticize their anxiety and emotional distress.

Even when a depressed mood is experienced, the depression itself may not have the same meaning in a nonwestern society. For example, generalized hopelessness and what westerners would call major depression can have a completely different meaning in South Asian Hindu and Buddhist cultural schemas. In this cultural context, depression is not an illness but an accomplishment, a spiritual insight about the true nature of the world (Castillo in Chapter 13; Obeyesekere, 1985).

From cross-cultural studies we can also see that depression can have a different subjective experience, idioms of distress, culture-based diagnosis, treatment, and outcome. For example, Catherine Lutz (1985), in her study of Micronesians, found that their subjective experience of depression is somewhat different from that of westerners. Depressive experience is not conceptualized by the Micronesians as an illness. If an individual has a longer than usual period of depressed mood following the loss of a personal relationship, the problem is defined by the Micronesians as that of an inadequate replacement of the lost relationship with another. This indigenous diagnosis of the problem is quite different from the disease-centered paradigm, and treatment also differs from disease-centered psychiatry. In the United States we recommend psychotherapy and antidepressant medications. This is appropriate in our highly egocentric society where the illness is viewed as being internal to the individual and persons are viewed

as being responsible for their own well-being. However, in the sociocentric society of Micronesia, the appropriate treatment is to get the person focused on remaining personal relationships or to replace the lost personal relationship with a new one. This reintegrates the sociocentric individual into the social life of the community and relieves the depressed mood.

Micronesians have been undergoing dramatic sociocultural change in recent decades resulting from cultural contact with the West. This has been correlated with an epidemic of suicide. In the years between 1960 and 1980 there was an eightfold increase in suicide rates for 15-to-24-year-old males on the island of Truk. This rate soared to 200 per 100,000 between 1974 and 1983, compared to a rate of 13.3 per 100,000 for all 15-to-24-year-olds in the United States in 1989 (Desjarlais, Eisenberg, Good, & Kleinman, 1995).

The disease-centered paradigm would tend to view the Truk suicides in terms of individual biological pathology. However, the client-centered approach would view each case within the sociocultural context. Micronesia has undergone rapid modernization with the introduction of a wage labor system, and traditional religious and social organizations have disappeared, leaving individuals with fewer traditional means of dealing with depressed emotions. This breakdown of traditional social support structures has resulted in alienation in the younger generation in a society that is highly sociocentric. In the local explanatory model, a completed suicide by a Micronesian teenager is viewed as an act expressing anger but also soliciting support, reconciliation, and nurturance (Desjarlais et al., 1995).

Although completed suicides are highly correlated with psychopathology in western societies (usually substance abuse, depression, or psychosis), in nonwestern societies in general, completed suicides are less likely to be associated with a psychiatric problem. For example, official statistics for suicide in India highlight social stressors. The top known causes of suicide in India for 1990 were: "Dreadful disease" (leprosy, etc.) "Quarrel with in-laws," "Quarrel with spouse," "Love affairs," "Insanity," "Poverty," and "Dowry dispute." Only 3% of suicides were attributed to "insanity," the only category of mental disorder on the list (Desjarlais et al., 1995).

Several other studies indicate that disruptions in social relationships are a strong predictor for suicide attempts (Grossi & Violato, 1992; Hart & Williams, 1987; Hawton, 1986; Magne-Igvar, Ojehagen, & Traskman-Bendz, 1992; Shaffer et al., 1988). Social factors can play a very important role in suicidal acts in nonwestern societies. In many of these cultures, depression arising from social stress is not seen as a psychiatric problem. For a clinician to view a suicide attempt strictly as the consequence of a psychiatric disorder may aggravate the situation. Psychiatric explanations are stigmatizing and may promote feelings of alienation, devaluation, and powerlessness (Kirmayer, 1994).

Suicidal acts relate to a range of social, political, and psychological factors and should not automatically be viewed as a symptom of major depression.

Diagnosing a major depressive episode outside of western culture can be problematic. The belief that depression is a psychiatric disorder appears to be a western cultural construction (Lutz, 1985; Obeyesekere, 1985). This may be tied to the peculiarly western notions of Cartesian dualism and the modern individual's right to the "pursuit of happiness." First, the Cartesian mind-body split that permeates throughout western thought appears to make westerners very mind- and mood-oriented as opposed to body- or group-oriented (Manson, 1995).

The pursuit of happiness has become the primary goal of western culture. "Are you happy?" is a question that people in the United States are constantly asking each other. In western culture, if you are not happy, or at least pursuing happiness with some degree of initiative, it is presumed that something is wrong with you. Moreover, the pursuit of happiness, which is virtually required of all people in Anglo American culture for them to be considered normal, is viewed as an individual right and responsibility. This egocentrism also structures the meaning of depression. Not all cultures are egocentric like the West. Most nonwestern cultures are sociocentric. This means an individual's personal identity is centered in the social group rather than in the self. In sociocentric societies, individual wants and desires are subjugated to the benefit of the group. Individual rights have very little meaning in this cultural context. Rather, individuals focus on personal obligations to the group. Self-sacrifice for the good of the group is usually seen as the greatest virtue and responsibility, not the pursuit of personal happiness. Thus, sadness in a sociocentric context is not usually seen as a psychiatric disorder, but as a disruption in social relations. Furthermore, sadness in this context need not be a personal event but could be a group experience. Rather than saying "I feel depressed," these individuals might say, "Our life has lost meaning" (Manson & Good, 1992).

An example of this sociocentric experience is the article in this chapter, Theresa O'Nell's study of depression and problem drinking among Native Americans on the Flathead Reservation in Montana. For the tribe as a whole, life has lost its traditional meaning. O'Nell concludes that while comorbidity of depression, alcoholism, and suicidality among Native Americans can indicate severe psychopathological distress, the creation, maintenance and disruption of social bonds are more important indicators for risk of suicidality than is an inner experience of depression. She found that depression and drinking could have positive meanings among the Indians at the Flathead Reservation based on the construction of depression, drinking, and suicide in the cultural meaning system of this society. She found that depression signified maturity and a recognition of the tremendous loss the tribe as a whole has experienced through domination and cultural destruction by Anglo American society.

REFERENCES

Barlow, D. H. (1988). *Anxiety and its disorders: The nature and treatment of anxiety and panic.* New York: Guilford Press.

Bebbington, P. (1993). Transcultural aspects of affective disorders. *International Review of Psychiatry, 5,* 145–156.

Beiser, M. (1985). A study of depression among traditional Africans, urban North Americans, and Southeast Asian refugees. In A. Kleinman & B. Good (Eds.), *Culture and depression: Studies in the anthropology and cross-cultural psychiatry of affect and disorder* (pp. 272–298). Berkeley: University of California Press.

Crittenden, K. S., Fugita, S. S., Bae, H., Lamug, C. B. et al. (1992). A cross-cultural study of self-report depressive symptoms among college students. *Journal of Cross-Cultural Psychology, 23,* 163–178.

Desjarlais, R., Eisenberg, L., Good, B., & Kleinman, A. (1995). *World mental health: Problems and priorities in low-income countries.* New York: Oxford University Press.

DiNardo, P. A., & Barlow, D. H. (1990). Syndrome and symptom comorbidity in the anxiety disorders. In J.D. Maser & C. R. Cloninger (Eds.), *Comorbidity of mood and anxiety disorders* (pp. 205–230). Washington, DC: American Psychiatric Press.

Ebert, D., & Martus, P. (1994). Somatization as a core symptom of melancholic type depression: Evidence from a cross-cultural study. *Journal of Affectve Disorders, 32,* 253–256.

Ebigbo, P. O. (1982). Development of a cultural specific (Nigeria) screening scale of somatic complaints indicating psychiatric disturbance. *Culture, Medicine and Psychiatry, 6,* 29–43.

Furnham, A., & Malik, R. (1994). Cross-cultural beliefs about "depression." *International Journal of Social Psychiatry, 40,* 106–123.

Grossi, V., & Violato, C. (1992). Attempted suicide among adolescents: A stepwise discriminant analysis. *Canadian Journal of Behavioural Science, 24,* 410–412.

Hart, E. E., & Williams, C. L. (1987). *Suicidal behavior and interpersonal network. Crisis, 8,* 112–124.

Hawton, K. (1986). *Suicide and attempted suicide among children and adolescents.* Newbury Park, CA: Sage.

Katon, W., Kleinman, A., & Rosen, G. (1982). Depression and somatization, a review: Part I. *American Journal of Medicine, 72,* 127–135.

Kirmayer, L. J. (1994). Suicide among Canadian aboriginal peoples. *Transcultural Psychiatric Research Review, 31,* 3–58.

Kleinman, A. (1982). Depression and neurasthenia in the People's Republic of China. *Culture, Medicine and Psychiatry, 6,* 1–80.

Kleinman, A. (1986). *Social origins of distress and disease: Depression, neurasthenia, and pain in modern China.* New Haven: Yale University Press.

Kleinman, A., & Kleinman, J. (1995). Remembering the Cultural Revolution: Alienating pains and the pain of alienation/transformation. In T. Y. Lin, W. S. Tseng, & E. K. Yeh (Eds.), *Chinese societies and mental health* (pp. 141–155). New York: Oxford University Press.

Lutz, C. A. (1985). Depression and translation of emotional worlds. In A. Kleinman & B. Good (Eds.), *Culture and depression: Studies in the anthropology and cross-cultural psychiatry of affect and disorder* (pp. 63–100). Berkeley: University of California Press.

Magne-Ingvar, U., Ojehagen, A., & Traskman-Bendz, L. (1992). The social network of people who attempt suicide. *Acta Psychiatrica Scandinavica, 86,* 153–158.

Manson, S. M. (1995). Culture and major depression: Current challenges in the diagnosis of mood disorders. *Psychiatric Clinics of North America, 18,* 487–501.

Manson, S. M., & Good, B. J. (1992). Cultural considerations in the diagnosis of DSM-IV mood disorders. In J. E. Mezzich, A. Kleinman, H. Fabrega, B. Good, G. Johnson-Powell, K. M. Lin, S. Manson, & D. Parron (Eds.), *Cultural proposals for DSM-IV* (pp. 87–103). Submitted to the DSM-IV Task Force by the Steering Committee, NIMH Group on Culture and Diagnosis. Pittsburgh: University of Pittsburgh.

Marsella, A. J., Sartorius, N., Jablensky, A., & Fenton, F. R. (1985). Cross-cultural studies of depressive disorders: An overview. In A. Kleinman & B. Good (Eds.), *Culture and depression: Studies in the anthropology and cross-cultural psychiatry of affect and disorder* (pp. 299–324). Berkeley: University of California Press.

Nolen-Hoeksema, S. (1987). Sex differences in unipolar depression: Evidence and theory. *Psychological Bulletin, 101,* 259–282.

Obeyesekere, G. (1985). Depression, Buddhism, and the work of culture in Sri Lanka. In A. Kleinman & B. Good (Eds.), *Culture and depression: Studies in the anthropology and cross-cultural psychiatry of affect and disorder* (pp. 134–152). Berkeley: University of California Press.

Ohara, K. (1973). The socio-cultural approach for the manic depressive psychosis. *Psychiatrica et Neurologica Japonica, 75,* 263–273.

Rao, A. (1973). Depression: A psychiatric analysis of thirty cases. *Indian Journal of Psychiatry, 15,* 231–236.

Sanderson, W. C., DiNardo, P. A., Rapee, R. M., & Barlow, D. H. (1990). Syndrome comorbidity in patients diagnosed with a DSM-III anxiety disorder. *Journal of Abnormal Psychology, 99,* 308–312.

Sartorius, N., Davidian, H., Ernberg, G., Fenton, F. R., Fujii, I., et al. (Eds.). (1983). *Depressive disorders in different cultures.* Geneva: World Health Organization.

Schieffelin, E. L. (1985). The cultural analysis of depressive affect: An example from New Guinea. In A. Kleinman & B. Good (Eds.), *Culture and depression: Studies in the anthropology and cross-cultural psychiatry of affect and disorder* (pp. 101–133). Berkeley: University of California Press.

Shaffer, D., Garland, A., Gould, M., Fisher, P., & Trautman, P. (1988). Preventing teenage suicide: A critical review. *Journal of the American Academy of Child and Adolescent Psychiatry, 27,* 675–687.

Shinfuku, N., Karasawa, A., Yamada, O., Tuasaki, S., Kanai, A., & Kawashima, K. (1973). Changing clinical pictures of depression. *Psychological Medicine, 15,* 955–965.

Tanaka-Matsumi, J., & Marsella, A. J. (1976). Cross-cultural variations in the phenomenological experience of depression: Word association. *Journal of Cross-Cultural Psychology, 7,* 379–396.

Terminsen, J., & Ryan, J. (1970). Health and disease in a British Columbian community. *Canadian Psychiatric Association Journal, 15,* 121–127.

Thornicroft, G., & Sartorius, N. (1993). The course and outcome of depression in different cultures: 10-year follow-up of the WHO collaborative study on the assessment of depressive disorders. *Psychological Medicine, 23,* 1023–1032.

Tseng, W. S., & Hsu, J. (1969). Chinese culture, personality formation and mental illness. *International Journal of Social Psychiatry, 16,* 5–14.

Ulusahin, A., Basoglu, M., & Paykel, E. S. (1994). A cross-cultural comparative study of depressive symptoms in British and Turkish clinical samples. *Social Psychiatry and Psychiatric Epidemiology, 29,* 31–39.

Weissman, M. M., Bruce, M. L., Leaf, P. J., Florio, L. P., & Holzer, C. (1991). Affective disorders. In L. N. Robins & D. A. Regier (Eds.), *Psychiatric disorders of America: The epidemiologic catchment area study* (pp. 53–80). New York: Free Press.

THERESA D. O'NELL

"Feeling Worthless"

An Ethnographic Investigation of Depression and
Problem Drinking at the Flathead Reservation

ABSTRACT. The study of depression, drinking and suicidality has long preoccupied students of American Indian life, in part because of the assumed connection between these specific forms of psychiatric distress and generalized demoralization. Given the significant variation in suicidal behavior and prevalence rates intertribally, this assumption deserves closer attention. Recently, researchers working with Western populations have sought to clarify the relationships among depression, alcohol abuse and suicidality through an explicit investigation of their comorbidity. Using data collected at the Flathead Reservation, this paper explores the degree to which the investigation of the comorbidity of these three disorders can validly reveal the relevant contours of psychopathological distress in a cross-cultural setting. The data show that while the comorbidity of problem drinking and depression can sometimes indicate severe psychopathological distress, measured in this case by suicidality, comorbidity cannot account for another group at high risk for suicide. The discrepancy is explicable with reference to the cultural construction of depression, drinking and suicidality in relation to the creation, maintenance and disruption of social bonds, rather than in relation to an internal state of demoralization.

INTRODUCTION

Anthropologists and other students of American Indian life have long demonstrated an interest in the problems of psychiatric disorder, alcohol abuse and suicide.[1] Despite convincing evidence of significant intertribal variation in suicidal behavior (Humphrey and Kupferer 1982; Levy 1965; Miller and Schoenfeld 1971; Shore 1975), in prevalence of psychiatric disorders (Roy et al. 1970; Sampath 1974; Shore et al. 1973) and in alcohol use (Levy and Kunitz 1971; May 1986; Weisner et al. 1984; Westermeyer 1974), some investigators and commentators continue to assume universally high rates across American Indian populations (Burd et al. 1987; Hochkirchen and Jilek 1985). The endurance of this assumption can be traced, in part, to a second and related assumption that alcohol abuse, suicide, and certain psychiatric disorders, particularly depression, are specific but related signs of the supposedly ubiquitous demoralization affecting American Indians (Foulks 1980; Guyette 1982; Hochkirchen and Jilek 1985; Shkilnyk 1985). This second assumption persists, again, despite studies that demonstrate that practices of drinking and suicide, for example, may carry meanings other than demoralization when located within their cultural contexts (Devereux 1961; Everett 1970; Levy 1965; Levy and Kunitz 1974; Pine 1981; Waddell 1975).

The pervasiveness of these assumptions and their face validity derive in part form the culturally-grounded common-sense notion in mainstream American society that depression, alcoholism and suicide are alternative, perhaps progressive, and perhaps sex-typed, expressions of demoralization. However, the relationships among depression, drinking and suicide are far from clear even within Western populations (Goodwin 1973; Guze and Robins 1970; Kielholz 1970; Schuckit 1979; Woodruff et al. 1973). Recent research on the comorbidity of psychiatric disorders has sought to clarify aspects of these relationships by directly questioning the frequency with which and the ways in which certain disorders overlap within populations, within the lifetimes of individuals, and in time for certain individuals (Berglund 1984; Black et al. 1987; Brown and Schuckit 1988; Hesselbrock et al. 1988; Hirschfeld et al. 1990; Jaffe and Ciraulo 1986; Meyer 1986; Meyer and Kranzler 1990).

Comorbidity, which by definition treats as problematic the relationships between and among psychiatric disorders, such as alcohol abuse and depression, impels us to examine our assumptions about the relationships between these behaviors among culturally diverse populations.

In this paper, the heuristic force of comorbidity, considered as an analytic tool for assessing psychopathological distress in American Indian populations, is examined with respect to the problems of depression, problem drinking and suicide among tribal members of two tribes living on a reservation in the inter-montane Plateau region of the northwest United States. Among these people, depression frequently is expressed as loneliness, a powerful idiom that can connote either a positive sense of belonging or a distressing sense of separation. In a similar way, drinking that appears pathological in psychiatric terms may or may not be evaluated negatively in local terms. At first glance, then, neither "depression" nor "problem drinking" straightforwardly express demoralization, suggesting that the relationship between depressive disorders and alcohol abuse may not be as alternative expressions of demoralization for these American Indian people. In this cross-cultural context, the question becomes, "To what extent can the investigation of the comorbidity of depression and alcohol abuse validly reveal the relevant contours of psychopathological distress in this population?"

THE SETTING

The data used to address the issues of comorbidity were "borrowed," in a sense, from my ethnographic and clinical study of depression among adult members of the Salish and Pend d'Oreilles tribes at the Flathead Reservation. The Flathead Reservation is home to about half of the approximately 6,000 enrolled members of the Salish, Pend d'Oreilles, and Kootenai, three tribes who were brought together when the reservation was created by the Hellgate treaty of 1855. Two of the tribes, the Salish and the Pend d'Oreilles, share the same native language and many cultural practices. It was among the people of these two tribes, to be referred to collectively throughout the remainder of the paper as the Flathead Indians, that my research on adult depression was conducted.[2]

The Flathead Reservation is one of the more beautiful locations in western Montana. Magnificent snow-capped mountains, a felt presence, line the reservation to the east, south and west. The spectacular Flathead Lake lies to the north. On the eastern side of the reservation, the fertile Flathead valley forms a north-south corridor through which a major state highway passes. On the west, the meandering Flathead river cuts through prairies, highly valued for the traditional food roots that continue to grow there. At one time nearly 90% of the original reservation acreage had been lost to non-Indians, much of it through the Flathead Allotment Act of 1904 in which "surplus" land was made available to white homesteaders (Confederated Salish and Kootenai Tribes n.d.). Today, however, as a result of an aggressive buy-back plan, about one-half of the reservation, including over 300,000 acres of forest lands, is held either by individual Indians or by the tribal government (Confederated Salish and Kootenai Tribes n.d.).

Nearly 20,000 people reside on the Flathead Reservation, making it one of the more densely populated areas, outside of the cities, in the state of Montana (Malone and Roeder 1976). According to the 1980 U.S. Census, Indians on the reservation made up slightly less than 20% of the total population (U.S. Bureau of the Census 1980). Another source estimates the percentage of Salish, Pend d'Oreilles and Kootenai Indians at an even lower rate of 18% (Salish-Kootenai College 1989). The Indian population is scattered across the reservation, with the Kootenai concentrating in the northern section around the lake, and Salish and Pend d'Oreilles living predominantly in the central and southern portions of the reservation. Although many tribal members live in trailers or houses on individual lots away from town, many also live in one of the seventeen small towns, that range in population from a few hundred to three thousand.

Prior to the arrival of whites, Flathead life had been ordered by the traditional hunting and gathering subsistence patterns common to the Plateau region (Flathead Culture Committee 1988; Spencer et al. 1977).[3] Historically, the Flathead tribes were known for the large number of horses they possessed and their warring relationship with the Blackfeet, a neighboring tribe (Bradley 1923; Haines 1938; Thompson 1971; Turney-High 1935). The Flathead people were also renowned among fur traders and early settlers for their piety and their friendliness (Chalfant 1974; DeSmet 1969; Fuller 1974; Philips 1974; Saum 1965). These qualities are often used by historians and by the Flathead people themselves to explain their rapid conversion to Catholicism in the mid-1800s and their high rates of intermarriage with whites and with members of other tribes (DeSmet 1969; Forbis 1951; Moyer 1961; Trosper 1976).

Today, horses no longer play an important role in tribal life, and warfare has been reduced to the purely symbolic level in which the Blackfeet are simply one of the favorite butts of Flathead jokes. However, friendliness and piety continue to mark self-definitions of tribal identity as well as the descriptive reports of visitors to the reservation. It is these two qualities, of heart and spirit, that help to define Flathead culture and the way in which contemporary reservation life is patterned and transformed. In particular, heart and spirit emphasize the ties of affection that grow out of and perpetuate the interdependence of all living beings. Within this context depression and drinking become meaningful in relation to the creation, maintenance, and disruption of social bonds, rather than in relation to an internal state.

THE STUDY

As part of my research project on adult depression, I conducted over 50 interviews with treatment providers, elders of the tribes, and other members of the reservation community over a period of eighteen months in 1987 and 1988. Twenty of those interviews, to be referred to as the "depressive experience interviews," form the basis for the following discussion of comorbidity. Although I began to collect the depressive experience interviews as early as five months into the research period, I conducted most in the final six months, after I had attained a degree of familiarity with the culture and social practices of the reservation community.

The depressive experience interviews, ranging in length from 45 minutes to $3\frac{1}{2}$ hours, were rich, culturally informed accounts about the phenomenological realities of depression for the respondents. The accounts were also sufficiently informative to enable me to make diagnostic decisions about the presence or absence of psychiatric disorders for each respondent using DSM-III criteria (American Psychiatric Association 1980).[4] The interviews were loosely structured around the respondents' experiences with depression, suicidality and help-seeking behaviors in a way that avoided posing direct questions, especially at the start of the interview, and thus avoided breaching local practices of respectful dialogue.[5]

Interviews opened with a general invitation for the respondent to describe the worst depression he or she had ever experienced, and each episode related by the respondent was probed for additional detail, often with merely a period of silence that encouraged the respondent to elaborate. The open-ended style was guided at times, however, by particular research interests, for example, in specific symptoms, treatment efficacy, drinking history, marital history, participation in the Indian community, or childhood experiences. Overall, however, respondents were encouraged to talk about what was important about their experiences with depression from their own perspective.

All twenty respondents were solicited for the study because they described themselves as having suffered with depression. They were solicited in varying ways. I approached eleven of the twenty respondents informally in private conversations at community events, such as a conference for Adult Children of Alcoholics, or in public places, such as at a bar, at the local college, or at another of the community gathering spots. Six of the respondents were longer-term acquaintances who agreed to be interviewed. The three elders who appear in the sample were invited to participate in the study during visits I made to their homes.

To the extent that respondents not only felt that they had experienced significant problems with depression and were interested in sharing that information, the sample resembles a clinical population. As in clinical studies, the problems of depression reported by respondents in the sample should not, and cannot, be assumed generalizable to all members of the community, or even to all who have experienced depression: this was not a "population" study. On the other hand, problems of depression are significant in the lives of many Flathead Indian people, and the cultural and behavioral patterns that are revealed in the study have value for understanding the experiences of depression in this population.[6]

As noted, respondents in the sample were not randomly drawn, but an effort was made to balance the sample in terms of age and sex during the period of research. The ten men and ten women in the sample ranged in age from 29 years to 79 years, with an average of 49 years and a median of 46 years. (See Table I.) One respondent was in his twenties; five respondents were in their thirties; five were in their forties; four were in their fifties; two were in their sixties; and three were in their seventies. The women were a slightly older group, ranging from 32 years to 79 years of age with an average of 52.8 years and a median of 50.5 years. The three oldest respondents in the sample were women. The men, on the other hand, accounted for the three youngest respondents. As a group, the men ranged in age from 29 years to 66 years and had an average age of 45.1 years and a median of 44.5 years.

Thirteen of the twenty respondents were single at the time of the interview by virtue of having been widowed (four respondents), being legally separated (three respondents), or being divorced (six respondents). (See Table I.) Of the remaining seven, five were legally married and two had been living with a partner for at least a year. The nineteen respondents who had been married at least once average two marriages each.

Of the sixteen respondents in the sample who were under the age of retirement, ten, or 62.5%, were employed full-time during the year preceding the interview. A 1980 Salish Kootenai College (S & K) survey of 922 community members produced a lower figure of 39% full-time employment (10–12 months) over the year, with 54% of their sample employed at the time of the survey (Salish and Kootenai College 1980). Most of the observed difference may be understood in terms of the difference in the age and sex composition of the two samples. In contrast to the interview sample, respondents in the S & K survey were overwhelmingly female (63%) and young (42% were under age 30). Young people, in general, are often unemployed or underemployed due to the difficulty of finding jobs at the reservation. In particular, young women who have children are often unemployed and receive public assistance.

Despite the fact that much of the difference between the S & K survey and the interview sample can be explained in terms of the age and gender composition of the respective groups of respondents, the interview sample probably does reflect higher

Table I
Interview sample characteristics

Case	Sex	Age (Yrs.)	Marital Status*	Employed Full-time over Last Year	Blood Quantum**
1	M	29	M (nl)		no info
2	M	30	D	X	D
3	M	30	M (s)		B
4	F	32	M (s)	X	B
5	F	33	D	X	C
6	F	34	D		B
7	M	43	W	X	A
8	F	43	D	X	A
9	M	44	M	X	A
10	M	45	D	X	C
11	F	47	D		C
12	M	50	M	X	C
13	F	54	M		B
14	M	55	M (nl)		A
15	M	59	M	X	A
16	F	61	M	X	B
17	M	66	M (s)		B
18	F	72	W		A
19	F	73	W		B
20	F	79	W		A

* M = married; M (nl) = married (not legal); M (s) = married (separated); D = divorced; W = widowed
** A = $3/4$ and up; B = $1/2$ to just under $3/4$; C = $1/4$ to just under $1/2$; D = under $1/4$

rates of full-time employment than the general Indian community. Employed persons were easier to solicit for the depressive experience interviews simply because they were more likely to be in public settings, a work site being a prime example, where a casual comment might suffice as a basis for self-introductions. On the other had, many unemployed people spent much of their time at home or visiting in the homes of relatives or friends where an attempt to solicit an interview without an introduction by a mutual acquaintance would be met with suspicion. While a sample that included more unemployed respondents might have produced a higher prevalence of serious pathology, it probably would have been similar to the actual interview sample in terms of lifetime incidence since most of the respondents in the sample had at other times in their lives also been unemployed or underemployed for significant periods of time.

In comparison to a sample of the enrolled membership, the interview sample was weighted toward higher degrees of blood quantum. (See Table II.) Seventy percent (70%) of the interview sample had blood quantum measurements *over* $1/2$ (categories A and B), compared to only 28.5% of the sample of enrolled mem-

bership. Conversely, only 25% of the interview sample had blood quantum measurements *less* than $1/2$ (categories C and D), compared to 71.5% of the enrolled membership sample. The preponderance of respondents with higher blood quantum measurements and of older respondents in the interview sample helps to explain the high proportion, relative to the community, of nine bilingual speakers of both Salish and English to eleven monolingual English speakers.

The almost reversed percentages of degrees of blood quantum between the interview sample and the enrolled membership sample is likely due in part to the exclusion of children from the interview sample. Children often have lower blood quantum measurements due to intermarriage between tribal members and non-tribal members. Furthermore, the enrolled membership sample includes a number of adults with lower blood quantum measurements (who were enrolled before changes in enrollment regulations in 1951 and 1960) who tended not to participate in the Indian community. In the investigator's estimation, the interview sample is probably more representative of the adult members of the Indian community than the enrolled membership sample.

Table II
Blood quantum distribution: enrolled membership sample and interview sample

	Degree of Blood Quantum				
	A *over 75%**	B *50%–74%*	C *25%–49%*	D *under 25%*	*Missing* *Data*
Enrollment sample N = 200	18% (36)	10.5% (21)	57.5% (115)	14% (28)	not applicable
Interview sample N = 20	35% (7)	35% (7)	20% (4)	5% (1)	5% (1)

* Blood quantum is usually expressed in a fraction, such as $^1/_2$, $^{11}/_{16}$, or $^{57}/_{64}$. Blood quantum is reported in the table in terms of percentages in order to simplify expression.

THE RESULTS

Like many places in the United States, the word depression is used at the reservation to talk about a variety of experiences, beyond simply clinical depression. This was evident in the fact that there were respondents in the sample who were neither clinically depressed with a major depressive disorder at the time of the interview nor seemed to have been at any point in their lives. However, as a whole, the group evinced significant levels of depressive psychopathology.

Twelve respondents in the sample of twenty, five men and seven women, were diagnosed by the researcher as suffering from *major depressive disorder* (MDD) at some point in their lives. Four of the twelve respondents, including three women and one man, were diagnosed with MDD at the time of the interview. (See Table III.) Two of the women were taking anti-depressant medication at the time of the interview. The third woman had stopped taking an anti-depressant medication about six months prior to the interview and seemed to be experiencing a recurrence of her depressive symptoms. The fourth respondent, a young man who was diagnosed with MDD at the time of the interview, was hospitalized and put on anti-depressants and anti-anxiety medication after a suicide attempt that took place within two months of the interview.

In addition to the four respondents who were suffering from MDD at the time of the interview, thirteen respondents were diagnosed with *dysthymic disorder* (DD) at the time of the interview. (See Table III.) Excluding for the moment the issue of alcohol abuse, only four respondents with DD did not receive an additional diagnosis. Seven of the thirteen respondents with DD had experienced at least one episode of MDD in their lifetimes. Since the presence of DD preceding each episode of MDD was not effectively determined in each interview, this figure reflects lifetime comorbidity only and does not necessarily imply a high rate of *concurrently* comorbid MDD and DD, better known as "double depression" (Keller and Shapiro 1982). Nonetheless, the prevalence of dysthymic disorder among the respondents with MDD suggests that "double depression" may be important at the reservation. In line with these indications in the data, Manson et al. (1985) reported that 50% of a clinic sample of Hopi respondents were found to be suffering from comorbid MDD and dysthymia.[7]

Three respondents were also diagnosed with non-affective disorders, again setting aside the issue of alcoholism for the moment. (See Table III.) In addition to an episode of MDD several years prior to the interview, one young male respondent (Case 1) was diagnosed with antisocial personality disorder. He also received a diagnosis of DD at the time of the interview that was probably secondary to his personality disorder. A male respondent in his sixties (Case 17) was diagnosed as suffering from both generalized anxiety disorder and DD. One female respondent in her thirties (Case 4) received a diagnosis of adjustment disorder with mixed emotional features (anxiety and depression) for a week-long episode occurring two years prior to the interview. She also was diagnosed at the time of the interview with DD that included the clear presence of anxiety symptoms.

Symptoms of anxiety were commonly reported. (see Table III.) Five of the twelve respondents who had lifetime diagnoses

Table III
Diagnoses in the interview sample

Case	MDD Lifetime	MDD Current	DD Current	Other Diagnosis
1	X*		X	1
2	X		X	
3	X*	X*	-	
4			X*	2
5			X	
6	X		X*	
7			X	
8	X*		X	
9	X		X	
10	X		X	
11	X*	on meds	-	
12				
13	X	X	-	
14			X*	
15				
16			X*	
17			X	3
18	X*			
19	X	on meds	-	
20	X		X	

*with anxiety symptoms;
1 - antisocial personality disorder;
2 - adjustment disorder with mixed emotional features;
3 - generalized anxiety disorder.

of MDD reported symptoms of anxiety in conjunction with episodes of depression including two cases with panic attacks. Four of the thirteen respondents with diagnoses of DD at the time of the interview also reported anxiety symptoms as part of their experiences. This last figure does not include the older male respondent with generalized anxiety disorder.

Table IV shows information collected on alcohol use among the depressive experience interview respondents.[8] For all practical purposes, no information pertaining to personal drinking histories was elicited from the three elders in the sample, beyond the facts that all had histories of drinking and that none were drinking at the time of the interview. Because the status of elder is morally inconsistent with a history of problem drinking, it would have been inappropriate to question an elder about his or her previous drinking patterns.[9] Summary descriptions of alcohol use in the sample exclude the three elders unless otherwise noted.

Every respondent reported periods of heavy, ego-dystonic drinking that involved blackouts and adverse consequences such as losing money, getting into a fight, wrecking a car, or being unable to make it into work on time because of a hangover. Despite the universality of problem drinking, however, respondents described varying degrees of trouble with their drinking. Based on their own descriptions, the severity of each respondent's difficulty with drinking has been grouped into one of three categories: mild, moderate and severe. (See Table IV.) The following examples and comparisons will help to clarify how assignments of severity were made. Only one respondent fell into the "mild" category. She described an incident in which she had gone out drinking with friends and ended up blacking out and losing both her friends and her car. However, she reported that she rarely drank to the point of intoxication and that episodes like this plagued her "less than once a year."

Each of the ten respondents who reported problem drinking of "moderate" severity described incidents similar to the one mentioned above but noted that they occurred with greater frequency. Moderate problem drinkers usually described one of

Table IV
Alcohol use in the interview sample

Case	Problem Drinking Lifetime	Severity	Age at First Drink	Drinking Currently	Years Sober	Treatment
1	X	moderate	under 10	X		(unknown)
2	X	moderate	under 12		13	yes
3	X	severe	early teens	X		yes
4	X	moderate	11		3	yes
5	X	mild	12	X		no
6	X	moderate	14		15	no
7	X	moderate	(unknown)		3	no
8	X	moderate	late teens	X		no
9	X	severe	16		10	(unknown)
10	X	severe	13		8	yes
11	X	moderate	12	X		yes
12	X	moderate	(unknown)		13	no
13	X	severe	under 10		1	no
14	X	moderate	late teens		5	no
15	X	severe	(unknown)		20	yes
16	X	moderate	(unknown)		5	no
17	X	severe	late teens	X		yes
18	X	(unknown)	(unknown)		(unknown)	(unknown)
19	X	(unknown)	(unknown)		(unknown)	(unknown)
20	X	(unknown)	(unknown)		(unknown)	(unknown)

two patterns of drinking: either heavy weekend drinking, that often involved round the clock drinking, or binge drinking lasting four or five days, usually during periods of unemployment. Drinking did not usually result in loss of employment for the respondents in this group, although job performance was often affected; for example, some reported arriving at work late due to a hangover, having left early to settle a legal difficulty, or having been absent due to accidental injury. Whether or not family members disapproved of the respondent's drinking or were, in fact, the principal drinking partners of the respondent, family difficulties, including resentment, concern, and some sexual and physical abuse, were common in this category of severity. However, they rarely reached the point of legal action, such as divorce or the removal of children from the respondent's home.

Of the six respondents who reported severe problem drinking, all described periods of drinking that extended for weeks and sometimes months at a time, with a few days "rest" scattered throughout the period. Severe problem drinkers reported examples of serious social impairment, such as serving time in jail or

prison for alcohol related offenses, neglecting family members or being unable to hold a job for longer than it took to make some money to purchase alcohol. These respondents were known locally during their drinking days as "hardcore" drinkers.

On the whole, respondents began drinking very early in their lives. The age at which the respondent had his or her first drink provides a rough barometer for when respondents began to drink regularly. Four respondents had their first drink in their late teens, six in their early teens, one when she was twelve, and two when they were under the age of ten. (See Table IV.)

Six respondents were drinking at the time of the interviewing process. The remaining eleven respondents had been sober for varying amounts of time, ranging from one to twenty years. The seven male respondents who had quit drinking had quit respectively around the ages of 17, 34, 37, 38, 40 and 50. The four female respondents who had quit drinking quit respectively around the ages of 19, 29, 53 and 55. The other three "sober" female respondents were elders for whom this information was lacking.[10] Seven respondents had been to treatment of some

Table V
Lifetime and concurrent comorbidity of MDD and problem drinking

Case	Drinking Lifetime	MDD Lifetime	Comorbidity Lifetime	Comorbidity Concurrent
1	X	X	X	
2	X	X	X	X
3	X*	X	X	X
6	X	X	X	
8	X	X	X	X
9	X*	X	X	X
10	X*	X	X	X
11	X	X	X	X
13	X*	X	X	X**
18	X	X	X	
19	X	X	X	
20	X	X	X	

* = severe problem drinking.
** = also experienced MDD during a period in which she was not actively drinking.

form or another, eight had not, and information was lacking for the remaining two.

Table V provides information on the comorbidity of the MDD and moderate or severe problem drinking in the sample. Since all twelve respondents with MDD had had difficulties with problem drinking at some point in their lives, lifetime comorbidity is simply a given in this sample. Concurrent comorbidity of MDD and problem drinking may be a more useful dimension for understanding individual variation in the sample. Out of the twelve respondents, six had MDD at a time when they were actively drinking. A seventh suffered from depression both in and out of drinking phases. The remaining five reported episodes of MDD that were clearly not comorbid in time with periods of drinking: one had been incarcerated for about three years, one had quit drinking three years before the onset of her depression, and the other three were elders who had not been drinking for a number of years.

For the most part, given the young ages at which most respondents began to drink, the onset of problem drinking preceded the onset of major depressive disorder or the two problems shared an insidious beginning. In three cases, all young men who began drinking heavily in their teens, there was clear evidence of problem drinking preceding the onset of depression. Two respondents, one man and one woman, described completely intertwined histories of drinking and depression beginning in their late teens and early twenties. In only one case, does a respondent describe heavy drinking that began *after* the onset of MDD. The woman, whose problems with depression

began when she was in her mid-thirties and going through a divorce while still grieving the loss of a parent, described a severe depression for which she was prescribed anti-depressant medication. Her depression cleared for a period of time but returned when she began "running around" after her divorce and started drinking very heavily. In a second case, another woman of the same age and in very similar circumstances, described the coincident onset of her depression and problem drinking.

Table VI reports information collected on suicide attempts among the interview respondents. A total of eight respondents, five men and three women, attempted suicide at least once. While two respondents had each attempted suicide several times, each of the remaining six had made only a single attempt. Four of the five male respondents who attempted suicide made their attempts when they were in their thirties. Two female respondents made their attempts when they were under twenty years of age, at 14 years of age and at 19 years of age, respectively. The two respondents who had attempted suicide on multiple occasions, did so at various ages. The male respondent made his first attempt at age 14, made two attempts in his twenties, and made an attempt at age 30. The female respondent began to make suicide attempts in her twenties and made her last attempt when she was 42.

Table VI shows that only three respondents made plans to take their own lives. The remainder insisted that their attempts followed at most after a few hours of deliberation. Half of the respondents ingested pills during their attempts to kill themselves. Two respondents intended to shoot themselves but did not pull

Table VI
Suicide attempts in the interview sample

Case	Sex	Age(s) at Attempt(s)	Method	Plan	Drinking	MDD
3	M	14, 20's 30	o.d., gun, o.d. & gun	X	X*	X
4	F	19	cut wrists		X	
6	F	14	o.d.		X	
9	M	32	o.d.		X*	X
10	M	32	cut wrists		X*	X
11	F	20's–40's	o.d.	X	X	X
12	M	34	gun	X	X	
15	M	38	jump out window		X*	

* = having "severe" problem drinking.

the trigger. One of the respondents who was going to use a gun had already ingested pills. Two other respondents cut their wrists, both severely enough to be hospitalized. One respondent contemplated jumping from a third floor window.

Tables VIIa, VIIb, and VIIc combine information of drinking, depression, and suicide attempts. Table VIIa compares males and females who were diagnosed with MDD on the basis of whether they attempted suicide or not. Table VIIb shows that of the eight respondents who attempted suicide none had MDD alone, four were drinking but did not have MDD, and four had concurrently comorbid MDD and problem drinking. Table VIIc is a two-by-two table that divides the interview sample into those who attempted suicide and those who did not and compares them on the basis of whether or not the two groups differed in terms of having concurrently comorbid MDD and problem drinking. Four out of the eight respondents who attempted suicide had both MDD and problem drinking whereas only two out of the twelve respondents who did not attempt suicide had comorbid MDD and problem drinking.

DISCUSSION

Analyzed from the perspective of the comorbidity of major depressive disorder and problem drinking, interview results of the study of adult depression at the Flathead Reservation indicate that comorbidity is relatively frequent in this sample of persons who identify themselves as having suffered "depression." Of the twelve in the sample who received diagnoses of MDD, seven were seen to have concurrent difficulties with moderate or severe problem drinking. Furthermore, there are suggestions in the data that the comorbidity of MDD and problem drinking is a

Table VIIa
Suicide attempts among respondents with MDD

	Suicide Attempt	No Attempt	Total
Males	4	1	5
Females	1	6	7
Total	5	7	12

Table VIIb
Comorbidity of MDD and problem drinking among respondents attempting suicide

	Drinking Only	MDD Only	Comorbid	Total
Males	2	0	3	5
Females	2	0	1	3
Total	4	0	4	8

Table VIIc
Suicide attempts among respondents with comorbidity of MDD and problem drinking and among respondents without comorbidity of MDD and problem drinking (n.s., Fisher exact probability test, one-tailed, p = 0.14)

	Suicide Attempt	No Attempt	Total
Comorbid	4	2	6
Not comorbid	4	10	14
Total	8	12	20

lethal combination. Half of the eight respondents who attempted suicide were diagnosable with concurrently comorbid MDD and problem drinking, whereas only two of the twelve respondents who had never attempted suicide were suffering from both MDD and problem drinking at the same time.

These provocative results indicate without question that additional research with larger numbers of respondents is warranted. Larger numbers by themselves, however, are insufficient to answer important questions about the comorbidity of MDD and problem drinking in this population. At one level, comorbidity holds out the promise of moving clinicians, diagnosticians, and researchers one step closer to grasping the phenomenological reality of psychopathological distress. Viewed from a cross-cultural perspective, however, comorbidity research presents the uncomfortable possibility of committing a "category fallacy" time two (Kleinman 1977). Furthermore, the process of establishing the cultural validity of comorbidity is complicated by a factor of three. Not only must each of the comorbid disorders be investigated ethnographically, but the connection of the specific form of comorbidity itself to local and individual signs of distress needs to be documented.

Researchers must be doubly cautious about comorbidity which, relying as it does on two or more diagnoses, carries the danger of transporting Western researchers from the already shaky ground of one potentially culturally inappropriate diagnosis to the even shakier ground of two or more potentially culturally inappropriate diagnoses. Comorbidity, just like any single psychiatric disorder, must be referenced to phenomenologically real pain in order to avoid the possibility of invalid results that can confuse ongoing research efforts. The experiential validity of comorbidity must also be established in order to avoid the possibilities of creating debilitating stereotypes and promoting medicalized demoralization, both of which increase rather than ameliorate personal distress.

Earlier, mention was made of heart and spirit as symbols central to an understanding to Flathead life. Briefly, heart signifies the profound and sentient awareness the Flathead people have of human dependence on one another, and spirit signifies the interdependence of human life with the power of the creator. Children do not have much heart or spirit, both of which take an awareness of suffering and pain that naturally develops with time and experience. It is a mark of maturity to feel profound loneliness when separated from loved ones, to feel sorrow for the pain one has caused others, and to feel pity for those who have nothing. Naturally, it is the elders whose hearts feel the most pain, for it is they who have suffered the most losses.

Depression, therefore, can be a positive expression of belonging in this milieu. To be sad is to be aware of human interdependence and the gravity of historical, tribal, familial and personal loss. To be depressed, and that includes tearfulness and sleep and appetite disturbances, is to demonstrate maturity and connectedness to the Indian world. A carefree attitude is often thought of as indicative of immaturity.

Life within the Flathead community is characterized, ideally, by close affective ties of kinship and friendship as well as by expectations of generous sharing among one's group of family and friends. It is also characterized at times, however, by feelings of loneliness, of not being cared for, of having nothing, or, worst of all, by fears of being abandoned. Loneliness is a term of distress that appeared at every turn in my study of adult depression at the Flathead Reservation. Thus, loneliness and depression can be the expressions of profound distress as well as the expressions of a positive moral virtue.

Loneliness always seems related to the disruption of affective and instrumental relationships but is a term that nonetheless seems to encompass three very different kinds of experiences. First, loneliness is used to talk about the feelings of grief that follow the death of a loved one. Feeling griefstricken often entails experiencing a sequence of tragic deaths that leave no time for recovery. Second, loneliness is used to talk about feelings of being aggrieved because of unfulfilled expectations of support or aid. Feeling aggrieved is usually described in terms of anger or irritability because of the undeserved shame of being treated so poorly. Finally, loneliness is used to talk about feelings of abandonment with an internalized sense of worthlessness. This final type of loneliness, feeling worthless, resonates with a statement made nearly sixty years ago by Turney-High (1937), in which he wrote, "One of the strongest Flathead insults indicates that no one wants you because you are of no more value than a wornout [sic] article. 'You are abandoned, thrown away!' is a very grave taunt."

Drinking is also a powerful element within this world. However, *its* meaning, like that of "depression," is not always pathological. Consonant with Flathead values, drinking, even drinking that passes threshold criteria for alcohol abuse in the DSM-III, is at times a positive expression of sociality, a reaffirmation of bonds of kinship and friendship through the sharing of resources and time. In this context, *not* drinking is sometimes seen as a slight against family and friends, and drinking is often used as a way to remain part of a group and to avoid loneliness.

On the other hand, as the interview material shows, drinking is far from a uniformly positive experience. Drinking, in spite of its possibilities for reaffirming and cementing affective ties, carries a tremendous potential for disrupting those very same ties. Because drinking can induce a state of "not caring about anything," people who are drinking often act in ways that are antithetical to proper social relations. The universality of claims of "blackouts" among the interview respondents underscores the moral ambivalence with which acts performed while intoxicated are viewed.

Given this brief exposition of Flathead culture and ethnopsychology, the question remains as to whether MDD, alcohol abuse, and the comorbidity of the two capture significant aspects of psychopathological distress at the Flathead Reservation. The answer, I believe, is "Yes, they do, but in somewhat complicated ways." MDD seems to be related in an essential way to feeling griefstricken and to feeling worthless, but not to feeling aggrieved. However, of the two types of loneliness that are associated with depression, feeling griefstricken was not associated with suicidality whereas feeling worthless was.

Table VIIa, showing suicide attempts among respondents with MDD, can be explained with reference to these two local signs of distress. Feeling griefstricken is a condition that is associated with older people whose hearts have felt loss and who are therefore more sensitive to loss. Suicide is not an option not only because it would wound those left behind but because suicide is a direct transgression against the words of the elders who have passed before. Feeling griefstricken was reported mostly by older women in the sample, explaining the relative lack of suicide attempts among female respondents with MDD.

Feeling worthless, on the other hand, was reported mostly by young men in the sample, explaining the relative preponderance of suicide attempts among male respondents with MDD. Feeling worthless is a condition marked by feelings of guilt for being selfish, acting without thought or regard for others. It is a condition, I would argue, that is to be expected in young men in their late twenties or thirties who are making the difficult transition from the status of "condoned irresponsibility," to put it crudely, to assuming roles as young leaders in their families and in the community. Finally, feeling aggrieved, which is most often associated with teenagers and jilted lovers, is not strongly related to MDD but is marked by suicidality, explaining why three of the eight respondents who attempted suicide do not appear in Table VIIa.[11]

Thus, MDD appears to capture a relevant dimension of distress at the reservation. It fails, however, to distinguish the profoundly important difference between respondents with MDD who are suicidal and those who are not. Comorbidity, on the other hand, seems to select that group of respondents whose intense "loneliness" is translated into a sense of feeling worthless and whose severe problem drinking no longer functions to strengthen relationships but merely induces a long-term state of "not caring." Yet neither MDD nor the comorbidity of MDD and problem drinking capture another group at relatively high risk for suicide attempt, those who are feeling aggrieved.

In conclusion, it would appear that depression, heavy drinking, and their comorbidity do sometimes indicate psychopathological distress among adults at the Flathead Reservation. However, the relationships among alcohol abuse, depression and suicidality are not entirely what Western researchers might assume.[12] Depression, drinking, and suicide each carry meanings

at the reservation beyond that of demoralization. Depression and drinking, in particular, can have positive connotations. Clearly, Western researchers would be well advised to approach the comorbidity of psychiatric disorders among American Indian populations with a critical alertness to the local, culturally-constituted signs of distress.

Acknowledgements

This paper has been authorized for publication by tribal representatives at the Flathead Reservation. The authorship of this paper was supported by the Mood, Anxiety and Personality Disorders Research Branch, Division of Clinical Research, NIMH. The research upon which the paper is based was supported by a Wenner Gren Dissertation Grant, a Sigma-Xi Grant-in-Aid of Research, and a National Center for American Indian and Alaska Native Mental Health Research Award. Special training in psychiatric diagnosis was supported by the NIMH-funded Training Program in Clinically Relevant Medical Anthropology (MH 18006), Department of Social Medicine, Harvard Medical School.

The author would like to thank members of the Flathead Culture Committee and staff of the Mental Health Program at the Flathead Reservation for their responses to a previous version of this paper. The author also would like to thank Carl W. O'Nell for comments on an earlier draft of this paper. I am also grateful to Byron Good for helpful comments.

NOTES

[1]See Kelso (1981) for a bibliography of mental health research among American Indians. See Shore (1983) and O'Nell (1989) for reviews of psychiatric investigations among American Indians. See Leland (1976) and Mail (1980) for bibliographies on alcohol use among American Indians. See Peters (1981), McIntosh (1981), and May (1990) for bibliographies on suicide among American Indians.

[2]The Kootenai are linguistically unrelated to the Salish and the Pend d'Oreilles, and have remained socially separated, to a degree, from the latter.

[3]Spencer et al. (1977) locate the Plateau culture area between the Rocky Mountains on the east and the Cascade mountains on the west, bounded on the north by the Frazer River and shading off to the south into the semi-desert of the Great Basin. The Flathead tribes live on the eastern side of the Plateau area and are held by the authors to exhibit Plains culture traits in addition to Plateau traits.

[4]The researcher received special training in psychiatric diagnosis prior to conducting this research and completed three internships at the Lindemann Hospital in Boston, MA, and with the Cambridge City Hospital and Cambridge Public School System in Cambridge, MA. Although this diagnostic process does not match the reliability of other processes, i.e., based on standardized instruments or replication, it goes beyond the clinical naivete of many fieldworkers.

[5]Direct questioning is often considered impolite except when the question stems directly from the questioner's misunderstanding of some information already given.

[6]My unwillingness to attach probabilistic assessments to my observations that would allow for generalizations about all Flathead adults follows from obvious inferential principles. Based as it is on a sample of convenience, any such claim would raise warning flags for those knowledgeable about the potentially deleterious effects of small sample size, self-selection, and violations of the assumptions of parametric statistics. If, however, I have done my ethnographic work well, this investigation will have isolated and determined important cultural aspects of these types of experiences in order to generate hypotheses for later probability-based empirical research. It is at this level that my efforts need to be judged.

[7]The Manson et al. research findings are on the high end of rates produced in three studies of treated samples drawn from the general population (Manson et al. 1985). Keller and Shapiro (1982) found that 26% of a sample of patients with MDD also exhibited chronic depression. In a separate study, Keller et al. (1983) reported a 25% figure. Finally, Rounsaville et al. (1980) noted a 36% rate of chronic depression in a sample of MDD outpatients. The prevalence of dysthymia among patients with MDD is echoed in the results of the community based ECA study. Weissman et al. (1988) reported that dysthymic respondents, about 3.1% of the sample, were at high risk for lifetime comorbidity with a number of other psychiatric disorders. Specifically, they found that 38.9% of persons found to be suffering from DD in the ECA study had a lifetime comorbidity with MDD.

[8]The data on alcohol use in this sample were gathered "naively" because the researcher had erroneously imagined being able to collect information on depression without having to deal directly with the issue of alcohol use and abuse. As a result, not only was the researcher unfamiliar with the DSM-III criteria used to differentiate alcohol abuse from alcohol dependence, but she was also unprepared to deal with the diagnostic and theoretical dilemmas attendant upon the 100% incidence of drinking problems in the depressive experience interviews. The "naive" approach had both benefits and drawbacks. On the down side, information about tolerance and withdrawal was not collected in the course of the interview process. On the other hand, the fact that alcohol abuse emerged as significant in every account, despite the researcher's original, if misguided, lack of interest, underscores its importance.

[9]In a review of this paper, some members of the reservation community who are working in the field of alcohol abuse and mental health challenged this statement. Working in a therapeutic capacity, their concern lay in the pragmatic task of eradicating barriers to treatment, including the effects of the "denial" of problems of this sort by high status individuals in the community. Thus, treatment providers are attempting to question elders more and more about their experiences with drinking and such questioning is becoming more appropriate as this perspective spreads across the reservation community. On the other hand, as a visitor to the reservation and a guest in the homes of the elders that I interviewed, I felt less comfortable about pushing the limits of this norm, in spite of its apparent transformation.

[10]These data lend some credence to Drew's claim that alcoholism is a self-limiting disease, despite the fact that his claim was made on the basis of a flawed interpretation of morbidity rates over age categories (Drew 1968).

[11]Suicidality attributed to anger or manipulation of others is reported by a number of researchers working with American Indians (Miller and Schoenfeld 1971; Curlee 1969; Levy 1965) and by researchers working in other parts of the world, most notably Malinowski among the Trobriand Islanders (Malinowski 1929). More recently, Robert Levy has written on aggressive suicide among the Tahitians, Catherine Lutz on justifiable anger as a cause of suicide among the Ifaluk, and Hollan on indignant suicide among the Toraja in Indonesia (Levy 1973; Lutz 1988; Hollan 1990).

[12]In the Japanese film *Tampopo*, images and vignettes of food, sex and violence abound in a curiously disconcerting way for many Western observers. Although food, sex and violence are meaningfully linked in Western culture, the linkages in *Tampopo* can startle and confuse western expectations. In a similar way, depression, alcoholism and suicide may be linked in most American Indian cultures, but in ways that might confuse Western observers.

REFERENCES

American Psychiatric Association (1980) Diagnostic and Statistical Manual of Mental Disorders, Third Edition. Washington, D.C.: APA.

Berglund, M. (1984) Suicide in alcoholism. Archives of General Psychiatry 41:888–891.

Black, D. W., G. Winokur, and A. Nasrallah (1987) Mortality in patients with primary unipolar depression, secondary unipolar depression, and bipolar affective disorder: A comparison with general population mortality. International Journal of Psychiatry in Medicine 17(4):351–360.

Bradley, Lt. J. H. (1923) Bradley manuscript. In A.M. Ouivey (ed.), Contributions to the Historical Society of Montana, Vol. 9.

Brown, S. A. and M. A. Schuckit (1988) Changes in depression among abstinent alcoholics. Journal of Studies on Alcohol 49(5):412–417.

Burd, L., T. E. Shea and H. Knull (1987) 'Montana Gin': Ingestion of commercial products containing denatured alcohol among Native Americans. Journal of Studies on Alcohol 48(4):388–389.

Chalfant, S. A. (1974) Aboriginal Territory of the Kalispel Indians. In E.O. Fuller, et al. (ed.), Interior Salish and Eastern Washington Indians, Vol. III. New York: Garland Publishing, Inc.

Curlee, W. V. (1969) Suicide and self-destructive behavior on the Cheyenne River reservation. Public Health Service Publication, No. 1903. National Institute of Mental Health and Indian Health Service.

Confederated Salish and Kootenai Tribes (n.d.) Flathead Reservation. An informational packet prepare by the Confederated Tribes.

DeSmet, Fr. P. (1969) Life, Letters and Travels of Father DeSmet. New York: Francis P. Harper (Arno Press).

Devereux, G. (1961) Mohave Ethnopsychiatry and Suicide: The Psychiatric Knowledge and Psychic Disturbances of an Indian Tribe. Washington D.C.: U.S. Government Printing Office.

Drew, L. R. H. (1968) Alcoholism as a self-limiting disease. Quarterly Journal of Studies of Alcohol 29:956–967.

Everett, M. W. (1970) Pathology in White Mountain Apache culture: A preliminary analysis. Western Canadian Journal of Anthropology 2(1):180–203.

Flathead Culture Committee (1988) A Brief History of the Flathead People. St. Ignatius, MT: Char-Koosta.

Forbis, R. (1951) The Flathead Apostasy: An Interpretation. Montana: Magazine of History 1:35–40.

Foulks, E. F. (1980) Psychological continuities: from dissociative states to alcohol use and suicide in Arctic populations. Journal of Operational Psychiatry 11(2):156–161.

Fuller, E. O. (1974) The Confederated Salish and Kootenai Tribes of the Flathead Reservation. *In* E.O. Fuller, et al. (eds.), Interior Salish and Eastern Washington Indians, Vol. III. New York: Garland Publishing, Inc.

Goodwin, D. W. (1973) Alcohol in suicide and homicide. Quarterly Journal of Studies on Alcohol 34:144–156.

Guyette, S. (1982) Selected characteristics of American Indian substance abusers. The International Journal of the Addictions 17(6):1001–1014.

Guze, S. B. and E. Robins (1970) Suicide and primary affective disorders. British Journal of Psychiatry 117:437–438.

Haines, F. (1938) The northward spread of horses among the Plains Indians. American Anthropologist 40(3):429–437.

Hesselbrock, M., V. Hesselbrock, K. Syzmanski and M. Weidenman (1988) Suicide attempts and alcoholism. Journal of Studies of Alcohol 49(5):436–442.

Hirschfeld, R. M. A., D. Hasin, M.B. Keller, J. Endicott and J. Wunder (1990) Depression and alcoholism: Comorbidity in a longitudinal study. *In* J.D. Maser and C. Robert Cloninger (eds.), Comorbidity of mood and anxiety disorders. Washington, D.C.: American Psychiatric Association, Inc.; pp. 293–303.

Hochkirchen, B. and W. Jilek (1985) Psychosocial dimensions of suicide and parasuicide in Amerindians of the Pacific Northwest. Journal of Operational Psychiatry 16(2):24–28.

Hollan, D. (1990) Indignant suicide in the Pacific: An example from the Toraja Highlands of Indonesia. Culture, Medicine and Psychiatry 14(3):365–379.

Humphrey, J. A. and H. J. Kupferer (1982) Homicide and suicide among the Cherokee and Lumbee Indians of North Carolina. International Journal of Social Psychiatry 28(2):121–128.

Jaffe, J. H. and D. A. Ciraulo (1986) Alcoholism and depression. *In* R. E. Meyer (ed.), Psychopathology and Addictive Disorders. New York: Guilford.

Keller, M. B., P. W. Lavori, C. E. Lewis et al. (1983) Predictors of relapse in major depressive disorder. Journal of the American Medical Association 250:3299–3304.

Keller, M. B. and R. W. Shapiro (1982) Double depression: superimposition of acute depression episodes on chronic depressive disorders. American Journal of Psychiatry 139(4):438–442.

Kelso, D. and C. Attneave (1981) Bibliography of North American Indian Mental Health. Westport, CT: Greenwood Press.

Kielholz, P. (1970) Alcohol and depression. British Journal of Addiction 65:187–193.

Kleinman, A. (1977) Depression, somatization, and the new cross-cultural psychiatry. Social Science and Medicine 11:3–10.

Leland, J. (1976) Firewater Myths: North American Indian Drinking and Alcohol Addiction. New Brunswick, N.J.: Journal of Studies on Alcohol, Incorporated.

Levy, J.E. (1965) Navajo suicide. Human Organization 24(4):308–318.

Levy, J. E. and S. J. Kunitz (1971) Indian reservations, anomie, and social pathologies. Southwestern Journal of Anthropology 27(2):97–128.

___. (1974) Indian Drinking: Navajo Practices and Anglo-American Theories. New York: John Wiley and Sons.

Levy, R. I. (1973) Tahitians. Chicago: University of Chicago Press.

Lutz, C. (1988) Unnatural Emotion. Chicago: University of Chicago Press.

Mail, P. D. and D. R. McDonald (1980) Tulapai to Tokay: A bibliography of alcohol use and abuse among Native Americans of North America. New Haven: HRAF Press.

Malinowski, B. (1929) The Sexual Life of Savages. New York: Harcourt, Brace & World, Inc.

Malone, M. P. and R. B. Roeder (1976) Montana: A History of Two Centuries. Seattle: University of Washington Press.

Manson, S., J. H. Shore and J. D. Bloom (1985) The depressive experience in American Indian communities: A challenge for psychiatric theory and diagnosis. *In* A. Kleinman and B. Good (eds.), Culture and Depression. Berkeley: University of California Press.

May, P. A. (1986) Alcohol and drug misuse prevention programs for American Indians: Needs and opportunities. Journal of Studies on Alcohol 47(3):187–195.

___. (1990) A bibliography on suicide and suicide attempts among American Indians and Alaska Natives. Omega 21(3):199–214.

McIntosh, J. L. and J. F. Santos (1980) Suicide among Native Americans: A compilation of findings. Omega 11(4):303–316.

Meyer, R. E. (1986) How to understand the relationship between psychopathology and addictive disorders: Another example of the chicken and the egg. *In* R.E. Meyer (ed.), Psychopathology and Addictive Disorders. New York: Guilford.

Meyer, R. E. and H. R. Kranzler (1990) Alcohol abuse/dependence and comorbid anxiety and depression. *In* J.D. Maser and C. Robert Cloninger (eds.), Comorbidity of Mood and Anxiety Disorders. Washington, D.C.: American Psychiatric Association, Inc.

Miller, S. I. and L. S. Schoenfeld (1971) Suicide attempt patterns among the Navaho Indians. International Journal of Social Psychiatry 17(3):189–193.

Moyer, J. M. (1961) Missionary-Indian alienation at St. Mary's Mission, 1841 to 1850. Unpublished student paper, Gonzaga University.

O'Nell, T. D. (1989) Psychiatric investigations among American Indians and Alaska Natives: A critical review. Culture, Medicine and Psychiatry 13:51–87.

Peters, R. (1981) Suicidal behavior among Native Americas: An annotated bibliography. White Cloud Journal 2(3):9–20.

Phillips, P. C. (1974) A History of the Confederated Salish and Kootenai Tribes of the Flathead Reservation. *In* E.O. Fuller, et al. (eds.), Interior Salish and Eastern Washington Indians, Vol. III. New York: Garland Publishing, Inc.

Pine, C. J. (1981) Suicide in American Indian and Alaska Native Tradition. White Cloud Journal 2(3):3–8.

Rounsaville, B .J., D. Sholomakas and B. A. Prusoff (1980) Chronic mood disorders in depressed patients. Journal of Affective Disorders 2:73–88.

Roy, C., A. Choudhuri and D. Irvine (1970) The prevalence of mental disorders among Saskatchewan Indians. Journal of Cross-Cultural Psychology 1(4):383–392.

Salish Kootenai College (1980) Salish Kootenai Vocational Education Program, 1981–84. A proposal submitted to the U.S. Department of Education. 1989 Salish Kootenai College Student Handbook. Pablo, MT: Char-Koosta Printing.

Sampath, H. M. (1974) Prevalence of psychiatric disorders in a southern Baffin Island Eskimo settlement. Canadian Psychiatric Association Journal 19(4):363–367.

Saum, L. O. (1965) The fur trader and the Indian. Seattle: University of Washington Press.

Schuckit, M. A. (1979) Alcoholism and affective disorders: diagnostic confusion. *In* D. W. Goodwin and C. K. Erikson (eds.), Alcoholism and Affective Disorders. New York: Spectrum Publications.

Shkilnyk, A. (1985) A Poison Stronger than Love. New Haven and London: Yale University Press.

Shore, J. H. (1975) American Indian suicide—fact and fantasy. Psychiatry 38:86–91.

Shore, J. H., J. D. Kinzie, J. L. Hampson and E. M. Pattison (1973) Psychiatric epidemiology of an Indian village. Psychiatry 36:70–81.

Shore, J. H. and S. Manson (1983) American Indian psychiatric and social problems. Trans-cultural Psychiatric Research Review 20:159–180.

Spencer, R. F., J. D. Jennings, et al. (1977) The Native Americans. New York: Harper & Row Publishers.

Thompson, D. (1971) Travels in Western North America, 1784–1812. Toronto: Macmillan Co. of Canada Limited.

Trosper, R. L. (1976) Native American boundary maintenance: The Flathead Indian Reservation 1860-1970. Ethnicity 3:256–274.

Turney-High, H. (1935) The diffusion of the horse to the Flatheads. Man 35:183–185.

___. (1937) The Flathead Indians of Montana, Memoirs, Vol. 48(4). American Anthropological Association.

U.S. Bureau of the Census (1980) Census Reports

Weisner, T. S., J. C. Weibel-Orlando and J. Long (1984) "Serious drinking," "white man's drinking" and "tee-totaling": Drinking levels and styles in an urban American Indian population. Journal of Studies on Alcohol 45(3):237–250.

Weissman, M. M., P. J. Leaf, M. L. Bruce and L. Florio (1988) The epidemiology of dysthymia in five communities: Rates, risks, comorbidity and treatment. American Journal of Psychiatry 145:815–819.

Westermeyer, J. (1974) "The drunken Indian": Myths and realities. Psychiatric Annals 4(9):29–36.

Woodruff, R. A., S. B. Guze, P. J. Clayton and D. Carr (1973) Alcoholism and depression. Archives of General Psychiatry 28:97–100.

CHAPTER THIRTEEN

Culture and Dissociation

Dissociation is characterized by a loss of the integration of faculties or functions that are normally integrated in consciousness. This lack of integration, or division, in consciousness can affect memory, sensory modalities, motor functions, cognitive functions, and personal identity or sense of self. Cultural schemas affect the subjective experience and expression of dissociation, with particular differences between societies that have a modern or scientific worldview and those with a premodern or supernatural worldview.

Dissociation is based in trance behavior, either spontaneous or voluntary. Trance and dissociation in themselves are not pathological. Institutionalized forms of trance have been identified in 437 societies, 89% of the societies for which adequate ethnographic data are available (Bourguignon, 1972). These are forms of trance that are voluntarily practiced within the context of cultural institutions, such as religious and healing rituals.

Culturally normative experiences of dissociation should not be considered to be cases of mental illness. Many people in premodern cultures can become highly skilled at dissociative experience. These are the shamans, mystics, and religious leaders found in premodern societies all over the world. Generally speaking, these people are not mentally ill, even though they may be permanently dissociated, hear voices of spirits, and believe they have supernatural powers. These can be normal experiences within their cultural contexts and can even form the normative structure of consciousness (see article by Roseman in Chapter 3). The unity of consciousness that is presumed in modern theories of psychology as a prerequisite for normality is simply not applicable in many premodern societies.

The first article in this chapter is by medical anthropologist Richard J. Castillo. This paper examines normative dissociative experiences deliberately induced by Hindu ascetics in India through meditative trance to overcome symptoms of depression. This demonstrates that dissociation can be used as a coping mechanism for dealing with emotional distress. The paper also discusses the psychological mechanics of trance, which are concluded to be based on focused attention. In the Indian cultural context, this type of dissociation is a highly valued religious experience and should not be considered pathological even though these individuals can develop permanently divided consciousness.

The major dissociative disorders in DSM-IV (American Psychiatric Association, 1994) are commonly found in modern societies but do not fit most dissociative syndromes found in premodern societies. For example, Saxena and Prasad (1989) reviewed the cases of 62 psychiatric outpatients in India whose symptoms fit the diagnostic criteria for dissociative disorders in DSM-III (APA, 1980), which are essentially the same in DSM-IV. Based on these criteria, 56 cases (90.3%) fell into the residual category of atypical dissociative disorder. The psychocultural differences between Anglo America and India are illustrated by the fact that only 10% of the Indian cases fit western diagnostic criteria. This is probably because of the difference in cultural schemas. India has an extensive cultural repertoire of supernatural beings (gods, ghosts, demons, and so forth) that are accepted as real entities by the vast majority of the population. The pathological dissociation cases in India typically center around some form of spirit possession. This is very different from modern cultural schemas and results in differences in subjective experience, idioms of distress, indigenous diagnoses, treatments, and outcomes.

As a result of observed cross-cultural differences in dissociative disorders, a new diagnostic category called *dissociative trance disorder* (DTD) was proposed for DSM-IV to accommodate premodern dissociative disorders. The spirit possession syndromes in India and elsewhere are examples of illnesses that would be appropriately diagnosed as DTD.

The diagnostic criteria for dissociative trance disorder in DSM-IV highlight the distinction between trance and possession trance made by Bourguignon (1973). DTD has a dual structure subsuming pathological dissociation of two overall types, trance syndromes and possession trance syndromes.

Trance, defined in DSM-IV as a temporary marked alteration of consciousness based on a narrowing of awareness, can manifest in a wide variety of symptoms and syndromes across cultures. Many syndromes would qualify for a diagnosis of DTD. For example, ataques de nervios, a Latin American trance syndrome characterized by trembling, heart palpitations, heat in the chest rising to the head, faintness, seizure-like episodes, and sometimes hallucinations, could be appropriately diagnosed as DTD in many cases. This syndrome is indigenously attributed to acute anxiety-provoking experiences, particularly related to family conflict, fear, and grief (Guarnaccia, De La Cancela, & Carrillo, 1989; Lewis-Fernandez, 1994).

Another syndrome that could be appropriately diagnosed as DTD is *latah*. *Latah* (which is usually thought of as a Malay-Indonesian syndrome, although similar syndromes are found elsewhere) is a trance syndrome characterized by an extreme response to startling stimuli. Attention becomes highly focused, and the person exhibits anxiety and trance-related behavior such as violent body movements, assumption of defensive postures, striking out, throwing or dropping held objects, mimicking observed movements, and sometimes extreme suggestibility or obedience (Kenny, 1978; Simons, 1985).

Another syndrome that could be diagnosed as DTD is *pibloktoq*. *Pibloktoq*, also sometimes called arctic hysteria, is a Polar Eskimo trance syndrome. It is characterized by short-lived episodes (5 minutes to 1 hour) of extreme anxiety responses in which the person will tear off his or her clothes and go running into the snow or across the ice, screaming incoherently. There is dissociative amnesia for these episodes. It is indigenously attributed to sudden fright, intense fear, and imagined or actual personal abuse (Foulks, 1985; Gussow, 1985).

Another possibility for a diagnosis of DTD is *amok*. *Amok*, a Southeast Asian trance syndrome, is characterized by a short-lived (a few minutes to several hours), sudden outburst of unrestrained violence, usually of a homicidal nature, preceded by a period of anxious brooding, and ending with exhaustion. There is dissociative amnesia for these episodes. It is indigenously attributed to interpersonal conflict, intolerably embarrassing or shameful situations, loss of honor, and personal abuse (Carr, 1985).

In contrast to trance syndromes, possession trance syndromes are characterized by replacement of the primary personality by a new identity, usually a ghost, demon, or deity. The behavior of persons with possession trance syndromes is usually more complex, with a more complete alternate personality whose behavior follows preestablished cultural patterns. An individual will behave as a particular spirit or demon from the indigenous cultural repertoire, in most cases speaking and performing actions as the spirit or demon, sometimes over lengthy periods of time.

There is no clear boundary between these two trance variations, and some syndromes fall in between. For example, spirit possession among female factory workers in Malaysia is characterized by extreme anxiety episodes in which the victims scream, cry, and flail about uncontrollably, with apparently great strength. This is attributed to spirit possession, but the behavior exhibited is comparatively simple compared to the elaborated behavioral characteristics of spirits that possess persons in India (Castillo, 1994; Lewis-Fernandez, 1994). The same thing can be said of *amok*. *Amok* is also attributed to spirit possession, but the behavior displayed is relatively simple in contrast to the fully developed supernatural personalities that carry on long negotiations with the families and healers of possessed persons in India, and who may remain in the victim for years.

Given the wide variety of possible symptoms, diagnosticians should not consider DTD to be a single disorder but a variety of disorders based on a common dissociative process with various types of cultural structuring. The symptoms of trance and possession trance syndromes that would be appropriately diagnosed as DTD can vary widely in different cultures. For example, North American Charismatic Christians can be possessed by satanic demons, but Taiwanese are possessed by local gods and ghosts. In the multi-ethnic population of India, symptoms will vary by religion, region, and caste.

What is clear is that populations form cultural repertoires of dissociative experience. A cultural repertoire of possessing agents may include stable characteristics of gender, personality, behavior, and social (supernatural or natural) status. Therefore, the cultural complexity of pathological trance syndromes should be noted in diagnosis and treatment of premodern forms of dissociative disorders.

Dissociative disorder not otherwise specified (DDNOS) is a residual category for syndromes that do not meet the full diagnostic criteria of the other dissociative disorders. The culture-bound syndromes described here illustrate the importance of dissociative trance disorder as an alternative diagnostic category appropriate to premodern societies. Unfortunately, DTD was not included as an independent diagnostic category in DSM-IV (APA, 1994) but was included as a variation of dissociative disorder not otherwise specified.

Placement of DTD within the category of DDNOS is probably inappropriate. Because a large portion of the world's population live in premodern societies that generally do not experience dissociation in the same way as modern psychiatric patients, DTD should have been an independent diagnostic category. Placing DTD within the category of DDNOS implies that the modern patterns of dissociation are normative and that the premodern syndromes are somehow "atypical." This is ethnocentric because the major DSM-IV dissociative disorders are generally limited to modern cultures and the modernized segments of premodern societies. This represents only a part of the world's population. Syndromes appropriate for a diagnosis of DTD are found in both premodern societies and those segments of modern societies holding a premodern worldview.

The second article in this chapter is by cross-cultural psychiatrist Roberto Lewis-Fernandez and reviews the literature supporting the inclusion of DTD in DSM-IV. DTD was originally called *trance and possession disorder*.

The third article in this chapter, by Indian psychiatrists A. N. Chowdhury, A. K. Nath, and J. Chakraborty, provides an example of illnesses that could be diagnosed as cases of DTD. They describe an epidemic of hysteria in Tripura, an eastern border state of India. Twelve people were affected in a span of ten days. Locally, the illness was called "wild madness" and was characterized by brief trance states in which the affected persons displayed extreme agitation, attempts at self-injury, running away, animal sounds, and dissociative amnesia. This example demonstrates that some dissociative disorders can be psychoculturally contagious and epidemic.

REFERENCES

American Psychiatric Association. (1980). *Diagnostic and statistical manual of mental disorders* (3rd ed.). Washington, DC: Author.

American Psychiatric Association. (1994). *Diagnostic and statistical manual of mental disorders* (4th ed.). Washington, DC: Author

Bourguignon, E. (1972). Dreams and altered states of consciousness in anthropological research. In F. K. L. Hsu (Ed.), *Psychological anthropology* (2nd ed.). Homewood, Ill: Dorsey Press.

Bourguignon, E. (1973). Introduction: A framework for the comparative study of altered states of consciousness. In E. Bourguignon (Ed.), *Religion, altered states of consciousness, and social change* (pp. 3–35). Columbus: Ohio State University Press.

Carr, J. E. (1985). Ethno-behaviorism and the culture-bound syndromes: The case of amok. In R. C. Simons & C. C. Hughes (Eds.), *The culture-bound syndromes: Folk illnesses of psychiatric and anthropological interest* (pp. 199–223). Dordrecht: D. Reidel.

Castillo, R. J. (1994). Spirit possession in South Asia, dissociation or hysteria? Part 2: Case histories. *Culture, Medicine and Psychiatry, 18,* 141–162.

Foulks, E. F. (1985). The transformation of arctic hysteria. In R. C. Simons & C. C. Hughes (Eds.), *The culture-bound syndromes: Folk illnesses of psychiatric and anthropological interest* (pp. 307–324). Dordrecht: D. Reidel.

Guarnaccia, P. J., De La Cancela, V., & Carrillo, E. (1989). The multiple meanings of ataques de nervios in the Latino community. *Medical Anthropology, 11,* 47–62.

Gussow, Z. (1985). Pibliktoq (hysteria) among the Polar Eskimo: An ethnopsychiatric study. In R. C. Simons & C. C. Hughes (Eds.), *The culture-bound syndromes: Folk illnesses of psychiatric and anthropological interest* (pp. 271–287). Dordrecht: D. Reidel.

Kenny, M. G. (1978). Latah: The symbolism of a putative mental disorder. *Culture, Medicine and Psychiatry, 2,* 209–231.

Lewis-Fernandez, R. (1994). Culture and dissociation: A comparison of *ataque de nervios* among Puerto Ricans and possession syndrome in India. In D. Spiegel (Ed.), *Dissociation: Culture, mind, and body* (pp. 123–167). Washington, DC: American Psychiatric Press.

Saxena, S., & Prasad, K. V. S. R. (1989). DSM-III subclassification of dissociative disorders applied to psychiatric outpatients in India. *American Journal of Psychiatry, 146,* 261–262.

Simons, R. C. (1985). The resolution of the latah paradox. In R. C. Simons & C. C. Hughes (Eds.), *The culture-bound syndromes: Folk illnesses of psychiatric and anthropological interest* (pp. 43–62). Dordrecht: D. Reidel.

RICHARD J. CASTILLO

Divided Consciousness and Enlightenment in Hindu Yogis

Yogis experience themselves as dual entities. That is, they have two coconscious selves—a self participating in the world, and an uninvolved observing self—both aware of each other. To yogis this is experienced as "true renunciation"—that is, the renunciation of the participating self through identification with the observing self. This subjective experience serves to illustrate the power of culture in the constitution of experience and behavior.

It is my position that this "true renunciation" of Hinduism is not a mere attitude of detachment, but is none other than a culture-bound subjective experience and public expression of divided consciousness. The Sanskrit texts speak consistently of two selves—one physical, impermanent, and engaged with the world—and the other nonphysical, permanent (immortal), an uninvolved witness of the physical self and the world. In the *jivanmukta* (a person who has achieved *moksha* [liberation] while still living) these two selves exist simultaneously side by side. One self (the participating self) performs actions in accordance with social norms. The second self (the observing self) is an uninvolved witness of the actions performed by the first self, and experiences those actions as if they were performed by someone else. For example, consider the description of the *jivanmukta* in the *Bhagavadgita*:

> 5:7 He who is disciplined in Yoga; whose self is purified; he who has conquered himself and has conquered the senses; whose self has become the Self of all beings; He is not involved even while he acts.[1]

In this verse, the person, who through the practice of Yoga meditation has "conquered himself" (*vijitatma*), and "conquered the senses" (*jitendriyah*), refers to a person who has transcended the ordinary self. He has divided consciousness and now has two selves, one ordinary self and one spiritual self. The spiritual self has conquered the ordinary self. The senses have been conquered and perception of the world has been altered. The person now identifies with the spiritual self, that is, the "Self of all beings." And when the ordinary self acts in the world, the spiritual self is uninvolved. It does not act in the world but is only a witness. From the perspective of the spiritual self the objects of the world are creations of senses which belong to the ordinary self. Thus, all actions and objects are ultimately not real. The spiritual self thinks "I do not act at all." For example, again consider the *Bhagavadgita*:

> 5:8-9 The Knower of Truth, fixed in Yoga, thinks, 'I do not act at all.' In seeing, hearing, touching, smelling, eating, walking, sleeping, breathing, speaking, excreting, seizing, and even in opening and closing the eyes; He thinks simply that the senses act among the objects of the senses.

Similar passages are found throughout classical and medieval Sanskrit literature and are too numerous to mention.[2] These conceptions of divided consciousness form the pre-existing reality of Hindu Yoga—that is, the system of culture-based cognitive categories that is internalized by the yogi in the process of enculturation and yogic training.

In the Hindu Yoga system, consciousness is seen in an inherently dual nature. It is assumed that both aspects of consciousness exist simultaneously, but that observing consciousness (*atman*) is only experienced as a separate entity when participating consciousness (*jiva*) is restrained. The whole practice of Yoga is designed to restrain the activities of the *jiva* so that the *atman* can be experienced as a separate entity. Ordinarily, according to the yogic doctrine, the *atman* is assimilated in the activities of the *jiva* and is therefore hidden, that is, it is not experienced as a conscious entity unto itself and only the *jiva* is experienced. The goal of yogic practice is to separate out *atman* from *jiva*, thus creating a division of consciousness in the individual (see YS 1:2-4).

The enlightened yogi has simultaneous coconsciousness of both *atman* and *jiva*. The *jiva* is comprised of the personal mind, thoughts, emotions, sensations, and memories. The *atman* is an uninvolved witness of the *jiva* and everything that the *jiva* does. The *atman* is an observing self. It watches what the *jiva* does and subjectively experiences those activities as the actions of another person. That is why, when the *jiva* performs actions in the world, the *atman* has the subjective experience, "I do not act at all," as described in the *Bhagavadgita*. The *atman* appears to itself as a nonphysical, unchanging, immortal, conscious being, not dependent on the physical body, and separate from personal consciousness.

My Indian yogi informants experienced this split in consciousness. But before I discuss their subjective experiences, I think it would be helpful to review Western experiences of a similar split in consciousness in order to provide some cultural contrast.

DEPERSONALIZATION

Western psychiatry conceptualizes this type of split in consciousness between a participating self and an observing self as *depersonalization*. DSM-III-R defines depersonalization as "(1) an experience of being as if detached from and an outside observer of one's mental processes or body; or (2) an experience of feeling like an automaton or as if in a dream" (1987:276).

Typically, depersonalization is a state in which an individual experiences a split in consciousness between a participating self and an observing self. The participating self is composed of body, thoughts, feelings, memories, and emotions. The observing self is experienced as a separate, uninvolved witness of the participating self, with the perception that all of the normal aspects of personality are somehow unreal and do not belong to the observing self. There is the experience of being split off from one's participating self and "watching" that self behave (Castillo 1990). The split between the two selves is clearly illustrated by descriptions of the experience given by Western psychiatric patients:

"I had the impression as though I led a double existence. Everything I did and said seemed to issue from one ego, yet I also had the definite impression that there was a second ego as well, and that this second ego looked on the activities of the first as though they belonged to a different being. . . . I could think of this [observed] ego as one thinks of an object and was often surprised at what it did. . . . What oppressed me most was this incessant observation by my second ego. I moved like a machine in a strange environment." (Taylor 1982:303)

"None of this makes any sense. I laugh but it's like someone else is laughing. It is as though there is a part of me watching and part of me doing it." (Torch 1981:250)

There are also secondary characteristics of depersonalization, which may include: feelings of dizziness, floating, or giddiness, a feeling of the participating self being "dead," a loss of affec-

tive responsiveness, and a feeling of calm detachment (Levy and Wachtel 1978).

Depersonalization, an experience in which the perception of the self is altered, is also commonly accompanied by a related experience conceptualized by Western psychiatry as *derealization*. Derealization is an experience in which one's perception of the environment is altered. In derealization the environment may take on a two-dimensional or "unreal" quality. Sometimes, normally stable, solid, inanimate objects may be seen to vibrate, or "breathe," to be unsolid, fluid, or alive. Shapes and sizes of objects may change, or objects may disappear altogether. Colors may be especially vivid, and some objects may be seen as "shimmering" (Castillo 1990).

Another possibility of depersonalization and derealization experience is a subjective merging with the physical environment. Laing cites the experience of a patient who had remained depersonalized for a number of years:

"I was about twelve, and had to walk to my father's shop through a large park, which was a long, dreary walk. I suppose, too, that I was rather scared. I didn't like it, especially when it was getting dark. I started to play a game to help pass the time. You know how as a child you count the stones or stand on the crosses on the pavement—well, I hit on this way of passing time. *It struck me that if I stared long enough at the environment that I would blend with it and disappear just as if the place was empty and I had disappeared. It was as if you get yourself to feel you don't know who you are or where you are.*" (Laing 1965:110, emphasis in original)

Patients frequently report an especially distinct separation between the observing self and mental activities. When these mental activities are cognitive in nature, the affected individuals complain that it seems as if they are not doing their own thinking, imaging, or remembering because they can observe an independent flow of these phenomena in their minds. There are also affective changes. In Western culture depersonalization is often linked with panic and anxiety (Kennedy 1976; Roth et al. 1965; Sheehan 1983; Sours 1965).

DSM-III-R includes a "Depersonalization Disorder" (300.60), which has as its diagnostic criteria:

A. Persistent or recurrent experiences of depersonalization as indicated by either (1) an experience of being as if detached from and an outside observer of one's mental processes or body; or (2) an experience of feeling like an automaton or as if in a dream. B. During the depersonalization experience reality-testing remains intact. C. The depersonalization is sufficiently severe and persistent to cause marked distress. D. The depersonalization experience is the predominant disturbance and not a symptom of another disorder, such

as Schizophrenia, Panic Disorder, or Agoraphobia without History of Panic Disorder but with limited symptom attacks of depersonalization, or temporal lobe epilepsy.
(1987:276–77)

Depersonalization may be present as a related symptom in all of
the above disorders as well as being an extremely common
symptom in MPD patients; and is thus a common experience in
psychiatric populations.

Depersonalization also occurs in the Western nonclinical
population. DSM-III-R estimates that single brief episodes of depersonalization may occur at some time in as many as 70% of
young adults. This estimate is supported by the findings of
Dixon (1963), Sedman (1966), and Trueman (1984). Dixon observed that over half of his college student subjects could recognize descriptions of depersonalization as something they had
experienced.

KAIVALYA

The ultimate goal of Yoga meditation is *kaivalya*. The term
kaivalya literally means "isolation," referring to the separating
out of the observing self from its assimilation in the participating
self. Thus creating the duality in consciousness of the *jivanmukta*. This observing self is considered to be the "True Self"
(*atman, purusha*), and the participating self and its actions are
thought to comprise a "false self" (*jiva*).

The *atman* (in orthodox Hinduism) is said to be one or identical with *brahman* (the Absolute, that is, consciousness and the
world in both manifest and unmanifest forms). The highest "truth
of the world order" (*ritam*) is said to be realized and subjectively
validated by the yogi in his experience of having his unembodied
"True Self" (*atman*) merge with the environment (*brahman*).

During my fieldwork in India (1986–1988) I found that yogis
do indeed have experiences of a split in consciousness characterized as a "false self" and a True Self" as well as the experience
of merging with their environment. However, their subjective
experiences, intellectual interpretations, and idioms of expression concerning these experiences are all consistent with the culturally specific symbolic system of Hindu Yoga. This is a
symbolic system radically different from that of Western psychiatry and Western popular culture. In contrast to Western psychiatric patients, whose experiences of divided consciousness are
characterized by panic and anxiety, the experiences of the yogis
are normal and normative religious experiences characterized by
ecstasy and bliss.

One of my informants, Swami Paramananda (pseudonym)
explained to me his experience of divided consciousness in the
following way.

"The True Self is the *drashta*—the Looker. When I am separate from my body and my mind, that is the *drashta*. That is
the *atman*. The Looker is there in the three states of mind—
waking, dreaming, sleeping. When the Looker is there all the
time during the three states of mind—that is *kaivalya* [libera-
tion]. The Looker is, you can say, a fourth state—*turiya*, we
call it. When the Looker witnesses everything in the world—
this ground, these trees, this river, these mountains, and all
people, and all other things, as *shakti* [the primordial energy
of the universe], the light, the energy; and also itself—this is
very important. Itself also is seen as *shakti* and nothing different. There is no Seer and seen, no Looker and looked—
they are One—That is *brahman* [the Absolute]. It's not just
on the level of the feelings or the mind—the *indriyas*, the
senses become one with *brahman*."

"This is done through different formulas. There are three
ways: *bhakti* [devotion], *karma* [action], and *jñana* [knowl-
edge]. They all do the same thing. They hold the mind still.
This is the key. They keep the mind on one thing. *Citta vritti
nirodha* [restraint of the activities of thought (from the *Yoga-
Sutra*)]—this is Yoga—keeping the mind still. This is how
the *paramatman* [higher Self] is known. The sannyasis have
more time to do this because they have renounced all responsibilities in the world, but anyone can do it."

"All the things in the world are just name and form—
name and form—everything is really one. All these things
that people think about—brother, sister, mother, father—
these are just thoughts. They are not ultimately real. They
have no meaning besides the meaning we give them in our
thoughts. . . . The key is to control the mind. Then you can
have peace."

"And you can have the experience [of the Looker] any-
time in any of the three stages of consciousness. There are
three stages—waking, dreaming, and deep sleep. Then, there
is a fourth stage. This is called *turiya*, the fourth stage. We
call this a fourth stage because you can have it by itself—in
meditation. But, also, you can have it in combination with
any of the other three stages. This is the experience of the
Looker. In the waking stage you can see some trees and some
mountains and some river, and you think, 'Oh, how nice.' Or
you can see some bad thing, some ugly thing and think, 'Oh,
how terrible.' This is the *jivatma* thinking. When you have
the experience of the Looker, the Looker is just watching it
all. This is *turiya* combined with waking stage. *Turiya* combined with dream stage is the same thing. You are dreaming.
In dreaming, you can be anywhere—in America—in Delhi—
doing so many things. This is the *jivatma* dreaming. The
paramatma doesn't dream. It watches. It knows the jivatma
is dreaming, but doesn't join in with it. It stays separate. It
watches the dream. Similarly, you can have *turiya* combined

with the deep sleep. The body is asleep. The mind is asleep. But, the *paramatma* is awake. It doesn't sleep, it watches the mind and the body sleep. It is only the *jivatma* that sleeps. The *paramatma* is unchanging. It is eternal. It doesn't go through all these stages. It can be covered-up, but it itself is unchanging."

Training in Yoga meditation involves the cultivation of the ability to finely focus attention. The focus of attention can be anything: a physical object, a sound, an image, an idea, a sensation, an emotion, a role, or a personality. In meditation the focus of attention gradually takes over all of consciousness until only the focus of attention exists—all else is pushed out of consciousness. In this training the yogi becomes very familiar with the intermediate stages of meditation in which attention is placed on the meditational focus of attention but also partially placed on the self and the environment. The yogi thus experiences a split in attention between these two poles and over the course of training becomes very adept at controlling the focus or foci of attention. Ordinarily, attention is placed on the self and environment, but the yogi learns to add a second focus of attention, the meditational focus, and maintain that focus even while he or she is not meditating. Thus even while the yogi is engaged in everyday activities there is a fixed focus partially away from the self and events of the world, to an inner experience which the yogi constantly maintains. The result is a division of consciousness in which the inner experience remains steady and constant, and the self and events of the world become dimmed, distant, and distorted. When the yogi enters into deep meditation, the self and the events of the world disappear completely and only the inner consciousness exists. It is this inner consciousness that yogis refer to as the *atman*, the "True Self," of the *sakshin*, "the Witness," or "Looker."

YOGA MEDITATION

Classical Yoga is the system of meditation codified in the ancient Sanskrit text, the *Yoga-Sutra* of Patañjali (c. 200 B.C.–200 A.D.). This text is the authoritative work on Yoga meditation consisting of a collection of pithy, terse aphorisms (*sutras*) expressing the main tenets of meditation practice. The goal of yogic practice is the transformation of consciousness, and the *Yoga-Sutra* (YS) is a guide to that transformation, constituting a map of internal experience. This ancient map describes a fundamental duality in consciousness, which I have earlier translated (Castillo 1985) as *personal consciousness* and *transpersonal consciousness*. According to the yogic system of cognitive categories, these two parts of consciousness are two separate entities which exist simultaneously but are normally fused in everyday

awareness such that they are subjectively experienced as a single entity. The goal of Yoga meditation is to separate these two entities in the subjective awareness of the individual. By accomplishing this the yogi thus becomes a dual personality or a person with divided consciousness.

The reason the yogi wants to establish this duality in consciousness is because according to the Hindu belief system, all persons do in fact have this dual nature but simply aren't aware of it. It is necessary to separate out transpersonal consciousness from its assimilation by personal consciousness in order for the individual to realize this dual nature in subjective experience. This separation is described as *moksha*—liberation—that is, liberation from the boundaries, limitations, and pains and suffering of life in the world. It is experienced as liberation from suffering because transpersonal consciousness, the newly isolated consciousness, is as if one step removed from the everyday events of life in the world. The events of the world are subjectively experienced as occurring to and around personal consciousness. Transpersonal consciousness only witnesses the events which happen to personal consciousness, but does not participate in them. Thus, by identifying his or her "True Self" as the observing consciousness, the yogi experiences the events of the world as if they were happening to someone else—"like a movie." The yogi is in effect "liberated" from ordinary life in the world. In the Hindu Yoga system, the life of the personal self is viewed and subjectively experienced as inherently painful and full of suffering, with salvation coming only from "liberation" (*moksha, kaivalya*).

The method of obtaining liberation in the Yoga system is through meditation. Yoga meditation has as its key dynamic the self-manipulation of attention. The *Yoga-Sutra* (YS) identifies three stages of meditation: fixed-attention (*dharana*), continuous-attention (*dhyana*), and coalescent-attention (*samadhi*).

Fixed-attention (*dharana*) is defined by the *Yoga-Sutra* as "binding personal consciousness to a particular place" (YS 3:1). This involves holding the attention of personal consciousness on a certain object. The object may be a spot on or within the body; a visual image; an image in the mind; a particular sound either verbalized, thought silently, or heard; an idea; the breath; or any external object. Attention is kept on the object of the meditation and brought back to the object when attention wanders.

Continuous-attention (*dhyana*) is defined by the *Yoga-Sutra* as "the unbroken continuity of mental content in that place" (YS 3:2). This is the successful holding of attention on the object of the fixed-attention. Continuous-attention differs from fixed-attention in that there is no wandering away from the object.

The final stage of meditation, coalescent-attention (*samadhi*), is defined by the *Yoga-Sutra* as "the same object only appearing, as if free of all self-consciousness" (YS 3:3). Coalescent-attention is awareness of some object, either external or internal, without awareness of anything else including the self (body and self-awareness). There is a complete forgetting of the self and anything external to the object of the meditation. That object is then all that exists in consciousness.

At the deepest level of meditation, attention becomes so concentrated that the subjective experience is one of loss of the world, loss of self, and even loss of the object of meditation. At this point the yogi slips into a void, a nothingness in which nothing exists except attention itself.

The goal of Yoga meditation is primarily the loss of self, that is, the loss of the body, senses, memory, and all else that goes to make up the normal experience of the self. It is this loss of self which yogis interpret as loss of personal consciousness, and the liberation of transpersonal consciousness which the *Yoga-Sutra* (YS:2:20) describes as "pure perception" or "pure attention" (*drishi-matra*).

This process is the isolation of transpersonal consciousness from personal consciousness, and if it is experienced often enough the yogi gains the ability to maintain awareness of transpersonal consciousness at all times, even while engaged in everyday activities. This ability is acquired because the yogi has learned how to master attention. He or she has learned how to continuously focus attention on an object of choice regardless of what else is happening in the environment. Thus the yogi is able to continuously keep enough attention on transpersonal consciousness to isolate this "witness" from personal consciousness, while simultaneously giving enough attention to personal consciousness to be engaged in everyday events. The yogi has mastered the ability to divide attention and thereby divide consciousness. By maintaining the constant existence of transpersonal consciousness in awareness, the yogi thereby attains a one step removal from the events of the world and thus gains liberation (*moksha*).

By accomplishing a permanent division of consciousness between the two selves, the yogi has not only permanently altered his perception, but subjectively validated the yogic worldview. Obeyesekere's insight (following Weber) that, "*cultural ideas are being constantly validated by the nature of subjective experience*" (1981:113), finds confirmation in the experiences of Hindu yogis. Similarly, Geertz' (1973) insight that cultural symbols are both models *of* and models *for* mental representation is demonstrated by the subjective experience of yogis. The Hindu cultural concept of *moksha* (liberation) serves as a model for subjective experience. Liberation from human existence is seen as the ultimate cure for the suffering inherent in the human condition.

Within the Hindu Yoga system, regardless of one's social status, life in the world is seen as nothing more than an endless pursuit of ephemeral pleasures in an oceanic swamp of hard work, social obligations, disease, death, sorrow, and ultimate despair and suffering (*duhkha*). *Kaivalya* is the means of escape. By achieving the constant presence in consciousness of the observing self, the yogi is able to completely repudiate and renounce the personal self, everything the personal self is and does, and the world which it inhabits. In this symbolic system, and therefore, in actual subjective experience, by achieving this division in consciousness and the experience of merging with the environment, the yogi achieves liberation (*kaivalya, moksha*) from ordinary life in the world and therefore freedom from suffering and despair (*duhkha*). Thus Yoga is used by the yogi to escape from his ordinary reality.

DEPRESSION

Madan (1987) has accused renouncers of fleeing from worldly life because of their own failures. According to Madan: "The hostility toward renouncers, which is paradoxically combined with reverence for them among householders, would seem to point to the vulnerability, if not also the inauthenticity, of the choice of renunciation if it flows from a sense of defeat rather than fulfilment" (1987:10). Thus, according to Madan, the suspicion arises among householders that individual renouncers have not renounced the world, but that the world has renounced them. Likewise, Masson (1976, 1980) sees the premonastic lives of renouncers as especially traumatic, resulting in despair and depression, and prompting the flight into yogic renunciation. This idea is consistent with many of the renouncers I met in India. For example, Swami Paramananda told me, "*Sannyasins* generally can't live in the regular world. They are frustrated in worldly life. Therefore they make a virtue out of necessity, that is, *having nothing is holy.*"

Masson (1976), in his interpretation of renunciation as a response to trauma in life, considers renouncers to be suffering from psychopathology—specifically, depression.

> I believe that the concern voiced ubiquitously by the ascetic in Indian literature—*vairâgya* or *nirveda*, "world weariness" or "disgust"—is an oblique reference to the affective disorder known as sadness when mild, depression when strong, and melancholia when severe. The most striking example of this phrase is one known to every Sanskritist: *yad ahar eva virajet, tad ahar eva pravrajet* ("On the very day that one conceives disgust for the world, on that very day should one set out to wander alone"). I do not think that in this context "depression" as a translation of *nirveda* or *vairâgya* would be very far off (cf. the near-synonymous *vaimanasya*). It is characteristic of the depressed individual to lose interest in his own family, his friends, his work, and his surroundings . . . no man sets about destroying his body systematically unless he is simultaneously destroying people from his past who are now lodged firmly within him. . . . Am I saying,

then, that all ascetics must have suffered from harsh and unloving parents in their childhoods? Yes. I should add however, that most analysts would disagree, and would qualify this by saying that often the harsh treatment was only imagined—often as retaliation for imagined evil in the little child himself, for his own destructive fantasies vis-à-vis his parents and siblings. In any case, asceticism is a means of—or rather, and attempt at (and one doomed to failure)—forcing love. But my own suggestion goes further; it is that *all ascetics* suffered massive traumas in their childhood in one of three ways: they were sexually abused, or they were the object of overt or covert aggression, or they lost those closest to them early in their lives. Their lives were pervaded with sadness; their rituals, their obsessive gestures of every kind, are an attempt to recapture the lost childhood they never had. (1976:618–623. emphasis in original)

My general impression of the personal histories of renouncers is consistent with that of Masson. Although I doubt that *all* renouncers had severe psychological traumas in their lives, the few renouncers that I got to know well in the course of my fieldwork certainly fit this pattern. For example, as a child Swami Paramananda was regularly beaten by his father. Another renouncer I got to know well had serious family problems as a child and ran away from home at age 15. Another suffered the traumatic loss of his mother at age seven. Thus, it is my impression that some type of psychological trauma is quite common in the personal backgrounds of renouncers. However, because of my small sample I would not want to generalize beyond this. Nevertheless, the impression that renouncers take to the ascetic life because of problems, failures, frustrations, and unhappiness in life is probably well taken. This general impression was also reported by Miller and Wertz (1976). Likewise, Tripathi (1978), in his large surveys of *sadhus*, reported that of 500 renouncers surveyed 81.6% took to the ascetic way of life for nonreligious reasons; 41.6% of these were because of sociofamilial factors.

Nevertheless, in relation to renouncers (and only for renouncers), I am in agreement with Obeyesekere (1985) in viewing depression in the South Asian cultural context as nonpathological. As Obeyesekere states, when considering persons filled with feelings of depression and hopelessness, "if it was placed in the context of Sri Lanka, I would say that we are not dealing with a depressive but a good Buddhist" (1985:134). Similarly, when dealing with Hindu renouncers one must realize that the cognitive categories of Yoga, which serve as models *of* and *for* subjective experience, identify life in the world as an endless field of suffering and pain (*duhkha*).[3]

In contrast to Western culture, which views depression as an illness, yogis view depression as an *accomplishment*—a realization or deep spiritual insight about the true nature of the world.

In fact, renouncers consider anyone who is not depressed about the nature of human life to be somehow deluded. It is at the point of their realization of the meaninglessness of life that they become ready for the practice of Yoga as a means of obtaining liberation from suffering.

I am convinced that yogis use meditation and the resulting division in consciousness to psychologically escape problems in life, as well as emotional distress and anxiety present in their primary personality. They create a secondary self through meditation which is removed from the problems and the emotional distress present in the life of the primary self. They thus escape from the suffering of their ordinary lives.

CONCLUSION

Hindu yogis experience a division in consciousness between a "participating self" and an "observing self." These two selves are experienced as separate conscious entities with their own identity and existence.

The participating self (*jiva*) is experienced as a temporary, constantly changing, physical and mental being, subject to the illness, pain and suffering (*duhkha*) inherent in human existence, and is considered to be ultimately unreal.

The observing self (*drashta, sakshin, atman, purusha*), is experienced as an eternal, unchanging, nonphysical and nonmental being—a pure witnessing consciousness that is not subject to the illness, pain and suffering of human existence, but only witnesses them. It is an uninvolved observer of the participating self. This observing self is considered to be the ultimate reality—one with the Absolute (*brahman*).

To have the experience of the observing self constantly—while engaged in waking activity, dreaming, and even while sleeping—is the stated goal of the yogis. The observing is considered by some to be a fourth state of consciousness (*turiya*), along with waking, dreaming, and sleeping, which can be experienced simultaneously along with those other states. This is the subjective experience of a duality in consciousness, with the participating self doing the waking, dreaming, and sleeping, while the observing self watches. The observing self can also be experienced by itself, in meditation (*samadhi*).

According to the yogis, meditation is the means by which the participating self is controlled, allowing the observing self to be uncovered or unassimilated from the activities of the participating self. A yogi who has accomplished this split in consciousness on a permanent basis is considered to have achieved liberation (*kaivalya, moksha*). This person is called a *jivanmukta*, that is, a person liberated while still living.

The experience of a division in consciousness in Hindu yogis is accomplished by the practice of meditative trance (*sanyama*).

This experience of a split in consciousness generally grows over time and is loosely correlated to how much time and effort is spent in meditating. In my informants the subjective experience, conceptualization, and verbal expression of this duality in consciousness is completely imbedded in the culture-based system of cognitive categories known as Vedanta-Yoga. I think it would be quite impossible at this point for them to experience it in any other way. In all cases the division in consciousness is a highly meaningful, sacred experience. The experience itself validates for the individual the yogic worldview and the Hindu reality in general. My informants experienced themselves as spiritual entities as understood in the Vedanta-Yoga system.

The experience of divided consciousness in Hindu yogis is contrasted with the experience of depersonalization and derealization in Western psychiatric patients. Depersonalized patients in the West also feel a distinct separation from the activities of their participating self, such that it appears to the observing self that it is an uninvolved witness (Laing 1965; Taylor 1982; Torch 1981). However, in Western patients, experiences of a split in consciousness between a participating self and an observing self are frequently associated with intense anxiety and panic attacks (Castillo 1990; Kennedy 1976; Sheehan 1983). Patients may feel they are going crazy.

I suggest that in both the Hindu yogis and the Western patients, that the ideational construction of the experiences, occurring in terms consistent with their own culture-based cognitive systems, shapes the experiences to the extent that in one cultural context a split in consciousness is subjectively experienced as a sacred event, while in the other it is subjectively experienced as an episode of mental illness.

In fact, in the case of the yogis, a deliberately induced division in consciousness is used as a means to escape what is commonly considered to be a mental illness in the West, that is, depression with associated symptoms of anxiety. However, as Obeyesekere (1985) has noted, general hopelessness with one's life in the world in the cultural context of South Asia is not seen as depression but simply the apprehension of the renouncer's realization that life is suffering (*duhkha*). This same realization is common to all the ascetic traditions of South Asia, and thus is an integral part of the Hindu Yoga symbolic system. In this system, life in the world for all people is considered to be ultimately painful and hopeless. It is just that the renouncers are the ones who have achieved (and it is considered to be an achievement) this realization in this particular lifetime, and have therefore renounced the world.

It has been noted that psychological traumas and sociofamilial problems are common in the personal histories of renouncers, and it is suggested that yogis use dissociation, in the form of a splitting into an observing self and a participating self, as a means of culture-based adaptation. Thus, Hindu Yoga, at least in

its more advanced stages, may be considered a psychoculturally specific, systematized, religious manifestation of psychotherapy.

The success of the Yoga system in overcoming generalized unhappiness and anxiety by inducing a split in consciousness, thus enabling the individual yogi to achieve a higher level of happiness, self-esteem, and social and occupational functioning (as observed in both renouncers and householder yogis), suggests that this type of divided consciousness should not be considered psychopathology. Thus, divided consciousness, while certainly abnormal in some cases such as multiple personality disorder in North America, cannot be considered universally abnormal. In the Indian cultural context, divided consciousness can be normal and even normative. That divided consciousness is seen in North America as psychopathology is certainly related to the American psychocultural context and should not be expanded to a universal model. The unity of the self which is generally assumed in Western psychological theories as a prerequisite for normality needs to be reassessed before it can be appropriately applied in cross-cultural research.

NOTES

Presented at the 90th Annual Meeting of the American Anthropological Association, Chicago, IL, November 20–24, 1991.

This work was supported by grants from the National Science Foundation, the Ford Foundation, and Harvard University.

[1] All passages from the *Bhagavadgita* and the *Yoga-Sutra* are translated from the Sanskrit by the author unless otherwise noted.

[2] Consider also *Bhagavadgita* 2:13-25, 3:27-28, 4:14-15, 4:18-21, 6:1-8, 6:20-23, 13:2, 13:24-26, 13:31-32; *Kena Upanishad* 1:1-8; *Mandukya Upanishad* 2-7; *Mundaka Upanishad* 2:1.2-10, 2:2.6-9, 3:1.1-9; *Ishavasya Upanishad* 4-17; *Katha Upanishad* 1:2.18-23, 1:3.10-15, 2:1.1-4, 2:2.8-13, 2:3.5-10; *Shvetashvatara Upanishad* 1:3-16; *Yoga-Sutra* 1:2-11, 2:5-28, 3:54, 4:4-6, 4:34; *Sankhya-Karika* 19-21, 65-66; *Viveka-Chudarmnani* 133-134, 156-159, 163-164, 210, 217, 269, 351, 377, 380-383, 494-495, 505-507, 543-546; *Drig-Drishya-Viveka* 1, 12, 16-19.

[3] However, I disagree with Obeyesekere when he states that in Western society the dysphoric affects of depression "are not anchored to an ideology and are therefore identifiable and conducive to labelling as illness" (1985:135). The Western illness of depression is of course tied to the cognitive categories of our popular and psychiatric culture—certainly an ideology. Severe unhappiness in itself is seen as an illness in Western culture even when there are readily identifiable reasons for unhappiness in the social environment (so-called "reactive depression"), as well as when there are no such factors (so-called "endogenous depression").

REFERENCES

American Psychiatric Association (1987) Diagnostic and Statistical Manual of Mental Disorders, 3rd ed., revised. Washington, DC: American Psychiatric Association.

Castillo, Richard J. (1985) The Transpersonal Psychology of Patañjali's Yoga-Sûtra (Book 1: Samâdhi): A Translation and Interpretation. Journal of Mind and Behavior 6:391–417.

___. (1990) Depersonalization and Meditation. Psychiatry 53:158–168.

Dixon, J.C. (1963) Depersonalization Phenomena in a Sample Population of College Students. British Journal of Psychiatry 109:371–375.

Geertz, Clifford (1973) The Interpretation of Cultures. New York: Basic Books.

Kennedy, R.B. (1976) Self-Induced Depersonalization Syndrome. American Journal of Psychiatry 133:1326–1328.

Lang, R.D. (1965) The Divided Self. New York: Penguin Books.

Levy, J.S., and P.L. Wachtel (1978) Depersonalization: An Effort at Clarification. American Journal of Psychoanalysis 38:291–300.

Madan, T.N. (1987) Non-renunciation: Themes and Interpretations of Hindu Culture. Delhi: Oxford University Press.

Masson, J.M. (1976) The Psychology of the Ascetic. Journal of Asian Studies 35:611–625.

Masson, J.M. (1980) The Oceanic Feeling: The Origins of Religious Sentiment in Ancient India. Dordrecht, Holland: D. Reidel.

Miller, D.M., and D.C. Wertz (1976) Hindu Monastic Life: The Monks and Monasteries of Bhubaneshwar, Montreal: McGill Queens University Press.

Obeyesekere, Gananath (1981) Medusa's Hair: An Essay on Personal Symbols and Religious Experience. Chicago: University of Chicago Press.

___. (1985) Depression, Buddhism, and the Work of Culture in Sri Lanka. *In* Culture and Depression: Studies in the Anthropology and Cross-Cultural Psychiatry of Affect and Disorder. A. Kleinman and B. Good, eds. Pp. 134–152. Berkeley: University of California Press.

Roth, M., R.F. Garside, and C. Gurney (1965) Clinical and Statistical Enquiries into the Classification of Anxiety States and Depressive Disorders. *In* Proceedings of Leeds Symposium on Behavioural Disorders. London: May and Baker.

Sedman, G. (1966) Depersonalization in a Group of Normal Subjects. British Journal of Psychiatry 112:907–912.

Sheehan, D.V. (1983) The Anxiety Disease. New York: Scribner's.

Sours, J.L. (1965) The "Break-off" Phenomenon. Archives of General Psychiatry 13:447–456.

Taylor, F.K. (1982) Depersonalization in the Light of Brentano's Phenomenology. British Journal of Medical Psychology 55:297–306.

Torch, E.M. (1981) Depersonalization Syndrome: An Overview. Psychiatric Quarterly 50:249–58.

Tripathi, B.D. (1978) The Sadhus of India: The Sociological View. Bombay: Popular Prakashan.

Trueman, D. (1984) Depersonalization in a Nonclinical Population. Journal of Psychology 116:107–112.

ROBERTO LEWIS-FERNÁNDEZ

The Proposed DSM-IV Trance and Possession Disorder Category

Potential Benefits and Risks[1]

"Non-Western" cultures, which make up 80% of the world and one-third of the population of the United States, exhibit culturally-patterned dissociative syndromes (characterized by prominent discontinuities of consciousness, memory, identity, and behaviour) which are phenomenologically distinct from the dissociative disorders described in DSM-III-R. Many of these indigenous syndromes, nevertheless, share several features in common with Western psychiatric disorders and thus can be formulated according to the DSM diagnostic format. That is, they are stable, discrete conditions in their societies of origin, commonly configured "descriptively" as relatively invariant clusters of symptoms[2]; they are usually characterized as afflictions resulting from heightened stress; and they often result in distress, impairment, and increased utilization of folk and professional health care resources. The distribution of these conditions is truly global and they are highly prevalent in very populous geographical regions, such as India, Malayo-Indonesia, Western Africa, and Latin America. Moreover, several "culture-bound" syndromes studied extensively over decades by anthropologists and cross-cultural psychiatrists are probably dissociative in nature. These include: *amok* in Malayo-Indonesia (Carr & Tan, 1976; Schmidt, Hill, & Guthrie, 1977; Prince, 1991); *ataques de nervios* among Puerto Ricans and other Latin Americans (Guarnaccia, 1989, in press; Lewis-Fernández, in press); "blacking-out" among Bahamians (Weidman, 1979; Rubin & Jones, 1979); "falling-out" among working class African-Americans in the Southern United States (Weidman, 1979; Lefley, 1979); *indisposition* in Haiti (Philippe & Romain, 1979; Charles, 1979); *latah* in Malayo-Indonesia (Simons, 1980, 1983; Kenny, 1983); *pibloktoq* among the native people of the Arctic (Gussow, 1960; Foulks, 1985); and various possession trance syndromes presenting with distinct but related traits in India (Varma, Srivastava & Sahay, 1970; Chandrashekar, 1989), Sri Lanka (Obeyesekere, 1970), Hong Kong (Yap, 1960), Taiwan (Kleinman, 1980), Malaysia (Ong, 1987), Niger (Stoller, 1989), South-

ern Africa (Gussler, 1973), Brazil (Pressel, 1977), Puerto Rico (Quiñones, 1991) and Haiti (Walker, 1972).

Yet, despite their widespread distribution, high prevalence, extensive ethnographic characterization, and high rates of distress and impairment, these dissociative conditions, so far, have found a place in the DSM nosology only as "Atypical" or "Not Otherwise Specified" variations of the Dissociative Disorders. In India, for example, a recent study found that over 90% of the dissociative disorders diagnosed at an out-patient psychiatry clinic failed to meet criteria for a specified category and instead received a DSM-III diagnosis of Atypical Dissociative Disorder (Saxena & Prasad, 1989).

It is time to correct this diagnostic dissonance. Syndromes that are over 90% of cases are not "atypical"—it is our diagnostic categories that need revision and expansion to incorporate these distinct cross-cultural dissociative phenomenologies. The current proposal for the inclusion of a new "Trance and Possession Disorder" diagnosis in the Dissociative Disorders section of the DSM-IV, which parallels an equivalent category already incorporated into ICD-10, is precisely directed to this purpose. Approval of this proposal would provide a Western nosological niche for these indigenous dissociative syndromes, thus facilitating their continued psychiatric and medical-anthropological investigation. It would constitute an important advance in the ongoing effort to increase the cross-cultural validity of the DSM (Mezzich, Kleinman, Fabrega, Good Johnson, Lin, Marson & Parion, 1992), which has been consistently criticized for its ethnocentric bias (Kleinman, 1988, 1992; Fabrega, 1989; Good & Kleinman, 1985; Rogler, 1989).

It is essential, however, that the cross-cultural validation of the professional nosology not result in a systematic misrepresentation of the categories of experience of other cultures. Embedded in every nosology are implicit understandings regarding what constitute "real" illness experiences, which include culturally-validated phenomenologies, etiologies and notions of causality, precipitants, courses, treatments, sick roles and social responses, and characteristic mixtures of materialist, psychological, social, ecological, and spiritual interpretations of illness. In recasting indigenous illness forms into a Western nosology, we risk substituting our ideas for theirs, fundamentally altering their experience in a Procrustean fashion, and falling into a "category fallacy" (Kleinman, 1977).

We run this risk now with this new proposed diagnosis, on three counts. First, because the local ways of distinguishing between experiences of health and illness which are embedded in the indigenous conditions constituting the new diagnosis are different from those of our biomedical nosology; this renders difficult the accurate psychiatric assessment of individual sufferers across cultures. Secondly, because the prototypical presentations of the indigenous syndromes cut across Western diagnostic boundaries distinguishing thought, affective, anxiety, dissociative, and somatoform disorders; this renders somewhat arbitrary any exclusive assignation of diagnostic status to the syndromes as global categories. Thirdly, because, although Trance and Possession Disorder may be misinterpreted as a single and uniform diagnostic construct, it is in fact a dual, composite category that was crafted for clinical and research purposes out of multiple indigenous syndromes which are phenomenologically diverse from both the emic and the etic perspectives. Thus, the new category may unwillingly suggest a greater degree of phenomenological uniformity than exists among the indigenous syndromes or, worse yet, it may induce the creation of a hybrid nosological entity without empirical validity.

THE IMPORTANCE OF CONTEXT IN DIAGNOSIS

Current psychiatric nosology categorizes experience as normal or pathological based mainly on the presence of descriptive indicators ("symptoms") and only secondarily on contextual characteristics, such as the appropriateness of the setting, the human circumstances, the provocation and the personal or social timing of the experience. Wary of "theoretical" etiologies, our current diagnostic system privileges a formal definition of pathology; Major Depressive Episode (MDE), for example, is defined according to a decontextualized symptom cluster, independent of precipitating factors (only acute bereavement, which usually preempts a diagnosis of MDE during its relatively brief duration, escapes this emphasis on pure description).

Most indigenous nosologies, on the other hand, distinguish pathology from normality at least as much on the basis of contextual characteristics as on descriptive ones. According to such indigenous systems, the signs of pathological possession trance,

for example, consist largely of assessments regarding the appropriateness of this kind of trance in the particular setting and at the specific time in question, of the relative sufficiency of the precipitating stressors, and of the nature and quality of the human relationships of the sufferer. Descriptive features are not neglected, however. Diagnosis is also based on the assessed normativity of the possession trance phenomenology, on the degree of distress and impairment of the sufferer, and on the course of the condition and its response to treatment. The similarity of these latter diagnostic methods to our own make it possible to formulate these syndromes as DSM categories and thus create a "Trance and Possession Disorder" category in DSM-IV (Lewis-Fernández, 1991, in press; Cardeña, Lewis-Fernández, Bear, Pakianathan & Spiegel, in press). But the contextual character of the diagnosis is equally fundamental although much harder to incorporate into psychiatric nosology, due precisely to the general acontextual stance of the DSM. As a result, context is represented only by criterion B of the disorder: "The trance or possession trance state is not authorized as a normal part of a collective cultural or religious practice" (APA Dissociative Disorders Committee, June 24, 1992, p. 12). This criterion essentially requires the Western clinician considering the new disorder to take into account the type of contextual assessment that is at least half of the indigenous healer's diagnostic art. In fact, it entails a rudimentary ethnographic evaluation—a brief review of the context of suffering and its local interpretation—which may require the assistance of cultural experts. However, a single contextuality criterion embedded in an otherwise descriptive nosological format may be too easily misinterpreted or overlooked. It is possible that the new disorder may be misapplied generally as a purely formal, decontextualized attribution of pathology.

We run the risk, therefore, of misattributing pathological status to all trance and possession trance states worldwide due to the misapplication of an overly formalistic nosological philosophy to phenomena which are delicately contextual in their native form. Trance and possession trance states in their indigenous cultures are not like the "Panic Disorder" category of the West. Most trance and possession trance states which adhere to the phenomenology described in the Disorder criteria, even when they occur frequently, are still normal, as long as they do not lead to distress or impairment, or do not fulfil the limited contextual requirements of criterion B. In fact, the overwhelming majority of trance states across cultures are normal, and probably represent the voluntary use of non-distressing dissociative ability for the purposes of culturally-accepted healing rituals, religious and philosophical practices, and secular rituals of various kinds (including rituals performed in order to negotiate changing interpersonal relationships or as expressions of sociopolitical resistance).

In sum, the first danger inherent in the new category is the potential misattribution of pathology to normal trancing subjects as a result of the discrepancy between psychiatric and indigenous nosological philosophies on the value of contextualization in the clinical assessment of experience.

NOSOLOGIES REFLECT DIFFERENT ORGANIZATIONS OF EXPERIENCE

Culturally-defined syndromes are different from DSM disorders in a second way: the configuration of their phenomenologies (Good & Delvecchio Good, 1982; Wig, 1983; Good & Kleinman, 1985; Kleinman, 1988; Weiss, 1991). The symptomatologies of *ataque de nervios* in Puerto Rico and "Possession Syndrome" in India—the prototypes for Trance and Possession Disorder—are composed of behavioral and experiential elements which are considered by Western nosologists to belong in separate diagnostic categories. The characteristic presentations of these conditions exhibit marked dissociative features, and, in addition, they may display diverse combinations of psychotic, anxiety, depressive, characterological and somatic symptoms (Lewis-Fernández, 1991, in press). There is also significant phenomenological variation among individual cases; rarely, the indigenous label may even be ascribed to someone with only minor dissociative symptoms.

This difference in phenomenological organization between psychiatric and indigenous categories ensures that the two nosologies are non-overlapping as global systems. From the psychiatric perspective, a cohort of individuals identified by a single indigenous label will prove to be diagnostically heterogeneous, or even nonpathological. The obverse is also true: homogeneous psychiatric cohorts will appear locally diverse. In creating the new disorder, a nomographic, one-to-one relationship between it and the indigenous syndromes is not intended. *A priori,* all *ataques de nervios* are not instances of Trance and Possession Disorder, and vice-versa. Individual *cases* of persons suffering from *ataques de nervios*, rather than the nosological category *per se,* are amenable to psychiatric evaluation and the possibility of diagnosis and treatment. A diagnosis of Trance and Possession Disorder is contemplated when the key presenting symptoms are consistent with the dissociative characteristics of a trance or possession trance state and the features of the case fulfil the other disorder criteria. It is expected that the majority of *ataque de nervios* cases will qualify for this diagnosis. Certain cases of *ataque de nervios*, on the other hand, only display minor dissociative features inconsistent with disorder criteria, and instead may fulfil criteria for Panic Disorder (which does contain minor dissociative symptoms among its features). Those cases of *ataque de nervios* should receive a diagnosis of Panic Disorder and not one of Trance and Possession Disorder. In turn, cases

with complex symptomatology fulfilling both sets of criteria should probably receive both diagnoses until further differentiating procedures are available. Moreover, the indigenous label of *ataque de nervios* should be preserved (perhaps in a cultural axis and/or a cultural formulation), as it provides invaluable clinical information on potential precipitants, etiological attributions, treatment expectations and compliance, family role, and even course and outcome of illness.

These arguments may appear invalid to some Western nosologists. But there is no getting around the fact that the indigenous syndromes are highly heterogenous from the perspective of our diagnostic system. It is arbitrary to attribute all cases of a syndrome by nosological fiat exclusively to a single psychiatric disorder. This would constitute an unwarranted homogenization ahead of the clinical facts, the summation into a privileged phenomenological prototype of what appear as diverse local presentations clustered around a single indigenous label. Instead, each case must be evaluated independently.

Therefore, the second danger raised by the new disorder is the invalid conclusion that it encompasses all the relevant phenomenological presentations of the indigenous syndromes, and could thus substitute for them in all respects, as their conceptual equivalent (or superior) and as their exclusive nosological replacement.

THE DIVERSITY OF SYNDROMES

Though clearly crafted as a composite category (a fact announced by the conjunction "and" in its title and by the bifurcation of its criteria into parallel descriptions of trance and possession trance), the new Trance and Possession Disorder may be misconstrued as describing a single uniform phenomenological entity. In fact, the various indigenous syndromes which make up this one category display significant etic and emic diversity.

Etically, the new disorder is dual. It subsumes the pathological cases of two distinct subcategories of dissociative state: trances and possession trances (Bourguignon, 1973). The distinction between these is set out in the criteria and elaborated in the text of the proposed DSM-IV draft. (See Appendix A of the article by Cardeña, *this issue*).

The proposed text distinguishes further between these two subcategories:

In general, pathological trance and possession trance states may be differentiated by the following diagnostic features: (1) during possession trance there is the appearance of one or several distinct alternate identities, with characteristic behaviors, memories, and attitudes, whereas, during trance, loss of customary identity is not associated with the appearance of alternate identities; (2) during possession trance, the activities performed by the person tend to be of greater complexity (e.g., coherent conversations; stereotyped behaviors culturally established as belonging to the particular possessing agent, such as characteristic gestures, facial expressions, and specific verbalizations) than the simpler actions performed during trance (e.g., convulsive movements, falling, running); and (3) following an episode of possession trance a definite report of full or partial amnesia is more reliably obtained than following an episode of trance (though reports of amnesia after trance states are not uncommon) (APA Dissociative Disorders Committee, June 24, 1992, pp. 4–5).

These distinctions are not totally rigid. Cases may present with a mixed phenomenology (e.g., conditions fulfilling criteria for pathological trance which are attributed to the effect of possession but do not show outright identity alteration or amnesia), or move between symptom clusters over time according to local cultural parameters. The key point, nevertheless, is that it is generally possible to distinguish etically between two distinct subcategories of experience, both of which are denoted by the new disorder. Presenting them together in one nosological entity makes clinical and research sense, but runs the risk of obscuring their significant phenomenological differences.

The etic duality outlined above constitutes only a bird's-eye view of the diversity encompassed by the new disorder. More detailed differences (as well as similarities) between the indigenous syndromes qualifying for a Trance and Possession Disorder diagnosis are registered when these are compared from an emic perspective, which analyzes each syndrome as a totality emerging from its particular culture of birth. Emic-based analysis picks out the clinical, epidemiological and anthropological correspondences and variances between the syndromes, both between those that are ascribed to different etic subcategories (e.g., trances vs. possession trances) as well as between those that are considered etically similar (e.g., diverse possession trances). An emic-based comparison of Puerto Rican *ataque de nervios* (a "trance") and Indian "Possession Syndrome" (a possession trance), the prototypes for the new disorder, clearly illustrates the phenomenological complexity underlying the category of Trance and Possession Disorder.

Ataques de nervios are characterized by an involuntary narrowing of awareness of the immediate surroundings, associated with shaking or convulsive movements, followed by hyperventilation and increased autonomic signs, screaming, semi-purposeful aggressive movements and agitation, and culminating in collapse and partial or full loss of consciousness. After the acute event, sufferers may complain of exhaustion and sometimes of partial or total amnesia for the episode (Guarnaccia, 1989; Lewis-Fernández, in press).

Cases of Possession Syndrome in India are characterized by a different configuration of dissociative features. In this condition,

the affected person starts to behave and speak in a manner consistent with an alternate identity usually easily recognized by members of the person's local culture as that of a spirit or god, even referring to the person's usual identity in the third person. Typically, special requests are solicited by the possessing agent (such as improvement of marital relations or cessation of abuse), followed by bursts of agitation or aggressive acts if these are not met. Complex negotiations may follow, until an arrangement is reached with the possessing spirit. Upon the departure of the alternate personality, the person returns to his/her usual identity after a brief period of disorientation and reports full or partial amnesia for the events (Chandrashekar, 1989; Lewis-Fernández, in press).

A thorough comparison of these conditions from the perspective of their emic particularities yields the following similarities and differences (Lewis-Fernàndez, in press):

Similarities between ataques and Possession Syndrome. Both syndromes stem from a dissociative reaction to a broad range of stressors (from mild to traumatic) occurring in the absence of firm emotional support and leading to distressing experiences of loss, grief, anger, fear and vulnerability. Phenomenologically, they share the following features: trance-like dissociations of consciousness, sensorimotor control and often also of memory (though this is less frequent in *ataque de nervios*), characterized by ego-dystonic acts and, occasionally, threatening gestures. These dissociations do not prevent marked responsivity to environmental cues. In both conditions, each dissociative shift lasts minutes to hours; exhaustion is typically reported immediately after an acute episode. Their course is variable, ranging from resolution after a single episode to years-long recurrence, distress and impairment, but it is typically relapsing, with a return to premorbid functioning between episodes. Both syndromes are more prevalent among women and may present as an epidemic when a community is exposed to a collective stressor—e.g., natural disaster (although endemicity is the more usual pattern for *ataque de nervios*). They are more prevalent as well among more disadvantaged social groups, those with limited formal education and the formerly married. In both conditions, there is debate whether they are due to hysteria or traumatically-induced dissociation, and both syndromes are associated with suicidality. They are often associated in epidemiological studies with non-dissociative psychopathology. Indigenously, they are seen as requiring some form of treatment, which may be home-based. When referred to specialized spiritual healers, they may receive similar treatments, including exorcism or admission into a trancing community. Anthropologically, both are associated with female gender, marginalized social status and with the social communication of resistance and a request for group solidarity but not with the expression of "mental illness," which in contrast, is heavily stigmatized. Finally, both show substantial historical variation in gender and age prevalence, and in their indigenous assessment of normality or health.

Differences between ataques and Possesion Syndrome.

Phenomenologically, the onset of an *ataque de nervios* tends to be more stereotyped (sudden shift in consciousness) than that of Possession Syndrome (which may have a somatoform prodrome before any acute shift in consciousness). *Ataques de nervios* are characterized uniformly by an affective storm congruent with the precipitating stimulus and associated with somatic alterations, whereas the display of prominent affective and somatic changes in Possession Syndrome is more variable and depends on the sufferer's reaction to his/her interpersonal environment during an attack. Unlike *ataques de nervios*, Possession Syndrome displays dissociative identity alteration (possession trance) with marked culture-specific features, which is usually associated with visual and auditory hallucinations of the possessing agent and with coherent vocalizations and demands during an attack. Loss of consciousness, disorientation and partial or total amnesia after an acute episode are typical of Possession Syndrome and apparently less frequent or less severe in *ataques de nervios*. Acute episodes of *ataque de nervios* are typically composed of a single shift in consciousness, whereas those of Possession Syndrome are frequently composed of many subsequent shifts of varying duration which can alternate for days or weeks. Perhaps correspondingly, *ataques* tend to be precipitated by sudden and discrete stressors, whereas the possession appears to result more often from gradually intensifying stress, following their respective cultural associations. Despite the fact that the prevalence of both syndromes can display an epidemic pattern, *ataque de nervios* is primarily endemic, whereas Possession Syndrome is frequently epidemic. Currently, *ataque de nervios* is more prevalent among the middle-aged (over 45) and Possession Syndrome among adolescents and young adults (under 30). Psychiatrically, *ataques de nervios* are markedly associated with depressive and anxiety conditions, whereas Possession Syndrome sufferers are more often given diagnoses of "Hysteria" and "Paranoid States". (However, this discrepancy may be the result of methodological differences and/or local diagnostic practices rather than actual psychopathological differences.) Anthropologically, the Indian syndrome—but not the Puerto Rican one—appears to be linked to social groups which symbolize the traversing of boundaries (such as castes who regularly cross geographical village borders or persons undergoing transitional life phases—e.g., marriage). Possession is also more closely associated with spiritual notions of causation (leading to the phenomenon of supernatural identity alteration) and, therefore, of spiritist treatment. *Ataques de nervios* usually present to multiple and diverse caregivers (including physicians), often at once, whereas sufferers of Possession Syndrome tend to prefer spiritual healers and avoid professional services.

Even within etic subcategories, the indigenous syndromes still display significant emic variability. Cross-culturally, different "trance" syndromes are associated with distinct behaviours performed during the altered state, and with the variable presence or absence of dissociative sensory alterations (e.g., blindness), among other differences. For example, in contrast to the characteristics of *ataque de nervios,* the diagnostic features of "falling-out," a trance disorder observed among working class African-Americans in the Southern United States, include more specific dissociative perceptual alterations. Falling-out is characterized by physical collapse either without warning or after momentary dizziness, accompanied by the inability to see, move or speak despite the ability to hear and understand. Afterwards, transient confusion may be reported, but amnesia appears to be rare (Weidman, 1979).

Alternatively, different "possession trance" syndromes vary across cultures according to the following: the identity of the specific agents of possession and the corresponding effects of their influence, the presence or absence of identity substitution and stereotyped behaviours characteristic of the possessing agent, and the degree of amnesia experienced following the altered state. For example, the features of "spirit possession" among female factory workers in Malaysia, a pathological possession trance condition, are distinct from those of Possession Syndrome in India. In these Malay cases, there is no global alteration of identity. Instead, sufferers describe a sudden vision of a terrifying, pouncing spirit which causes them to scream in fright; subsequently, they report amnesia for the succeeding events. The sufferers are then observed to sob or shriek, flail against objects and persons (sometimes with reportedly "superhuman" strength), and require restraining to prevent self-harm. They are clearly thought to be possessed by the spirit they perceived, which is considered the true agent of their uncharacteristic actions. However, their individual identities appear not to be supplanted; a new personality is neither portrayed nor verbalized (Ong, 1987).

A "Trance and Possession Disorder" diagnostic category should not be used to moot the etic and emic complexity of the various related indigenous dissociative syndromes that influenced its creation. The major etic distinction between trance and possession trance is in fact preserved quite clearly in its title and criteria. The purpose of the new category, instead, is to set out a Western nosological niche for a whole class of dissociative illness experiences previously unaccounted for by the DSM system. The existence of this niche should facilitate, not hinder, continued psychiatric and medical-anthropological characterization of the significant cross-cultural diversity of illness forms encompassed by the new disorder.

In sum, the third risk presented by the proposed category is the unwarranted minimization, in the name of a superficial nosological uniformity, of the considerable emic and etic phenomenological diversity of pathological trance and possession trance states existing across cultures.

CONCLUSION

The foregoing may be misunderstood as arguments against the acceptance of Trance and Possession Disorder into DSM-IV. This is far from the case. I believe the new category is absolutely necessary, because it brings into official nosology a salient class of illness experiences affecting millions of individuals worldwide which currently receives insufficient clinical and research attention. Its professional recognition would contribute to the growing cultural sensitivity and internationalization of the DSM and, specifically, to its rapprochement with the ICD. This class of illness forms is amenable to formulation in descriptive psychiatric terms, and the primacy of its dissociative syndromes places it in that larger diagnostic category. My comments, instead, are meant to articulate a debate about the risks inherent in our attempts to craft a global nosological system.

The three dangers outlined above represent some of the possible ways in which the subtlety of cross-cultural differences may be left out in the process of creating diagnostic entities. This would be an unnecessary and deleterious omission. Anthropology in general, and clinical ethnography in particular, can contribute uniquely to descriptive psychiatry. These disciplines can provide clinicians with essential data on the motivations, conflicts and contextual variables of illness experience embedded in indigenous syndromes, especially when evaluation and therapy is carried out across cultural boundaries. This task is different from, and complementary to, that of the formal nosologist, and both are equally important for effective therapeutic intervention. To illustrate: evaluation and treatment of a case of Malayo-Indonesian *amok,* one of the syndromes typically qualifying for inclusion in Trance and Possession Disorder, requires both an appreciation of the formal features of the case—its "symptoms" (for example, the degree and form of dissociation and/or psychosis, of associated depression, anxiety, etc.)—and of the social messages entailed by the sufferer's behaviour—that is, the culturally-understood adequacy of his motivation and precipitants, the possibility of relapse given the community reaction, the personal and social point of the behaviour, and so on. Assessment of the former yields a psychiatric formulation and diagnosis; the latter is explicated by the intracultural comparisons afforded by ethnographic analysis. The task of psychiatric formulation is facilitated by the inclusion of the new disorder in DSM-IV. My point is that the indigenous particularities of the ethnographic analysis should not be pushed aside and neglected by clinicians or by totalizing nosologies. If, however, the operant Western nosology does not contain a diagnostic niche for *amok* which accurately portrays the psychiatric fea-

tures of the condition, then the clinical evaluation is flawed, and competent performance of the main mandate of psychiatry is seriously compromised.

The integrity of both the psychiatric and the indigenous perspectives can be preserved by retaining the conceptual separation between their representative nosologies. Trance and Possession Disorder does not render obsolete the categories of *amok, pibloktoq,* etc. They complement each other, as cultural systems which are only partially-overlapping and which emphasize different views of human phenomena. We should keep and develop both, and for that we need the iterative cross-fertilization and development of two of the relevant Western disciplines. Psychiatry, in order to be truly global and etic, needs a "Trance and Possession Disorder." The indigenous syndromes, on the other hand, in order to be accurately represented, need the emic complexity and contextuality of ethnographic analysis.

NOTES

[1]Support for this work was provided by an NIMH Fellowship in Clinically-Relevant Medical Anthropology (1991–92) (RER-25 T32 MH18006-07), by the MacArthur Foundation Research Network on Mind-Body Interactions, and by the Cummings Foundation. The author appreciated many helpful conversations that contributed to the ideas expressed in this essay with Arthur Kleinman, David Spiegel, Mitchell Weiss, Byron Good, Mary-Jo Good, Etzel Cardeña, Peter Guarnaccia, Laurence Kirmayer, Goretti Almeida, and the Dissociation Group and Medical Anthropology Fellows at Harvard. Responsibility for the shortcomings of the views expressed herein are of course the author's own.

[2]"Trance and Possession Disorder" does not encompass indigenous syndromes organized (a) along "etiological" parameters—by attributed causation—or (b) according to ascribed treatment modality (cf. Good & Delvecchio Good, 1982).

REFERENCES

APA Dissociative Disorders Committee. (R. Lewis-Fernández, E. Cardeña, and D. Spiegel, drafters.) (1992, June 24th). "Proposed text for the Trance and Possession Disorder category in DSM-IV." Unpublished manuscript, 4th revision

Bourguignon, E. (1973). Introduction: A framework for the comparative study of altered states of consciousness. In E. Bourguignon (Ed.), *Religion, altered states of consciousness, and social change* (pp. 3–35). Columbus, Ohio: Ohio State University Press.

Cardeña, E., Lewis-Fernández, R., Bear, D., Pakianathan, I. & Spiegel, D. (in press). Dissociative disorders. In *DSM-IV sourcebook,* Washington, D.C.: APA Press.

Carr, J.E. & Tan, E.K. (1976). In search of the true *amok: Amok* as viewed within the Malay culture. *American Journal of Psychiatry, 133*(11), 1295–1299.

Chandrashekar, C.R. (1989). Possession syndrome in India. In C.A. Ward (Ed.), *Altered states of consciousness and mental health* (pp. 79–95). Newbury Park: Sage.

Charles, C. (1979). Brief comments on the occurrence, etiology and treatment of *Indisposition. Social Science and Medicine, 13*B, 135–136.

Fabrega, H. (1989). An ethnomedical perspective on Anglo-American psychiatry. *American Journal of Psychiatry, 146,* 588–596.

Foulks, E.F. (1985). The transformation of 'Arctic Hysteria.' In R.C. Simons & C.C. Hughes (Eds.), *The culture-bound syndromes* (pp. 307–324). Dordrecht: Reidel.

Good, B.J. & Delvecchio Good, M-J. (1982). Toward a meaning-centered analysis of popular illness categories: 'Fright-Illness' and 'Heart Distress' in Iran. In A.J. Marsella & G.M. White (Eds.), *Cultural conceptions of mental health and therapy* (pp. 141–166). Dordrecht: Reidel.

Good, B.J. & Kleinman, A. (1985). Culture and anxiety: Cross-cultural evidence for the patterning of anxiety disorders. In H. Tuma & J. Mazur (Eds.), *Anxiety and the anxiety disorders* (pp. 297–323). New York: L. Erlbaum.

Guarnaccia, P.J., De La Cancela, V. & Carrillo, E. (1989). The multiple meaning of *ataques de nervios* in the Latino community. *Medical Anthropology, 11,* 47–62.

Guarnaccia, P.J., Canino, G., Rubio-Stipec, M., & Bravo, M. (in press). The prevalence of *ataques de nervios* in the Puerto Rico Disaster Study: The role of culture in psychiatric epidemiology. *Journal of Nervous and Mental Disease.*

Gussler, J. (1973). Social change, ecology, and spirit possession among the South African Nguni. In E. Bourguignon (Ed.), *Religion, altered states of consciousness, and social change* (pp. 88–126). Columbus, Ohio: Ohio State University Press.

Gussow, Z. (1960). *Pibloktoq* (Hysteria) among the Polar Eskimo. *The Psychoanalytic Study of Society, 1,* 218–236.

Kenny, M.G. (1983). Paradox lost: The *latah* problem revisited. *Journal of Nervous and Mental Disease, 171*(3), 159–167.

Kleinman, A. (1977) Depression, somatization and the "New cross-cultural psychiatry." *Social Science and Medicine, 11,* 3–10.

Kleinman, A. (1980). *Patients and healers in the context of culture: An exploration of the borderland between anthropology, medicine, and psychiatry.* Berkeley: University of California Press.

Kleinman, A. (1988). *Rethinking psychiatry: From cultural category to personal experience.* New York: The Free Press.

Kleinman, A. (in press) How culture is important for DSM-IV? In J. Mezzich (Ed.), *Culture and psychiatric diagnosis.* Washington D.C.: APA Press.

Lefley, H.P. (1979). Prevalence of potential Falling-out cases among the Black, Latin and non-Latin White populations of the city of Miami. *Social Science and Medicine, 13*B, 113–114.

Lewis-Fernández, R. (1991, October). *The indigenous dissociative syndromes: Evidence in support of the proposed Trance and Possession Disorder category for DSM-IV.* Working document submitted to the APA Dissociative Disorders Committee in October, 1991. Unpublished manuscript.

Lewis-Fernández, R. (in press). The role of culture in the configuration of dissociative states: A comparison of Puerto Rican *ataque de nervios* and Indian 'Possession Syndrome.' In D. Spiegel (Ed.), *Dissociation: Culture, mind and body.* Washington, D.C.: APA Press.

Obeyesekere, G. (1970). The idiom of demonic possession: A case study. *Social Science and Medicine, 4,* 97–111.

Ong, A. (1987). *Spirits of resistance and capitalist discipline: Factory women in Malaysia.* Albany, NY: State University of New York Press.

Mezzich, J.E., Kleinman, A. Fabrega, H., Good, B., Johnson-Powell, G., Lin, K-M., Manson, S. & Parron, D. (1992, April). *Cultural Proposals for DSM-IV.* Working document submitted to the DSM-IV Task Force by the Steering Committee, NIMH-Sponsored Group on Culture and Diagnosis. April, 1992. Unpublished manuscript.

Philippe, J. & Romain, J.B. (1979). *Indisposition* in Haiti. *Social Science and Medicine, 13*B, 129–133.

Pressel, E. (1977). Negative spirit possession in experienced Brazilian Umbanda spirit mediums. In V. Crapanzano & V. Garrison (Eds.), *Case studies in spirit possession* (pp. 333–364). New York: Wiley.

Prince, R. (1991). Amok then and now. *Transcultural Psychiatric Research Review, 28,* 219–229.

Quiñones, S. (1991). Exorcism: A therapeutic intervention. In L.N. Allende *et al.* (Eds.), *Claves psicológicas en nuestra América: Visión puertorriqueña* (pp. 221–29). San Juan: Libros Homines.

Rogler, L.H. (1989). The meaning of culturally sensitive research in mental health. *American Journal of Psychiatry, 146,* 296–303.

Rubin, J.C. & Jones, J. (1979). Falling-out: A clinical study. *Social Science and Medicine, 13*B, 117–27.

Saxena, S. & Prasad, K.V.S.R. (1989). DSM-III subclassification of Dissociative Disorders applied to psychiatric outpatients in India. *American Journal of Psychiatry, 146*(2), 261–262.

Schmidt, K., Hill, L. & Guthrie, G. (1977). Running *amok. International Journal of Social Psychiatry, 23*(4), 264–274.

Simons, R.C. (1980). The resolution of the *latah* paradox. *Journal of Nervous and Mental Disease, 168*(4), 195–206.

Simons, R.C. (1983). Latah II—Problems with a purely symbolic interpretation: A reply to Michael Kenny. *Journal of Nervous and Mental Disease, 171*(3), 168–175.

Stoller, P. (1989). *Fusion of the worlds: An ethnography of possession among the Songhay of Niger.* Chicago: University of Chicago Press.

Varma, L.P., Srivastava, D.K., & Sahay, R.N. (1970). Possession syndrome. *Indian Journal of Psychiatry, 12,* 58–70.

Walker, S.S. (1972). *Ceremonial spirit possession in Africa and Afro-America: Forms, meanings, and functional significance for individuals and social groups.* Leiden: Brill.

Weidman, H.H. (1979). Falling-out: A diagnostic and treatment problem viewed from a transcultural perspective. *Social Science and Medicine, 13*B, 95–112.

Weiss, M.G. (1991). Culture and the diagnosis of Somatoform and Dissociative Disorders: Comments and considerations based on González and Griffith. Paper presented at the "Cultural Issues and Psychiatric Diagnosis" Conference, Pittsburgh, PA, April 11–12.

Wig, N.N. (1983). DSM-III: A perspective from the Third World. In R.L. Spitzer, J.B.W. Williams & A.E. Skodol (Eds.), *International perspectives on DSM-III* (pp. 79–89). Washington, D.C.: American Psychiatric Press.

Yap, P.M. (1960). The Possession Syndrome: A comparison of Hong Kong and French findings. *The Journal of Mental Science, 106,* 114–137.

A. N. CHOWDHURY, A. K. NATH, AND J. CHAKRABORTY

An Atypical Hysteria Epidemic in Tripura, India

This paper reports an atypical hysteria epidemic in a tribal village of the State of Tripura, India. Twelve persons, eight female and four male, were affected in a chain reaction within a span of ten days. The cardinal feature was an episodic trance state of 5 to 15 minutes duration with restlessness, attempts at self-injury, running away, inappropriate behaviour, inability to identify family members, refusal of food and intermittent mimicking of animal sounds. The illness was self-limiting and showed an individual course of one to three days duration. Sociocultural aspects of the epidemic are discussed.

Tripura is a land-locked Eastern border state of India and is bounded by Bangladesh in the North, South and West. To the East, it borders on the Indian states of Assam and Mizoram (Figure 1). Agartala is the State capital. It is a terrain of hills and valleys; the hills are covered with dense forests. The climate is generally hot and humid, with plenty of rainfall occurring mainly from June to September during monsoon. The main occupation is agriculture and tea plantation.

The population is a mixed one, with tribal and Bengali groups comprising the majority and Christian and Muslims contributing significant minorities. The life of the people living in the valleys and plains is related to Bengali Hindu culture. In contrast, the tribal people, living mostly in the hill areas, have their own dialects, and social, recreational and health customs and rituals. Tripura has a rich heritage of tribal monarchy.

The present epidemic was confined to a small village "Garopara" situated two kilometres away from the Natunbazar Primary Health Centre (PHC) of the Amarpur area in the South District of Tripura (Figure 1). The village has a population of about 350, distributed among 35 families. They are mainly tribes of *Tripura* and *Marak* lines. The latter tribes are more concentrated in the Garo hill region of neighbouring State, Meghalaya.

THE EPIDEMIC

On the 27th August 1992, a radiogram message was received by the Health Department from the Natunbazar PHC reporting the outbreak of a "strange madness" in the nearby locality. A representation for urgent medical intervention was given to the PHC doctors by the Tripura Upajati Kalyan Samity (Tribal Welfare Organization) members on this day. Two psychiatrists (AKN and JC) from G.B. Hospital, Agartala immediately rushed to the spot (127 kilometres from Agartala) for investigation and medical intervention.

A total of 12 persons, eight female and four male were affected (Table 1). Locally, the illness was called "wild madness." The index case was a 20-year old single female. The clinical picture was a trance-like state of 5 to 15 minutes duration, starting

Figure 1
Map of Tripura. (Not drawn to scale.)

Table 1
Characteristics of consecutive cases in an epidemic of hysteria.

Case No.	Sex	Age (Yrs.)	Marital Status	Education	Occupation
1.	Female	20	Single	X Class	Student
2.	Female	16	Single	Illiterate	Nil
3.	Female	17	Single	Illiterate	Nil
4.	Female	18	Married	Illiterate	Housewife
5.	Female	35	Married	Illiterate	Housewife
6.	Male	7	Single	Illiterate	Nil
7.	Female	40	Married	Illiterate	Housewife
8.	Male	35	Married	Illiterate	Farmer
9.	Male	9	Single	Illiterate	Nil
10.	Male	60	Married	Illiterate	Nil
11.	Female	20	Married	Illiterate	Housewife
12.	Female	27	Married	Illiterate	Housewife

with extreme restlessness, throwing about of limbs and attempts at self-injury (slapping the face, strangulation by hand or clothing, hitting the head against the bamboo pillars or mud wall of the hut), staring and inability to identify family members, motor hyperactivity and a tendency to run away. This state persisted for four to six minutes to be followed by a loud shouting of different animal calls (e.g., dog, horse, cow, monkey, fox and crow) either singly or in combination. There was no consistent choice of any particular call. Sometimes the calls were of a single animal (mostly dog) with pauses and sometimes multiple calls, following one after another with different intonations. At this stage the patient appeared highly excited and was kept seated forcibly by others. One male child patient mimicked a galloping horse with a loud neigh. After this spell of five to ten minutes, the patient appeared exhausted and gradually became calm and silent. Cold water was sprinkled over the patient's head and face during this period. Within half an hour, patients gradually returned to their normal senses whereupon they could not recall the episode. Behaviour between the spells was absolutely normal except for feelings of weakness. The 12 cases were affected by a chain reaction within a time span of ten days. The average duration of the illness for an individual was two to three days with a frequency of spells of five to six times a day. No spell occurred during the night.

Mental status examination of the cases revealed no psychiatric abnormality except focal amnesia for the event. The patients failed to furnish reasons for the animal call and it appeared as if the question was unwanted. Their behaviour seemed manipulative and attention seeking; the impression of the attending psychiatrists was that they were quietly enjoying the gesture. The extraordinary village-wide magico-religious rituals pro-

voked by the epidemic made heroes of the victims and they were the focus of great community attention.

THE INDEX CASE

The index case was a single, 20-year old female. She was a student of class ten and the only educated patient. She was referred from Natunbazar PHC to G.B. Hospital, Agartala on the 4th of June 1992 with an uncertain diagnosis of epilepsy with mild fever. She was admitted in the hospital from the 4th to 13th of June and was diagnosed as a case of hysterical fit. Her skull x-ray and routine blood and urine examinations were normal. She was prescribed alprazolam tablets (0.25 mg) and B-vitamins.

After discharge, she had a few fits at home. During the last week of July, the frequency of her fits increased and this caused great concern among family members and villagers. By virtue of the good treatment facilities at G.B. Hospital and owing to the reputation of the hospital in caring for and treating the sick, there is a common conviction that anyone who does not benefit from being treated in this hospital has a grave prognosis. As the girl's fits continued, it was the overwhelming opinion of the villagers that her illness was running a serious course which might eventually culminate in death.

At the end of July she was having frequent fits, during which she made an abnormal loud noise, similar to a dog's bark. A series of traditional healing rituals with an *ojha* (village charmer) was done but the *mantras* and *tabij* failed to decrease the frequency of fits. A *tantrik* (charmer of higher rank) living in the same village was called in and he performed a lengthy religious ritual with *home* (holy fire) and *mantras* for two days. The *tantrik* then gave the verdict that this "wild madness" was inflicted by an envious neighbour through black magic and charms. He further advocated that the conspirator did this evil by secretly keeping some carcass bones, fortified with magical power, under the soil of the house. With elaborate religious and *tantrik* rituals, he discovered these bones by digging to one foot depth at a corner of the house yard. He identified bones of different dead animals including horse, cow, crow, monkey and fox. This magical discovery of charmed carcass bones caused a severe panic in the whole village and all the villagers were apprehensive that some great havoc would occur shortly. Every household started performing religious rituals, even in the face of extreme economic hardship, to abet the impending ill-effects of black magic. Within a few days the illness became a contagious one and it infected other villagers. This caused another panic reaction and the *tantrik* was forced to disclose the name of the "envious neighbour," whereupon he named an *ojha* of the village. This *ojha* was immediately beaten almost to death by the villagers but ultimately was rescued by the police. Another series of religious rituals and prayers started in every household and, in at least three affected families, the younger male members fled from their homes and took shelter elsewhere in fear of infection by this "evil madness." For a few days, this tiny tribal village became a seat of extreme fear and agony and people were pauperized because of the high cost of religious rituals and worship offerings. People from the neighbouring villages also stopped visiting for fear of evil infection and madness.

DISCUSSION

Sociopolitical and economic stress have often been implicated as causal factors in psychiatric outbreaks of "mass hysteria." Prince (1992) analyzed the background of several *koro* epidemics in the light of ethnic minority stress of various origins. In particular, rapid social change has often been regarded as detrimental to the survival of ethnoreligous minority cultures. Murphy (1982) stressed that loss of cultural identity and livelihood are matters of serious ethnic concern. Teoh, Soewondo and Sidharta (1975) stated that mass hysteria is common in transitional societies undergoing rapid social change in the midst of multiple stresses and tensions. They viewed mass hysterical behaviour as a byproduct of culture shock resulting from modernization. The analysis of this tribal epidemic in Tripura reveals some important facts in this regard.

The first relevant issue is the generalized background of sociopolitical tension and conflict prevalent in the region. Conflict between tribal and nontribal groups is a long-standing problem

in the State, causing many political upheavals in the past and is at the root of current extremist activity. Generalized hostility, often reaching the level of paranoia is common in this segment of the population. A majority of the tribal people believe that their gradual displacement from the present urban situation to interior lands and their loss of property are directly caused by the growth of the non-tribal population of the State. A rural-urban conflict has been brewing whereby many tribal clans view the towns, the urban non-tribals and their prosperity as signs of the waning of their cultural identity and socioeconomic supremacy. These feelings have been given vehement expression in sociopolitical movements based on ethnic solidarity.

The index case, an educated girl, was an economic asset to her tribal community. Her illness caused great concern among the villagers and it was widely believed that she might easily be the victim of a conspiracy. Her illness then became an issue of broad social concern and initiated a two-fold response. First, strong magico-religious beliefs promoted paranoid cognition and helped to transmit fear to vulnerable individuals so that new cases appeared. Murphy (1982) stressed the importance of the index case in such hysterical epidemics where the pattern of symptom presentation by the initial case determines the symptoms of subsequent victims. The symptom pattern of animal calls gained community acceptance because it was consistent with folk beliefs. The isolated small village pockets in the midst of forest and hills have a variety of folk-beliefs that animal-ghost possession can lead to madness. The malevolent character of ghosts of animals like cow (*godana*) and horse (*ghodana*) is well accepted. The crow is viewed as a bird with unholy and magical influence. Some believe that a venomous jungle spider can inflict madness by its bite. These cultural beliefs strengthened the paranoid attribution of illness etiology.

In relation to mass hysterical outbreaks, Raymond and Ackerman (1980) identified a similar concept in the world view of a Malay community which places heavy stress on supernatural and spirit possession in the causation of abnormal behaviour. Prince (1992), in a recent analysis of the epidemiology of *koro*, described the role of "fox spirit" as a cultural belief in Hainan Island, China. Belief in magical power often plays an important cognitive role in epidemic hysterical behaviour as is apparent in the account of magical penis loss by supernatural forces in Nigeria (Ilechukwu, 1992).

The loud sounds mimicking animal calls are of special interest here. Langness (1965) reported a hysterical psychotic episode, *negi negi*, in the Bena Bena people of New Guinea where he found a cry of "loud, piercing, unnatural sounds" in three successive turns in the affected victim which he described as an "insane cackle." Bena culture holds that *negi negi* is due to malevolent ghosts. Carothers (1959) discussed the role of sounds from a psychiatric anthropological perspective:

Sounds are in a sense dynamic things, or at least are always indicators of dynamic things—of movements, events, activities, for which man, when largely unprotected from the hazards of life in bush or veldt, must be ever on the alert. Whatever form they take—thunder, the burble of running water, the snapping of twigs, the cries of animals, the beating of drums, the voice or music of man—they are usually of direct significance, and often even of peril, for the hearer.

The significance of sound, he asserted, plays an important role in a "large array of ethnopsychological and ethnopsychiatric facts," especially among the rural, nonliterate people of the world.

Small and Nicholi (1982) stressed the preponderance of young women in epidemic hysterical illness and the importance of the transmission of illness by sight and/or sound. All these features are present in the current outbreak. The loud animal call of the cases reported here served at least three intelligible functions: (1) to signify animal-ghost possession (consistent with cultural beliefs); (2) to evoke community fear and anxiety (to gain social attention); and (3) to act as an acceptable model for other vulnerable individuals (the contagious aspect).

The second social response to the illness was the mobilization by the community of its healing resources to combat this malady. This response to the epidemic followed two paths: (1) a major effort was to take recourse in medio-religious healing rituals with performances of rites by a *tantrik*. This also addressed intra-community conflicts inasmuch as the *tantrik* identified another medicine man (*ojha*) of this community as the conspirator. (2) Another path of response was followed by the Tribal Welfare Organization who sought medical intervention from the nearby treatment centre. Kirmayer (1992) suggests this type of resort to biomedicine might be an attempt at "medical legitimation" of distress. Medical help-seeking was also emphasized by the previous history of hospital admission and treatment of the index case.

Mass hysterical outbreaks are not uncommon in this region. In June 1992, an episode of a mass trance-like state with religious identification (involving the clan priest "Guru") was noted in Sachan village in the Udaypur area. The index case was a middle-aged housewife who one morning identified herself with the male priest Babamoni and went into a prolonged trance state. She refused her normal diet except fruit during this period. She claimed that the divine spirit of Babamoni was being transmitted into her soul and she exhibited a stereotyped swinging movement for hours at a time. Her husband (42 years old), one son (24) and one daughter (18) all went into a similar trance state and believed that they also possessed the divine soul of their clan priest. Consequently, seven females (four married, three unmarried), two adult males (26 and 40 years old) and two male children (seven and eight) of this locality developed the same transformation. The whole episode lasted for two weeks.

A few years ago another mass hysterical outbreak occurred in the Teliamura town (40 km from Agartala) involving more than 60 people. The chief complaint was the loss of power and sensation in the limbs, especially the lower limbs, thus making the affected individuals lame. The illness was locally called "*Jhinjhine*" and predominantly affected females. An intervention by a medical team checked the spread of the illness in the locality.

In conclusion, the cases in the hysterical epidemic reported here might be diagnosed with an atypical form of somatoform disorder involving animal calls and alterations of consciousness.[1] At a social level, the epidemic may be understood as the expression of ethnic anxiety through traditional cultural illness beliefs.

NOTE

[1]Lukianowicz (1967) discussed the different forms of body image disturbances (shape) in schizophrenics which he termed as "zoophilic metamorphosis" and his findings are worth mentioning here. He cited case histories of the patients experiencing different transformations involving animals like dog, cat, crab, lion and monkey, either as a whole or in some portions of their body (dog's body, crab's hand, cat's paw, lion's head and monkey's curly tail) but without exhibiting any explicit animal behaviour. Moreover, they had clear insight into the unreality of their experiences.

REFERENCES

Carothers, J.C. (1959). Culture, psychiatry, and the written word. *Psychiatry, 22,* 307–320.

Ilechukwu, S.T.C. (1992). Magical penis loss in Nigeria: Report of a recent epidemic of a *koro*-like syndrome. *Transcultural Psychiatric Research Review, 29*(2), 91–108.

Kirmayer, L.J. (1992). From the Witches' Hammer to the Oedipus complex: Castration anxiety in Western society. *Transcultural Psychiatric Research Review, 29*(2), 133–158.

Langness, L.L. (1965). Hysterical psychosis in the New Guinea highlands: A Bena Bena example. *Psychiatry, 22,* 258–277.

Lukianowicz, N. (1967). "Body image" disturbances in psychiatric disorders. *British Journal of Psychiatry, 113,* 31–47.

Murphy, H.B.M. (1982). *Comparative psychiatry: The international and intercultural distribution of mental illness.* New York: Springer-Verlag.

Prince, R. (1992). *Koro* and the fox spirit on Hainan Island (China). *Transcultural Psychiatric Research Review, 29*(2), 119–132.

Raymond, L.M. & Ackerman, S.E. (1980). The sociocultural dynamics of mass hysteria: A case study of social conflict in West Malaysia. *Psychiatry, 43,* 78–88.

Small, G.W. & Nicholi, A.M. (1982). Mass hysteria among school children. *Archives of General Psychiatry, 39,* 721–724.

Teoh, J.I., Soewondo, S. & Sidharta, M. (1975). Epidemic hysteria in Malaysian school: An illustrative episode. *Psychiatry, 38,* 258–268.

CHAPTER FOURTEEN

Culture and Schizophrenia

Cultural meaning systems shape the experience of self through the construction of cultural schemas, as well as structuring the physical and social environments. The most fundamental consequence of recognizing this cultural influence is the fact that symptomatic manifestations may be interpreted differently by individuals, healers, and societies. This is especially true when dealing with schizophrenic symptoms such as hallucinations and delusions. These symptoms do not stand alone as universally pathological phenomena but depend on the prevailing cultural schemas and social relationships of the persons involved. The meanings of schizophrenia are constructed within a sociocultural context with important implications for adaptive functioning, subjective experience, idioms of distress, culture-based diagnoses, treatments, and outcomes.

The World Health Organization has conducted two major international comparisons of persons with psychoses: International Pilot Study of Schizophrenia (WHO, 1973) and Determinants of Outcome of Severe Mental Disorders (WHO, 1979). These two studies were carried out in nine and ten countries, respectively, and represented both economically developed and less developed societies. These studies found important cross-cultural differences in symptomatology. Overall, paranoid schizophrenia was the most commonly diagnosed subtype, followed by undifferentiated and acute. However, in less developed societies, acute schizophrenia was found almost twice as often (40%) as paranoid schizophrenia (23%). Catatonic schizophrenia was found in 10% of the cases in less developed societies but in only a handful of cases in developed societies. In contrast, undifferentiated schizophrenia was found in 13% of the cases from developed societies and in only 4% of the cases from less developed societies. Thus, the WHO researchers have found significant differences in symptomatology across cultures. These differences are most likely attributable to the cognitive structuring of cultural schemas producing different cultural experiences of the self, illness, and the environment.

The most important finding of these studies was that the clinical course and social impairment of schizophrenia are more benign in less developed societies, regardless of the nature of onset or type of presenting symptoms. This finding was especially true in the least economically developed nations in the study (Nigeria and India).

Patients in the less developed countries had a better course and outcome than did patients in the most economically developed countries (Great Britain, United States, and Denmark). This finding was confirmed during both two-year and five-year follow-up studies (Leff et al., 1992; Sartorius et al., 1986; WHO, 1979). In the economically developed countries, only 25% of the patients were classified in the best two outcome categories, and 65% were classified in the worst two outcome categories. In contrast, in the economically less developed countries, 39% were classified in the best two categories, and only 38% were in the worst two categories (Sartorius et al., 1986). Full recoveries from schizophrenia are not unknown in economically developed societies (Angst, 1988; Harding et al., 1987; McGlashan, 1988), but they are more common in less developed societies.

In the area of social impairment, 43% displayed no or mild impairment, and 56% displayed moderate or severe impairment in the developed countries. In contrast, in the less developed countries, 65% displayed no or mild impairment, and only 33% displayed moderate or severe impairment (Sartorius et al., 1986).

A similar benign course and outcome for schizophrenia was found in previous studies in the developing nations of Mauritius (Murphy & Raman, 1971) and Sri Lanka (Mendis, 1986).

Also, in subsequent analyses of the WHO data, Susser and Wanderling (1994) found that the incidence of nonaffective psychoses with acute onset and full recovery was about twice as high in women across the various research centers, and about *ten times* higher in the less developed societies versus the developed societies. Thus, there is a strong preponderance of evidence to indicate that psychoses including schizophrenia have a more benign course and better outcome in less developed nations. Moreover, prevalence rates for schizophrenia are much higher in economically developed societies than in agrarian or hunter-gatherer societies. In fact, schizophrenia seems to be relatively uncommon in any society without a system of wage labor (Warner, 1985). The chances of developing schizophrenia are higher for persons raised in cities compared to those raised in rural areas (Lewis et al., 1992).

The reasons for the differences in prevalence, course, and outcome of schizophrenia across cultures remain unclear. However, the differences appear to be related to social relations and the distinctions between sociocentric and egocentric societies, and premodern versus modern cultural meaning systems.

The concept of *expressed emotion* (EE) has been developed to describe the influence of family life on the patient with schizophrenia (Brown et al., 1962). Expressed emotion refers to criticism, hostility, and emotional over-involvement directed at the patient by his or her family. Numerous studies have shown that schizophrenic patients who live in homes with high levels of EE are significantly more likely to suffer relapses of psychotic symptoms (Jenkins, 1991, 1992; Karno et al., 1987; Leff, 1989; Leff & Vaughn, 1985; Martins, de Lemos, & Bebbington, 1992; Vaughn & Doyle et al., 1992; Vaughn & Leff, 1976; Vaughn & Snyder et al., 1984; Wig et al., 1987a, b).

Levels of EE in families with a schizophrenic member appear to vary by culture. In cultural groups studied thus far, families in India have shown the lowest rates of high EE (23%), followed by Mexican Americans (41%), British (48%), and Anglo Americans (67%); (Karno et al., 1987; Vaughn & Leff, 1976; Wig et al., 1987). The highly significant difference between Indians, Mexican Americans, and Anglo Americans on levels of EE appears to provide support for the hypothesis that behavioral factors within the family are affecting course and outcome of schizophrenia across cultures (Karno et al., 1987).

Low levels of EE could be one of the reasons schizophrenia has a relatively benign course and outcome in economically less developed countries, which tend to be sociocentric, meaning that the sense of self, personal identity, and sense of well-being are all centered in the extended family. The ill person has a larger and more effective social support network than do persons living in egocentric societies. In a sociocentric context, a schizophrenic person will receive more personal attention and caring because there are typically much larger families with more individuals available to care for the sick person. Thus, the patient is less likely to be perceived as an undue burden, as he or she might be in the small nuclear family typical of egocentric societies. Therefore, there is likely to be less hostility and criticism of the patient in a sociocentric family, and more hostility and criticism in an egocentric family (Karno & Jenkins, 1993).

The autistic withdrawal characteristic of schizophrenia is less acceptable and more noticeable in a sociocentric family, and it is quickly identified and treated. In an egocentric family, individuals are more isolated and have more personal latitude to withdraw into themselves as long as they do not become occupationally impaired. Thus, autistic withdrawal may proceed further, with more deterioration in the patient's condition, before it is perceived to merit treatment (El Islam, 1979).

In addition, the presence of modern versus premodern meaning systems may also be related to levels of EE. In a family with a premodern meaning system, psychotic symptoms are likely to be conceptualized within their own indigenous illness categories, such as witchcraft, sorcery, or demonic possession. In such cases, the cause of the illness is always *external* to the patient. This means that the illness is not the patient's fault. It is assumed that the patient was attacked by some external force and is not responsible for his or her behavior or for being sick in the first place. Also, because the cause of the illness is cognized as external, the cure is seen as relatively simple, and the illness is not expected to be chronic but *short-lived* (Waxler, 1974, 1979). Thus, hostility and criticism are less likely to be directed at the patient than in a family with a modern meaning system.

In the modern egocentric families of Anglo American society, schizophrenia is typically cognized as *internal* to the patient and almost always *incurable*. This is consistent with disease-centered explanations of schizophrenia. Moreover, because a high degree of independence and self-sufficiency is expected of all individuals in egocentric Anglo American society, these patients are viewed as personally inadequate and therefore stigmatized. Family hostility and criticism directed at patients are more likely in this sociocultural context. The very high levels of EE reported in Anglo American families with a schizophrenic member is perhaps a manifestation of these cultural factors. The high level of hostility and criticism is correlated with a more serious course and poor outcome for schizophrenia in modern societies such as the United States.

The article in this chapter is by medical anthropologist Nancy Scheper-Hughes. In this article she discusses the cultural meanings of schizophrenia in a working class community of south Boston. She points out that the subjective experience of schizophrenia and the social response to schizophrenic outpatients varies by ethnic group. In particular, the Irish Americans of this community structure their illness experiences in concepts that are important in their religion and highly egocentric social relations. In this egocentric society, individuals are allowed to withdraw and deteriorate in their mental functioning to a greater extent than they would be in a sociocentric society. Also, the families of the Irish American outpatients respond toward their schizophrenic relatives with high levels of hostility and rejection. This essentially leaves the mentally ill person without a social support network other than that provided by social service agencies. This rejection by families could be promoting relapse and a more serious course of illness.

REFERENCES

Angst, J. (1988). European long-term follow up studies of schizophrenia. *Schizophrenia Bulletin, 14,* 501–513.

Brown, G. E., Monck, E., Carstairs, G., et al. (1962). Influence of family life on the course of schizophrenic illness. *British Journal of Prevention and Social Medicine, 16,* 55–68.

El Islam, M. F. (1979). A better outlook for schizophrenics living in extended families. *British Journal of Psychiatry, 135,* 343–347.

Harding, C. M., Brooks, G. W., Ashikaga, T., et al. (1987). The Vermont Longitudinal Study of Persons with Severe Mental Illness. II. Long-term outcome of patients who retrospectively met DSM-III criteria for schizophrenia. *American Journal of Psychiatry, 144,* 727–735.

Jenkins, J. H. (1991). Anthropology, expressed emotion, and schizophrenia. *Ethos, 19,* 387–431.

Jenkins, J. H. (1992). Too close for comfort: Schizophrenia and emotional overinvolvement among Mexicano families. In A. D. Gaines (Ed.), *Ethnopsychiatry: The cultural construction of professional and folk psychiatries* (pp. 203–221). Albany: State University of New York Press.

Karno, M., & Jenkins, J. H. (1993). Cross-cultural issues in the course and treatment of schizophrenia. *Psychiatric Clinics of North America, 16,* 339–350.

Karno, M., Jenkins, J. H., de la Selva, A., et al. (1987). Expressed emotion and schizophrenic outcome among Mexican-American families. *Journal of Nervous and Mental Disease, 175,* 143–151.

Leff, J. (1989). Family factors in schizophrenia. *Psychiatric Annals, 19,* 542–547.

Leff, J., Sartorius, N., Jablensky, A., Korten, A., et al. (1992). The international pilot study of schizophrenia: Five-year follow-up findings. *Psychological Medicine, 22,* 131–145.

Leff, J., & Vaughn, C. (Eds.). (1985). *Expressed emotion in families.* New York: Guilford Press.

Lewis, G., David, A., Andreasson, S., & Allsbeck, P. (1992). Schizophrenia and city life. *Lancet, 340,* 137–140.

Martins, C., de Lemos, A., & Bebbington, P. E. (1992). A Portuguese/Brazilian study of expressed emotion. *Social Psychiatry and Psychiatric Epidemiology, 27,* 22–27.

McGlashan, T. H. (1988). A selective review of recent North American long-term follow-up studies of schizophrenia. *Schizophrenia Bulletin, 14,* 515–542.

Mendis, N. (1986). The outcome of schizophrenia in Sri Lanka—A ten-year follow-up study. *Ceylon Medical Journal, 31,* 119–134.

Murphy, H. B. M., & Raman, A. C. (1971). The chronicity of schizophrenia in indigenous tropical peoples: Results of a twelve-year follow-up survey in Mauritius. *British Journal of Psychiatry, 118,* 489–497.

Sartorius, N., Jablensky, A., Korten, A., Ernberg, G., et al. (1986). Early manifestations and first-contact incidence of schizophrenia in different cultures: A preliminary report on the initial evaluation phase of the WHO collaborative study on determinants of outcome of severe mental disorders. *Psychological Medicine, 16,* 909–928.

Susser, E., & Wanderling, J. (1994). Epidemiology of nonaffective acute remitting psychosis vs. schizophrenia: Sex and sociocultural setting. *Archives of General Psychiatry, 51,* 294–301.

Vaughn, C., Doyle, M., McConaghy, N., et al. (1992). The relationship between relatives' expressed emotion and schizophrenia relapse: An Australian replication. *Social Psychiatry and Psychiatric Epidemiology, 27,* 10–15.

Vaughn, C., & Leff, J. (1976). The influence of family and social factors on the course of psychiatric illness: A comparison of schizophrenic and depressed neurotic patients. *British Journal of Psychiatry, 129,* 125–137.

Vaughn, C., Snyder, K., Jones, S., et al. (1984). Family factors in schizophrenic relapse. Replication in California of British research on expressed emotion. *Archives of General Psychiatry, 41,* 1169–1177.

Warner, R. (1985). *Recovery for schizophrenia: Psychiatry and political economy.* New York: Routledge & Kegan Paul.

Waxler, N. E. (1974). Culture and mental illness: A social labeling perspective. *Journal of Nervous and Mental Disease, 159,* 379–395.

Waxler, N. E. (1979). Is outcome for schizophrenia better in nonindustrialized societies? The case of Sri Lanka. *Journal of Nervous and Mental Disease, 167,* 144–158.

WHO. (1973). *International pilot study of schizophrenia.* Geneva: World Health Organization.

WHO. (1979). *Schizophrenia: An international follow-up study.* Chichester, NY: Wiley & Sons.

Wig, N. N., Menon, D. K., Bedi, H., et al. (1987a). Expressed emotion and schizophrenia in North India, 1: Cross-cultural transfer of ratings of relatives' expressed emotion. *British Journal of Psychiatry, 151,* 156–160.

Wig, N. N., Menon, D. K., Bedi, H., et al. (1987b). Expressed emotion and schizophrenia in North India, 2: Distribution of expressed emotion components among relatives of schizophrenic patients in Aarhus and Chandigarh. *British Journal of Psychiatry, 151,* 160–165.

NANCY SCHEPER-HUGHES

"Mental" in "Southie"

Individual, Family, and Community Responses
to Psychosis in South Boston

ABSTRACT. The deinstitutionalization of psychiatric patients is a deeply cultural as well as political task. It entails the sharing of responsibility for human distress with family and community. Consequently, the locus of social control has also shifted from psychiatric and medical expertise to community and legal institutions. Diagnosis and treatment models must be more compatible with lay explanatory models. This paper explores the various meanings of "going 'mental'" and "being 'mental'" in the white, working class, ethnic neighborhood of South Boston. The data are extracted from a study of the impact of deinstitutionalization on a cohort of middle-aged, psychiatric patients discharged from Boston State Hospital in the attempt to return them to community living. Individual, family, and community responses to, and interpretations of, the symptoms of mental distress are discussed. The study indicates that even seriously disturbed individuals are sensitive to cultural meanings and social cues regarding the perception, expression, and content of psychiatric episodes. While madness invariably disenfranchises, it does not necessarily deculturate the individual.

INTRODUCTION:
WHY COMMUNITY PSYCHIATRY
NEEDS THE ANTHROPOLOGIST*

There are several compelling reasons for psychiatrists to entertain more than an academic curiosity about cultural influences on behavior, affect and cognitive style. For one, the process of psychiatric labeling and diagnosis begins not in the psychiatrist's office but in the community. Each patient initially presenting for psychiatric consultation, either voluntarily or involuntarily, has usually had a long and complex history of negotiations with family, co-workers, and neighbors about the possible meanings of his or her erratic behaviors. Second, attendant to the policy of psychiatric deinstitutionalization (*see* Scull 1984), more and more

serious psychiatric disorder will be managed in the community setting and, often, within the family context. Hence, the locus of social control has shifted from psychiatric and medical expertise to community and legal institutions. Increasingly, diagnosis and treatment plans involve the psychiatrist in delicate negotiations with family members, police, clergy, social workers, disability counsellors, teachers, and other concerned community members.

While the benefits of the so-called deinstitutionalization "movement" are many (not least of which is the sharing of responsibility for psychiatric suffering), one unintended side-effect has been a calling into question of psychiatric expertise, including the scientific validity of diagnosis categories (Scheff 1975; Lovell and Scheper-Hughes 1986). A growing realization of the importance of lay perspectives on madness has eventuated in the wake of community-based, deprofessionalized, and demedicalized programs for the so-called chronically mentally ill. Public psychiatrists working in these new community settings have become aware of the need to make diagnosis and treatment more compatible with lay explanatory models. Finally, it is incumbent upon hospital-based psychiatrists to make culturally informed and appropriate decisions about the timing of psychiatric discharges and the community placements of the ex-patients of psychiatric facilities.

This paper explores various cultural influences on individual, family, and community interpretations of the meanings of going and being crazy in the tough, economically deteriorating, white, working class, "ethnic" inner-city neighborhood of South Boston ("Southie" to its residents). The data are extracted from a larger community study of the impact of deinstitutionalization on a cohort of fifty-five chronic "revolving door" psychiatric patients, discharged, again and again, from Boston State Hospital in a largely futile attempt to return these hapless souls to some semblance of "community living" (see Scheper-Hughes 1981, 1983). During the time of the study (1979–1980, with brief return visits for several weeks in 1981 and 1982) the individuals in

---

SOURCE: From *Culture, Medicine and Psychiatry, 11,* 1987, 53–78. Copyright © 1987 Kluwer Academic Publishers B.V. Reprinted with permission.

the sample were all out-patients attending a day hospital program in South Boston. In addition to participant-observation in the daily events of the day hospital program, I visited the clients in their homes and in various ex-patient "hang-outs" (the Jolly Donut Shop, for one) after hours. In addition, I contacted family members of the clients and interviewed them in person when possible, and by phone and letter correspondence when face-to-face interviewing was impossible or unwanted. Finally, I interviewed residents of the South Boston community at large about their thoughts and feelings on the subjects of madness, deviance, alcoholism, family and community norms and values. And, with the help of several community key informants, I was able to complete a telephone survey on community responses to psychiatric symptoms and to deinstitutionalized mental patients among seventy-six South Boston residents randomly selected from the Boston telephone directory.

"SOUTHIE": COMMUNITY UNDER SIEGE

The original Irish immigrants who settled on the marshy peninsula south of Boston proper during the early decades of the 19th century left an indelible cultural stamp on the community of South Boston. Despite subsequent waves of Italian, Polish, Russian, Lithuanian, and Albanian immigrants in the early decades of the 20th century, and despite the fact that the Irish, today, constitute less than the majority, this community is stereotyped by both residents and outsiders in Boston as one of that city's archetypic "Irish-Catholic" neighborhoods. Irish cultural dominance is staunchly maintained and defended. The Irish of Southie live scattered throughout every section of the South Boston community, from the shrinking upper middle class (i.e., "Waterford crystal" Irish) section known as the Upper End, to the middle class (i.e., "lace curtain" Irish) waterfront section known as the "Irish Riviera", to the lower-class (i.e. "Shanty" Irish) housing projects of the "Lower End." By contrast, the other ethnic groups are geographically and politically contained in their own small two or three block square enclaves. Local civil, political, religious, and educational institutions in "Southie" are conspicuously Irish, and Saint Patrick's day is a community-wide "open-house" that celebrates the ethnic origins and solidarity of the South Boston community. The community boasts its own green and white flag with its symbols of the shamrock and a local fortress. A mimeographed flier, distributed by hand, describes the fort as ". . . symbolic of our need to guard our community against outside elements." The outsiders menacingly alluded to here are the Blacks and Puerto Ricans who have tried, with varying degrees of success, to integrate public housing projects and public schools in "Southie" under the Boston school desegregation order (*see* Sheehan 1984; Lupo 1977; Lukas 1985).

In the face of perceived threats to community survival, both *legal-political* (i.e., forced school desegregation and busing) and *economic* (i.e., the flight of industry from South Boston, waterfront decay, and the gentrification plans of Boston "Back Bay Brahmins" for Southie's largely run-down, residential beachfront property), the residents of Southie have recently banded together against their common enemies. The Irish, Poles, Lithuanians, Italians and Russians of South Boston have put aside long-standing ethnic antagonisms and regrouped around a new, common ethos—a white ethnic, working-class, Catholic social identity, which residents refer to as "Southie Pride." One observer (Novak, n.d.) has used the term "ethclass" to describe the fusion of the dominant Irish cultural ethos with the more general working class interests of South Boston residents. The people of Southie see themselves today as cast in bold and dramatic roles, the courageous victims of sham W.A.S.P. (White Anglo Saxon Protestant) liberalism on the one hand, as Protestant liberals from affluent suburbs are seen as forcing integration on a community least able "to defend" itself, and of Jewish "radicalism" on the other (as psychiatrists and mental health professionals are seen as forcing unwanted mental health programs and mental patients form Boston state Hospital on the community (*see* Scheper-Hughes 1981:96–97). Meanwhile, the most common jobs in South Boston—dockworker, policeman, fireman, utilities worker, and civil service worker (City of Boston 1975)—have become scarce and increasingly difficult to pass on from father-to-son in the traditional manner. The result is that common class interests now compete with older ethnic loyalties as the main source of social self identity in contemporary South Boston.

Within this current political-cultural climate one proceeds with an analysis of cultural influences on behavior with great caution and bearing in mind that much is shared among the residents of Southie regardless of ethnic background. I must also add another disclaimer before proceeding with the analysis. I do not wish to suggest that the deviant patterns of behavior, communication, or family interaction that I am about to describe for this small sample of chronically mentally afflicted individuals and their families are in any way generalizable to the Irish, Lithuanian, and Italian populations at large in South Boston or elsewhere. It must be absolutely clear that my sample is a skewed one, comprising people in acute pain and in deep predicament. Madness affects not only the individual, but the entire family and larger social network, its symptoms producing and reproducing distortions in human relations so that after many years of dealing with psychosis both the individual and their significant others are radically changed. The illness experience intrudes upon and transforms ordinary cultural patterns and relationships. We are not dealing, then, with norms, but rather with cultural patterns and beliefs as they are refracted through and changed by one of the most devastating assaults on person-hood: psychosis. Nevertheless, there is no doubt that cultures do provide some guidelines and social scripts for how to behave when crazy and how to respond to madness in others. It is this small aspect of culture that I am examining here.

THE PSYCHIATRIC SAMPLE

Boston State (Psychiatric) Hospital, originally located in South Boston, opened its wards in the later 19th century just in time to help manage the mental problems of poor Irish immigrants who came to Boston during the waves of immigration following the series of potato famines beginning in the 1820s and culminating in the Great Hunger of 1845–1849. Boston State was a typical custodial institution with a characteristically bad reputation in the community, even after the hospital was relocated to the neighboring section of Dorchester in Boston. Local residents still tell apocryphal stories about their immigrant ancestors who were locked up without just cause, and of Protestant "bounty hunters" who reportedly received a sack of potatoes for every "mad" Irishman rounded up on the streets of Boston and deliv-ered to psychiatrist-jailers at Boston State. The psychiatric hos-pital remains to this day a feared institution, and psychiatrists remain an alien and mistrusted profession among a people still more comfortable with traditional and Irish forms of social con-trol: i.e., the Catholic clergy, the police and criminal justice sys-tem. To this day the residents of South Boston avoid psychiatric care, and almost all referrals to Boston State Hospital from the community are involuntary ones. The stigma of having been hospitalized at "Mattapan" (as residents refer to Boston State) is very great, and attaches to the family and extended kin of a men-tal patient, which in part accounts for the length of stays of many of the older patients in my now "deinstitutionalized" sample. As will be discussed at greater length below, once institutionalized, many ex-patients were subsequently abandoned and cut off by their mortified relatives.

Under the mandate to initiate deinstitutionalization, the su-perintendents of Boston State Hospital, beginning with Barton in the 1950s and most vigorously pursued by superintendent Nelson in the 1970s, reduced the hospital census from an aver-age of 3,000 inmates to an average of 300 inmates today (Scheper-Hughes 1981:93). In order to facilitate this process wards were reorganized so that neighborhood affiliation (rather than acuteness or chronicity of the illness) became the main cri-teria for ward assignment. In this way it was hoped that long-term inmates could begin the process of "resocialization" to "community living" prior to actual discharge. Hence, most of the fifty-five ex-patients in my sample had been inmates of "Foggy Bottom," the nickname given to the South Boston-Dorchester ward of South Boston Hospital, and most had been discharged with the same follow-up treatment plan: 8 A.M.–3 P.M. day care at the South Boston Day Hospital.

The ethnic, class, and religious affiliations of the deinstitu-tionalized cohort reflect the general demography of the South Boston community. Like most residents of Southie, the vast ma-jority of the ex-patients (81%) are Roman Catholic; the minority were divided among Russian, Albanian, and Greek Orthodox churches, and a few Protestants. All the day hospital clients were white, and 33 of the 55 clients described themselves as Boston Irish Catholics. Eleven of the clients were Eastern Europeans (mainly first generation Lithuanians), four were Italian-Ameri-cans, three were French-Canadians, and three were self-defined "WASP's." One day hospital client claimed "inter-planetary" ethnicity only, and nothing about his family heritage was known by the staff. The Irish were somewhat over-represented, in this sample, and the Italians were under-represented, reflecting dif-ferences in mental health utilization patterns. Likewise, the sam-ple was skewed in terms of sex ratio: 41 of the clients were women at the time of the study. The majority came from second or third generation immigrant backgrounds, and with two excep-tions all came from working or lower class families. Less than half the clients had a high school diploma. The day hospital served a very chronically mentally ill population—the average age of the clients was 50.2 years, and most had experienced mul-tiple hospitalizations at Boston State. Six of the clients had more than fifteen separate commitments ranging in length of time from a few days to several years. Most clients had spent three or more years in hospital, although not continuously. Eighty per-cent of the clients had been diagnosed as schizophrenic (chronic, undifferentiated, or schizo-affective). There were no significant diagnostic differences by ethnicity (see Table I).

The life histories of the day hospital clients were uniformly wretched, characterized by sometimes extreme poverty and de-privation, family violence, alcoholism, abandonment, and abuse. Yet the lives of these patients seem to be no more wretched than those of the average poorer residents of Southie living in the D-Street projects, judging from a Felt Need Survey conducted there in 1974 (Sigal n.d.), and from the autobiographical essays that I assigned to South Boston high school students during fieldwork in 1980. The life histories of these ex-patients almost justified a community psychiatrist's wry profile of the "typical" Irish-American family in Southie as: "An alcoholic father, a de-pressed masochistic mother, a good dose of violence and a dash of incest." I would add the proviso, however, that much the same could be said of other poor white ethnic families living in the Lower End of South Boston today. One Italian-American day hospital client who was reared with her eleven siblings in a four-room apartment in the Italian section of Southie, described her early life to me as follows:

Living in want. Dealing with difficulty. My story is here. Where? Somewhere on the jagged journey for shelter, food, clothing, and that luxury, soap. Mother kept our window panes very clean so that our lives and our disgrace were visible to everyone. Didn't she know that we needed blinds and shades, knives and forks, separate cots? In reality maybe it wasn't so bad, but the horror, the horror was real.

The majority of ex-patients came from families with histories of multiple psychiatric and social problems, including madness, child abuse, alcoholism, drug addiction, crime, suicide. Like marginalized and excluded peoples everywhere they shared a number of social psychological problems that intersected, among these: chronic un- or underemployment; broken and single parent families with a great deal of father absenteeism; truncated childhoods with early initiation into adult behavior and into a highly conflicted and (in this staunchly Irish Catholic community) guilt-ridden sexuality; depression and alcoholism related to feelings of deprivation and loss, powerlessness, and despair.

RECOGNITION AND LABELING OF PSYCHIATRIC SYMPTOMS

In formulating the propositions relating to his social reaction or "labeling theory" of mental illness, Thomas Scheff (1966) suggested at the outset that *psychiatric* labeling would most likely constitute the last resort of sympathetic but exasperated family and friends. According to Scheff most "deviant" behavior is ignored, rationalized away, or denied by those close to the individual rule-breaker. Little empirical research, however, has followed in order to test Scheff's proposition, and little is known about individual, family and community differences with respect to reactions to psychotic-like symptoms.

In this sample the Irish sub-group was distinguished by the extent to which "denial" (to borrow, for the moment, a psychiatric interpretation) was mobilized by the patient, his/her family, and the Irish-American community at large as a characteristic response to the threatening symptoms of psychiatric disorder. In this my sample conforms to previous studies of Irish-Americans in Boston and New York City which indicate that the Irish are generally stoical about physical and mental suffering, that they do not always seek out medical help even when they are quite ill, that they have a rather high tolerance for pain, and that they tend toward confusion and inaccuracy in describing their symptoms and are generally unexpressive and uncomplaining about discomfort and illness even among immediate family members (*see* Sternbach 1965; Zborowski 1964; Zola 1966).[1]

The case histories and life history profiles of the Irish patients in this study were notable for the extent to which the immediate family members of patients were able to ignore distress signals to the point of serious crisis—one usually involving the intervention of the police and consequently public scandal. I interviewed eleven family members of ten Irish-American day hospital clients in person, by telephone, or by an exchange of letters (the latter incidentally providing a very rich source of data from otherwise extremely research-shy subjects). All were asked to reconstruct the events that led up to their first suspicions that their relative might be having severe mental problems. All mentioned at least one florid symptom of psychosis, which often followed months or years of erratic or eccentric behavior that had often been studiously "over-looked." In most cases the referral to a psychiatric treatment facility came neither from the individual nor from family members, but through the intervention of police, the courts, or social workers. The most frequently mentioned disturbing behaviors that led to family members' suspicions that something might be seriously wrong with the patient were: extreme reclusiveness and social withdrawal (i.e., refusing to leave the room or the house); suicidal gestures; vagrancy and

Table I
Diagnosis by Ethnicity*

	Chronic, Undifferentiated Schizophrenia	Schizoaffective	Depression	Bipolar	Borderline
Irish	22	4	4	2	1
Italian	4	—	—	—	—
Eastern European	7	1	2	1	—
Other	4	—	2	—	1
Totals	37	5	8	3	2

*Diagnostic labels are periodically renegotiated in the day hospital program and over the years correspond to fluctuations in current styles and usage.

homelessness; violent aggressiveness involving a public disturbance; florid hallucinations.

Although the comparison group is far too small to be anything more than merely suggestive, the eight family members of Eastern European and Italian clients at the day hospital were more likely to cite the premorbid behavioral or personality characteristics of the patient that had worried them, including: school adjustment problems; nervousness; anxiety and depressions; lack of interest in personal appearance and grooming; poor social skills, especially with respect to dating and relations with the opposite sex; immaturity and over-dependence on parents, etc.

The following vignettes illustrate how long erratic behavior can go unnoticed and unlabeled in some South Boston Irish-American families.

Terry's[2] spinster aunt Mary, an Irish immigrant who worked all her adult life in downtown Boston as a chamber maid in a hotel, lived on the same street as her nephew and his family but was never very "cozy" with her kin. She was a loner who enjoyed her independence. Following retirement, however, Mary's behavior changed radically and she began to visit her nephew's household frequently, often dropping in without warning. She became "eccentric," said Terry, citing her undignified outbursts of laughter, her fits of talkativeness, her suspiciousness of banks and shopkeepers. She withdrew her money from the bank and began carrying her life savings on her person. Convinced that the grocer had poisoned her meat, she stopped eating most foods and became emaciated. Still, Terry saw no grounds for real concern until a crisis erupted:

I could see that she was very changed. Her face had gotten old—red and weather-beaten—like maybe she was spending a lot of time walking the streets. But then she started talking about going home to Ireland. We didn't pay any attention to it. But we finally had to call the police when she climbed to the roof of her apartment where she insisted she was waiting for an Aer Lingus [Irish airlines] plane to come and take her away.

Robert's older sister, a middle aged matron living in the Boston suburbs, wrote to me of her first inkling that her younger brother might have some serious mental problems (Robert is a street person who has been in and out of Boston State Hospital for more than ten years):

I think it began when he was about forty. He had lost his job, had no income, and was without any place to live. He couldn't handle money at all, and when I would give him some he would have it all spent in a few days and then he'd be back out on the streets again. I guess he was drinking a lot during this time as well. He had some delusions and was acting strange. Once he came out to my house with a telephone

cord in his pocket and he kept going off into corners to reach his "contacts." I knew then that something was really wrong.

The mother of twenty-four year old Dennis wrote to me about the following sequence of events that led to the initial recognition of mental disorder in her son:

I first suspected that Dennis needed some help when he stopped talking to us altogether, and he acted like he was afraid of us. It was so bad he couldn't even stay in the same room when his cousins or other relatives came to the house. Because he was so afraid of people we couldn't get him out of the house to look for a job or anything. Then he started to hear people talking to him when he and I were the only ones in the room. Then he began to talk about wanting to kill himself, and he began to cut his body because he said he didn't like it. He said people were always talking about him. He locked himself in his room and he wouldn't come out at all. Then I got so frightened I talked to some people at church and they told me about the day care program [the South Boston Day Hospital]. I believed that it saved my son's life and his Mind (sic). God bless them forever!

Eileen's mother told me during a home visit that she was "shocked beyond belief" to be told by a psychiatrist at Boston State Hospital that her daughter (who had been arrested and involuntarily committed) was "mental." She angrily protested to me: "Such a thing never entered my mind. I never even *thought* about such an existence." Eileen understood her mother's need for denial and she explained to me during a lengthy life history session: "You see, I *couldn't* be mentally ill as a child (even though she reported having hallucinations since kindergarten). Mental illness wasn't available to me. There was a fear of mental people in my family." In fact, throughout much of South Boston, there was a tendency to dichotomize more understandable and less threatening "emotional" problems from greatly feared "mental" problems. However, it appeared that emotional problems consisted of virtually anything people suffered from *outside* the mental hospital. *Mental* problems were suffered by "mental cases," those who were carted off to Boston State Hospital, almost always against their will, often with unseemly displays of force, much to the shame of their families. In short, in this community, mental hospitals made mental cases. Prior to hospitalization even very "crazy" behavior can be absorbed and rationalized by the family and the community at large.

The ability of segments of the South Boston community to tolerate or, depending on point of view, to "deny" mental problems is at least in part a function of family dynamics. In the working class Irish American households of South Boston individual family members are allowed a great deal of personal space (physically and psychologically) despite often very congested living quarters. There is in many Irish-American households a high regard for the individual's privacy. Family dynamics tends to conform to Salvador Minuchin's model of "distanced" (as opposed to enmeshed) family relations (1967). While Irish-American family loyalties are strong indeed, intimacy is generally avoided, and many deeply experienced personal feelings are never articulated. A Boston family therapist, John Pearce, who specializes in the treatment of Irish-American families has the following to say on this subject based on his years of experience with these clients:

> The paradox of their general articulateness and their inability to express inner feelings can be puzzling for a therapist, who may have difficulty figuring out what is going on in the Irish family. Family members may be so out of touch with their feelings that their inexpressiveness in therapy is not a sign of resistance, as it would be for other cultural groups, but rather a reflection of their blocking off inner emotions, even from themselves. Thus, although the Irish have a marvelous ability to tell stories, when it comes to their emotions they have no words (McGoldrick and Pearce 1981:226).

Indeed, in the Irish-American families I was able to visit it was quite clear that many topics are simply not open for discussion. During a visit to one extremely disturbed client's mother, the woman painted a glowing picture of her daughter's early childhood, one seriously at odds with that the daughter had told me herself. When I broached the topic of Kathleen's breakdown at the age of twenty and her subsequent decade as a "revolving door" and extremely suicidal patient, tears sprung to the mother's eyes and she said that it was all a great mystery to her, that only God knew what had gone wrong to ruin her daughter's life. The mother denied knowing that Kathleen had been periodically mutilating herself throughout her teenage years. I asked how Kathleen had managed to hide the wounds that she inflicted on herself with razor blades, and the mother replied: "She was mature by then. I wouldn't ever see her undressed, or barge in on her in the bathroom or her bedroom. We weren't *that* kind of family." The blood-soaked rags that turned up in the wastepaper basket in the toilet were mistaken for menstrual rags, bringing up another subject that was "impossible" to discuss openly, even between mother and daughter, in this particular household.

The other side of the coin, however, was the way in which "denial" could lead to symbiotic relationships between parents and very disturbed children. There were, for example, clients at the day hospital who, prior to the attention of social workers or mental health workers, had been kept secreted away at home in a kind of limited status as disabled household servants.

One might also refer to a kind of collective, community-wide denial with respect to the perception of mental problems. There is, for example, almost a code of silence with respect to the very visible presence of newly deinstitutionalized and frequently still very disturbed ex-patients living in rooming houses and community residence programs in South Boston. This attitude has actually contributed to some ex-patients' perceptions of "Southie" as a good place to be "mental." Sally, a middle-aged chronically ill client of the day hospital described Southie as a "fine place," a place where she could wander the length of Broadway [Southie's main street] without being "picked on" or "pointed out." She said:

> They pretty much leave us alone here, and so we just blend in with the drunks and bums along Broadway.

Initially the politics of "community mental health" in South Boston during the initial stage of "deinstitutionalization" (roughly 1965–1970) was dominated by protests against plans to open various community mental health services in 'Southie' on the grounds that there were *no* mental health problems in the community that couldn't be taken care of by families and by the Church. Residents complained that mental health clinic would bring deviants and "mentals" into Southie from *other* communities. Finally, members of the South Boston Neighborhood Improvement Association protested that if the State really wanted to improve mental health in Southie, it should end forced integration and school busing which represented in their view a real cause of anxiety, depression, and nervousness in the community. When questioned in mental health felt needs surveys conducted by the Community Mental Health Catchment Area Board in the late 1960s and early 1970s (Schmitt 1972; Sigal n.d.), South Boston residents showed a remarkable lack of familiarity with the terms used to describe the more common forms of mental problems, they denied that alcoholism was a "problem" in their community, and expressed the opinion that most personal problems were best kept to oneself. Psychiatric services were neither needed nor wanted in the community.

Hence the earliest attempts to open alcohol detoxification program and a "drop in" psychiatric (crisis) clinic were violently protested in community-wide demonstrations, some individuals carrying banners that read, "Keep Mental Health Out of Southie," much to the amusement of some Massachusetts mental health professionals. Anti-liberal, anti-communist, and anti-semitic sentiments were directed at the new mental health professionals who represented to the Irish Catholics of Southie the latest assault on their autonomy, and an insult to their pride in being able "to take care of their own." As the protests died down and more than twenty community mental health programs gradually opened (often covertly attached to social centers, church programs, health centers, and with euphemistic titles that obscured the "mental" or psychiatric focus of the programs), the community simply responded with characteristic denial. Most residents were unaware of the number and nature of these programs in Southie, as documented in the telephone survey of seventy-six residents. Meanwhile, the residents of a large public housing project located directly across from the South Boston Day Hospital, frequently replied when questioned, that the day hospital was some kind of job-training program for "deadbeats" and "down-and-outs." That these "deadbeats" often talked loudly to themselves, sat and rocked on street corners, or dressed in outlandish clothing seemed to pass unnoticed. The owner of a submarine sandwich shop frequented by day hospital clients replied to my inquiries about just who his customers were: "Well, I guess maybe some of them could maybe have had nervous breakdowns or something like that." Then he asked me, somewhat anxiously, "You don't think any of them could be '*mental,*' do you?" I replied by drawing on the local vernacular which the clients used to describe themselves: "No, I think they're just a bit *emotional.*" The shopkeeper nodded his head in obvious relief and agreement.

MADNESS, CULTURE, AND ETHNIC STEREOTYPES: SELF-PERCEPTIONS AMONG PATIENTS

Despite the fact that the experience of chronic psychiatric disorder and, in many cases, multiple hospitalizations united the day hospital clients into a grim "alliance of the damned," ethnicity (or, as the patients would say "nationality") remained a salient category among even very psychotic clients. As many ethnopsychiatrists have pointed out with respect to the non-western world, psychoses are never devoid of cultural content or meanings. In South Boston ethnicity shaped the way in which chronically mentally ill patients behaved and the way they interacted with others. Like other members of the South Boston community, the day hospital clients tended to explain peoples' behavior in terms of ethnic stereotyping. Clients were not only acutely aware of each other's ethnicity, but they tended to evaluate each other in these terms. Ethnic slurs were a common cause of dissension in the otherwise tranquillized milieu of the day room.

A Lithuanian client of the day hospital said that she needed help finding a new roommate, and that she couldn't continue to live with a very quiet, regressed, and hallucinatory Irish client of the same program: "She's haughty and stuck up like all the Irish," said the woman. And when Lucia, a young Italian client got frustrated with the landlady of her group home and angrily shattered a window, she explained in her own defense: "I didn't know that this wasn't allowed. I have to be *taught* how to behave. I came up from the bottom, from a big, loud, Italian family."

The staff of the day hospital program tolerated a certain amount of the ethnic slurs that would erupt in the daily group

therapy sessions on the grounds that such attitudes were appropriate to the community to which they had been returned. Within the program, as in the community at large, Irish ethnicity was dominant, celebrated in the Irish flag hanging conspicuously in the day room. Irish cultural dominance was also expressed in the self-deprecatory comments of non-Irish clients, as when a Lithuanian client retorted to another: "What do you expect from a slob [Slav] like me?" and when an Italian patient goaded "Patrick" from across the day room: "Did you hear that they found out Saint Patrick was a Jew after all?" But the most compelling demonstration of the salience of ethnicity to this psychiatric population was to be found in a graph charting annual psychiatric hospital readmissions. These tended to cluster around the Roman Catholic and Russian Orthodox liturgical calendar with Ash Wednesday, Good Friday, Easter Sunday and ethnic holidays representing particularly troublesome times. The period around Saint Patrick's Day, March 17th, was the time of greatest risk for the day hospital clients who, one staff member quipped, "just decompensate all over the place" on that day.

Characteristic of the day hospital patients in general, but of the Irish cohort in particular, was an anxious and often ambivalent attachment to the local community, which one staff member glossed as "neighborhood psychosis." It was expressed in clients' fears of crossing the little bridge that separated "Southie" from Boston proper. Field trips into Boston generated a great deal of diffuse anxiety during the planning stages, and many clients would stay home rather than confront the short bus or subway ride downtown. On each of the few field trips I ventured with the clients a "neighborhood psychosis" would flare up in a phobic or panic-flight response. On one occasion a thirty-year old male client bolted from the subway at the first stop and had to be chased by a staff member. He said he got disoriented and just wanted to go home. On another field trip a woman client expressed her anxiety in a constant barrage of questions: "Are we *still* in South Boston?" "How far are we from Broadway?" "Can we go home soon?" The insularity of the day hospital clients was, in fact, a general neighborhood trait, particularly of women, many of whom claimed they hadn't been out of Southie for months and, in a few cases, for years. The attachment of clients to the home community and neighborhood is all the more poignant since, for most, they have been subject to frequent forced removals "all the way to Dorchester," as one woman described her frightening trip by police car to Boston State Hospital at the time of her last involuntary commitment.

A number of personality characteristics distinguished the Irish-American clients at the day hospital, among them: reserve and propriety, secretiveness, religiosity, a damning sense of guilt and 'inner badness', and a tendency to defuse anxiety-provoking situations with humor and often very clever "double-talk." The reluctance of Irish clients to share "family secrets" seemed to me more pronounced, as I learned in trying to elicit "privileged" information. A middle-aged first generation Irish-American client reneged on her original promise to be interviewed by saying:

I don't know exactly what it is you want from us, but my mother said to stay away from you. Look, it's all there, everything you think—the drinking, the beatings, the father in and out of jail, the mother in and out of "Mattapan." I told my story a thousand times, but it doesn't make anything different or better. It only gives us shame and makes me feel rotten.

Another client postponed my interview with the following statement:

We all have a story to tell. But should I tell it? The things I think about are: how much do you want to just forget about it and close the door? Won't you ever let the case rest? And, am I stepping on somebody's toes? Maybe I want to say: I'm separate, I'm different, and I hate you. I hope I didn't hurt your feelings, Dr. Hughes.

The characteristic traits of reserve and respectability among the Irish clients at the day hospital meant that few presented any significant behavioral problems for the staff, with the exception of occasional suicide threats and gestures. In the history of the day hospital program most of the suicides were by young, quiet, single Irish males. The landlady who supervised a community residence where several day hospital clients were living at the time of my study, commented that she preferred single Irish males to any other residents because they were so little trouble and were so well behaved. "My only fear with them," she said, "is that one may decide to quietly climb to the roof some evening and jump off." She actually spoke from such an experience which had occurred while she was away visiting relatives for the Christmas holidays. But she said that with the Irish patients one could usually apply to their enormous sense of respectability. She told of the case of a young man who became very depressed and suicidal:

I warned him that if he committed suicide in my house he would give me, the Irish, and mental illness a bad name in the community. He took my words very much to heart and when his situation deteriorated he checked himself into Boston State Hospital where he quietly and privately took his life.

In the milieu of the day hospital the Irish patients behaved in a generally decorous manner and tended to be rather judgmental of those who "acted out." D., a very regressed and almost continuously hallucinatory client, always arrived at the day hospital carefully groomed and neatly, if idiosyncratically, dressed. When I complimented her on her neat appearance, she replied:

Well everyone has their own set of behaviors. Mine is alone and lonely and sad. One set I especially hate is called "dirty and crazy." Like A., over there, she uses her craziness to cover her dirt and laziness. That's something I really hate because crazy or not crazy, there is still a responsibility to be clean.

"Are there any other 'sets' you hate?" I probed, to which she replied:

Yes, there's the jerky set. When J. does this [and she demonstrates with grotesque gestures the tremors induced by long-term use of psychotrophic medication]. He can get himself out of that when he wants. You can *be* crazy but you don't have to *look* crazy.

Even during a psychotic episode the working class Irish-American clients manifested that concern with propriety that one observer of the Irish (Corry 1977) referred to as the "... curse of the Irish since they came to America, building respectability layer on layer." Public comportment was particularly problematic for ex-patients. M., a client born into a large and well-known Irish American family in Southie, was continually mortified by the company she was forced to keep at the day hospital and she would refuse to accompany staff and patients on walks to the public library or bowling alley because she said she didn't want to be seen in public "with a bunch of nuts." This same person took offense when during a day hospital group meeting a young patient became upset and ran sobbing from the room. She turned to me and said primly:

What's wrong with that girl? Doesn't she know how very upsetting that is for us? Why can't she just sit still and quietly hallucinate like the rest of us?

In order to preserve the vestiges of their respectability several day hospital clients pose in public as recovering alcoholics, a more acceptable form of deviance in South Boston. During one day hospital meeting a patient told of her acute anxiety when, the night before, she had been called to "testify" at an Alcoholic Anonymous meeting. "Did you do O.K.?" another patient inquired to which J. responded: "I think so. At least they still think I'm just a drunk" (i.e. and not "crazy").

SYMPTOM EXPRESSION

The Irish and Irish-Americans have frequently been the subjects of cross-cultural psychiatric inquiry not only because of their particularly high rates of psychiatric hospitalization within Ireland (Walsh 1968; Murphy 1975; Scheper-Hughes 1979), but because of the identification of what appears to be a "culture-bound" expression of schizophrenic symptomatology (Opler and

Singer 1959; Fantil and Shiro 1959; Wylan and Mintz 1976). Compared to Italian-American schizophrenic patients, Irish-American patients tend to be more delusional, hallucinatory, and fantasy-indulging, as well as more outwardly conforming in their overt behavior and general deportment (as illustrated above). In addition, Irish "schizophrenics" tend to be more guilt-ridden and conflicted about sexuality than other patients. In all, the Irish expression of schizophrenia seems to elicit more "paranoid" features, and its course is marked by a tendency toward social isolation, and a generally poor prognosis (Opler and Singer, *op. cit.*). By contrast, the Italian schizophrenics observed in Opler and Singer's study exhibited many schizo-affective features marked by a tendency toward talkativeness, hyperactivity, excitement and pronounced mood swings.

It has been suggested that the differences in symptom expression might be reflection of the kinds of behaviors that are either allowed or disallowed in the family (Wylan and Mintz 1976). The question, then, is whether or not there is a greater tolerance for psychotic *ideation* (delusion, hallucination) in the Irish-American family, and a greater tolerance for psychotic *affect* (mood swings, emotional outburst, acting out) in Italian families. I attempted to answer this in two ways: by observation and interview with the family members of day hospital clients, and in the telephone survey of randomly selected South Boston residents.

In reply to the question, "Which symptoms of N. (the patient) most worry or upset you these days?" the eleven Irish-American family members interviewed were less likely to mention the patient's lack of contact with reality than to mention "inappropriate" appearance or deportment. The following responses are illustrative: "the anger"; "her life of indolence"; "his disheveled appearance"; "when she gets out of control"; "the bad words." Rarely did family members complain of hallucinations, delusions, nonsensical language or other cognitive symptoms of psychosis. In fact, in at least some quarters of Southie, alternative "folk" meanings compete with psychiatric interpretations of hallucinations. One day hospital client complained that her parents refused to see that she was seriously troubled as a child:

> I was always lost in a world of my own, talking to imaginary playmates. When anyone tried to say anything about me to my mother she would quiet them and say, "Leave the girl alone. Can't you see she walks with God?"

In some families the symptoms of psychotic ideation are interpreted as creativity, signs of genius rather than madness. This was the case with one day hospital client, R., whose large, extended Irish family "coddled" and nurtured his delusions (and self-delusions). His sister wrote me an impassioned letter in which she defended the sanity of a brother who had been in and out of Boston State Hospital for more than fifteen years:

R. was the child genius of the family. Unfortunately our parents didn't know how to deal with him. And many of the people who came into his life later on didn't know either. It is a terrible thing to waste such a mind, but I have a marvelous hope that someday R., even at the age of fifty will once more return to his Creative Self (sic) and become the writer-genius that he was destined to be. He has such a gift to offer the world!

Since R.'s life for many years has consisted of sleeping, chain smoking, and nursing the wounds inflicted on his psyche by a world that has refused to recognize his genius, it is not at all clear that there are grounds for his sister's optimism. Rather, one might conclude that both R. and his sister are heir to that Irish trait which McGoldrick and Pearce refer to as "the dreaming," the retreat from humiliation and failure into a heroic and impossibly unrealistic fantasy or family myth (McGoldrick and Pearce 1981:226).

The high tolerance for psychotic ideation is also a characteristic of South Boston residents at large, revealed in their responses to the charge to rank order from *most* to *least* threatening the following commonly attributed traits of "mental illness":[3] hallucinations (described as seeing or hearing things that other people don't); too many mixed-up emotions; unpredictability; dirty or slovenly appearance; strange behaviors and gestures; talking without making any sense; potential for violence. The results, coded by ethnicity of the respondents, are as in Table II.

In each group (but especially for the Irish) the cognitive symptoms—hallucination and deviant speech—were ranked as least upsetting or less upsetting than other symptoms, some of which (like the potential for violence) represent common stereotypes rather than actual symptoms of psychosis. The results of this survey have particular relevance to a paradox created by the medical treatment of psychosis. Although powerful drugs like Prolixin and Thorazine are routinely administered to the chronically mentally ill patients of the day hospital in order to reduce the florid symptoms of psychosis—hallucinations and delusions—their side-effects often produce the bizarre gestures and tics of tardive dyskenesia that may be actually more upsetting to the self-esteem of some of the patients than their primary symptoms, and which may result in even greater rejection and stigmatization in the South Boston community.

RELIGIOUS CONTENT OF PSYCHIATRIC SYMPTOMS

In a community where people still identify themselves by parish it is not altogether surprising that Catholicism should leave a

Table II
Rank order of most to least disturbing psychiatric symptoms

n = 76 Irish (n = 49)	Italian (n = 12)	Eastern European (n = 8)	White Protestant (n = 8)
1. Unpredictability	Violence	Violence	Violence
2. Violence	Unpredictability	Unpredictability	Unpredictability
3. Strange Behaviors	Hallucinations	Strange Behaviors	Strange Behaviors
4. Mixed-up Emotions	Strange Behaviors	Slovenly Appearance	Hallucinations
5. Slovenly Appearance	Mixed-up Emotions	Talks Nonsense	Slovenly Appearance
6. Hallucinations	Talks Nonsense	Hallucinations	Mixed-up Emotions
7. Talks Nonsense	Slovenly Appearance	Mixed-up Emotions	Talks Nonsense

stamp on the content and expression of psychotic symbolization. This was true of the day hospital population in general, and not just of the large Irish Catholic sub-group. Themes of sin, guilt, atonement, and redemption predominated in the anxieties, delusions, hopes, wishes and fears of the South Boston Day Hospital patients. This was so strong a characteristic of the patient population that it struck me as patently absurd that so few staff members knew anything about Roman Catholicism or Easter Orthodoxy, which led them to frequently mistake religious beliefs for delusions, and to not recognize when religious beliefs *had* taken on a delusional quality. The following vignettes are illustrative of the fusion of religious belief and delusion in this population.

E., a seminarian before this first breakdown, believes that he has cancer of the brain resulting from his "dirty" habit of masturbation. He is driven crazy, he says, by a constant babbling in his head, telling him that he has a "bad, bad brain." C. believes that God has punished her for her bad thoughts by closing her body orifices: her mouth so that she can speak no evil, her vagina so that she can't have sexual intercourse with her husband, and her anus so that she cannot defecate. F. believes that she is being chased by God as the "Hound of Heaven" and she once ran away from her six fatherless children and hid out in an abandoned building in order to elude Him. L. is certain that a distinct odor of rancid meat comes from her pores and so she carries around a small room atomizer in order to freshen the air that her evil flesh has fouled. But T. has managed to bypass all that [is] tainted, and earthy, and dirty for he was born on the Crystal Planet where there is neither male nor female, no sex, no death, and where everything is pure and crystal clear.

For some of these clients their faith sustains as well as torments them. Belief in God and His providence gives shape and meaning to their suffering. Some believe that their illness is a sign that God has chosen them above others:

This morning I felt very close to God. Sometimes he tempts me with despair. Now, for example, I'm feeling alone and frightened, like I don't know what else He has in store for me. I try hard to pray, to ask God for forgiveness. Mostly, I offer up my suffering for the poor souls in Purgatory, those who have no one to pray for them. I believe that God afflicts those He loves the most, and that my sickness is the cross I was asked to bear in this life.

Pain, confusion, depression, and other forms of psychological suffering were accepted by some day hospital clients as their fate. A sense of the imperfectability of humans, and of their own flaws and "inner badness" made their suffering understandable, and in a way less chaotic, less random, less disorganizing. Many did not dwell on *why* they had been afflicted; their Catholic socialization had, in a sense, left them with a high expectation of, and, hence, resignation to, human suffering (see also Mc-Goldrick and Pearce 1981).

CHRONICITY: "MAKING IT CRAZY"[4] IN SOUTH BOSTON

Although all the day hospital clients were revolving door or "chronic" mental patients whose low expectancies of recovery reflected the pessimism of their psychiatrists and counsellors, they differed with respect to their adaptations outside of hospital. Since discharge plans today are not contingent upon full remission of symptoms, adjustment in this group generally means learning how to "make it" or at least how to "fake it" while still very "crazy." Ethnic families in Southie also responded differently to the challenge to welcome home their "deinstitutionalized" relatives.

The South Boston Irish in this sample, although seemingly reluctant to label a family member as "mental" or "crazy," were more likely to sever ties completely with a close relation once that person had been hospitalized at Boston State. The public shame resulting from outside intervention into their generally very closed and private domestic lives, and the stigma from association with "Mattapan" were often more than these beleaguered families could stand. The assault to their fragile family respectability was simply too great. Hence, the hapless mental patient from such a family was often subject to a characteristically Irish interactional strategy known in the vernacular as the "cut-off" (see Scheper-Hughes 1979; McGoldrick and Pearce 1981). The cut-off individual is socially and emotionally disinherited. For all practical purposes he or she no longer exists, except perhaps as a negative example. I am reminded, for example, of one elderly alcoholic and frequently hallucinatory ex-patient who spent a good deal of time on the streets of South Boston although he counted among his relations a powerfully political family from the Upper End. His one remaining role in the family was that of emblematic "Blacksheep," an all too visible warning to his many nieces and nephews of the evils of the bottle. One nephew, an aspiring young politician, told me that on many a stormy winter's night when he was still a boy, his mother would tuck him into bed saying, "Think of poor old Uncle Ed sleeping out on a doorstep somewhere in the Lower End, and say a prayer that you will never wind up like him."

In some of the Irish families in this sample there appeared to be a tendency to move from a position of denying the *problem* to one of denying the *person* with the problem. One demonstrable result was the greater social isolation of the ex-patients from Irish families. After their discharge from Boston state these patients often "came home" to live in rooming houses and in community residency programs, not with family members or even within the borders of their home parishes.[5] Among these patients their natal community had evaporated and virtually all of their interactions and social relations were with other ex-patients or with mental health professionals.

Even the local Catholic clergy let these often devoutly religious individuals exist on the very fringes of parish life. They tended to attend very early Masses and to sit in darkened corners of the church. Except for weekly Bingo games, the ex-patients avoided all parish-related activities, saying that their presence would only make "regular" parishioners uncomfortable. Another key neighborhood institution that was "off-limits" to ex-patients was the famous James Michael Curley public bath house (the "L Street Baths"), an Irish social center, working class spa, and hotbed of local political activism. I could not convince ex-patients to come with me to "the baths" where they were convinced they were unwelcome, and where they feared they might run into relatives or old acquaintances. Some day hospital clients expressed anger and hurt at the implicit mandate to render themselves socially invisible:

> My relatives wish I would just disappear. I suppose I'm just an "eye-sore" to them. They don't want to see me any more than a "bad penny."

Another one said:

> All my life I've been poor and crazy. I just have to remind myself that when my relatives see me they think, "What does this loafer want now?"

Hence, pride often keeps them away from situations and places where they might be seen and recognized, and they tend to hold on to and cherish the occasional phone call or holiday greeting from a relative who may live just a few blocks away. *Unsolicited* attention from old friends and relatives was the most precious commodity—and the scarcest—among these ex-patients.

The "cut-off" ex-patient, living in a traditional white ethnic neighborhood where relatives tend to double for friend and where sociability rarely extends beyond family and old friend networks, is left with few opportunities for social interaction. S/he can spend the day dozing on a couch at the day hospital, sitting on a park bench or in a laundromat or in a donut shop until asked to leave. Of all the clients at the day hospital it was the single, middle aged, Irish male who was most isolated, most often left to his own (weak) inner resources and to his characteristic defenses of withdrawal, fantasy, and "the dreaming." A 43 year old male residing in a half-way house in Southie kept a journal in which he recorded the non-activities of his life as a "deinstitutionalized" mental patient. The following is a typical set of entries:

> *Monday.* Record playing is a good recreation if you are losing interest. It might work. Sometimes you might read, or play cards. Take a load off your feet. Well, nothing to complain about today. Everything is going well, except the plumbing.
> *Thursday.* The simple life is good, providing you don't become too simple. Try to be basic. A coffee break or a cigaret will keep you going. Not that life needs to be any more simple.

This does not mean to imply, however, that Italian or Lithuanian ex-patients are not also often lonely, isolated, and reduced to a very "basic" existence. The results of weekend summary files that I kept on thirty clients during 1979–1980 indicated that the most common leisure and weekend activities of the day hospital clients were, in order of frequency: watching T.V., cooking, cleaning house, sleeping, attending Mass, Bingo, and visiting with each other (Scheper-Hughes 1981:97). However, rarely were Italian and Eastern European clients actually severed from family, friends, and neighbors following hospitalization. In fact, eight of the eleven Eastern European clients in my sample were living at home with relatives. Some were active members of the local Lithuanian Club, and one was a member of a Lithuanian cultural organization and a frequent contributor to the organization's literary journal where she published some of her startling and dramatic verses on madness, suicide and lesbianism.

Among the small sample of Italian ex-patients neither did their status as veterans of Boston State Hospital result in family ostracism. Quite to the contrary, their presence at important family gatherings was often mandatory. One very psychotic woman from a large, extended Italian family that was no longer contained within the South Boston neighborhood, complained that the demands for her participation in family functions were overly taxing to her fragile grasp on realty. (This same woman confided that the only time she didn't actually hallucinate was when she could daydream black). She said that she would have to spend a day of preparation before a family visit, resting and doing special breathing exercises to increase her hold on reality. Since the members of her family lived dispersed throughout the greater Boston area she would often have to take long subway and bus rides which sometimes "unhinged" her before arriving. Once at the gathering she would try to behave as unobtrusively as possible by watching peoples' expressions and laughing whenever they did even though the humor often eluded her. If the "unreality" (as she referred to her persistent hallucinations) would begin to descend on her, she would excuse herself and lie down in a bedroom or take a taxi home, excusing herself with the complaint of a severe migraine headache.

Another Italian ex-patient, the eldest of four siblings, had her first psychotic episode following the early death of her mother. Although L. has been in and out of Boston State Hospital for the past ten years she never entirely gave up her role as surrogate mother to her younger siblings. Upon the death of her father, L. quietly checked herself into Boston State Hospital for the highly stressful days of the wake, but then checked herself out again in order to attend the funeral Mass and burial. Her absence, she felt, would have been inexcusable regardless of her state of mind. She remained out of the hospital long enough to make some important family decisions following the death, but once these were taken care of she lapsed into a seriously psychotic state that lasted for several weeks during which she remained hospitalized. In this case, L's family claims included demands on her tenuous sanity, and she complied to the fullest extent possible. Against this we would contrast the way in which the Irish clients were frequently abandoned to their own "unreality."

CONCLUDING REMARKS

These vignettes drawn from the life experiences of a small cohort of chronically mentally ill patients in South Boston indicate the relevance of cultural analysis to the new work that community psychiatrists have carved out for themselves. This very preliminary and exploratory study indicates that even chronically disturbed and floridly psychotic individuals respond to cultural cues regarding the perception, expression, timing, and meaning of psychiatric symptoms. Madness invariably disenfranchises, but it does not necessarily *deculturate* the individual. Some awareness of the cultural shaping of the experience of chronic mental illness is useful not only in the initial diagnostic encounter, but also during the much longer phase of therapy, rehabilitation, and resocialization.

Deinstitutionalization is a deeply cultural as well as political task. It challenges us all to reconsider what madness is, and what part culture and history play in the ways in which we respond to those who are labeled mad, crazy, psychotic, or schizophrenic. The laudable movement to close down state institutions—those crumbling Victorian "monasteries for the mad" (Scull 1984)—must now be accompanied by the more difficult task of *opening up* communities. We have returned mental patients to our city streets but not necessarily to our consciousness. The majority of ex-patients remain an invisible, marginalized, and mute cultural minority.

While the success of deinstitutionalization depends primarily on the goodwill and common human decency of ordinary citizens—the relatives, friends, co-workers, and neighbors of the deinstitutionalized patient—mental health professionals can help by putting themselves squarely on the side of the ex-patients to help them negotiate the culturally-constructed (and sometimes harmful) beliefs, stereotypes, responses and defenses that have been marshalled against them. This cultural task for an enlightened practice of public psychiatry is one which has, until now, received but scant attention.

NOTES

*With due courtesy to Edward Sapir's seminal article, "Why Cultural Anthropology Needs the Psychiatrist" (1938).

[1]Elsewhere I have suggested that a fundamental ambivalence toward the body, communicated to children through a non-nurturant early socialization and inculcation with the vestiges of Irish Catholic Jansenism, may contribute to the tendency of the rural Irish of County Kerry to likewise misread physical signs and to deny unpleasant psychological or somatic states (*See* Scheper-Hughes 1978; 1979, chapter 5).

[2]All personal names are pseudonyms, and many identifying features have been altered in these excerpts from case histories.

[3]The list of "symptoms" was generated from discussions with community leaders in South Boston: teachers, priests and nuns, social workers, etc.

[4]With acknowledgment to Sue E. Estroff, *Making it Crazy: An Ethnography of Psychiatric Clients in An American Community* (1981, University of California Press).

[5]In South Boston residents identify themselves in terms of their parish communities. There are a half dozen Catholic and a couple of Eastern Orthodox parishes within "Southie".

REFERENCES

City of Boston (1975) South Boston: Background Information, Planning Issues, Boston: Boston Redevelopment Authority.

Corry, J. (1977) The Golden Clan. Boston: Houghton-Mifflin.

Fantl, B. and J. Schiro (1959) Cultural Variables in the Behavioral Patterns and Symptom Formation of 15 Irish and 15 Italian Female Schizophrenics. International Journal of Social Psychiatry 4:245–259.

Lovell, A. M. and N. Scheper-Hughes (1986) Breaking the Circuit of Social Control: Lessons in Public Psychiatry from Italy and Franco Basaglia. Social Science and Medicine 23:159–178.

Lukas, J. Anthony (1985) Common Ground. New York: Alfred Knopf.

Lupo, Alan (1977) Liberty's Chosen Home: The Politics of Violence in Boston. Boston: Little, Brown.

McGoldrick, M. and J. Pearce (1981) Family Therapy With Irish-Americans. Family Process 20(2):223–224.

Minuchin, S., et al. (1967) Families of the Slums. New York: Basic Books.

Murphy, H. B. M. (1975) Alcoholism and Schizophrenia in the Irish: A Review. Transcultural Psychiatric Research Review 12:116–139.

Novak, D. (n.d.) Ethnicity in South Boston: Emergent National Origin. (manuscript)

Opler, M. K. and J. Singer (1957) Ethnic Differences in Behavior and Psychopathology: Italian and Irish. International Journal of Social Psychiatry 1:11–17.

Sapir, Edward (1938) Why Cultural Anthropology Needs the Psychiatrist. Psychiatry 1:7–12.

Scheff, T. J. (1966) Being Mentally Ill. Chicago: Aldine.

___. (1975) Labeling Madness. Englewood Cliffs: Prentice-Hall.

Scheper-Hughes, N. (1978) Disarming the Irish: Reflections on Irish Body Image. Kroeber Anthropological Society Papers 54:58–70.

___. (1979) Saints, Scholars, and Schizophrenics: Mental Illness in Rural Ireland. Berkeley: University of California Press.

___. (1981) Dilemmas in Deinstitutionalization. Journal of Operational Psychiatry 12(2): 90–99.

___. (1983) 'Benevolent Anarchy': A Proposal For the Aftercare of Chronic Mental Patients. Medical Anthropology Quarterly 14(2):11–15.

Schmitt, P. (1972) Needs Assessment: A Working Manual. Tufts-New England Medical Health Center, Bay Cove Community Mental Health Center, October 19.

Scull, A.T. (1984) Decarceration: Community Treatment and the Deviant—A Radical View. New Brunswick, NJ: Rutgers University Press.

Sheehan, Brian (1984) The Boston School Integration Dispute. New York: Columbia University Press.

Sigal, G. (n.d.) D. Street Felt Need Survey. (manuscript)

Sternbach, R. (1965) Ethnic Differences Among Housewives in Psychophysical and Skin Potential Responses to Electric Shock. Psychophysiology 1/3:241–246.

Walsh, D. (1968) Some Influences on the Intercounty Variation in Irish Psychiatric Hospitalization Rates. British Journal of Psychiatry 114:15–20.

Wylah, L. and N. Mintz (1976) Ethnic Differences in Family Attitudes Towards Psychotic Manifestations, With Implications for Treatment Programmes. International Journal of Social Psychiatry 22(2):86–95

Zborowski, M. (1964) People in Pain, San Francisco: Jossey Bass.

Zola, I. (1966) Culture and Symptoms: An Analysis of Patients Presenting Complaints. American Sociological Review 31:615–630.

CHAPTER FIFTEEN

Culture, Mind-Brain, and Mental Illness

The realization has slowly dawned that the etiology, structure, course, and outcome of mental disorders are far more complexly integrated than previously imagined. It is now becoming clear that mental disorders need to be defined in a holistic manner that includes the interactions of the patient's sociocultural environment and the effects of diagnosis and treatment on the patient's brain. All of these factors combine and interact to produce an actual illness experience in a given patient.

The modern disease-centered paradigm in psychiatry is now being expanded to include the neurobiology of brain adaptation to the environment. This theoretical expansion includes the effects of neural changes in the brain resulting from psychotropic medications, psychotherapy, internalization of cultural meanings, a person's habitual patterns of thought, and the effects of social stress on the mind-brain.

The first article in this chapter is by the late Nobel laureate neuroscientist Roger W. Sperry, describing the theoretical significance of recent advances in the neurosciences concerning causal determinism of mind and brain. According to Sperry, microdeterministic concepts of brain function are giving way to macrodeterministic explanations with the view that consciousness is causal. That is, a person's habitual patterns of thought, experience, and behavior alter the brain. This is just the opposite of earlier views, which assumed that thought and behavior were exclusively dependent on microlevel physiological processes in the brain. Sperry argues that the concept of *downward causation*

from consciousness to brain is now accepted in neuroscience, but the implications of this new view are not being fully appreciated throughout the rest of science. Many researchers are still microdeterministic in their views, conceptualizing thought and behavior as being determined exclusively by functions at the molecular or cellular level. The concept of downward causation reinstates mind. Cultural meanings and social environment are then important and ineliminable factors in understanding brain function and dysfunction, including mental illness, in the monistic concept of mind-brain.

The second article in this chapter is by anthropologist Margery Wolf. It is an ethnographic case study of a mentally ill woman in a Taiwanese village. The woman was hallucinating, and according to the cultural meanings present in this village, she was either being called by a god to speak for him (thus become a shaman) or was going crazy. However, because she was a woman in a highly male dominated society and her family was new to the community, her status in the village was low. Her low status disallowed the formal training in shamanic techniques that would have permitted her to become a successful shaman, and thus avoid being labeled crazy. If this woman had possessed a higher social status, she might have avoided serious mental illness. In the end, the woman was labeled crazy and took on the social role of a seriously mentally ill person. This article demonstrates the kinds of effects the meanings of madness can have on mental illness and presumably on the mind-brain.

R. W. SPERRY

Structure and Significance of the Consciousness Revolution

The recent swing in psychology from behaviorism to a more subjective mentalist (or cognitive) paradigm is interpreted to be more than a mere Zeitgeist phenomenon and to represent a fundamental conceptual shift to a different form of causal determinism. Traditional microdeterministic conceptions of brain function are replaced by an explanatory view that gives primacy to macrodeterminism. It is argued that the key factor among numerous contributing influences was the appearance in the 1960s of an emergent, functional, interactionist concept of consciousness that gives subjective mental phenomena a causal role in brain processing and behavior. Whereas the basic behaviorist philosophy of science could be adjusted to accommodate advances in computer simulation, information theory, cognitive process research, linguistic and other cognitive developments in the 1960s, behaviorism could not adapt to the new concept of consciousness as causal. The two views, at bedrock, are mutually exclusive and irreconcilable. It is suggested that the new macrodeterminist view represents a more valid paradigm for all science.

The so-called consciousness revolution of the 1970s in the behavioral sciences, referred to also as the "cognitive," "mentalist" or "humanist" revolution, is widely evident and well documented (Block, 1981; Boneau, 1974; Davidson and Davidson, 1980; Dember, 1974; Ferguson, 1980; Gardner, 1985; Heinen, 1980; Hilgard, 1980; Kantor, 1977; Manicas and Secord, 1983; Matson,

The work was supported in part by the F.P. Hixon Fund of the California Institute of Technology. For helpful comments on an earlier draft of the manuscript I thank Joseph Bogen, Erika Erdmann, Charles Hamilton, S. Harnad, W.T. Jones, Thomas Natsoulas, Howard Slaatte, and Colwyn Trevarthen. I am indebted to Erika Erdmann for library research and compiling references and to Margaret Limm and Jessica Madow for assistance with revisions and the typing. Requests for reprints may be sent to R.W. Sperry, Ph.D., Division of Biology, California Institute of Technology, Pasadena, California 91125.

1971; Pylyshyn, 1973; Segal and Lachman, 1972; Simon, 1982). Behaviorist doctrine, which had dominated psychology since the 1920s, gave way rather abruptly in the early seventies to a more subjective, cognitive or mentalist paradigm manifest in practice as a direct turnabout with respect to the scientific recognition and treatment of mental states and events. Subjective phenomena, including mental images, feelings, thoughts, memories and other cognitive contents of inner experience that had long been banned from scientific explanation by rigorous objective behaviorist and materialist principles, suddenly made a strong comeback and became widely used and accepted as legitimate explanatory constructs. The accepted role of conscious experience in brain function and behavior changed from that of a noncausal, epiphenomenal, parallel or identical status (and something best ignored or excluded from scientific explanation) to that of an ineliminable causal, or interactional role.

In describing the revolution in question preference is given here to "consciousness" over "cognitive" because in current usage "cognitive" has become ambiguous in that it may or may not imply consciousness and the subjective. One can speak of the incremental rise of a new cognitive science on the one hand (Gardner, 1985), and on the other, of the revolutionary about-face in the scientific treatment of conscious experience. The two are related in many ways—but to combine and mix the two without clear distinctions easily leads to unnecessary confusion. For similar reasons the term "mental" will be used here in preference to cognitive because mental more generally tends to connote processing in the living brain.

In the following we deal specifically with the more narrowly defined development referred to as "the new legitimacy of the subjective" (Stryker, 1981) and exemplified in the interpretation of mental events and imagery, not as epiphenomenal to brain processing but as functional, interactional or causative (Block 1981). The new legitimacy of the subjective is evident not only in the current conceptions of psychology but also in the kinds of experiments and writings undertaken, the kinds of questions asked, journals and societies formed, conferences held and so on which would all have been discouraged under former behaviorist principles as being something less than scientific.

Whereas this turnabout in the scientific treatment and conception of the subjective is today well recognized and accepted, its root causes and meaning remain much less clear. In fact, the change appears to have meant many different things to different scientific communities. For example, the humanistic psychologists refer to the "humanist," "third" or "third force" revolution (the first two "revolutions" having been associated respectively with Watson and Freud) and perceive the new outlook as a realization of the holistic-subjective principles proclaimed by Abraham Maslow, Carl Rogers, and others. (For references see more detailed discussion in sections that follow.) Similarly the cognitive psychologists and phenomenologists point to their own, even longer history of quarrels with behaviorist doctrine in which they have traditionally favored much the same cognitivist or mentalist framework that has become today the majority position. Meantime the computerologists, especially in artificial intelligence, are inclined to see the key to the new outlook in analogies between mental and computer programs and recent developments in computer science. Related thinking credits the new outlook to information theory. Others cite "functionalist philosophy" and "transformational linguistics." General systems theorists tend to perceive it as an intrinsic development of general systems theory, while disciples of the "consciousness raising" and "self awareness" movements of the sixties see an impelling role in these and related social activist trends. Others credit advances in the research on perception and imagery—and the list continues, as explained in more detail below.

Many scientists accept the swing to mentalism as simply an outcome of the trends of the times, a Zeitgeist phenomenon with a fadlike quality impelled by many diffuse sociological influences. One commonly hears that "the time was ripe," that after more than 50 years of domination by behaviorist principles and practice, "psychology was ready for a change." At another extreme I ascribe the consciousness revolution in what follows to a specific change in mind-brain theory. According to this view, the shift from behaviorism to mentalism represents a changeover to a revised form of causal determinism, in essence a shift from an exclusive microdeterminist paradigm to one that emphasizes "macro," "molar" or "emergent" determinism.

The new mentalist paradigm is deduced to be a more valid paradigm for all science, not just psychology, and to represent a new "middle way" position in philosophy which integrates positivistic thought with phenomenology (Slaate, 1981). The result is a revised scientific description of human nature and also nonhuman nature and of the kinds of forces in control, a changed world outlook that brings a new era in the science-values relation, a resolution of the freewill-determinism issue and other promising developments in the long standing worldview conflicts between science and the humanities. These and other far reaching humanistic as well as scientific implications call for deeper understanding of the causes and structure of the consciousness revolution and what it signifies.

Mind-brain issues are involved as well as those of the holist-reductionist dispute, both of which easily become entangled in philosophic abstractions and semantics and already have been subject to endless debate without resolution. The consciousness revolution on the other hand is an actual historical occurrence, the nature and causes of which should be subject to some definite answers. By focusing on those factors that actually did convince hundreds, even thousands of minds to reverse their reasoning about consciousness and to relinquish behaviorism in favor of mentalism we thereby bypass innumerable possibly fruitless empty approaches to center in on ideas that already have been proven to count in practice. A pragmatic reference frame is thus obtained for some notoriously elusive philosophic issues with possibilities for fresh diagonals through the time-worn perspectives on mind and brain, emergence and reductionism.

GENERAL PRESUPPOSITIONS

It may be taken for granted that a majority of the scientific community involved in the changeover from behaviorism to mentalism did not make special efforts to analyze underlying forces or conceptual foundations but simply followed what they saw others doing. When some authority known to be knowledgeable in such matters is seen to defy behaviorist tradition by using "mental images," "feelings" or other subjective phenomena as explanatory causes of behavior, many others quickly reason that if the authority has found justification they can do the same. The more peers observed to adopt the new practice the greater the tendency for others to follow suit. Such a self-feeding, amplifying, cascade process may be presumed to have played a strong role in helping to bring about the current swing to mentalism.

Another set of factors of undoubted influence includes a variety of what can be referred to as "subjectivist pressures" that have tended to favor the subjective approach against the dictates of behaviorist doctrine ever since behaviorism first appeared. One source, common experience, includes the natural tendency to perceive our behavior as being directed and caused by subjective mental states, i.e., by our subjectivist desires, intentions, needs, values, percepts, thoughts, and the like. Added to this pressure from common experience are the more formal professional or disciplinary influences in cognitive, clinical, and humanistic doctrine, reinforced also in psychotherapy, psychiatry, and all the other subdisciplines obliged by the nature of their work to rely heavily on introspection, including such research fields as those involving perception, emotion, and memory.

These various subgroups in behavioral science have for the most part been able to reconcile their findings and thinking with an ultimate objective behaviorist or neuronal explanation. Nevertheless a strong inclination exists to favor any theoretical justification for cognitive explanation and what Carl Rogers (1964a) used to call "subjective knowing." The common dissatisfaction with behaviorism's renunciation of the subjective represents an example of what Kuhn (1970) describes as an invariable antecedent of scientific revolutions, "a common awareness that something has gone wrong" with prior theory. In any case these subjectivist pressures, natural and formal, along with the above-mentioned tendency to follow suit, mutually reinforcing each other, can largely be held responsible for the suddenness with which the general acceptance of subjective explanation occurred once it got started, a suddenness described by Pylyshyn (1973) as having "exploded into fashion."

The specialists meantime are quick to seek out new ideas and titles in their field and are finely tuned to apprehend even subtle conceptual changes. Any new developments quickly became incorporated into their writing with or without references. It is highly unlikely, once and idea for paradigmatic change gets into the literature, that it will go unnoticed among the specialists. The specialists, however, often with strong professional investments in earlier positions, may tend to resist acknowledging innovation until swayed by majority opinion. Many other related subtle and complex forces may be recognized that, following Kuhn (1970), can be classified under the heading of sociological factors.

Another invariant of scientific revolutions, recognized by Kuhn but perhaps not given enough emphasis, is the appearance of a conceptual innovation that challenges the preexisting paradigm and is incompatible with its foundational concepts. The new concept must also be capable of competing successfully in the open market with the preceding rival view. This would seem to be the *sine qua non* for major revolutions in science: a new concept or theory so incompatible with preexisting theory that the preceding paradigm cannot be stretched to include it. Evident in the Copernican, Newtonian, Darwinian and other recognized revolutions, such a conceptual innovation is the central basic change around which the sociologic and other phenomena revolve and depend.

Sociologic factors may be important but the paradigms of science are not subject to change like fashions in headwear. They tend to be adhered to because of reason, logic and mathematics, and regardless of seeming counterintuitiveness. For example, the rigorous objective tenets of what Skinner (1964) refers to as the behaviorist "philosophy of science" successfully kept in abeyance for over half a century the widespread intuitive pressures favoring subjectivism. This in itself suggests that the switch to mentalism, when it finally did occur, was more than just a diffuse sociological or Zeitgeist trend and had to be based

upon revisions in the underlying conceptual foundations. Thus, the effort to understand the consciousness revolution boils down primarily to a search for a critical change in the conceptual foundations of psychology, more specifically for rival new theoretical concepts incompatible with behaviorist doctrine.

Unlike the situation in the Copernican, Darwinian and most scientific revolutions, the rival concepts involved in the consciousness revolution never became generally explicit. This means that the sociologic forces must have played a correspondingly greater role—as evident in the lack of any consensus even today regarding the rationale and the diverse interpretations still being favored among different special interest groups. Even so, these sociological dynamics could have taken a different direction or could have remained anchored in behaviorism. The question is whether it may be possible to uncover, by critical analysis, the underlying rival theory responsible for steering the sociologic trends in the mentalist direction.

KEY FACTOR: A CAUSAL CONCEPT OF CONSCIOUSNESS

A key development that seems to fit the foregoing requirements and to have been responsible for the 1970s' swing to mentalism, according to the present analysis, was the emergence during the 1960s of concepts of brain function and consciousness that introduced a causal view of subjective qualities in brain processing (e.g., Fodor, 1968; Miller, Galanter, and Pribram, 1960; Neisser, 1967; Popper, 1965; Putnam, 1960; Sperry, 1965, 1969b). The result was in direct conflict with and undermined the most basic tenets of behaviorist doctrine. At the same time the new interpretation provided a long-sought logical determinist basis for cognitive, clinical and humanistic psychology. Essentially, the new theory conceived subjective qualities to be emergent properties of brain processes that interact causally at their own cognitive level and also at the same time exert downward causal control in a supervening sense over the activity patterns of the neuronal components.

These revised mind-brain concepts shared with behaviorism the assumption that mental phenomena are determined by physicochemical processes. However, they directly countered the conviction of behaviorism that there is no way these physicochemical processes can be causally influenced by the qualities of subjective experience. In direct contradiction to the behaviorist paradigm, subjective mental and cognitive phenomena were given a causal, functional or interactionist role in brain processing and thereby a new legitimacy in science as autonomous *ineliminable* explanatory constructs. This logical turn-around from a passive to a functional interactional status for subjective experience was further reinforced by the prevailing ambient "subjective pressures" already mentioned and also by a new appreciation of the control role of cognition gained from computer science. The combined effect led to a rapid rise of the new mentalist-cognitive outlook as the dominant paradigm in behavioral science.

The terms "interaction" and "interactionism" are used here in the way these have been applied historically to the mind-brain relation, i.e., as used by Popper and Eccles (1977) when they refer to "dualist and psycho-neural interactionism" and by Natsoulas (1984, 1987) when he refers to "monist interactionism." Mind-brain interaction is taken to mean that mental states are causally influenced by brain states and vice versa. The usage in this context does *not*, however, imply an interaction of the mental and physical *within* a given level in the brain hierarchy but rather *inter*level causal influences. Mind-brain interaction is used as a contrast to mind-brain parallelism.

This changed interactional view of the mind-brain relation applied emergent and functionalist thinking in combination with the concept of downward causation (as explained below) to describe a view of consciousness that not only refutes behaviorist doctrine, but contradicts also traditional reasoning in neuroscience. It counters claims that a complete account of brain and behavior can be given, in principle, in strictly objective, stimulus-response and neuronal terms without reference to subjective awareness—as expressed by Sir John Eccles:

> We can, in principle, explain all our input-output performance in terms of activity of neuronal circuits; and consequently, consciousness seems to be absolutely unnecessary! ... [A]s neurophysiologists we simply have no use for consciousness in our attempts to explain how the nervous system works. (Eccles, 1966, p. 248)

The only available counterargument for this traditional reasoning seems to be that of emergent interaction with downward control which serves to distinguish between the causal role of the mental qualities per se and that of their neuronal infrastructure, providing for the causality of the former as well as the latter. On both counts the emergent downward control concept is critical for upholding mentalism over behaviorism. In these terms the subjective aspects of brain processing can no longer be ignored or excluded in scientific explanation.

Thus interpreted the mentalist paradigm clearly leans heavily on holistic doctrine with extensive antecedents in earlier writings on emergence, holism and epistemology (e.g., Herrick, 1956; Morgan, 1923; Polanyi, 1962; Ritter, 1919; Sellars, 1922, 1943; Smuts, 1926 and others). The mentalist movement of the 1970s, however, represents the first occasion in which emergent reasoning has gained acceptance to the extent of becoming the dominant

paradigm for a large scientific discipline. What needs to be explained is why the anticipatory threads of holistic thinking changed from the status of occasional, scattered, personal and often obscure philosophy, or at most minority science, into the majority practicing paradigm of the behavioral sciences. The new success I believe is attributable primarily to the combining of emergentist thought with the concept of downward determinism and with the functionalist view of the subjective applied where they count most, i.e., to consciousness and mind-brain interaction.

Behaviorism had not been threatened by earlier emergent views as applied to biological evolution or in Gestalt psychology where no mind-brain interaction was implied. Behaviorism had not been threatened either by previous conceptions of the mind-brain relation including identity theory, epiphenomenalism, double aspect theory, dualism or dismissal of the mind-brain question as a pseudoproblem (Skinner, 1964, 1971). Dualism posed contradictions, of course, but its status in science from the 1920s through the 1960s was so weak that it represented no real threat. On the other hand, behaviorism could not coexist with the new causal interpretation of consciousness which was explicitly antibehavioristic.

THE COMPUTER PROGRAM ANALOGY

Other views of the consciousness-cognitive revolution have ascribed a major role to developments in information theory and computer science, particularly to artificial intelligence and computer program analogy (e.g. Gardner 1985; Hilgard 1980; MacKay 1982; Neisser 1967). Although the computer developments forced adjustments in behaviorist policy in regard to cognition they did not demand an abandonment of its founding philosophy. The behaviorist philosophy of science could live with the computer program model of cognition much as it had with the "cognitive behaviorism" of Tolman (1925, 1926) decades earlier. In a number of ways computer simulation can be seen (Rosenberg, 1986), not as refuting behaviorism but as doing the reverse: demonstrating that a concrete objective explanation of mental processing is possible in science without recourse to introspection or conscious awareness. Since neither computers nor their programs were generally supposed to be conscious, the computer model was not taken initially as a model of subjective experience and did not represent a threat either to basic behaviorist philosophy nor to the general microdeterminist paradigm prior to parallel processing models (Rumelhart, McClelland, and PDP Research Group, 1986).

With regard to the causal determinist issue (see below), the computer model was neutral and could be interpreted either way. It was neutral also on the issue of whether mind and brain interact, or run in parallel, or are identical. Much depends on its validity as a model for mind and brain and this has come increasingly to be questioned (Churchland and Churchland, 1983; Libet, 1980; Natsoulas, 1980; Rosenberg, 1986; Searle, 1980). Much depends also on how the causal relation between program and hardware is to be interpreted, i.e., whether merely sequential and feedback, or top-down etc. The computer models, further, can be readily interpreted in terms of the identity and "double aspect" views of Feigl (1958), as stressed by MacKay (1984) and others, and thus hardly require a new mentalist paradigm in which subjective qualities per se have explanatory legitimacy. All things considered it would appear that the paradigm shift in the early 1970s from behaviorism to mentalism had to come from other resources.

TWO DIFFERING VIEWS OF CAUSAL DETERMINISM

It is important to remember in this context that the basic behaviorist philosophy as propounded by Watson, Kantor, Skinner and others still remains a powerful explanatory paradigm and is upheld by a strong minority within psychology (see Catania and Harnad, 1984; Natsoulas, 1983). It is still claimed by its supporters to be quite applicable, in ways that have worked for decades, to all the modern findings in cognitive science, including the recent observations on imagery (Block, 1981) and artificial intelligence (Skinner, 1984, 1985). In the final analysis, we come down to two opposing views of physical reality, two different worldviews, each claiming to provide in principle a complete and valid explanation.

The strength by which behaviorism succeeded in dominating psychology for over half a century stemmed in no small measure from its firm entrenchment in 20th century scientific materialism or microdeterminist doctrine. This made behavioral science consistent with the rest of natural science. To topple behaviorism at its base required therefore that the conventional reductive microdeterminist reasoning of science itself must be toppled also. Only the principle of emergent or molar determinism (as discussed in more detail below) appears to qualify. Whereas the basic behaviorist paradigm was not jeopardized by computer science nor by other cognitive developments of the 1960s, it could not cope with this causal concept of consciousness. If the new interactionist view of consciousness were correct, the opposed behaviorist philosophy of science had to be wrong.

The changeover in behavioral science to mentalism (and thereby to emergent principles of causal determinism) has not been accompanied meantime by a similar shift in the more exact sciences such as physics, chemistry and molecular biology. These have continued to adhere in majority opinion and practice, to traditional reductionist, materialist doctrine. The result is that we have in science today two major conflicting doctrines of causal

control, two conflicting scientific descriptions of the kinds of forces that govern ourselves and the world. The classic view reduces everything to physics and chemistry and ultimately to quantum mechanics or some even more elemental, unifying theory. Everything is supposed to be governed from below upward following the course of evolution. Science, in this traditional microdeterminist view, presents a value-devoid, strictly physically driven cosmos and conscious self, governed by the elemental forces of physics and chemistry, ultimately by quantum mechanics. By this long dominant physicalist-behaviorist paradigm there is no real freedom, dignity, purpose or intentionality. These are only aspects or epiphenomena of mind which in no way influence the course of physical events in the real world or in the brain.

According to the new mentalist view, by contrast, things are controlled not only from below upward by atomic and molecular action but also from above downward by mental, social, political and other macro properties. Primacy is given to the higher level controls rather than to the lowest. The higher, emergent, molar or macro phenomena and their properties throughout nature supersede the less evolved controls of the components. The concepts of physical reality and the kind of cosmology upheld by science in the two conflicting views thus differ vastly, particularly with respect to their psychological and humanistic implications.

Both sides in the debate agree on the existence and prevalence of microdeterminism. The question at issue is whether things are determined *exclusively* from below, upward or whether downward causation is also operating. If the control of a system is exclusively in terms of its elements, then a complete account of conscious brain function is logically possible without including conscious experience, as behaviorism and neuroscience have long maintained. Conversely, if the principle of emergent interaction with downward determinism is valid then the emergent subjective properties become ineliminable explanatory causal constructs.

A main overriding concern in attempts to better understand the consciousness revolution relates to its bearing on this ongoing macro versus micro debate. In the final analysis the arguments stand or fall on the issue of micro versus macro determinism. We need to know if the shift from behaviorism to cognitivism is an endorsement of macrodeterminism. Is the consciousness revolution a revolution for all science? I believe it is and that the behavioral sciences may be leading the way to a more valid paradigm for science in general.

EMERGENT INTERACTION AND DOWNWARD CONTROL

The concept of downward control and how it works in emergent interaction is critical for the present claim that fundamental concepts of causation are at stake. The fact that downward, top-down, emergent, molar or macro causation continues to be contested, especially in the exact sciences, but also in philosophy (e.g. Kim, 1983; Klee, 1984; MacKay, 1982), indicates that it either has not been adequately explained or that fails to hold up under examination. Because it lies at the heart of our present thesis some further explanation is in order before proceeding.

Downward determinism has been illustrated in terms of biological hierarchies (Campbell, 1974; Sperry, 1964); the mind-brain relation (Sperry, 1965), using simple physical examples such as a wheel rolling down hill (Klee, 1984; Sperry, 1969b); and in terms of its theoretical logic (Sperry, 1981). In the brain it includes the control by the higher mental activity over the lower neuronal activity—expressed in 1964 as follows:

> . . . a molecule in many respects is the master of its inner atoms and electrons. The latter are hauled and forced about in chemical interactions by the overall configurational properties of the whole molecule. At the same time, if our given molecule is itself part of a single-celled organism such as paramecium, it in turn is obliged, with all its parts and its partners, to follow along a trail of events in time and space determined largely by the extrinsic overall dynamics of *Paramecium caudatum.* When it comes to brains, remember that the simpler electric, atomic, molecular, and cellular forces and laws, though still present and operating, have been superseded by the configurational forces of higher-level mechanisms. At the top, in the human brain, these include the powers of perception, cognition, reason, judgment and the like, the operational, causal effects and forces of which are equally or more potent in brain dynamics than are the outclassed inner chemical forces. (Sperry, 1964, p. 20)

Spelled out more fully, in the following year (in relation to consciousness and evolution—with direct implications for freewill, values, and the worldview of science [Popper 1965; Sperry 1965]), this emergent control concept was presented as a new solution to the mind-body problem. It was also described by Popper as a new view of evolution and a different view of the world. Perceived to lead to a compromise or middle way philosophic outlook that is neither dualism nor traditional materialism, it denied that the mental can exist apart from the functioning brain. At the same time it accepted the objective causal reality of mental states at their own level as subjectively experienced. The downward control aspect, later dubbed "downward causation" (Campbell, 1974; Popper, 1978; Popper and Eccles, 1977) has also been referred to as "emergent causation," "holistic control" and "molar determinism" (Klee 1984; Sperry 1986) in opposition to the traditional microdeterminism of materialist doctrine.

Because the concept is critical for the idea of a more valid scientific paradigm and continues to be disputed, some further explanation is attempted in the following passage using simpler examples which will serve also to emphasize the universality of the principle. As such an illustration, consider a molecule in an airplane leaving Los Angeles for New York. Our molecule, say in the water tank or anywhere in the structure, may be jostled or held by its neighbors—but, these lower level actions are relatively trivial compared to the movement across the country. If one is plotting the space-time trajectory of the given molecule, those features governed from above by the higher properties of the plane as a whole, make those governed at the lower molecular level insignificant by comparison.

The same principle applies throughout nature at all levels. The atoms and molecules of our biosphere, for example, are moved around, not so much by atomic and molecular forces as by the higher forces of the varied organisms and other entities in which they are embedded. The atomic, molecular and other micro forces are continuously active but at the same time they are enveloped, submerged, superseded, "hauled and pushed around" by, or "supervened" by an infinite variety of other higher molar properties of the systems and entities in which the micro elements are embedded—without interfering with the physico-chemical activity of lower levels.

Reductionists claim that the entire flight of the plane from Los Angeles to New York can be accounted for in terms of the collective atomic and molecular activity, eventually quantum mechanics. The "macro" answer asserts there is no way that quantum mechanics can describe the multinested spatial features of the plane's structure which govern the flight as much as the molecular components per se. Similarly, the timing factors, as in its various motors, could not be accounted for by quantum mechanics. The plane will have radio, computer, and TV circuits. If one were to disconnect two elements in these circuits and reconnect them in reverse manner, the whole system would fail. The particular connections of the circuit plan cannot be determined from quantum mechanics; the laws for circuit design come from a higher level. In general, subatomic physics fails to give a full account of these higher organizational features.

The same applies to the circuit plan and function of the nervous system. If one were to plot the firing pattern for a given cortical neuron involved in cognitive function, the bursts of activity would, of course, be correlated with the local excitatory and inhibitory inputs to the given cell. At the same time, the timing of the neuron's firing, as well as that of its local input, would also be found to be determined predominantly by the train of mental events that happens to be in process. A change in mental programming brings corresponding major changes in the given neuron's activity pattern.

Most everyone agrees that neuronal events determine the cognitive events, but it is also true that the mental events, once they emerge, interact with other mental events at their own level and in the process also exert downward control to determine concomitantly the firing pattern of their neuronal constituents. The controls work both ways, upward and downward as well as sequentially. In "emergent interaction" or "emergent determinism" the mental events control neuronal activity at the same time that they are determined by them. The downward control view contends that the higher emergent forces and properties are more than the collective effect of the lower because critical novel space-time factors are not included in the laws governing the components (see Rumelhart et al., 1986).

It may be objected that examples of interlevel causation in which both levels are physical are no help to explain the mind-brain relation where one level is mental and thus by definition nonphysical. Our present thesis discounts such objections claiming the pertinent causal principles are the same. Brain processes have many unconscious as well as conscious emergent properties. Just because some emergent properties are subjective does not mean their basic interlevel causal control relationships are therefore different. Identity theory disposes of this issue semantically by calling the subjective properties physical properties.

In probing further the micro versus macro dispute it may help, at the risk of being repetitive, to focus on a simple familiar example, such as the downward control exerted by a molecule of water over its hydrogen and oxygen atoms. It usually is agreed that the laws defining the behavior of the atoms, particularly their course through time and space, become quite different after the atoms become joined together as a molecule. Although the atomic properties in the main are preserved, the atoms, once joined, are obliged to follow a new space-time course determined predominantly by the higher properties of the water molecule as a whole.

Many reductionists concur but argue that the new properties of the molecule are themselves determined entirely by those of the atoms and in fact can be completely predicted from the atomic properties. The macrodeterminist answer holds that predictability is not the issue here. Being able to predict the formation of novel emergent properties does not make the new properties go away or make them any less real, less novel or less important and powerful as causal determinants. The macrodeterminist can accept that the entire course of evolution is predictable, *in principle,* starting from subatomic properties, but this does not change the argument that evolution *does* occur, that new properties and control forces *do* emerge and that when they do, they exert downward control over their constituents which, as a result, are thereafter governed by new scientific laws.

The old reductionist claim that the properties of the molecule are nothing but the collective effects of the constituent atomic properties usually becomes qualified, these days, by the addition of some phrase to include the new organizational or spatio-temporal relations. With very simple entities, like the water molecule, the spacing and timing may be closely determined by the atomic properties themselves—but this does not hold for more complex entities, as in our airplane, for example, where the coherent configuration may be a product of anything from chaos to an inventor's insight. Again, however, to be able to describe how the formation of the new properties was determined does not provide scientific descriptions or laws for the new entities. The point is that the new emergent entity with its new spatio-temporal arrangement and resultant new properties, once it has come into existence, deserves to be treated and recognized in its own form for what it is—not solely as a collection of its elements in a special new space-time arrangement.

For an accurate, complete, scientific description of nature, the *spacing* and *timing* of all the multinested elements at all levels must be included. Science has laws for the behavior of the material, mass-energy elements but in general does not have laws for the complex multilevel space-time components. The space-time, or pattern factors, however, are *automatically incorporated* in the laws for the macrophenomena, as for example, in classical mechanics. Properties manifest at subatomic levels tend to be bound up and controlled by properties at higher levels. If an uncertainty principle is operating at sub-atomic levels this does not necessarily imply that this uncertainty operates in the whole natural order at large, or characterizes the essence of reality.

It is frequently objected that if science has been wrong on this issue, how could it have been so eminently successful? It needs to be remembered in this connection that microdeterminism in itself is very valid. It is not contradicted by the acceptance of emergentism and downward control; neither is the value of the analytic, reductive methodology of science. It is only the *exclusion* of macrodeterminism that is claimed to be in error, and science has not excluded macrodeterminism in *practice,* only in its philosophy, theory and outlook. The microbiologist, for example, consistently relies on macrodeterminism and downward control in the treatment of molecular activity. It is in treating organisms, not molecules, that biology usually becomes reductionistic. The laws of classical mechanics are heavily macrodeterminist. In general, science has always depended on macrodeterminist principles though this has usually remained tacit and unrecognized.

RISE OF MENTALISM: CHRONOLOGICAL CORRELATES

The deduction that the mentalist overthrow of behaviorism involved a paradigmatic shift to changed concepts of causation as described in the foregoing gains added support from chronological considerations. It is commonly agreed that the new acceptance of the cognitive in behavioral science was greatly aided by developments during the 1950s in information theory and computer science, which became widely disseminated in psychology particularly through the 1960 volume of Miller, Galanter, and Pribram and later through the 1967 textbook on *Cognitive Psychology* by Ulrich Neisser. Information theory and the computer program analogy were already well developed by the end of the 1950s (Ashby, 1956; Feigenbaum and Feldman, 1963; Von Neumann, 1958) and had become familiar in psychology by the mid 1960s. The major changeover from behaviorism to mentalism, however, did not take place until some five years later. Although the timing of developments in computer science by no means excludes these as a possibly important influence, the correlation does not appear to have been particularly close or direct.

The thinking in computer science as it existed during the 1950s into the early 1960s is well represented in the 1963 book, *Computers and Thought*, edited by E.A. Feigenbaum and J. Feldman. As discussed earlier, one searches in vain for any principles that overturn behaviorism's microdeterminist philosophy or the materialist reasoning in neuroscience, or otherwise explain the later turnabout on consciousness. An intensive examination of related hierarchy theory and interlevel controls almost a decade after (Dewan, 1976; Wimsatt, 1976) indicates that relevant antibehaviorist, downward control ideas were only then beginning to be applied in this area. The current mentalist-functionalist philosophy of the new cognitive science (Fodor, 1981; Gardner, 1985) thus does not appear to have been applied to the computer program model (Neisser, 1967) until after it had already been stated in reference to the mind-brain relation. In other words it was only after the consciousness revolution had already appeared in mind-brain science that the corresponding concepts became applied in computer science.

Cognitive psychology, humanistic psychology, and the phenomenological school can argue in each case that behavioral science has simply come around at last to recognize and accept the relative merits of their respective, long expressed oppositions to behaviorism. These schools, however, and their respective arguments had been present for many years, even decades, without bringing down the reign of behaviorism. Cognitive theory and phenomenology extended back at least to the 1920s to Tolman and Husserl and was updated in work such as that of Miller, Galanter, and Pribram (1960). All this had failed, however, prior to the mid sixties to overthrow the opposing, and firmly ensconced, behaviorist contention that a full scientific account of behavior can best be provided in strict, objective terms consistent with physiochemical science and without recourse to subjective experience.

The humanistic movement, though more recent, is based in holistic, emergent and gestalt principles which also go back into the 1920s and 1930s and had likewise failed for many years to shake the behaviorist logic. The writings of Abraham Maslow and Carl Rogers up to and into the mid 1960s did not invoke

downward causation or other deterministic principles that could refute behaviorist reasoning, or that of neuroscience as expressed above by Eccles. Well into the 1960s proponents of both phenomenology and behaviorism were still vigorously debating their opposed philosophies without significant give on either side (Kantor, 1969; Koch, 1964, 1969; Maslow, 1968; Rogers, 1964a, 1969; Skinner, 1964, 1971; Wann, 1964). The situation as it still stood in the mid 1960s was summarized by Carl Rogers at the close of his 1964 "Humanist of the Year" address as "two sharply divergent and irreconcilably contradictory points of view [the behavioristic and the humanistic]. If in response to this you say, 'But these views *cannot* both be true,' my answer is, 'This is a deep paradox with which we must learn to live'" (Rogers, 1964b, p. 40).

Despite the apparent explanatory value and seeming causal potency of cognitive phenomena as commonly used in humanistic, cognitive, phenomenologic and also evolutionary reasoning, neuroscience and psychology could always claim that it is only the underlying neural correlates of these subjective states that are causative and that these objective physiological elements are what real science and evolution are based on, not on the correlated epiphenomena. The continued coexistence of the two very different—in many respects incompatible—explanations of human nature had come to be accepted *in practice* despite their being despaired of *in theory* as an unfathomed paradox. Something new and different, therefore, over and above what had existed through the 1950s and early 1960s, seems needed to account for the explosive turnabout that occurred in the early seventies.

Setbacks in corollary aspects of behaviorist doctrine, not directly involving its central tenets concerning subjectivity and introspection, are sometimes associated with the downfall of behaviorism. These include the espousal of an extreme environmentalism, an "empty cranium," stimulus-response peripheralism and also behaviorism's earlier pro-nurture, anti-inheritance stance, all of which suffered major corrective revisions prior to the 1970s (e.g. Bruner, 1964; Chomsky, 1959; Koch, 1954; Stevens, 1951; Tolman, 1952). Although contributing to a general disillusionment with behaviorism, none of these negated the central core of behaviorist philosophy nor called for the acceptance of subjective phenomena as explanatory constructs. Along with inadequate correlations in timing, this would seem to disqualify these ancillary developments as having been essential factors in the rise of the new mentalism.

Among various developments that might satisfy both the temporal and logical requirements, it is not easy to find anything more direct than the emergence during the mid and late 1960s of the interactionist concept of the mind-brain relation in which conscious experience was conceived to play a causal role in brain function and behavior. While the behaviorist philosophy could encompass most of the 1960s' advances in cognitive science, this was not true with the new emergent causal or interactionist view of consciousness which points up a critical shortcoming at the core of the behaviorist paradigm and also that of traditional neuroscience.

Described from the start as a mentalist (but not dualist) view (Fodor 1968; Sperry, 1965), and invoking emergence (Popper, 1965), functionalism (Fodor, 1968; Putnam, 1960; Sperry, 1952), downward causation (Sperry, 1964, 1965) and psycho-neural interaction (Bindra, 1970; Sperry, 1969a, 1969b, 1970a, 1970b), this changed concept of consciousness directly confronted and negated the central founding precepts of the behaviorist philosophy of science. Correlations with the ensuing swing to mentalism, which manifested its greatest momentum in the early 1970s, could hardly have been more close and direct with respect to both the conceptual relevance and also the timing. Further distinctions in the analysis and appraisal of the shift to mentalism are drawn below in reference to some other interpretations.

ALTERNATIVE VIEWS

Research in perception and mental imagery has undergone recent developments in conjunction with computer science and mentalist philosophy with a result that a causal role is now being ascribed to mental images, percepts and related subjective phenomena (Block, 1981). It is claimed that the new empirical findings require an active causal participation of mental images. Developments in this area, including the establishment of the *Journal of Mental Imagery,* are taken in some quarters to have had a significant influence in helping to bring about the new acceptance of the subjective.

Perceptual phenomena have always been considered to be causal in the language of the subjective but with no implication that a complete explanation is not also possible in objective neuronal terms. It is difficult to see that the new findings about perception are any more than this, or that they present, any more than Gestalt psychology, for example, fundamental new obstacles to an objective interpretation in terms of the neural correlates. The recent findings of Paivio (1981), Shepard (1975), Kosslyn (1980), and others are, of course, more readily explained in terms of mental images and other mental constructs. However, this did not deter the behaviorist-materialist-reductive approach in the past. As summarily stated by Ned Block (1981, p. 8), "The claim that image-experiences are epiphenomenal rather than functional is no more challenged by Kosslyn's and Shepard's empirical data than traditional epiphenomenalism is challenged by the fact that pains are followed by groans [that] seem to be caused by them." The same reasoning applies as well to other recent findings on cognitive processes in general. The

new results, like those in the past, remain open to explanation on either the traditional microdeterminist or the new macromentalist basis.

The information processing paradigm, although already touched on in reference to computer simulation, is sometimes singled out in a special theoretic sense, as having generated key ideas behind what Simon (1982) describes as "the new way of looking at things." Donald M. MacKay in particular has persistently applied information theory, communication engineering and computer science to arrive at a "flow of information" view which, as currently presented (MacKay, 1982, 1984), poses a direct challenge to the present thesis. Explicitly rejecting emergent interaction and put forward as a more valid mind-brain solution than the one favored here and with strong support in neuroscience (Szentagothai, 1984), MacKay's position would seem to demand some accounting in the present context.

During the 1950s and 1960s MacKay propounded a *double aspect* position popular in mind-brain theory at the time in which the mental and the physical were described as "complementary internal and external aspects of one and the same situation" (MacKay, 1966). A strict physical determinacy of brain function was stressed. "No physical action waits on anything but another physical action" (MacKay, 1966, 438). With the burgeoning of the new mentalism in the 1970s, MacKay's presentation correspondingly became more pro-mentalist until in the 1980s it is hardly distinguishable in many salient features from that supported here. Points of agreement seem to include (a) the casual efficacy of mental activity (MacKay, 1978; Sperry, 1965, 1969b), (b) the rejection of dualism on the one side and of traditional physicalism on the other (MacKay, 1982; Sperry, 1965, 1969b), (c) the arrival at a mid-way compromise philosophy (MacKay, 1982; Sperry, 1965, 1969b), (d) the assertion that this middle-way position means that classical physics does not reduce to quantum mechanics, hence no overthrow of classical physical theory is required (MacKay, 1982; Sperry, 1981), (e) the claim that subjective unity, perceptual constancy and other subjective qualities depend, not on isomorphic mind-brain correlations but on *functional* interaction in brain processing (MacKay, 1982; Sperry, 1952).

Despite the extensive congruence, however, some very critical differences remain: downward causation is rejected by MacKay along with any interaction between the mental and the physical. Like Feigl (1958, 1967), MacKay conceives the two to be distinct non-interactive categories, each a causally complete description within itself. Like Feigl he refers to "two languages," "two logics," "two stories," for one and the same thing (MacKay 1966, 1978, 1982)—with the recent curious assertion that each is in itself causally "complete" but, at the same time, "inadequate" (MacKay, 1982). The acceptance by MacKay since the mid 1970s of "the causal efficacy of mental activity"

(MacKay, 1978) is later explained to have been only *within* the mental level, not in an interactional sense (MacKay, 1982), and is no more than has always had commonplace acceptance. Thus, although MacKay's sophisticated terminology often leads the reader to believe otherwise, he seems to come back to a consistent dual aspect mind-brain parallelism. E.M. Dewan (1976), like MacKay, also uses control systems engineering but arrives at a quite different model for consciousness fully consistent with emergent interaction.

General systems theory is frequently referred to as lending conceptual support to the new holistic outlook. Systems, involving wholes and parts, are easily related to emergence, whole-part relations, holism, etc. The doctrines of emergence and holism, however, antedate general systems theory by at least several decades. Originally general systems theory centered in the idea that systems of different types have much in common in the way of laws and abstract principles governing the interrelationships of the components (von Bertalanffy, 1956). It was theorized that if these principles are learned for one type of system they would then apply to other types of systems in other sciences. The theory, however, has not lived up to early expectations because the interrelations of the parts in different systems, especially in different sciences, have proven to be so different that few useful commonalities could be found. The situation was summarized by Herbert Simon (1962, p. 467).

> A number of proposals have been advanced in recent years for the development of "general systems theory" which, abstracting from properties peculiar to physical, biological, or social systems, would be applicable to all of them. We might well feel that, while the goal is laudable, systems of such diverse kinds could hardly be expected to have any non-trivial properties in common.

The outstanding exception, of course, that has proven to be far from trivial is the relationship of a whole system to its parts and vice versa. As a result, systems theory has turned increasingly in recent times to the field of part-whole and hierarchic problems and the kinds of holistic and emergent control issues raised here (Bahm, 1984).

Consciousness raising movements along with counterculture activism of the sixties, plus related books of the period such as *The Psychology of Consciousness* by Robert Ornstein (1972) may also be mentioned as having been thought to have contributed in different ways to the swing to mentalism. Although these developments reflect and enhance general subjectivist pressures, they do not appear to have introduced any new mind-brain theory, logic, basic scientific principles or other conceptual grounds that would be adequate to overthrow behaviorist-materialist doctrine. A 1980 volume devoted to the paradigm

shift and its multiple manifestations and portent (Ferguson, 1980, p. 18) interprets the broad paradigm change of the seventies as a "historic synthesis" combining "the social activism of the 1960's and the 'consciousness revolution' of the early 1970's." An extensive collection of signs of socio-ideologic change is brought together emphasizing the far reaching influence of the new outlook plus other related and unrelated developments, but no attempt is made at discriminative analysis or evaluation.

FURTHER REPERCUSSIONS

It is not surprising that a major about-face in the conception and treatment of consciousness, at the epicenter of all knowledge and understanding, should have extensive ramifications and repercussions. The new mentalist paradigm has been entwined, directly and indirectly, with a number of associated developments of the past fifteen years. These concern more the meaning and significance of the new paradigm than they do its origins—though in some instances they have been inferred to have also had an influence in generating the new outlook.

One of the more direct and obvious of these is the extension from the human to the animal mind. The new acceptance of consciousness along with the changed concept of the mind-brain relation applies also to the animal mind and brain with consequences for the treatment of animal awareness and behavior. Some of the many ramifications in this realm are ably reviewed and evaluated in a recent comprehensive work by Donald Griffin (1981).

By the mid seventies John Eccles had begun to espouse and support a new mind-brain logic (Eccles, 1973, 1976, 1980; Popper and Eccles, 1977) that directly reversed his prior reasoning about the apparent superfluousness of consciousness and which he defined as being essentially the same as that presented here as emergent interactionism (Popper and Eccles, 1977, p. 374). Eccles, however, combined this view of mind-brain interaction with dualist doctrine calling the combination "dualist interactionism." His additions included the 1968 "World Two and Three" concepts of Popper, speculations about possible cerebral mediating mechanisms supported by recent research literature plus personal convictions concerning the mind-brain interface and supernatural influences in the fetal acquisition of consciousness and in its survival after brain death. These differently derived components were merged and presented as a unit. Sound arguments can be seen (Natsoulas, 1984; Puccetti, 1977; Sperry, 1980) against Eccles' inclusion of the emergent interactionist concept as a form of dualism. Nevertheless, Eccles' extensive promotion of an openly antimaterialist position has had a significant influence in helping to question traditional microdeterminist thinking and in stimulating increased awareness of the issues and of the relevance of brain research.

The philosopher Mario Bunge in the latter 1970s added notable support for the emergentist view, describing it as emergent materialism (Bunge, 1977, 1980). He provides a comprehensive philosophic account but does not include the functionalist and downward control features and mistakenly lists my own position as dualistic. Although the old terminology of philosophy becomes ambiguous and often misleading in the light of the new mentalist position, other specialists (e.g., Dewan, 1976; Engelhardt, 1977; Natsoulas, 1984, 1987; Puccetti, 1977; Ripley, 1984; Slaatte, 1983; Weimer, 1977; Wimsatt, 1976) have not been similarly misled. Bunge's support of emergent materialism came quite late and would appear to be better perceived as a consequence rather than a cause of the new mentalism. Another emergentist view appeared in philosophy in the 1970s under the label "supervenience," which appears to agree with the notion that the mental properties do not *inter*vene but *super*vene (Davidson, 1970, 1973; Kim, 1978; Rosenberg, 1978). A recent discussion of supervenient causation (Kim, 1983), however, indicates that despite the updated terminology, the underlying issues are basically largely where they stood in the mid 1960s prior to the introduction of downward causation.

What seems to be much the same mind-brain position upheld by the new mentalism in psychology has recently been defended by John Searle (Searle, 1980, 1983). Searle similarly rejects both the dualist and the strictly physicalist answers and affirms the reality and causal efficacy of the mental: "I think there really are such things as intrinsic mental phenomena which cannot be reduced to something else. . . . There really are pains, tickles . . . thoughts, feelings and all the rest" (Searle, 1983, p. 262). Restating the mentalist contentions of the 1960s, Searle affirms that "mental states which are caused by brain states can also cause further brain states and mental states." His mind-brain view and the emergent interactionist view appear to differ only superficially. Like Davidson, Searle comes to the mentalist position directly without invoking supporting logic to refute the decades of specific materialist and positivist counterreasoning in neuroscience, biology, psychology and philosophy. As a result, both the functionalist derivation of subjective meaning and the notion of downward causation appear to be relatively neglected.

Mind-brain identity theory has undergone important developments with respect to the causal efficacy of the mental in the late 1960s and 1970s. In its current form it has wide support, can be reconciled with the causal concept of consciousness and also is considered by some advocates to be a reasonable candidate for a root cause of the current mind-brain outlook. Acceptance of mind as a causative property of brain function along with related consequences and implications has transformed identity theory until it is hardly recognizable today as related to its original pre-

1965 form (Natsoulas, 1987; Peacocke, 1979; Ripley, 1984; Uttal, 1978). Herbert Feigl, the father of mind-brain identity theory, described his view in the fifties as a "two languages" or "double knowledge" (of one and the same thing) theory (also as a "double language" or *"two-fold access"* theory) [Feigl, 1967]. As late as 1967, Feigl still continued to deplore any acceptance of emergentism. "If future scientific research should lead to the adoption of one or another form of emergentism (or—*horrible dictu!*—dualistic interactionism), then most of my reflections will be reduced to the status of a logical (I hope not illogical!) exercise within the frame of an untenable presupposition" (Feigl, 1967 p. 160). Needless to say, Feigl would hardly recognize his own theory as currently supported.

The contributions of identity theory have always seemed primarily semantic, making no difference to the practice of either neuroscience or of psychology. In shifting from a noncausal parallelistic view (Feigl, 1967) to the current causal view of mind (Armstrong and Malcolm, 1984) identity theory has followed and reconciled itself with the changing trend of opinion but seems not, in itself, to have introduced anything that would logically force a shift from behaviorism to mentalism, or from micro to macrodeterminism.

A functionalist view of mental states has become in recent years a prominent feature of contemporary cognitive philosophy (Fodor, 1981; Gardner, 1985). Applied to the mind-brain problem in the 1950s, it proposed that subjective meaning derives, not from an isomorphic, topologic, or an "identity" correspondence in the substrate of neural processes, but rather from the overall *functional* interactions (Sperry, 1952, pp. 307–309). According to this early theory: "the same psychic meaning may be obtained from brain patterns the neuronal details of which differ considerably on different occasions. . . . Its is only in the overall functional or operational effect that their essential similarity resides. Conscious unity is conceived . . . as a functional or operational derivative." It follows that the functionally derived subjective properties must therefore, by definition, have causal efficacy in conscious cerebral action. The functionalist view was developed further by Putnam (1960) and Fodor (1968) with implications that support emergentist rather than microdeterminist principles. This early thread of functionalist thought is believed to have played a significant role in the swing to mentalism, not so much as a direct impetus but as a logical precursor to viewing consciousness as causal.

In its currently expanded form functionalist philosophy (Fodor, 1981; Gardner, 1985) appears to have much in common with the early emergent interactionist mind-brain theory deduced here to have been the key factor behind the 1970's overthrow of behaviorism. The current functionalism (i.e. Fodor 1968, 1981; Gardner 1985) and emergent interactionism (Sperry, 1952, 1965, 1969a, 1969b) are both described as being mentalistic. Both positions recognize the existential reality of mental states and endow mental events with causative power to affect brain processing and to interact functionally with other mental events. Both reject dualism and both deny that mentalism is equivalent to dualism. Both reject radical behaviorism, reductivism, epiphenomenalism, identity theory and double aspect parallelism. Both agree on the functional contextual derivation of subjective meaning and define mental entities in terms of causal relations. Both sustain supervenient determinism. Both recognize the special difficulties for the functionalist interpretation posed by raw sensory qualities such as color or pain. Both stress the innate basis of consciousness and of cognition and behavior in general. Both are directed to understanding the unknown, largely inherent "brain code." Both claim to be midway philosophic positions that resolve the prior dualist-materialist dichotomy and its modern offsprings and both claim to retain what is most valid from each side of the old dichotomy.

Along with these many broad similarities one finds a few differences: contemporary cognitive philosophy is inclined to go further, firstly, in stressing the independence of cognitive processes from the mediating infrastructure and, secondly, in treating the mind as a device for computation and processing symbols leading to greater emphasis on linguistics and computation. This latter appears to be in large part a consequence of current tendencies to identify the mind-brain problem with problems associated with a flow of information (e.g., Fodor 1981; MacKay 1982; Gardner 1985).

Information processing, in addition to intrinsic complications of its own, involves added dimensions of complexity in the relationship of the symbols, on the one hand, to what they represent and, on the other, to the interpreter of the information. The mind-brain problem is difficult enough in its simplest form without complicating matters further by concentrating on one of its most complex manifestations. The concern with information processing seems to be in large part responsible for diverting current mind-brain theory away from what had seemed a more profound issue raised initially by the functionalist approach (Sperry, 1952, p. 301), namely, that of whether to view the correlated brain process as a representation of the perceived or imagined object, or as a special form of interaction with or upon it.

Many more examples could be cited from a continuing series of ideologic, philosophic and even theological contributions that have appeared since the sixties in which a new world outlook is upheld rejecting both traditional mechanistic approaches on the one hand and supernatural explanations on the other in favor of a midway holistic or emergentist position. The logical underpinnings of these varied proposals appear, in final analysis, to rest on a common basis similar to that of the new mentalist outlook in psychology. They all boil down to an acceptance, not of many or several, but of one major paradigm change, involving a core principle of causal determinism with wide application to rational explanation in general, not only in science but also in the humanities.

IS THE NEW MENTALISM A MODIFIED MATERIALISM?

Since the early 1970s a general trend can be seen in which different mind-brain theories have evolved in directions that tend to converge onto forms of mentalism that are both emergent or molar, and causative. Despite the growing convergence, debate continues to wage over whether the basic target position should be called materialistic. Proponents of identity theory and materialism reason that if the subjective qualities are properties of material brain processes and are inseparable form them, the view must therefore be materialist.

Others of us prefer to not use the materialist label, regardless of the foregoing, for reasons that include the following: the original basic distinction between mind and matter, the mental and the physical, is a useful and sound distinction and is based in immediate direct experience in a way that deserves priority over historical turns in philosophical and other disciplinary semantics. It was the latter that led us, all through the materialist-behaviorist era, to throw out consciousness along with the supernatural and the dualistic. To try now to rectify things by defining materialism to be synonymous with monism appears to be a further error leading into conflict with long accepted *a priori* differences between the mental and material. Our new mentalist paradigm allows finer classifications than formerly were possible when mentalism meant dualism and monism meant materialism for lack of finer distinctions.

Additional strong reasons for rejecting the materialist label are found in the long history of close association between scientific materialism and reductionist "nothing but" reasoning, such that the one has for a long time almost implied the other. By contrast, the mentalist position is emergent, holistic, and antireductionist. These changed views of mind and matter in the new outlook need to be emphasized, rather than deemphasized by belatedly twisting the material label in order to include its historically recognized prime antonym, the "mental."

Materialist philosophy by definition has always been distinguished by an emphasis on the material mass-energy aspects of nature at the expense of the nonmaterial. The new view, in contrast, gives primacy to the immaterial spacing and timing of the elements, i.e., to forms, patterns, organizational properties and also to strictly mental qualities such as abstractions and other "things of the mind" that go beyond mass, with attributes and influences not readily measured, weighed or counted (Williams, 1984). Since the material components and the space-time features can be separated only with much difficulty, if at all, it becomes in practice a matter of emphasis. Both are needed, but there seems good reason today for taking the stand that the long-term, one-sided emphasis on the exclusivity of material, mass-energy determinacy needs to be corrected.

Nor does it seem right to call a position "materialist" if its origination and prime reason for being have been from the outset to contest the materialist brand of thinking that dominated both scientific and philosophic thought up to the mid sixties and which, as late as 1968, was still trying to tell us that "man is nothing but a material object, having non but physical properties," and that "science can give a complete account of man in physicochemical terms" (Armstrong, 1968).

It needs to be emphasized again that the acceptance of macrodeterminism as a principle would not devalue the conventional reductive, analytic methodology of science. It only affects the reductionist descriptions, outlooks and beliefs commonly deduced therefrom. Nor would it invalidate traditional microdeterminist principles, only the claim that these are exclusive and can ultimately account for and determine everything.

Since the mid 1970s many of the implications of the new macro outlook (Sperry, 1983) have been gaining recognition in writings about the "new science," "the new paradigm," "the new realism," "the new cosmology," "the new philosophy of science," "the new era in the science-value relation," "a contagion of reperception," "the reconception of theology" (Kaufman, 1985), and so on. This is not the place to more than just refer to the many developments of this nature, other than to note that the abundant evidence of their precipitous increase in recent years lends credence to the contention that the consciousness revolution in behavioral science represents a fundamental correction applying not only to all the sciences but also to the humanities and to contemporary thought in general.

The idea that the new mentalism might be the prime source in this movement has been challenged from physics. It has recently been claimed that advances in subatomic physics and relativity theory have brought a similar paradigm "shift from the mechanistic to a holistic conception of reality. . . . This new vision includes the emerging systems view of life, mind, consciousness and evolution" (Capra, 1982, p. 16). If in fact science is in the midst of a paradigm change that provides a "new way of looking at things," as many sources now proclaim, it becomes of some urgency to determine whether this new outlook has its basis in physics or in behavioral science or perhaps in both, or whether the base in both is the same.

Many things point to the conclusion that the new holistic outlook described by Capra originated primarily in the behavioral and mind-brain sciences and could hardly have come from subatomic physics. This in no way detracts, of course, from the importance of the new physics *qua* physics or its changed concepts

of the cosmos. The holistic, axiological, social and other humanistic implications follow directly and logically from the changed concept of consciousness. On the other hand, it is not legitimate, according to macrodeterminist principles, to directly transpose properties of subatomic matter to the macro world as in the reasoning of Capra (1975) and also of Bohm (1973, 1980) to a lesser extent. Macrodeterminism, in contrast to reductive physics leads to a view of physical reality in which the proverbial solid table is no less solid, nor any less different from soft pudding than classical physics affirmed—regardless of changed interpretations in the subatomic theory. One can point also to the long interval between the referred-to advances in physics, already well established by the 1930s, and the relatively recent emergence of the new holistic outlook in the early 1970s. It is difficult to believe that the implications in physics were not appreciated or understood until comparisons were drawn with mysticism and Eastern religion.

Wide ranging humanistic implications, on the other hand, are a natural logical consequence of the changed concepts of brain and consciousness. More than advances in subatomic physics and relativity theory, the recent turnabout in the conception of the conscious mind, along with the corresponding macrodeterminist extension to the rest of reality, profoundly alter the kind of universe in which science would have us believe.

REFERENCES

Armstrong, D.M. (1968). *A materialist theory of mind.* London: Routledge & Kegan Paul.

Armstrong, D.M., and Malcolm, N. (1984). *Consciousness and causality.* Oxford: Basil Blackwell.

Ashby, W.R. (1956). *An introduction to cybernetics.* New York: Wiley.

Bahm, A.J. (1984). Holons: Three conceptions. *Systems Research, 1*(2), 145–150.

Bertalanffy, L. von (1956): General systems theory. In L. von Bertalanffy and A. Rapaport (Eds.), *General systems*, Yearbook, Vol. 1 (pp. 1–10). Louisville, Kentucky: Society for General Systems Research.

Bindra, D. (1970). The problem of subjective experience: Puzzlement on reading R.W. Sperry's "A modified concept of consciousness." *Psychological Review, 77,* 581–584.

Block, N. (Ed.). (1981). *Imagery.* Cambridge, Massachusetts: MIT Press.

Bohm, D. (1973). Quantum theory as an indication of a new order in physics. B. Implicate and explicate order in physical law. *Foundations of Physics, 3,* 139–168.

Bohm, D. (1980). *Wholeness and the implicate order.* New York: ARK paperbacks.

Boneau, C.A. (1974). Paradigm regained: Cognitive behaviorism restated. *American Psychologist, 29,* 297–309.

Bruner, J.S. (1964). The course of cognitive growth. *American Psychologist, 19,* 1–15.

Bunge, M. (1977). Emergence and the mind. *Neuroscience, 2,* 501–509.

Bunge, M. (1980). *The mind-body problem.* New York: Pergamon Press.

Campbell, D.T. (1974). Downward causation in hierarchically organized biological systems. In F.J. Ayala and T. Dobzhansky (Eds.), *Studies in the philosophy of biology* (pp. 139–161). Berkeley: University of California Press.

Capra, F. (1975). *The Tao of physics.* East Lansing, Michigan: Shambala Publications.

Capra, F. (1982). *Turning point.* New York: Simon & Schuster.

Catania, A.C., and Harnad, S. (Eds.). (1984). Canonical papers of B.F. Skinner. *The Behavioral and Brain Sciences, 7,* 473–724.

Chomsky, N. (1959). [Review of *Verbal behavior* by B.F. Skinner]. *Language, 35,* 26–58.

Churchland, P.S., and Churchland, P.M. (1983). Stalking the wild epistemic engine. *Nous, 17,* 5–18.

Davidson, D. (1970). Mental events. In L. Foster and J.W. Swanson (Eds.), *Experience and theory* (pp. 79–101). Amherst: University of Massachusetts Press.

Davidson, D. (1973). The material mind. In P. Suppes (Ed.), *Logic, methodology and the philosophy of science* (pp. 709–722). Amsterdam: North Holland Publishing Company.

Davidson, R.J., and Davidson, J.M. (1980). Introduction: The scientific study of human consciousness in psychobiological perspective. In J.M. Davidson (Ed.), *The psychobiology of consciousness* (pp. 1–10). New York: Plenum Press.

Dember, W.N. (1974). Motivation and the cognitive revolution. *American Psychologist, 29,* 161–168.

Dewan, E.M. (1976). Consciousness as an emergent causal agent in the context of control system theory. In G.G. Globus, G. Maxwell, and I. Savodnik (Eds.), *Consciousness and the brain* (pp. 179–198). New York: Plenum Press.

Eccles, J.C. (1966). Discussion after "Consciousness" by E.D. Adrian. In J.C. Eccles (Ed.), *Brain and conscious experience* (p. 248). New York: Springer.

Eccles, J.C. (1973). Brain, speech and consciousness. *Naturwissenschaften, 60,* 167–176.

Eccles, J.C. (1976). Brain and free will. In G.G. Globus (Ed.), *Consciousness and the brain* (pp. 99–121). New York: Plenum Press.

Eccles, J.C. (1980). *The human psyche.* Berlin: Springer International.

Engelhardt, H.T. Jr. (1977). Splitting the brain, dividing the soul, being of two minds: An editorial concerning mind-body quandaries in medicine. *The Journal of Medicine and Philosophy, 2,* 89–100.

Feigenbaum, E.A., and Feldman, J. (Eds.). (1963). *Computers and thought.* New York: McGraw-Hill.

Feigl, H. (1958). The "mental" and the "physical". In H. Feigl, M. Scriven, and G. Maxwell (Eds.), *Minnesota studies in the philosophy of science,* Vol. 2 (pp. 370–497). Minneapolis: University of Minnesota Press.

Feigl, H. (1967). *The "mental" and the "physical"* (with "postscript after ten years"). Minneapolis: University of Minnesota Press.

Ferguson, M. (1980). *The aquarian conspiracy.* Los Angeles: Tarcher.

Fodor, J.A. (1968). *Psychological explanation: An introduction to the philosophy of psychology.* New York: Random House.

Fodor, J.A. (1981). The mind-body problem. *Scientific American, 244*(1), 114–123.

Gardner, H. (1985). *The mind's new science.* New York: Basic Books.

Griffin, D. (1981). *The question of animal awareness: Evolutionary continuity of mental experience.* New York: Rockefeller University Press.

Heinen, J.R.K. (1980). Psychological theory: Evaluation and speculations. *The Journal of Psychology, 106,* 287–301.

Herrick, C.J. (1956). *The evolution of human nature.* Austin: University of Texas Press.

Hilgard, E.R. (1980). Consciousness in contemporary psychology. *Annual Review of Psychology, 31,* 1–26.

Kantor, J.R. (Observer) (1969). Comments and queries. *The Psychological Record, 19,* 143–146.

Kantor, J.R. (Observer) (1977). Comments and queries concerning cognitive reversionism in psychology. *The Psychological Record, 27,* 351–354.

Kaufman, G.D. (1985). *Theology for a nuclear age.* Philadelphia, Pennsylvania: Westminster Press.

Kim, J. (1978). Supervenience and nomological incommensurables. *American Philosophical Quarterly, 15,* 149–156.

Kim, J. (1983). Supervenience and supervenient causation. *Southern Journal of Philosophy, 22,* 45–56, Supp. 83.

Klee, R.L. (1984). Micro-determinism and concepts of emergence. *Philosophy of Science, 51,* 44–63.

Koch, S. (1954). Clark L. Hull. In W.K. Estes (Ed.), *Modern learning theory* (pp. 1–176). Englewood Cliffs, New Jersey: Appleton-Century-Crofts.

Koch, S. (1964). Psychology and emergent conceptions of knowledge as unitary. In T.W. Wann (Ed.), *Behaviorism and phenomenology* (pp. 1–45). Chicago: University of Chicago Press.

Koch, S. (1969). Value properties: Their significance for psychology, axiology and science. In M. Grene (Ed.), *The anatomy of knowledge* (pp. 119–148). Amherst: University of Massachusetts Press.

Kosslyn, S.M. (1980). *Image and mind.* Cambridge, Massachusetts: Harvard University Press.

Kuhn, T. (1970). *The structure of scientific revolutions.* Chicago: University of Chicago Press.

Libet, B. (1980). Mental phenomena and behavior [Commentary to Searle, J.R.]. *The Behavioral and Brain Sciences, 3,* 434.

MacKay, D.M. (1966). Cerebral organization and the conscious control of action. In J.C. Eccles (Ed.) *Brain and conscious experience* (pp. 422–455). New York: Springer.

MacKay, D.M. (1978). Selves and brains. *Neuroscience, 3,* 599–606.

MacKay, D.M. (1982). Ourselves and our brains: Duality without dualism. *Psychoneuroendocrinology, 7,* 285–294.

MacKay, D.M. (1984). Science and moral priority: Book review. *Neuropsychologia, 22,* 385–389.

Manicas, P.T., and Secord, P.F. (1983). Implications for psychology of the new philosophy of science. *American Psychologist, 3,* 399–413.

Maslow, A. (1968). *Toward a psychology of being.* Princeton, New Jersey: Van Nostrand.

Matson, F.W. (1971). Humanistic theory: The third revolution in psychology. *The Humanist, 31*(2), 7–11.

Miller, G.A., Galanter, E.H., and Pribram, K.H. (1960). *Plans and the structure of behavior.* New York: Holt, Rinehart & Winston.

Morgan, C.L. (1923). *Emergent evolution.* London: Williams and Norgate Ltd.

Natsoulas, T. (1980). The primary source of intentionality [Commentary to Searle, J.R.]. *Behavioral and Brain Sciences, 3,* 440–441.

Natsoulas, T. (1983). Perhaps the most difficult problem faced by behaviorism. *Behaviorism, 11,* 1–26.

Natsoulas, T. (1984). Gustav Bergmann's psychophysiological parallelism. *Behaviorism, 12,* 41–69.

Natsoulas, T. (1987). Roger W. Sperry's monist interactionism. *The Journal of Mind and Behavior, 8,* 1–22.

Neisser, U. (1967). *Cognitive psychology.* New York: Appleton-Century-Crofts.

Neumann, J. von (1958). *The computer and the brain.* New Haven: Yale University Press.

Ornstein, R.E. (1972). *The psychology of consciousness.* New York: W.H. Freeman.

Paivio, A. (1971). *Imagery and verbal process.* New York: Holt, Rinehart & Winston.

Peacocke, A.R. (1979). *Creation and the world of science.* Oxford: Clarendon Press.

Polanyi, M. (1962) Tacit knowing: Its bearing on some problems of philosophy. *Reviews of Modern Physics, 34,* 601–616.

Popper, K. (1965). *Of clouds and clocks.* Second Arthur Holly Compton Memorial Lecture, presented at Washington University on 21 April 1965. Reprinted in Karl Popper (Ed.), *Objective knowledge,* (pp. 206–255). Oxford: Clarendon Press.

Popper, K. (1978). Natural selection and the emergence of mind. *Dialectica, 32,* 339–355.

Popper, K.R., and Eccles, J.C. (1977). *The self and its brain.* New York: Springer International.

Puccetti, R. (1977). Sperry on consciousness: A critical appreciation. *Journal of Medicine and Philosophy, 2,* 127–144.

Putnam, H. (1960). Minds and machines. In S. Hook (Ed.), *Dimensions of mind* (pp. 138–164). New York: Collier.

Pylyshyn, Z.W. (1973). What the mind's eye tells the mind's brain: A critique of mental imagery. *Psychological Bulletin, 80,* 1–24.

Ripley, C. (1984). Sperry's concept of consciousness. *Inquiry, 27,* 399–423.

Ritter, W.E. (1919). *The unity of the organism.* Boston: The Gorham Press.

Rogers, C.R. (1964a). Toward a science of the person (discussion following the paper). In T. Wann (Ed.), *Behaviorism and phenomenology* (pp. 109–140). Chicago: University of Chicago Press.

Rogers, C.R. (1964b). Freedom and commitment. *The Humanist, 29*(2), 37–40.

Rogers, C.R. (1969). *Freedom to learn.* Columbus, Ohio: Merrill Publishing Company.

Rosenberg, A. (1978). The supervenience of biological concepts. *Philosophy of Science, 45,* 368–386.

Rosenberg, D.N. (1986). The fundamental incompatibility between computerism and humanism. *Contemporary Philosophy, 11*(2), 4–6.

Rumelhart, D.E., McClelland, J.L., and the PDP Research Group. (1986). *Parallel distributed processing.* (Vols. 1 and 2). Cambridge, Massachusetts: MIT Press.

Searle, J.R. (1980). Minds, brains, programs. *Behavioral and Brain Sciences, 3,* 427–457.

Searle, J.R. (1983). *Intentionality.* New York: Cambridge University Press.

Segal, E.M., and Lachman, R. (1972). Complex behavior or higher mental process? Is there a paradigm shift? *American Psychologist, 27,* 46–55.

Sellars, R.W. (1922). *Evolutionary naturalism.* Chicago: The Open Court Publishing Company.

Sellars, R.W. (1943). Causality and substances. *Philosophical Review, 52,* 1–27.

Shepard, R.N. (1975). Form, formation, and transformation of internal representatives. In R.L. Solso (Ed.), *Information processing and cognition: Theories in cognitive philosophy* (pp. 87–122). New York: Wiley.

Simon, H.A. (1962). The architecture of complexity. *Proceedings of the American Philosophical Society, 106,* 467–482.

Simon, H.A. (1982). Unity of the arts and sciences: The psychology of thought and discovery. *Bulletin of the American Academy of Arts and Sciences, 35*(6), 26–53.

Skinner, B.F. (1964). Behaviorism at 50. In T. Wann (Ed.), *Behaviorism and phenomenology* (pp. 79–108). Chicago: University of Chicago Press.

Skinner, B.F. (1971). *Beyond freedom and dignity.* New York: Alfred A. Knopf.

Skinner, B.F. (1984). Canonical papers of B.F. Skinner (Special issue). *The Behavioral and Brain Sciences, 7*(4), 473–724.

Skinner, B.F. (1985). Cognitive science and behaviourism. *British Journal of Psychology, 76,* 291–301.

Slaatte, H.A. (1981). The existential creativity of consciousness. *Contemporary Philosophy, 8*(8), 24.

Slaatte, H.A. (1983). *The creativity of consciousness.* Lanham, Maryland: University Press of America.

Smuts, J.C. (1926). *Holism and evolution.* New York: Macmillan.

Sperry, R.W. (1952). Neurology and the mind-brain problem. *American Scientist, 40,* 291–312.

Sperry, R.W. (1964). *Problems outstanding in the evolution of brain function.* James Arthur Lecture. New York: American Museum of Natural History.

Sperry, R.W. (1965). Mind, brain and humanist values. In J.R. Platt (Ed.), *New views of the nature of man* (pp. 71–92). Chicago: University of Chicago Press. Reprinted in: *Bulletin of the Atomic Scientists,* (1966), 22(7), 2–6; and in *Science and moral priority.* New York: Praeger (1985).

Sperry, R.W. (1969a). Toward a theory of mind (Abstract). *Proceedings of the National Academy of Sciences, U.S.A., 63,* 230–231.

Sperry, R.W. (1969b). A modified concept of consciousness. *Psychological Review, 76,* 532–536.

Sperry, R.W. (1970a). Perception in the absence of the neocortical commissures. *Perception and Its Disorders, 48,* 123–138.

Sperry, R.W. (1970b). An objective approach to subjective experience: Further explanation of a hypothesis. *Psychological Review, 77,* 585–590.

Sperry, R.W. (1980). Mind-brain interaction: Mentalism, yes; dualism, no. *Neurosciences, 5,* 195–206. Reprinted in: A.D. Smith, R. Llinas, and P.G. Kostyuk (Eds.), *Commentaries in the neurosciences* (pp. 651–662). Elmsford, New Jersey: Pergamon Press (1980); and in, *Science and moral priority.* New York: Praeger (1985).

Sperry, R.W. (1981). Changing priorities. *Annual Review of Neuroscience, 4,* 1–5. Reprinted in: *Science and moral priority.* New York: Praeger (1985); and in *Journal of Humanistic Psychology,* (1986), 26, 8–23.

Sperry, R.W. (1983). Changed concepts of brain and consciousness: Some value implications. 1982–83 Isthmus Foundation Lecture Series. *Perkins Journal, 36*(4), 21–32. Reprinted in: *Zygon*, (1985), 20, 41–57.

Sperry, R.W. (1986). Discussion: Macro- versus micro-determinism. *Philosophy of Science, 53,* 265–270.

Stevens, S.S. (Ed.) (1951). *Handbook of experimental psychology.* New York: Wiley.

Stryker, S. (1981). Social psychology: Trends, assessment, and prognosis. *American Behavioral Scientist, 24,* 386–406.

Szentagothai, J. (1984). Downward causation? *Annual Review of Neuroscience, 7,* 1–11.

Tolman, E.C. (1925). Behaviorism and purpose. *Journal of Philosophy, 22,* 36–41. Reprinted in: E.C. Tolman: *Collected papers in psychology* (pp. 32–37). Berkeley: University of California Press (1951).

Tolman, E.C. (1926). A behavioristic theory of ideas. *Psychological Review, 33,* 352–369. Reprinted in: E.C. Tolman: *Collected papers in psychology* (pp. 48–62). Berkeley: University of California Press (1951).

Tolman, E.C. (1952). A cognition motivation model. *Psychological Review, 59,* 389–400.

Uttal, W.R. (1978). *Psychology of mind.* New York: Erlbaum.

Wann, T.W. (Ed.). (1964). *Behaviorism and phenomenology.* Chicago: The University of Chicago Press.

Weimer, W.B. (1977). A conceptual framework for cognitive psychology: Motor theory of the mind. In R. Shaw and J. Bransford (Eds.), *Perceiving, acting and knowing: Toward an ecological psychology* (pp. 267–311). New York: Erlbaum.

Williams, R.J. (1984). Can we integrate moral principles with science and learning? *Texas Humanist,* November-December, 23–26.

Wimsatt, W.C. (1976). Reductionism, levels of organization, and the mind-body problem. In G.G. Globus (Ed.), *Consciousness and the brain* (pp. 199–267). New York: Plenum Press.

MARGERY WOLF

The Woman Who Didn't Become a Shaman

When a Taiwanese village woman began to display shamanistic behavior, her neighbors had to decide whether she was being called by a god to speak for him, possessed by a ghost, exploited by her husband, or crazy. Although she had many of the attributes of a successful *tang-ki*, or shaman, she was finally labeled crazy because of her marginal status in the community and in the male ideology. [China, Taiwan, gender, shamans, self]

In the spring of 1960 in a then-remote village on the edge of the Taipei basin in northern Taiwan, a young mother of three lurched out of her home, crossed a village path, and stumbled wildly across a muddy rice paddy. The cries of her children and her own agonized shouts quickly drew and excited crowd out of what had seemed an empty village. Thus began nearly a month of uproar and agitation as this small community resolved the issue of whether one of their residents was being possessed by a god or was suffering from a mental illness. For Mrs. Chen, it was a month of misery and exultation; for the residents of Peihotien, it was a month of gossip, uncertainty, and heightened religious interest; for the anthropologists in the village, it was a month of confusion and fascination.

Mrs. Chen herself had less influence over the outcome of the month of trial than a foreign observer might expect. Even Wang Ming-fu, a religious specialist who lived nearby and who was given credit for making the final decision, was only one factor in a complex equation of cultural, social, ritual, and historical forces. In the pages that follow, I will attempt to reconstruct the events of that spring from field notes, journal entries, and personal recollections and evaluate what happened from the perspective of the anthropologist. I am not concerned here with shamanism per se, but with the social and cultural factors that were brought to bear by various members of the community in deciding whether Mrs. Chen was being approached by a god who wished to use her to communicate with his devotees, whether an emotional pathology included fantasies of spirit possession, or whether, as a few maintained, her feckless husband hoped to use her as a source of income.

In the hours following Mrs. Chen's precipitous trip into the mud of the rice paddies, an enormous amount of information

traveled through the village about her recent behavior, her past, and the attitude of her family and neighbors. The day before, she had taken her six-month-old baby to her sister's house and left her. She had been complaining to her husband that there was a fever in her heart. She had beaten herself on the chest, pleading to be left in peace, and had jumped up and down on the bed so violently that it had broken. Her husband, commonly referred to in the village as Dumb T'ien-lai, had told one of their neighbors that she was probably going crazy "again." Nonetheless, he had done nothing about it until her very public display. Informants who were in the crowd that gathered as neighbors pulled her out of the paddy and took her back to her house reported that she begged to be allowed to go to the river to "meet someone" who was calling her. The nearby river is considered a dangerous place, full of ghosts who have either accidentally drowned or committed suicide. Water ghosts are infamous for trying to pull in the living to take their place in the dark world of unhappy ghosts.

As the long afternoon wore on, I heard other reports. People said that she pleaded with her husband, Chen T'ien-lai, to give her incense so that she could apologize to "the god who crossed the water." When he lit the incense for her, she began to tremble all over, her eyes glazed, and she began to talk in a loud male voice. One of the oldest women in the village, a woman known for her religious knowledge, came to see her and told T'ien-lai that he should call in a *tang-ki* (shaman)[1] to see if she had met a ghost. By then, however, Mrs. Chen's husband had finally taken some action on his own, and the ranting woman was hauled off under some kind of restraint in a pedicab to what was described to me as a "mental hospital" in the nearby market town.

During the three days that Mrs. Chen was out of the village, the Chen family was part of every conversation. Arthur Wolf, our assistant Wu Chieh, and I collected information about the Chens whether we wanted it or not. We discovered that even though the family was extremely poor, Mrs. Chen went regularly to the temple in Tapu and visited other temples within walking distance. Whenever her children were ill she consulted *tang-ki* in Tapu and neighboring areas. At home, she burned incense and made offerings daily to both her husband's ancestors and a variety of spirits and gods. We learned that although she was painfully shy (we had had much less contact with her than with most other villagers), Mrs. Chen was a fiercely protective mother who had quarreled in recent months with a woman from the Lin household when Mrs. Chen's young son had been slugged by a Lin boy. The Chens had lived in the village for early ten years, but by village tradition they were still considered newcomers—it took at least a generation for a new family to be accepted among those whose grandparents and great-grandparents had been born in Peihotien. Until then, newcomers were expected to behave like guests, and guests were expected to watch their hosts' faces. It was a Lin village.

When Mrs. Chen returned to the village, pale and drugged, her mother, Mrs. Pai, was called in by Chen T'ien-lai to "help out." Mrs. Pai had none of her daughter's shyness, and the villagers soon learned from her that her daughter had had one previous "episode" of this kind of behavior. When she was a young adolescent the family had come upon hard times and had been forced to give her away "in adoption" to a family in need of a servant. The girl had done fairly well until "something happened" about which the mother was vague in detail but implied that a member of the family had either raped or attempted to rape her. The girl had run away to her mother, been returned to her adoptive family, and within a few weeks been sent back to her parents by the adoptive family because "she was crazy." She stayed with her natal family until her marriage. There had been, according to her mother, no recurrence of erratic behavior.

Mrs. Pai also cast new light on what might have precipitated her daughter's current distress. It seems that a couple of weeks earlier a sizable sum of money had been lost from the pocket of her jacket. Mrs. Chen's son said he had seen his father take it before he went out to gamble one night, but Chen T'ien-lai denied it. Mrs. Chen blamed herself for the loss, but at times seemed convinced that it had been stolen by someone from the Lin household. At some point in the days that followed, the money was miraculously found (probably supplied by sympathetic villagers), but the expectation that this would end the problem was disappointed.

Within 48 hours of her return to Peihotien, Mrs. Chen was again drawing crowds. First, she told her mother that she must *bai-bai* (worship) to "the god who crossed the ocean," a god unknown to Mrs. Pai. The old woman I mentioned earlier informed Mrs. Pai that this was probably Shang Ti Kung (a local god) and that it cost only one New Taiwan dollar (a few cents) per day to rent an image. She also urged her to bring in Shang Ti Kung's *tang-ki* to ask what was wanted. All of this was done the next day and, according to a neighbor, the *tang-ki* said that Mrs. Chen had met a ghost. Later that afternoon the image of another god, Wang Yeh, was brought in, but Mrs. Chen still was not at peace. The next day, Mrs. Chen, according to her husband, leapt

out of bed shouting that the god was in her body and that T'ien-lai must go at once to get the god's image so that she could *bai-bai* to him. They tried to humor her and finally, because she was getting more and more frantic, agreed to purchase the image. However, neither Chen T'ien-lai nor his mother-in-law recognized the god she described. As Chen T'ien-lai was discussing this problem with some neighbors, his mother-in-law came out of her daughter's bedroom and announced that the daughter, using a strange voice, had told her the exact place to purchase the god's image. She sent her son-in-law on his way and, according to my informants, Mrs. Chen calmed down and went to sleep as soon as she heard that he had gone to purchase "the right god."[2]

Once the new god was put on the Chen household alter, however, the activities in the Chen courtyard changed dramatically. Mrs. Chen began to "dance" like a *tang-ki*, speak in a strange language, and make oracle-like statements. For nearly a week, whenever she came out of the house, crowds would gather and she would "perform." We did not attended all of her sessions, but we were told that she revealed knowledge about people's personal lives that "only a god" would have. She behaved and spoke in ways that were most uncharacteristic of the withdrawn, depressed woman to whom the village was accustomed.

One session in which our research assistant was involved is a good example. I quote from our field notes:

Mrs. Chen suddenly jumped up and pointed at Lin Mei-ling and told her to approach. Lin Mei-ling had been chatting with some other women about some medicine she had put on her eyes, which appeared to be infected. She looked quite scared, and the others had to push her forward toward Mrs. Chen, saying, "Go on, see what she has to say." As soon as Lin Mei-ling reached her, Mrs. Chen touched her eyes and said, "All right. This one will be well." She sounded as if she were reading a formal notice. Mrs. Chen then returned to making *bai-bai* motions with her hands, saying: "Your husband is a good man. He has a kind heart. He took me home one night on his bicycle. Your family will have peace and won't have any troubles." Lin Mei-ling was holding her baby, who began to cry very loudly. Her mother-in-law came up and tried to take Mrs. Chen's hands off Mei-ling, telling her that the baby was crying because she had to urinate. Mrs. Chen pushed her aside and said in a loud commanding voice, "Never mind." She then began to handle the baby, saying, "You will have peace and you won't have any trouble. It doesn't matter. It doesn't matter." To Mei-ling she said, "In these days everything will be all right for you. Everything will be all right." She made more *bai-bai* motions and then told Mei-ling to go home and not speak with anyone on the way. "Do you understand?" she asked. Mei-ling was still smiling, but she was probably quite frightened, for her face had turned white. She left and Mrs. Chen knelt on the threshold, making more *bai-bai* motions. She called our assistant, Wu Chieh, to come to her.

Wu Chieh was frightened and didn't want to go forward. She asked another woman what to do and was urged to comply. She was told, "Nothing is wrong. The god is in her body, that's all." Several people pushed Wu Chieh, including Mrs. Pai, Mrs. Chen's mother. Mrs. Chen moved her hands over Wu Chieh's body and face and then took her hands and began to "jump" like a *tang-ki*. Some of the people in the crowd laughed and said, "She wants to dance with you, Wu Chieh." Mrs. Chen said, "Older Sister, you come and you are very kind to all of the children. From the top of the village to the bottom, all of the children call you Older sister. Do you like that? Do you like that?" Wu Chieh was speechless with fear. Mrs. Chen's mother told her to say something, and Wu Chieh blurted out, "Yes." Mrs. Chen hugged her close and put her face against Wu Chieh's. Mrs. Pai said, "She wants to kiss you." Mrs. Chen shouted, "No, no, no!" Her mother quickly said, "No, I am wrong. I am just an old lady who doesn't understand."

Mrs. Chen told the crowd through gestures (reaching in her pocket, smacking her lips, and so forth) that Wu Chieh gives the children candy. "Children, adults, and old people are all the same. You know that, right? Wu Chieh nodded. Mrs. Chen then began to make wide, sweeping *bai-bai* gestures and pronounced, "People should not be judgmental, saying this person is good and that person is bad." Then she began to jump around the yard, and an older woman hissed at Wu Chieh, "Stupid child, aren't you going to run away now?" Some little boys were giggling and saying, "This crazy lady is dancing and poor Wu Chieh is going to have to wash all of her clothes." (Mrs. Chen was dirty from kneeling and falling in the dusty courtyard.) Mrs. Chen immediately turned on the boys and shouted, "Go away if you don't believe. Go away." She waved them off as if they were curious chickens, and they scattered like chickens. She turned again to Wu Chieh and rubbed her hands, telling her that everything would be peaceful with her.

As she talked, she continued to make *bai-bai* motions and to jump about, and finally she fell over backward on the ground. She lay there for some time, and Wu Chieh said that when Mrs. Chen opened her eyes, only the whites were visible. After a bit, Mrs. Chen got up and told everyone to go away, saying, "If you don't and you meet something bad [by implication, a ghost], don't blame me." People moved off to edge of the yard, some of them whispering, some of them laughing, but after a bit the crowd slowly began to edge back toward the house. Mrs. Chen told Wu Chieh, "Because they bully me, I am not willing to continue. Do you understand?

You must take me out. Do you understand that?" Wu Chieh kept agreeing at the urging of Mrs. Chen's mother, but she wasn't at all sure what was expected of her.

Mrs. Chen told Wu Chieh to go home again and not to talk with anyone she met on the way. "Listen to what I say or it won't go well for me. After you go home, then come back and take me into the house." People urged Wu Chieh to leave then, so she started to walk away, but Mrs. Chen called her back one more time. "I haven't finished talking to you yet," she said. "If you don't listen to me things will go badly for you. Do you understand? Now, hurry up and go home and then come back and take me to my room. Will you do that? If you don't, I will come to your house and find you." She repeated these instructions several times and added, "When you come back, if I am still talking to these women, you stand here and don't say anything, do you hear?" This was all said in a loud commanding voice, totally unlike her normal voice, according to Wu Chieh. Mrs. Chen grabbed both of Wu Chieh's hands in one of hers and gestured with the other in the "counting" motions of a *tang-ki* who is "calculating" what goes on in the world. (This is considered an indication of the god's omniscience.)

Wu Chieh finally extricated herself from this session, but returned in a few minutes and led Mrs. Chen, still gesturing and talking oddly, into her bedroom, where she got her to lie down. Wu Chieh then fled, but Mrs. Chen did not forget her. She called for her attendance several times over the next few days. Unlike Mrs. Chen, who had spent ten years in the village and was still an outsider, Wu Chieh in the year she had lived in the village had become everyone's confidante, everyone's friend, even Mrs. Chen's.

I have included this long quote from our field notes to give the reader a sense of Mrs. Chen's performances to compare with the description of the session of an experienced *tang-ki* that will be quoted below, and also to provide a glimpse of the way in which some of the villagers responded to this event. Village opinion was divided at best. Before Mrs. Chen was finally taken away "for a rest" by her mother, several village women reported smelling "puffs of fragrant air" in her room, a sure sign that a god was present; several others reported that she had told them things that only a god could know about their family affairs; she had tormented the Lin family, who had treated her so harshly over the quarrel between their children; she had been visited by a doctor who had given her heavy doses of tranquilizers; and she had held many sessions not unlike the one described above. Finally, old Wang Ming-fu, who was considered the expert in the region on matters of religion and ritual, came to talk with her. Their conversation, of which we never got a complete report, was not a happy one. He left in a huff.

We began to detect a change in village attitudes shortly after Wang Ming-fu's visit. Dumb T'ien-lai was enjoying the spectacle far too much and talking openly about how expensive it was for him to have his wife providing free advice to anyone who asked for it. Mrs. Chen spoke too often and too much about herself as Mrs. Chen rather than behaving as a vehicle who was unaware of her pronouncements while "in trance"; her speeches rambled on too long and lost the enigmatic quality that brings authority to the *tang-ki*. And the fact that Wang Ming-fu was unlikely to recommend that she go to a temple where other *tang-ki* got training and experience seemed to end the matter. Within a week, people had begun to refer to her as "poor Mrs. Chen," to regard her displays as a nuisance, and to pressure members of her family "to do something."

Before I explore in more detail how and why this decision was reached, some background on shamanism, or spirit possession, in China and Taiwan and its role in folk religion is necessary. I will not try to sort out the peculiar amalgam of Buddhism, Taoism, and Confucianism that is involved in folk religion in Taiwan in particular and China in general. Suffice it to say that there are Buddhist temples and monasteries and that their adherents and practitioners are distinguished by dress and diet. There are no Taoist temples, but folk temples devoted to local gods are usually the locus of the activities of Taoist priests and of the lowly spirit mediums (Jordan 1972:29). The average Taiwanese citizen will make use of Buddhist and Taoist practitioners as the need arises, sometimes entertaining both during funeral rituals. Temples nearly always have at least one Buddhist worthy on their altars, and Buddhist temples sometimes have shrines for local gods in side alcoves. Too add to the confusion, spirit mediums in rural areas often provide services from their own home in front of their ancestral altar—which is also a shrine to their particular god—or in the home of the family requesting the help of their god. In urban areas some *tang-ki* have shop-front shrines to their gods, and the most successful have cults of followers who may themselves perform in trance (Kleinman 1980:232).

In his study of folk religion in a Taiwanese village, David K. Jordan describes the function of the *tang-ki* at the village level:

> The *tang-ki* are the prime rural religious arbiters. It is they who diagnose a given case of familial or village disharmony as caused by ghosts; it is they who explore the family tree of the village forts for possible ghosts and their motivations; it is they who prescribe the cure. Spirit mediums drive harmful ghosts from the village; spirit mediums perform exorcisms; and spirit mediums represent the august presence of the divine at rites performed in their name. It is likely that in the past it was the spirit mediums who had the final voice in alliances between villages [in local wars]. [1972:85]

But, as Jordan goes on to warn:

> The *tang-ki* is not a free man [*sic*], and his imitation of the gods is not a matter of his own caprice. Not only must he perform in trance (and therefore presumably not be guided by capricious desires but only by unconscious directives), but he is subject to charges of being possessed by ghosts rather than by gods should he become incredible. [1972:85]

And if the *tang-ki* is deemed possessed by a ghost, like any other villager, he or she will have his or her soul called back by another practitioner, essentially ending his or her legitimacy as a shaman.

My own experience with shamans in Taiwan was much more limited than that of Jordan, in part because religion was not the primary focus of my research or that of my coreseacher, Arthur Wolf, and in part because the villages we worked in did not have a resident *tang-ki*. In Peihotien, villagers used the services of an itinerant spirit medium who visited the area every few weeks or, late in our stay, of a young man who was attached to a temple in a nearby market town. Neither of these men seemed to have the kind of influence as "religious arbiter" that Jordan describes. Our field notes and the cases the staff recorded of visits to *tang-ki* certainly show that most villagers were "true believers," but we also heard a good deal of the cynicism that Jack Potter (1974) described when villagers assigned self-serving motives to some of the in-trance pronouncements of local shamans. I do not mean to suggest in any sense that I doubt Jordan's analysis for Bao-an, but only that our informants judged shamans on the basis of their success in solving individual problems—on how *ling* (strong) their gods were. Had I had the foresight to interview more widely, I might have found that spirit mediums had more influence on community matters than I assumed at the time. Considering the case I am discussing here, this would have been an extremely valuable piece of information.

In northern Taiwan, the source of my data and much of the secondary material to which I refer, the village shaman is considered simply a conduit between a god and his or her petitioners. During festivals celebrating the god, the shaman is expected to put on a display of bodily abuse, such as lying on a bed of nails or lacerating the body with swords or a prickball. Although this often called "mortification" in the literature (Jordan 1972:78), the purpose is not to subjugate the flesh as in early Christian ritual, but to prove that the god does not allow his vehicle to feel pain from these injuries and will protect him or her from permanent damage. The injuries do seem to heal rather quickly, and most observers comment on the absence of any expression of pain. Some shamans draw blood during each session, others only at major public events. In private sessions they rarely stage such ordeals, but they always trance.

In the literature there are a number of excellent descriptions of the performances of Chinese shamans. Some focus on the more spectacular (and bloody) feats of *tang-ki* on festival days, when they are showing off the power of their gods (see, for example, Elliott 1955), but a few give us a village perspective. Potter (1974) provides a particularly full picture of what amounts to a villagewide seance in the New Territories in Hong Kong, a seance in which the spirit medium travels through the underworld of spirits, chatting with the departed relatives of fellow villagers and allowing them to convey messages, warnings, threats, and reassurances to the living. A description by Katherine Gould-Martin (1978:46–47) of a *tang-ki's* session in a market town not far from Mrs. Chen's home captures the relaxed familiarity of Taiwan shamanism. The god who speaks in Gould-Martin's account is Ong-la-kong, and a cult has formed around the image of him in the living room of a very devout but otherwise not unusual family. The *tang-ki*, a laborer in his forties who lives two doors away from this family, trances every night after dinner. While petitioners, believers, or just neighbors gather to observe, comment, or seek help, the *tang-ki* wanders about the room, lights a cigarette for the god, exchanges a few words with him, and chats with friends in the crowd. In time an assistant begins to burn spirit money and to chant. As the tempo of the chant increases, the *tang-ki* begins to shake, tremble, and then to jump about, finally banging his head on a table. As Gould-Martin describes it:

> Once the *tang-ki's* head comes down, the assistant stops chanting and begins to read off the first case: "believing man or woman," name, birthdate, address, problem. During the reading the *tang-ki* starts to make sounds in a strange falsetto. He continues for some time. This is considered to be the god speaking in his native dialect, i.e., that which was spoken in his area of the Chinese mainland in the T'ang Dynasty. No one can understand these sounds. The acute advice is given in Taiwanese in a voice similar to the *tang-ki's* normal speaking voice, but deeper, more forceful, more inflected. The sentences of advice are often followed by, "Do you understand that?" They are interspersed with the falsetto noises. Often there is some discussion. The patient asks the god or the *tang-ki* helper a question. The god speaking through the *tang-ki* may reply or, if it is simple or the god seems annoyed, then the helper or even another patient or listener may answer the question. The god does not like to repeat himself and will be annoyed at that, but he will answer further questions. At the end the god, speaking through the *tang-ki,* says, "next case" and lapses into soft falsetto while the data of the next case are read to him. [1978:46]

Once the *tang-ki* has completed the evening's requests to Ong-la-kong, he is brought out of his trance by the assistant's burning of more spirit money, washes his hands and face, and chats with whomever is left in the crowd; his evening's work is then over. The money contributed is divided up among the assistant, the *tang-ki*, the host family, and a money-box designated for the god's birthday celebration and a temple the group hopes to build in his honor.

The problems brought to *tang-ki* are varied, ranging from illnesses in humans and animals to economic setbacks to marital disputes to fears of infertility. In 1958–1959, Arthur Wolf and his field staff collected more than 500 observations of villagers' visits to a local *tang-ki*. Over half of the problems brought to the *tang-ki* concerned illness: 53 percent of the women asked about their own or a family member's ill health, and 56 percent of the male visitors sough help for illness. Another 16 percent of the women inquired about domestic discord, and 15 percent of the women inquired about their fortune and/or asked to have it changed. Male clients did not ask as much about family disputes (4 percent) and were more interested in having their fortune tended to (14 percent), seeking help with sick animals (12 percent), or getting advice on financial decisions (8 percent). The following examples indicate the kid of information and acuity required of a practicing *tang-ki*:

> An old lady asked for advice about her husband, who was seriously ill. The shaman said: "He should have been dead by now. Your husband should have been dead yesterday. However, due to 'strengthened fortune and added longevity' [perhaps from earlier treatment?], he has been able to reach the age of 73. His original life was for only 69 years. Even so, it looks to me as if he were supposed to have died yesterday. If he survives the first day of the coming month, he will have great fortune. You can then come to me to further strengthen his fortune, but not before." He gave her a *hu-a* [charm paper].

> A 17-year-old boy asked about a large protuberance under one of his knees. The shaman said: "You have disturbed some ghosts at night." People in the boy's family admitted that he often ran around outside in the evening and said that the swelling had become larger and more painful in recent days. The shaman gave him a *hu-a* and told him to see a doctor.

> An old lady inquired about her lost gold chain. She said she had come several days earlier, but after four days of searching, she had still not found the chain. The shaman said: "Members of your family do not get along with one another and are quarreling. It doesn't matter that you have lost this chain. The quarreling is more important. Take this *hu-a* home and burn it to ashes, mix the ashes in water, and sprinkle it on the roof. You will be in harmony and only then will the chain reappear."

A middle-aged man asked about his chickens: "I have raised some chickens and they seem to have a lot of sickness lately. I don't know whether they have offended some dirty thing or there is some epidemic." The shaman said: "You did not choose a good date when you built the chicken house. Besides, you have offended the fox ghost. Cleanse the chicken house three ties with *hu-a* ashes in water. Offer sacrifices to make the fox ghost go away. Then, everything will be all right."

As Kleinman (1980:218ff.) also notes, a client's interview with a shaman often takes only a few minutes (although as much as two hours may be spent talking with the assistants and bystanders). In order to address the problems brought before her or him, a *tang-ki* must have a quick mind as well as a keen understanding of human motivation. Most *tang-ki* recommend medical help for obvious illness and, where appropriate, are also likely to recommend the assistance of other ritual specialists, such as geomancers and herbalists. They also practice a certain amount of psychotherapy (Kleinman 1980). In the examples above, the old woman with the seriously ill husband needed resignation coupled with a bit of hope; the boy clearly needed to see a doctor; a dirty chick house *might* have been causing the man's chickens to get sick; and the old lady who came back because the *tang-ki's* last bit of advice hadn't helped her recover her gold chain needed distraction—and all families have quarrels.

A successful *tang-ki* must be quick-witted and alert to the needs of his or her clients ("guests" is the literal translation of the term used). Other researchers (Elliott 1955:92; Gould-Martin 1978:59; Kleinman 1980:217; Potter 1974:210, 214) have suggested that *tang-ki's* successes often rest on their knowledge of the social and economic background of their clients. Kleinman (1980), who interviewed and observed urban *tang-ki* in Taipei, comments extensively on their sensitivity to potential tensions in the Chines family, even if the particular client/patient does not happen to be known to them.

These "job qualifications" are, obviously, derived from the observation of professional, experienced shamans. My concern in this article is why Mrs. Chen was eventually considered not to be *tang-ki* material, why she was never allowed to reach this stage. A number of scholars have discussed the means by which spirit mediums are identified in China, and they report pretty much the same set of expectations (Elliott 1955; Jordan 1972; Kleinman 1980; Potter 1974). *Tang-ki* come from modest socioeconomic backgrounds; they are preferably illiterate; they must be sincere and honest; they must display clear indications that a god has chosen them to be his vehicle. People fated to become shamans are originally fated to have short, harmless, unimportant lives, but their lives are extended by the gods who possess them in order that their bodies may be put to good use.

Many spirit mediums tell of illnesses in which they were brought back from the dead, after which they are troubled by a god who sends them into trances. Nearly all *tang-ki* in Taiwan report that they struggled against possession as long as they could but finally had to give in to the god's will. In Singapore, according to Elliott, some young men choose the life and train for it, but only after "something happens" to convince them that a god wants to enter them (1955:163). *Tang-ki*, incidentally, must not charge money for their services, but it is assumed that reasonable gifts will be made by grateful clients. I suspect that in rural Taiwan, few *tang-ki* receive enough in contributions to support themselves without another source of income (Gould-Martin 1978:62–32; Jordan 1972:75). As Jordan reports, in rural Taiwan there are few "divine rascals" because the living is too poor (1972:75).

Anthropologists frequently entertain the theory that spirit possession serves to provide a role for the emotionally disabled, the psychotic, or the epileptic. Kleinman, who studied the *tang-ki* in Taiwan primarily as healers, dismisses this explanation as impossible because of the complex behavior required of shamans:

Shamanistic healing clearly demands personal strengths and sensitivities incompatible with major psychopathology, especially chronic psychosis. Thus my findings argue against the view that shamanism provides a socially legitimated role for individuals suffering from schizophrenia or other severe psychiatric or neurological disorders. [1980:214]

Kleinman has extensive case material that includes detailed observations of *tang-ki* sessions as well as interviews with both shamans and their clients. His conclusions and those of others who have studied the Taiwan *tang-ki* are in accord with my own observations.

Nonetheless, the behavior of the beginning *tang-ki* and even of experienced *tang-ki* when they are going into trance might well be confused with that of a person who is deranged. (See, for example, the description by Elliott [1955:63]). And Kleinman himself provides us with a long case study (followed over three years) of a Hakka businessman suffering from acute anxiety and a variety of debilitating physical symptoms, who solved (to his and the shaman's satisfaction) his problems by "accepting the god" of the shrine, trancing, and essentially playing the role of lay shaman in the cult (1980:333–374). What Western observers might classify as mental illness is not necessarily so classified in Taiwan or China. The Hakka businessman in Taipei was treated for his problems for some time before he was defined as "troubled by the god" who wished to use him as a vehicle. Another of Kleinman's cases, one he classified as "acute, recurrent psychosis associated with normal inter-ictal behavior and provoked by acute stress producing extreme fear," was that of a 34-year-old mother of three who frequently attended *tang-ki* sessions (1980:166–169). When she began to trance regularly at one of the shrines and "asked that shrine's *tang-ki* if she could become a shaman . . . he told her no (an unusual response), because it was 'too early' and she was 'not yet ready.'" According to Kleinman, the *tang-ki* did so because "the patient was unable to control her trance behavior and acted inappropriately during her trances" (1980:167). The Hakka businessman seemed to have similar difficulties at the outset, but nonetheless was accepted readily as a lay shaman.

Mrs. Chen, our heroine from Peihotien, was eventually deemed "crazy" by her community, or, as Kleinman might more delicately phrase it, to be showing signs of psychopathology. Why? She had as many shamanistic characteristics as others who went on to full *tang-ki* status. Her origins were humble; she was functionally illiterate; she was sincere, devout, and kind-hearted; she had led a harmless and unimportant life; she had a history of psychological breakdown that could be attributed to the god's attempt to make her his vehicle; she had resisted as long as she could; she went into trances and spoke in a voice other than her own. For a fortnight she convinced a fair number of respectable villagers that a god was making his wishes known to them through her. Her lack of finesse in her public performance seemed no more inappropriate than that of other novices described in the literature.[3] Why, then, did she not qualify as a likely apprentice for training?

Unfortunately, we must depend on anthropological hindsight and the randomly recorded voices of villagers for the answers to these questions. Had Mrs. Chen become a *tang-ki* in Peihotien, we would have pages of field notes on her subsequent career, for having a *tang-ki* in one's village is a source of considerable prestige (Jordan 1972:81) and certainly something that an anthropologist would want to document, no matter how peripheral ritual behavior might be to his or her project. But having a near miss became close to a nonevent. We recorded some conversations and asked a few questions, and then quickly turned to other issues. However, even without focused and detailed interviews with Mrs. Chen's neighbors, we can explore some of the reasons why her misery was not validated as divine visitation. From the perspective of her village neighbors, the question was not merely whether she was hallucinating the voice of a god or the god was in fact speaking to her. The question included another (for many villagers) more likely alternative: that a malicious ghost rather than a god was tormenting her. When another practitioner diagnosed her illness as a ghost problem this might have ended the matter, but his treatment appeared to have no effect on Mrs. Chen whatsoever, indicating to her would-be followers that his diagnosis was wrong and the god-possession theory was still the best explanation for her behavior.

To understand why Mrs. Chen was not accepted as a vehicle for her god, we must look more closely at her position in her community. A diagnosis of "mental illness" is even less likely to produce a response of care and concern among Chinese villagers than it is among Americans. As long as a family member's oddities can be hidden or explained away, they will be; and whatever they may think privately, the neighbors will go along, for, after all, they, their parents, and their grandparents have lived and worked side by side with this family, sometimes for centuries. Condemning someone with whom your family has had that kind of relationship to a status that removes him or her from participation in society as a fully adult human is not done lightly. One might say that the person's genealogical legitimacy in the community is too high.

In the hierarchy of attributes of legitimacy, Mrs. Chen simply did not rank highly enough to protect her from dismissal as a "crazy"; for the same reason, various members of the community who might have recognized her as a potential *tang-ki* decided it was not worth the risk. To begin with, her gender was against her. There are respected female *tang-ki*, but not very many of them. *Tang-ki* are expected to be and do things inappropriate for women, and even though the extraordinary circumstances of a god's demand should make it all right, the sheer incongruity of the expectations of a god's behavior and those of a woman's behavior are enough to create misgivings. *Tang-ki*, even when not in trance and speaking with a god's voice, must be assured and competent individuals. Mrs. Chen's everyday behavior did not inspire this kind of confidence, nor did that of the only known male relative associated with her, Dumb T'ien-lai.

Even had Mrs. Chen been male, I suspect that her legitimacy would still have received closer scrutiny than that of most men in the village. As noted above, the Chens were "outsiders" in a Lin village. They had no relatives in the area whose genealogy would vouch for their respectability. They were better off than the one or two mainlanders who lived nearby and who were considered totally untrustworthy because they had no family anywhere in Taiwan who could be called to account for whatever transgressions their sons might commit. Nonetheless, the Chens by virtue of their newcomer status remained objects of suspicion, people who were considered slightly dangerous because they had no family whose face their misbehavior could ruin. The arrival of Mrs. Chen's mother helped, but the presence of her father and his brothers would have helped even more. And here again, her gender was against her, for women are considered only adjunct members of the husbands' families and temporary members of their natal families. There is no solidity, no confidence in ties through females to families about whom one knows nothing.

At another level of abstraction, Mrs. Chen's failure to be judged a *tang-ki* in the making comes down to her ambiguous status in terms of the Chinese concept of the family. Any *tang-ki* treads dangerously near the edge of respectability in relation to Chinese notions of filiality, and Mrs. Chen's situation tipped her into the area of violation. From the point of view of the Chinese villager, an individual is only part of a more important unit, the family, and the individual's personal inclinations must be subordinated to the needs of that family. Choice of education, occupation, marriage partner, even of medical attention, should be determined by family elders in terms of what is best for the group—and often that group is conceived of as a long line of ancestors stretching into a hazy past and an equally long line of descendants stretching into an unknowable future. The individual is expected to be selfless—even his or her own body is the property of the ancestors. I have seen innumerable village children harshly punished by their parents for playing so carelessly as to fall and injure themselves, thus damaging the body that belongs to the family. Jordan (1972:84) also mentions this idea in relation to *tang-ki* who regularly slash, cut, and otherwise mutilate their bodies in service to their god. Although divine intervention is supposed to prevent any permanent damage to the ancestors' property, the *tang-ki* nonetheless violates one tenet of filial piety.

More important, *tang-ki* as *tang-ki* are serving another master. They are expected to be totally selfless in that role as well, submitting themselves fully to the god's will in order to enable the god to solve his followers' problems. In fact, the needs of the ancestors and of the possessing god rarely come into conflict, for when out of a trance, the *tang-ki* can fulfill all of his or her obligations to parents, grandparents, and so forth.[4] However, in theory, the *tang-ki* has given his or her person to a god to do with as he will. Thus, the *tang-ki* submits to the god that which belongs to the ancestors. This may make the *tang-ki's* filial piety suspect, but it also highlights the sacrifice the god requires of his vessel. Mrs. Chen's assumed (although demonstrably inaccurate) rootlessness may very well have served to devalue the selflessness of her generosity in submitting to the will of the god.

Had Mrs. Chen been a wife or daughter of a Lin, there might actually have been strong pressures on her to accept the nomination of the god whether she wished to or not. In an intriguing study of shamanism in contemporary China, Ann Anagnost describes the social pressure put on a woman to assume the role of shaman (1987:52–54). During a period of failing health, Zhu Guiying exhibited symptoms that were interpreted as spirit possession. Sought out be fellow villagers as a healer, she at first resisted, but finally submitted to the social expectations of her neighbors. As Anagnost puts it, "To refuse this role would have been tantamount to a denial of social ties and the forms of reciprocity and obligation that bound the community together" (1987:53).

I wish I had been able to pursue Mrs. Chen's case in the years that followed this incident in Peihotien. It is conceivable

that in another setting, one where she was known in the context of a family, she might in fact have been encouraged to continue her interactions with the god who approached her in Peihotien. If, for instance, she had moved to Taipei and become involved in some of the cults surrounding well-known urban *tang-ki,* she might have continued to go into trance and might have become a valued member of one of the groups that Kleinman (1980) describes, thereby finding peace and status. In Peihotien she was too low in all of the hierarchies to achieve legitimacy as a full member of her community. As a result, she was not able to overcome her anomaly in either world—that of the village or that of the possessed.

Mrs. Chen failed to become a shaman, by one set of measures, because of the structural context in which she lived; she was an outsider—socially and genealogically. But her failure might be accounted for by another set of reasons, reasons even more intimately associated with her gender. Feminist theorists, exploring the construction of the gendered self in white middle-class North Americans, suggest that the male self is based on a set of oppositional categories (good/bad, right/wrong, nature/culture, and so forth) and that males selves are more rigidly bounded, more conscious of a distinction between the self and the other than female selves are (Chodorow 1974; Gilligan 1982, 1988; Hartsock 1983; Martin 1988). A female—perhaps because, as Chodorow (1974) suggests, the female infant does not need to transfer her identity from her original female caretaker—has a less bounded self. It is not tied into oppositions between self and other, but is constructed instead from connectedness and continuities.[5] A good *tang-ki* must be able to separate his or her behavior as a *tang-ki* from his or her everyday behavior. With a self constructed out of dualisms, a male may find it easier to keep his relations with his deity separate from his conscious mental life. Mrs. Chen clearly could not.

In time, Mrs. Chen might have been able to achieve this separation—other female *tang-ki* have. But Mrs. Chen had a special problem. Elsewhere I have explored the construction of the Chinese female self and have suggested that it is highly dependent on the meaning given to the individual by others (Wolf 1989). Whereas the Chinese male is born into a social and spiritual community that has continuity not only in life but after death, the Chinese female is born into a social community of which she is only a temporary resident, and her spiritual community after death depends upon whom she marries or, more important, whose ancestors she gives birth to. A Chinese boy's self is defined by this certainty, this continuity. A girl's sense of self develops in an environment of uncertainty—if she isn't sufficiently modest, she won't find a good family; it she isn't obedient, no mother-in-law will want her; if she is willful, she will have trouble with some unknown husband. She reads *who* she is in the approving or disapproving faces of those around her. The trauma of Chinese marriage, in which a very young woman is transferred to a distant village where she knows no one, not even her husband, creates for a woman a crisis of identity that is only resolved by the gradual acquisition of a new set of mirrors in which she can identify herself. Mrs. Chen. came to Peihotien a stranger, and a stranger she remained. There was no family to smile or frown, no mother-in-law to approve or disapprove of her behavior, and only a husband who was himself a stranger. Without ties to a family that had an accepted place in the village social system, when Mrs. Chen was no longer a novelty, she ceased to have an identity. She was an outsider who was neither dangerous nor useful, and she was more or else ignored. She was in fact nameless, having lost her personal name at marriage (Watson 1986). Unlike other brides, her self was never reconstructed, and her mirrors remained cloudy, except for the self she saw reflected in her children and in the conversations she had with the various gods she visited.

I continue to wonder whether or not Mrs. Chen, on that fateful day when she threw herself into the rice paddy, was not, as some claimed, trying to get to the river. Suicide (often by drowning) is a solution for many (younger) Chinese women who have trouble creating a new self in a strange place. Perhaps when she was pulled out of the muck of the paddy, she made one final attempt to join the social world of the village by way of a god who had more reality for her than the people among whom she lived. Unfortunately, her self was so poorly established that she could not carry it off. The self that spoke with the gods could not be used to construct a self that could survive in a social world constructed by strangers.

NOTES

Acknowledgments. I am grateful to my field assistant, Wu Chieh (fictitious name), who played a central role in the events discussed here, for her patience and persistence. I also want to thank Arthur Wolf, who made me a part of that first field experience. Mac Marshall and three anonymous reviewers have made suggestions that improved this manuscript significantly. I appreciate their help.

[1] I use shamanism and spirit possession interchangeably and refer to the practitioners as shamans, spirit mediums, or *tang-ki*, the last being the local term in Taiwan.

[2] We never did get a name for this god, who needed a special paint job (with half his face black and half white) but still looked and acted very much like Shang Ti Kung to some of the people in the village who knew about such things.

[3] Jordan describes the initiation of another village woman: "Throngs of village people looked on as she flailed her back, shouting, sputtering, drooling, and muttering. When it was over, she was, willy-nilly, a *tang-ki* (1972:167).

[4] Gary Seaman (1980:67) reports that early in their careers shamans are ritually adopted by the gods who possess them—these gods literally buy the young shamans from their parents. I had not heard of this in northern Taiwan.

[5] I am keenly aware of the dangers of applying theoretical concepts developed from Western data to the analysis of personalities constructed in a very different culture. This hypothesis in particular seems fraught with cultural pitfalls: among them the fact that Chinese children, unlike white middle-class American children, usually have a *variety* of female caretakers during their early childhood. Whether or not the explanations hypothesized by Chodorow (1974), Gilligan (1982, 1988), and others have cross-cultural viability remains to be seen, but some aspects of the resulting gender differences they describe in adults do appear to translate. See, for example, Martin's (1988:173ff.) description of a female ideology in funeral ritual that emphasizes "the unity of opposites" in contrast to a male ideology that shows "constant efforts to separate opposites"; see also Watson (1986), who uses personal naming practices in China as evidence of differences in personhood. Gender differences in personhood and the construction of the self in Chinese society are a much neglected topic. Much of the research either asserts that there are no differences (for example, Tu 1985) or ignores gender completely (for example, Yang 1989), by default taking the male self to be the Chinese self. I have begun to explore some of these ideas elsewhere (Wolf 1989 and in a manuscript in progress), and it is a rich area for investigation.

REFERENCES CITED

Anagnost, Ann S. (1987) Politics and Magic in Contemporary China. Modern China 13(1):40–61.

Chodorow, Nancy (1974) Family Structure and Feminine Personality. *In* Woman, Culture, and Society. Michelle Z. Rosaldo and Louise Lamphere, eds. pp. 43–66. Stanford, CA: Stanford University Press.

Elliott, Alan J. A. (1955) Chinese Spirit Medium Cults in Singapore. London School of Economics and Political Science Monographs on Social Anthropology, No. 14. London: University of London.

Gilligan, Carol (1982) In a Different Voice: Psychological Theory and Women's Devlopment. Cambridge, MA: Harvard University Press.
___. (1988) Adolescent Development Reconsidered. *In* Mapping the Moral Domain. C. Gilligan, J. V. Ward, and J. M. Taylor, eds. pp. vii–xxxviii. Cambridge, MA: Harvard University Press.

Gould-Martin, Katherine (1978) *Ong-la-kong:* The Plague God as Modern Physician. *In* Culture and Healing in Asian Societies: Anthropological, Psychiatric and Public Health Studies. Arthur Kleinman, Peter Kunstadter, E. Russell Alexander, and James L. Gate, eds. pp. 41–67. Boston: G. K. Hall & Co.

Hartsock, Nancy (1983) Money, Sex, and Power: Toward a Feminist Historical Materialism. Boston: Northeastern University Press.

Jordan, David K. (1972) Gods, Ghosts, and Ancestors: The Folk Religon of a Taiwanese Village. Berkeley: University of California Press.

Kleinman, Arthur (1980) Patients and Healers in the Context of Culture: An Exploration of the Borderland between Anthropology, Medicine, and Psychiatry. Berkeley: University of California Press.

Martin, Emily (1988) Gender and Ideological Differences in Representations of Life and Death. *In* Death Ritual in Late Imperial and Modern China. James L. Watson and Evelyn S. Rawski, eds. pp. 164–179. Berkeley: University of California Press.

Potter, Jack M. (1974) Cantonese Shamanism. *In* Religion and Ritual in Chinese Society. A. P. Wolf, ed. pp. 207–231. Stanford, CA: Stanford University Press.

Seaman, Gary (1980) In the Presence of Authority: Hierarchical Roles in Chinese Spirit Medium Cults. *In* Normal and Abnormal Behavior in Chinese Culture. Arthur Kleinman and T. Y. Lin, eds. pp. 61–74. Boston: D. Reidel.

Tu, Wei-ming (1985) Confucian Thought: Selfhood as Creative Transformation. Albany: State University of New York Press.

Watson, Rubie S. (1986) The Named and the Nameless: Gender and Person in Chinese Society. American Ethnologist 13:619–631.

Wolf, Margery (1989) The Self of Others, the Others of Self: Gender in Chinese Society. Paper presented at the conference "Perceptions of the Self: China, Japan, India," August, East-West Center, University of Hawaii, Honolulu.

Yang, Mayfair Mei-hui (1989) The Gift Economy and State Power in China. Comparative Studies in Society and History 31(1):25–54.